Fodor's 92
France

SO-AEZ-027

Fodor's Travel Publications, Inc.
New York and London

Fodor's France

Editor: Nancy van Itallie
Area Editor: Simon Hewitt
Editorial Contributors: Judy Allen, Donna Dailey, Suzanne De Galan, James Etheridge, John P. Harris, Andrew Heritage, Holly Hughes, Amanda Jacobs, Philip Joseph, Ann O'Connor, Carla Power, Marcy Pritchard, Linda K. Schmidt, Richard Smart, Caroline B.D. Smith, Anne Willan
Art Director: Fabrizio La Rocca
Cartographer: David Lindroth
Illustrator: Karl Tanner
Cover Photograph: Jean-Paul Nacivet/Leo de Wys, Inc.

Design: Vignelli Associates

Special Sales

Fodor's Travel Publications are available at special discounts for bulk purchases (100 copies or more) for sales promotions or premiums. Special editions, including personalized covers, excerpts of existing guides, and corporate imprints, can be created in large quantities for special needs. For more information, write to: Special Marketing, Fodor's Travel Publications, 201 East 50th Street, New York, NY 10022; or call 800/800–3246. Inquiries from the United Kingdom should be sent to: Fodor's Travel Publications, 20 Vauxhall Bridge Rd., London, England SW1V 2SA.

Contents

Foreword *vi*

Highlights '92 *ix*

Fodor's Choice *xvi*

Introduction *xxiv*

1 Essential Information *1*

Before You Go *2*

Government Tourist Offices *2*
Tour Groups *2*
Package Deals for Independent Travelers *3*
When to Go *4*
Festivals and Seasonal Events *5*
What to Pack *6*
Taking Money Abroad *7*
Getting Money from Home *8*
French Currency *8*
What It Will Cost *8*
Passports and Visas *9*
Customs and Duties *10*
Traveling with Film *11*
Language *12*
Staying Healthy *12*
Insurance *13*
Renting or Leasing Cars *14*
Rail Passes *15*
Student and Youth Travel *16*
Traveling with Children *17*
Hints for Disabled Travelers *19*
Hints for Older Travelers *20*
Further Reading *21*

Arriving and Departing *22*

From the U.S. by Plane *22*
From the U.S. by Ship *23*
From the U.K. by Plane, Car, Train, and Bus *24*

Staying in France *26*

Getting Around France *26*
Telephones *28*
Mail *29*
Tipping *29*
Opening and Closing Times *30*
Shopping *30*
Sports and Fitness *30*
Beaches *31*
Dining *31*

Lodging *32*
Credit Cards *33*

Great Itineraries *33*

2 **Portraits of France** *41*

France at a Glance: A Chronology *42*
The Art of French Cooking *48*
A Survey of French Architecture *54*
An Introduction to French Wine *59*

3 **Paris** *66*

4 **Ile de France** *134*
Versailles, Chartres, Fontainebleau

5 **The Loire Valley** *166*

6 **Brittany** *196*

7 **Normandy** *223*
Rouen to Mont-St-Michel

8 **Champagne and the North** *252*

9 **Alsace-Lorraine** *278*
Strasbourg, Nancy

10 **Burgundy** *310*

11 **Lyon and the Alps** *337*

12 **Provence** *366*

13 **The Riviera** *400*
St-Tropez to Monaco

14 **Corsica** *435*

15 **Toulouse and the Midi-Pyrénées** *456*

16 **The Atlantic Coast** *485*
Bordeaux, Biarritz

Conversion Tables *515*

French Vocabulary *516*

Menu Guide *521*

Index *527*

Maps and Plans

France *xx–xxi*
World Time Zones *xxii–xxiii*
Wine Regions *60–61*
Paris Metro *70–71*
Paris Arrondissements *74–75*
Paris *76–77*
Montmartre *98*
Paris Shopping *112–113*
Paris Dining *118–119*
Paris Lodging *126–127*
Ile de France *140–141*
Versailles *142*
Fontainebleau *155*
The Loire Valley *170*
Tours *177*
Orléans *184*
Brittany *200–201*
Nantes *214*
Normandy *228–229*
Rouen *230*
Champagne and the North *256–257*
Reims *267*
Alsace *282*
Strasbourg *284–285*
Lorraine *295*
Nancy *299*
Burgundy *314*
Troyes *316*
Dijon *325*
Lyon and the Alps *342–343*
Lyon *344*
Provence *371*
Nîmes *372*
Avignon *381*
Marseille *387*
The Riviera *404–405*
Nice *414*
Monaco *420*
Corsica *440*
Ajaccio *445*
Midi-Pyrénées *462–463*
Toulouse *464*
The Atlantic Coast *489*
Bordeaux *501*

Foreword

We'd like to express our gratitude to Simon Hewitt, our Area Editor, for his help in preparing this edition.

Special thanks also to Marion Fourestier of the French Tourist Office in New York; Colette Martin of Paris's Tourist Board; Jean-Pierre Martinetti, head of A.R.T.L., Corsica's regional tourist agency; Alexandre Lévy of the Toulouse-Midi-Pyrénées regional tourist board; and also to Brigitte Doignon and Florence Danjean.

While every care has been taken to ensure the accuracy of the information in this guide, the passage of time will always bring change and, consequently, the publisher cannot accept responsibility for errors that may occur.

All prices and opening times quoted here are based on information supplied to us at press time. Hours and admission fees may change, however, and the prudent traveler will avoid inconvenience by calling ahead.

Fodor's wants to hear about your travel experiences, both pleasant and unpleasant. When a hotel or restaurant fails to live up to its billing, let us know and we will investigate the complaint and revise our entries where the facts warrant it.

Send your letters to the editors of Fodor's Travel Publications, 201 East 50th Street, New York, NY 10022.

Highlights'92 and Fodor's Choice

Highlights '92

Olympics and Disney: those promise to be the words on everyone's lips in France in 1992, as the winter Olympics come to the Alps and Disneyworld comes to Paris.

One million spectators are expected in the French Alps in February 1992 as France hosts the **winter Olympics** for the third time. After Chamonix (site of the very first winter games, in 1924) and Grenoble (1968), the town of Albertville (population 18,000) in Savoie will be at the center of world sporting attention from February 8 through 23.

Thirteen venues, most within 64 kilometers (40 miles) or so of Albertville, will host the Olympic events. The opening and closing ceremonies, as well as the skating program, will take place in Albertville itself. Former French ski champion Jean-Claude Killy has played a big part in organizing the games and designing the ski runs, so spectacular action is guaranteed at Val d'Isère (men's giant slalom, Super G, and downhill), Les Menuires (men's slalom) and Méribel (women's slalom, giant slalom, Super G, downhill, and ice hockey). The other venues are Les Arcs (speed skiing), Courchevel (ski jumping and nordic combined), La Plagne (luge and bobsled, with a new 1500-meter run), Pralognan (curling), and Tignes (freestyle skiing).

Albertville is less than 4 hours by TGV train from Paris and just one hour from Lyon, Grenoble, and Geneva. The rail line has been electrified up the Tarantaise Valley from Albertville to Bourg St-Maurice, near several of the major venues. The new, spectacular Lyon–Albertville A43 expressway has been completed and the region's other main highways widened.

Free shuttle buses will ferry visitors to and from events. Fourteen hotels are being built (notably in Les Arcs, Chamonix, Courchevel, Meribel, and La Plagne), providing an additional 8,000 new beds. Olympic tickets and packages are being handled by Olson-Travelworld (100 N. Sepulveda, Suite 1010, El Segundo, CA 90245, tel. 800/874–1992).

Ski facilities in the French Alps—arguably the best in the world—have been further improved: 200 new snow guns and 15 new ski lifts were installed in 1991. Other Alpine innovations include an open-air skating rink at Avoriaz, an underground funicular at Tignes (powering skiers to slopes 3000 meters above sea level), and a helicopter liaison between Geneva and Val d'Isère. The famous Aiguille du Midi cable car, linking Chamonix to Mont Blanc (originally opened in 1954), has undergone a $10 million modernization, increasing its capacity from 400 to 600 persons an hour.

Heavy snowfalls throughout the winter meant that the 1991 ski season was the best in France in several years. Torrential rains elsewhere helped replenish the country's reservoirs, empty after the droughts of 1989 and 1990.

Eleven million vistors a year are expected at the $4.4 billion **EuroDisney**, set to open April 12, 1992, at Marne-la-Vallée, 32 kilometers (20 miles) east of Paris.

As we went to press (June 1991), 6 hotels and 29 attractions were rising above the rolling wheatfields of the Ile de France. Crowning them all: the turreted castle of Sleeping Beauty, soaring 140 feet. Other heroes of European fairy tales and mythology—including Lancelot, Snow White, Pinocchio, Peter Pan, and Alice in Wonderland—will loom large in Fantasyland, one of the five theme parks. Marvelous machines inspired by Leonardo da Vinci, Jules Verne, and H. G. Wells will animate Discoveryland; pirates, Arabian nights, and Treasure Island bring Adventureland to life. Elsewhere, EuroDisney will be determinedly American. Frontierland will evoke the canyons and mountains of Gold Rush country, while horse-drawn streetcars, a steam train, shops, restaurants, and classic automobiles enliven Main Street U.S.A. Admission prices had not been fixed as we went to press, although a special commemorative Disney Passport was on sale for 200 francs.

A golf course and five hotels will ring man-made Lake Buena Vista. Deluxe accommodation (1100–1950 francs per room, depending on the season) can be had at the Victorian-style Disneyland Hotel or the Manhattan-style New York Hotel. Slightly less pricey (750–1100 francs) are the Newport Bay Club, with the flavor of a New England resort, and the Rocky Mountain–style Sequoia Lodge. Budgeteers can choose between the Wild-West feel of the Cheyenne Hotel or the Mexican mood of the Sante Fe Hotel (550–750 francs). All rooms are designed for up to four guests, and rooms for nonsmokers and disabled travelers will be available in each hotel. Campers, meanwhile, can book a cabin at the Davy Crocket Campground (575–875 francs for 4–6 persons).

Each hotel has its own restaurants, all under the eye of Michel Grobon, trained at Lenôtre and Maxim's in France before acquiring American experience in Chicago, Las Vegas, and Palm Springs. He will be responsible for a taste-numbing 50,000 meals a day.

Getting to EuroDisney from Paris will be no problem, Disney moguls having persuaded the French government to provide the site with its own expressway access (off the Strasbourg-bound A4) and RER station (the rail journey from central Paris will take 35 minutes). The high-speed TGV-North will stop at EuroDisney beginning in 1994, putting Brussels at 90 minutes and London at 3¼ hours away.

Shuttle buses will ply between EuroDisney and the nearby international airports at Roissy and Orly.

Work on the **TGV-North,** with new tracks laid between Paris and the Channel Coast, continues on schedule; French and English workers met up midway under the English Channel in December 1990. The much-awaited Paris–London service will be operational in 1993. The TGV-Atlantic service to Bordeaux, meanwhile, was inaugurated in 1990, slashing journey time from 4¼ to 3 hours. The Gare Montparnasse, extended to act as Paris terminus for the new TGV trains, has emerged as a concrete showcase of postmodern industrial architecture.

On the road, seatbelts are now compulsory for back-seat passengers, and speed limits in towns have been reduced from 60 kilometers per hour (37 miles per hour) to 50 kilometers per hour (31 miles per hour). Broken speed limits are rare in Paris, though, where chronic traffic congestion has caused many of the principal thoroughfares to be declared *axes rouges* and all parking prohibited. At the same time, underground parking lots have been springing up—or rather down—across the capital. But parking remains a headache and traveling around Paris by car is not recommended.

The Paris metro will be extended west, from Pont de Neuilly to La Défense (where it will connect with the regional RER network), in 1992.

On the political front, May 1991 saw socialist Edith Cresson become France's first woman prime minister. Cresson was expected to make few major policy changes and to pursue the economic rigor favored by her predecessor, Michel Rocard. Inflation remains a modest annual 3.5% and the traditionally volatile French franc has achieved exchange-rate stability (at around 6 francs to the dollar and 10 francs to the pound during 1991).

As the 1993 deadline for "Greater Europe" approaches, France has abolished passport and customs checks at its borders with Belgium, Germany, and Luxembourg.

After years of new building activity, Paris appears to be entering a period of consolidation, with particular attention lavished on the majestic vista between the Arc de Triomphe and the Louvre. Mayor Jacques Chirac has launched a campaign to restore elegance to the Champs-Elysées and vowed to put an end to garish signs and chaotic parking. New trees will be planted; sidewalks widened; and harmoniously designed benches, street lights, and waste bins installed.

Across Place de la Concorde, the intimate Jeu de Paume museum, former home to the work of the Impressionists, reopened in June 1991 as home to temporary exhibitions of contemporary art. The nearby Tuileries are also due for a face lift, with new trees, flower beds, and fountains. At the far end of the gardens, the "new" Louvre is up and running beneath its glass pyramid, but work continues on cleaning its lengthy facades and converting the Rue de Rivoli wing (once home to the finance ministry) into extra museum space.

The other big museum news of 1991 concerned the Musée Marmottan, which finally recovered five Impressionist pictures stolen in 1985—including Claude Monet's watershed view of Westminster, *Impression: Soleil Levant*, that gave the art movement its name, in 1872.

The smartest newcomer to the Paris restaurant scene, called simply 15 Montaigne after its address, is perched on top of the Théâtre des Champs-Elysées, close to the Seine. Panoramic views and state-of-the-art decor complement the cuisine. For a less formal lunch, the top-floor café at the Virgin Megastore on the Champs-Elysées has become an overnight hit, thanks to an imaginative but inexpensive menu that blends Gallic savoir faire with the influence of American fast food and Spanish tapas.

In nearby Versailles, the top-ranking Trianon Hotel reopened in 1991, after massive renovation by its new Japanese owners, with award-winning chef Gérard Vié (he made his name across town at Les Trois Marches) called in to man the kitchens. A stylish new hotel, the Pullman Place d'Armes, opened close to the Château of Versailles early in 1991.

The 1992 Winter Olympics: The Savoie

by Richard Smart

Albertville (population 17,537), a largely industrial town, was selected to host the 1992 Winter Olympics because it's the train- and roadway hub for much of the French Alps. Take the train from Paris (for schedule and prices, call Rail Europe Inc. in the U.S., tel. 914/682–5172 or 800/345–1990) or fly to Lyons or Geneva and take a bus (France-on-Call, tel. 900/990–0040). All Olympic resorts are within 90 minutes of Albertville by bus or train. France-on-Call can provide phone numbers and information for all resorts, as well as the names of tour operators. The sole U.S. agent for Olympic ticket sales is Olson-Travelworld, Ltd. (tel. 800/874–1992).

In a radical departure from past Winter Games, the French are distributing the competitions among no fewer than 13 resorts in an area stretching from Les Saisies to Les Menuires, and from Tignes to Albertville. That's more than 968 square kilometers (600 square miles) of Alps to cover, but the organizing committee says not to worry: *pas de problème!* Two thousand athletes to move about, a pro-

---

This article was originally published in different form in Condé Nast Traveler.

jected million spectators going in and out, 300,000 tourist beds, with more on the way. With the cost of the competition and support facilities being built across this far-flung area, of the difficult logistics, and of administration and promotion, the XVI Winter Olympic Games carry a $790 million price tag. Nobody is greatly alarmed by this. Transforming a sports event into a regionwide economic development program does not come cheap, but the government will pick up 20% of the tab, the TV people are paying $244 million for world-wide broadcast rights, and there are the many sponsoring corporations that, in return for their $226 million worth of benevolence, will be licensed to sport the Olympic logo in their advertising. The commercial spin-offs to finance these games are endless. There are also 800,000 event tickets to be sold.

For those who buy them, it may be easier to find a place to sleep than to get from place to place when awake, because, despite the organizing committee's denial of *le problème*, travel between widely dispersed events will exact a heavy toll in time, energy, and patience. In the most benign conditions, the round trip between Les Menuires and Val d'Isère is a good three hours; during the games' congestion, you might well have to double that. Despite a planned fleet of shuttle buses, the committee rather oddly emphasizes that it is not discouraging the use of private cars, and there's no way for a bus to exceed the speed of a mountain-road traffic jam.

This does not mean you should stay home. Even with the games' disjointed geography, if you choose your base camp very carefully and don't plan on wandering too far afield in a vehicle, you can get a full plate of impossibly beautiful mountains and exciting competitions, but you're going to have to preselect a manageable menu. For me, the highest pitch of excitement always emanates from the Alpine skiing events, but this time the race courses are designed for competitor challenges and spectator thrills the likes of which haven't been seen for decades. It is the vision of a man remembering how the sport used to be, in his own glory days, and determined to make it that way again: Jean-Claude Killy, copresident of the organizing committee and the driving force behind the games. And, not incidentally, the most naturally gifted skier who ever lived.

Those who witnessed Killy's spectacular sweep of the three Alpine gold medals at the Grenoble Olympics in 1968 speak of it as though they had been present at the Second Coming. Today, Killy's imprint is most felicitous on the design of the downhill courses. The fashion, in recent years, has been to bulldoze away a mountain's natural contours—to "manufacture" a steep slope with unduly flat surfaces, favoring the raw speed of runaway-truck–type skiers while devaluing the skills of a subtler, more technically gifted athleticism. Killy, having none of that, enlisted the like-minded Swiss great, Bernhard Russi—the 1972 downhill champion at Sapporo—to do it right. The Killy-Russi heresy—actually a throwback to more pristine times—is to take the mountain on its own terms, largely as nature made it; to identify the most challenging skiable way down and let the skiers have at it. The result, on Val d'Isère's Face de Bellevarde, is a classic, technique-demanding course of the old school: 9,844 feet long with a vertical drop of 3,045 feet, richly endowed with serpentine twists, swift chutes, and great natural bumps that will return the breathtaking jumps to downhill racing.

The same philosophy has shaped the women's downhill course at Méribel, where a 2,717-foot vertical drop has been certified, breaking the rule limiting a women's downhill to a drop of 2,297 feet.

At both sites, planning genius has contrived to make the downhill, Super G, giant slalom, and combined races all end up at a common finish area. With all of the Super G and giant slalom and 80% of the downhill visible from there, it is a bountiful spectator feast.

So, with all this action going on, where to bed down in 1992? Three criteria: reasonably convenient access to a good number of exciting competitions, resort ambience, and, assuming you're coming there not just to watch but to ski, slopes that suit your skills. For most, these requirements should exclude Val d'Isère. There's gorgeous terrain, but much of it is for very advanced skiers; for mere mortals, it's a good place to break a neck. The resort itself has little charm, and aside from the men's Alpine races, the only events close by are freestyle skiing at Tignes and speed skiing at Les Arcs—both entertaining, but not mainstream events.

For maximum Olympic action, Les Trois Vallées is the place to be—preferably at Méribel, 4,759 feet high in the heart of the middle valley, or at one of its adjacent villages, Belvédère or Mottaret. Alone among the major Olympic resorts, Méribel, while thriving and expanding with the others in the postwar ski boom, has rigorously retained an authentic Savoyard mountain character—all chalet-type hotels with facades of stone and simple larch-wood siding bare of gingerbread. There's nothing flashy about the place; its strength is a relaxed, understated charm that makes for a perfect family resort (its mood much of what the old Aspen had before the infamous Alien Invasions from Park Avenue and Beverly Hills). Most compelling, though, is immediately accessible ski terrain so vast and varied that, on first sight, it absolutely boggles the mind and stuns the eye.

These three valleys—each with its own distinct character but linked together by an incredible network of 200 chair lifts, gondolas, cable cars, and poma lifts—add up to the most extensive integrated ski area in the world. From Courchevel's eastern valley to Les Menuires—Val Thorens' western one, with Méribel in the middle, you've got an astonishing 483 kilometers (300 miles) of trails, and you can ski each and every mile of them without once stepping into a car or onto a bus.

Given this lay of the land, the Méribel-based spectator-skier can catch the women's Alpine races and the ice hockey right in town and, passing over terrain of enthralling beauty en route, *ski* to other event in the adjacent valleys: ski jumping and Nordic combined at Courchevel, the men's special slalom (the only men's Alpine event not held at Val d'Isère) at Les Menuires–Val Thorens. If you've an appetite for more, Albertville's speed and figure skating are reachable by road.

Despite its bleak facade, Val Thorens offers a good choice of luxe and comfortable midpriced accommodations; after either Méribel's valley or Courchevel, it's your next-best choice, even with its sometimes dicey weather. The men's special slalom will begin a short ski away, and Méribel's high-voltage events are also within easy reach.

The finish of the slalom is at Les Menuires, a place better left unmentioned; but, because of its widespread advertising that trumpets low prices, I feel a moral obligation to warn you away. Fortunately, Les Menuires is not the standard, and in rebellion against the '60s' boom of slapdash modern construction, there's been a strong return to traditional mountain architecture. Still, 200,000 skiers an hour going up Les Trois Vallées' mountains by way of machinery is rather a lot.

Yet, if the area is an environmentalist's bane, it is undeniably a skier's paradise. The French are transportation junkies, and as with their SST and high-speed train, their advanced-technology ski lifts move people astonishingly fast. Despite the huge crowds, nowhere do we wait more than minutes—in most places less than five. And then there is this: Once you're atop a peak, the crush thins out. In every direction, as far as the eye can see, mountains of awesome grandeur, inaccessible and unskiable, fold forever on as if the entire earth were made only of Alps.

In 1992 we'll thrill to the slalom racers' twisting speed and the ski jumpers' skyward reach, roar with the crowd at the hockey players' mayhem, and go breathless at the ice dancers' balletic grace—along with the hundreds of thousands of others captivated by the world's greatest winter athletes in spectacular competition for a piece of Olympic gold.

Fodor's Choice

No two people will agree on what makes a perfect vacation, but it's fun—and can be helpful—to know what others think. We hope you'll have a chance to experience some of Fodor's Choices yourself while you're visiting France. For detailed information about each entry, refer to the appropriate chapters within this guidebook.

Hotels

La Cour des Loges, Lyon (*Very Expensive*)

Crillon, Paris (*Very Expensive*)

Le Palais, Biarritz (*Very Expensive*)

Westminster, Le Touquet (*Very Expensive*)

Angleterre, Paris (*Expensive*)

Grand Hôtel de Cala Rossa, Porto-Vecchio (*Expensive*)

Mas du Langoustier, Ile de Porquerolles (*Expensive*)

Château de Bellecroix, Chagny (*Moderate*)

L'Hostellerie du Vieux Cordes, Cordes (*Moderate*)

Louvre, Nîmes (*Moderate*)

Restaurants

Boyer-Les Crayères, Reims (*Very Expensive*)

L'Espérance, Vézelay (*Very Expensive*)

Georges Blanc, Vonnas (*Very Expensive*)

Le Grand Véfour, Paris (*Very Expensive*)

Joël Robuchon, Paris (*Very Expensive*)

Le Centenaire, Les Eyzies-de-Tayac (*Expensive*)

Château d'Esclimont, near Maintenon (*Expensive*)

Hiély-Lucullus, Avignon (*Moderate*)

Mas de la Chapelle, Arles (*Moderate*)

Au Gourmet sans Chiqué, Strasbourg (*Inexpensive–Moderate*)

Historic Towns and Villages

Les Baux de Provence

Beaune

Cluny

Cordes

Laon

Rocamadour

St-Emilion

Troyes

Vendôme

Drives

The Seine Valley from Mantes-la-Jolie to Rouen

The Voie Express Georges-Pompidou (Paris) along the north bank of the Seine

Through the Beauce from Chartres to Vendôme

Along the Route du Vin (wine road) in Alsace

Along the banks of the Loire between Blois and Saumur

Across the Marais Poitevin from Niort to La Rochelle

The Gorges du Verdon in the Alpes de Haute-Provence

Across the Camargue from Aigues-Mortes to Saintes-Maries-de-la-Mer

Along the Scali di Santa Regina (D84) from inland Corsica to the coast at Piana

Museums

Musée des Beaux-Arts, Dijon

Musée Condé, Chantilly

Musée Ingres, Montauban

Musée Matisse, Le Cateau-Cambrésis

Musée National de l'Automobile and Musée Français du Chemin de Fer (National Car and Train Museums), Mulhouse

Musée de l'Oeuvre Notre-Dame, Strasbourg

Musée d'Orsay, Paris

Musée Unterlinden, Colmar

Works of Art

Apocalypse Tapestry, Angers (castle museum)

Bayeux Tapestry, Bayeux (Musée de la Tapisserie)

Géricault's *Raft of the Medusa*, Paris (Louvre)

Grünewald's *Issenheim Altarpiece*, Colmar (Musée Unterlinden)

Janmot's *Poem of the Soul* painting cycle, Lyon (Musée des Beaux-Arts)

Rodin's sculpture *The Burghers of Calais*, Calais

Sculpted tombs, Dreux (Chapelle Royale)

Stained glass, Chartres (cathedral)

Churches and Abbeys

Abbey of St-Savin, St-Savin

Basilica of Ste-Madeleine, Vézelay

Cathedral, Amiens

Cathedral, Bourges

Mont-St-Michel

Notre-Dame, Guebwiller

Notre-Dame-la-Grande, Poitiers

Ste-Foy, Conques

St-Urbain, Troyes

Gardens

Château of Vaux-le-Vicomte

Château of Versailles

Château of Villandry

Jardin du Thabor, Rennes

Jardin des Tuileries, Paris

Musée Rodin, Paris

Orangerie, Strasbourg

Claude Monet's Garden, Giverny

Streets and Squares

Cours Mirabeau, Aix-en-Provence

La Croisette, Cannes

Main street, Riquewihr

Place de la Bourse, Bordeaux

Place du Capitole, Toulouse

Place Stanislas, Nancy

Place Vendôme, Paris

Place des Vosges, Paris

Châteaus and Castles

Chambord, Loire Valley

Chenonceau, Loire Valley

Fontainebleau, Ile de France

Hautefort, Périgord

Josselin, Brittany

Pierrefonds, Oise

Vitré, Brittany

France

N

ENGLAND

La Manche
(English Channel)

Boulogne

Cherbourg

Dieppe

Amie

Le Havre

Rouen

Roscoff

Caen

Seine

Brest

St-Malo

Morlaix

St-Brieuc

Chartres

Quimper

Rennes

Le Mans

Orl

Lorient

Vannes

Angers

Blois

Nantes

Loire Tours

ATLANTIC
OCEAN

Poitiers

La Rochelle

Niort

Saintes

Limoges

Bay of Biscay

Angoulême

Périgueux

Brive-la-Gaillarde

Bordeaux

Garonne

Dordogne

Langon

Cahors

Montauban

Albi

Bayonne

Toulouse

Biarritz

Pau

Tarbes

Carcassonne

SPAIN

ANDORRA

World Time Zones

Numbers below vertical bands relate each zone to Greenwich Mean Time (0 hrs.).
Local times frequently differ from these general indications,
as indicated by light-face numbers on map.

Algiers, **29**
Anchorage, **3**
Athens, **41**
Auckland, **1**
Baghdad, **46**
Bangkok, **50**
Beijing, **54**

Berlin, **34**
Bogotá, **19**
Budapest, **37**
Buenos Aires, **24**
Caracas, **22**
Chicago, **9**
Copenhagen, **33**
Dallas, **10**

Delhi, **48**
Denver, **8**
Djakarta, **53**
Dublin, **26**
Edmonton, **7**
Hong Kong, **56**
Honolulu, **2**

Istanbul, **40**
Jerusalem, **42**
Johannesburg, **44**
Lima, **20**
Lisbon, **28**
London (Greenwich), **27**
Los Angeles, **6**
Madrid, **38**
Manila, **57**

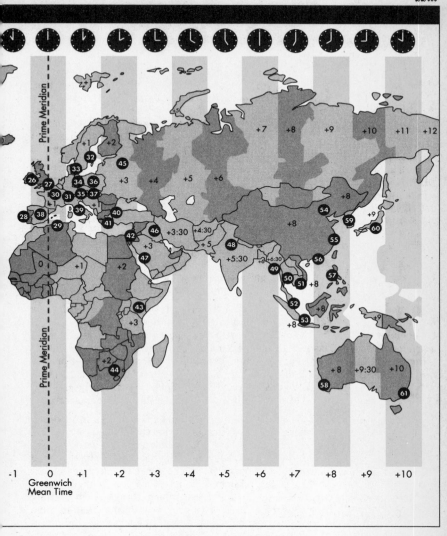

Mecca, **47**

Mexico City, **12**

Miami, **18**

Montreal, **15**

Moscow, **45**

Nairobi, **43**

New Orleans, **11**

New York City, **16**

Ottawa, **14**

Paris, **30**

Perth, **58**

Reykjavík, **25**

Rio de Janeiro, **23**

Rome, **39**

Saigon, **51**

San Francisco, **5**

Santiago, **21**

Seoul, **59**

Shanghai, **55**

Singapore, **52**

Stockholm, **32**

Sydney, **61**

Tokyo, **60**

Toronto, **13**

Vancouver, **4**

Vienna, **35**

Warsaw, **36**

Washington, DC, **17**

Yangon, **49**

Zürich, **31**

Introduction

by John P.
Harris

*Born in England,
John P. Harris
has lived in a
small village in
the south of
France since
1975. He has
written numerous
articles for both
French and
British
newspapers and
magazines,
including the
London* Times,
*and is the author
of* France—a
Guide for the
Independent
Traveler
(*Macmillan,
London 1987*).

France is neither too hot nor too cold, neither too wet nor too dry, neither too flat nor too crammed with inconvenient mountains. At any rate, that is what the French say. They think that countries should be hexagonal in shape and about 600 miles across. Spain is too square, Norway is frayed at the edges, l'Angleterre (which is what they usually call Great Britain) is awkwardly surrounded by cold water, Switzerland landlocked and too small, and the United States too large (you cross three time zones and then get the same depressing dinner). After God created France, He belatedly realized that He had gone too far: It was too near perfection. "How can I restore the balance?" He asked Himself. Then He saw what to do—He created the French. That is a French story. The French enjoy grumbling about themselves or, rather, about other French people, but in the same breath they admit that there is only one civilized way for people to live, and that is the French way, *la civilisation française*.

On the other hand, a chorus tells us that the French are a nation of individualists, and, indeed, at each corner of *l'hexagone*, there are people speaking strange languages—Basque, Breton, Flemish, Alsatian, Provençal, and Catalan—many of whom (especially Bretons) get rather prickly if you call them French. And yet almost all of them feel that nonhexagonal ways of life are deviations from the civilized norm: barbarous, if not verging on the extraterrestrial.

My wife and I have lived in France for more than 15 years, and we have come to the conclusion that there is something to be said for this view. Our fellow villagers are kind, patient, and friendly, behaving with natural dignity and good manners, like most of the other French people we meet (except Parisians in the rush hour). If we were to try to live in outlandish ways, doing the wrong things at the wrong times, we might meet with greater tolerance than in some other countries, but our life would be less easy and pleasant. Visitors to France, whether they stay a week or a year, will have a better time if they "go native" as far as they find it practicable—and when and where they don't, they should be philosophically aware of the drawbacks of trying to behave as in dear old Birmingham (AL or U.K.). This essay is about the French way of life as it impinges on the visitor, particularly the Anglo-Saxon visitor. (I am using the word "Anglo-Saxon" as the French use it. To them, Louis Armstrong, Robert Burns, James Joyce, and Frank Sinatra are representative Anglo-Saxons; Beowulf and King Alfred have nothing to do with it.)

Let's look at the French timetable. Most of them are up early, gulping a *café au lait* and getting to work by 8. By 10, Parisian executives are fuming because their London contacts haven't yet answered the phone (it's only 9 in England). There is no coffee break.

At noon, they are hungry. Work stops for two hours or longer. Museums and small shops close. *Le déjeuner* (called *le dîner* in the country) is a sacred rite. Fast-food outlets have multiplied, but the norm is a proper meal, taking an hour and a half; a surprising number, even of those who work in central Paris, manage to get home for it. However, the increasing number of women at work means that six lunches out of ten are eaten at restaurants or canteens—substantial, freshly cooked affairs, eaten with serious critical attention. The French grew rich in the '60s: Back in 1920, they each ate nearly three pounds of bread a day—now it is just under a pound, with a corresponding increase in the consumption of meat, fish, and cheese. Less wine is drunk, but more of it is of higher quality. Quality is important. Bread, butter (margarine is for Americans and such), eggs, chickens, and cheese—basic things like these—can be had in perfection in France if you take time and trouble and pay the price. Rich and poor alike pay as much attention to bread and butter and eggs and the contents of the water jug as rich Anglo-Saxons might pay to the choice of steak and claret.

There is a typical restaurant in our nearest market town (pop. 6,000). It has only one menu: copious hors d'oeuvres, a fish dish or a light meat dish, a more serious meat dish, vegetables in season, a good cheese board, fruit or ice cream. It's always full by 12:30. A couple from San Francisco who stayed in a rented cottage in our village were hardly ever able to use it. They used to get up at 9 and have an Anglo-Saxon sort of breakfast, and so they were hopelessly out of phase with the commercial travelers (up at 6) who form the restaurant's main clientele. You can't start your lunch there at 1:30 or 2, and there are no doggy bags in France. We are in the Midi, where an early start and a siesta are convenient (many of the shops don't reopen until 3:30). However, the couple happily developed the picnic habit: France is God's own country for picnicking, if only you get to the *charcuterie* and the *boulangerie* and the *pâtisserie* well before they close at noon.

Back to work for another four-hour stretch. No tea or coffee break. Are the French mighty toilers? Yes and no. I have conducted oral language examinations in France and in England. The French expect me to keep on examining nonstop from 8 to 12:30 and again from 2 to 6:30. The merciful (lazy?) English think six hours of attentive interviewing per day, with breaks mid-morning and mid-afternoon, are all the human mind can stand. French schoolchildren have a much longer day than do Anglo-Saxon ones and have more to learn (enormously more than American children, who seem to the French to leave serious learning until university, if then; U.S. postgraduate degrees are respected, though).

On the other hand, wage earners and schoolchildren have many leisure days. In the '80s, the average industrial worker put in 1,872 hours of work in the United States, 1,750 in Great Britain, but only 1,650 in France. Five weeks' paid vacation is the official minimum, and there are many public holidays. The children have Europe's longest school day, but they also have the longest vacations. The French have become addicts of leisure in the past two decades. They are the world's champions in ownership of *résidences secondaires:* One family in ten has a second house in the country, where they go on weekends and vacations, causing astounding traffic jams as they flee the cities.

But many French people want to be their own bosses. The price of independence is hard work. A motorized grocer comes to our village on Tuesday and Saturday. He and his wife seem happy working a 70-hour week. He takes one week's vacation a year. To him, company men seem featherbedded: 50% of all who work have secure tenure in their jobs, 27% buy their enterprise's products at reduced rates (electricity workers are given current almost free, for example), 24% get automatic promotion by seniority, 24% get six weeks' paid vacation or more; and there are all kinds of fringe benefits. But our grocer clings to independence. So do small family enterprises: the modest hotels, restaurants, little shops, and garages that give such good service on a personal basis.

I f he finishes his day's work at 6 or 6:30, will our average Frenchman call in at his favorite café for a chat and an aperitif on his way home? Probably not, nowadays. In the past, the café was used as a sort of extra living room for meeting friends or professional contacts, or even for writing novels if you were Jean-Paul Sartre or Simone de Beauvoir. But today an average of two hours and 50 minutes is spent watching television at home, which reduces the time available for social life.

This is sad. The number of cafés has diminished. Fortunately, there are still a lot left, and how convenient they are for the visitor! Anglo-Saxon bars and pubs may be seen by the French as somber haunts where customers take refuge from the wife and children while getting soused as rapidly as possible. On the terrace of a French café, you can bask in the sun or enjoy the shade of a multicolored parasol, sipping a cool beer and keeping an eye on life's passing show, while your near and dear toy with popsicles or write letters. A small black coffee entitles you to spend an hour or two—no hurry. But in our market town, the cafés do good business only in the summer, when the tables are set out under the plane trees in the avenue, and then half the customers are "foreigners"—Parisians, Britons, the Dutch. . . .

While we are on the subject: It seems odd to the Anglo-Saxon that in France beer is generally considered a non-alcoholic drink. When you tell the French that some people at home succeed in getting nastily drunk on it, they say, "But they must drink several glasses!" Indeed. A Frenchman will spend half an hour sipping a quarter of a liter. One sees few drunks in France, except in the north.

Nonetheless, alcoholism exists. The cause, usually, is excessive regular consumption of wine. The average is 73 liters a year, but it is those who drink substantially more than a liter a day who pay the price; they don't get rowdy, they succumb at last to cirrhosis of the liver. Let's not be gloomy. The French live fractionally longer than do Americans or Britons, and a moderate amount of daily wine is thought to be good for the health.

I mentioned the aperitif hour to talk not only about cafés but about friendliness. Some people—notably Americans—complain that the French are inhospitable and standoffish. The fact is that they are great respecters of privacy. If the Englishman's home is his castle, the Frenchman's apartment or house is his lair. People simply do not pop into one another's lairs, drinking casual cups of coffee and borrowing half a pound of sugar. They need a neutral place in which to socialize. Britons (more or less, depending on whether they live in the north or the south) come somewhere between typical French people and the American middle class. According to Paul Fussell (*Caste Marks*, 1983): "Among the [American] middles there's a convention that erecting a fence or even a tall hedge is an affront." And he quotes William H. Whyte, Jr., who was told: "The street behind us is nowhere near as friendly. They knock on doors over there."

It's different in France. People in the Midi, where we live, just love to talk, and even to listen. But our village neighbors are timid about entering our house. If they want to ask us something they will wait until we meet, or stay on the doorstep, or phone (from 50 yards away). They penetrate our house, and we penetrate theirs, when specifically invited—for aperitifs or dinner—and the occasion is rather formal. No potluck meals on the spur of the moment. That is how they behave among themselves, too. It's not because we are foreigners.

So when do we talk? If there were a café in our village, that would be the place, but the village is too small. Fortunately, there are only a few days in the year when open-air life is impossible, and there are benches everywhere, in the sun and in the shade. The villagers—and we—sit there for hours, chatting. Are you staying in a small country hotel or renting a vacation place? The locals really are interested in you, your habits and tastes, the number and ages of your children, your work, where you come from, and so forth, and are longing to impart a discreet selection of their own personal details. Of course you *may* be invited home. There are no rules about this sort of thing. And if there were, the French would take pleasure in breaking them.

When talking with the French, there are conventions that should be observed if you don't want to be thought a barbarian by people who are unaware of Anglo-Saxon attitudes. You must say *Bonjour*, followed by *Monsieur, Madame, Mademoiselle, Messieurs, Mesdames,* or *Messieurs-dames* much more often than you would think necessary (on entering a small shop, for instance) and *Au revoir, Monsieur* (etc.). Hands are shaken frequently (by colleagues at work, morning and evening, and by the most casual acquaintances). *Bon appétit* can replace *Au revoir* shortly before mealtimes. On going through a door, a certain amount of *après-vous*-ing is normal, with *Pardon* if you go through first, turning your back. Getting on first-name terms is a sign of much greater intimacy than in England or the United States. Rush-hour Parisian life is more brutal, of course, and, as elsewhere in the world, the driving seat of a car exerts a malign influence. In England, a headlight flash sometimes means "After you"; in France, it means either "After me" or "I am a criminal and I expect you are, too, so watch it, chum, the cops are round the corner."

Back home from the café, there is, of course, television, about which the French have mixed feelings. At one and the same time, they envy the number of channels available to American viewers and feel superior about the low intellectual quality of American television, as reported by French sources. Old movies are the favorites. Lengthy and serious discussion programs have a wide audience.

Le dîner (called *le souper* in the country) is served around 8, for rich and poor. It's a lighter meal than at midday, with soup replacing hors d'oeuvres. The schoolchildren will have finished their homework by then. Bed follows not long after. But the movies, after a sharp fall as television established itself in every home, have resisted well. Except in Paris, films are dubbed into French, a practice deplored by intellectuals. (Visitors to Paris who want to see a movie in the language in which it was made should look for the abbreviation *v.o.*, meaning *version originale;* otherwise, they'll experience such shocks as seeing the space traveler in *"2001, A Space Odyssey"* pressing the button marked "English" at the satellite debriefing computer, only to receive the question *"Quelle est votre nationalité?"* to which the able astronaut replies, without blinking an eyelid, *"Américain."*)

Almost all employed people now have a two-day weekend, usually Saturday and Sunday, but Sunday and Monday for many shop workers. Schoolchildren have Wednesday free. In recent years, the French have revolutionized their leisure habits: Jogging, swimming, soccer, gymnastics, tennis, and vigorous bicycling (for fun, not transport) are practiced, mainly on weekends, by large numbers of all social classes.

Sunday is a day for enjoying oneself. Though 85% of the population declare themselves Catholics, only 15% of those go to church every week. There is a fairly strong anti-Church sentiment among many, even among those who say they are Catholics (but the traditional warfare between priest and primary-school teacher, the one reactionary and the other attached to Republican ideals, is a thing of the past). Divorce, the pill, and safe legal abortion are widely accepted, even by practicing Catholics, who politely conceal their smiles when celibate ecclesiastics denounce such facilities.

The great Sunday ritual takes place at noon or soon after. Four out of 10 will visit friends or relations. Sixty percent of families do more cooking on Sundays than on other days. This is also a big day for restaurants that feature a special Sunday menu (with somewhat higher prices). Half the French end their Sunday lunch with a fresh fruit tart or some sort of *gâteau*, which is why the pastry shops are open in the morning and why you see Frenchmen carefully carrying flat cardboard boxes. Then a quarter of the population takes a little siesta.

An essay such as this has to contain rash generalizations, unless it is to be five times the length, hedging every statement with ifs, buts, and exceptions. Is there an average French person? Obviously not. There are the rich and the poor, for example. But in the Anglo-Saxon world, there seem to be more class differences, apart from money, than in France. The Anglo-Saxon blue-collar worker—to speak only of food, an important enough subject—chooses different meals from the élite and eats them at different times. Not so in France, where, however, income differences can be greater. The poor, in France, like champagne, oysters, and foie gras, but they get them less often than do the rich. The same is true of other aspects of life. The gulf between one class and another is not one of tastes and aspirations; rich and poor are in broad agreement on what constitutes a pleasant life. The poor are simply further away from it than are the rich.

Many people who constitute the unskilled sector and the unemployed are North African immigrants, a reminder of France's colonial past. Frictions develop in rundown areas that have turned into ghettos. Extreme right-wing groups, notably the *Front National* under Le Pen, have picked up racist votes, capitalizing on the fear of insecurity. Theft and violent robbery have increased, but not as much as awareness of them. French enthusiasts for bringing back the death penalty are incredulous when told that the number of murders in France today is no greater than it was in 1825, when the population was half its present size. You are in no more danger of being murdered in France than in Britain, and in nine times less danger than in the United States.

Changing France . . . I was there in 1947, and I said to myself: "How wonderful! But it can't last." On the whole it has. The surge of prosperity in the '60s brought improvements to French life, with some drawbacks (traffic in Paris, for example), but basic traditions die hard. The young ape foreign fashions, with a fast-food/motorcycle/mid-Atlantic pop noise/comic-strip culture, but they grow out of it. Official morality has changed. Contraception used to be forbidden; Paris was famed for its elegant brothels, but women had to go to London for diaphragms and to Switzerland for abortions. All that has gone. In 1988, the rise of AIDS caused a quickly smothered quarrel among bishops about the sinfulness of condoms, which are readily available. *Le topless* is seen on most beaches, and total nakedness on some. But the family remains a powerful, cohesive unit.

What do they think of us? Corresponding to the Anglo-Saxon stereotype that depicts all Frenchmen wearing berets and pointed beards, waving their arms wildly and being saucy with the girls, the French picture Americans as rich, generous, overweight, and likely in world politics or personal relationships to behave like well-meaning bulls in china shops and the English as either tall, silent, inhibited, masochistic, and scrupulously honest or as drunken, sadistic, soccer-watching vandals. Of course nobody really believes any of this, but if you are going to attach a national label to yourself, you might as well be aware of the cliché lurking at the back of the mind.

"Happy as God in France" say the Germans, exaggerating a bit. Anglo-Saxons come in two sorts: those who love France and those who don't. It's a matter of taste and character. The former find it easy to slip into the French way of life for a week or a month or permanently. The latter are better off in Paris or on the Riviera. There, at a price, arrangements can be made to suit inflexible millionaires from Texas or the Middle East; you might even be able to get a classic dish served with milky breakfast coffee at three in the afternoon, shielded from the shudders of the natives. But really, the French are canny operators when it comes to enjoying *la douceur de vivre*, the sweetness of life. If you follow their example while in France, you can't go far wrong. (One way of going wrong might be to quote almost any paragraph from this essay to them; at any rate, it will start a vigorously French argument.)

1 Essential Information

Before You Go

Government Tourist Offices

Contact the French Government Tourist Offices for information on all aspects of travel to and in France.

In the U.S. 610 Fifth Ave., New York, NY 10020 (tel. 212/315–0888); 645 N. Michigan Ave., Chicago, IL 60611 (tel. 312/337–6301); 2305 Cedar Springs Rd., Dallas, TX 75201 (tel. 214/720–4010); 9454 Wilshire Blvd., Suite 303, Beverly Hills, CA 90212 (tel. 213/271–6665); 1 Hallidie Plaza, Suite 250, San Francisco, CA 94102 (tel. 415/986–4174).

In Canada 1981 McGill College, Suite 490, Montreal, Quebec H3A 2W9 (tel. 514/288–4264); 1 Dundas St. W., Suite 2405, Box 8, Toronto, Ontario M5G 1Z3 (tel. 416/593–4723).

In the U.K. 178 Piccadilly, London W1V OAL England (tel. 071/491–7622).

Tour Groups

Care to balloon over the Loire Valley, sip wine with a countess in Burgundy, or just hop aboard a whistle-stop tour of the country's most famous highlights? Then you may want to consider a package tour. Creative itineraries abound, offering access to places you may not be able to get to on your own as well as the more traditional spots. They also tend to save you money on airfare and hotels. If group outings are not your style, check into independent packages; somewhat more expensive than package tours, they are also more flexible.

When considering a tour, be sure to find out exactly what expenses are included (particularly tips, taxes, side trips, additional meals, and entertainment); governmental ratings of all hotels on the itinerary and the facilities they offer; cancellation policies for both you and the tour operator; and, if you are traveling alone, the price of the single supplement. Most tour operators request that bookings be made through a travel agent (there is no additional charge for doing so). Below is a sampling of the many tour options available. Contact your travel agent or the French Government Tourist Office for additional resources.

General-Interest Tours **American Express Vacations** (Box 5014, Atlanta, GA 30302, tel. 800/241–1700 or, in Georgia, 800/637–6200) is a veritable supermarket of tours; you name it—they've either got it packaged or will customize a package for you. **Globus-Gateway** (150 S. Los Robles Ave., Suite 860, Pasadena, CA 91101, tel. 818/449–0919 or 800/556–5454) offers the hectic but comprehensive 15-day "La France." **Jet Vacations** (775 Broadway, Suite 2405, New York, NY 10019, tel. 212/247–0999 or 800/JET–0999) features "Paris & Châteaux Country" and "Paris, Burgundy, Provence & the Riviera." **Trafalgar Tours** (21 E. 26th St., New York, NY 10010, tel. 212/689–8977 or 800/854–0103) offers a moderately priced, two-week "Best of France" program. **Olson-Travelworld** (100 N. Sepulveda Blvd., Suite 1010, El Segundo, CA 90245, tel. 800/421–2255, 800/421–5785 in CA or 213/615–0711) has comprehensive three- and five-star tours of France. **Maupintour** (Box 807, Lawrence, KA 66044, tel. 800/

255–4266 or 913/843–1211) hits the highlights of France within 12 days.

Special-Interest Tours
Wine/Cuisine
Travel Concepts (373 Commonwealth Ave., Suite 601, Boston, MA 02115–1815, tel. 617/266–8450) serves up such specialties as "Champagne and Cuisine with Mrs. Charles Heidsieck" (of Heidsieck Champagne fame), "Burgundy: History, Wine & Cuisine with Countess De Loisy," and, for the serious wine-lover, a week-long seminar at the University of Wine in the Rhône Valley.

Art/Architecture
Past Times Arts and Archaeological Tours (800 Larch Lane, Sacramento, CA 95864–5042, tel. 916/485–8140) escorts the curious through the strange world of prehistoric cave art in southern France. Its "Paris Art Museums and Historic Neighborhoods" is a tour that tells as well as shows.

Cycling
Sobek Expeditions (Box 1089, Angels Camp, CA 95222, tel. 209/736–4524) gets the blood flowing with its "Tour de France" ride through the French countryside from Burgundy to the Bay of Biscay.

Ballooning
Buddy Bombard Balloon Adventures (6727 Curran St., McLean, VA 22101–3804, tel. 703/448–9407 or 800/862–8537) takes groups of a dozen or fewer into the gentle breezes above Burgundy and the Loire Valley during its three- to six-night tours. Fine dining back on the ground is an added touch.

Barge Cruising
Drift in leisure and luxury through Burgundy, Champagne country, and other scenic areas on any of four tours with **Floating Through Europe** (271 Madison Ave., New York, NY 10016, tel. 212/685–5600).

Singles and Young Couples
Trafalgar Tours (*see* General-Interest Tours, above) offers "Club 21–35," faster-paced tours for travelers who are not afraid of a little physical activity—whether it's bike riding or discoing the night away.

Music
Dailey-Thorp Travel (315 W. 57th St., New York, NY 10019, tel. 212/307–1555) offers deluxe opera and music tours, including "French Festivals." Itineraries vary according to available performances.

Package Deals for Independent Travelers

Self-drive tours are popular in France, and **The French Experience** (370 Lexington Ave., Suite 812, New York, NY 10017, tel. 212/986–1115) has put together eight different routes, including "The Châteaux Experience," with stays at private châteaus and manor houses. Accommodations at country cottages, Paris apartments, and bed and breakfasts can also be arranged. **Abercrombie & Kent International** (1420 Kensington Rd., Oak Brook, IL 60521, tel. 708/954–2944 or 800/323–7308) adds the option of a chauffeur to its somewhat pricier deluxe driving tours. **Air France** (666 Fifth Ave., New York, NY 10103, tel. 212/247–0100) offers week-long air/hotel packages to Paris and the Riviera. **Pan Am Holidays** (800/THE–TOUR) and **TWA Vacations** (800/GETAWAY) have similar flexible packages. "France à la Carte" is a menu of hotel packages available in Paris and Nice from **The French Experience** (*see* above). **Globus-Gateway** (*see* General-Interest Tours, above) gives you a week in Paris, including airport transfers, local host service, half-day sightseeing, and shopping discounts.

When to Go

On the whole, June and September are the best months to be in France, since both are free of the mid-summer crowds. June offers the advantage of long daylight hours, while slightly lower prices and frequent Indian summers (often lasting well into October) make September an attractive proposition.

Try to avoid the second half of July and all of August, or be prepared for inflated prices and huge crowds on the roads and beaches. Don't travel on or around July 14 and August 1, 14, and 31. July and August in southern France can be stifling. Paris can be stuffy in August, too, but it is pleasantly deserted (although many restaurants, theaters, and small shops are closed).

The skiing season in the Alps and Pyrenees lasts from Christmas to Easter; do not go in February if you can avoid it (vacation time for schoolchildren). Anytime between March and November will offer you a good chance to soak up the sun on the Riviera, though, of course, you'll tan quicker between June and September. If Paris and the Loire are among your priorities, remember that the weather is unappealing before Easter. If you're dreaming of Paris in the springtime, May (not April) is your best bet.

Climate The following are average daily maximum and minimum temperatures for Paris and Nice.

Paris	Jan.	43F	6C	May	68F	20C	Sept.	70F	21C
		34	1		49	10		53	12
	Feb.	45F	7C	June	73F	23C	Oct.	60F	16C
		34	1		55	13		46	8
	Mar.	54F	12C	July	76F	25C	Nov.	50F	10C
		39	4		58	15		40	5
	Apr.	60F	16C	Aug.	75F	24C	Dec.	44F	7C
		43	6		58	15		36	2

Nice	Jan.	55F	13C	May	68F	20C	Sept.	77F	25C
		39	4		55	13		61	16
	Feb.	55F	13C	June	75F	24C	Oct.	70F	21C
		41	5		61	16		54	12
	Mar.	59F	15C	July	81F	27C	Nov.	63F	17C
		45	7		64	18		46	8
	Apr.	64F	18C	Aug.	81F	27C	Dec.	55F	13C
		46	8		64	18		41	5

Current weather information for more than 750 cities around the world may be obtained by calling **WeatherTrak** information service at 900/370–8728 (cost: 95¢ per minute). A taped message will tell you to dial the three-digit access code for the destination in which you're interested. The code is either the area code (in the United States) or the first three letters of the foreign city. For a list of all access codes, send a stamped, self-addressed envelope to Cities, 9B Terrace Way, Greensboro, NC 27403. For further information, phone 800/247–3282.

Public Holidays January 1, Easter Monday, May 1 (Labor Day), May 8 (VE Day—a new holiday and one not observed as extensively as the others), Ascension Day (five weeks after Easter), the Monday after Pentecost, July 14 (Bastille Day), August 15 (Assumption), November 1 (All Saints), November 11 (Armistice), and Christmas Day. If a public holiday falls on a Tuesday or a Thursday, many businesses and shops and some restaurants close on the Monday or Friday, too.

Festivals and Seasonal Events

Top seasonal events in France include the Monte Carlo Motor Rally in January, February's Carnival in Nice, the Cannes Film Festival in May, Paris's French Open Tennis Championships in May, the Festival du Marais in Paris in July, July's Bastille Day, and the September Autumn Festival in Paris. Contact the French Government Tourist Office for exact dates and further information.

Jan. International Circus Festival, featuring top acts from around the world, is held in Monaco.

Mid- to late Jan. Monte Carlo Motor Rally, one of the motoring world's most venerable races, has its finish line in the streets of Monaco.

Mid- to late Feb. Carnival of Nice provides an exotic blend of parades and revelry during the weeks leading up to Lent.

Late Mar. to early Apr. Prix du President de la République takes place at Auteuil Racecourse in Paris.

Mid- to late Apr. Monte Carlo Open Tennis Championships get under way at the ultraswanky Monte Carlo Country Club.

Apr. to Sept. Sound and Light Shows (son-et-lumière), historical pageants featuring special lighting effects, are held at many châteaus in the Loire Valley.

Mid- to late May. Cannes Film Festival sees two weeks of star-studded events.

Mid-May. International Marathon of Paris leaves from the place de la Concorde and ends at the Château de Vincennes, in Paris's eastern suburb. **Monaco Grand Prix** races through the streets of Monaco.

Late May to mid-June. Lyon International Festival spells three weeks of artistic celebrations, held at various locations in Lyon.

Late May to early June. French Open Tennis Championships get under way at Roland Garros Stadium in Paris.

Mid-June to mid-July. Festival du Marais, including everything from music to dance to theater, is held in Paris. (Tickets: 68 rue François-Miron, 75004 Paris, tel. 48–87–74–31.)

Mid-June. Strasbourg International Music Festival features concerts in various city cathedrals and halls. (Tickets: 24 rue de la Mésange, 67081 Strasbourg, tel. 88–56–04–77.) **Grand Steeplechase de Paris** is a popular horse race at Auteuil Racecourse, Paris.

Late June. Grand Prix de Paris, a major test for equine three-year-olds, gets under way at Longchamp Racecourse.

Early July to early Aug. Festival of Avignon affords almost an entire month of top-notch theater throughout Avignon. (Tickets: Bureau de Festival, 8-bis rue de Mons, 84000 Avignon, tel. 90–82–67–08.)

Mid-July. Grand Parade of Jazz provides nearly two weeks of musical entertainment in Nice.

July 14. Bastille Day, a national holiday commemorated throughout the country, celebrates the Storming of the Bastille in 1789—the start of the French Revolution.

Mid- to late July. Festival of Lyric Art and Music brings nearly three weeks of musical entertainment to Aix-en-Provence. (Tickets: Palais de l'Ancien Archevêché, 13100 Aix-en-Provence, tel. 42–23–11–20.)

Mid-July to late Sept. Festival Estival of Paris hosts classical concerts in churches, museums, and concert halls throughout the city. (Tickets: 20 rue Geoffroy-l'Asnier, 75004 Paris, tel. 48–04–98–01.)

Mid-July to early Aug. International Fireworks Festival features spectacular displays of pyrotechnics in Monaco.

Late July. Tour de France, the world's most famous bicycle race, has its finish line on the Champs-Elysées on the last Sunday in July; all Paris turns out to cheer.

Sept. Music Festival of Besançon and Franche-Comté hosts a series of chamber music concerts in and around Besançon. (Tickets: 2d rue Isenbart, 25000 Besançon, tel. 81–80–73–26.)

Mid-Sept. to Dec. Festival of Autumn is a major arts festival held throughout Paris. (Tickets: 156 rue de Rivoli, 75001 Paris, tel. 42–96–96–94.)

Early Oct. Prix de l'Arc de Triomphe, a venerable annual horse race, is held at Longchamp Racecourse in Paris.

Oct. *Vendanges* (grape harvest) **festivals** are held in the country's wine regions.

Late Nov. Les Trois Glorieuses is Burgundy's biggest wine festival, featuring the year's most important wine auction and related merriment in several Burgundy locations.

Dec. 24 Shepherd's Festival, a Christmas celebration, featuring midnight mass and picturesque "living crèches," is held in Les Baux, Provence.

Late Dec. to early Jan. Christmas in Paris spells celebrations, especially for children, during the school holiday. A giant crèche is set up on the square in front of the Hôtel de Ville (City Hall), and there are automated window displays in the *grands magasins* (department stores) on boulevard Haussmann.

What to Pack

Pack light: Baggage carts are scarce in airports and railroad stations, and luggage restrictions on international flights are tight. (*See* Carry-on Luggage and Checked Luggage, below, for exact specifications.)

Clothing   What you pack depends more on the time of year than on any particular dress code. Northeastern France is hot in the summer and cold in the winter. You'll need a raincoat or an umbrella for Paris anytime of the year and a sweater or warm jacket for the Mediterranean areas during the winter.

For the cities, pack as you would for an American city: cocktail outfits for formal restaurants and nightclubs, casual clothes for sightseeing. Jeans, as popular in France as anywhere else, are acceptable for sightseeing and informal dining. However, a jeans-and-sneakers outfit will cause raised eyebrows at theaters or expensive restaurants or when visiting French families. The rule here is to dress up rather than down. The exception is in young or bohemian circles, where casual dress is always acceptable.

Men and women who wear shorts will probably be denied admission to churches and cathedrals, although there is no longer any need for women to cover their heads and arms. For the beach resorts, pack something to wear over your bathing suit when you leave the beach (wearing bathing suits on the street is frowned upon).

Most casinos and nightclubs along the Riviera require jackets and ties. They are the place for chic cocktail dresses and tuxedos, if you like to dress formally. Casual dresses and slacks outfits are also appropriate.

Miscellaneous You'll need an adapter for hair dryers and other small appliances. The electrical current in France is 220 volts and 50 cycles. If you are staying in budget hotels, take along small bars of soap; many do not provide soap or limit guests to one tiny bar per room.

Carry-on Luggage Airlines generally allow each passenger one piece of carry-on luggage on international flights from the United States. The bag cannot exceed 114.3 centimeters (45 inches)—length + width + height—and must fit under the seat or in the overhead luggage compartment.

Checked Luggage Passengers are generally allowed to check two pieces of luggage, neither of which can exceed 157.5 centimeters (62 inches)—length + width + height—or weigh more than 31.5 kilograms (70 pounds). Baggage allowances vary slightly among airlines, so be sure to check with the carrier or your travel agent before departure.

Taking Money Abroad

Traveler's checks and major U.S. credit cards—particularly Visa, often going under the name of France's domestic equivalent, Carte Bleue—are accepted in the larger towns and tourist areas. In small towns and rural areas, you'll need cash. Even in the larger cities, many small restaurants and shops operate on a cash basis. You won't get as good an exchange rate at home as abroad, but it's wise to change a small amount of money into French francs before you go to avoid long lines at airport currency-exchange booths. Most U.S. banks will change your money into francs. If your local bank can't provide this service, you can exchange money through **Deak International.** To find the office nearest you, contact the headquarters (630 Fifth Ave., New York, NY 10111, tel. 212/635–0515).

For safety and convenience, it's always best to take traveler's checks. The most widely recognized traveler's checks are **American Express, Barclay's, Thomas Cook,** and those issued through major commercial banks such as **Citibank** and **Bank of America.** Some banks will issue the checks free to established customers, but most charge a 1% commission fee. Buy part of the traveler's checks in small denominations to cash toward the end of your trip. It will save you from having to cash a large check and ending up with more francs than you need. You can also buy traveler's checks in francs, a good idea if the dollar is falling and you want to lock in the current rate. Don't forget to take the addresses of offices where you can obtain refunds for lost or stolen traveler's checks.

Getting Money from Home

There are at least three ways to get money from home: (1) Have it sent through a large commercial bank with a branch in the town where you're staying. The only sticking point is that you must have an account with the bank; if you don't, you'll have to go through your bank, and the process will be slower and more expensive. (2) Have it sent through American Express. If you are a cardholder, you may cash a personal check or a counter check at an American Express office for up to $1,000; up to $500 will be in cash and $500 in traveler's checks. There is a 1% commission on the traveler's checks. American Express has a new service, **American Express MoneyGram,** available in France and most major cities worldwide. Through this service, even non-cardholders can receive up to $10,000 in cash. It works this way: You call home and ask someone to go to an American Express office or an American Express MoneyGram agent located in a retail outlet and fill out an American Express MoneyGram (it can be paid for with cash or any major credit card). The person making the payment is given a reference number and telephones you with that number. The American Express MoneyGram agent calls an 800 number and authorizes the transfer of funds to an American Express office or a participating agency in the town where you're staying. In most cases, the money is available immediately on a 24-hour basis. You pick it up by showing identification and giving the reference number that was phoned to you by the person who purchased the American Express MoneyGram. Fees vary according to the amount of money sent. For sending $300, the fee is $30; for $5,000, $195. (For the American Express MoneyGram location nearest your home and for locations overseas, call 800/543–4080.) You do not have to be a cardholder to use this service. (3) Have it sent through **Western Union** (U.S. number: 800/325–6000). If you have a MasterCard or Visa, you can have money sent for any amount up to your credit limit. If not, have someone take cash or a certified cashier's check to a Western Union office. The money will be delivered to a bank in the city where you're staying within two business days. Fees vary with the amount of money sent. For sending $1,000, the fee is $69; for $500, $59.

French Currency

The units of currency in France are the franc (fr.) and the centime. Bills are in denominations of 500, 200, 100, 50, and 20 francs. Coins are 10, 5, 2, and 1 francs, and 50, 20, 10, and 5 centimes. At press time (spring '91), the exchange rate was about 5.20 francs to the U.S. dollar, 4.50 to the Canadian dollar, and 10 to the pound sterling.

What It Will Cost

Inflation in France was low during the late '80s, around 3% annually. Air and car travel in France can be expensive (gas prices are above average and tolls are payable on most highways). Train travel, though, is a good value.

Hotel and restaurant prices compensate for the expense of travel. Prices are above average in Paris, on the Riviera, and in the Alps during the skiing season (worst here in February). But even in these areas, you can find pleasant accommodations and excellent food at moderate prices. Hotel prices in the Loire Valley can be reasonable, but try to book well ahead in summer.

Taxes All taxes must be included in posted prices in France. The initials TTC (toutes taxes comprises—taxes included) sometimes appear on price lists but, strictly speaking, are superfluous. By law, restaurant and hotel prices must include 18.6% taxes and a service charge. If you discover that these have rematerialized as additional items on your bill, kick up a fuss.

Sample Prices The following prices are for Paris; other cities/areas are often cheaper.

Coffee in a bar: 4 francs (standing), 7 francs (seated); beer in a bar: 6 francs (standing), 9 francs (seated); Coca Cola: 6–10 francs a can; ham sandwich: 12–15 francs; one-mile taxi ride: 25–30 francs; movie-theater seat: 35–45 francs (30% cheaper on Monday); foreign newspaper: 8–10 francs.

Passports and Visas

Americans All U.S. citizens are required to have a valid passport for entry into France. Applications for a new passport must be made in person; renewals can be obtained in person or by mail (*see* below). First-time applicants should apply to one of the 13 U.S. Passport Agency offices well in advance of their departure date. In addition, local county courthouses, many state and probate courts, and some post offices accept passport applications. Necessary documents include (1) a completed passport application (Form DSP–11), (2) proof of citizenship (birth certificate with a raised seal or naturalization papers), (3) proof of identity (unexpired driver's license, employee identification card, or any other document with your photograph and signature), (4) two recent, identical, two-inch-square photographs (black and white or color) with a white or off-white background, (5) $42 application fee for a 10-year passport (those under 18 pay $27 for a five-year passport). If you pay cash, you must have exact change; no change is given. Passports are mailed to you in about 10 working days.

To renew your passport by mail, you'll need completed Form DSP–82, two recent, identical passport photographs, a recent passport less than 12 years old from the date of issue, and a check or money order for $35. For further information, contact the Embassy of France, 4101 Reservoir Rd., N.W., Washington, D.C. 20007, tel. 202/944–6000.

U.S. citizens do not need a visa to enter France for a period of 90 days.

Canadians All Canadians are required to have a passport for entry into France. Send a completed application (available at any post office or passport office) to the Bureau of Passports, (Suite 215, West Tower, Guy Favreau Complex, 200 René Lévesque Blvd. W., Montreal, Que. H2Z 1X4). Include $25, two photographs, a guarantor, and proof of Canadian citizenship. Applications may be made in person at the regional passport offices in Edmonton, Halifax, Montreal, Toronto, Vancouver, or Winnipeg. Passports are valid for five years and are nonrenewable.

Visas are not required of Canadian citizens to enter France. Obtain details regarding length of stay from the French Consulate or the French National Tourist Office.

Britons All British citizens need passports, for which applications are available from travel agencies or a main post office. Send the completed form to a regional Passport Office or apply in person at a main post office. You'll need two photographs and will be charged a £15 fee. The occasional tourist might opt for a British Visitors Passport. It is valid for one year, costs £7.50, and is nonrenewable. You'll need two passport photographs and identification. Apply at your local post office.

Visas are not required for British citizens entering France.

Customs and Duties

On Arrival There are two levels of duty-free allowance for travelers entering France: one for those coming from an EC country and the other for those coming from anywhere else.

In the first category, you may import duty-free: 300 cigarettes or 150 cigarillos or 75 cigars or 400 grams of tobacco; five liters of table wine and (1) 1½ liters of alcohol over 22% volume (most spirits), (2) two liters of alcohol under 22% by volume (fortified or sparkling wine), or (3) three more liters of table wine; 90 milliliters of perfume; 375 milliliters of toilet water; and other goods to the value of 2,400 francs (620 francs for those under 15).

In the second category, you may import duty-free: 200 cigarettes or 100 cigarillos or 50 cigars or 250 grams of tobacco (these allowances are doubled if you live outside Europe); two liters of wine and (1) one liter of alcohol over 22% volume (most spirits), (2) two liters of alcohol under 22% volume (fortified or sparkling wine), or (3) two more liters of table wine; 60 milliliters of perfume; 250 milliliters of toilet water; and other goods to the value of 300 francs (150 francs for those under 15).

Any amount of French or foreign currency may be brought into France, but foreign currencies converted into francs may be reconverted into a foreign currency only up to the equivalent of 5,000 francs. Similarly, no more than 5,000 francs may be exported and no more than the equivalent of 2,000 francs in foreign currency may be exported.

On Departure
U.S. Customs U.S. residents who are bringing any foreign-made equipment from home, such as cameras, would be wise to carry the original receipt with them or register it with U.S. Customs before leaving home (Form 4457). Otherwise you may end up paying duty on your return. You may bring home duty-free up to $400 worth of foreign goods, as long as you have been out of the country for at least 48 hours and you haven't made an international trip in 30 days. Each member of the family is entitled to the same exemption, regardless of age, and exemptions may be pooled. For the next $1,000 worth of goods, a flat 10% rate is assessed; above $1,400, duties vary with the merchandise. Included for travelers 21 or older are one liter of alcohol, 100 cigars (non-Cuban), and 200 cigarettes. Only one bottle of

perfume trademarked in the United States may be brought in. However, there is no duty on antiques or art over 100 years old. Anything exceeding these limits will be taxed at the port of entry and may be taxed again in the traveler's home state. Gifts valued at under $50 may be mailed to friends or relatives at home duty-free, but no more than one package per day may be sent to any one addressee and no perfumes costing more than $5, tobacco, or liquor may be mailed.

Canadian Customs Exemptions for returning Canadians range from $20 to $300, depending on length of stay out of the country. For the $300 exemption, you must have been out of the country for one week. For any given year, you are allowed one $300 exemption. You may bring in duty-free up to 50 cigars, 200 cigarettes, 2.2 pounds of tobacco, and 40 ounces of liquor, provided these are declared in writing to customs on arrival and accompany the traveler in hand or in checked-through baggage. Personal gifts should be mailed as "Unsolicited Gift—Value under $40." Request the Canadian Customs brochure *I Declare* for further details.

U.K. Customs British residents have two different allowances: one for goods bought in a duty-free shop in France and the other for goods bought anywhere else in France.

In the first category, you may import duty-free: 200 cigarettes or 100 cigarillos or 50 cigars or 250 grams of tobacco (these allowances are doubled if you live outside Europe); two liters of table wine and (1) one liter of alcohol over 22% by volume (most spirits) or (2) two liters of alcohol under 22% by volume (fortified or sparkling wine) or (3) two more liters of table wine; 60 milliliters of perfume; 250 milliliters of toilet water; and other goods up to a value of £32, but no more than 50 liters of beer or 25 lighters.

In the second category, you may import duty-free: 300 cigarettes or 150 cigarillos or 75 cigars or 400 grams of tobacco; five liters of table wine and (1) 1½ liters of alcohol over 22% volume (most spirits) or (2) three liters of alcohol under 22% by volume (fortified or sparkling wine) or (3) three more liters of table wine; 90 milliliters of perfume; 375 milliliters of toilet water; and other goods to a value of £265, but no more than 50 liters of beer or 25 lighters.

No animals or pets of any kind may be brought into the United Kingdom without a lengthy quarantine. *The penalties are severe and strictly enforced.*

Traveling with Film

If your camera is new, shoot and develop a few rolls of film before leaving home. Pack some lens tissue and an extra battery for your built-in light meter. Invest about $10 in a skylight filter and screw it on the front of your lens. It will protect the lens and reduce haze.

Film doesn't like hot weather. If you're driving in summer, don't store film in the glove compartment or on the shelf under the rear window. Put it behind the front seat on the floor, on the side opposite the exhaust pipe.

On a plane trip, never pack unprocessed film in check-in luggage; if your bags get X-rayed, your pictures will be ruined. Always carry undeveloped film with you through security and ask to have it inspected by hand. (It helps to isolate your film in a plastic bag, ready for quick inspection.) Inspectors at American airports are required by law to honor requests for hand inspection; abroad, you'll have to depend on the kindness of strangers.

The old airport scanning machines—still in use in some Third World countries—use heavy doses of radiation that can turn a family portrait into an early morning fog. The newer models— used in all U.S. airports—are safe for anything from five to 500 scans, depending on the speed of your film. The effects are cumulative; you can put the same roll of film through several scans without worry. After five scans, though, you're asking for trouble.

If your film gets fogged and you want an explanation, send it to the National Association of Photographic Manufacturers (550 Mamaroneck Ave., Harrison, NY 10528). The association will try to determine what went wrong. The service is free.

Language

The French study English for a minimum of four years at school (often longer) but to little general effect. English is widely understood in major tourist areas, however, and, no matter what the area, there should be at least one person in most hotels who can explain things to you if necessary. Be courteous and patient and speak slowly: The French, after all, have plenty of other tourists and are not massively dependent for income on English-speaking visitors. And while it may sound cynical, remember that the French respond quicker to charm than to anything else.

Even if your own French is terrible, try to master a few words: The French are more cooperative when they think you're making at least an effort to speak their language. Basic vocabulary: *s'il vous plaît* (please), *merci* (thanks), *bonjour* (hello—until 6 PM), *bonsoir* (good evening), *au revoir* (goodbye), *comment ça va* (how do you do), *oui* (yes), *non* (no), *peut-être* (maybe), *les toilettes* (toilets), *l'addition* (bill/check), *où* (where), *anglais* (English), *je ne comprends pas* (I don't understand).

Refer to the Traveler's Vocabulary and Menu at the back of the book.

Staying Healthy

There are no serious health risks associated with travel in France. However, the Centers for Disease Control (CDC) in Atlanta cautions that most of southern Europe is in the "intermediate" range for risk of contracting traveler's diarrhea. Part of this risk may be attributed to an increased consumption of olive oil and wine, which can have a laxative effect on stomachs used to a different diet. The CDC also advises all international travelers to swim only in chlorinated swimming pools, unless they are certain the local beaches and freshwater lakes are not contaminated.

If you have a health problem that might require purchasing prescription drugs while in France, have your doctor write a prescription using the drug's generic name. Brand names vary widely from country to country.

The **International Association for Medical Assistance to Travelers (IAMAT)** is a worldwide association that publishes a list of approved English-speaking doctors whose training meets British and American standards. For a list of French physicians and clinics that are part of this network, contact IAMAT (417 Center St., Lewiston, NY 14092, tel: 716/754–4883. **In Canada:** 40 Regal Rd., Guelph, Ontario N1K 1B5. **In Europe:** 57 Voirets, 1212 Grand-Lancy, Geneva, Switzerland. Membership is free).

Shots and Medications Inoculations are not needed to enter France. The American Medical Association recommends Pepto Bismol for minor cases of traveler's diarrhea.

Insurance

Travelers may seek insurance coverage in three areas: health and accident, loss of luggage, and trip cancellation. Your first step is to review your existing health and home-owner policies: Some health insurance plans cover health expenses incurred while traveling, some major medical plans cover emergency transportation, and some home-owner policies cover the theft of luggage.

Health and Accident Several companies offer coverage designed to supplement existing health insurance for travelers:

Carefree Travel Insurance (Box 310, 120 Mineola Blvd., Mineola, NY 11501, tel. 516/294–0220 or 800/343–3553) provides coverage for medical evacuation. It also offers 24-hour medical phone advice.
International SOS Assistance (Box 11568, Philadelphia, PA 19116, tel. 215/244–1500 or 800/523–8930) does not offer medical insurance but provides medical evacuation services to its clients, who are often international corporations.
Travel Guard International, underwritten by Transamerica Occidental Life Companies (1145 Clark St., Stevens Point, WI 54481, tel. 715/345–0505 or 800/782–5151), offers reimbursement for medical expenses with no deductibles or daily limits and emergency evacuation services.
Wallach and Co. Inc. (243 Church St. NW, Suite 100D, Vienna, VA 22180, tel. 703/281–9500 or 800/237–6615) offers comprehensive medical coverage, including emergency evacuation, for trips of 10–90 days.

Trip Cancellation and Luggage The loss of luggage is usually covered as part of a comprehensive travel insurance package that includes personal accident, trip-cancellation, and sometimes default and bankruptcy insurance. Several companies offer comprehensive policies:

Access America Inc., a subsidiary of Blue Cross–Blue Shield (P.O. Box 11188, Richmond, VA 23230, tel. 800/284–8300 or 800/334–7525). **Near Services** (450 Prairie Ave., Suite 101, Calumet City, IL 60409, tel. 708/868–6700 or 800/654–6700). **Travel Guard International** (*see* Health and Accident Insurance, above).

Flight Flight insurance is often included in the price of a ticket when paid for with American Express, Visa, and other major credit and charge cards. It is usually included in combination travel insurance packages that are available from most tour operators, travel agents, and insurance agents.

Renting or Leasing Cars

Renting If you're flying into Paris or some other city in France and are planning to spend time there, save money by arranging to pick up your car in the city the day you depart; otherwise, arrange to pick up and return your car at the airport. You'll have to weigh the added expense of renting a car from a major company with an airport office against the savings on a car from a budget company with offices in town. You could waste precious hours trying to locate the budget company in return for only a small financial savings. If you're arriving and departing from different airports, look for a one-way car rental with no return fees. If you're traveling to more than one country, make sure your rental contract permits you to take the car across borders and that the insurance policy covers you in every country you visit. Be prepared to pay more for cars with automatic transmissions. Since they are not as readily available as those with manual transmissions, reserve them well in advance.

Rental rates vary widely, depending on the size and model, the number of days you use the car, insurance coverage, and whether special drop-off fees are imposed. In many cases, rates quoted include unlimited free mileage and standard liability protection. Not included are Collision Damage Waiver (CDW), which eliminates your deductible payment if you have an accident, personal accident insurance, gasoline, and European Value-Added Taxes (VAT). The VAT on car rentals in France is among the highest in Europe.

Driver's licenses issued in the United States and Canada are valid in France. You may also take out an International Driving Permit before you leave to smooth out difficulties if you have an accident or as an additional piece of identification. Permits are available for a small fee through local offices of the **American Automobile Association** (AAA) and the **Canadian Automobile Association** (CAA), or from their main offices (AAA, 1000 AAA Dr., Heathrow, FL 32746–0001, tel. 800/336–4357; CAA, 2 Carlton St., Toronto, Ontario M5B 1K4, tel. 416/964–3170).

It's best to arrange a car rental before you leave. You won't save money by waiting until you arrive in France, and you may find that the type of car you want is not available at the last minute. Rental companies usually charge according to the exchange rate of the dollar at the time the car is returned or when the credit-card payment is processed. Three companies with special programs to help you hedge against the falling dollar, by guaranteeing advertised rates if you pay in advance, are **Budget Rent-a-Car** (3350 Boyington St., Carrollton, TX 75006, tel. 800/527–0700), **Connex Travel International** (983 Main St. Peekskill, NY 10566, tel. 800/333–3949), and **Cortell International,** 17310 Red Hill Ave., Suite 360, Irvine, CA 92714, tel. 800/228–2535). Other budget rental companies serving Europe include **Europe by Car** (1 Rockefeller Plaza, New York, NY 10020, tel. 212/245–1713, 800/223–1516, in 800/252–9401), **Auto Europe** (Box 1097 Sharps Wharf, Camden, ME 04843, tel. 800/223–5555, in Maine 800/342–5202, in Canada 800/237–2465), **Foremost Euro-Car** (5430 Van Nuys Blvd., Van Nuys, CA 91404, tel. 800/423–3111), and **Kemwel** (106 Calvert St. Harrison, NY 10528, tel. 800/678–0678). Others with European rentals include **Avis** (tel. 800/331–1212), **Hertz** (tel. 800/223–6472, in New York 800/654–3001), and **National** or **Europcar** (tel. 800/ CAR–RENT).

Leasing For trips of 21 days or more, you may save money by leasing a car. With the leasing arrangement, you are technically buying a car and then selling it back to the manufacturer after you've used it. You receive a factory-new car, tax-free, with international registration and extensive insurance coverage. Rates vary with the make and model of the car and the length of time it is used. Car-leasing programs in France are offered by Renault, Citroën, and Peugeot. Delivery is free to downtown Paris and to the airports in Paris. There is a small fee for deliveries to other parts of France. Before you go, compare long-term rental rates with leasing rates. Remember to add taxes and insurance costs to the car rentals, something you don't have to worry about with leasing. Companies that offer leasing arrangements include **Kemwel, Europe by Car,** and **Auto Europe,** all listed above.

Rail Passes

The **French Flexipass** (formerly the **France-Vacances Rail Pass**) is a good value for those who plan to do a lot of their traveling by train. The Flexipass allows you to stagger your train travel time instead of having to use it all at once. For example, the four-day pass ($179 in first class, $119 in second) may be used on any four days within a 15-day period. Similarly, the nine-day pass ($309 in first class, $209 in second) may be used on any nine days within one month.

You must buy the French Flexipass before you leave for France. It is obtainable through travel agents or through **Rail Europe** (610 Fifth Ave., New York, NY 10020, tel. 800/345–1990).

The **EurailPass,** valid for unlimited first-class train travel through 17 countries, including France, is an excellent value if you plan to travel around the Continent.

The ticket is available for periods of 15 days ($390), 21 days ($498), one month ($616), two months ($840), and three months ($1,042). For two or more people traveling together, a 15-day rail pass costs $298. Between April 1 and September 30, you need a minimum of three in your group to get this discount. For those younger than 26 years old, there is the **Eurail Youthpass,** for one or two months of unlimited second-class train travel at $425 and $560. The **BritFrance Rail Pass** allows you to travel for any five of 15 days in France and Britain (including Channel crossing by Hovercraft) for $199 (second class) or $269 (first class), or for any 10 days in a 30-day period ($299/$399). You can obtain the pass from travel agencies or Rail Europe.

For travelers who like to spread out their train journeys, there is the **Eurail Flexipass.** With the 15-day Flexipass ($230), travelers get 5 days of unlimited first-class train travel but can spread that travel out over 15 days; a 21-day pass gives you 9 days of travel ($398), and a one-month pass gives you 14 days ($498).

The EurailPass is available only if you live outside Europe or North Africa. The pass must be bought from an authorized agent before you leave for Europe. Apply through your travel agent or through **Rail Europe** (address above).

Student and Youth Travel

The **International Student Identity Card (ISIC)** entitles students to youth rail passes, special fares on local transportation, Intra-European Student Charter flights, and discounts at museums, theaters, sports events, and many other attractions. If the ISIC is purchased in the **United States,** its $14 cost also includes $3,000 in emergency medical insurance, plus $100 a day for up to 60 days of hospital coverage. Apply to the **Council on International Educational Exchange** (CIEE) (205 E. 42nd St., 16th floor, New York, NY 10017, tel. 212/661–1414). **In Canada,** the ISIC is available for CN $12 from **Travel Cuts** (187 College St., Toronto, Ont. M5T 1P7, tel. 416/979–2406).

The **Youth International Educational Exchange Card** (YIEE), issued by the Federation of International Youth Travel Organizations (FIYTO, 81 Islands Brugge, DK-2300 Copenhagen S, Denmark), provides similar services to nonstudents under age 26. **In the United States,** the card is available from CIEE (address above) or from ISE (Europa House, 802 W. Oregon St., Urbana, IL 61801, tel. 217/344–5863). **In Canada,** the YIEE is available from the Canadian Hostelling Association (CHA) (1600 James Naismith Dr., Suite 608, Gloucester, Ont. K1B 5N4, tel. 613/748–5638).

An **International Youth Hostel Federation** (IYHF) membership card is the key to inexpensive dormitory-style accommodations at thousands of youth hostels around the world. Hostels provide separate sleeping quarters for men and women at rates ranging from $7 to $20 a night per person, and are situated in a variety of facilities, including converted farmhouses, villas, and restored castles, as well as specially constructed modern buildings. There are more than 5,000 hostel locations in 68 countries around the world. IYHF memberships, which are valid for 12 months from the time of purchase, are available in the United States through **American Youth Hostels** (AYH, Box 37613, Washington, DC 20013, tel. 202/783–6161). The cost for a first-year membership is $25 for adults ages 18 to 54. Renewal thereafter is $15. For youths (under 18) and senior citizens (55 and older), the rate is $15. Family membership is available for $35. Every national hostel association arranges special reductions for members visiting their country, such as discounted rail fare or free bus travel, so be sure to ask for an international discounts list when you buy your membership.

Economical **bicycle tours** for small groups of adventurous, energetic students are another popular AYH student travel service. For information on these and other AYH services and publications, contact AYH at the address listed above.

Council Travel, a CIEE subsidiary, is the foremost U.S. student travel agency, specializing in low-cost charters and serving as the exclusive U.S. agent for many student airfare bargains and student tours. CIEE's 80-page *Student Travel Catalog* and *Council Charter* brochure are available free from any Council Travel office in the United States (enclose $1 for postage if ordering by mail). In addition to CIEE headquarters (205 E. 42nd St., New York, NY 10017) and a branch office (35 W. 8th St. in New York, NY 10009), there are Council Travel offices in Berkeley, La Jolla, Long Beach, Los Angeles, San Diego, and San Francisco, CA; Chicago, IL; Amherst, Boston, and Cambridge, MA; Portland, OR; Providence, RI; Austin and Dallas, TX; and Seattle, WA, among other cities.

The **Educational Travel Center,** another student travel specialist worth contacting for information on student tours, bargain fares, and bookings, may be reached at 438 N. Frances St., Madison, WI 53703, tel. 608/256–5551.

Students who would like to work abroad should contact **CIEE's Work Abroad Department** (205 E. 42nd St., New York, NY 10017, tel. 212/661–1414, ext. 1130). The council arranges various types of paid and voluntary work experiences overseas for up to six months. CIEE also sponsors study programs in Europe and publishes many books of interest to the student traveler. These books include *Work, Study, Travel Abroad: The Whole World Handbook* ($10.95 plus $1 book-rate postage or $2.50 first-class postage); or *Volunteer! The Comprehensive Guide to Voluntary Service in the U.S. and Abroad* ($6.95 plus $1 book-rate postage or $2.50 first-class postage).

The Information Center at the **Institute of International Education** (IIE) has reference books, foreign university catalogues, study-abroad brochures, and other materials that may be consulted by students and nonstudents alike free of charge. The Information Center (809 UN Plaza, New York, NY 10017, tel. 212/984–5413) is open from 10 AM to 4 PM weekdays and until 7 PM Wednesday evenings. It is not open on weekends or holidays.

IIE administers a variety of grant and study programs offered by U.S. and foreign organizations, and publishes a well-known annual series of study-abroad guides, including *Academic Year Abroad, Vacation Study Abroad,* and *Study in the United Kingdom and Ireland.* The institute also publishes *Teaching Abroad,* a book of employment and study opportunities overseas for U.S. teachers. For a current list of IIE publications with prices and ordering information, write to Publications Service, Institute of International Education (809 UN Plaza, New York, NY 10017). Books must be purchased by mail or in person; telephone orders are not accepted.

General information on IIE's programs and services is available from its regional offices in Atlanta, Chicago, Denver, Houston, San Francisco, and Washington, DC.

For information on the **Eurail Youthpass,** *see* Rail Passes, above.

Traveling with Children

Publications   *Family Travel Times* is an 8–12-page newsletter published 10 times a year by **TWYCH** (Travel with Your Children, 80 8th Ave., New York, NY 10011, tel. 212/206–0688). Subscription includes access to back issues and twice-weekly opportunities to call in for specific advice.

Family Travel Organizations   **American Institute for Foreign Study** (AIFS, 102 Greenwich Ave., Greenwich, CT 06830, tel. 203/869–9090) offers family vacation programs in France for high school- and college-aged students as well as interested adults. Programs for high school students are handled by **Educational Travel Division, American**

Council for International Studies (19 Bay State Rd., Boston, MA 02215, tel. 617/236–2015 or 800/825–AIFS). For information on programs for college students, contact AIFS (102 Greenwich Ave., Greenwich, CT 06830, tel. 203/869–9090).

Families Welcome! (Box 16398, Chapel Hill, NC 27516, tel. 800/326–0724) is a travel agency that arranges French tours brimming with family-sensitive choices and activities. Two other travel arrangers that understand families' needs (and can even set up short-term rentals) are **Paris Accueil** (231 Spruce St., New Windsor, NY 12550, tel. 914/565–6951) and **The French Experience** (370 Lexington Ave., New York, NY 10017, tel. 212/986–3800).

Hotels
The **Novotel** hotel chain allows up to two children under 15 to stay free in their parents' room. Many Novotel properties have playgrounds. (For international reservations call 800/221–4542). **Sofitel** hotels offer a free second room for children during July and August, and over the Christmas holidays. (For international reservations call 800/221–4542.) **Club Med** (40 W. 57th St., New York, NY 10019, tel. 800/CLUB–MED) has a "Baby Club" (from age four months) at its resort in Chamonix; "Mini Clubs" (for ages four to six or eight, depending on the resort), and "Kids Clubs" (for ages eight and up during school holidays) at all its resort villages in France except in Val d'Isere. In general, supervised activities are scheduled all day long. Some clubs are only French-speaking, so check first.

Villa Rentals
At Home Abroad, Inc., 405 E. 56th St., Suite 6H, New York, NY 10022, tel. 212/421–9165. **Villas International,** 71 W. 23rd St., New York, NY 10010, tel. 212/929–7585 or 800/221–2260. **Hideaways, Int'l.,** Box 1270, Littleton, MA 01460, tel. 508/486–8955. **B. & D. de Vogue,** 1830 S. Mooney Blvd. 113, Visalia, CA 93277, tel. 209/733–7119 or 800/727–4748. **Vacances en Campagne,** Box 297, Falls Village, CT 06031, tel. 203/824–5155 or 800/553–5405.

Home Exchange
Exchanging homes is a surprisingly low-cost way to enjoy a vacation abroad, especially a long one. The largest home-exchange service, **International Home Exchange Service** (Box 190070, San Francisco, CA 94119, tel. 415/435–3497) publishes three directories a year. Membership costs $45 and entitles you to one listing and all three directories. **Loan-a-Home** (2 Park La., Apt. 6E Mount Vernon, NY 10552, tel. 914/664–7640) is popular with the academic community on sabbatical and with businesspeople on temporary assignments. Although there's no annual membership fee or charge for listing your home, one directory and a supplement cost $35.

Getting There
On international flights, children under two not occupying a seat pay 10% of the adult fare. Various discounts apply to children 2 to 12 years of age. Regulations about infant travel on airplanes are in the process of changing. Until they do, however, if you want to be sure your infant is secure and traveling in his or her own safety seat, you must buy a separate ticket and bring your own infant car seat. (Check with the airline in advance; certain seats aren't allowed.) Some airlines allow babies to travel in their own car seats at no charge if there's a spare seat available, otherwise safety seats are stored and the child has to be held by a parent. (For the booklet *Child/Infant Safety Seats Acceptable for Use in Aircraft*, write to the Federal Aviation Administration, APA-200, 800 Independence Ave. SW, Wash-

ington, DC 20591, tel. 202/267–3479.) If you opt to hold your baby on your lap, do so with the infant outside the seat belt so he or she doesn't get crushed in case of a sudden stop.

Also inquire about special children's meals or snacks. The February 1990 and 1992 issues of *Family Travel Times* include *TWYCH's Airline Guide,* which contains a rundown of the children's services offered by 46 airlines.

Getting Around The **French National Railways** (SNCF) accommodates family travel by allowing children under four to travel free (provided they don't occupy a seat) and by allowing children four to 11 to travel at half fare. There is also the *Carte Kiwi,* costing 360 francs, which allows children under 16 and up to four accompanying adults to travel at half fare.

Baby-sitting Services First check with the hotel concierge for recommended childcare arrangements. Paris agencies: **American University of Paris** (31 av. Bosquet, 75007 Paris, tel. 45–55–91–73); **Baby Sitting Express** (157 rue de Bercy, 75012 Paris, tel. 43–43–35–55); **Allo Service Maman** (21 rue de Brey, 75017 Paris, tel. 42–67–99–37); **Home Service** (5 rue Yvon-Villarceau, 75116 Paris, tel. 45–00–82–51); **Institut Catholique** (21 rue d'Assas, 75006 Paris, tel. 45–48–31–70).

Miscellaneous Contact the **CIDJ** (Centre d'Information et de Documentation pour la Jeunesse, 101 quai Branly, 75015 Paris, tel. 45–67–35–85) for information about activities and events for youngsters in France.

Hints for Disabled Travelers

In France Facilities for the handicapped in France are better than average. The French government is doing much to ensure that public facilities provide for disabled visitors, and it has produced an excellent booklet—*Tourists Quand Même*—with an English glossary and easily understood symbols detailing, region by region, facilities available to the disabled in transportation systems and museums and monuments. The booklet is available from French national tourist offices and from the main Paris Tourist Office, or from the **Comité National Français de Liaison pour la Réadaptation des Handicapés** (38 blvd. Raspail, 75007 Paris, tel. 45–48–90–13).

A number of monuments, hotels, and museums—especially those constructed within the past decade—are equipped with ramps, elevators, or special toilet facilities. Lists of regional hotels include a symbol to indicate which hotels have rooms that are accessible to the disabled. Similarly, the SNCF has special cars on some trains that have been reserved exclusively for the handicapped and can arrange for wheelchair-bound passengers to be escorted on and off trains and assisted in catching connecting trains (the latter service must be requested in advance).

A helpful organization in Paris is the **Association des Paralysés de France** (17 blvd. Auguste-Blanqui, 75013 Paris, tel. 45–80–82–40), which publishes a useful hotel list.

Free baby-sitting for physically and mentally handicapped children is provided by the **Fondation Claude Pompidou** (42 rue du Louvre, 75001 Paris, tel. 45–08–45–15; phone between 2 and 6). Services are available at all times.

In the U.S. Tours that are especially designed for handicapped travelers generally parallel those for nonhandicapped travelers, albeit at a more leisurely pace. For a complete list of tour operators who arrange such travel, write to the **Society for the Advancement of Travel for the Handicapped** (26 Court St., Penthouse, Brooklyn, NY 11242, tel. 718/858–5483). Annual membership costs $45, or $25 for senior citizens and students. Send a stamped, self-addressed envelope.

Moss Rehabilitation Hospital (1200 W. Tabor Rd., Philadelphia, PA 19141–3009, tel. 215/456–9600; TDD 215/456–9603) answers inquiries regarding specific cities and countries and provides toll-free telephone numbers for airlines with special lines for the hard of hearing and, again, listings of selected tour operators.

The **Information Center for Individuals with Disabilities** (Fort Point Pl., 1st floor, 27–43 Wormwood St., Boston, MA 02210, tel. 617/727–5540; TDD 617/727–5236) offers useful problem-solving assistance, including lists of travel agents that specialize in tours for the disabled.

Mobility International USA (Box 3551, Eugene, OR 97403, tel. 503/343–1284) has information on accommodations, organized study, and so forth around the world.

The Itinerary (Box 2012, Bayonne, NJ 07002, tel. 201/858–3400) is a bimonthly travel magazine for the disabled. *Access to the World: A Travel Guide for the Handicapped* by Louise Weiss offers tips on travel and accessibility around the world. It is available from Henry Holt & Co. for $12.95 (tel. 800/247–3912; the order number is 0805001417).

Hints for Older Travelers

The **American Association of Retired Persons** (AARP, 1909 K St. NW, Washington, DC 20049, tel. 202/662–4850) has two programs for independent travelers: (1) *The Purchase Privilege Program,* which offers discounts on hotels, airfare, car rentals, and sightseeing, and (2) the *AARP Motoring Plan,* provided by Amoco, which offers emergency aid and trip-routing information for an annual fee of $33.95 per couple. The AARP can also arrange group tours, including apartment living in Europe. AARP members must be 50 or older. Annual dues are $5 per person or per couple.

When using an AARP or other identification card, ask for a reduced hotel rate at the time you make your reservation, not when you check out. At participating restaurants, show your card to the maitre d' before you're seated since discounts may be limited to certain set menus, days, or hours. When renting a car, be sure to ask about special promotional rates that might offer greater savings than the available discount.

Elderhostel (75 Federal St., 3rd floor, Boston, MA 02210, tel. 617/426–7788) is an innovative educational program for people 60 and older. Participants live in dorms on some 1,200 campuses around the world. Mornings are devoted to lectures and seminars; afternoons to sightseeing and field trips. All-inclusive fees for two- to three-week trips, including room, board, tuition, and round-trip transportation, range from $1,800 to $4,500.

Travel Industry and Disabled Exchange (TIDE, 5435 Donna Ave., Tarzana, CA 91356, tel. 818/368–5648) is an industry-based organization with a $15 per person annual membership fee. Members receive a quarterly newsletter and information on travel agencies and tours.

National Council of Senior Citizens (925 15th St. NW, Washington, DC 20005, tel. 202/347–8800) is a nonprofit advocacy group with some 5,000 local clubs across the country. Annual membership is $12 per person or per couple. Members receive a monthly newspaper with travel information and an identification card for reduced-rate hotels and car rentals.

Mature Outlook (6001 N. Clark St., Chicago, IL 60660, tel. 800/336–6330), a subsidiary of Sears Roebuck & Co., is a travel club for people over 50, offering hotel and motel discounts and a bimonthly newsletter. Annual membership is $9.95 per couple. Instant membership is available at participating Holiday Inns.

In France Senior citizens (men over 62 and women over 60) enjoy reduced museum admission (usually 50%) and cheap train tickets (the **Carte Vermeil,** available at stations throughout France; the Carte Vermeil costs 139 francs a year and entitles the holder to discounts of up to 50%, depending on when you travel). Senior citizens should keep their passport or an identification card with them at all times.

Further Reading

An erudite, perceptive, and witty survey of France and its people is Theodore Zeldin's *The French* (Pantheon); Joseph T. Carroll's *The French—How They Live and Work* (David & Charles) is in a similar vein. A summary of recent social, political, and economic developments is provided by John Ardagh's *France Today* (Penguin).

Nancy Mitford's *The Sun King* (Crown) is a readable approach to the regal grandeur of the 17th century, while Alfred Cobban's *History of Modern France* (Pelican) provides workmanlike coverage of trends and events from the death of Louis XIV up to 1962. If you prefer your history in a fictional setting, pick up Victoria Holt's fictional memoir of Marie Antoinette, *The Queen's Confession* (Doubleday).

Books about French wine are numerous, but Steven Spurrier's pocket-size *French Country Wines* (Putnam) is unusual in its thorough treatment of lesser-known (and often good-value) wines. Architecture buffs should read Henri Focillon's *The Art of the West* (Cornell U. Press) for a thoughtfully illustrated, scholarly exposé of Romanesque and Gothic architecture.

Charles Dickens, in a *Tale of Two Cities* (Bantam), and Ernest Hemingway, notably in *A Moveable Feast* (Scribner's), are just two authors who have written about Paris in English. One author whose descriptive powers and latterday relevance seldom disappoint is Emile Zola. His novels are situated mostly in Provence or in Paris—by and large the Paris we know today, emerging from mid-19th-century reconstruction amid backstreet squalor and brash glamour, all tellingly depicted in such works as *La Curée, L'Assommoir,* and *Nana* (Penguin).

Historian and archaeologist Dorothy Carrington has written the well-documented *Granite Island: A Portrait of Corsica,* which gives a thoughtful insight into the islanders' archaic beliefs, infamous vendettas, and complicated internal politics.

Several good thrillers set in France include the following: *Assignment in Brittany* (Fawcett), by Helen MacInnes; Pierre

Salinger's *The Dossier* (Doubleday); Philip Loraine's *Death Wishes* (St. Martin); and *Most Secret* (Amereon) by Nevil Shute.

Arriving and Departing

As the air routes between North America and France are among the world's most heavily traveled, passengers have many airlines and fares to choose from. But fares change with stunning rapidity, so consult your travel agent on which bargains are currently available.

From the U.S. by Plane

Be certain to distinguish among (1) nonstop flights—no changes, no stops; (2) direct flights—no changes but one or more stops; and (3) connecting flights—two or more planes, one or more stops.

Airports and Airlines The U.S. airlines that serve France are **TWA** (tel. 800/892–4141), **American Airlines** (tel. 800/433–7300), **Delta** (tel. 800/241–4141), and **Pan Am** (tel. 800/221–1111). All fly to Paris's Charles de Gaulle (Roissy) Airport (tel. 48–62–22–80) and Orly (tel. 49–75–52–52). Pan Am also flies to Nice.

Flying Time to Paris From New York: 7½ hours. From Chicago: 9 hours. From Los Angeles: 11 hours.

Discount Flights The major airlines offer a range of tickets that can increase the price of any given seat by more than 300%, depending on the day of purchase. As a rule, the further in advance you buy the ticket, the less expensive it is and the greater the penalty (up to 100%) for canceling. Check with the airlines for details.

The best buy is not necessarily an APEX (advance-purchase) ticket on one of the major airlines. APEX tickets carry certain restrictions: They must be bought in advance (usually 21 days); they restrict your travel, usually with a minimum stay of seven days and a maximum of 90; and they penalize you for changes— voluntary or not—in your travel plans. But if you can work around these drawbacks (and most travelers can), they are among the best-value fares available.

Charter flights offer the lowest fares but often depart only on certain days, and seldom on time. Though you may be able to arrive at one city and return from another, you may lose all or most of your money if you cancel your ticket. Don't sign up for a charter flight unless you've checked with a travel agent about the reputation of the packager. It's particularly important to know the packager's policy concerning refunds if a flight is canceled. One of the most popular charter operators is **Council Charter** (tel. 212/661–0311 or 800/223–7402), a division of **CIEE** (Council on International Educational Exchange). Other companies advertise in Sunday travel sections of newspapers.

Somewhat more expensive—but up to 50% below the cost of APEX fares—are tickets purchased through companies, known as consolidators, that buy blocks of tickets on scheduled airlines and sell them at wholesale prices. Here again, you may lose all or most of your money if you change your plans, but at least you will be on a regularly scheduled flight with less risk of cancellation than a charter. Once you've made your reservation, call the airline to make sure you're confirmed. Among the best-known consolidators are **UniTravel** (Box 12485, St. Louis, MO 63132, tel. 314/569–2501 or 800/325–2222) and **Access International** (101 W. 31st St., Suite 1104, New York, NY 10001, tel. 212/465–0707 or 800/825–3633). Others advertise in the Sunday travel sections of newspapers as well.

Yet another option is to join a travel club that offers special discounts to its members. Three such organizations are **Moment's Notice** (425 Madison Ave., New York, NY 10017, tel. 212/486–0503); **Discount Travel International** (Suite 205, 114 Forrest Ave., Narberth, PA 19072, tel. 215/668–7184); and **Worldwide Discount Travel Club** (1674 Meridian Ave., Miami Beach, FL 33139, tel. 305/534–2082). These cut-rate tickets should be compared with APEX tickets on the major airlines.

Enjoying the Flight If you're lucky enough to be able to sleep on a plane, it makes sense to fly at night. Many experienced travelers, however, prefer to take a morning flight to Europe and arrive in the evening, just in time for a good night's sleep. Since the air on a plane is dry, it helps, while flying, to drink a lot of nonalcoholic liquids; drinking alcohol contributes to jet lag, as does eating heavy meals on board. Feet swell at high altitudes, so it's a good idea to remove your shoes while in flight. Sleepers usually prefer window seats to curl up against; those who like to move about the cabin should ask for aisle seats. Bulkhead seats (located in the front row of each cabin) have more legroom, but seat trays are attached to the arms of your seat rather than to the back of the seat in front. Bulkhead seats are generally reserved for the elderly, the disabled, or parents traveling with babies.

Smoking Smoking is banned on all scheduled routes within the 48 contiguous states; within the states of Hawaii and Alaska; to and from the U.S. Virgin Islands and Puerto Rico; and on flights of under six hours to and from Hawaii and Alaska. The rule applies to the domestic legs of all foreign routes but does not affect international flights.

On a flight where smoking is permitted, you may request a nonsmoking seat during check-in or when you book your ticket. If the airline tells you there are no seats available in the nonsmoking section on the day of the flight, insist on one: Department of Transportation regulations require that U.S. carriers find seats for all nonsmokers, provided they meet check-in time restrictions. Avoiding smoke can be a serious problem on non-U.S. carriers.

From the U.S. by Ship

The *Queen Elizabeth 2 (QE2)* is the only ocean liner that makes regular transatlantic crossings. However, the *Vistafjord* of the Cunard Line sails between Fort Lauderdale, Florida, and Marseille, France, in repositioning crossings. These crossings occur when cruise ships are taken to or from North America and Europe as one season ends and another begins. Some sail straight across, often at reduced rates to passengers. Others stop at several ports of call before heading to open sea. Arrangements can be made to cruise one way and fly one way. Because itineraries can change at the last minute, check with the cruise lines for the latest information.

Cunard Line (555 Fifth Ave., New York, NY 10017, tel. 800/221–4770, in New York 212/880–7545) operates four ships, including the *QE2* and *Vistafjord*. The *QE2* makes regular crossings from April through December, between Baltimore, Boston, and New York City and Southampton, England. Arrangements for the *QE2* can include one-way airfare. The *Sea Goddess I* and *Sea Goddess II* sail to and from Madeira, Portugal, and St. Thomas, the U.S. Virgin Islands, for their repositioning crossings. Cunard Line offers fly/cruise packages and pre- and postland packages. For the European cruise season, ports of call include Southhampton; Madeira; Marseille; Hamburg, Germany; Genoa, Rome, Venice, and Naples, Italy; Monte Carlo, Monaco; Malaga, Spain; Piraeus (Athens), Greece; Copenhagen, Denmark; and Stockholm, Sweden. Ports of call vary with the ship.

Royal Viking Line (750 Battery St., San Francisco, CA 94111, tel. 800/634–8000) has three ships that cruise out of European ports. Two of the ships make repositioning crossings between Fort Lauderdale, Florida, and Lisbon, Portugal. Fly/cruise packages are available. Major ports of call, depending on the ship, are Copenhagen, Denmark; Stockholm, Sweden; Bergen, Norway; Hamburg, Germany; Leningrad, USSR; Barcelona, Spain; Venice, Italy; Dubrovnik, Yugoslavia; Villefranche, France; Corfu, Greece; and Lisbon, Portugal.

American Star Lines (660 Madison Ave., New York, NY 10021, tel. 800/356–7677, in New York 212/644–7900) makes transatlantic crossings in spring and fall to and from Greece and Barbados, British West Indies. The crossings are regular cruises, with ports of call in Portugal, Italy, Turkey, and the Greek Islands. Summer cruises are from Piraeus (Athens), Greece, to the Greek Islands and Turkey. Fly/cruise packages are available.

Check the travel pages of your Sunday newspaper for other cruise ships that sail to Europe.

From the·U.K. by Plane, Car, Train, and Bus

By Plane Some of the airlines operating between the United Kingdom and France are **Air France** (tel. 081/759–2311), **British Airways** (tel. 081/897–4000), and **Caledonian Airways** (tel. 0293/36321), the charter division of British Airways.

The route from London to Paris (journey time: one hour) is the busiest in Europe, with up to 17 flights daily from Heathrow (Air France/British Airways) and four or five from Gatwick (Air France), all to Charles de Gaulle (also known as Roissy). There are also regular flights—geared mainly to businesspeople—from the new London City Airport in the Docklands; direct flights to Paris from several regional U.K. airports, including Manchester, Birmingham, Glasgow, Edinburgh, and Southampton; and flights from London to Nice, Lyon, Bordeaux, Marseille, Clermont-Ferrand, Caen, Quimper, Nantes, Montpellier, and Toulouse, as well as from Manchester to Nice. Remember, though, flying to France is often absurdly expensive. Charter flights (contact **Nouvelles Frontières**, 1–2 Hanover St., London W1R 9WB, tel. 071/629–7772), including Caledonian Airways' service between Gatwick and Beauvais, north of Paris, offer the best value.

By Car There is no shortage of Channel crossings from England to France; all boats (and Hovercraft) welcome motor vehicles. The quickest and most frequent routes are between Dover/Folkestone and Calais/Boulogne: Sealink and P & O run about 16 daily services in summer and at least 10 in winter. The Dover-Calais journey time is 75 minutes.

Each of the other routes has geographic advantages to offset its comparative slowness. Ramsgate-Dunkirk (Sally Line: 2½ hours) offers excellent restaurant and duty-free facilities, plus minimum fuss at port terminals; Newhaven-Dieppe (Sealink: 4½ hours) lands you in pretty Normandy; Portsmouth-Caen/St-Malo (Brittany Ferries: six hours) can take you either to Brittany (St-Malo) or within striking distance of Paris (Caen); while Portsmouth-Le Havre/Cherbourg (P & O: six hours), Plymouth-Roscoff (Brittany Ferries: eight hours), and Poole/Weymouth-Cherbourg (Brittany Ferries: eight hours) all cater to drivers from Wales and southwestern England.

The Ramsgate-Dunkirk service operates several times daily, the rest at least once a day (Weymouth-Cherbourg summer only). The Hoverspeed crossings between Dover and Boulogne/Calais take just over half an hour but are suspended during heavy winds and, therefore, unreliable in winter. Whichever route you choose, it is advisable to book ahead. Prices and time-tables vary according to season, time of day, and length of stay, so contact the relevant ferry operator for details: **Sealink** (tel. 0233/647047), **Sally Line** (tel. 0843/595566), **Brittany Ferries** (tel. 0705/827701), **P & O** (tel. 0171/734–4431), and **Hoverspeed** (tel. 0304/240241).

Beginning in 1993 cars will be able to reach France through the Channel Tunnel, aboard special double-decker trains that will shuttle between Folkestone and Sangatte every 15 minutes.

By Train Until the Channel Tunnel is opened in 1993 (journey time will be slashed to 3½ hours), traveling by train from London to Paris and other French cities means hassle—in the form of purposeless waiting, lengthy lines, and a pervading air of either dilapidation (British Rail) or indifference (French officialdom). If there are no unforeseen delays, the journeys from London to Paris via Dover or Folkestone take around seven hours. The trip via Newhaven-Dieppe—offering the cheapest prices to those aged under 26—takes nine hours. Check train/ferry prices with Sealink/British Rail, as there are numerous variations, depending on the time, season, crossing, and length of travel. The faster and more convenient Hovercraft service via Dover-Boulogne takes under six hours, but remember that Hovercraft are more affected by high winds and are relatively expensive (around £46 each way, although five-day mini-vacations are a good value at just around £60). There are also good-value five-day trips to such destinations as Lyon, Avignon, and Cannes. For more information contact Sealink or British Rail.

Paris is the hub of the French train system and a change, both of train and station, is often necessary if your destination lies farther afield. There are, however, direct trains from London to Strasbourg, Lyon, the Alps, the Riviera, and the Pyrenees.

By Bus If you prefer bus to train travel, a London-to-Paris bus journey can be a rewarding experience (and costs only a little over £40 round-trip). **Eurolines** (tel. 071/730–0202), the international affiliate of **National Express,** runs four daily *Citysprint* buses in summer from Victoria Coach Station to the rue Lafayette in Paris near the Gare du Nord; these buses use the Hovercraft crossing, and the journey time is around 7½ hours. Three daily buses from Victoria to the Porte de la Villette on the outskirts of Paris use traditional ferries for the Channel crossing and take a bit longer (9 to 10 hours).

Eurolines has buses to the Riviera, leaving Victoria three times a week for such resorts as Nice and Cannes. The round-trip fare to Cannes is £99. The Atlantic coast is also served by Eurolines, with two buses a week to Bordeaux and Biarritz in mid-summer (journey time 24 hours; price approximately £92 round-trip); the Bordeaux service can be extended to Lourdes via Tarbes. There is also regular service from London to Chamonix and the Alps (22½ hours; around £85 round-trip).

In addition, Eurolines (tel. 071/730–0202) operates an express service that runs overnight to Grenoble, where there are connecting services to Nice and Marseille (return trip to Nice costs around £99), as well as a fast bus service to Lyon six days a week in summer, leaving London mid-evening and reaching Lyon the following afternoon (around £75 round-trip).

Staying in France

Getting Around France

By Plane France's domestic airline service is called **Air Inter,** with flights from Paris to all major cities and many interregional flights. For long journeys—from Paris to the Riviera, for instance—air travel is a time saver, though train travel is always much cheaper. Most domestic flights from Paris leave from **Orly Airport** (tel. 49–75–15–15). For details, check with the local airport or call Air Inter (tel. 45–39–25–25).

By Train The SNCF is generally recognized as Europe's best national train service: It's fast, punctual, comfortable, and comprehensive. The high-speed TGVs, or *Train à Grande Vitesse* (average 255 kph/160 mph on the Lyon/southeast line, 300 kph/190 mph on the Bordeaux/southwest line), are the best domestic trains, operating between Paris and Lyon/Switzerland/the Riviera, and Angers/Nantes and Tours/Poitiers/Bordeaux. As with other mainline trains, you may need to pay a small supplement when taking a TGV at peak hours. Unlike other trains, the TGV *always* requires a seat reservation—easily obtained at the ticket window or from an automatic machine. Seat reservations are reassuring but seldom necessary on other mainline French trains, except at certain busy holiday times.

If you are traveling from Paris (or any other station terminus), get to the station half an hour before departure to ensure yourself a good seat. The majority of intercity trains in France consist of open-plan cars and are known as *Corail* trains. They are clean and extremely comfortable, even in second class. Trains on regional branch lines are currently being spruced up but lag behind in style and quality. Food in French trains can be good, but is poor value for the money.

It is possible to get from one end of France to the other without resorting to overnight train travel. Otherwise you have the choice between high-priced *wagons-lits* (sleeping cars) and affordable (around 75 francs) *couchettes* (bunks), six to a compartment (sheet and pillow provided). Special summer night trains from Paris to Spain and the Riviera, geared to younger people, are equipped with disco and bar to enable you to dance and talk the night away.

Fares Various reduced fares are available. Senior citizens (over 60) and young people (under 26) are eligible for the **Carte Vermeil** (139 francs) and **Carré/Carte Jeune** (165 francs) respectively, with proof of identity and two passport photos. The SNCF offers 50% reductions during "blue" periods (most of the time) and 20% the rest of the time ("white" periods: noon Friday through noon Saturday; 3 PM Sunday through noon Monday). On major holidays ("red" periods), there are no reductions. A calendar of red/white/blue periods is available at any station, and you can buy tickets at any station, too. Note that there is no reduction for buying a round-trip *(aller-retour)* ticket rather than a one-way *(aller simple)* ticket.

By Bus France's excellent train service means that long-distance buses are rare; regional buses, too, are found mainly where the train service is skimpy. Excursions and bus holidays are organized by the SNCF and other tourist organizations, such as **Horizons Européens.** Ask for the brochure at any major travel agent, or contact **France-Tourisme** (3 rue d'Alger, 75001 Paris, tel. 42–61–85–50).

By Car Roads marked A *(Autoroutes)* are expressways. There are ex-
Road Conditions cellent links between Paris and most French cities, but poor ones between the provinces (principal exceptions: the A62 between Bordeaux and Toulouse; and the A9/A8 that runs the length of the Mediterranean). It is often difficult to avoid Paris when crossing France; this need not cause too many problems if you steer clear of the rush hours (7–9:30 AM and 4:30–7:30 PM). Most expressways require you to pay a toll *(péage);* the rates vary and can be steep. The N *(Route Nationale)* roads and D *(Route Départementale)* roads are usually wide, unencumbered, and fast (you can average 80 kph/50 mph with luck). The cheap, informative, and well-presented regional yellow Michelin maps are an invaluable navigational aid.

Rules of the Road You may use your home driver's license in France but must be able to prove you have third-party insurance. Drive on the right. Be aware of the erratically followed French tradition of giving way to drivers coming from the right, unless there is an international stop sign. Seat belts are obligatory, and children under 12 may not travel in the front seat. Speed limits: 130 kph (81 mph) on expressways; 110 kph (68 mph) on major highways; 90 kph (56 mph) on minor rural roads; 50 kph (31 mph) in towns. French drivers break these limits and police dish out hefty on-the-spot fines with equal abandon.

Parking Parking is a nightmare in Paris and often difficult in large towns. Meters and ticket-machines (pay and display) are commonplace (be sure to have a supply of 1-franc coins). In smaller towns, parking may be permitted on one side of the street only, alternating every two weeks: Pay attention to signs. The French park as anarchically as they drive, but don't follow their example: If you're caught out of bounds, you could be due for a hefty fine and your vehicle may be unceremoniously towed away to the dreaded compound (500 francs to retrieve it).

Gas Gas is more expensive on expressways and in rural areas. Don't let your tank get too low (if you're unlucky, you can go for many miles in the country without hitting a gas station) and keep an eye on pump prices as you go. These vary enormously: anything between 4.80 and 6 francs/liter. At the pumps, opt for "super" (high-grade/4-star) rather than "essence" (low-grade/2-star).

Breakdowns If you break down on an expressway, go to the nearest roadside emergency telephone and call the breakdown service. If you break down anywhere else, find the nearest garage or, failing all else, contact the police (dial 17).

By Boat France has Europe's densest inland waterway system, and canal and river vacation trips are popular. You can take an all-inclusive organized cruise or simply rent a boat and plan your own leisurely route. Contact a travel agent for details or ask for a *Tourisme Fluvial* brochure in any French tourist office. Some of the most picturesque stretches are found in Brittany, Burgundy, and the Midi. The Canal du Midi between Toulouse and Sète, constructed in the 17th century, is a historic marvel. Request further information from French national tourist offices, or try **France-Anjou Navigation** (Quai National, 72300 Sablé-sur-Sarthe) or **Bourgogne Voies Navigables** (1 quai de la République, 89000 Auxerre).

By Bicycle There is no shortage of wide, empty roads and flat or rolling countryside in France suitable for biking. The French themselves are great bicycling enthusiasts. Bikes can be hired from many train stations (ask for a list at any station) for around 30 francs a day; you need to show your passport and leave a deposit of around 200 francs (unless you have Visa or Mastercard). You must usually return the bike to a station within the same *département* (county or region). Bikes may be sent as accompanied luggage from any station in France; some trains in rural areas transport them without any extra charge.

Telephones

Local Calls The French telephone system is modern and efficient. Telephone booths are plentiful; you will nearly always find them at post offices and often in cafés. A local call costs 73 centimes for the first minute plus 12 centimes per additional minute; half-price rates apply weekdays between 9:30 PM and 8 AM, from 1:30 PM Saturday, and all day Sunday.

Pay phones work principally with 50-centime, 1- and 5-franc coins (1 franc minimum). Lift the receiver, place the coin or coins in the appropriate slots, and dial. Unused coins are returned when you hang up. A vast number of French pay phones are now operated by cards *(télécartes)*, which you can buy from post offices and some tobacco shops, or *tabacs* (cost: 40 francs for 50 units; 96 francs for 120).

All French phone numbers have eight digits; a code is required only when calling the Paris region from the provinces (add 16–1 for Paris) and for calling the provinces from Paris (16 then the number). The number system was changed only in 1985; therefore, you may still come across some seven-digit numbers (in Paris) and some six-digit ones (elsewhere). Add 4 to the beginning of such Paris numbers, and the former two-figure area code to provincial ones.

International Calls	Dial 19 and wait for the tone, then dial the country code (1 for the United States and Canada; 44 for the United Kingdom), area code (minus any initial 0) and number.

Approximate daytime rate, per minute: 9.50 francs for the United States and Canada; 4.50 francs for the United Kingdom. Reduced rates, per minute: United States and Canada, 5.75 francs (2–noon daily) or 7.25 francs (noon–2 PM and 8 PM–2 AM weekdays, noon–2 AM Sunday); U.K., 3 francs (9:30 PM–8 AM/2 AM–8 PM Saturday/all-day Sunday and holidays).

Operators and Information	To find a number in France or to request other information, dial 12. For international inquiries, dial 19–33 plus the country code.

Mail

Postal Rates	Airmail letters to the United States and Canada cost 3.80 francs for 20 grams, 6.40 francs for 30 grams, 6.70 francs for 40 grams, and 7.00 francs for 50 grams. Letters to the United Kingdom cost 2.30 francs for up to 20 grams. Letters cost 2.30 francs within France; postcards cost 2.10 francs within France and if sent to Canada, the United States, the United Kingdom, and Common Market countries; 3.50 francs if sent airmail to North America. Stamps can be bought in post offices and cafés sporting a red TABAC sign outside.

Receiving Mail	If you're uncertain where you'll be staying, have mail sent to **American Express** (tel. 800/543–4080 for a list of foreign offices) or to the local post office, addressed as **Poste Restante**. American Express has a $2 service charge per letter.

Tipping

The French have a clear idea of when they should be tipped. Bills in bars and restaurants include service, but it is customary to leave some small change unless you're dissatisfied. The amount of this varies: 30 centimes if you've merely bought a beer or a few francs after a meal. Tip taxi drivers and hairdressers about 10%. Give ushers in theaters and movie theaters 1 or 2 francs. In some theaters and hotels, coat check attendants may expect nothing (if there is a sign saying *Pourboire Interdit*—Tips Forbidden); otherwise give them 5 francs. Washroom attendants usually get 5 francs, though the sum is often posted.

If you stay in a hotel for more than two or three days, it is customary to leave something for the chambermaid—about 10 francs per day. In expensive hotels you may well call on the services of a baggage porter (bell boy) and hotel porter and possibly the telephone receptionist. All expect a tip: Plan on about 10 francs per item for the baggage boy, but the other tips will depend on how much you've used their services—common sense must guide you here. In hotels that provide room service, give 5 francs to the waiter (this does not apply to breakfast served in your room). If the chambermaid does some pressing or laundering for you, give her 5 francs on top of the charge made.

Gas-station attendants get nothing for gas or oil, and 5 or 10 francs for checking tires. Train and airport porters get a fixed sum (6–10 francs) per bag, but you're better off getting your own baggage cart if you can (a 10-franc coin—refundable—is sometimes necessary). Museum guides should get 5–10 francs after a guided tour, and it is standard practice to tip tour guides (and bus drivers) 10 francs or more after an excursion, depending on its length.

Opening and Closing Times

Banks Banks are open weekdays but have no strict pattern regarding times. In general, though, hours are from 9:30 to 4:30. Most banks, but not all, take a one-hour, or even a 90-minute, lunch break.

Museums Most museums are closed one day a week (usually Tuesday) and on national holidays. Usual opening times are from 9:30 to 5 or 6. Many museums close for lunch (noon–2); many are open afternoons only on Sunday.

Shops Large stores in big towns are open from 9 or 9:30 until 6 or 7 (without a lunch break). Smaller shops often open earlier (8 AM) and close later (8 PM) but take a lengthy lunch break (1–4). This siesta-type schedule is routine in the south of France. Corner groceries, often run by immigrants (*"l'Arabe du coin"*), frequently stay open until around 10 PM.

Shopping

If you ask any Frenchman to identify a region by product, he'd probably think first in alcoholic terms—of such local wines and brandies as cognac, armagnac, calvados, and marc (brandy made from grape skins). Food would be next on the list: foie gras in the southwest, mussels and oysters on the Channel and Atlantic coasts, olives and herbs in Provence, sausages and sauerkraut in Alsace, and nougat in Montélimar. Most regions have their own cheeses.

As for clothes, Paris is the firm fashion capital. Traditional regional strongholds (Lille for textiles, Calais for lace) have little clout these days, though good clothes can be bought everywhere and are invariably cheaper outside Paris (*see* Shopping in individual chapters for details).

VAT Refunds A number of shops, particularly large stores and shops in holiday resorts, offer VAT refunds to foreign shoppers. You are entitled to an Export Discount of 20–30%, depending on the item purchased, often only applicable if your purchases in the same store reach a minimum 2,800 francs (for U.K. and Common Market residents) or 1,200 francs (other residents, including U.S. and Canadian).

Bargaining Shop prices are clearly marked and bargaining isn't a way of life. Still, at outdoor markets and flea markets and in antique stores, you can try your luck. If you're thinking of buying several items, you've nothing to lose by cheerfully suggesting to the storeholder, *"Vous me faites un prix?"* ("How about a discount?").

Sports and Fitness

France has no shortage of sports facilities. Many seaside resorts are well equipped for **water sports,** such as windsurfing and waterskiing, and there are swimming pools in every French town. In winter, the Alps and (somewhat cheaper) the

Pyrénées and Vosges boast excellent **skiing** facilities—both for downhill (*ski alpin*) and cross-country (*ski de fond*).

Biking (*see* Getting Around by Bicycle in Staying in France, above) is a popular pastime and, like horseback riding (*equitation*), possible in many rural areas. The many rivers of France offer excellent **fishing** (check locally for authorization rights), and **canoeing** is popular in many areas. **Tennis** is phenomenally popular in France, and courts are everywhere: Try for a typical *terre battue* (clay) court if you can. **Golf** and **squash** have caught on recently; you may be able to find a course or a court not too far away. The French are not so keen on **jogging**, but you'll have no difficulty locating a suitable local park or avenue.

The sport that is closest to French hearts is ***boules*** or ***pétanque***—an easy-to-grasp version of bowling, traditionally played beneath plane trees with a glass of *pastis* (similar to anisette) at hand. The local *boulodrome* is a social focal point in southern France.

Beaches

It is ironic that France's most famous coastline should possess the country's worst beaches. But there it is: Sand is in shorter supply along the Riviera than pebbles. There are sandy beaches, of course, but they are seldom large or particularly clean, as the Mediterranean behaves like a large lake, with minimal tide to wash away the litter.

By far the best French beaches are those facing north (toward the Channel) and west (toward the Atlantic). Many are so vast that you can spread out even at the most popular resorts (like Biarritz, Royan, Dinard, or Le Touquet). The most picturesque beaches are those of Brittany; the Brétons, the most seafaring of French people, will provide a hearty and well-equipped welcome to sailing enthusiasts.

Best bets for family vacations include the coast west of Bordeaux around Arcachon (good choice of accommodations and amusements), and the northern coast between Calais and Le Touquet (for a more invigorating climate and tranquil beachcombing). The larger resorts are invariably equipped with landlubbing sports facilities like golf, tennis, and horseback riding; Le Touquet is unbeatable for this.

Dining

Eating in France is serious business. This is two-big-meals-a-day country, with good restaurants around every corner. If you prefer to eat lighter, you can try a *brasserie* for rapid, straightforward fare (steak and french fries remains the classic), a picnic (a *baguette* loaf with ham, cheese, or pâté makes a perfect combination), or one of the fast-food joints that have mushroomed in cities and towns over recent years. Snack possibilities—from pastry shops (*patisseries*) to pancake/roast chestnut streetsellers—are legion.

French breakfasts are relatively skimpy: good coffee, fruit juice if you request it, and croissants. You can "breakfast" in cafés as well as hotels. If you're in the mood for bacon and eggs, however, you're in trouble.

Mealtimes   Dinner is the main meal and usually begins at 8 PM. Lunch—starting at 12:30 or 1—can be as copious as you care to make it.

Precautions   Tap water is safe, though not always appetizing (least of all in Paris). Mineral water—there is a vast choice of both still (*eau plate*) and fizzy (*eau gazeuse*)—is a palatable alternative. Perhaps the biggest eating problem in France is saying no: If you're invited to a French family's home, you will be encouraged, if not expected, to take two or three servings of everything offered.

Ratings   Highly recommended restaurants are indicated by a star ★.

Category	Cost*: Major City	Cost*: Other Areas
Very Expensive	over 450 francs	over 350 francs
Expensive	250–450 francs	200–350 francs
Moderate	150–250 francs	100–200 francs
Inexpensive	under 150 francs	under 100 francs

per person for a three-course meal, including tax (18.6%) and tip but not wine

Lodging

France has a wide range of accommodations, ranging from rambling old village inns that cost next to nothing to stylish converted châteaus that cost the earth. Prices must, by law, be posted at the hotel entrance and should include taxes and service. Prices are always by room, not per person (ask for a *grand lit* if you want a double bed). Breakfast is not always included in this price, but you are usually expected to have it and are often charged for it regardless. In smaller rural hotels you may be expected to have your evening meal at the hotel, too.

Hotels   Hotels are officially classified from one-star up to four-star/deluxe. France is not dominated by big hotel chains; examples in the upper price bracket include **Frantel, Holiday Inn, Novotel,** and **Sofitel.** The **Ibis** and **Climat de France** chains are more moderately priced; the new **Formula 1** chain provides basic comfort for up to three persons per room for 120 francs a night. Chain hotels, as a rule, lack atmosphere, with the following exceptions: **Logis de France** has small, inexpensive hotels that can be relied on for minimum standards of comfort, character, and regional cuisine. Look out for the distinctive yellow-and-green signs. The Logis de France paperback guide is widely available in bookshops (cost: around 50 francs) or from Logis de France, 83 av. d'Italie, 75013 Paris. **France-Accueil** is another friendly low-cost chain (free booklet from France-Accueil, 85 rue Dessous-des-Berges, 75013 Paris). You can stay in style at any of the 150 members of the prestigious **Relais et Châteaux** chain of converted châteaus and manor houses. Each hotel is distinctively furnished, provides top cuisine, and often stands in spacious grounds. A booklet listing members is available in bookshops or from Relais et Châteaux (9 av. Marceau, 75016 Paris).

Self-catering   Best bets are the **Gîtes Ruraux,** which offer a family or group the possibility of a low-cost, self-catering vacation in a furnished cottage, chalet, or apartment in the country; rentals are by the week or month. For details contact either the **Maison des Gîtes de France** (35 rue Godot de Mauroy, 75009 Paris), naming which region interests you, or the **French Government Tourist Office** in London (178 Piccadilly, W1V OAL, tel. 01/491-7622), which runs a special reservation service.

Bed and Breakfast B&Bs, known in France as *Chambres d'Hôte*, are becoming increasingly popular, especially in rural areas. Check local tourist offices for details.

Youth Hostels Given that cheap hotel accommodations in France are so easy to find, there is scarcely any economic reason for staying in a youth hostel, especially since standards in France don't come up to those in neighboring countries. If you enjoy a hostel ambience, however, you may care to note the address of the French headquarters (**Fédération Unie des Auberges de Jeunesse,** 10 rue Notre-Dame-de-Lorette, 75009 Paris).

Villas The French Government Tourist Offices in New York and London publish extensive lists of agencies specializing in villa rentals. You may also write to **Rent-a-Villa Ltd.** (3 W. 51st St., New York, NY 10019) or, in France, **Interhome** (15 av. Jean-Aicard, 75011 Paris).

Camping French campsites have a high reputation for organization and amenities but tend to be jam-packed in July and August. More and more campsites now welcome advance reservations; if you're traveling in summer, it makes good sense to book ahead. A guide to the country's campsites is published by the **Fédération Française de Camping et de Caravaning** (78 rue de Rivoli, 75004 Paris).

Ratings Highly recommended hotels are indicated by a star ★.

Category	Cost*: Major City	Cost*: Other Areas
Very Expensive	over 1,000 francs	over 750 francs
Expensive	500–1,000 francs	350–750 francs
Moderate	250–500 francs	200–350 francs
Inexpensive	under 250 francs	under 200 francs

All prices are for a standard double room for two, including tax (18.6%) and service charge.

Credit Cards

The following credit card abbreviations are used: AE, American Express; DC, Diners Club; MC, MasterCard; and V, Visa.

Great Itineraries

Great Gothic Cathedrals

Medieval cathedrals are among France's most precious heritage, and some of the best ones are conveniently close to Paris. After paying homage to Notre-Dame, venture into the dowdy northern suburb of **St-Denis,** where the kings of France are buried in a cathedral-size basilica with a nave and the earliest Gothic choir (1140s). Head north along A1 to **Senlis,** with its slender spire, then on to **Noyon,** whose muscular bulk attests to the pervading influence of the Romanesque style that preceded Gothic. Check out the ruined facade of the abbey of St-Jean des Vignes at **Soissons** after visiting its cathedral, then head to **Laon** and admire its many-towered silhouette and dynamic facade.

The kings of France were crowned at **Reims** Cathedral, where the facade is richly sculpted. Late Gothic is on display at the cathedral in nearby **Châlons-sur-Marne,** where the old church of Notre-Dame-en-Vaux and the flamboyant basilica of Notre-Dame de l'Epine, 10 kilometers (6 miles) east, also deserve scrutiny. There are several churches of note at **Troyes;** both the cathedral and St-Urbain contain improbable vistas of stained glass. The journey south from Champagne into Burgundy leads to **Sens,** one of France's oldest cathedrals and the home of the country's leading archbishop. A trip cross-country to **Chartres** is rewarded by spires and glass of unparalleled splendor. A taste for intricate late-medieval embellishment becomes apparent as you continue north into Normandy, at the cathedral of **Evreux,** then at St-Maclou in **Rouen**—whose cathedral and St-Ouen abbey (perhaps France's finest 14th-century building) contain much to admire. The 13th-century cathedral of **Beauvais** is the highest in France—but its nave was never built! **Amiens,** its neighbor and contemporary, is almost as high and counts as the largest completed French Gothic cathedral.

Length of Trip 8 days.

Getting Around
By Car Cars can be rented in Paris. A car is essential to follow this itinerary.

By Train There are trains from Paris to virtually all the cathedral towns on this itinerary, but there are few cross-country services (Rouen/Amiens/Laon/Reims/Châlons).

The Main Route **Two nights: Paris.** Visit Notre-Dame and the Basilica St-Denis, then head north to Senlis and Noyon.

One night: Laon. Explore the cathedrals of Laon, Soissons, and Reims.

One night: Châlons-sur-Marne. See the Châlons cathedral and the church of Notre-Dame-en-Vaux. Visit L'Epine.

One night: Troyes. See Troyes cathedral and the town's several churches. Make an excursion to Sens.

One night: Chartres. Visit Chartres cathedral, then head north to Rouen via Evreux.

One night: Rouen. Explore Rouen cathedral, the Abbaye St-Ouen, and the church of St-Maclou.

One night: Beauvais. See Beauvais and Amiens cathedrals.

Information *See* chapters on the Ile de France, Champagne and the North, and Normandy.

Burgundy

Burgundy is one of France's best-known wine-making regions. While the opportunity to try some of the world's most celebrated wines is a major drawing card, visitors will also enjoy the region's irresistible combination of rolling hills, picturesque towns, impressive churches, and outstanding restaurants.

The cathedral town of **Sens** is the gateway to Burgundy as you approach from Paris. The attractive Yonne Valley leads south toward Auxerre, although a short detour to the austere old abbey of **Pontigny** is recommended. Old, pretty **Auxerre** captures the unhurried flavor of Burgundian life that will be strongly apparent as you continue along the Yonne to sleepy **Clamecy,** a hilltop market town with narrow streets and many small shops. A few miles east is the Romanesque basilica of **Vézelay,** one of Europe's leading early-medieval buildings. The tiny surrounding village remains unspoiled by invading tourist crowds; so does the lush patchwork of meadowland that can be surveyed from the basilica's hilltop site. There are more fine views from the ramparts at neighboring **Avallon,** where you veer south toward ancient **Saulieu** in the heart of the lake-spangled Morvan Forest.

Away to the east is **Dijon,** Burgundy's capital and the opulent home of the once-mighty grand dukes (their palace now houses an exceptional art museum) and several superb restaurants. The 40-kilometer (25-mile) stretch south toward **Beaune** contains the most prestigious parts of the Burgundy vineyards. Some of its exorbitantly priced wines can be sampled cheaply in historic Beaune, a stylish town whose multicolored tile roofs are a regional landmark. Keep going south to **Tournus,** another quaint town on the banks of the Saone, before heading inland to **Cluny**—once the most powerful church in the world and now a motley assemblage of imposing ruins nestling alongside an undisturbed, centuries-old village. Continue south into the **Beaujolais** region—renowned for its fruity young wine—and end your trip in **Lyon,** a large commercial city that retains much charm in the form of restored medieval areas and numerous fine restaurants and museums.

Length of Trip 5–8 days.

Getting Around Sens is 110 kilometers (70 miles) southeast of Paris via A6/N6.
By Car The rural charms of Burgundy can be appreciated only by car.

By Train Sens, Auxerre, Clamecy, Beaune, and Tournus can be reached by a regular (if sluggish) train service. The superfast TGV reaches Dijon within 90 minutes from Paris, and Lyon (430 kilometers/270 miles away) within just two hours.

The Main Route **One to two nights: Auxerre.** See Sens and the Abbey of Pontigny.

One night: Vézelay. Visit the basilica. Make excursions to Clamecy, Avallon, and the Morvan Forest.

One to two nights: Dijon. Visit the city's museums, churches, and restaurants. Take the wine road south.

One night: Beaune. Sample some wines at the Marché aux Vins. Drive to Cluny. Explore the hills and vineyards of Beaujolais on the way to Lyon.

One to two nights: Lyon. Eat and drink well, and visit the museums and medieval town.

Information *See* chapters on Burgundy, Lyon, and the Alps.

Châteaus of the Loire Valley

The Loire Valley provides a fascinating three-dimensional overview of French history, thanks to the hundreds of châteaus that dot its wooded terrain. A cathedral and museum make Orléans an interesting place from which to start your tour, but the first châteaus you encounter are farther west, at **Beaugency** and **Chambord**—the largest of all the Loire châteaus and surrounded by an extensive forest. Nearby **Cheverny** was one of the last Loire châteaus to be built, as its formal neoclassicism testifies. The attractive town of **Blois** has churches and narrow streets, as well as a château that was built over several periods. **Chaumont** and **Amboise** both offer terrific views across the Loire and, at Amboise, you may visit the Clos-Lucé and its display of models based on designs by Leonardo da Vinci (who died here in 1519). **Chenonceau,** built across the River Cher, has an unforgettable setting.

Tours is the principal city of the Loire Valley, and despite heavy bombing in 1944, it retains its picturesque old quarter and superb cathedral. It makes a sensible base for exploring such nearby châteaus as **Villandry** (with its formal Renaissance gardens and tree-lined avenues), fortresslike **Langeais,** romantic **Azay-le-Rideau,** and Ussé (said to have inspired Perrault's fairy tale *Sleeping Beauty*). **Chinon** is, or was, an authentic castle; its ruined walls tower high above a delightful town. A medieval abbey at **Fontevraud** and a famous riding school at **Saumur** (home of another opulent château) add variety to the tour. **Angers** has a castle and two fine museums—one with the colossal, vividly colored 14th-century *Apocalypse* tapestry, the other showcasing the sculpture of 19th-century local David d'Angers.

Length of Trip 6–8 days.

Getting Around
By Car Orléans is a 90-minute drive (120 kilometers/75 miles) south of Paris via A10. Picturesque roads run along both banks of the Loire.

By Train A respectable train service runs down the valley from Orléans to Angers, stopping at Blois, Amboise, Tours, and Saumur. Combining train travel with local bus excursions makes it possible to visit many of the sites covered in this itinerary.

The Main Route **One to two nights: Orléans.** See the cathedral. Stop at Beaugency. Explore Chambord.

Two to three nights: Blois. Stop off at Chaumont and Cheverny. Visit Amboise and Chenonceau on the way to Tours.

Two nights: Tours. Make excursions to Villandry, Langeais, Azay-le-Rideau, and Ussé.

One night: Saumur. Tour Chinon and the abbey at Fontevraud. Visit Angers.

Information *See* chapter on the Loire Valley.

The Vineyards of the Southwest

This tour will appeal to anyone who enjoys fine wines and brandies. Not only will you get to see the towns and vineyards that produce your favorites, but you'll also have ample opportunity to buy them on the spot. The pretty harbor of **La Rochelle** is a good place to start your trip—and a reminder of the crucial role ships played in establishing the international demand for these local wines and brandies. **Rochefort,** built as a naval base by Sun King Louis XIV, is worth a quick visit before you head southeast along the charming banks of the River Charente to **Saintes,** with old churches and Roman remains. As you carry on east toward **Cognac,** vines become ever more common—although grapes from as far afield as La Rochelle can be used in making cognac brandy. The towns of Cognac and drowsy **Jarnac** (a few miles upstream) are home to most of the leading cognac firms; a visit to Hennessy, Martell, Otard, Hine, or Courvoisier should be a priority. The graceful, chalky hills south of Cognac yield the region's top brandy.

Farther southeast are the wine-producing vineyards of Bordeaux. One of the most famous names—**St-Emilion**—is also a beautifully preserved town with ramparts and tumbling streets. **Bordeaux** itself is just an hour away. This elegant city oozes wine-induced affluence and makes a pleasant base for exploring the neighboring vineyards: dusty **Médoc** to the north, which produces the country's best claret; **Graves** to the west, home of both red and white wines; verdant **Entre-Deux-Mers** to the southeast, with its crisp white wines; and the rolling hills of **Sauternes** to the south, whose sweet white wines (notably those of Château d'Yquem, which you can visit) can fetch astronomical prices. Some 80 kilometers (50 miles) south of Sauternes, around the quaintly named towns of **Eauze, Auch, Condom,** and **Vic-Fezensac,** lies the region that produces Armagnac brandy. Family producers (not big firms) hold sway here.

Length of Trip 5–6 days.

Getting Around La Rochelle lies 512 kilometers (320 miles) southwest of Paris
By Car via A10/N11.

By Train It is possible to visit only the larger towns by train (La Rochelle, Rochefort, Saintes, Cognac, Bordeaux).

The Main Route **One night: La Rochelle.** Drive the pretty river road (D124/D114) from Rochefort to Saintes.

One to two nights: Cognac. Visit firms in Cognac and Jarnac and see the surrounding vineyards. Explore St-Emilion.

Two nights: Bordeaux. Visit the vineyards surrounding Médoc, Graves, Sauternes, and Entre-Deux-Mers.

One night: Condom. Explore the surrounding Armagnac vineyards.

Information *See* chapters on the Atlantic Coast, Toulouse, and the Midi-Pyrénées.

The Lot Valley

The Lot River valley is one of the country's most dramatically scenic areas, meandering through steep gray-rock escarpments and beneath promontories topped by medieval villages. Start your trip at **Cahors,** once an opulent Gallo-Roman town and later, in the Middle Ages, Europe's leading banking center. Today it is famous for its excellent red wines. You could easily while away a weekend here, wandering the picturesque little streets leading off rue Nationale and rue de l'Université, where Jacques Dueze, better known as Pope John XXII, founded the university in 1332. From Cahors, take N20 north until it meets D677, a prettier road, to **Gramac** and **Rocamadour.** Avoid visiting Rocamadour in July or August, when crowds of tourists outnumber the thousands of pilgrims who used to make this one of their main stops on their trek from Conques to Santiago de Compostela in Spain. The medieval town seems to defy the laws of gravity as it surges out of the cliffs overlooking the narrow gorge of the River Alzou. Risk sore muscles to climb the stair carved into the cliffs. Your reward: Place St-Amadour, with its bevy of churches (seven in all). The area around Rocamadour is riddled with underground caves and grottoes. One of the best-known, the **Gouffre de Padirac,** is just 16 kilometers (10 miles) north of town.

N140 leads southeast from Rocamadour to **Figeac,** a charming old market town built around a 9th-century abbey. Many houses here date from the 14th, 15th, and 16th centuries, and have preserved their strange octagonal chimneys, ground-floor archways, and *soleilho* (open attics), used for drying flowers (or laundry) and for stocking wood. From Figeac, head west along D662, which winds along the River Lot back to Cahors. Stop off at **St-Cirq-Lapopie,** perched atop the steep escarpment opposite an arc of high, white cliffs. Despite numerous sieges, the village has survived almost intact and is now a picturesque center for arts and crafts; it also offers a couple of fine hotels and restaurants.

Length of Trip 3–5 days.

Getting Around *By Car* The Lot Valley is almost impossible to see without a car. Cahors lies 590 kilometers (350 miles) south of Paris.

By Train Cahors, Rocamadour, and Figeac are accessible by train. For Rocamadour, take the train from Figeac.

The Main Route **One to two nights: Cahors.** Explore the town, visiting the 14th-century fort, Cathédrale St-Étienne, and the Pont Valentré, a fine medieval bridge. Fit in a wine tasting.

One to two nights: Rocamadour. Visit the Musée Roland-le-Preaux. Climb the 200-step staircase to place St-Amadour. Explore the surrounding countryside. See the towering peak of Gouffre de Padirac.

One night: Figeac. Wander the narrow streets to admire the picturesque buildings. Take in the Saturday-morning market. Visit St-Cirq-Lapopie.

Information *See* Toulouse and the Midi-Pyrénées.

The West Coast of Corsica

Thousands of visitors flock to Corsica's western coast, where the island's long sandy beaches and wild terrain act as a rejuvenating tonic. Start your tour at **Calvi,** one of Corsica's most popular resorts, on the island's northwest tip. Spend the day lounging under an umbrella pine on the 4-mile stretch of white-sand beaches; the early evening wandering around the Genoese citadel on its promontory overlooking the bay; and the evening and most of the night at Chez Tao, a well-known nightclub.

From Calvi, take D51 south past the little villages of Balagne, scattered in the foothills of the mountains leading up to the Monte Cinto, Corsica's highest peak. The road takes you through the island's national park, lined with forests and Corsica's famous *maquis* undergrowth. (The coast road [D81] is a bit longer and just as pretty.) The road (now joined with D81) winds its way to **Porto** and climbs to the Col de Palmarella and

Col de la Croix passes—both offering stupendous maritime views. Porto itself is little more than an artificial village, built so tourists can enjoy the superb setting created by its fjord-shaped bay and steep, jagged cliffs.

The main attraction of your trip lies just a couple of miles up the road from Porto: the Calanche, a natural rock formation hewn into extraordinary shapes that conjure up magical men and monsters. The road then cuts across the rocky peninsula down to **Cargese:** Its two churches—one Latin, one Greek—glare at each other across the village. D81 then runs the length of the coast to **Ajaccio,** the island's capital and the birthplace of the most famous Corsican—Napoleon Bonaparte.

From Ajaccio, take D55, which climbs through the Forest of Chiavari past **Filitosa** and around the Golfe de Valinco. Stop off in Sartène, where a medieval town lies hidden behind the modern-day ramparts created by a wall of six-story houses. The 55-kilometer (35-mile) run down to **Bonifacio,** on the island's southern tip, is an easy drive on the picturesque N196—especially when you compare it with Corsica's usually tortuous roads.

Length of Trip	5–7 days.
Getting Around *By Car*	A rented car is the only possible means of visiting Corsica's western coast.
The Main Route	**One to two nights: Calvi.** Relax on the beach and explore the cliffs. Visit the citadel. Spend an evening at Chez Tao.
	One night: Porto or Piana. See the Calanche at sunset. Take a morning swim in the Golfe de Porto.
	One to two nights: Ajaccio. Visit Napoleon's birthplace and the Musée Fesch. Drive to Sartene.
	Two nights: Bonifacio. Explore the old town and citadel. Take a boat trip around the cliff caves.
Information	*See* Corsica.

2 Portraits of France

France at a Glance: A Chronology

c 3500 BC Megalithic stone complexes erected at Carnac, Brittany

c 1500 BC Lascaux cave paintings executed (Dordogne, southwest France)

c 600 BC Greek colonists found Marseille

after 500 BC Celts appear in France

58–51 BC Julius Caesar conquers Gaul; writes up the war in *De Bello Gallico*

52 BC Lutetia, later to become Paris, is built by the Gallo-Romans

46 BC Roman amphitheater built at Arles

14 BC The Pont du Gard, the aqueduct at Nîmes, is erected

AD 212 Roman citizenship conferred on all free inhabitants of Gaul

406 Invasion by the Vandals (Germanic tribes)

451 Attila invades, and is defeated at Châlons

The Merovingian Dynasty

486–511 Clovis, king of the Franks (481–511), defeats the Roman governor of Gaul and founds the Merovingian Dynasty. Great monasteries, such as those at Tours, Limoges, and Chartres, become centers of culture

497 Franks converted to Christianity

567 The Frankish kingdom is divided into three parts—the eastern countries (Austrasia), later to become Belgium and Germany; the western countries (Neustria), later to become France; and Burgundy

732 Arab expansion checked at the Battle of Poitiers

The Carolingian Dynasty

768–778 Charlemagne (768–814) becomes king of the Franks (768); conquers northern Italy (774); and is defeated by the Moors at Roncesvalles in Spain, after which he consolidates the Pyrénées border (778)

c 782 Carolingian renaissance in art, architecture, and education

800 The pope crowns Charlemagne Holy Roman Emperor in Rome. Charlemagne expands the kingdom of France far beyond its present borders and establishes a center for learning at his capital, Aix-la-Chapelle (Aachen, in present-day Germany)

814–987 Death of Charlemagne. The Carolingian line continues until 987 through a dozen or so monarchs, with a batch called Charles (the Bald, the Fat, the Simple) and a sprinkling of Louis. Under the Treaty of Verdun (843), the empire is divided in two—the eastern half becoming Germany, the western half France

The Capetian Dynasty

987   Hugh Capet (987–996) is elected king of France and establishes the principle of hereditary rule for his descendants. Settled conditions and the increased power of the Church see the flowering of the Romanesque style of architecture in the cathedrals of Autun and Angoulême

1066   Norman conquest of England by William the Conqueror (1066–87)

1067   Work begins on the Bayeaux Tapestry, the Romanesque work of art celebrating the Norman Conquest

c 1100   First universities in Europe include Paris. Development of European vernacular verse: *Chanson de Roland*

1140   The Gothic style of architecture first appears at St-Denis and later becomes fully developed at the cathedrals of Chartres, Reims, Amiens, and Notre-Dame in Paris

c 1150   Struggle between the Anglo-Norman kings (Angevin Empire) and the French; when Eleanor of Aquitaine switches husbands (from Louis VII of France to Henry II of England), her extensive lands pass to English rule

1194   Chartres Cathedral is begun; Gothic architecture spreads throughout western Europe

1204   Fourth Crusade: Franks conquer Byzantium and found the Latin Empire

1257   The Sorbonne university is founded in Paris

1270   Louis IX (1226–70), the only French king to achieve sainthood, dies in Tunis on the seventh and last Crusade

1302–07   Philippe IV (1285–1314), the Fair, calls together the first States-General, predecessor to the French Parliament. He disbands the Knights Templars to gain their wealth (1307)

1309   Papacy escapes from a corrupt and disorderly Rome to Avignon in southern France, where it stays for nearly 70 years

The Valois Dynasty

1337–1453   Hundred Years' War between France and England: episodic fighting for control of those areas of France gained by the English crown following the marriage of Eleanor of Aquitaine and Henry II

1348–1350   The Black Death rages in France

1428–31   Joan of Arc (1412–31), the Maid of Orleans, sparks the revival of French fortunes in the Hundred Years' War but is captured by the English and burned at the stake at Rouen

1434   Johannes Gutenberg invents the printing press in Strasbourg, Alsace

1453   France finally defeats England, terminating the Hundred Years' War and the English claim to the French throne

1475   Burgundy at the height of its power under Charles the Bold

1494   Italian wars: beginning of Franco-Habsburg struggle for hegemony in Europe

1515–47 Reign of François I, who imports Italian artists, including Leonardo da Vinci (1452–1519), and brings the Renaissance to France. The palace of Fontainebleau is begun (1528)

1558 France captures Calais, England's last territory on French soil

1562–98 Wars of Religion (Catholics versus Protestants/Huguenots) within France

The Bourbon Dynasty

1589 The first Bourbon king, Henri IV (1589–1610), is a Huguenot who converts to Catholicism and achieves peace in France. He signs the Edict of Nantes, giving limited freedom of worship to Protestants. The development of Renaissance Paris gets under way

c 1610 Scientific revolution in Europe begins, marked by the discoveries of mathematician and philosopher René Descartes (1596–1650)

1643–1715 Reign of Louis XIV, the Sun King, an absolute monarch who builds the Baroque power base of Versailles and presents Europe with a glorious view of France. With his first minister, Colbert, Louis makes France, by force of arms, the most powerful nation-state in Europe. He persecutes the Huguenots, who emigrate in great numbers, nearly ruining the French economy

1660 Classical period of French culture: writers Molière (1622–73), Jean Racine (1639–99), Pierre Corneille (1606–84), and painter Nicolas Poussin (1594–1665)

c 1715 Rococo art and decoration develop in Parisian boudoirs and salons, typified by the painter Antoine Watteau (1684–1721) and, later, François Boucher (1703–70) and Jean-Honoré Fragonard (1732–1806)

1700 onward Writer and pedagogue Voltaire (1694–1778) is a central figure in the French Enlightenment, along with Jean-Jacques Rousseau (1712–78) and Denis Diderot (1713–84), who, in 1751, compiles the first modern encyclopedia. The ideals of the Enlightenment—for reason and scientific method and against social and political injustices—pave the way for the French Revolution. In the arts, painter Jacques Louis David (1748–1825) reinforces revolutionary creeds in his severe neoclassical works

1756–63 The Seven Years' War results in France losing most of her overseas possessions and England becoming a world power

1776 The French assist in the American War of Independence. Ideals of liberty cross the Atlantic with the returning troops to reinforce new social concepts

The French Revolution

1789–1804 The Bastille is stormed on July 14, 1789. Following upon early Republican ideals comes the Terror and the administration of the Directory under Robespierre. There are widespread political executions—Louis XVI and his queen, Marie Antoinette, are guillotined in 1793. Reaction sets in, and the instigators of the Terror are themselves executed (1794). Napoleon Bonaparte enters the scene as the champion of the Directory (1795–

99) and is installed as First Consul during the Consulate (1799–1804)

The First Empire

1804 Napoleon crowns himself Emperor of France at Notre-Dame in the presence of the pope

1805–12 Napoleon conquers most of Europe. The Napoleonic Age is marked by a neoclassical style in the arts, called Empire, as well as by the rise of Romanticism—characterized by such writers as Chateaubriand (1768–1848) and Stendhal (1783–1842), and the painters Eugène Delacroix (1798–1863) and Théodore Géricault (1791–1824)—which is to dominate the arts of the 19th century

1812–14 Winter cold and Russian determination defeat Napoleon outside Moscow. The emperor abdicates and is transported to Elba in the Mediterranean (1814)

Restoration of the Bourbons

1814–15 Louis XVIII, brother of the executed Louis XVI, regains the throne after the Congress of Vienna is held to settle peace terms

1815 The Hundred Days: Napoleon returns from Elba and musters an army on his march to the capital, but lacks national support. He is defeated at Waterloo (June 18) and exiled to the island of St. Helena in the South Atlantic

1821 Napoleon dies in exile

1830 Bourbon king Charles X, locked into a prerevolutionary state of mind, abdicates. A brief upheaval (Three Glorious Days) brings Louis-Philippe, the Citizen King, to the throne

1840 Napoleon's remains are brought back to Paris

1846–48 Severe industrial and farming depression contribute to Louis-Philippe's abdication (1848)

Second Republic and Second Empire

1848–52 Louis-Napoleon (nephew and step-grandson of Napoleon I) is elected president of the short-lived Second Republic. He makes a successful attempt to assume supreme power and is declared Emperor of France, taking the title Napoleon III

c 1850 The ensuing period is characterized in the arts by the emergence of realist painters—Jean-François Millet (1814–75), Honoré Daumier (1808–79), Gustave Courbet (1819–77)—and late-Romantic writers—Victor Hugo (1802–85), Honoré de Balzac (1799–1850), and Charles Baudelaire (1821–87)

1853 Baron Haussmann (1809–91) re-creates the center of Paris, with great boulevards connecting important squares, or *places*

1863 Napoleon III inaugurates the Salon des Refusés in response to critical opinion. It includes work by Edouard Manet (1832–83), Claude Monet (1840–1926), and Paul Cézanne (1839–1906) and is commonly regarded as the birthplace of Impressionism and of modern art in general

The Third Republic

1870–71 The Franco-Prussian War sees Paris besieged, and Paris falls to the Germans. Napoleon III takes refuge in England. The Commune is established, an attempt by the extreme left to seize power. France loses Alsace and Lorraine to Prussia before the peace treaty is signed

1871–1914 Before World War I, France expands her industries and builds up a vast colonial empire in North Africa and Southeast Asia. Sculptor Auguste Rodin (1840–1917), musicians Maurice Ravel (1875–1937) and Claude Debussy (1862–1918), and writers such as Stéphane Mallarmé (1842–98) and Paul Verlaine (1844–96) set the stage for Modernism

1874 Emergence of the Impressionist school of painting: Monet, Pierre Auguste Renoir (1841–1919), and Edgar Degas (1834–1917)

1889 The Eiffel Tower is built for the Paris World Exhibition. Centennial of the French Revolution

1894–1906 Franco-Russian alliance (1894). Dreyfus affair: the spy trial and its anti-Semitic backlash shocks France

1898 Pierre and Marie Curie (1859–1906, 1867–1934) observe radioactivity and isolate radium

1904 The Entente Cordiale: England and France become firm allies

1907 Exhibition of Cubist painting in Paris

1914–18 During World War I, France fights with the Allies, opposing Germany, Austria-Hungary, and Turkey. Germany invades France; most of the big battles (Vimy Ridge, Verdun, Somme, Marne) are fought in trenches in northern France. French casualties exceed 5 million. With the Treaty of Versailles (1919), France regains Alsace and Lorraine and attempts to exact financial and economic reparations from Germany

1918–39 Between wars, Paris attracts artists and writers, including Americans—Ernest Hemingway (1899–1961) and Gertrude Stein (1874–1946). France nourishes major artistic movements: Constructivism, Dadaism, Surrealism, and Existentialism

1923 France occupies the Ruhr, a major industrial area in Germany's Rhine valley

1939–45 At the beginning of World War II, France fights with the Allies until invaded and defeated by Germany in 1940. The French government, under Marshal Pétain (1856–1951), moves to Vichy and cooperates with the Nazis. French overseas colonies split between allegiance to the legal government of Vichy and declaration for the Free French Resistance, led (from London) by General Charles de Gaulle (1890–1970)

1944 D-Day, June 6: The Allies land on the beaches of Normandy and successfully invade France. Additional Allied forces land in Provence. Paris is liberated in August 1944, and France declares full allegiance to the Allies

1944–46 A provisional government takes power under General de Gaulle; American aid assists French recovery

The massive and stocky Romanesque style that succeeded Carolingian differed in various ways—with its stone (as opposed to wooden) ceilings or vaults, its introduction of windows high up the walls, and its preference for stone sculpture over such superficial ornaments as mosaic and painting. Many 10th- and 11th-century Romanesque buildings survive in Burgundy, Alsace, the Auvergne, and western France: The city of Poitiers is particularly rich in Romanesque architecture; notably the intricately carved west front of the church of Notre-Dame-la-Grande.

The airier Gothic style of the great French cathedrals built between the 12th and 16th centuries represented a fundamental departure from Romanesque. The most obvious visual change was that pointed arches replaced round ones. Just as important, though, was a new vaulting structure based on intersecting ribbed vaults, which sprang across the roof from column to column. Outward thrust was borne by flying buttresses, slender arches linking the outer walls to free-standing columns, often topped by spiky pinnacles. Where Romanesque architecture had thick, blocky walls with little room for window space, Gothic architecture, technically more sophisticated, replaced stone with stained glass.

Most medieval churches were built in the form of a cross, with two arms, or transepts, that intersect at the crossing (often topped by a tower in Romanesque churches). The nave, divided into bays (the spaces between each column) and flanked on either side by side aisles, formed the main body of the church, with the east end, known as the chancel, containing the choir and altar. Many Gothic churches also have a number of small chapels behind the high altar, forming an outline known as the *chevet*, or apse.

Romanesque and Gothic churches are divided into three or four distinct vertical sections, like strata. Forestlike rows of pillars, topped by carved capitals, spring from the ground either to a gallery or triforium (an arcade of small columns and arches, originally of stone, later filled with glass), then to a clerestory (row of windows) above.

The Romanesque facade was intended as an ornate screen and was sometimes fronted by a large porch (or narthex). The tympanum, a large sculpted panel above the central doorway (usually representing Christ in Judgment or Glory), was retained in the Gothic facade, which also featured huge portals, a circular rose window, a statue gallery, and lofty towers. Other towers, over the crossing or alongside the transepts, gradually lost favor: The stone bulls on top of the many-towered cathedral of Laon mourn a dying breed.

Pointed arches and ribbed vaults were first used in the Gothic style during the 1130s at Sens and at St-Denis—home of Abbot Suger, the leading political figure of his day. Within a decade, local bishops had followed Suger's lead, and huge Gothic cathedrals were under way at Noyon, Senlis, and Laon. As France expanded during the early Middle Ages from its Parisian epicenter, Gothic went with it. But the Gothic style did not displace the Romanesque overnight. Many Romanesque churches survive as crypts beneath later buildings (as at Dijon Cathedral, for example); similarly, Romanesque naves were conserved at Mont-St-Michel, Vézelay, and Le Mans despite the addition of new Gothic chancels, while at Strasbourg Cathedral, the reverse is true and a Romanesque chancel survives.

As the Gothic style evolved, less and less stone was used, and churches came to assume a delicate, almost skeletal framework. Paris's Sainte Chapelle is the most famous example, though, as a stained-glass showcase, its scale doesn't match that of Metz Cathedral.

Height was another Gothic quest. Roofs soared higher and higher—until that at Beauvais Cathedral came crashing down in 1284. Notre-Dame of Paris is 106 feet high, but later cathedrals are even loftier: Chartres is 114 feet; Bourges, 120 feet; Reims, 124 feet; Amiens, 137 feet; and Beauvais an ill-fated 153 feet (it was never completed, so Amiens reigns as the country's largest cathedral).

The circular rose window was one feature that lasted throughout the Middle Ages, evolving from 13th-century geometric splendor at St-Denis and Notre-Dame in Paris, to a petal-like fluidity during the first half of the 16th century.

The Chambiges family, last in a long line of great Gothic master-masons and glaziers, played a major role in the development of the Flamboyant style. When the Bishop of Beauvais was planning a grandiose transept for his cathedral he sent for Martin Chambiges, tempting him away from Sens and keeping him jealously at Beauvais for 30 years. Some see in the flamelike Flamboyant style the last neurotic shrieks of Gothic decadence. But while its decorative profusion sometimes smacks of sculptural self-indulgence (St-Pierre in Caen is a good example), there are several admirable Flamboyant churches, notably St-Séverin in Paris, and St-Nicolas de Port near Nancy.

In the 16th century, Gothic architecture was subject to the influx of Renaissance ideas, given official encouragement when François I (1515–47) invited the Italian painters and architects Il Rosso, Primaticcio, and Leonardo da Vinci to his court. Renaissance architecture was marked by a return to Classical Roman styles and existed side by side with Gothic throughout the 16th century; in a number of Paris churches you will see Classical columns and ornaments superimposed on Gothic structures (St-Etienne-du-Mont, St-Gervais, and St-Eustache are the best examples). While Gothic was first and foremost an ecclesiastical style, many of the chief creations of Renaissance architecture had a civil setting: the châteaus of noblemen, princes, and kings. In the Loire Valley, for instance, fortified medieval castles like Chinon gradually yielded to ideals of comfort and luxury (Cheverny, for example). Along the way, Renaissance proportion and daintiness were mingled with medieval massiveness, as at the châteaus of Azay-le-Rideau and Amboise. One of the loveliest showcases of Renaissance architecture is the place des Vosges in Paris, a square whose huge, steep-sloping roofs are a recurring trait of French buildings of the 16th and 17th centuries.

To contrast the Renaissance style with the Baroque, its successor, compare the pink-brick arcades of the place des Vosges (1612) with the solemn and dignified stone of the place Vendôme, built in 1685 a couple of miles across town. A similar difference can be observed between the intimate château of Fontainebleau (mid-16th century) and the immense palace of Versailles (late 17th century).

Baroque imbued the Classical style with drama and a sense of movement: Take a look at Mansart's dome surging above Paris's Hôtel des Invalides, or the powerful rhythms of Charles Perrault's Louvre facade. Yet only in northern France, under the temporary influence of Spanish occupiers, did Latin exuberance find an outlet, typified in the soaring curves and curls on the colossal belfry of St-Amand-les-Eaux near Lille. The overblown fantasies to which Baroque lent itself in Italy, Spain, southern Germany, and Austria—wild curves, broken outlines, and sculptural overkill—were held firmly in check by the French love of discipline. Whole towns survive to remind us: The rigid planning and identical houses of Richelieu, south of Chinon, are restrained and austere.

The 18th century saw several major provincial building programs in the neoclassical style—a more literal, toned-down interpretation of antique precedent. The state rooms of Strasbourg's Château des Rohan, the charming place Stanislas in Nancy, and the Grand Théâtre and place de la Bourse in Bordeaux are top examples. A number of the more affluent châteaus in the Bordeaux vineyards also date from this time.

Baroque, however, continued to dominate church building until the early 19th century (witness the cathedrals of Nancy and Arras). Many clerics commissioned architects to dress up Gothic buildings in Classical apparel, sticking pilasters on columns or transforming pointed arches into rounded ones. Louis XIV set the tone by remodeling the choir of Notre-Dame in Paris in 1708, but Autun Cathedral—revamped throughout—is the most extreme example of this kind of architectural rethink. Stained-glass windows were even ripped out—an act of stylistic vandalism surpassed only during the French Revolution when thousands of churches were wrecked in the name of the Age of Reason.

Napoleon ushered in the 19th century with the Arc de Triomphe, which remained unfinished for 20 years—typifying the hesitations of a century that was bereft of original ideas. Iron made its appearance—most obviously at the Eiffel Tower, most frequently accompanied by glass in train stations and covered markets.

The 19th century bequeathed us Paris as we know it, with Baron Haussmann carving boulevards through the city. Luckily, Haussman's seven-story buildings have proved sufficiently large and imposing to withstand the rapacious onslaughts of modern developers, and central Paris has remained unchanged for a hundred years. But it's not surprising that the showpiece of Haussmann's Paris, the Opéra, is a pompous jumble of styles.

Things perked up in the 20th century. While such Paris landmarks as the Grand and Petit Palais and opulent town halls throughout the country were faithful to conservative taste, Emile Gallé and Hector Guimard led an artistic revolution known as Art Nouveau, with sinuous, nature-based forms. The Paris Métro, ornamented by iron railings and canopies, is the most familiar example. A reaction occurred in the straighter lines of art deco, which first turned up at the Théâtre des Champs-Elysées in 1913. At the same time, the French developed a taste for reinforced concrete that they have never lost. Its most imaginative exponent was Swiss-born Le Corbusier, an architectural Picasso whose best work (like the chapel at Ronchamp in eastern France) obeys few established rules.

In the first half of the 20th century, much energy was spent repairing the damage of two world wars: Many towns are now lackluster copies of their former selves. Efforts were lavished on restoring cathedrals and other landmarks, a pursuit instigated a century before by Eugène Viollet-le-Duc, without whom any number of cathedrals and churches might have crumbled away.

The most visited postwar building in France is Paris's futuristic Pompidou Center. Its pipes and workings are on the outside, ensuring that the interior is uncluttered to a fault (the fault being that the exterior is going rusty). In terms of size and mass appeal, the equivalents of cathedrals today may well be sports stadiums; here France again sets the lead, with Paris's Parc des Princes a model for the Olympic arenas of Montreal and Seoul.

Paris's latterday skyscrapers have—with the exception of the Tour Montparnasse—been banished to the city outskirts, notably to La Défense. There, finished only in 1989, the giant glass and concrete arch known as La Tête Défense has cemented a vista that stretches along the avenue de la Grande Armée, past the Arc de Triomphe, down the Champs-Elysées, across the place de la Concorde, and over the Tuileries to the gleaming glass pyramid of the Louvre.

tails are published in the weekly magazines *Pariscope* and *L'Officiel des Spectacles* under the heading "Conférences." You can sometimes make advance reservations for walking tours organized by the **Caisse Nationale des Monuments Historiques,** Bureau des Visites/Conférences (Hôtel de Sully, 62 rue St-Antoine, 4e, tel. 42–74–22–22).

Personal Guides **Espace Limousines** (48 rue Sarrette, 14e, tel. 45–45–53–30) has guides with luxury cars or minibuses (taking up to seven passengers) who will take you around Paris and the environs for a minimum of three hours. Reservations are required, and the cost is about 250 francs per hour.

Exploring Paris

Numbers in the margin correspond with points of interest on the Paris map.

Orientation

The best method of getting to know Paris is on foot. With this in mind, we've divided our coverage of Paris into six tours. Use our routes as a base; concentrate on the areas that are of particular interest to you; and, above all, enjoy to the full the sights, sounds, and smells of this exciting city.

Highlights for First-time Visitors

Arc de Triomphe and Champs-Elysées, Tour 3
Eiffel Tower, Tour 4
The Louvre, Tour 1
Musée de Cluny, Tour 5
Musée d'Orsay, Tour 4
Notre-Dame, Tour 1
Place Vendôme, Tour 3
Beaubourg (Pompidou Center), Tour 2
Sacré Coeur, Tour 6
Sainte-Chapelle, Tour 1

Tour 1: The Historic Heart

Of the two islands in the Seine—the Ile St-Louis and Ile de la Cité—it is the latter that forms the historic heart of Paris. It was here that the earliest inhabitants of Paris, the Gaulish tribe of the Parisii, settled around 250 BC. Whereas the Ile St-Louis is largely residential, the Ile de la Cité remains deeply historic: It is the site of the great, brooding cathedral of Notre-Dame. Few of the island's other medieval buildings have survived, most having fallen victim to Baron Haussmann's ambitious rebuilding of the city in the mid-19th century. Among the rare survivors are the jewel-like Sainte Chapelle, a vision of shimmering stained glass, and the Conciergerie, the grim former city prison.

The tour begins at the western tip of the Ile de la Cité, at the ❶ sedate **Square du Vert Galant.** The statue of the *Vert Galant* himself, literally the "vigorous [by which was really meant the amorous] adventurer," shows Henri IV sitting sturdily on his horse. Henri, king of France from 1589 until his assassination

Paris Arrondissements

COURBEVOIE

CLICHY

ST. OUEN

LEVALLOIS-
PERRET

Blvd. Berthier

Blvd. Bessières

Av. de Clichy

Av. de St. Ouen

LA
DEFENSE

Pl. de Neuilly

Av. Charles de Gaulle

NEUILLY-SUR-
SEINE

17e

Av. de Villiers

Blvd. des Batignolles

R. d'Amsterdam

Blvd.

Av. de Wagram

Blvd. de Courcelles

Av. de La Grande
Armée

Parc
Monceau

**Gare
St-Lazare**

Av. Foch

Arc de
Triomphe

Av. Friedland

Blvd.

Haussmann

Av. des Champs

8e

La Madeleine

Opéra

Av. Victor Hugo

Av. Kléber

Av. George V

-Elysées

Av. E. D. Roosevelt

Av. Marceau

Pl.
Vendôme

Pl. de la
Concorde

R. de Rivoli

Av. du Pres. Wilson

Pl. du
Trocadéro

Quai d'Orsay

Jardin des
Tuileries

Bois de Boulogne

16e

PASSY

**Palais
de Chaillot**

**Eiffel
Tower**

Av. la Bourdonnais

7e

Blvd.

Av. du Pres. Kennedy

Av. de Suffren

Av. de Breteuil

**Hôtel des
Invalides**

R. de Sèvres

6e

Av. du Général Sarrail

Blvd. Murat

Blvd. Exelmans

AUTEUIL

Blvd. de Grenelle

Av. Emile Zola

R. de la Convention

R. Lecourbe

R. de Vaugirard

Blvd. Raspail

Blvd. du Montparnasse

Blvd.
Exelmans

Av. F. Faure

15e

R. de Vaugirard

**Gare
Montparnasse**

Av. du Maine

Blvd. Victor

R. de Vaugirard

R. d'Alésia

14e

Blvd. Gallieni

R. Ernest Renan

Blvd. Lefebvre

Av. du Gt. Leclerc

Av. Victor Cresson

VANVES

Blvd. Brune

Blvd.

ISSY-LES-
MOULINEAUX

MONTROUGE

Paris

Arc de Triomphe, **27**

Archives Nationales, **17**

Beaubourg, **16**

Bibliothèque Nationale, **8**

Bourse du Commerce, **10**

Carrefour de Buci, **47**

Closerie des Lilas, **54**

Comédie-Française, **6**

Cour Carré, **3**

Ecole Nationale des Beaux-Arts, **50**

Eglise de la Madeleine, **31**

Eiffel Tower, **41**

Forum des Halles, **12**

Grand Palais, **28**

Hôtel Carnavalet, **21**

Hôtel des Invalides, **40**

Hôtel des Monnaies/ Institut de France, **49**

Hôtel et Musèe de Cluny, **58**

Hôtel de Sens, **25**

Hôtel de Ville, **15**

Ile St-Louis, **26**

Jardin des Plantes, **61**

Jardin des Tuileries, **34**

Louvre, **4**

Musée de l'Art Moderne de la Ville de Paris, **45**

Musée Bricard de la Serrure, **18**

Musée Cognacq-Jay, **20**

Musée Eugène Delacroix, **51**

Musée Guimet, **43**

Musée d'Orsay, **37**

Musée Picasso, **19**

Musée Rodin, **39**

Notre-Dame, **14**

Opéra, **36**

Orangerie, **33**

Palais Bourbon, **38**

Palais de Chaillot, **42**

Palais de l'Elysée, **30**

Palais Galliera, **44**

Palais de Justice, **13**

Palais du
Luxembourg, **55**

Palais de la
Mutualité, **60**

Palais Royal, **7**

Panthéon, **57**

Petit Palais, **29**

Place de la Bastille, **23**

Place de la
Concorde, **32**

Place St-Michel, **46**

Place Vendôme, **35**

Place des Victoires, **9**

Place des Vosges, **22**

Procope, **48**

St-Eustache, **11**

St-Germain-
l'Auxerrois, **2**

St-Germain-
des-Prés, **52**

St-Gervais-
St-Protais, **24**

St-Roch, **5**

St-Séverin, **59**

Sorbonne, **56**

Square du Vert
Galant, **1**

Tour Maine-
Montparnasse, **53**

of a dashing figure as well as a canny

té, just behind the Vert Galant, is the
nfusingly called the **Pont Neuf,** or New
e early 17th century, it was the first
uilt without houses lining either side.
oss the river, turn left again and walk
oligny, opposite the massive eastern
ore heading for the museum, howev-
sidewalk and duck into the church of
his was the French royal family's
fore the Revolution, when the Lou-
a museum. The fluid stonework of
ence of 15th-century Flamboyant
fling of the Gothic before the Clas-
takeover of the Renaissance. Note the unusual double
aisles and the exceptionally wide windows—typical of the
style. The triumph of Classicism is evident, however, in the
18th-century fluted columns around the choir, the area surrounding the altar.

The Louvre colonnade across the road screens one of Europe's
3 most dazzling courtyards, the **Cour Carré,** a breathtakingly
monumental, harmonious, and superbly rhythmic ensemble. In
the crypt below, excavated in 1984, sections of the defensive
towers of the original, 13th-century fortress can be seen.

Saunter through the courtyard and pass under the **Pavillon de
l'Horloge,** the Clock Tower, and you'll come face-to-face with I.
M. Pei's **glass pyramid,** surrounded by three smaller pyramids.
The pyramid marks the new entrance to the Louvre and houses
a large museum shop, café, and restaurant. It is also the termi-
nal point for the most celebrated city view in Europe—a majestic vista stretching through the Arc du Carrousel, the Tuileries
Gardens, across place de la Concorde, up the Champs-Elysées
to the towering Arc de Triomphe, and ending at the giant modern arch at La Tête Défense, a further 2½ miles away. Needless
to say, the architectural collision between Classical stone
blocks and pseudo-Egyptian glass panels has caused a furor.

4 Today's **Louvre** is the end product of many generations of work.
It began in the early 13th century, when Philippe Auguste
built it as a fortress to protect the city's western flank. The earliest parts of the current building date from the reign of François I at the beginning of the 16th century, while subsequent
monarchs—Henri IV (1589–1610), Louis XIII (1610–43), Louis XIV (1643–1715), Napoleon (1802–14), and Napoleon III
(1851–70)—all contributed to its construction. The open section facing the Tuileries Gardens was once the site of the Palais
des Tuileries, the main residence of the royal family in Paris.

Over the centuries, the Louvre has been used as both a royal
residence and a home for minor courtiers; at one point, it was
taken over by a rabble of artists who set up shop and whose
chimneys projected higgledy-piggledy from the otherwise severe lines of the facades. After a stint as headquarters of the
French Revolution, the Louvre was finally established, in
Napoleon's time, as a museum, though the country's last three
monarchs continued to make it their home.

The number-one attraction for most visitors is Leonardo da Vinci's enigmatic *Mona Lisa*, "La Joconde" to the French; be forewarned that you will find it encased in glass and surrounded by a mob of tourists. The collections are divided into seven sections: Oriental antiquities; Egyptian antiquities; Greek and Roman antiquities; sculpture; paintings, prints, and drawings; furniture; and objets d'art. Unless you enjoy masochistic 10-hour slogs around museums, don't try to see it all at once. Try, instead, to make repeat visits—the Louvre is half-price on Sundays. Some highlights of paintings, in addition to the *Mona Lisa*, are *The Inspiration of the Poet*, by Nicolas Poussin (1594–1665); *The Oath of the Horatii*, by Jacques-Louis David (1748–1825); *The Raft of the Medusa*, by Théodore Géricault (1791–1824); and *La Grande Odalisque*, by Jean-Auguste Dominique Ingres (1780–1867). Probably the best-loved bit of sculpture is Michelangelo's pair of *Slaves*, intended for the tomb of Pope Julius II, while the French crown jewels (in the objets d'art section) include the mind-boggling 186-carat Regent diamond. *Palais du Louvre. Admission: 30 frs. adults, 15 frs. ages 18–25 and on Sun.; children under 18 free. Open daily 9–6, Mon. and Wed. until 9:45; closed Tues.*

Stretching westward from the main entrance to the Louvre and the glass pyramid is an expanse of stately, formal gardens. These are the **Jardins des Tuileries** (*see* Tour 3: From the Arc de Triomphe to the Opéra, below).

Time Out Good-value meals and snacks are hard to come by in this upscale area of Paris, so why not try the **Self-Service Tuileries** (near place des Pyramides), reader-recommended for cleanliness and pleasant, English-speaking service. *206 rue de Rivoli.*

Running the length of the Louvre's northern side is Napoleon's arcaded rue de Rivoli. Cross it and you're in **place des Pyramides,** face-to-face with its gilded statue of Joan of Arc on horseback. Walk up rue des Pyramides and take the first left, ❺ rue St-Honoré, to the Baroque church of **St-Roch.** The church was completed in the 1730s, the date of the cool, Classical facade. It's worth having a look inside to see the bombastically Baroque altarpiece in the circular Lady Chapel.

Return to rue des Pyramides and follow rue St-Honoré to **place André-Malraux,** with its exuberant fountains. The Opéra building is visible down the avenue of the same name, while, on one ❻ corner of the square, at rue Richelieu, is the **Comédie-Française,** the time-honored setting for performances of classical French drama. The building dates from 1790, but the Comédie-Française company was created by Louis XIV in 1680. If you understand French and have a taste for the mannered, declamatory style of French acting, you will appreciate an evening here (*see* The Arts and Nightlife, below).

To the right of the theater (as you face it from the Louvre) is the ❼ unobtrusive entrance to the gardens of the **Palais Royal.** The buildings of this former palace date from the 1630s and are royal only in that the builder, Cardinal Richelieu (1585–1642), magnanimously bequeathed them to Louis XIII. Today the Palais Royal is home of the French Ministry of Culture and is not open to the public. But don't miss the **gardens,** divided by rows of perfectly trimmed little trees, a surprisingly little-known oasis in the gray heart of the city. There's not much chance that you'll miss the black-and-white striped columns in the courtyard or the revolving silver spheres that slither around in the two fountains at either end, the controversial early-1980s work of architect Daniel Buren. Walk to the end, away from the main palace, and peek into the opulent, Belle-Epoque, glass-lined interior of **Le Grand Véfour** (*see* Dining, below). One of the swankiest restaurants in the city, it's probably the most sumptuously appointed, too.

Around the corner, on rue de Richelieu, stands France's national library, the **Bibliothèque Nationale,** containing over 7 million printed volumes. Visitors can admire Robert de Cotte's 18th-century courtyard and peep into the 19th-century reading room. *58 rue de Richelieu. Open daily noon–6.*

Time Out Wine bars, which sprang to prominence in London a decade ago, have caught on less quickly in Paris. A splendid trendsetter is English-run **Willi's,** behind the Palais-Royal. Sample a glass of wine on a stool at the bar or eat a sit-down meal in the cute restaurant behind (the inexpensive menu changes daily). *13 rue des Petits-Champs.*

From the library, walk along rue des Petits-Champs to the circular **place des Victoires.** It was laid out by Mansart, a leading proponent of French 17th-century Classicism, in 1685, in honor of the military victories of Louis XIV. You'll find some of the city's most upscale fashion shops here and on the surrounding streets.

Head south down rue Croix-des-Petits-Champs. The second street on the left leads to the circular 18th-century **Bourse du Commerce,** or Commercial Exchange. Alongside it is a 100-foot-high fluted column, all that remains of a mansion built here in 1572 for Catherine de' Medici. The column is said to have been used as a platform for stargazing by her astrologer, Ruggieri.

You can easily spot the bulky outline of the church of **St-Eustache,** away to the left. It is a huge church, the "cathedral" of Les Halles, built, as it were, as the market people's Right Bank reply to Notre-Dame. Under construction from 1532 to 1637 and modified over the centuries, the church is a curious architectural hybrid. Its exterior flying buttresses, for example, are solidly Gothic, yet its column orders, rounded arches, and comparatively simple window tracery are unmistakably Classical. Few buildings bear such eloquent witness to stylistic transition.

If Notre Dame and the Louvre represent Church and State, respectively, Les Halles (pronounced "lay al") stands for the common man. For centuries, this was Paris's central market. Closed in 1969, it was replaced by a striking shopping mall, the **Forum des Halles.** The surrounding streets have since undergone a radical transformation, much like the neighboring Marais, and the shops, cafés, restaurants, and chic apartment buildings make it an example of successful urban redevelopment.

Time Out A few blocks south of Les Halles and just north of place du Châtelet is **Le Trappiste,** where 20 different international beers are available on draught, along with well over 180 bottled. Mussels and french fries are the traditional accompaniment, although various other snacks (hot dogs and sandwiches) are also available. There are tables upstairs and on the pavement. *4 rue St-Denis.*

From place du Châtelet cross back over the Seine on the Pont-au-Change to the Ile de la Cité. To your right looms the imposing **Palais de Justice,** the Courts of Law, built by Baron Haussmann in his characteristically weighty Classical style around 1860. The main buildings of interest on the Ile de la Cité, however, are the medieval parts of the complex, spared by Haussmann in his otherwise wholesale destruction.

The **Conciergerie,** the northernmost part of the complex, was originally part of the royal palace on the island. Most people know it, however, as a prison, the grim place of confinement for Danton, Robespierre, and Marie Antoinette during the French Revolution. Inside you'll see the guardroom (the Salle des Gens d'Armes), a striking example of Gothic monumentality; the cells, including the one in which Marie Antoinette was held; and the chapel, where objects connected with the ill-fated queen are displayed. *Admission: 23 frs. adults, 12 frs. children, students, and senior citizens. Joint ticket (with Ste-Chapelle): 36 frs. (19 frs.). Open daily 9–6 (9:30–5 in winter).*

The other perennial crowd-puller in the Palais de Justice is the **Sainte-Chapelle,** the Holy Chapel, one of the supreme achievements of the Middle Ages. It was built by the genial and pious Louis IX (1226–70) to house what he took to be the Crown of Thorns from Christ's crucifixion and fragments of the True Cross. Architecturally, for all its delicate and ornate exterior decoration, the design of the building is simplicity itself; in essence, no more than a thin, rectangular box much taller than it is wide. Some clumsy 19th-century work has added a deadening touch, but the glory of the chapel—the stained glass—is spectacularly intact: The walls consist of at least twice as much glass as masonry. Try to attend one of the regular, candle-lit concerts given here. *Admission: 23 frs. adults, 12 frs. children under 17. Open daily 9:30–6 (5 in winter).*

Take rue de Lutèce opposite the Palais de Justice down to place Louis-Lépine and the bustling **Marché aux Fleurs,** the flower market. Around the corner is the most enduring symbol of Paris, the cathedral of **Notre-Dame.** The building was started in 1163, with an army of stonemasons, carpenters, and sculptors working on a site that had previously seen a Roman temple, an early Christian basilica, and a Romanesque church. The chancel and altar were consecrated in 1182, but the magnificent sculptures surrounding the main doors were not put into position until 1240. The north tower was finished 10 years later. Despite various changes in the 17th century, principally the removal of the rose windows, the cathedral remained substantially unaltered until the French Revolution, when much destruction was wrought, mainly to statuary.

Place du Parvis, in front of the cathedral, is the perfect place from which to gaze at the building's famous facade, divided neatly into three levels. At the first-floor level are the three main entrances, or portals, the Portal of the Virgin on the left; the Portal of the Last Judgment in the center; and the Portal of St. Anne on the right. Above this level are the restored statues of the kings of Israel, the Galerie des Rois (which took a beating during the French Revolution). Above the gallery is the great rose window and, on top of that, the Grande Galerie, at the base of the twin towers. The south tower houses the great bell of Notre-Dame, as tolled by Quasimodo, Victor Hugo's fictional hunchback.

The interior of the cathedral, with its vast proportions, soaring nave, and gentle, multicolored light filtering through the stained-glass windows, inspires awe, despite the inevitable throngs of tourists. On the south side of the chancel is the **Treasury**, with a collection of garments, reliquaries, and silver and gold plate. (Admission: 15 frs. adults, 10 frs. students and senior citizens, 3 frs. children. Open Mon.–Sat. 10–6, Sun. 2–6). The 387-step climb to the top of the towers is worth the effort for the close-up view of the famous gargoyles and the expansive view over the city. (Entrance via the north tower. Admission: 27 frs. adults, 12 frs. students and senior citizens, 5 frs. children. Open daily 10–5.)

If your interest in the cathedral is not yet sated, duck into the **Musée Notre-Dame,** which displays artwork and documents tracing the cathedral's history. *10 rue du Cloître Notre-Dame. Admission: 10 frs. Open Wed. and weekends only, 2:30–6.*

Tour 2: The Marais and Ile St-Louis

The history of the Marais began when Charles V, king of France in the 14th century, moved the French court from the Ile de la Cité. However, it wasn't until Henri IV laid out the place Royale, today the place des Vosges, in the early 17th century that the Marais became *the* place to live. Following the French Revolution, however, the Marais rapidly became one of the most deprived, dissolute areas in Paris. It was spared the attentions of Baron Haussmann, the man who rebuilt so much of Paris in the mid-19th century, so that, though crumbling, its ancient golden-hued buildings and squares remained intact. Today's Marais once again has staked a convincing claim as the city's most desirable district.

⓯ Begin your tour at the **Hôtel de Ville** (City Hall), overlooking the Seine. It was in the square on the Hôtel de Ville's south side that Robespierre, fanatical leader during the period of the French Revolution known as the Reign of Terror, came to suffer the fate of his many victims when a furious mob sent him to the guillotine in 1794. Following the accession of Louis-Philippe in 1830, the building became the seat of the French government, a role that came to a sudden end with the uprisings in 1848. In the Commune of 1871, the Hôtel de Ville was burned to the ground. Today's exuberant building, based closely on the Renaissance original, went up between 1874 and 1884.

From the Hôtel de Ville, head north across rue de Rivoli and up rue du Temple. On your right, you'll pass one of the city's most popular department stores, the **Bazar de l'Hôtel de Ville,** or BHV as it's commonly known. The first street on your left, rue de la Verrerie, will take you to the stores, restaurants, and galleries of the rue St-Martin.

⓰ The Centre National d'Art et de Culture Georges Pompidou, known as the **Beaubourg,** is next. The center hosts an innovative and challenging series of exhibits, in addition to housing the world's largest collection of modern art. Its brash architectural style—it has been likened to a gaudily painted oil refinery—has caused much controversy, however. Many critics think it is beginning to show its age (it only opened in 1977) in a particularly cheap manner: Witness the cracked and grimy plastic tubing that encases the exterior elevators, and the peeling, skeletal interior supports. Probably the most popular thing to do at the Beaubourg is to ride the escalator up to the roof to see the Parisian skyline unfolding as you are carried through its clear plastic piping. There's a sizable restaurant and café on the roof. Aside from the art collection (from which American painters and sculptors are conspicuously absent), the building houses a movie theater; a language laboratory; an extensive collection of tapes, videos, and slides; an industrial design center; and an acoustics and musical research center. *Plateau Beaubourg, tel. 42–77–12–33. Admission free. Admission to Modern Art museum: 23 frs. Open Wed.–Mon. noon–10 PM, weekends 10–10; closed Tues. Guided tours: weekdays 3:30, weekends 11.*

Time Out   Don't leave the plateau without stopping for coffee at the **Café Beaubourg** on the corner of rue St-Merri. A staircase takes you up from the first floor to a *passerelle*, or foot bridge, linking the two sides of a mezzanine. The severe, high-tech design is lightened by the little glass-top tables, which are gradually being covered with artists' etchings.

Leave plateau Beaubourg by its southwestern corner and head down little rue Ste-Croix de la Bretonnerie to visit the Marais's Jewish quarter, lately rather cloistered as a result of recent bomb attacks. You'll see the more obvious of the area's historical highlights if you take rue Rambuteau, which runs along the north side of the center (to your left as you face the building). The **Quartier de L'Horloge,** the Clock Quarter, opens off the plateau here. An entire city block has been rebuilt, and despite the shops and cafés, it retains a resolutely artificial quality. The mechanical clock around the corner on rue Clairvaux will amuse children, however: St. George defends Time against a dragon, an eagle-beaked bird, or a monstrous crab (symbolizing earth, air, and water, respectively) every hour, on the hour. At noon, 6 PM, and 10 PM, he takes on all three at once.

You are now poised to plunge into the elegant heart of the Marais. The historic homes here are now private residences, but don't be afraid to push through the heavy doors, or *portes-cochère*, to glimpse the discreet courtyards that lurk behind.

From the little market on rue Rambuteau, take the first left, up rue du Temple, to the 17th-century **Hôtel de Montmor,** at no. 79. It was once the scene of an influential literary salon—a part-social, part-literary group—that included the philosopher Descartes (1596–1650) and the playwright Molière (1622–73).

Take rue de Braque (opposite) down to the Hôtel de Soubise, now the **Archives Nationales** (its collections form part of the Musée de l'Histoire de France). The museum's highlights are the papers dating from the revolutionary period, including Marie Antoinette's last letter, the pattern book from which she would select a new dress every morning, and Louis XVI's diary that contains his sadly ignorant entry for July 14, 1789, the day the Bastille was stormed at the start of the French Revolution: *Rien* (nothing), he wrote. You can also visit the apartments of the Prince and Princess de Soubise: Don't miss them if you have any interest in the lifestyles of 18th-century French aristocrats. The Archives buildings also include the elegant **Hôtel de Rohan,** built for the archbishops of Strasbourg in 1705 (open only during temporary exhibits). *60 rue des Francs-Bourgeois, tel. 40–27–62–18. Admission: 12 frs. adults, 8 frs. children. Open Wed.–Mon. 1:45–5:45; closed Tues.*

Turn right into rue des Archives, then take first right into rue des Quatre-Fils, which becomes rue de la Perle. At No. 1 is the **(18) Musée Bricard de la Serrure,** the Lock Museum. The museum's sumptuous building is perhaps more interesting than the assembled locks and keys within; it was built in 1685 by Bruand, the architect of Les Invalides. If you have a taste for fine craftsmanship, you will appreciate the intricacy and ingenuity of many of the older locks. One represents an early security system—it would shoot anyone who tried to open it with the wrong key. *Hôtel Bruand, 1 rue de la Perle. Admission: 10 frs. Open Tues.–Sat. 10–noon and 2–5; closed Mon., Aug., and last week of Dec.*

From here it is but a step to the Hôtel Salé, built between 1656 **(19)** and 1660, and today the popular **Musée Picasso;** be prepared for long lines. The collection encompasses pictures, sculptures, drawings, prints, ceramics, and other assorted works of art given to the French government after the painter's death, in 1973, in lieu of death duties. What's notable about it—other than its being the world's largest collection of works by Picasso—is that these were works that the artist himself owned and especially valued. There are works from every period of his life, as well as paintings by Paul Cézanne, Joan Miró, Pierre Auguste Renoir, Georges Braque, Edgar Degas, Henri Matisse, and others. The palatial surroundings add greatly to the visit. *5 rue de Thorigny, tel. 42–71–25–21. Admission: 21 frs. Open Wed. 9:15 AM–10 PM, Thurs.–Mon. 9:15–5:15; closed Tues.*

Cut across place Thorigny and take rue Elzévir. Halfway down **(20)** on the left is the **Musée Cognacq-Jay,** transferred here in 1990 from its original home near the Opéra. The museum is devoted to the arts of the 18th century: furniture, porcelain, and paintings (Watteau and Boucher notably). The Hôtel Donon, a 15th-century mansion, was virtually in ruins before its tasteful transformation by the City of Paris. *8 rue Elzévir, tel. 42–74–33–66. Admission: 12 frs. Open Tues.–Sun. 10–5:30.*

Continue down rue Elzévir to rue des Francs-Bourgeois, **(21)** where the substantial **Hôtel Carnavalet** became the scene, in the late 17th century, of the most brilliant salon in Paris, presided over by Madame de Sévigné. She is best known for the hundreds of letters she wrote to her daughter during her life; they've become one of the most enduring chronicles of French high society in the 17th century. In 1880, the hotel was transformed into the **Musée de l'Histoire de Paris;** its extraordinary exhibits of the Revolution, which have now moved to the neighboring Hôtel Peletier St-Fargeau, include some fascinating macabre models of guillotines. *23 rue de Sévigné, tel. 42–72–21–13. Admission: 15 frs. adults, 8.50 frs. children and senior citizens. Open 10–5:30; closed Mon.*

(22) Now walk along to **place des Vosges,** a minute or two farther along rue des Francs-Bourgeois. Place des Vosges, or place

Royale as it was originally known, is the oldest square in Paris:
Laid out by Henri IV at the beginning of the 17th century, it is
the model for all the later city squares on which most French
urban developments are based. The harmonious balance of the
square, with its symmetrical town houses of pale pink stone,
makes it a pleasant place to spend a hot summer's afternoon. At
no. 6 is the **Maison de Victor Hugo,** which commemorates the
workaholic French writer.

From place des Vosges, follow rue du Pas-de-la-Mule and turn
㉓ right down rue des Tournelles until you reach **place de la Bastille,** site of the infamous prison. Until 1988, there was little
more to see at place de la Bastille than a huge traffic circle and
the **Colonne de Juillet,** the July Column. As part of the country-
wide celebrations held in July 1989, the bicentennial of the
French Revolution, a 3,000-seat **opera house** boasting five moving stages and a gleaming curved-glass facade has been put up
on the south side of the square. Redevelopment projects have
changed what was formerly a humdrum neighborhood into one
of the city's most chic and attractive.

The **Bastille** was built by Charles V in the late 14th century and
destroyed in 1789 during the French Revolution. The ground
plan is marked by paving stones set into the modern square.
The Bastille was originally intended not as a prison but as a fortress to guard the eastern entrance to the city. By the reign of
Louis XIII (1610–43), however, it was used almost exclusively
to house political prisoners, including, in the 18th century, Voltaire and the Marquis de Sade. This obviously political role led
the "furious mob" (in all probability no more than a largely un-
armed rabble) to break into the prison on July 14, 1789, kill the
governor, steal what firearms they could find, and set free the
seven remaining prisoners.

Return toward the Hôtel de Ville down rue St-Antoine, forking
㉔ off left down rue François-Miron to the church of **St-Gervais-St-Protais,** named after two Roman soldiers martyred by
the Emperor Nero in the 1st century AD. The original church—
one of the earliest in Paris; no trace remains of it now—was
built in the 7th century. The present building, a riot of Flamboyant decoration, went up between 1494 and 1598, making it
one of the last Gothic constructions in the country. Pause before you go in to look at the facade, put up between 1616 and
1621. While the interior is late Gothic, the exterior is one of the
earliest examples of the Classical, or Renaissance, style in
France.

Don't cross the Seine to Ile St-Louis yet. Take rue de l'Hôtel de
Ville to where it meets rue de Figuier. The painstakingly re-
㉕ stored **Hôtel de Sens** (1474) on the corner is one of a handful of
Parisian homes to have survived since the Middle Ages. With
its pointed corner towers, Gothic porch, and richly carved decorative details, it is a strange mixture, half defensive stronghold, half fairytale château. Built at the end of the 15th century
for the archbishop of Sens, it was once the home of Henri IV
and his queen, Marguerite, philanderers both. While Henri
dallied with his mistresses—he is said to have had 56—at a series of royal palaces, Marguerite entertained her almost equally large number of lovers here. Today the building houses a fine
arts library, the **Bibliothèque Forney** (admission free; open
Tues.–Fri. 1:30–8:30, Sat. 10–8:30).

26 Cross pont Marie to the residential **Ile St-Louis,** the smaller of the two islands in the heart of Paris, linked to the Ile de la Cité by pont St-Louis. There are no standouts here and no great sights, but for idle strolling, window shopping, or simply sitting on one of the little quays and drinking in the views, the Ile St-Louis exudes a quintessentially Parisian air.

Time Out **Berthillon** has become a byword for delicious ice cream. Cafés all over Ile St-Louis sell its glamorous products, but the place to try them is still the little shop on rue St-Louis-en-l'Ile. Expect to wait in line. *31 rue St-Louis-en-l'Ile. Closed Tues.*

Tour 3: From the Arc de Triomphe to the Opéra

This tour takes in grand, opulent Paris; the Paris of imposing vistas; long, arrow-straight streets; and plush hotels and jewelers. It begins at the Arc de Triomphe, standing sturdily at the top of the most famous street in the city, the Champs-Elysées.

Place Charles-de-Gaulle is known by Parisians as **l'Etoile,** the star—a reference to the streets that fan out from it. It is one of Europe's most chaotic traffic circles, and short of a death-defying dash, your only way of getting to the Arc de Triomphe in the middle is to take an underground passage from the Champs-Elysées or avenue de la Grande-Armée.

27 The colossal, 164-foot **Arc de Triomphe** was planned by Napoleon to celebrate his military successes. Unfortunately, the great man's strategic and architectural visions were not entirely on the same plane: When it was required for the triumphal entry of his new empress, Marie Louise, into Paris in 1810, it was still only a few feet high. To save face, he ordered a dummy arch of painted canvas to be put up. (The real thing wasn't finished until 1836.) After recent, extensive cleaning, its elaborate relief sculptures are magnificent. The highlight is the scene by François Rude, illustrated to the right of the arch when viewed from the Champs-Elysées. Called *Departure of the Volunteers in 1792,* it's commonly known as *La Marseillaise* and depicts *La Patrie,* or the Motherland, with outspread wings exhorting the volunteers to fight for France.

If you like views, go up to the viewing platform at the top of the monument, from which you can admire the vista down the Champs-Elysées toward place de la Concorde and the distant Louvre. A small museum halfway up the arch is devoted to its history. France's *Unknown Soldier* is buried beneath the archway; the flame is rekindled every evening at 6:30. *Pl. Charles-de-Gaulle. Admission: 27 frs. adults, 15 frs. children and senior citizens. Open daily 10–6; 10–5 in winter.*

Laid out by landscape gardener Le Nôtre in the 1660s as a garden sweeping away from the Tuileries, the cosmopolitan **Champs-Elysées** occupies a central role in French national celebrations. It witnesses the finish of the Tour de France cycle race on the last Sunday of July and is the site of vast ceremonies on Bastille Day, July 14 (France's national holiday), and November 11, Armistice Day. Start by walking down from l'Etoile on the left, where 300 yards down, at no. 116-B, is the famous **Lido** nightclub: Foot-stomping melodies in French and English, and champagne-soaked, topless razzamatazz pack in the crowds every night. Opposite, avenue George-V leads down to the **Prince de Galles** (Prince of Wales) at no. 33 (with the red awning) and the **George V** (with the blue awning), two of the city's top hotels. Continue down avenue George-V, and turn right down Pierre-Ier-de-Serbie to the church of **St-Pierre de Chaillot** on avenue Marceau. The monumental frieze above the entrance, depicting scenes from the life of St. Peter, is the work of Henri Bouchard and dates from 1937. Returning to avenue George-V, continue toward the slender spire of the **American Cathedral of the Holy Trinity,** built by G. S. Street between 1885 and 1888. *Open weekdays 9–12:30 and 2–5, Sat. 9–noon. Services: weekdays noon, Sun. 9 AM and 11 AM; Sun. School and nursery.*

At the bottom of avenue George-V is the place de l'Alma and the Seine. Just across the Alma bridge, on the left, is the entrance to **Les Egouts,** the Paris sewers (admission: 22 frs. adults, 17 frs. students and senior citizens; open Sat.–Wed. 11–4). Or stay on the Right Bank and head down the sloping side road to the left of the bridge, for the embarkation point of the *Bâteaux Mouches* motorboat tours of the Seine.

Stylish avenue Montaigne leads from the Seine back toward the Champs-Elysées.

Time Out   Although power brokers and fashion models make up half the clientele at the **Bar des Théâtres,** its blasé waiters refuse to bat an eyelid. This is a fine place for an aperitif or a swift, more affordable lunch than what you'll find around the corner at the luxury restaurants on place de l'Alma. *Opposite the Théâtre des Champs-Elysées at 6 av. Montaigne.*

---

28   Two blocks east, along the Champs-Elysées and on the side of avenue Winston-Churchill, sit the **Grand Palais** and the Petit Palais, erected before the Paris World Fair of 1900. Like the Eiffel Tower, there was never any intention that these two buildings would be anything other than temporary additions to the city. Together they recapture the opulence and frivolity of the Belle Epoque. Today the atmospheric iron-and-glass interior of the Grand Palais plays regular host to major exhibitions. *Av. Winston-Churchill. Admission varies according to exhibition. Usually open 10:30–6:30, often until 10 AM on Wed.*

29   The **Petit Palais** has a beautifully presented permanent collection of lavish, 17th-century furniture and French 19th-century painting, with splendid canvases by Courbet and Bouguereau. Temporary exhibits are often held here, too. The sprawling entrance gallery contains several enormous turn-of-the-century paintings on its walls and ceiling. *Av. Winston-Churchill. Admission: 12 frs. adults, 6 frs. children. Open Tues.–Sun. 10–5:30.*

Cross the Champs-Elysées and head down avenue de Marigny to **rue du Faubourg St-Honoré,** a prestigious address in the world of luxury fashion and art galleries. High security surrounds the French president in the **Palais de l'Elysée.** This "palace," where the head of state lives, works, and receives official visitors, was originally constructed as a private mansion in 1718. It has known presidential occupants only since 1873; before then, Madame de Pompadour (Louis XV's influential mistress), Napoleon, Josephine, and Queen Victoria all stayed here. Today the French government, the *Conseil des Ministres*, meets here each Wednesday. *Not open to the public.*

Continue down to rue Royale. This classy street, lined with
③ jewelry stores, links place de la Concorde to the **Eglise de la
Madeleine.** With its rows of uncompromising columns, the Madeleine's sturdy neoclassical edifice looks more like a Greek temple than a Christian church. The only natural indoor light
comes from three shallow domes. The inside walls are richly
and harmoniously decorated, and gold glints through the
murk. The church was designed in 1814 but not consecrated until 1842. The portico's majestic Corinthian colonnade—cleaned
and renovated in 1991—supports a gigantic pediment with a
sculptured frieze of the *Last Judgment.* From the top of the
steps, stop to admire the view down rue Royale across the
Seine.

At the far end of the rue Royale, on the right (as you look from
La Madeleine), is the legendary **Maxim's** restaurant. Unless
you choose to eat here—an expensive and not always rewarding experience—you won't be able to see the interior decor, a
riot of crimson velvet and florid Art Nouveau furniture.

Time Out **L'Ecluse,** on the west side of the square around the church, is a
select, wood-paneled wine bar where you can order a whole
range of Bordeaux by the glass. Stylish snacks, such as foie
gras or carpaccio, make this a great place for a light lunch. *15
pl. de la Madeleine. Open noon–2 AM.*

There is a striking contrast between the gloomy locked-in feel
③② of the high-walled rue Royale and the broad, airy **place de la
Concorde.** This huge square is best approached from the
Champs-Elysées: The flower beds, chestnut trees, and sandy
sidewalks of the avenue's lower section are reminders of its
original leafy elegance. Place de la Concorde was built in the
1770s, but there was nothing in the way of peace or concord
about its early years. From 1793 to 1795, it was the scene of
over a thousand deaths by guillotine; victims included Louis
XVI, Marie Antoinette, and Danton. The obelisk, a present
from the viceroy of Egypt, was erected in 1833. The handsome,
symmetrical, 18th-century buildings facing the square include
the deluxe **Hôtel Crillon** (far left), though there's nothing so
vulgar as a sign to identify it—just an inscribed marble plaque.
Facing one side of place de la Concorde are the Tuileries Gardens. Two smallish buildings stand sentinel here. To the left,
nearer rue de Rivoli, is the **Jeu de Paume,** fondly known to many
as the former home of the Impressionists (now in the Musée
d'Orsay). It underwent extensive renovation in 1990–91 and
was slated to become a temporary exhibition center as we went
to press. The other identical building nearer the Seine is the re-
③③ cently restored **Orangerie,** containing some early 20th-century
paintings by Monet and Renoir, among others. *Pl. de la
Concorde. Admission: 23 frs. (12 frs. Sun.). Open Wed.–Mon.
9:45–5:15; closed Tues.*

③④ As gardens go, the formal and greatly patterned **Jardin des Tuileries** is typically French, a charming place to stroll and survey
the surrounding cityscape. Leave the Tuileries by the rue de
Rivoli gateway across from rue de Castiglione and the hefty
bronze column of place Vendôme.

③⑤ **Place Vendôme** is one of the world's most opulent squares, a
perfectly proportioned example of 17th-century urban architecture (by Mansart), now holding numerous upscale jewelers

and the **Ritz.** Napoleon had the square's ce
from the melted bronze of 1,200 cannons ca
of Austerlitz in 1805. That's him standing v

36 The **Opéra,** begun at the behest of Napoleo
in 1875 by Charles Garnier, typifies the pompous ~~bee~~
pire style of architecture. The monumental foyer and staircase
are a stage in their own right where, on first nights, celebrities
preen and prance. If the lavishly upholstered auditorium (ceiling painted by Marc Chagall in 1964) seems small, it is only because the stage is the largest in the world—more than 11,000
square yards. The **Opéra museum,** containing a few paintings
and theatrical mementos, is unremarkable. *Admission: 17 frs.
Open daily 11–4:30; closed occasionally. Tel. 47–42–57–50.*

Tour 4: From Orsay to Trocadéro

The Left Bank has two faces: the cozy, ramshackle Latin Quarter (*see* Tour 5: The Left Bank, below) and the spacious, stately
Seventh Arrondissement, covered in this tour. The latest addi-
37 tion to this area is already the most popular: the **Musée d'Orsay,**
a stylishly converted train station housing key Impressionist
works, as well as important examples of other 19th- and 20th-
century schools. The chief artistic attraction here is the collection of Impressionist works, featured on the top floor. Highlights include Monet's *Waterlilies* and Renoir's *Le Moulin de la
Galette.* The Post-Impressionists—Paul Cézanne, Vincent Van
Gogh, Paul Gauguin, and Henri de Toulouse-Lautrec—are all
also represented on this floor.

On the first floor, you'll find the work of Edouard Manet and the
delicate nuances of Edgar Degas. Pride of place, at least in art-
history terms, goes to Manet's *Déjeuner sur l'Herbe,* the painting that scandalized Paris in 1863. If you prefer modern developments, head for the exhibit of paintings by the early 20th-
century group known as the *Fauves* (meaning wild beasts, as
they were dubbed by an outraged critic in 1905)—particularly
Henri Matisse, André Derain, and Maurice de Vlaminck.
Sculpture at the Orsay means, first and foremost, Auguste
Rodin. Two further highlights are the faithfully restored Belle
Epoque restaurant and the model of the entire Opéra quarter,
displayed beneath a glass floor. Prepare for huge crowds: The
best times for relatively painless viewing are at lunchtime or on
Thursday evening. *1 rue de Bellechasse. Admission: 30 frs., 15
frs. Sun., children under 18 free. Open Tues.–Sun. 10–5:30
(Thurs. 10–9:15); closed Mon.*

Continue along the left bank of the Seine to the 18th-century
38 **Palais Bourbon** (directly across from place de la Concorde),
home of the Assemblée Nationale (French Parliament). The
colonnaded facade was commissioned by Napoleon. Though it's
not open to the public, there is a fine view from the steps across
to place de la Concorde and the church of the Madeleine.

Head south to rue de Varenne and the Hôtel Biron, better
39 known as the **Musée Rodin.** The splendid house, with its spacious vestibule and light, airy rooms, retains much of its 18th-
century atmosphere and makes a handsome setting for the
sculpture of Rodin (1840–1917), including the famous *Thinker*
(le Penseur) and *Kiss.* Don't leave without visiting the garden:
It is exceptional, both for its rosebushes (over 2,000) and its
sculptures. *77 rue de Varenne, tel. 47–05–01–34. Admission:*

20 frs., 10 frs. Sun. Open Tues.–Sun. 10–6, 10–5 winter; closed Mon.

40 From the Rodin Museum, you can see the **Hôtel des Invalides** along rue de Varenne, founded by Louis XIV in 1674 to house wounded (or "invalid") veterans. Only a handful of old soldiers live there today, but the building houses one of the world's foremost military museums, **Musée de l'Armée,** with a vast collection of arms, armor, uniforms, banners, and military pictures. The **Musée des Plans-Reliefs,** housed on the fifth floor of the right-hand wing, contains a fascinating collection of scale models of French towns made to illustrate the fortifications planned by the 17th-century military engineer Sébastien de Vauban. The largest and most impressive is Strasbourg, which takes up an entire room.

The museums are not the only reason for visiting the Invalides, however. The building itself is an outstanding monumental ensemble in late 17th-century Baroque, designed by Libéral Bruant (1635–97) and Jules Hardouin-Mansart (1646–1708). The main, cobbled courtyard is a fitting scene for the parades and ceremonies still occasionally held here. The most impressive dome in Paris towers over the **Eglise du Dôme** (Church of the Dome). The Dôme church was designed by Mansart and built between 1677 and 1735. The remains of Napoleon are here, in a series of six coffins, one inside the next, within a bombastic tomb of red porphyry. Among others commemorated in the church are French World War I hero Marshal Foch and fortification-builder Vauban, whose heart was brought to the Invalides at Napoleon's behest. *Hôtel des Invalides. Admission: 25 frs. adults, 13 frs. children. Open daily 10–6, 10–4:45 winter. A son-et-lumière (sound-and-light show) in English is held in the main courtyard on evenings throughout the summer.*

Turn right out of the Dôme church and follow avenue de Tourville to the Champ de Mars. At the far end looms Paris's

41 best-known landmark, the **Eiffel Tower.** Built by Gustave Eiffel for the World Exhibition of 1889, the centennial of the French Revolution, it was still in good shape to celebrate its own 100th birthday. Such was Eiffel's engineering wizardry that even in the strongest winds, his tower never sways more than 4½ inches. Today it exudes a feeling of mighty permanence. As you stand beneath its huge legs, you may have trouble believing that it nearly became 7,000 tons of scrap iron when its concession expired in 1909. Only its potential use as a radio antenna saved the day; it now bristles with a forest of radio and television transmitters. The energetic can stride up the stairs as far as the third deck. If you want to go to the top, 1,000 feet up, you'll have to take the elevator. *Pont d'Iéna. Cost by elevator: 2nd floor, 16 frs.; 3rd floor, 30 frs.; 4th floor, 47 frs. Cost by foot: 8 frs. (2nd and 3rd floors only). Open daily 10 AM–11 PM; mid-Mar.–Aug., Fri. and Sat. 10 AM–midnight.*

Visible just across the Seine from the Eiffel Tower, on the

42 heights of Trocadéro, is the massive, sandy-colored **Palais de Chaillot,** a cultural center built in the 1930s. The gardens between the Palais de Chaillot and the Seine contain an aquarium and some dramatic fountains, and the terrace between the two wings of the palace offers a wonderful view of the Eiffel Tower.

The Palais de Chaillot contains four large museums, two in each wing. In the left wing (as you approach from the Seine) are the **Musée de l'Homme,** an anthropological museum, with primitive and prehistoric artifacts from throughout the world (Admission: 16 frs. adults, 8 frs. children. Open Wed.–Mon. 10–5), and the **Musée de la Marine,** a maritime museum with exhibits on French naval history right up to the age of the nuclear submarine (Admission: 22 frs. adults, 10 frs. children. Open Wed.–Mon. 10–6).

The other wing is dominated by the **Musée des Monuments Français,** without question the best introduction to French medieval architecture. Its long first-floor gallery pays tribute to French buildings, mainly of the Romanesque and Gothic periods (roughly AD 1000–1500), in the form of painstaking copies of statues, columns, archways, and frescoes. Substantial sections of a number of French churches and cathedrals are represented here, notably Chartres and Vézelay. Murals and ceiling paintings—copies of works in churches around the country—dominate the other three floors. *Admission: 15 frs., 8 frs. on Sun. Open Wed.–Mon. 9–6.*

The **Musée du Cinema,** tracing the history of motion pictures from the 1880s, is located in the basement. *Admission: 20 frs. adults, 12 frs. children and senior citizens. Open Wed.–Mon., guided tours only, on the hour at 10, 11, 2, 3, and 4.*

43 The area around the Palais de Chaillot offers a feast for museum lovers. The **Musée Guimet** has three floors of Indo-Chinese and Far Eastern art, including stone Buddhas, Chinese bronzes, ceramics, and painted screens. *6 pl. d'Iéna. Admission: 15 frs., 8 frs. on Sun. Open Wed.–Mon. 9:45–5:10; closed Tues.*

44 Nearby is the **Palais Galliera,** home of the **Musée de la Mode et Costume** (Museum of Fashion and Costume), a late 19th-century town house that hosts revolving exhibits. *10 av. Pierre-Ier-de-Serbie. Admission: 21 frs. Open Tues.–Sun. 10–5:40.*

45 The **Musée de l'Art Moderne de la Ville de Paris** has both temporary exhibits and a permanent collection of modern art. Among the earliest works in the vast galleries are Fauvist paintings by Vlaminck and Derain, followed by Picasso's early experiments in Cubism. Other highlights include works by Robert Delaunay, Georges Braque, and Amedeo Modigliani. There is also a large room devoted to Art Deco furniture and screens; a pleasant, if expensive, museum café; and an excellent bookshop with many books in English. *11 av. du Président-Wilson. Admission: 15 frs., free Sun. for permanent exhibitions only. Open Tues.–Sun. 10–5:40, Wed. 10–8:30.*

Tour 5: The Left Bank

References to the Left Bank have never lost their power to evoke the most piquant images of Paris. Although the bohemian strain the area once nurtured has lost much of its vigor, people who choose to live and work here today are, in effect, turning their backs on the formality and staidness of the Right Bank. As a matter of fact, President Mitterrand himself lives here.

The Left Bank's geographic and cerebral hub is the Latin Quarter, which takes its name from the university tradition of studying and speaking in Latin, a practice that disappeared at the time of the French Revolution. The area is populated mainly by students and academics from the Sorbonne, the headquarters of the University of Paris.

46 **Place St-Michel** is a good starting point for exploring the rich slice of Parisian life that the Left Bank offers. Leave your itineraries at home and wander along the neighboring streets lined with restaurants, cafés, galleries, old bookshops, and all sorts of clothing stores, from tiny boutiques to haute-couture showrooms. If you follow quai des Grands Augustins and then quai de Conti west from St-Michel, you will be in full view of the Ile de la Cité, the Louvre, and the Temple de l'Oratoire (built in 1621 and once one of the most important churches in France) across the Seine.

For an alternative route crowded more with humanity than with traffic, pick up the pedestrian rue St-André des Arts at the southwest corner of place St-Michel. Just before you reach the carrefour de Buci crossroads at the end of the street, turn onto the cour du Commerce St-André. Jean-Paul Marat printed his revolutionary newspaper, *L'Ami du Peuple*, at no. 8, and it was here that Dr. Guillotin conceived the idea for a new "humane" method of execution that, apparently to his horror, was used during the French Revolution.

47 Continue to the **carrefour de Buci,** once a notorious Left Bank landmark. By the 18th century, it contained a gallows, an execution stake, and an iron collar for punishing troublemakers. Many Royalists and priests lost their heads here during the bloody course of the French Revolution. Nearby rue de Buci has one of the best markets in Paris. The stands close by 1 PM and do not open at all on Monday.

Several interesting, smaller streets of some historical significance radiate from the carrefour de Buci. Rue de l'Ancienne-Comédie, which cuts through to the busy place de l'Odéon, is so named because no. 14 was the first home of the now legendary French theater company, the *Comédie-Française*. Across the **48** street sits the oldest café in Paris, the **Procope** (now a classy restaurant). Opened in 1686, it has been a watering hole for many of Paris's literati, including Voltaire, Victor Hugo, and Oscar Wilde. Ben Franklin was a patron, as were the fomenters of the French Revolution—Marat, Danton, Desmoulins, and Robespierre. Napoleon's hat, forgotten here, was encased in a glass dome.

Stretching north toward the Seine is the rue Dauphine, the street that singer Juliet Greco put on the map when she opened the **Tabou jazz club** here in the '50s. The club attracted a group of young intellectuals who were to become known as the Zazous, a St-Germain movement prompting the jazz culture, complete with all-night parties and "free love."

The next street that shoots out of the carrefour (moving coun- **49** terclockwise) is rue Mazarine, housing the **Hôtel des Monnaies,** the national mint. Louis XVI transferred the Royal Mint to this imposing mansion in the late 18th century. Although the mint was moved in 1973, weights and measures, and limited-edition coins are still made here. You can see the vast collection of coins, documents, engravings, and paintings at the **Musée Monétaire.** *11 quai Conti. Admission: 15 frs. adults, 10 frs.*

children and senior citizens. Open Tues., Thurs.–Sun. 1–6, Wed. 1–9.

Next door is the **Institut de France,** one of France's most revered cultural institutions and one of the Left Bank's most impressive waterside sights, with its distinctive dome and commanding position overlooking the quai. It was built as a college in 1661; in the early 19th century, Napoleon stipulated that the Institut de France be transferred here from the Louvre. The **Académie Française,** the oldest of the five academies that comprise the Institut de France, was created by Cardinal Richelieu in 1635. Its first major task was to edit the French dictionary; today, among other functions, it is still charged with safeguarding the purity of the French language. Membership is the highest literary honor in France. Not until 1986 was a woman, author Marguerite Yourcenar, elected to its ranks. *Guided visits are reserved for cultural associations only.*

50 Just west along the waterfront, on quai Malaquais, stands the **Ecole Nationale des Beaux-Arts,** whose students can usually be seen painting and sketching on the nearby quais and bridges. The school, once the site of a convent, was established in 1816. Allow yourself time to wander into its courtyard and galleries to see the casts and copies of the statues that were once stored here, or stop in at one of the temporary exhibitions of professors' and students' works. *14 rue Bonaparte. Open daily 1–7.*

Tiny **rue Visconti,** running east–west off rue Bonaparte (across from the entrance to the Beaux-Arts), has a lot of history packed into its short length. In the 16th century, it was known as Paris's "Little Geneva"—named after Europe's foremost Protestant city—because of the Protestant ghetto that formed here. Jean Racine, one of France's greatest playwrights and tragic poets, lived at no. 24 until his death in 1699. Honoré Balzac set up a printing shop at no. 17 in 1826, and the fiery Romantic artist Eugène Delacroix (1798–1863) worked here from 1836 to 1844.

Time Out The terrace at **La Palette** beckons as you reach the rue de Seine, at the end of rue Visconti. This popular café has long been a favorite haunt of Beaux-Arts students. One of them was allowed to paint an ungainly portrait of the patron, François, which rules over the shaggy gathering of clients with mock authority. *43 rue de Seine.*

Farther down the gallery-lined rue de Seine, swing right onto the pretty rue Jacob, where both Wagner and Stendhal once lived. Then turn left onto rue de Fürstemberg, which leads to one of Paris's most delightful and secluded little squares, the place Fürstemberg. Delacroix's studio here has been turned **51** into the charmingly tiny **Musée Eugène Delacroix;** it contains a small collection of sketches and drawings, while the garden at the rear is almost as interesting. *Pl. Fürstemberg. Admission: 11 frs. adults, 6 frs. youths 18–25 and senior citizens over 60, children under 18 free. Open Wed.–Mon. 9:15–12:30 and 2–5:15; closed Tues.*

52 **St-Germain-des-Prés,** Paris's oldest church, began as a shelter for a relic of the True Cross brought back from Spain in 542. Behind it, rue de l'Abbaye runs alongside the former **Abbey Palace,** dating from 990. Interesting interior details include the colorful 19th-century frescoes in the nave by Hippolyte

Flandrin, a pupil of the Classical painter Ingres. The church stages superb organ concerts and recitals; programs are displayed outside and in the weekly periodicals *Officiel des Spectacles* and *Pariscope*.

Across the cobbled place St-Germain-des-Prés stands the celebrated **Deux Magots** café, still thriving on its '50s reputation as one of the Left Bank's prime meeting places for the intelligentsia. These days, you're more likely to rub shoulders with tourists than with philosophers, but a sidewalk table still affords a perfect view of Left Bank life.

In the years after World War II, Jean-Paul Sartre and Simone de Beauvoir would meet "The Family"—their intellectual clique—two doors down at the **Café de Flore,** on the boulevard St-Germain. Today the Flore has become more of a gay hangout, but it is a scenic spot that never lacks for action, often in the form of the street entertainers performing in front of the church.

If you now pick up the long rue de Rennes and follow it south, you'll soon arrive in the heart of Montparnasse. The opening of
❺❸ the **Tour Maine-Montparnasse** in 1973 forever changed the face of this former painters' and poets' haunt. The tower, containing offices and a branch of the Galeries Lafayette department store, was part of a vast redevelopment plan that aimed to make the area one of Paris's premier business and shopping districts. As Europe's tallest high rise, it claims to have the fastest elevator in Europe and affords stupendous views of Paris. *Admission: 34 frs. adults, 20 frs. children 5–14, under 5 free. Open daily 10 AM–11 PM, weekdays 10 AM–10 PM in winter.*

Up boulevard du Montparnasse and across from the Vavin métro station are two of the better-known gathering places of Montparnasse's bohemian heyday, the **Dôme** and **La Coupole** brasseries. La Coupole opened in 1927 and soon became a home away from home for some of the area's most famous residents, such as Guillaume Apollinaire, Max Jacob, Jean Cocteau, Erik Satie, Igor Stravinsky, and the inevitable Ernest Hemingway.

Continue along boulevard du Montparnasse, to the intersection with boulevard St-Michel, where the verdant avenue de l'Observatoire sweeps down to the Luxembourg Gardens. Here you'll find perhaps the most famous bastion of the Left Bank
❺❹ café culture, the **Closerie des Lilas** (*see* Dining, below). Now a pricey but pretty bar/restaurant, the Closerie remains a staple on all literary tours of Paris, not least because of the commemorative plaques fastened onto the bar, marking the places where renowned writers used to sit. Charles Baudelaire, Paul Verlaine, Ernest Hemingway, and Guillaume Apollinaire are just a few of the names.

Walk down avenue de l'Observatoire to the **Jardin du Luxembourg** (the Luxembourg Gardens), one of the city's few large parks. Its fountains, ponds, trim hedges, precisely planted rows of trees, and gravel walks are typical of the French fondness for formal gardens. At the far end is the **Palais du Luxembourg** itself, gray and formal, built, like the park, for Maria de' Medici, widow of Henri IV, at the beginning of the 17th century. The palace remained royal property until the French Revolution, when the state took it over and used it as a prison. Danton, the painter Jacques Louis David, and American political philosopher and author Tom Paine (1737–1809) were all detained here. Today it is the site of the French Senate and is not open to the public.

If you follow rue Vaugirard (the longest street in Paris) one block east to boulevard St-Michel, you will soon be at the place de la Sorbonne, nerve center of the Left Bank's student population. The square is dominated by the **Eglise de la Sorbonne,** whose outstanding exterior features are its 10 Corinthian columns and cupola. Inside is the white marble tomb of Cardinal Richelieu. (The church is open to the public only during exhibitions and cultural events.) The university buildings of La Sorbonne spread out around the church from rue Cujas down to the visitor's entrance on rue des Ecoles.

56 The **Sorbonne** is the oldest university in Paris—indeed, one of the oldest in Europe—and has for centuries been one of France's principal institutions of higher learning. It is named after Robert de Sorbon, a medieval canon who founded a theological college here in 1253 for 16 students. By the 17th century, the church and university buildings were becoming dilapidated, so Cardinal Richelieu undertook to have them restored; the present-day Sorbonne campus is largely a result of that restoration. For a glimpse of a more recent relic of Sorbonne history, look for Puvis de Chavannes's painting of the *Sacred Wood* in the main lecture hall, a major meeting point during the tumultuous student upheavals of 1968.

Behind the Sorbonne, bordering its eastern reach, is the rue St-Jacques. The street climbs toward the rue Soufflot, named **57** in honor of the man who built the vast, domed **Panthéon,** set atop place du Panthéon. One of Paris's most physically overwhelming sites—it was commissioned by Louis XV as a mark of gratitude for his recovery from a grave illness in 1744—the Panthéon is now a seldom-used church with monumental frescoes by Puvis de Chavannes and a crypt that holds the remains of such national heroes as Voltaire, Emile Zola, and Jean-Jacques Rousseau. *Admission: 23 frs. adults, 18–24 12 frs., 17 and under 5 frs. Open daily 10–5:30.*

Up rue St-Jacques and left on the rue des Ecoles is the square Paul-Painlevé; behind it lies the entrance to the inimitable **58** **Hôtel et Musée de Cluny.** Built on the site of the city's enormous Roman baths, the Musée de Cluny is housed in a 15th-century mansion that originally belonged to the monks of Cluny Abbey in Burgundy. But the real reason anyone comes to the Cluny is to see its superb tapestry collection. The most famous series is the graceful *Dame à la Licorne* (the *Lady and the Unicorn*), woven in the 15th or 16th century, probably in the southern Netherlands. There is also an exhibition of decorative arts from the Middle Ages; a vaulted chapel; and a deep, cloistered courtyard with mullioned windows, set off by the *Boatmen's Pillar*, Paris's oldest sculpture, at its center. *Admission: 15 frs. Open Wed.–Mon. 9:45–12:30 and 2–5:15; closed Tues.*

Above boulevard St-Germain, rue St-Jacques reaches toward the Seine, bringing you past the elegant proportions of the **59** church of **St-Séverin,** the parish church of the entire Left Bank during the 11th century. Rebuilt in the 16th century and noted for its width and its Flamboyant Gothic architecture, the church dominates a close-knit neighborhood filled with quiet squares and pedestrian streets. Note the splendidly deviant spiraling column in the forest of pillars behind the altar. *Open weekdays 11–5:30, Sat. 11–10.*

Running riot around the relative quiet of St-Séverin are streets filled with restaurants of every description and serving everything from take-out souvlaki to five-course haute cuisine. Rue de la Huchette is the most heavily trafficked of the restaurant streets and is especially good for its selection of cheaper Greek food houses and Tunisian patisseries.

Time Out If you are in the mood for entertainment with your supper, duck into **Le Cloître** (19 rue St-Jacques). This old, heavily wood-beamed bar has a one- and sometimes two-woman revue in the cellar, performing songs of old Paris from the '20s, '30s, and '40s. For a quieter diversion, stop at **Pub St-Jacques** (11 rue St-Jacques), where you can drink whiskey until the wee hours.

Cross to the other side of rue St-Jacques. In square René-Viviani, which surrounds the 12th-century church of **St-Julien-le-Pauvre,** stands an acacia that is supposedly the oldest tree in Paris (although it has a rival claim from another acacia at the Jardin des Plantes). This tree-filled square also gives you one of the more spectacular views of Notre-Dame.

Behind the church, to the east, are the tiny, elegant streets of the recently renovated Maubert district, bordered by quai de Montebello and boulevard St-Germain. Rue de Bièvre, once filled with tanneries, is now guarded at both ends to protect President Mitterrand's private residence.

60 Public meetings and demonstrations have been held in place Maubert ever since the Middle Ages. Nowadays, most gatherings are held inside or in front of the **Palais de la Mutualité** on the corner of the square, also a venue for jazz, pop, and rock concerts. On Tuesday, Thursday, and Saturday, it is transformed into a colorful outdoor food market.

61 The **Jardin des Plantes,** several blocks southeast, is an enormous swath of greenery containing spacious botanical gardens and a number of natural-history museums. It is stocked with plants dating back to the first collections of the 17th century and has since been enhanced by subsequent generations of devoted French botanists. The garden claims to shelter Paris's oldest tree, an *Acacia robinia*, planted in 1636. It also contains a small, old-fashioned zoo, an alpine garden, an aquarium, a maze, and a number of hothouses. *Admission: 12–25 frs. Open Wed.–Mon. 2–5; closed Tues.*

Time Out At the back of the gardens, in place du Puits-de-l'Hermite, you can drink a restorative cup of sweet mint tea in **La Mosquée,** a beautifully kept, white mosque, complete with minaret. The Moslem restaurant here serves copious quantities of couscous. The sunken garden and tiled patios are open to the public—the prayer rooms are not—and so are the luxurious *hammams,* or Turkish baths (open Fri. and Sat. 11–7 men only; Mon., Wed., and Thurs. 11–7 women only). *Admission: 10 frs. adults, 6 frs. students and senior citizens. Open Sat.–Thurs., guided tours 9–12 and 2–6.*

Tour 6: Montmartre

Numbers in the margin correspond with points of interest on the Montmartre map.

On a dramatic rise above the city is **Montmartre,** site of the basilica of Sacré-Coeur—Paris's best-known landmark after the Eiffel Tower—and home to a once-thriving artistic community, now reduced to gangs of third-rate painters clustered in the area's most famous square, the place du Tertre. Despite their presence, and the fact that the fabled nightlife of old Montmartre has fizzled down to some glitzy nightclubs and porn shows, the area still exudes a sense of history.

62 Begin your tour at **place Blanche,** site of the Moulin Rouge. Place Blanche (White Square) takes its name from the clouds of chalky dust churned up by the windmills that once dotted Montmartre. The windmills were set up here not just because the hill was a good place to catch the wind—at over 300 feet, it's the highest point in the city—but because Montmartre was covered with cornfields and quarries right up to the end of the 19th century. Today only two of the original 20 windmills are intact. The most famous, immortalized by painter Toulouse-Lautrec, is the **Moulin Rouge,** or Red Windmill, built in 1885 and turned into a dance hall in 1900; the place is still trading shamelessly on the notion of Paris as a city of sin (*see* Arts and Nightlife, below).

For a taste of something more authentically French than the Moulin Rouge's computerized light shows, walk up rue Lepic, site of one of the most colorful and tempting **food markets** in Paris (closed Mon.).

Turn left onto rue des Abbesses and walk along to the small **Montmartre cemetery.** It contains the graves of many prominent French men and women, including Edgar Degas and Adolphe Sax, inventor of the saxophone. The Russian ballet dancer Vaslav Nijinsky is buried here as well.

63 Walk along rue des Abbesses, then turn into rue Tholoze, which leads to the **Moulin de la Galette,** one of the two remaining windmills in Montmartre, now unromantically rebuilt. To reach it you pass **Studio 28:** This seems no more than a scruffy little movie theater, but when it opened in 1928, it was the first *art et essai,* or experimental theater, in the world, and has shown the works of such directors as Jean Cocteau, François Truffaut, and Orson Welles before the films' official premieres.

64 Return to rue des Abbesses, turn left, and walk to **place des Abbesses.** Though commercial, the little square has the kind of picturesque and slightly countrified architecture that has made Montmartre famous.

There are two competing attractions just off the square. Theater buffs should head down the tiny rue André-Antoine. At no. 37, you'll see what was originally the **Théâtre Libre,** the Free Theater, which was influential in popularizing the groundbreaking works of naturalist playwrights Henrik Ibsen and August Strindberg. The other attraction is **rue Yvonne-le-Tac,** scene of a vital event in Montmartre's early history and linked to the disputed story of how this quarter got its name. Some say the name Montmartre comes from the Roman temple to Mercury that was once here, called the Mound of Mercury, or

Montmartre

N

Basilique du Sacré-
Coeur, **69**

Bateau-Lavoir, **66**

Chapelle du
Martyre, **65**

Lapin Agile, **71**

Moulin de la
Galette, **63**

Musée de l'Art Juif, **72**

Musée du Vieux
Montmartre, **70**

Place des
Abbesses, **64**

Place Blanche, **62**

Place Jean-Baptiste
Clément, **67**

Plâce du Tertre, **68**

Mons Mercurii. Others contend that it was an adaptation of *Mons Martyrum,* a name inspired by the burial here of Paris's first bishop, St-Denis. (The popular yet implausible version of his martyrdom is that he was beheaded by the Romans in AD 250 but arose to carry his severed head from rue Yvonne-le-Tac to an area four miles north, now known as St-Denis.) St-Denis

65 is commemorated by the 19th-century **Chapelle du Martyre** at no. 9. It was in the crypt of the original chapel that the Italian priest Francis Xavier founded the Jesuit order in 1534, a decisive step in the efforts of the Catholic Church to reassert its authority in the face of the Protestant Reformation.

From rue Yvonne-le-Tac, retrace your steps through place des Abbesses. Take rue Ravignon on the right, climbing to the summit via place Emile-Goudeau, an enchanting little cobbled

66 square. Your goal is the **Bateau-Lavoir,** or Boat Wash House, at its northern edge. Montmartre poet Max Jacob coined the name for the old building on this site, which burned down in 1970: Not only did it look like a boat, he said, but the warren of artists' studios within were always paint-spattered and in need of a good hosing down. The drab, present-day concrete building also contains art studios, though none so illustrious as those of Cubist painters Picasso and Braque, which were housed here in years gone by.

67 Continue up the hill to **place Jean-Baptiste Clément.** The Italian painter and sculptor Modigliani (1884–1920) had a studio here at no. 7. Some people have claimed that he is the greatest Italian artist of the 20th century, the man who fused the genius of the Italian Renaissance with the modernity of Cézanne and Picasso. Modigliani claimed he would drink himself to death—he eventually did—and chose the wildest part of town in which to do it. Most of the old-time cabarets are gone now, though, and only the Moulin de Paris still reflects a glimmer of the old atmosphere.

Rue Norvins, formerly rue des Moulins, runs behind and parallel to the north end of the square. Turn right, walk past the

68 bars and tourist shops, and you'll reach **place du Tertre.** At most times of the year, you'll have to fight your way through the crowds to the southern end of the square and the breathtaking view over the city. The real drawback here, though, is the swarm of artists clamoring to dash off your portrait. Most are licensed, but there is a fair share of con men. If one produces a picture of you without having asked first, you're under no obligation to buy it!

La Mère Catherine, the restaurant at the north end of the square, was a favorite with the Russian cossacks who occupied Paris after Napoleon's 1814 exile to the island of Elba. Little did the cossacks know that when they banged on the tables and shouted "bistro," the Russian word for "quick," they were inventing a new breed of French restaurant. Now fairly touristic, La Mère Catherine is surprisingly good, though prices are high.

Time Out **Patachou** sounds the one classy note in place du Tertre. It offers exquisite, if expensive, cakes and teas.

It was in place du Tertre that one of the most violent episodes in French history began, one that colored French political life for generations. Despite popular images of later 19th-century

France—and Paris especially—as a time of freedom and prosperity, the country was desperately divided into two camps for much of this period: a militant underclass, motivated by resentment of what they considered an elitist government, and a reactionary and fearful bourgeoisie and ruling class. In March 1871, the antimonarchist Communards clashed with soldiers of the French government leader, Adolphe Thiers. The Communards formed the Commune, which ruled Paris for three months. Then Thiers ordered his troops to take the city, and upwards of 10,000 Communards were executed after the Commune's collapse.

Looming behind the church of St-Pierre on the east side of the square, the **Basilique du Sacré-Coeur** was erected in 1873 (after Thiers's death) as a kind of guilt offering for the ruthless killing of the Communards. Even so, the building was to some extent a reflection of political divisions within the country, financed by French Catholics fearful of an anti-clerical backlash and determined to make a grand statement on behalf of the Church. Stylistically, the Sacré-Coeur borrows elements from Romanesque and Byzantine models, fusing them under its distinctive Oriental dome. The gloomy, cavernous interior is worth visiting for its golden mosaics; climb to the top of the dome for the view over Paris.

More of Montmartre beckons north and west of the Sacré-Coeur. Take rue du Mont-Cenis down to rue Cortot, site of the **Musée du Vieux Montmartre.** Like the Bateau-Lavoir, the building that is now the museum sheltered an illustrious group of painters, writers, and assorted cabaret artists in its heyday toward the end of the 19th century. Foremost among them were Pierre-Auguste Renoir and Maurice Utrillo, who was the Montmartre painter par excellence. Taking the gray, crumbling streets of Montmartre as his subject matter, Utrillo discovered that he worked much more effectively from cheap postcards than from the streets themselves. Look carefully at the pictures in the museum here and you will see the plaster and sand he mixed with his paints to help convey the decaying buildings of the area. The next best thing about the museum is the view over the tiny vineyard on neighboring rue des Saules. *12 rue Cortot. Admission: 20 frs. adults, 10 frs. children and senior citizens. Open Tues.–Sat. 2:30–6, Sun. 11–6.*

There's an equally famous Montmartre landmark on the corner of rue St-Vincent, just down the road: the **Lapin Agile,** or the Nimble Rabbit. It's a bar-cabaret, originally one of the raunchiest haunts in Montmartre. Today it manages against all odds to preserve at least something of its earlier flavor, unlike the Moulin Rouge.

Behind the Lapin Agile is the **St-Vincent Cemetery,** whose entrance is off little rue Lucien Gaulard. It's a tiny graveyard, but serious students of Montmartre might want to visit to see Utrillo's burial place. Continue north on rue des Saules, across busy rue Caulaincourt, and you'll come to the **Musée de l'Art Juif,** the Museum of Jewish Art, containing devotional items, models of synagogues, and works by Camille Pissarro and Marc Chagall. *42 rue des Saules. Admission: 15 frs. adults, 10 frs. students and children. Open Sun.–Thurs. 3–6; closed Aug., Fri., and Sat.*

Excursion: Rueil-Malmaison

Rueil-Malmaison is today a faceless, if pleasant, western suburb of Paris, but the memory of star-crossed lovers Napoleon and Josephine still haunts its Malmaison château on avenue Napoléon-Bonaparte. To get there by car, take N13 from Porte Maillot; or, alternatively, catch the RER to La Défense, then switch to the 158A bus, which stops right by the château.

Built in 1622, **La Malmaison** was bought by the future Empress Josephine in 1799 as a love nest for Napoleon and herself (they had married three years earlier). After the childless Josephine was divorced by the heir-hungry emperor in 1809, she retired to La Malmaison and died here on May 29, 1814.

The château has 24 rooms furnished with exquisite tables, chairs, and sofas of the Napoleonic period; of special note are the library, game room, and dining room. The walls are adorned with works by contemporary artists of the day, such as Jacques-Louis David, Pierre-Paul Prud'hon, and Baron Gérard. Take time to admire the clothes and hats belonging to Napoleon and Josephine, particularly the display of the empress's gowns. Their carriage can be seen in one of the garden pavilions, and another pavilion contains a unique collection of snuffboxes donated by Prince George of Greece. The gardens themselves are delightful, especially the regimented rows of spring tulips. *Av. du Château. Admission: 21 frs., 11 frs. Sun. Open Wed.–Mon. 10–noon and 1:30–5; closed Tues.*

The **Bois Préau,** which stands close to La Malmaison, is a smaller mansion dating back to the 17th century. It was acquired by Josephine in 1810, after her divorce, but subsequently reconstructed in the 1850s. Today its 10 rooms, complete with furniture and objects from the Empire period, are devoted mainly to souvenirs of Napoleon's exile on the island of St. Helena. *Entrance from av. de l'Impératrice. Admission: 23 frs. Open Wed.–Mon. 10–noon and 1:30–5; closed Tues.*

For other excursions from Paris, *see* the Ile de France chapter.

Paris for Free

Unfortunately, Paris doesn't offer many organized sights that can be enjoyed without first digging deep into your pockets. That said, the city is one of the world's most scenic and exciting capitals, and just strolling along, breathing in its rich, romantic atmosphere, is an occupation in which every visitor will want to indulge. A **walk along the Seine** is at the top of the list, whether you're on your first trip or your 51st. One of the rewarding sections is the quayside on the Ile St-Louis, notably the **quai de Bourbon,** at the west end facing Ile de la Cité, from which you'll get some memorable views of Notre-Dame. The streets of **Montmartre** are also rich in Gallic charm, though don't be surprised by the crowds or the many steep streets and flights of steps you'll encounter.

Paris's many parks and gardens can be enjoyed free of charge (the **Tuileries** and the **Jardin du Palais-Royal** are especially delightful), and, of course, the churches of **Sacré-Coeur, La Madeleine,** and **St-Germain-des-Prés** won't break the bank either.

A trip to the city's largest and most attractive cemetery, the 19th-century **Cimetière du Père-Lachaise,** is also a freebie: Cobbled avenues, steep slopes, and lush vegetation contribute to its powerful atmosphere, while inhabitants include Frédéric Chopin, Jean-Baptiste Molière, Honoré de Balzac, and Oscar Wilde, among other luminaries.

A number of museums are free on Sunday, including the Petit Palais, the Paris Museum of Modern Art, the Musée Carnavalet, and the homes of Honoré de Balzac and Victor Hugo.

Except for its modern art museum and those galleries with temporary exhibitions, the vast halls of the **Beaubourg** are always open free of charge. Outside, on the plateau Beaubourg, you can be entertained for hours by the fire-eaters, Indian rope tricksters, musicians, mimes, and clowns who gather here during summer months. Similar entertainment can be found on the square in front of St-Germain-des-Prés, on the Left Bank.

And while this isn't strictly speaking free: The price of a cup of coffee will guarantee you a ringside seat in any of Paris's sidewalk cafés, where you can amuse yourself for hours watching the world go by.

What to See and Do with Children

Amusement Parks **Jardin d'Acclimatation.** This charming children's play park in the Bois de Boulogne boasts a miniature train, boat rides, and a zoo. *Admission: 7.50 frs. adults, 3.50 frs. children. Open daily 10–6. Métro: Les Sablons.*

Parc Floral de Paris. The east Paris equivalent of the Jardin d'Acclimatation, the Parc Floral is situated in the Bois de Vincennes, near the château. It features a miniature train, a games area, and miniature golf. *Rte. de la Pyramide, Vincennes. Admission: 8 frs. adults, 4 frs. children, under 6 free. Open daily, summer 9:30–8; winter 9:30–5. Métro: Château de Vincennes.*

Aquariums Fish gazing is a soothing, mesmerizing experience for young and old alike. There are two principal aquariums in Paris: **Centre la Mer et des Eaux** (195 rue St-Jacques, 5e. Admission: 18 frs. adults, 10 frs. children. Open Tues.–Fri. 10–12:30 and 1:15–5:30; weekends 10–5:30. RER: Luxembourg) and **Aquarium Tropical** (293 av. Daumesnil, 12e. Admission: 20 frs., 10 frs. Sun. Open Wed.–Mon. 10–noon and 1:30–5. Métro: Porte Dorée). Don't forget the new **Parc Océanique,** a high-tech, though overpriced, display center devoted to marine life dreamed up by the famous ocean explorer Captain Jacques Cousteau (Forum des Halles, 1er. Admission: 75 frs. adults, 50 frs. children. Open Sat.–Thurs. 12–7. Métro: Les Halles).

Boat Trips An hour on the Seine on a *Bateau Mouche* or *Vedette* is a fun way to get to know the capital. The cost is 35 francs for adults, 20 francs for children under 10. Departures: every half hour from **Square du Vert Galant** (1er. Métro: Pont-Neuf), **Eiffel Tower** (7e. Métro: Bir-Hakeim), and **Pont de l'Alma** (8e. Métro: Alma-Marceau).

Boating Rowboats can be rented at the **Lac Inférieur** in the Bois de Boulogne and at **Lac des Minimes** and **Lac Daumesnil** in the Bois de Vincennes.

Circus There's no need to know French to enjoy a circus. Tickets range from 40 francs to 180 francs. There are evening and weekend matinee performances. Check for details with **Cirque Pauwels** (Jardin d'Acclimatation, Bois de Boulogne, tel. 48–05–44–39;

Métro: Les Sablons) or **Cirque d'Hiver** (110 rue Amelot, 11e, tel. 48–78–75–00; Métro: Chemin Vert).

Museums **Cité des Sciences et de l'Industrie de la Villette.** Children love this extensive and imaginatively laid out museum devoted to industry. *Parc de la Villette. Admission: 35 frs., planetarium 15 frs. extra. Open Thurs. and Fri. 10–6; Tues., Wed. and weekends noon–8. Métro: Porte de la Villette.*

Musée de la Femme et Collection d'Automates. The collection of automata and clockwork dolls bursts into life each afternoon. It's well worth making the short trip to Neuilly, especially since the Jardin d'Acclimatation (*see* above) and Bois de Boulogne are close at hand. *12 rue du Centre, Neuilly. Admission: 12 frs. adults, 6 frs. children and senior citizens. Guided tours Wed.–Mon. 3 PM. Métro: Pont de Neuilly.*

Musée Grévin. The long-established boulevard Montmartre museum concentrates on waxwork imitations of the famous, the newer one in Halles on recapturing the Belle Epoque. *10 blvd. Montmartre, 9e. Admission: 42 frs. adults, 28 frs. children under 14. Métro: Rue Montmartre. Forum des Halles, 1er. Admission: 36 frs. adults, 22 frs. children under 14. Métro: Les Halles. Both open Mon.–Sat. 10:30–7, Sun. 1–8 (the blvd. Montmartre museum is closed mornings in winter).*

Puppet Shows On most Wednesday, Saturday, and Sunday afternoons, **Guignol,** the French equivalent of Punch and Judy, performs at various parks, including the Tuileries and the Luxembourg.

Zoos Monkeys, deer, birds, and farm animals star at the **Jardin d'Acclimatation** (*see* above), while the **Ménagerie** in the Jardin des Plantes boasts elephants, lions, and tigers. *57 rue Cuvier, 5e. Admission: 22 frs. adults, 10 frs. children. Open daily 9–6 (9–5 in winter). Métro: Jussieu.*

Paris's biggest zoo is in the **Bois de Vincennes;** in addition to wild beasts, it includes a museum, films, and exhibitions. *53 av. de St-Maurice, 12e. Admission: 30 frs. adults, 15 frs. children. Open daily 9–6 (9–5 in winter). Métro: Porte Dorée.*

Off the Beaten Track

Buttes-Chaumont. This immensely picturesque park in the downbeat 19th arrondissement of northeast Paris boasts a lake, waterfall, and clifftop folly, or "belvedere." Until town planner Baron Haussmann got his hands on it in the 1860s, the area was a rubbish dump and quarry—hence the steep slopes. *Rue Botzaris. Métro: Buttes-Chaumont, Botzaris.*

Les Catacombes. The Catacombs consist of an extensive underground labyrinth founded by the Romans, who tunneled under much of the Left Bank and into the near suburbs. They were subsequently used to store bones from disused graveyards; then, during World War II, they became the headquarters of the French Resistance. You are well advised to take a flashlight with you. *1 pl. Denfert-Rochereau. Admission: 15 frs., 8.50 frs. students and senior citizens. Open Tues.–Fri. 2–4, weekends 9–11 and 2–4. Guided tours on Wed. at 2:45, 20 frs. extra. Métro and RER: Denfert/Rochereau.*

Sightseeing Checklists

Historical Buildings and Sites

Arc de Triomphe. *See* Tour 2. Métro; Bastille.

Bateau-Lavoir. *See* Tour 6. Métro: Abbesses.

Bibliothèque Nationale. *See* Tour 1. Métro: Bourse, Pyramides.

Bourse. The Paris Stock Exchange, a serene, colonnaded 19th-century building, is a far cry from Wall Street. Take your passport if you want to tour it. *Pl. de la Bourse. Guided tours Mon.–Sat. every half hour, 11–1. Métro: Bourse.*

Carrefour de Buci. *See* Tour 5. Métro: Odéon.

Comédie-Française. *See* Tour 1. Métro: Palais-Royal.

Conciergerie. *See* Tour 1. Métro: Cité.

Ecole Militaire. Still used as a military academy, the École Militaire, overlooking the Champ de Mars and the Eiffel Tower, is not open to visitors, but you can admire its harmonious 18th-century architecture from the Champ de Mars. Métro: École Militaire.

Ecole Nationale des Beaux-Arts. *See* Tour 5. Métro: St-Germain-des-Prés.

Eiffel Tower. *See* Tour 4. Métro: Bir Hakeim.

Hôtel de Beauvais. A Renaissance-era *hôtel particulier* (town house) dating from 1655, located on rue François-Miron in the Marais. Métro: St-Paul.

Hôtel Carnavalet. *See* Tour 2. Métro: St-Paul-le-Marais.

Hôtel des Invalides. *See* Tour 4. Métro: Latour-Maubourg, Varenne.

Hôtel Matignon. The French prime minister's residence is obviously not open to visitors, but the courtyard of this elegant mansion, built in 1721, is worth a discreet peek. Métro: Varenne.

Hôtel de Sens. *See* Tour 2. Métro: Pont Marie.

Hôtel de Sully. This superb 17th-century mansion houses the Caisse Nationale des Monuments Historiques, which organizes some excellent guided tours of and conferences on historical monuments throughout the city. *62 rue St-Antoine. Open daily 10–6. Métro: St-Paul.*

Hôtel de Ville. *See* Tour 2. Métro: Hôtel de Ville.

Institut de France. *See* Tour 5. Métro: Pont Neuf.

La Malmaison. Rueil-Malmaison. Excursion.

Mémorial de la Déportation. Located at Square de l'Ile-de-France at the tip of the Ile de la Cité is a modern crypt dedicated to French men and women who died in Nazi concentration camps. It was once the city morgue. *Admission: free. Open daily. Métro: Maubert-Mutualité.*

Opéra. *See* Tour 3. Métro: Opéra.

Opéra de la Bastille. *See* Tour 4. Métro: Bastille.

Panthéon. *See* Tour 5. Métro: Luxembourg.

Palais Bourbon. *See* Tour 4. Métro: Assemblée Nationale.

Palais de l'Elysée. *See* Tour 3. Métro: Champs-Elysées-Clemenceau.

Palais de Justice. *See* Tour 1. Métro: Cité.

Palais Royal. *See* Tour 1. Métro: Palais-Royal.

Place de la Concorde. *See* Tour 3. Métro: Concorde.

Place du Tertre. *See* Tour 6. Métro: Abbesses.

Place Vendôme. *See* Tour 3. Métro: Opéra, Tuileries.

Place des Vosges. *See* Tour 2. Métro: St-Paul, Chemin-Vert.

Pompidou Center. *See* Tour 2. Métro: Rambuteau.

Sorbonne. *See* Tour 5. Métro: Cluny-La Sorbonne, Luxembourg.

Théâtre National de l'Odéon. *See* Tour 5. Métro: Odéon.

Museums and Galleries

Archives Nationales. *See* Tour 2. Métro: Rambuteau.

Atelier Gustave Moreau. The town house and studio of painter Gustave Moreau (1826–98), doyen of the Symbolist movement, features works of extravagant colors and flights of fantasy and provides some of the strangest artistic experiences in Paris. *14 rue de la Rochefoucauld. Admission: 15 frs., 8 frs. on Sun. Open Wed.–Sun. 11–1 and 2–5:15. Métro: Trinité.*

Cité des Sciences et de l'Industrie de la Villette. *See* What to See and Do with Children. Métro: Porte de la Villette.

Grand Palais. *See* Tour 3. Métro: Champs-Elysées-Clemenceau.

L'Historial. A wax museum specializing in Montmartre history. *Rue Poulbot. Admission: 22 frs. Open daily 11–6:30. Métro: Abbesses.*

Institut du Monde Arabe. This new addition to the Left Bank, opposite the east end of the Ile St-Louis, does for Arab culture what the Beaubourg does for modern art. *23 quai St-Bernard. Admission: free. Open Tues.–Sun. 1–8. Métro: Cardinal-Lemoine.*

Maison de Balzac. This was the Paris home of one of France's greatest 19th-century novelists. It contains a wide range of exhibits charting his tempestuous life. *47 rue Rayounard, tel. 42–24–56–38. Admission: 15 frs. Open Tues.–Sun. 10–5:40. Métro: Passy.*

Maison de Victor Hugo. *See* Tour 2. Métro: St-Paul.

Maison de la Vigne. *See* Tour 3. Métro: Franklin-Roosevelt.

Musée de l'Affiche. The history of posters and other advertising material is covered in this small museum. *107 rue de Rivoli. Admission: 20 frs. Open Wed.–Mon. 10–6. Métro: Palais-Royal.*

Musée de l'Armée. *See* Tour 4. Métro: Latour-Maubourg.

Musée de l'Art Africain et des Arts Océaniques. Artifacts from Africa and the South Seas are intriguingly displayed in this sizable museum. *293 av. Daumesnil. Admission: 20 frs., 10 frs. on Sun. Open Wed.–Mon. 10–12 and 1:30–5:30. Métro: Porte-Dorée.*

Musée de l'Art Juif. *See* Tour 6. Métro: Lamarck-Caulaincourt.

Musée d'Art Moderne de la Ville de Paris. *See* Tour 4. Métro: Iéna.

Musée National d'Art Moderne. *See* Tour 2. Métro: Rambuteau.

Musée de l'Art Naïf. A substantial collection of naive paintings; many people love it. *2 rue Ronsard. Admission: 25 frs. adults, 18 frs. children and senior citizens. Open Tues.–Sun. 10–6. Métro: Anvers.*

Musée des Arts et Traditions Populaires. Preindustrial objects from all regions of France. *6 rue Mahatma-Gandhi, Bois de Boulogne. Admission: 15 frs. Open Wed.–Mon. 10–5. Métro: Les Sablons.*

Musée Bricard de la Serrure. *See* Tour 2. Métro: St-Paul-le-Marais.

Musée Cernuschi. This collection of Chinese art ranges from Neolithic pottery (3rd century BC) to funeral statuary, painted 8th-century silks, and contemporary paintings. *7 av. Vélasquez. Admission: 9 frs. Open Tues.–Sun. 10–5:40. Métro: Monceau.*

Musée Cognacq-Jay. *See* Tour 2. Métro: St-Paul.

Musée de la Chasse et de la Nature. Some may find the assembled paintings, guns, and traps here unpleasant; others will love them. *60 rue des Archives. Admission: 30 frs. Open Wed.–Mon. 10–12:30 and 1:30–5:30. Métro: Rambuteau.*

Musée du Cinéma. *See* Tour 4. Métro: Trocadéro.

Musée de Cluny. *See* Tour 5. Métro: Cluny-Sorbonne.

Musée Eugène Delacroix. *See* Tour 5. Métro: St-Germain-des-Prés.

Musée de la Femme et Collection d'Automates. *See* What to See and Do with Children. Métro: Pont de Neuilly.

Musée Guimet. *See* Tour 4. Métro: Iéna.

Musée de l'Histoire de Paris. *See* Tour 2. Métro: St-Paul-le-Marais.

Musée de la Holographie. The museum of holography—a photographic method of producing futuristic, three-dimensional images—has a suitably modern setting in the Forum des Halles. *15 Grand Balcon, Forum des Halles. Admission 28 frs. adults, 24 frs. students and senior citizens. Open Mon.–Sat. 10–7, Sun. 1–7. Métro: Les Halles.*

Musée de l'Homme. *See* Tour 4. Métro: Trocadéro.

Musée Jacquemart-André. A sumptuous 19th-century town house is the setting for this little-known museum that contains a rich collection of Renaissance and 18th-century art. *158 blvd. Haussmann. Admission: 15 frs. Open Wed.–Sun. 1–6. Métro: St-Philippe-du-Roule.*

Musée du Louvre. *See* Tour 1. Métro: Palais-Royal.

Musée de la Marine. *See* Tour 4. Métro: Trocadéro.

Musée Marmottan. One of the most underestimated museums in Paris. The chief attraction here is the fabulous collection of Impressionist paintings, chiefly by Claude Monet. *2 rue Louis-Boilly. Admission 25 frs. Open Tues.–Sun. 10–5:30. Métro: La Muette.*

Musée de La Mode et Costume. *See* Tour 4. Métro: Iéna.

Musée des Monuments Français. *See* Tour 4. Métro: Trocadero.

Musée de la Musique Mécanique. A pleasantly rustic museum near the Pompidou Center, featuring mechanical musical instruments (hourly tours with working demonstrations). *Impasse Berthaud. Admission: 25 frs. adults, 15 frs. children under 12. Open weekends 2–7. Métro: Rambuteau.*

Musée Nissim de Camondo. This stylish, aristocratic Parisian mansion, in the style of Louis XVI, dates from the last days of the regal Ancien Regime. *63 rue de Monceau. Admission: 15 frs. Open Wed.–Sun. 10–noon and 2–5. Métro: Monceau.*

Musée de Notre-Dame. *See* Tour 1. Métro: Cité.

Musée de l'Opéra. *See* Tour 3. Metro: Opéra.

Musée de l'Orangerie. *See* Tour 3. Métro: Concorde.

Musée de l'Ordre de la Libération. The Order of Liberation was created by General de Gaulle after the fall of France in 1940 to honor those who made outstanding contributions to the Allied victory in World War II. Some 200 display cabinets evoke various episodes of the war. *51 bis blvd. de Latour-Maubourg. Admission: 5 frs. Open Mon.–Sat. 2–5. Metro: Latour-Maubourg.*

Musée d'Orsay. *See* Tour 4. Métro: Musée d'Orsay, Solférino.

Musée Picasso. *See* Tour 2. Métro: St-Sébastien-Froissart.

Musée des Plans-Reliefs. *See* Tour 4. Métro: Latour-Maubourg.

Musée Rodin. *See* Tour 4. Métro: Varenne.

Musée du Sport. A sports museum housed at the French national stadium in southwest Paris, featuring posters, trophies, equipment, and other sporting paraphernalia. *Parc des Princes, 24 rue du Commandant-Guilbaud. Admission: 20 frs. adults, 10 frs. children and senior citizens. Open Sun.–Tues., Thurs., and Fri. 9:30–12 and 2–5. Métro: Porte de St-Cloud.*

Musée des Transports. A collection of more than 100 vehicles dating back to the 17th century, including horse-drawn carriages and trams. *60 av. Ste-Marie, Saint-Mandé. Admission: 15 frs. adults, 8 frs. students and senior citizens. Open Apr.–Oct., weekends 2:30–6. Métro: Porte Dorée.*

Musée de Vieux Montmartre. *See* Tour 6. Métro: Lamarck-Caulaincourt.

Musée du Vin. Wine museum, with tastings. *Rue des Eaux. Admission: 25 frs. Open Tues.–Sun. 12–6. Métro: Passy.*

Palais de la Découverte. *See* Tour 3. Métro: Champs-Elysées-Clemenceau.

Petit Palais. *See* Tour 3. Métro: Champs-Elysées-Clemenceau.

Churches Paris is rich in churches of two architectural styles: late Gothic (the Flamboyant style of the 14th and 15th centuries with its intricate stone tracery) and 17th-century Baroque (columns, rounded arches, and smaller windows inspired by Classical antiquity and the Italian Renaissance). Another feature is the phenomenal number of wall paintings, to be found mainly inside chapels and dating, for the most part, from the first half of the 19th century.

Most churches are open 9–noon and 2–5, but there are no set hours. Some have daily services at lunchtime.

American Cathedral of the Holy Trinity. *See* Tour 3. Métro: Alma-Marceau.

American Church in Paris. A neo-Gothic church built between 1927 and 1931. *65 quai d'Orsay, tel. 47–05–07–99. Métro: Alma-Marceau.*

Basilique du Sacré-Coeur. *See* Tour 6. Métro: Anvers.

Cathédrale Notre-Dame. *See* Tour 1. Métro: Cité.

Chapelle du Martyre. *See* Tour 6. Métro: Abbesses.

Eglise du Dôme. *See* Tour 4. Métro: St-François-Xavier.

Eglise de la Madeleine. *See* Tour 3. Métro: Madeleine.

Eglise de la Sorbonne. *See* Tour 5. Métro: Cluny-La Sorbonne.

Mosquée de Paris. Not far from the Jardin des Plantes, you can plunge yourself into a Muslim atmosphere beneath the arcades and minaret of an authentic mosque built between 1922 and 1925, decorated in Hispano-Moorish style. The gardens are overgrown, but the French-speaking tour guides are there to fill you in on Islam, not horticulture. *Pl. du Puits de l'Ermite. Open Sat.–Thurs. 2–5. Métro: Monge.*

Notre-Dame des Victoires. You'll want to visit this 17th-century church, built between 1666 and 1740, to see the 30,000 ex-voto tablets that adorn its walls. *Pl. des Petits-Pères. Métro: Sentier.*

St-Alexander-Nevsky. The onion domes of the Russian Orthodox Cathedral of Paris are one of the most distinctive landmarks of the city. *12 rue Daru. Métro: Courcelles.*

Sainte-Chapelle. *See* Tour 1. Métro: Cité.

Ste-Clothide. This neo-Gothic church (1846–58) is chiefly of note for its imposing twin towers, visible from across the Seine. *Rue Las-Cases. Métro: Solférino.*

Ste-Croix-St-Jean. This much-restored church, erected in 1624, is now the Armenian Cathedral of Paris. Its chancel contains some splendid 18th-century gilded paneling. *Rue du Perche. Métro: Rambuteau.*

St-Denys-du-St-Sacrement. This severely neoclassical edifice (close to the Picasso Museum in the Marais) dates from the 1830s. Notice the *grisaille* (colorless) frieze and gilt fresco above the semicircular apse and the Delacroix *Deposition* (1844) in the front right-hand chapel as you enter. *Rue de Turenne. Métro: St-Sébastien.*

St-Elisabeth. This studied essay in the Baroque style (1628–46) has a pleasantly unpretentious feel. There are brightly restored wall paintings and a wide apse around the choir with stupendous, carved, 17th-century wood paneling. *Rue du Temple. Métro: Temple.*

St-Etienne-du-Mont. This church (1492–1632), in the shadow of the Pantheon, has a mishmash facade, but its curly, carved screen-rood (1525–35), separating nave and chancel, is the only one of its kind in Paris. *Pl. Ste-Geneviève. Métro: Cardinal-Lemoine.*

St-Eustache. *See* Tour 1. Métro: Les Halles.

St-Germain l'Auxerrois. *See* Tour 1. Métro: Louvre.

St-Germain-des-Prés. *See* Tour 5. Métro: St-Germain-des-Prés.

St-Gervais-St-Protais. *See* Tour 2. Métro: Hôtel-de-Ville.

St-Jean l'Evangéliste. An innovative, 1904 essay in art-nouveau concrete, subsequently clad in red brick. *Pl. des Abbesses. Métro: Abbesses.*

St-Julien-le-Pauvre. *See* Tour 5. Métro: St-Michel.

St-Louis-des-Invalides. The original church at Les Invalides. Métro: Latour-Maubourg.

St-Louis-de-la-Salpêtrière. Built between 1670 and 1677 according to the designs of architect Libéral Bruant, the church is shaped like a Greek cross and boasts a lantern-topped, octagonal dome. *Blvd. de l'Hôpital. Métro: Gare d'Austerlitz.*

St-Médard. The nave and facade, with its large late-Gothic window, date from the late 15th century. The 17th-century choir is in the contrasting Classical style. A picturesque churchyard lines rue Censier. *Square St-Médard. Métro: Censier-Daubenton.*

St. Michael's English Church. A modern building with a friendly welcome. *5 rue d'Aguesseau, tel. 47–42–70–88. Open Thurs.–Tues. 9:30–5:30. Services Thurs. 12:30 and Sun. 10:30 and 6:30. Métro: Madeleine.*

St-Nicolas-des-Champs. Here's another Parisian example of the Gothic colliding with the Renaissance style: The round-arched, fluted Doric capitals in the chancel date from 1560 to 1587, a full century later than the pointed-arched nave. There is a mid-17th-century organ and a fine *Assumption* above the high altar by Simon Vouet (1629). *Rue St-Martin. Métro: Arts et Métiers.*

St-Nicolas-du-Chardonnet. The first church on the site was built in a field of thistles (*chardons*); in recent years, St-Nicolas has been a thorn in the side of the Catholic Church by refusing to abandon the Latin mass. This pleasant Baroque edifice (1656–1709) on the Left Bank houses a Corot study for the *Baptism of Christ* in the first chapel on the right and a *Crucifixion* by Peter Brueghel the Younger in the sacristy. *Rue St-Victor. Métro: Maubert-Mutualité.*

Ste-Odile. The colossal, dark-brick tower of this modern church (1938–46) is reminiscent of Stalinist Russia, but the inside is influenced by Scandinavian architecture, with its harmony, simple lines, and decorative restraint. The modern stained glass is first-rate. *Av. Stéphane-Mallarmé. Métro: Porte de Champerret.*

St-Pierre. *See* Tour 6. Métro: Pigalle.

St-Roch. *See* Tour 1. Métro: Tuileries.

St-Séverin. *See* Tour 5. Métro: St-Michel.

St-Sulpice. Built between 1646 and 1780, this is the "Cathedral of the Left Bank." *Pl. St-Sulpice. Métro: St-Sulpice.*

Temple Ste-Marie. Constructed between 1632 and 1634 by François Mansart as the chapel of the Convent of the Visitation, this is now a Protestant church. The dome above the distinctive nave-rotunda is one of the earliest in Paris and is said to have influenced Christopher Wren when he was planning St. Paul's Cathedral in London. *Rue St-Antoine. Métro: Bastille.*

Parks and Gardens

Bois de Boulogne. In the 1850s, Baron Haussmann designed these 2,200 acres of woodland on Paris's western outskirts. The gardens are full of amenities, including two lakes, stadiums, cafés, and restaurants. Walking and even driving are inadvisable after dark, however. *Métro: Porte Dauphine (east), Les Sablons (north), and Port d'Auteuil (south).* Worth seeing is the spectacular **Bagatelle**, a floral park with vast lawns and 18th-century buildings. *Entrance: Route de Sèvres à Neuilly, or off Allée de Longchamp (bus no. 44 or Métro: Pont de Neuilly). Admission: 8 frs.* On the north edge of the Bois is the Jardin d'Acclimatation, a children's amusement park (*see* What to See and Do with Children, above). *Blvd. des Sablons. Métro: Les Sablons. Admission: 8 frs. Open daily 10–6.*

Bois de Vincennes. This is another vast area of woodland, but on the southeast outskirts of Paris, with a sprawling castle, a zoo, and a floral park. Métro: Château de Vincennes.

Buttes-Chaumont. In the 1860s, Baron Haussmann transformed this one-time, steep-sloped quarry into an immensely picturesque park with a lake, waterfalls, and an oft-painted belvedere. It also has a charming restaurant. *Rue Botzaris. Métro: Buttes-Chaumont.*

Champ-de-Mars. This long, formal garden, landscaped at the turn of the century, lies between the Eiffel Tower and Ecole Militaire. Métro: Ecole Militaire.

Jardin Albert-Kahn. On the Paris side of the Seine, across from St-Cloud park, these gardens add a surprising note of Oriental greenery to the undistinguished suburb of Boulogne. *1 rue des Abondances, Boulogne. Admission: 10 frs. Open daily 11–7 (dusk in winter). Métro: Boulogne-Pont de St-Cloud.*

Jardin des Halles. This new urban park near the church of St-Eustache is geared mainly for children, with an old-fashioned carousel and rhino-shaped bushes. Métro: Les Halles.

Jardin du Luxembourg. *See* Tour 5. Métro: Odéon, Luxembourg.

Jardin du Palais-Royal. *See* Tour 1. Métro: Palais-Royal.

Jardin des Plantes. *See* Tour 5. Métro: Monge, Jussieu.

Jardin des Tuileries. *See* Tour 3. Métro: Tuileries.

Moorish Gardens (Mosquée de Paris). *See* Tour 5. Métro: Monge.

Parc Monceau. An 18th-century park with lake, rotunda, and mock ruins. Métro: Monceau.

Parc Montsouris. Very pretty, English-style gardens in the south of the city, with cascades, a lake, and a meteorological observatory disguised as a Tunisian Palace. Métro: Cité Universitaire, Glacière.

Parc de St-Cloud. This wooded park on a hill to the southwest of Paris offers some superb views of the city. Métro: Boulogne-Pont de St-Cloud.

Park de la Villette. A vast new park now surrounds the glimmering science and industry museum complex, with a children's play area, the Inventorium. Located in the once-unfashionable 19th arrondissement in the northeast of Paris, it's a pleasant place for a stroll near the Canal de l'Ourcq. Métro: Porte de Pantin, Porte de la Villette.

Cemeteries This listing is not as macabre as it sounds. The cemeteries of Paris are remarkable for their statues, elaborate monuments, tombs of the famous, and melancholy disrepair. They are usually open from 7:30 to 6 in summer, and from 8 till dusk in winter.

Cimetière de Montmartre. Situated on the west side of the Montmartre hill, this cemetery, built in 1795, houses the tombs of the writers Zola and Stendhal, the composer Hector Berlioz, the painter Degas, and the French film director François Truffaut. *Av. Rachel. Métro: Place de Clichy.*

Cimetière de Montparnasse. High walls encircle the Montparnasse cemetery, a haven of peace in one of Paris's busiest shopping and business areas. You can visit the tombs of Jean-Paul Sartre, Baudelaire, Frédéric-Auguste Bartholdi—who designed the Statue of Liberty—and André Citroën. *Blvd. Edgar-Quinet. Métro: Raspail, Edgar-Quinet.*

Cimetière du Père-Lachaise. This cemetery, the largest in Paris, is also the most attractive. It houses the tombs of the French author Colette, the composer Frédéric Chopin, the playwright Jean-Baptiste Molière, writers Honoré de Balzac, Marcel Proust, and Oscar Wilde, the popular French actress Simone Signoret, and rock star Jim Morrison, among many others. *Av. Gambetta. Open daily 8–6, 8–5 in winter. Métro: Père-Lachaise.*

Shopping

Paris lives up to its reputation as one of the world's great shopping capitals. The city boasts great names in haute couture, perfume, and accessories, as well as countless boutiques and department stores. Prices are generally higher than in London or New York, so you may prefer to limit yourself to window shopping.

Shopping Districts A general rule of thumb is that the Left Bank is geared more to small, specialty shops and boutiques, while the Right Bank is home to the high-fashion houses, the most ostentatious shops, and the large department stores.

On the Left Bank, **St-Germain-des-Prés** has long been a center for bookshops, ready-to-wear fashion stores, and specialty shops. The nearby **rue de Grenelle** has seen the arrival of chic designers, including Sonia Rykiel and Charles Jourdan. Shoe and fabric shops crowd the **rue des Saints-Pères,** while the **rue de Rennes,** running from St-Germain to Montparnasse, is packed with a variety of clothing stores, many quite inexpensive. The **Montparnasse Tower** contains several department stores.

On the Right Bank, the modern, three-tiered **Forum des Halles** has recently become a popular shopping spot. The area around the mall contains numerous shops with knick-knacks and clothes. **Place des Victoires** is one of the leading centers of avant-garde Parisian fashion, while the **rue du Faubourg St-Honoré** and the area around the **Champs-Elysées** offer numerous haute-couture houses.

The **Opéra** district contains landmark department stores. The **place Vendôme** and the surrounding streets glitter with the city's swankiest jewelry stores.

Shopping Arcades   The various shopping arcades scattered around Paris often date to the 19th century. Many have been splendidly restored, with arching glass roofs, marble flooring, and brass lamps set off to full advantage. Most are conveniently located in the 1st and 2nd arrondissements on the Right Bank.

The **Galerie Vivienne** (4 rue des Petits Champs, 2e), between the Bourse (Stock Exchange) and Palais Royal, is a delightful place in which to amble.

Galerie Véro-Dodat (19 rue Jean-Jacques Rousseau, 1er) has painted ceilings and slender copper pillars.

Passage des Panoramas (11 blvd. Montmartre, 2e) is the granddaddy of them all, opened in 1800. You can window-shop here until about 9 PM, when the ornamental gates at either end are closed.

Department Stores   Paris has a good selection of department stores, several of which are conveniently grouped on the Right Bank around the Opéra. **Printemps** (64 blvd. Haussmann, 9e) claims to be the "most Parisian department store." Its main rival is **Galeries Lafayette** (40 blvd. Haussmann, 9e), and competition is fierce. Both go out of their way to cater to foreign visitors, and each offers excellent services, including multilingual hostesses, bureaux de change, and sales. For visitors in a hurry, both stores have the added attraction of a series of designer boutiques.

Two other department stores are located on the Right Bank, nearer the Seine. **Samaritaine** (19 rue de la Monnaie, 1er) is the largest department store in Paris, offering a vast range of goods at reasonable prices. As the name implies, the **Bazar de l'Hôtel de Ville** (52 rue de Rivoli) is located across from the Hôtel de Ville (City Hall). Familiarly known as the B.H.V. (pronounced bay-ash-vay), it is great for clothes and good-quality household goods.

The Left Bank's sole department store is **Au Bon Marché** (22 rue de Sèvres), at the corner of rue de Sèvres and rue du Bac. It's not trendy but has an excellent antiques section and a terrific grocery store, complete with cheese, pastry, bread, wine, and prepared-food sections.

The budget **Monoprix** and **Prisunic** stores are cheap and cheerful. The largest Prisunic outlets are at 109 Champs-Elysées, on the corner of rue La Boétie, 8e; and 25 av. des Ternes. Monoprix's handiest outlet for tourists is at 21 av. de l'Opéra, 1er.

Markets   Every *quartier* in Paris boasts an open-air food market, if only for a few days a week. Sunday mornings, until 1 PM, is usually a good time to go; Monday is the most likely closing day. The local markets usually concentrate on food, but they always have a few brightly colored flower stalls. Some markets have stalls that sell antiques, clothing, household goods, and secondhand books. Their lively—sometimes chaotic—atmosphere makes them a sight worth seeing even if you don't want to buy anything.

Many of the better-known markets are located in areas you'd visit for sightseeing. Our favorites are on **rue de Buci,** 6e (open

A la Mère de Famille, **26**
A La Ville du Puy, **14**
Annick Goutal, **23**
Au Bon Marché, **48**
La Bagagerie, **12**
Bazar de l'Hôtel de Ville, **41**
Bouchara, **16**
Cacharel, **32**
Carel, **47**
Carré Rive Gauche, **44**
Cartier, **19**
Chanel, **9**
Chaumet, **22**
Chauvet, **37**
Chipie, **40**
Christian Dior, **3**
Christian Lacroix, **5**
Claude Montana, **29**
Daniel Hechter, **38**
Didier Aaron & Perrin, **6**
Fauchon, **11**
Galeries Lafayette, **18**
Galerie Véro-Dodat, **34**
Galerie Vivienne, **28**
Givenchy, **1**
Guy Laroche, **2**
Hediard, **10**
Hermès, **8**
Jean Laporte, **20**
Karl Lagerfeld, **7**
Kenzo, **31**
Léon, **24**
Lolita Lempicka, **42**
Louvre des Antiquaires, **33**
Maud Frizon, **46**
Le Monde en Marché, **43**
Monoprix, **25**
Naf Naf, **36**
Passage des Panoramas, **27**
Pierlot, **35**
Printemps, **15**
Prisunic, **4**
Pucinella, **13**
Samaritaine, **39**
Sephora, **17**
Sonia Rykiel, **45**
Tati, **49**
Van Cleef and Arpels, **21**
Victoires, **30**

Paris Shopping

blvd. Haussmann
av. Friedland
rue du Faubourg St-Honoré
rue la Boétie
blvd. Malesherbes
av. des Champs Elysées
av. George V
rue François 1er
av. Montaigne
av. F. D. Roosevelt
Matignon
av.
Elysée Palace
La Madeleine
av. Boissy d'Anglas
rue Jean Goujon
pl. de l'Alma
pl. de la Concorde
pont del'Alma
pont de la Concorde
quai d'Orsay
rue de l'Université
blvd. St-Germain
av. Bosquet
rue St-Dominique
rue de Bellechasse
rue Grenelle
av. de la Tour Maubourg
blvd. des Invalides
rue de Varenne
Piquet
Parc du Champ de Mars
av. de la Motte
rue de Babylone
Naf Naf
av. de Lowenthal
av. de Ségur
av. de Breteuil
blvd. des Invalides
rue Vaneau
blvd. Garibaldi
pl. de Breteuil
rue de Sèvres
blvd. Montparnasse

0   550 yards
0   500 meters

daily); **rue Mouffetard,** 5e; and **rue Lepic** in Montmartre. (The latter two are best on weekends.) The **Marché d'Aligre** (open Sat., Sun., and Mon. mornings) is located beyond the Bastille on rue d'Aligre in the 12th arrondissement. It's not very touristic, but Parisians from all over the city know and love it.

Paris's main **flower market** is located right in the heart of the city on Ile de la Cité, between Notre-Dame and the Palais de Justice. It's open every day except Monday. On Sunday, it becomes a bird market.

The huge **Marché aux Puces** on Paris's northern boundary (Métro: Porte de Clignancourt) is the city's largest flea market. It's not as cheap as it was in days of yore, but it remains a great place to barter, browse, and maybe even buy. The century-old labyrinth of alleyways is packed with antiques dealers and junk stalls. *Open weekends and Mon.*

Specialty Stores
Gift Ideas

Those wishing to take home china and crockery should head for the **rue du Paradis,** 10e; it's lined with china shops selling goods at a wide range of prices. If you need something to put on your dishes, you can procure posh nosh from all over the world at **Fauchon** (no. 26) and **Hédiard** (no. 21), two upmarket grocers on place de la Madeleine, 8e. Hard-core sweet-tooths can satisfy cravings at **À la Mere de Famille** (35 rue du Fbg. Montmartre, 9e).

Shoppers looking for fabrics should try **Bouchara** (54 blvd. Haussmann, 9e; 57 rue de Passy, 16e; and 10 av. des Ternes, 17e), the best-known name in Paris for high-quality fabric. Those on a more limited budget may like the wide range of souvenir shops on the **rue de Rivoli,** selling porcelain boxes, imitation Sèvres china, busts of Napoleon, and Eiffel Tower memorabilia. **Léon,** at no. 222, has been in business for over a century.

For children, try **Le Monde en Marché** (34 rue Dauphine, 6e), which has a great selection of wooden toys, puppets, and miniatures.

Antiques

Louvre des Antiquaires (2 pl. du Palais Royal, 1er) features 250 antiques dealers under one roof. On the rue du Faubourg St-Honoré are the internationally known antiques dealers **Didier Aaron & Perrin** and **Alexandre Poniatowski.**

Carré Rive Gauche is a prime hunting ground for antiques on the Left Bank. A number of small dealers are grouped along the narrow, atmospheric streets of rue du Bac, rue de Beaune, rue de Lille, rue de l'Université, rue des Sts-Pères, rue Jacob, and quai Voltaire. These streets also have small, discreet art galleries—with wares at upscale prices.

Accessories

World-famous **Hermès** (24 rue du Faubourg St-Honoré, 8e) is known for exquisite silk scarves, leather goods, jewelry, and haute couture, and has opened a perfume boutique around the corner at 6 rue Royale.

Place Vendôme is renowned for having the best and most expensive jewelry stores in town, counting **Van Cleef and Arpels** and **Chaumet** among its occupants. **Cartier** is just around the corner, at 13 rue de la Paix.

Pulcinella (10 rue Vignon, 9e) has a delightful selection of old jewelry.

For bags and belts, try **La Bagagerie** (outlets at 41 rue du Four, 6e; 11 rue du Fbg. St-Honoré, 8e; and 12 rue Tronchet, 8e).

Rue des Sts-Pères is one place to go in search of shoe shops: **Carel** has been at no. 78 for ages, and **Maud Frizon,** at no. 79, carries numerous styles at well-heeled prices.

Clothing Chic and pricey young-designer creations can be found at **À La Ville du Puy** (36 rue Tronchet, 9e).

Lolita Lempicka (corner of rue des Rosiers and rue Paveé, 4e) is one of the newest stars of French ready-to-wear, with a junior collection, **Lolita Bis,** located on the opposite corner.

Pierlot (4 rue du Jour, 1er) is a favorite shopping spot for young French career girls, while **Naf Naf** (10 rue du Jour) and **Chipie** (31 rue de la Ferronerie, 1er) offer sporty, trendy clothes.

For the city's cheapest threads, try **Tati,** a Parisian institution (140 rue de Rennes, 6e).

Those looking for something at the other end of the price range might try the **place des Victoires,** where **Victoires** houses the creations of young stylists, and where **Kenzo, Cacharel,** and **Claude Montana** have boutiques.

Sonia Rykiel's small boutique (6 rue de Grenelle, 6e) is highly popular for upscale women's clothes.

Haute couture fiends will head for **rue du Faubourg St-Honoré,** where **Christian Lacroix** (no. 73) and **Karl Lagerfeld** (no. 19) keep shop.

Av. Montaigne, near the Champs-Elysées, offers such hardy perennials as **Christian Dior** (11 rue François-1er), **Guy Laroche** (29 av. Montaigne), and **Givenchy's** boutique for men (56 rue François-1er).

Rue Cambon, in the Opéra district, boasts one of the finest **Chanel** (no. 29) boutiques.

For men, try **Chauvet** (28 pl. Vendôme) or **Daniel Hechter** in Forum des Halles.

Perfume This tried-and-true Parisian gift is available at **Annick Goutal's** exquisite boutique (14 rue de Castiglione, 1er) or at the chain **Sephora** (outlets at 66 rue Chaussée d'Antin, 9e; 30 av. de l'Italie, 13e; 46 av. Général-Leclerc, 14e; and 50 rue de Passy, 16e). **Jean Laporte** has two highly original boutiques (5 rue des Capucines, 1er, and 84 bis rue Grenelle, 7e).

Sports and Fitness

Biking The Bois de Boulogne and the Bois de Vincennes, with their wide, leafy avenues, are good places for biking. Bikes can be rented from **Paris Vélo** (4 rue du Fer à Moulin, 5e, tel. 43–37–59–22) for around 80 francs a day or 130 francs a weekend.

Fitness Centers The best hotel-fitness facilities are in the newer properties on the edges of the city center. The Vitatop Club on the top floors of the **Sofitel Paris** (8 rue Louis Armand, 15e, tel. 45–54–79–00) offers a 15-meter pool, sauna, steamroom, and Jacuzzi, plus a stunning view of the Paris skyline. Next door is the **Parc Suzanne Lenglen,** with plenty of room for running, plus indoor and outdoor tennis courts. The **Bristol** (112 rue du Faubourg St-Honoré, 8e, tel. 42–66–91–45) has a large pool, plus a sauna.

The new **Aquaboulevard** complex (46 rue Louis-Armand, 15e, tel. 40–60–10–00), opened in 1989, has gyms, Turkish baths, a solarium, and the city's finest swimming pool, complete with a giant slide and a wave machine.

Gyms and aerobic centers have mushroomed in Paris. One of the leading names is **Garden Gym** (65 Champs-Elysées, 8e, tel. 42–25–87–20; 147 bis rue St-Honoré, 1er, near Palais-Royal; and 2 rue Drouot, 9e, near the Opéra).

Jogging The best inner-city running is in the **Champ-de-Mars**, next to the Eiffel Tower, measuring 1½ miles around the perimeter. Shorter and more crowded routes are found in the **Luxembourg Gardens,** with a one-mile loop just inside the park's fence; in the **Tuileries,** also measuring about one mile; and in the **Parc Monceau,** which has a loop of two-thirds of a mile. The **Bois de Boulogne,** on the western edge of Paris, offers miles of trails through woods, around lakes, and across grassy meadows. The equally bucolic **Bois de Vincennes,** on the eastern side of the city, offers a nine-mile circuit or a one-mile loop around the château de Vincennes itself.

Tennis There are few tennis courts in Paris. Your best bet is to try the public courts in the **Luxembourg Gardens.** There is also a large complex of courts at the "Polygone" sportsground in the **Bois de Vincennes.** It's a 20-minute walk down route de la Pyramide from the château de Vincennes métro stop. There are also 11 covered courts (and six squash courts) at **Aquaboulevard** (*see* above).

The **French Open** is held during the last two weeks in May at the **Roland Garros** stadium on the eastern edge of the Bois de Boulogne (take the métro to Porte d'Auteuil). Center-court tickets are difficult to obtain, especially for the second week; try your hotel or turn up early in the morning (play starts at 11) and buy a general ground ticket.

Dining

Our restaurant recommendations have been compiled under the direction of Jean-Marc Blanchot, editor of UP Magazine, a prestigious bilingual publication distributed in hotels throughout Paris and the Riviera.

Eating out is one of the perennial delights of this most civilized of cities. Some complain that the French capital is overrated gastronomically and that the Parisian restaurateur is resting complacently on his or her laurels. Of course, not every restaurant offers a gastronomic adventure, and bad meals at unconscionable prices are no more unknown in Paris than at home. The important point to remember is that the city's restaurants exist principally to cater to the demanding needs of the Parisians themselves, and any restaurant that fails to meet their high standards is unlikely to stay in business long.

It's dangerous to generalize on such a complex subject, but Paris's most expensive and formal restaurants offer either classical food (characterized by rich sauces) or nouvelle cuisine (characterized by light, fresh produce artfully arranged on your plate); many serve a judicious mixture of the two. In less expensive places—especially the numerous bistros and brasseries—the food veers more toward classical styles, though it will almost always be less intimidatingly rich than in the temples of classical cuisine. Different regional cuisines are also widely available, most commonly from Normandy.

Almost all restaurants offer two basic types of menu: à la carte and fixed-price (*un menu* to the French). The fixed-price menu will almost always offer the best value, though you will have to eat three or sometimes four courses, and choices will be limited. There's nothing to stop you from choosing only one or two dishes from the à la carte menu, but only the most thick-skinned will want to try this in a top restaurant, especially if it's busy: The wilting look of a Parisian waiter is not something many can happily endure.

Lunch is usually served from noon to 2. You shouldn't have difficulty getting a table in all but the best restaurants if you arrive by 12:30; after 1, however, you may have problems, especially if you want a full three-course meal. Dinner is rarely served before 8, and 9:30 is not considered unduly late.

Highly recommended restaurants are indicated by a star ★.

Category	Cost*
Very Expensive	over 500 francs
Expensive	250–500 francs
Moderate	150–250 francs
Inexpensive	under 150 francs

per person for a three-course meal, including tax (18.6%) and tip but not wine

1st Arrondissement   **Le Carré des Feuillants.** Anyone with pretensions to be numbered among *le beau monde* will already know that this elegant restaurant offers one of the city's most talked-about dining experiences. Try for a table in the largest of the three dining rooms; it has a memorable fireplace. The food is predominantly from the southwest of France, one of the richest gastronomic regions of the country. Foie gras, truffles, and young pigeon number among the specialties. The wine list is fabulous. *14 rue de Castiglione, tel. 42–86–82–82. Reservations advised. Dress: neat but casual. AE, DC, MC, V. Closed Sat. lunch, Sun., and weekends in July and Aug. Very Expensive.*

★ **Le Grand Véfour.** Located under the elegant neoclassical colonnades at the north end of the gardens of the Palais Royal, Le Grand Véfour has a convincing claim to be regarded as the most sumptuously decorated restaurant in the city. The elegantly incised and painted early 19th-century mirrors reflect the crisp white linen of the tablecloths. Haute cuisine is prepared in the traditional manner; this is not a place for lovers of nouvelle cuisine. Breton lobster with artichokes is a perennial favorite. The fixed-price menu, available only at lunch, offers good value. *17 rue de Beaujolais, tel. 42–96–56–27. Reservations required; book 1 week in advance for Fri. and Sat. dinner. Jacket and tie required. AE, DC, MC, V. Closed Sat. lunch, Sun., and Aug. Very Expensive.*

★ **Chez Paul.** Lovers of the authentic Parisian bistro—and they don't come much more authentic than this—rejoice at the survival of Chez Paul. It's located on the Ile de la Cité, between the Pont Neuf and the Palais du Justice, on one of the prettiest squares in Paris. Dining on the terrace is an experience to remember. The food is sturdily traditional, with snails, and calf's head in shallot sauce as long-time favorites. Readers recommend this restaurant. *15 pl. Dauphine, tel. 43–54–21–48. Res-*

Au Clocher du
Village, **1**
L'Assommoir, **11**
Beauvilliers, **13**
Bistrot d'André, **32**
Brasserie Lipp, **27**
Le Carré des
Feuillants, **6**
Chartier, **9**

Chez Papa, **25**
Chez Paul, **18**
Closerie des Lilas, **29**
Coconnas, **15**
La Colombe, **17**
Le Coupe-Chou, **22**
Da Graziano, **10**
Dôme, **30**
Drouant, **7**

Le Grand Véfour, **8**
Jean-Claude
Ferrero, **2**
Joël Robuchon, **3**
Jules Verne, **31**
Lucas-Carton, **5**
Mansouria, **14**
Le Maquis, **12**
Petit St-Benoit, **26**

La Petite Chaise, **28**
Le Procope, **23**
Saumoneraie, **21**
Taillevent, **4**
Tour d'Argent, **19**
Trumilou, **16**
Vagenende, **24**
Villars Palace, **20**

*ervations required. Dress: casual. No credit cards. Closed
Mon., Tues., and Aug. Moderate.*

**2nd
Arrondissement**

Drouant. This elegant restaurant and café is a Paris institution,
where France's highest literary prize, the Prix Goncourt,
has been awarded since 1914. The glamorous café serves rather traditional bourgeois cuisine, with the accent on seafood. The
more sophisticated restaurant offers excellent nouvelle dishes.
Try the warm oysters with caviar, the rabbit with spices, or
lobster fricassee. *18 rue Gaillon, tel. 42–65–15–16. Reservations advised. Dress: neat but casual; jacket and tie required in
restaurant. AE, DC, MC, V. Closed weekends. Expensive.*

4th Arrondissement

Coconnas. With its warm Italian decor and early 18th-century
paintings of beautiful place des Vosges, the little Coconnas has
won plaudits from critics and humble diners alike. Depending
on your mood, you can choose either nouvelle dishes or cuisine *à
l'ancienne*, solid 19th-century fare with not so much as a hint of
nouvelle innovation. Owned and run by the proprietors of the
Tour d'Argent (*see* below), the Coconnas has a considerable
reputation to live up to. If the overbooking is anything to go by,
it obviously does. *2 bis pl. des Vosges, tel. 42–78–58–16. Reservations required. Dress: casual. AE, DC, MC, V. Closed Mon.,
Tues., and mid-Dec.–mid-Jan. Moderate.*

La Colombe. "The Dove" lives up to its name and is home to 14
white doves. It also offers one of the most charming dining experiences in Paris. The restaurant is set in a beautiful 13th-cen-
tury house on the Seine, right near Notre-Dame. Try to secure
a table on the leafy terrace. The food is predominantly classic,
but with nouvelle touches. The good-value fixed-price lunch
menu is also available for dinner before 9 PM. *4 rue de la
Colombe, tel. 46–33–37–08. Reservations advised. Dress: casual. AE, DC, MC, V. Closed Sun. and Mon. lunch. Moderate.*

★ **Trumilou.** Overlooking the Seine opposite the Ile St-Louis, this
very French little bistro is a real find. Despite the harsh lighting, the mood is boisterous and welcoming, with many regulars
among the diners. Bright and splashy paintings line the walls.
The food is resolutely traditional, with such time-honored favorites as *boeuf bourguignon* and sweetbreads. *84 quai de
l'Hôtel de Ville, tel. 42–77–63–98. Reservations accepted.
Dress: casual. MC, V. Closed Mon. Inexpensive.*

5th Arrondissement

Tour d'Argent. The Tour d'Argent is the sort of temple to haute
cuisine that has serious gourmets quivering in expectation. It
offers a complete dining experience, very much in the grand
manner. You come not simply for the food—though, after some
years of noticeably falling standards, new chef Manuel Martinez has restored this to its previous high peaks—but for the
perfect service, the discreetly understated decor, the immense
wine list, and the fabled view of Notre-Dame. *15 quai de la
Tournelle, tel. 43–54–23–31. Reservations at least 1 week in
advance. Jacket and tie required. AE, DC, MC, V. Closed
Mon. Very Expensive.*

Le Coupe-Chou. Located in an alley at the foot of the Montagne
Ste-Geneviève and the Panthéon, Le Coupe-Chou has uneven
floors, bare stone walls, and candlelit alcoves. The mood
throughout is great for romantic dining. The food is competent
rather than memorable, but it's the magical setting that
counts. Have your coffee and *digestif* in the small, fire-lit sitting room. *9 rue Lanneau, tel. 43–54–36–54. Reservations ad-*

vised. Jacket and tie required. MC, V. Closed Sun lunch. Expensive.

★ **Villars Palace** and **Saumoneraie.** Fish lovers should make for rue Descartes, halfway up the Montagne Ste-Geneviève, to the Villars Palace and the Saumoneraie. They belong to the same owner and, until recently, shared the same entrance. The Villars Palace is the more sophisticated and expensive. Its tasteful modern decor is enhanced by wall mosaics and two aquariums—one freshwater, one seawater—where your dinner swims, oblivious of its fate. The Saumoneraie is a more traditional bistro-style haunt, with bare stone walls. Salmon dominates the wide range of fish and seafood dishes. There's also a good-value fixed-price menu. *Villars Palace, 8 rue Descartes, tel. 43–26–39–08. Reservations advised. Dress: casual. AE, DC, MC, V. Expensive. Saumoneraie, 6 rue Descartes, tel. 46–34–08–76. Reservations required. Dress: casual. MC, V. Moderate.*

6th Arrondissement

★ **Closerie des Lilas.** On the corner of boulevard St-Michel and boulevard du Montparnasse, the Closerie des Lilas has been an essential part of the Left Bank scene since it opened in 1907. Hemingway was here so regularly that a plaque commemorates his favorite spot at the bar. Though the lilacs—*les lilas*—may long since have disappeared from the terrace, the place is just as popular as it was during its salad days in the '30s. Straightforward traditional fare is the staple: Try the oysters. The adjoining brasserie offers much the same food at lower prices. *171 blvd. du Montparnasse, tel. 43–26–70–50. Reservations advised. Dress: casual elegant. AE, DC, MC, V. Expensive.*

Brasserie Lipp. The Brasserie Lipp is perhaps *the* Left Bank restaurant. It's been a favorite haunt of politicians, journalists, and assorted intellectuals for longer than most people can remember. Try for a table on the first floor, but don't be surprised to find yourself relegated to the second-floor dining room. Food, service, and atmosphere are polished. *151 blvd. St-Germain, tel. 45–48–53–91. No phone reservations; expect lines. Dress: casual. AE, DC. Closed mid-July–mid-Aug. Moderate.*

Chez Papa. The refreshing open-plan decor of Chez Papa makes a pleasant change from the bustle and tightly packed tables of most St-Germain restaurants. A shiny-black baby-grand piano, surrounded by a host of plants, stands out against the white walls and high ceiling. There's soft music from 9 every evening. The cuisine is surprisingly light, considering that the dishes themselves are usually associated with the sturdiest French traditional food: snails, cassoulet, and pot-au-feu. A good fixed-price lunch menu makes Chez Papa an ideal lunch spot. *3 rue St.-Benoît, tel. 42–86–99–63. Reservations advised. Dress: casual. AE, DC, MC, V. Closed Sun. Moderate.*

Le Procope. Founded in 1686 by an Italian, Francesco Procopio, Le Procope is said to be the oldest café in Paris. It was a meeting place for Voltaire in the 18th century and for Balzac and Victor Hugo in the 19th. In 1987 it was bought by the Blanc brothers, owners of a number of other popular brasseries. Though they have given the Procope something of a face-lift, they have promised, practically on pain of death, not to change the busy and bustling mood or to tamper with the solid *bourgeoise* food. *13 rue de l'Ancienne-Comédie, tel. 43–26–99–20.*

Reservations advised. Dress: casual. AE, DC, MC, V. Moderate.

Vagenende. Dark woods, gleaming mirrors, and super-professional waiters—perfect in their black jackets and white aprons—take the Vagenende dangerously close to turn-of-the-century pastiche. Nonetheless, the superior brasserie food—seafood and hearty *cuisine bourgeoise*—and the busy atmosphere make this a restaurant to take seriously. The homemade fois gras and the chocolate-based desserts are outstanding. *142 blvd. St-Germain, tel. 43–26–68–18. Reservations advised. Dress: casual. AE, MC, V. Moderate.*

★ **Petit St. Benoît.** This is a wonderful place—small, amazingly inexpensive, always crowded, and with decor that's plain to the point of barely existing. The food is correspondingly basic, but quite good for the price. Expect to have to share a table. *4 rue St-Benoît. No phone reservations. Dress: casual. No credit cards. Closed weekends. Inexpensive.*

7th Arrondissement **Jules Verne.** Those who think that the food in a restaurant with a view is bound to take second place to that view should head *tout de suite* for the Jules Verne, located, memorably, on the third floor of the Eiffel Tower. The view, of course, is fantastic, but the food, too, is superb, featuring inventive combinations of classic and nouvelle cuisine. Specialties include baked turbot in vinegar and tarragon, and veal in lemon and vanilla. *Eiffel Tower, tel. 45–55–61–44. Reservations required; book at least 3 weeks in advance. Jacket and tie required. AE, DC, MC, V. Very Expensive.*

La Petite Chaise. What was once a coaching inn, opened in 1680, has since become one of the most popular restaurants in the city. While the decor may be on the musty side, the simple, good-value food, with such specialties as seafood pancakes and avocado mousse, is the important factor here. *36 rue de Grenelle, tel. 42–22–13–35. Reservations advised. Dress: casual. MC, V. Inexpensive.*

8th Arrondissement **Lucas-Carton.** Many gastronomes maintain that the Lucas-Carton is absolutely *the* best restaurant in Paris. Are they right? Who can say? What's beyond doubt, however, is that Lucas-Carton offers a gastronomic experience equaled in no more than a handful of restaurants around the world. The decor is strictly Belle Epoque, all glinting mirrors and crimson seats. The food, by contrast, is strictly nouvelle, though nouvelle at its subtle best, which some may find an acquired taste. But duck with honey and spices or sweetbreads with mixed vegetables prepared by master chef Alain Senderens will probably be a once-in-a-lifetime experience. *9 pl. de la Madeleine, tel. 42–65–22–90. Reservations required; book at least 3 weeks in advance. Jacket and tie required. MC, V. Closed weekends, Christmas–New Year's, and most of Aug. Very Expensive.*

Taillevent. The exquisite mid-19th-century mansion that houses Taillevent provides the perfect, discreet setting for some of the most refined nouvelle food in the city. Such specialties as stuffed baby pigeon on a bed of cabbage à la Taillevent provide the sort of gastronomic experience you'll never forget. The wine list boasts over 500 vintages; it's said to be the most extensive in Paris. *15 rue Lamennais, tel. 45–63–39–94. Reservations at least 1 week in advance. Jacket and tie required. MC, V. Closed weekends, and July 20–Aug. 20. Very Expensive.*

9th Arrondissement **Chartier.** Low prices, simple decor, and classic fare have earned Chartier an enviable reputation as one of the best-value places to eat in Paris. The choice isn't wide, but the food is always hearty and filling. Try the steak tartare if it's on the menu and you're feeling adventurous. *7 rue du Fbg. Montmartre, tel. 47–70–86–29. No reservations. Dress: casual. No credit cards. Inexpensive.*

11th Arrondissement **Mansouria.** Despite its off-the-beaten-track location, to the west of place de la Bastille, Mansouria is worth the trip if you have any interest in Moroccan food—it's in a class of its own. The decor is fresh and modern, and the service is friendly and relaxed. Try any of the *tagines*, a range of sophisticated spicy Moroccan "stews," and the pigeon "pie" with sugar. *11 rue Faidherbe, tel. 43–71–00–16. Reservations required. Dress: casual. MC, V. Closed Aug., Tues., and Wed. lunch. Moderate.*

14th Arrondissement **Dôme.** In the heart of Montparnasse, the Dôme still reigns as one of the city's classic brasseries. Have a drink outside on the terrace before venturing into the ebullient Belle Epoque interior to enjoy one of the excellent fresh-fish platters or the steaming bouillabaisse. Unfortunately, service can seem offhand, and no allowance is made for nonsmokers. *108 blvd. du Montparnasse, tel. 43–35–25–81. Reservations advised. Dress: casual. AE, DC, MC, V. Closed Mon. Expensive.*

15th Arrondissement ★ **Bistrot d'André.** This classic bistro, not far from Aquaboulevard (*see* Fitness Centers in Sports and Fitness, above), stands close to the former site of the Citroën automobile factory, and car mementos—mainly plaques and old photos—line the walls. The wooden chairs and maroon-velvet benches conjure up a mood of pre-war Paris, and jovial Hubert Gloaguen, the mustached *patron* hosts half the quartier most nights. Bistro cooking at its sturdiest and most reliable includes snails, *andouillette* (pork sausage), *confit de canard* (duck preserved in its fat), and chicken with tarragon. An aperitif (try the kir with red wine) and four courses plus coffee comes to under 150 francs, while a decent bottle of Burgundy won't push your check skyward either. *232 rue St-Charles, tel. 45–57–89–14. Reservations advised. Dress: casual. MC, V. Closed Sat. lunch and Sun. Inexpensive.*

16th Arrondissement **Jean-Claude Ferrero.** The chic habitués of the upscale 16th arrondissement feel very much at home in this oh-so-classy restaurant. Nouvelle cuisine reigns supreme. Any of the mushroom dishes is excellent; otherwise, try the beef in crusty pastry. The restaurant is located in a stately town house and has a charming, plant-filled courtyard. *38 rue Vital, tel. 45–04–42–42. Reservations required. Jacket and tie required. AE, DC, MC, V. Closed Sat., Sun., May 1–10, 3 weeks in Aug., and Christmas. Very Expensive.*

★ **Joël Robuchon.** Without a doubt, this is one of the very best restaurants in Paris. Joël Robuchon is a chef known for his personalized and exceptionally creative cuisine—*langoustine* (prawn) ravioli with cabbage, potato purée, roasted pig's head, and other dishes are impeccably served in this refined and delightfully decorated restaurant. Reservations must be made months in advance. *32 rue de Longchamp, tel. 47–27–12–27. Jacket and tie required. MC, V. Closed weekends and July. Very Expensive.*

★ **Au Clocher du Village.** The simple, country-villagelike interior of the Clocher du Village, with old posters on the walls, wine presses hanging from the ceiling, lace curtains, and a gleaming brass coffee machine on the bar, provides the perfect complement to simple, well-prepared classic French cuisine. Service is straightforward and friendly. It's a place like this that can make eating out in Paris special. There's nothing very fancy here, yet the whole place exudes that inimitable Gallic culinary flair. *8 bis rue Verderet, tel. 42–88–35–87. Reservations advised. Dress: casual. MC, V. Closed weekends and Aug. Moderate.*

18th Arrondissement

Beauvilliers. This is the best luxury restaurant in Montmartre. Chef Michel Deygat has won lavish praise for his nouvelle-inspired dishes; red mullet in green peppers and veal kidneys in a truffle-based sauce are among his specialties. An excellent fixed-price menu (lunch only) keeps prices, which can otherwise be high, within reach. Blooming bouquets of fresh flowers add colorful touches to the formality of the three main dining rooms, and there's a tiny terrace for summer evenings. *52 rue Lamarck, tel. 42–54–54–42. Reservations required. Jacket and tie required. MC, V. Closed Sun., Mon. lunch, and first 2 weeks in Sept. Very Expensive.*

L'Assommoir. L'Assommoir is known not just for its subtle cuisine—there's a superb range of sophisticated fish dishes—but for the personality of owner and chef Philippe Larue, who speaks English to perfection and has a tremendous sense of humor. He has covered the walls of his charming little bistro with samples from his vast collection of paintings. L'Assommoir also has the advantage of being on a peaceful little street away from crowded place du Tertre. *12 rue Girardon, tel. 42–64–55–01. Reservations advised. Dress: neat but casual. MC, V. Closed Sun., Mon., Aug., and Christmas. Moderate.*

Da Graziano. Located right under one of the neighborhood's remaining windmills, Da Graziano offers an exquisite taste of Italy in the heart of Montmartre. Owner Federighi Graziano is as chic as his restaurant—chandeliers, mirrors, and flowers proliferate—and as Tuscan as the cuisine. His fresh pasta is memorable. He also offers a range of French dishes, some named after stars who have dined here. Try the smoked beef *à la* Jean Marais. The inexpensive fixed-price lunch menu makes the climb up the hill well worthwhile. *83 rue Lepic, tel. 46–06–84–77. Reservations required. Dress: neat but casual. MC, V. Closed Feb. Moderate.*

Le Maquis. Visitors often miss this spot on the little-traveled north side of Montmartre. But locals know it, and come often. They come for the warm, friendly atmosphere created by owner-chef Claude Lesage, as well as for his excellent, traditional French cuisine. The reasonably priced, superb lunchtime fare (the menu changes daily) usually has the place packed at midday, so it's best to book a table before you head for Montmartre. In the evenings try the blanquette of veal, salted pork with lentils, or chicken with garlic, followed by a homemade cake. *"Patissier hors pair"* (pastrycook without equals), M. Lesage also makes the breads that accompany each dish. *69 rue Caulaincourt, tel. 42–59–76–07. Reservations advised. Dress: casual. MC, V. Moderate.*

Lodging

At last count, the Paris Tourist Office's official hotel guide listed 1,090 hotels in 20 inner-city districts, or *arrondissements*, alone. Despite this huge choice, you should always be sure to make reservations well in advance, except, paradoxically, during July and August, when the trade fairs, conventions, and conferences that crowd the city the rest of the year come to a halt.

Our listings have been compiled with the aim of identifying hotels that offer maximum atmosphere, convenience, and comfort. We do not include many chain hotels for the simple reason that those in Paris are little different from those in other major cities. We prefer to list special, one-of-a-kind hotels that will, in themselves, contribute greatly to the charm of your stay. For the most part, hotels on the Right Bank offer greater luxury, or at any rate formality, while those on the Left Bank are smaller and offer more in the way of a certain, old-fashioned Parisian charm.

Other than in the largest and most expensive hotels, almost all Parisian hotels have certain idiosyncrasies. Plumbing can be erratic, though rarely to the point where it becomes a problem. Air-conditioning is the exception rather than the rule. This can cause difficulties chiefly because of noise in summer, when on stuffy, sultry nights you may have no choice but to open the windows. Ask for a room *sur cour*—overlooking the courtyard (almost all hotels have one)—or, even better, if there is one, *sur le jardin*—overlooking the garden.

There is almost always an extra charge for breakfast, anything from about 20 francs per person in the least expensive hotels to 90 francs per person in the most expensive. If you want more than the standard French breakfast of *café au lait* (coffee with milk) and a croissant, the price will almost certainly be increased.

Highly recommended hotels are indicated by a star ★.

Category	Cost*
Very Expensive	over 1,000 francs
Expensive	500–1,000 francs
Moderate	250–500 francs
Inexpensive	under 250 francs

All prices are for a standard double room for two people, including tax (18.6%) and service charge.

1st Arrondissement
★

Inter-Continental. An aura of elegant luxury reigns throughout this exquisite late-19th-century hotel, which was designed by the architect of the Paris Opéra, Garnier. Three of its opulent public rooms are official historic monuments. In summer, breakfast on the patio is a delicious experience. Service is impeccable. There are two year-round indoor restaurants—*La Rôtisserie Rivoli* and the *Café Tuileries;* in summer, you can also eat outdoors at the *Terrasse Fleurie. 3 rue de Castiglione, tel. 44–77–11–11. 450 fully equipped rooms and suites, many*

Bradford, **1**
Crillon, **2**
Deux-Iles, **10**
Elysa, **12**
Gaillon-Opéra, **5**
Grand, **4**
L'Hôtel, **15**
Hôtel d'Angleterre, **16**
Inter-Continental, **3**
Marronniers, **14**
Montpensier, **6**
Normandy, **7**
Pavillon, **18**
Place des Vosges, **9**
Royal, **13**
Sorbonne, **11**
Université, **17**
Vieux Marais, **8**

Paris Lodging

with Jacuzzis. *Facilities: 2 restaurants, bar, patio. AE, DC, MC, V. Very Expensive.*

Normandy. For a combination of Belle Epoque elegance and an excellent central location near the Palais Royal, the Normandy is hard to beat. Rooms are individually decorated and vary considerably in size. Some of the least expensive ones have showers only. There's a restaurant and a wood-paneled, English-style bar. *7 rue de l'Echelle, tel. 42–60–30–21. 130 rooms, plus 4 large and 4 small suites, most with bath. Facilities: restaurant (closed weekends). AE, DC, MC, V. Expensive.*

2nd Arrondissement
★

Gaillon-Opéra. The oak beams, stone walls, and marble tiles of the Gaillon-Opéra single it out as one of the most charming hotels in the Opéra neighborhood. To add to the charm, there are plants throughout and a flower-filled patio. There's a small bar but no restaurant. *9 rue Gaillon, tel. 47–42–47–74. 26 rooms and 1 suite, all with bath. Facilities: bar. AE, DC, MC, V. Expensive.*

Montpensier. This handsome 17th-century mansion was transformed into a hotel in 1874. It offers the kind of small-hotel charm and character for which Paris is known, as the clientele, many of them regulars, will testify. All the rooms are individually decorated and vary greatly in size. Those on the top floor, for example, are tiny and modern. The location, on an attractive street running parallel to the gardens of the Palais Royal, is ideal. There's no restaurant or bar. *12 rue Richelieu, tel. 42–96–28–50. 37 rooms with bath, 6 without bath. MC, V. Moderate.*

4th Arrondissement
★

Deux-Iles. This cleverly converted 17th-century mansion on the residential Ile St-Louis has long won plaudits for charm and comfort. Flowers and plants are scattered around the stunning hall. The fabric-hung rooms, though small, have exposed beams and are fresh and airy. Ask for a room overlooking the little garden courtyard. There's no restaurant, but drinks are served in the cellar bar until 1 AM. The lounge is dominated by a fine chimneypiece and doubles as a second bar. *59 rue St-Louis-en-Ile, tel. 43–26–13–35. 8 rooms with bath, 9 with shower. Facilities: bar (closed Sun.). No credit cards. Expensive.*

Place des Vosges. A loyal American clientele swears by the small, historic Place des Vosges, which is located on a charming street just off the exquisite square of the same name. The entrance hall is imposingly grand and is decorated in Louis XIII-style, but some of the rooms are little more than functional. A number of the smaller ones fall into the inexpensive category. There's no restaurant, but there is a welcoming little breakfast room. *12 rue de Birague, tel. 42–72–60–46. 11 rooms with bath, 5 with shower. AE, DC, MC, V. Expensive.*

Vieux Marais. As its name implies, this charming, two-star hotel lies in the heart of the Marais. It dates to the 16th century; today an elevator takes the strain out of coping with six floors. The rooms and bathrooms are simply decorated in light, refreshing colors and are impeccably clean. Try to get a room overlooking the courtyard. Breakfast is served in a pretty, corn-colored lounge. The staff is exceptionally courteous. *8 rue de Plâtre, tel. 42–78–47–22. 22 rooms with bath, 8 with shower. MC, V. Moderate.*

5th Arrondissement

Elysa. The Elysa is what the French call a *"hôtel de charme."* Though the building is not large, most rooms are surprisingly spacious, and all have been renovated; cream-colored furniture is set against pale blue or pink fabrics. There's no restaurant or bar, but you'll find a minibar in every room and a breakfast lounge serving Continental or buffet breakfasts. Moreover, the Elysa is one of the rare hotels in the city with a sauna. Readers have recommended this hotel as well. *6 rue Gay-Lussac, tel. 43–25–31–74. 25 rooms with bath, 5 with shower. Facilities: sauna. AE, DC, MC, V. Expensive.*

Sorbonne. This pretty, early 18th-century hotel, located right by the Sorbonne, was transformed in 1988 when its handsome stone facade was cleaned. As part of the cleanup, fresh flowers are now put into every room, augmenting their existing simple elegance. There's no restaurant or bar, but the receptionist is English, so you'll have no trouble making dining and entertainment plans. Try for a room overlooking the little garden. *6 rue Victor-Cousin, tel. 43–54–58–08. 10 rooms with bath, 27 with shower. MC, V. Moderate.*

6th Arrondissement

★ **L'Hôtel.** The reputation of the oh-so-chic L'Hôtel shows no sign of waning. This is the place to stay for anyone with aspirations to being numbered among the real sophisticates of Paris. The stunning hall, which is decked out with lavish and cool marbles and features an elegant curved staircase, sets the tone. There are two suites—one, Le Jardin, has a terrace filled with flowers and views of the church of St-Germain-des-Près. Here you can stay in the room where Oscar Wilde died ("I am dying beyond my means") or where music-hall star Mistinguette liked to reside (authentic Art Deco furniture and mirrors crowd the room). Not only is there a restaurant (Le Belier)—which is most unusual for a small Left Bank hotel—but it's one of the best in the city, offering delicate nouvelle cuisine. What's more, there's a tree growing up through the ceiling. *Le tout Paris* gathers in the bar—it stays open till 1 —especially when the pianist is on duty. *13 rue des Beaux-Arts, tel. 43–25–27–22. 19 rooms and suites, all with bath; 8 rooms with shower. Facilities: restaurant, bar. AE, DC, MC, V. Very Expensive.*

★ **Hôtel d'Angleterre.** Some claim the Hôtel d'Angleterre is the ultimate Left Bank hotel—a little small and shabby, but elegant and perfectly managed. The 18th-century building was originally the British ambassador's residence; later, Hemingway made it his Paris home. Room sizes and rates vary greatly, though all rooms are individually decorated. Some are imposingly formal, others are homey and plain. Ask for one overlooking the courtyard. There's no restaurant, but a small bar has been installed. *44 rue Jacob, tel. 42–60–34–72. 29 rooms with bath. Facilities: bar. AE, DC, MC, V. Expensive.*

★ **Marronniers.** There are few better places in Paris than the Marronniers for great value and atmosphere. Located on appealing rue Jacob, the hotel is reached through a small courtyard. All rooms are light and full of character. Those on the attic floor have sloping ceilings, uneven floors, and terrific views over the church of St-Germain-des-Près. The vaulted cellars have been converted into two atmospheric lounges. There's a bar but no restaurant. *21 rue Jacob, tel. 43–25–30–60. 37 rooms with bath. Facilities: bar. No credit cards. Moderate.*

7th Arrondissement

Université. This appealingly converted 18th-century town house is located between boulevard St-Germain and the Seine. The rooms have their original fireplaces and are decorated with English and French antiques. Ask for one of the two rooms with a terrace on the sixth floor. Though there's no restaurant, you can rent the vaulted cellar for parties. Drinks and snacks are served all day in the bar or, in good weather, in the courtyard. *22 rue de l'Université, tel. 42–61–09–39. 28 rooms with bath. Facilities: bar. No credit cards. Expensive.*

Pavillon. The entrance to the family-run Pavillon lies behind a garden at the end of an alley off rue St–Dominique, guaranteeing peace and quiet. Although some rooms in this former 19th-century convent are tiny, all have been redecorated and feature Laura Ashley wallpaper and old prints. Breakfast is served in the little courtyard in summer. There's no restaurant or bar, but snacks can be served in your room. *54 rue St-Dominique, tel. 45–51–42–87. 18 rooms, most with shower. MC, V. Moderate.*

8th Arrondissement
★

Crillon. There can surely be no more sumptuous a luxury hotel than this regal mansion overlooking place de la Concorde. The Crillon was founded in 1909 by the Champagne family Taittinger (who still run it), with the express intention of creating the best hotel in the city. They chose as their setting two adjoining town houses built by order of Louis XV. Renovations in the '80s have added comfort—all rooms are air-conditioned—though not at the expense of the original imposing interior. Mirrors, marbles, tapestries, sculptures, great sprays of flowers, and glistening floors are found in all the public rooms. The expansive bedrooms have judicious mixtures of original and reproduction antiques. The bathrooms are, of course, marble. If you want to enjoy the amazing view over place de la Concorde to the National Assembly, you'll have to reserve one of the palatial suites. Of the three restaurants, the best is Les Ambassadeurs, housed in what was originally the Grand Salon and offering the best hotel food in the city. *10 pl. de la Concorde, tel. 42–65–24–24. 189 rooms and suites, all with bath. Facilities: 3 restaurants, bars, private reception rooms. AE, DC, MC, V. Very Expensive.*

Bradford. The Bradford prides itself on providing slightly old-fashioned, well-polished service in an appealing, fusty atmosphere, the kind that has many repeat guests coming back year after year. It's no surprise that this is a family-run hotel. An old wooden elevator takes you up from the flower-filled lobby to the rooms. Some are vast, with brass beds and imposing fireplaces. Hardly any have a TV; that's not the Bradford style. Drinks are served in the soothing, Louis XVI–style lounge on the first floor; there's no restaurant. *10 rue St-Philippe-du-Roule, tel. 43–59–24–20. 36 rooms with bath, 12 with shower. MC, V. Expensive.*

9th Arrondissement

Grand. The recent restoration of the Grand's reception area and honey-colored facade put the final touches on a lengthy renovation program that has transformed this 19th-century palace on place de l'Opéra. All rooms have been lavishly redecorated in Art Nouveau style and are now air-conditioned. The hotel prides itself on its exemplary business facilities, not the least of which are its three restaurants. The Opéra is the most formal and imposing, while the Relais Capucines offers less intimidatingly grand meals; Le Patio serves buffet lunches and breakfast. *2 rue Scribe, tel. 42–68–12–13. 515 rooms and suites with bath. Facilities: 3 restaurants, 2 bars, 13 conference rooms, secretarial services, travel agency, shops, parking. AE, DC, MC, V. Very Expensive.*

14th Arrondissement **Royal.** This small hotel, set in a late 19th-century building on attractive boulevard Raspail, has already won much praise, especially from American guests. The mood throughout is stylish yet simple, with salmon-pink rooms and a wood-paneled, marble-floored lobby filled with plants. You can sit in the small conservatory, where drinks are served; there's no bar or restaurant. *212 blvd. Raspail, tel. 43–20–69–20. 33 rooms and suites with bath, 15 with shower. AE, MC, V. Expensive.*

The Arts and Nightlife

The Arts

The weekly magazines *Pariscope* and *L'Officiel des Spectacles*, published on Wednesday, give detailed entertainment listings, as does *Figaroscope*, a free supplement to the Wednesday edition of the daily newspaper *Le Figaro. Paris Free Voice* gives monthly listings in English—you can find it in bilingual bookstores or at the American Church (65 quai d'Orsay). The best place to buy tickets is at the venue itself; otherwise, try your hotel or a travel agency such as **Paris-Vision** (214 rue de Rivoli). Tickets for some events can be bought at the **FNAC** stores (there are special ticket counters in branches at 26 av. de Wagram, near the Arc de Triomphe; and at the Forum des Halles). Half-price tickets for many same-day theater performances are available at the booth next to the Madeleine church.

Theater A number of theaters line the grand boulevards between Opéra and République, but there is no Paris equivalent to Broadway or London's West End. Shows are mostly in French. Classical drama is performed at the **Comédie-Française** (Palais-Royal, tel. 40–15–00–00). You can reserve seats in person about two weeks in advance or turn up an hour beforehand and wait in line for returned tickets.

A completely different sort of pleasure is to be found near place St-Michel at the tiny **Théâtre de la Huchette** (23 rue de la Huchette, 5e, tel. 43–26–38–99), where Ionesco's short plays make a deliberate mess of the French language.

Concerts The **Salle Pleyel** (252 rue du Fbg. St-Honoré, tel. 45–63–88–73), near the Arc de Triomphe, remains Paris's principal home of classical music. Paris isn't as richly endowed as New York or London when it comes to orchestral music, but the city compensates with a never-ending stream of inexpensive lunchtime and evening concerts in churches. The candlelit concerts held in the **Sainte-Chapelle** are outstanding—make reservations well in advance. Notre-Dame is another church where you can combine sightseeing with good music.

Opera The **Opéra** itself (tel. 47–42–53–71) is a dramatically flamboyant hall, and, with Rudolf Nureyev as artistic director, its ballet choreography has reached new heights. But getting tickets is not always easy. The **Opéra Comique** (the French term for opera with spoken dialogue), close by (5 rue Favart, 2e, tel. 42–86–88–83), is more accessible.

The **Théâtre Musical de Paris** (pl. du Châtelet, tel. 42–33–00–00) offers opera and ballet for a wider audience at more reasonable prices. The **Opéra-Bastille** (Place de la Bastille, tel. 40–01–16–16), which opened in early 1990, stages both traditional opera and symphony concerts under its dynamic young Korean director Myung-Whun Chung.

Dance   Apart from the traditional ballets sometimes on the bill at the Opéra, the highlights of the Paris dance year are the visits of major foreign troupes, usually to the **Palais des Congrès** at Porte Maillot (tel. 40–68–22–22) or the **Palais des Sports** at the porte de Versailles (tel. 48–28–40–48). The annual **Festival de la Danse** is staged at the **Théâtre des Champs-Elysées** on avenue Montaigne (tel. 47–20–36–37) in October.

Films   There are hundreds of movie theaters in the city, and a number of them show English films. Look for the initials "V.O."—they mean original version (not dubbed). Cinema admission runs from 35 to 45 francs. There are reduced rates on Monday; programs change Wednesday. Old and rare films are often screened at the **Pompidou Center** and **Musée du Cinéma** at Trocadéro.

Nightlife

Paris's nightclubs are household names, at least among foreign tourists. Prices can range from 200 francs (simple admission plus one drink) to 600 francs (dinner plus show). For 400 francs, you can get a good seat plus half a bottle of champagne.

Cabaret   The **Crazy Horse** (12 av. George-V, 8e, tel. 47–23–32–32) is one of the best known for pretty girls and *risqué* dance routines, lots of humor and little clothing.

The **Moulin Rouge** (pl. Blanche, 18e, tel. 46–06–00–19) is an old favorite at the foot of Montmartre.

Nearby is the **Folies-Bergère** (32 rue Richer, 9e, tel. 42–46–77–11), not as "in" as it once was, but still renowned for its glitter and its vocal numbers.

The **Lido** (116 bis av. des Champs-Elysées, 8e, tel. 45–63–11–61) stars the famous Bluebell Girls and tries to win you over through sheer exuberance.

Bars and   The more upscale Paris nightclubs tend to be both expensive
Nightclubs   (1,000 francs for a bottle of gin or whiskey) and private—in other words, you'll usually need to know someone who's a member to get through the door.

If **Crescendo** (40 rue du Colisée, 8e) is not too full and if you look sufficiently slick, you may be allowed in.

Club 79 (79 av. des Champs-Elysées, 8e) is probably the handiest bet for dancing the night away.

For a more leisurely evening, in an atmosphere that's part pub, part gentleman's club, try **Harry's Bar** (5 rue Daunou, 2e), a cozy, wood-paneled hangout for Americans, journalists, and sportsmen, that still reeks with memories of Ernest Hemingway, F. Scott Fitzgerald, and Gertrude Stein.

Other places for a fun evening out include:

Caveau des Oubliettes. Traditional folk singing and ballads are performed in a medieval cellar with Gothic arches and heavy beams. It's very popular with tourists, but still full of energetic charm. *1 rue St-Julien-le-Pauvre, 5e.*

Le Lapin Agile. This is a touristy but picturesque Montmartre setting: hard wooden benches, brandied cherries, and thumping great golden French oldies. *22 rue des Saules, 18e. Admission: 90 frs. Open 9 PM–2 AM.*

La Rôtisserie de l'Abbaye. French, English, and American folk songs are sung to the accompaniment of a guitar in a medieval setting. The action starts around 8 PM; come early or you won't get in. You can dine here, too. *22 rue Jacob, 6e. Closed Sun. Admission (including dinner): 150–350 frs.*

Jazz Clubs Paris is one of the great jazz cities of the world, with plenty of variety, including some fine, distinctive local coloring. For nightly schedules, consult the magazines *Jazz Hot* or *Jazz Magazine.* Remember that nothing gets going until 10 or 11 PM and that entry prices can vary widely from about 30 francs to over 100 francs.

The Latin Quarter is a good place to track down Paris jazz. The **Caveau de la Huchette** (5 rue de la Huchette, 5e) offers Dixieland in a hectic, smoke-filled atmosphere.

Le Petit Opportun (15 rue des Lavandières-Ste-Opportune, 1er) is a converted Latin Quarter bistro with a cramped, atmospheric basement that sometimes features top-flight American soloists with French rhythm sections. At street level, there is a pleasant bar with recorded music and less-expensive drinks.

On the Right Bank is **New Morning** (7 rue des Petites-Ecuries, 10e), a premier venue for visiting American musicians and top French bands.

Discos **Club Zed** (2 rue des Anglais, 5e) boasts lively dancing and some rock-only evenings.

The long-established **Balajo** (9 rue de Lappe, 11e) is crowded and lots of fun, with plenty of nostalgic '60s sounds some nights.

Les Bains (7 rue du Bourg-l'Abbé, 3e), once a public bathhouse, now specializes in New Wave music and features live music on Wednesday.

4 Ile de France

Versailles, Chartres, Fontainebleau

Introduction

Paris is small as capital cities go, with just under 2 million inhabitants. The Paris region, however, contains about 10 million people—almost one-fifth of France's entire population. That type of statistic conjures up visions of a gray, never-ending suburban sprawl. Nothing could be further from the truth.

The official name for the region sets the tone. "Ile de France" has a poetic ring to it; there is no island here, but the region is figuratively isolated from the rest of France by the three rivers—the Seine, Oise, and Marne—that weave majestic, meandering circles around its limits.

The juxtaposition of the broad, ambling waters of those rivers, along with a quiver of brooks and streams, both defend the area and make it lush. This precious combination has always enticed settlers; an entire country was to spring from the Ile de France fountainhead. Indeed, the kings and clerics who ruled the medieval roost refused to be sequestered in Paris: Castles and palaces went up in the towns of Vincennes, St-Germain-en-Laye, and Provins; abbeys and cathedrals sprang skyward in Chartres, Senlis, and Royaumont.

Ile de France never lost favor with the powerful, partly because its many forests—large chunks of which still stand—harbored sufficient game for even bloated, cosseted monarchs to achieve a regular kill. First Fontainebleau, in humane Renaissance proportions, then Versailles, on a minion-crushing, Baroque scale, reflected the royal desire to transform hunting lodges into palatial residences.

The 17th century was a time of prodigious building in the Ile de France—a period that bequeathed a vast array of important sights to admire and explore. The château, gardens, and well-preserved town of Versailles should not be overlooked. But do not neglect Versailles's slightly lesser neighbors; Vaux-le-Vicomte, Dampierre, Rambouillet, and Chantilly would bask in superstar status anywhere else. And, after the crowds of Versailles in midsummer, you will welcome the relative tranquillity of these smaller châteaus.

By way of contrast, April 1992 sees the opening of Euro Disney near Marne-la-Vallée, 20 miles east of Paris. The allure of Mickey Mouse and Donald Duck is expected to attract visitors from all over Western Europe, and a massive complex of hotels and restaurants has been built alongside the new leisure park to accommodate them.

On the whole, however, the architectural impact of the 20th century is discreet in the Ile de France, and you may find it disorienting that so many rural backwaters exist within 30 minutes' drive of the capital. There is no miracle involved with this, however, just some commonsensical forethought: With the Gallic mania for centralized planning, new developments are assigned to restricted areas. Modern architecture students may find food for thought in such so-called new towns as St-Quentin-en-Yvelines (near Versailles), and sociologists won't lack material in the concrete ghettoes of the "red belt" north of Paris (so called because its working-class population votes heavily communist), but the average visitor can comfortably avoid them.

Essential Information

Important Addresses and Numbers

Tourist Information
The regional tourist office for the Ile de France (written inquiries only) is the **Comité Régional de Tourisme d'Ile de France** (73 rue Cambronne, 75015 Paris, tel. 45–67–89–41). Local offices are in the following towns: **Barbizon** (41 rue Grande, tel. 60–66–41–87), **Chartres** (pl. de la Cathédrale, tel. 16/37–21–50–00), **Fontainebleau** (31 pl. Napoléon-Bonaparte, tel. 64–22–25–68), **Rambouillet** (8 pl. de la Libération, tel. 34–83–21–21), and **Versailles** (7 rue des Réservoirs, tel. 39–50–36–22).

Travel Agencies
American Express (11 rue Scribe, Paris, 9e, tel. 42–66–09–99); **Wagons-Lits** (32 rue du 4 September, 2e, tel. 42–63–48–48).

Car Rental
Avis (tel. 45–62–18–68); **Hertz** (tel. 45–51–20–37); **Europcar** (tel. 30–43–82–82). All in Paris.

Arriving and Departing

By Plane
Visitors to the Ile de France can arrive at either of Paris's two airports: **Charles de Gaulle** (Roissy), 25 kilometers (16 miles) northwest of the city (tel. 48–62–22–80) or **Orly**, 16 kilometers (10 miles) south (tel. 49–75–15–15).

Getting Around

By Car
Although a comprehensive rail network ensures that most towns in the Ile de France can make comfortable day excursions from Paris, the only way to crisscross the region without returning to the capital is by car. There is no shortage of expressways or fast highways, but be prepared for delays close to Paris and during the morning and evening rush hours.

By Train
Many of the sights mentioned in our exploring text can be reached by train from Paris. Both regional and mainline (Le Mans-bound) trains leave the **Gare Montparnasse** for Chartres; the former also stop at Versailles, Rambouillet, and Maintenon. Gare Montparnasse is also the terminus for trains to Dreux (Granville line) and for the suburban trains that stop at Montfort-l'Amaury, the nearest station to Thoiry.

Some mainline trains from **Gare St-Lazare** stop at Vernon and Mantes-la-Jolie on their way to Rouen and Le Havre. Mantes and Pontoise are termini for the frequent suburban trains from St-Lazare, most of which stop at Conflans-Ste-Honorine. Suburban trains leave St-Lazare for Maisons-Laffitte and Versailles, and the **Gare du Nord** for L'Isle-Adam and Beaumont-sur-Oise. Chantilly is on the main north-bound line from Gare du Nord (Senlis can be reached by bus from Chantilly) and Provins on the Swiss-bound line from **Gare de l'Est**. Fontainebleau—or, rather, neighboring Avon, 1½ miles away (there is a frequent bus service)—is 45 minutes from **Gare de Lyon**.

St-Germain-en-Laye is a terminus of the **RER-A express metro** that tunnels through Paris (main stations at Etoile, Auber, and Les Halles). The handiest of Versailles's three train stations is the one reached by the **RER-C** (main stations at Austerlitz, St-Michel, and Invalides).

Guided Tours

Orientation **Paris Vision** (214 rue de Rivoli, 1e, tel. 42–60–31–25) and
Cityrama (4 pl. des Pyramides, 1e, tel. 42–60–30–14) organize
guided visits to a number of sites in the Ile de France region,
departing Paris from the place des Pyramides (off rue de Rivoli
at the Louvre end of the Tuileries Gardens). Both run half-day
trips to Chartres on Tuesday and Saturday afternoons (230
francs), full-day trips to Chartres plus Versailles (360 francs),
and half-day trips to Fontainebleau and Barbizon (departures
1:30 Wednesday, Friday, and Sunday; price 245 francs).

Guided excursions to Giverny are organized by **American Express** (11 rue Scribe, 9e, tel. 42–66–09–99) and the **RATP** (Paris
Transport Authority): either half-day or full-day when combined with Rouen. The RATP also has guide-accompanied excursions in and around Paris. Inquire at its Tourist Service on
the place de la Madeleine (8e, to the right of the church as you
face it) or at its office (53 quai des Grands-Augustins, 6e); both
are open daily.

Personal Guides For touring in style, get in touch with **International Limousines**
(182 blvd. Péreire, 17e, tel. 45–74–77–12). Guides with luxury
cars or a minibus (taking up to seven passengers) will take you
around Paris or the surrounding area for a minimum of three
hours for around 250 francs an hour (though call to check details
and prices). Advance reservations are obligatory.

Exploring the Ile de France

*Numbers in the margin correspond with points of interest on
the Ile de France and Versailles maps.*

Orientation

Our three tours take you southeast to Fontainebleau, north to
Chantilly, and west—the most favored point on the regional
touring compass—to Versailles, Chartres, and Giverny. We
have occasionally transgressed the administrative limits of Ile
de France along the way: Bear in mind that phone numbers in
several of the towns—Chartres, Dreux, Giverny, Chantilly,
and Senlis—must be prefixed by "16" when you dial from Paris
(where applicable, we have included the code). Though they are
within striking distance of Paris, the towns of Reims, Laon,
Compiègne, and Beauvais are officially part of northern
France, and are described in that chapter.

Highlights for First-time Visitors

Chartres Cathedral, Tour 1
Château of Chantilly, Tour 2
Château of Fontainebleau, Tour 3
Claude Monet's house and gardens at Giverny, Tour 1
Château of Vaux-le-Vicomte, Tour 3
Château and gardens of Versailles, Tour 1
Thoiry—château and safari park, Tour 1

Tour 1: West to Versailles, Chartres, Giverny, and Thoiry

No visit to Paris is complete without an excursion to Versailles—easy to get to either by train (*see* Getting Around in Essential Information, above) or car (A13 expressway from Porte d'Auteuil) in about 25 minutes. On this tour, however, Versailles is only the starting point for a trip through the west of the Ile de France, a region of forests, wheat fields, lush valleys, and imposing châteaux.

If, after days of museum lines and crowded métros, you feel a sense of escape as you leave Paris, you won't be the first. Back in the 17th century, Louis XIV, the Sun King, was barely out of his teens when he began to cast his cantankerous royal eye over the Ile de France in search of a new power base. Marshy, inhospitable **Versailles**, 24 kilometers (15 miles) to the west of Paris, was the place of his dreams. Down came its modest royal hunting lodge and up, up, and along went the new château.

Today the **château** of Versailles seems outrageously big—but it wasn't nearly big enough for the sycophantic army of 20,000 noblemen, servants, and hangers-on who moved in with Louis. A new capital had to be constructed from scratch. Tough-thinking town planners dreamed up vast Baroque mansions and avenues broader than the Champs-Elysées.

It is hardly surprising that Louis XIV's successors soon felt out of sync with their architectural inheritance. Louis XV, who inherited the throne from the Sun King in 1715, transformed the royal apartments into places to live rather than pose in. The unfortunate Louis XVI—reigning monarch at the time of the French Revolution—cowered at the Petit Trianon in the leafy depths of Versailles park, well out of the mighty château's shadow. His queen, Marie Antoinette, had lost her head well before her trip to the guillotine in 1793, by pretending to be a peasant shepherdess amid the ersatz rusticity of her cute hamlet.

The château was built by French architects Louis Le Vau and François Mansart between 1662 and 1690. Enter through the gilt iron gates from the huge place d'Armes. On the first floor of the château, right in the middle as you approach across the sprawling cobbled forecourt, is Louis XIV's bedchamber. The two wings were occupied by the royal children and princes of the blood, with courtiers making do in the attics.

The highlight for many on the guided tour of the palace is the **Galerie des Glaces** (Hall of Mirrors), fully restored to sparkling glory. It was here, after France's capitulation, that Prince Otto von Bismarck proclaimed the unified German Empire in 1871, and here, too, that the controversial Treaty of Versailles, asserting Germany's responsibility for World War I, was signed in 1919.

The **Grands Apartements** (State Rooms) that flank the Hall of Mirrors retain much of their original Baroque decoration: gilt stucco, painted ceilings, and marble sculpture. Perhaps the most extravagant of these rooms is the **Salon d'Apollon,** the former throne room, dedicated to the sun god Apollo, Louis XIV's mythical hero. Equally interesting are the **Petits Apartements,** where the royal family and friends lived in (relative) intimacy.

In the north wing of the château can be found the solemn white-and-gold **chapel,** designed by François Mansart and completed in 1710; the miniature **opera house,** the first oval room in France, built by J. A. Gabriel for Louis XV in 1770; and, connecting the two, the 17th-century **Galleries,** with exhibits retracing the château's history. The south wing contains the wide, lengthy **Galerie des Batailles** (Gallery of Battles), lined with gigantic canvases extolling French military glory. *Admission: 27 frs. adults, 14 frs. students and senior citizens. Open Tues.–Sun. 10–7; closed Mon.*

After the awesome feast of interior decor, the **park** outside is an ideal place to catch your breath. The gardens were designed by the French landscape architect Le Nôtre, whose work here represents formal French landscaping at its most rigid and sophisticated. The 250-acre grounds include woods, lawns, flower beds, statues, artificial lakes, and fountains galore. They are at their golden-leafed best in the fall, but are also enticing in summer—especially on those Sundays when the fountains are in full flow. They become a spectacle of rare grandeur during the **Fêtes de Nuit** floodlighting and fireworks shows held in July and September. *The grounds are free and open daily. Tel. 39–50–36–22 for details of the fountains and Fêtes de Nuit.*

If you wander too far into the park woods you can easily get lost. Follow signs to skirt the numerous basins (or ponds) until you reach the **Grand Canal.** Move down the right bank, along gravelly paths beneath high-plinthed statues, until you discover that the canal is in the form of a cross—with two smaller arms known as the **Petit Canal.** At the crossing, bear right toward the Grand Trianon (in all, about a mile from the château).

❸ The **Grand Trianon,** built by Mansart in 1687, is a scaled-down, pink-marble pleasure palace, now used to entertain visiting heads of state. When it is not in use, the palace is opened so that visitors can admire its lavish interior and early 19th-century furniture. *Admission: 16 frs. adults, 8 frs. students and senior citizens; joint ticket for the two Trianons 20 frs. (10 frs. students and senior citizens). Open Tues.–Sun. 10–noon and 2–5; closed Mon.*

❹ The **Petit Trianon,** close by, was built by architect Gabriel in the mid-18th century. It is a mansion, not a palace, and is modest by Versailles standards—though still sumptuously furnished. It contains mementos of its most illustrious inhabitant, Marie Antoinette. Look for her initials wrought into the iron railings of the main staircase.

Beyond the Petit Trianon and across the Petit Lac, which looks more like a stream as it describes a wriggly semicircle, is the **❺** queen's so-called hamlet **(Hameau).** With its watermill, genuine lake (Grand Lac), and pigeon loft, this phony village is outrageously pretty; it was here that Marie Antoinette lived out her romanticized dreams of peasant life. *Admission: 11 frs. adults, 6 frs. students and senior citizens; joint ticket for the two Trianons 20 frs. (10 frs. students and senior citizens). Open Tues.–Sun. 2–5; closed Mon.*

The town of Versailles is attractive, and its spacious, leafy boulevards make agreeable places to stroll. Facing the château are

Ile de France

Cathédrale St-Louis, **7**
Château, **2**
Eglise Notre-Dame, **8**
Grand Trianon, **3**
Hameau, **5**
Musée Lambinet, **9**
Petit Trianon, **4**
Royal Stables, **6**

6 the **royal stables,** buildings of regal dimensions and appearance. Take avenue de Sceaux, to the right, and turn right again along **7** rue de Satory, which leads to the **Cathédrale St-Louis,** an austere edifice built between 1743 and 1754 by Mansart's grandson, with notable paintings and an organ loft.

Turn right out of the cathedral, then left down avenue Thiers, which cuts through the town's three major boulevards—avenues de Sceaux, de Paris, and de St-Cloud—to the ancient mar- **8** ket square, where rue de la Paroisse heads left to the **Eglise Notre-Dame.** This sturdy Baroque monument was built from 1684 to 1686 by Mansart (and is therefore older than the cathedral) as parish church for the Sun King's new town. Louis XIV himself laid the foundation stone.

Behind the church, in an imposing 18th-century mansion on **9** boulevard de la Reine, is the **Musée Lambinet,** a museum with a wide-ranging collection—a maze of cozy, finely furnished rooms replete with paintings, weapons, fans, and porcelain. *54 blvd. de la Reine. Admission free. Open Tues.–Sun. 2–6; closed Mon.*

The fast N10 heads down from Versailles to another famous château town—Rambouillet (*see* below). But if you're in no rush, take the attractive D91 south from Versailles through the glades and folds of the Chevreuse Valley to the unspoiled vil- **10** lage of **Dampierre,** 18 kilometers (11 miles) away.

The **château** of Dampierre is a handsome, stone-and-brick structure, surrounded by a moat and set 100 yards back from the road behind 18th-century iron railings. Rebuilt in the 1670s by Mansart for the Duc de Luynes, it is still the family seat. Much of the interior has kept its 17th-century decoration—portraits, wood-paneling, furniture, and works of art. But the main staircase, with its trompe-l'oeil murals, and the richly gilded Salle des Fêtes date from the last century. The Salle des Fêtes, on the second floor, contains a huge wall painting by the celebrated artist Jean Auguste Ingres (1780–1867): a mythical evocation of the Age d'Or (Golden Age). The large park was designed by Le Nôtre. *Admission: 36 frs. adults, 26 frs. children and senior citizens. Open Apr.–Oct., daily 2–6:30; closed Nov.–Mar.*

From Dampierre take D58 (signposted to Chevreuse) for 2½ kilometers (1½ miles) before forking off toward N306. A couple of miles farther south (follow signs), close to the village of Choisel, is the steep-roofed château of **Breteuil**. Like the Luynes of Dampierre, the Breteuil family have owned and lived in their château since the early 17th century. And, like the Panouses of Thoiry (*see* below), they have been innovative in their attempts to woo visitors: Life-size wax figures—including the English Queen Victoria's son King Edward VII and onetime guest Marcel Proust, the French novelist (1871–1922)—lurk in many of the rooms.

Interior highlights range from Swedish porcelain to Gobelin tapestries and a richly inlaid Teschen table, encrusted with pearls and precious stones—an 18th-century present to the Breteuils from Austrian Empress Maria Theresa. The basement kitchens contain a gleaming array of copper pots and pewterware, while the vast wooded park offers picnic areas and playgrounds. *Admission (château): 40 frs. adults, 28 frs. children and senior citizens. Admission (grounds): 19 frs. adults, 13 frs. children and senior citizens. Château open daily 2:30–5:30; grounds open daily 11–5:30.*

Get back onto N306 and head southwest to **Rambouillet**, 14 kilometers (9 miles) away. Surrounded by a huge forest, Rambouillet is a haughty town, once favored by kings and dukes. Today it is home to affluent gentry and, occasionally, President Mitterrand. When the president is not entertaining visiting bigwigs, the château and its grounds are open to all.

Leave your car in the spacious parking lot next to the **Hôtel de Ville** (town hall), an imposing Classical building in red brick, and wander around the corner to the **château**. Most of the buildings you see date from the early 18th century, but the muscular **Tour François I** (Tower of François I), named after the king who breathed his last therein in 1547, once belonged to a 14th-century castle. *Admission: Grounds free; château (guided tours only): 25 frs. Open Wed.–Mon. 10–noon and 2–6; closed Tues.*

If your appetite for château interiors has already been satisfied, you'll be able to forgo Rambouillet's without feeling too guilty. The château's exterior charms are hidden as you arrive, but if you head to the left of the buildings—and if nature is in bloom—you are in for two pleasant surprises. A splendid lake, with several enticing islands, spreads out for you, beckoning you to explore the extensive grounds beyond. Before you do, however, turn around: There, behind you, across trim flower beds awash with color, is the facade of the château—a sight of unsuspected serenity, asymmetry, and, as more flowers spill from its balconies, cheerful informality.

If time allows, veer left around the lake and carry on until you reach two interesting groups of outbuildings: the **Laiterie de la Reine** (built as a dairy for Marie Antoinette), with its small temple, grotto, and shell-lined **Chaumière des Coquillages** (Shell Pavilion); and the **Bergerie Nationale** (National Sheepfold), site of a more serious agricultural venture; the merino sheep reared here, prized for the quality and yield of their wool, are descendants of beasts imported from Spain by Louis XVI in 1786. *Admission: 15 frs. (Laiterie), 12 frs. (Bergerie). Laiterie open Jan.–Apr., Thurs.–Mon. 10–noon and 2–6; May–Nov., 10–noon and 2–4; closed Dec. and Tues., Wed. The Bergerie can be visited Fri.–Sun. 2:30–5:30 (Sun. only in winter).*

🔟③ D906 links Rambouillet to the town of **Maintenon**, 24 kilometers (15 miles) west. The Renaissance **château** of Maintenon once belonged to Louis XIV's mistress, Madame de Maintenon, whose private apartments form the hub of the short interior visit. A round brick tower (14th century) and a 12th-century keep are all that remain of the buildings on the site. The formal gardens ease their way back from the château to the unlikely ivy-covered arches of a ruined aqueduct, one of the Sun King's most outrageous projects. His aim: to provide Versailles (some 50 kilometers/30 miles away) with water from the River Eure. In 1684, 30,000 men were signed up to construct a three-tiered, 3-mile aqueduct as part of the project. Many died of fever in the process, and construction was called off in 1688. *Admission: 24 frs. Open Easter–Oct., Wed.–Sat. 2:30–6, Sun. 10–noon and 2:30–6; Nov.–Easter, Sat. 2:30–6, Sun. 10–noon and 2:30–6, closed weekdays.*

🔟④ The River Eure, accompanied by picturesque D6, snakes southwest from Maintenon to **Chartres**, 19 kilometers (12 miles) away. Try to spot the noble, soaring spires of **Chartres Cathedral** before you reach the town; they form one of the most famous sights in western Europe.

Worship on the site of the cathedral goes back to before the Gallo-Roman period; the crypt contains a well that was the focus of Druid ceremonies. In the late 9th century, Charles II (known as the Bald) presented Chartres with what was believed to be the tunic of the Virgin, a precious relic that attracted hordes of pilgrims. Chartres swiftly became a prime destination for the Christian faithful; pilgrims trek here from Paris to this day.

Today's cathedral dates primarily from the 12th and 13th centuries, having been built after the previous, 11th-century edifice burned down in 1194. A well-chronicled outburst of religious fervor followed the discovery that the Virgin's relic had miraculously survived unsinged, and reconstruction moved ahead at a breathtaking pace: Just 25 years were needed for the cathedral to rise from the rubble.

The lower half of the facade is a survivor of the earlier Romanesque church: This can be seen most clearly in the use of round arches rather than the pointed Gothic type. The main door (**Portail Royal**) is richly sculpted with scenes from the Life of Christ, and the flanking towers are also Romanesque. The taller of the two spires (380 feet versus 350 feet) dates from the start of the 16th century; its fanciful Flamboyant intricacy contrasts sharply with the stumpy solemnity of its Romanesque counterpart across the way.

The **rose window** above the main portal dates from the 13th century, while the three windows below it contain some of the finest examples of 12th-century stained glass in France.

The interior is somber, and your eyes will need time to adjust to the murk. The reward: the gemlike richness of the stained glass, with the famous deep "Chartres blue" predominating. The oldest window is arguably the most beautiful: **Notre Dame de la Belle Verrière,** in the south choir. *Pl. Notre-Dame.*

Just behind the cathedral stands the **Musée des Beaux-Arts** (Museum of Fine Arts), a handsome 18th-century building that used to be the Bishop's Palace. Its varied collection includes Renaissance enamels; a portrait of the Dutch scholar Erasmus by German painter Hans Holbein; tapestries; armor; and some fine, mainly French paintings dating from the 17th to the 19th century. There is also an entire room devoted to the forceful 20th-century land- and snowscapes of Maurice de Vlaminck, who lived in the region. *29 cloître Notre-Dame. Admission: 10 frs. adults, 5 frs. students and senior citizens. Open Wed.-Mon. 10–11:45 and 2–5:45; closed Tues.*

The **museum gardens** overlook the old streets that tumble down to the River Eure. Take rue Chantault down to the river, cross over, and head right along rue de la Tannerie (which, in turn, becomes rue de la Foulerie) as far as rue du Pont St-Hilaire. From here, there is a picturesque view of the roofs of old Chartres nestling beneath the cathedral. Cross over the bridge and head up to the **Eglise St-Pierre,** whose magnificent windows date to the early 14th century. There is more stained glass (17th century) to admire at the **Eglise St-Aignan** nearby, just off the rue St-Pierre. Wander at will among the steep, narrow surrounding streets, using the spires of the cathedral as your guiding landmark.

15 Thirty-two kilometers (20 miles) northwest of Chartres (via N154) is the charming and ancient town of **Dreux.** The downtown area has several old houses and monuments, notably the **Eglise St-Pierre** on place Métézeau, and the **Beffroi** (Belfry) just across the road. St-Pierre, an interesting jumble of styles with good stained glass and a 17th-century organ loft, presents a curious silhouette, with its unfinished Classical towers, cut off in mid-column. The Beffroi, standing at one end of a lively shopping square, is a hefty tower built between 1512 and 1531; there is a fine view from the top. *Pl. Métézeau. Admission: 3 frs. Open Wed., Fri.–Mon. 10–11:30 and 2–5; closed Tues. and Thurs.*

Dreux was a prosperous place in the 16th century—it was awarded the title of Royal Borough in 1556—but the early 19th century conferred lasting glory on the town. In 1816, the Orléans family, France's ruling house from 1830 to 1848, began the construction of a chapel-mausoleum on the hill behind the center of town. The circular chapel, known as the **Chapelle Royale de St-Louis,** is built in the sugary but not unappealing neo-Gothic style: Superficial ornament rather than structure recalls the medieval style. Unfortunately, the sumptuously decorated interior can be visited only with a French-speaking guide, but no linguistic explanations are needed to prompt wonder at either the Sèvres-manufactured "stained glass"— thin layers of glass coated with painted enamel (an extremely rare, fragile, and vivid technique)—or the funereal statuary. Some of the tombs—an imploring hand reaching through a window to a loved one, or an infant wrapped in a cloak of transparent gauze—may evoke morbid sentimentality, but their technical skill and compositional drama belie sculpture's reputation as one of the fustier visual arts. *Rue de Billy. Admission: 24 frs. Open daily 9–11:30 and 2–5 (4 in winter).*

16 D928 runs straight through the **Forest of Dreux** to the tiny village of **Anet**, 16 kilometers (10 miles) to the north. Only picturesque ruins now remain of what was reputedly the finest **château** of the French Renaissance, begun in 1548 for Henri II's mistress Diane de Poitiers. Her bedchamber can be visited in the Left Wing, the finest surviving building with its 17th-century **Escalier d'Honneur** (Grand Staircase) and tapestries in the **Salle des Gardes** (Guard Room), depicting the adventures of the Huntress Diana. The chapel is of note, thanks to its 16th-century dome, one of the earliest in France. *Admission: 25 frs. Open Easter–Oct., Mon., Wed.–Sat. 2–6:30, Sun. 10–11:30 and 2–6:30, closed Tues.; Nov.–Easter., Sat. 2–5, Sun. 10:30–11:30 and 2–5, closed weekdays.*

17 From Anet, keep to the road that winds along the River Eure (D836) and follow signs north to Pacy-sur-Eure, 24 kilometers (15 miles) away. Here D181 heads off to the pleasant old town of **Vernon**, 13 kilometers (8 miles) distant. Together with its pleasant riverside location on the Seine, Vernon boasts several medieval timber-frame houses; the best of these has been chosen by local authorities to house the Tourist Office, in rue Carnot. Alongside is the arresting rose-windowed facade of **Notre-Dame** church. The facade, like the high nave, dates from the 15th century, but the rounded Romanesque arches in the choir attest to the building's 12th-century origins. The church is a fine sight when viewed from behind—Impressionist painter Claude Monet painted it several times from across the Seine.

A few minor Monet canvases, along with other late 19th-century paintings, can be admired in the **Musée Poulain** (Town Museum) at the other end of rue Carnot. This rambling old mansion is seldom crowded, and the helpful curators are happy to explain local history to visitors who are intrigued by the town's English-sounding name. *Rue du Pont. Admission: 8 frs. (free Wed.). Open Tues.–Sun. 2–5:30; closed Mon.*

18 Most people stop off at Vernon simply because of its proximity to the village of **Giverny** across the Seine (turn right along D5 after the bridge). A place of pilgrimage for art lovers, this was the village where Claude Monet lived for the second half of his life and died in 1926 at age 86. After decades of neglect, his pretty pink-washed house, with its green shutters, studios, and, above all, the wonderful garden with its famous lily pond, have been lovingly restored.

Monet was brought up in Normandy, in northwestern France, and, like many of the Impressionists, was stimulated by the soft light of the Seine Valley. After several years at Argenteuil, just north of Paris, he moved downriver to Giverny in 1883, along with his two sons, mistress Alice Hoschedé (whom he later married), and her own six children. By 1890, a prospering

Monet was able to buy the house outright; three years later, he purchased another plot of land across the road to continue his gardening experiments, diverting the little River Epte to make a pond.

Soon the much-loved and oft-painted waterlilies and Japanese bridges were special features of Monet's garden. They readily conjure up the image of the grizzle-bearded brushman dabbing cheerfully at his canvas—pioneering a breakup of form that was to have a major impact on 20th-century art.

Provided you steer clear of the tourist battalions that tramp through Giverny on weekends and hot summer days, Monet's house—which you enter from the modest country lane that masquerades as Giverny's major thoroughfare—feels refreshingly like a family home after the formal French châteaus. The rooms have been restored to Monet's original designs: the kitchen with its blue tiles, the buttercup-yellow dining room, Monet's bedroom containing his bed and desk. Walls are lined with the Japanese prints Monet avidly collected, as well as with reproductions of his works.

The exuberant **garden** breaks totally with French tradition, with flowers spilling over the paths. You can reach the enchanting **water garden,** with its lilies, bridges, mighty willow, and rhododendrons, via an attractively decorated tunnel. *84 rue Claude-Monet. Admission: 28 frs. (garden only, 16 frs.). Open Apr.–Oct., Tues.–Sun. 10–noon and 2–6 (garden open 10–6); closed Mon. and Nov.–Mar.*

South of Giverny, the French road network has difficulty matching the extravagant bends of the meandering Seine. If you follow the signs to Mantes, you will next encounter the river at the charming village of **La Roche-Guyon**, dominated by chalky cliffs and its Classical **château** (not open to the public).

A few miles farther on, just after the tumbling village of **Vétheuil**, with its **12th-century church,** the road (now D147) again abandons the riverbank until it reaches prettily named **Mantes-la-Jolie**, these days a sullen suburban town but once favored by 19th-century landscape artist Camille Corot. Corot would set up his easel within sight of the town's principal attraction, the 12th-century church of **Notre-Dame.** The small, circular windows that ring the east end are a rare local characteristic; you may have noticed them at the church of nearby Vétheuil.

N183 runs 13 kilometers (8 miles) south of Mantes to Septeuil, where we suggest that you head east along D11 (follow signs to Versailles) to **Thoiry**, 9 kilometers (5½ miles) away.

The **château** of Thoiry, just 40 kilometers (25 miles) west of Paris, makes an excellent day outing in its own right, especially if you are traveling with children. Owners Vicomte de La Panouse and his American wife, Annabelle, have restored the château and park to their former glory, opening both to the public. The result is a splendid combination of history, culture, and adventure. The superbly furnished 16th-century château has archive and gastronomy museums and overlooks a safari park, where you can picnic with the bears and lions.

The château was built in 1564. Its handsome Renaissance facade is set off by gardens landscaped in typically disciplined French fashion by Le Nôtre. The discipline has unexpected justification: The château is positioned to be directly in line with the sun as it rises in the east at the winter solstice (December 21) and as it sets in the west at the summer solstice (June 21). To heighten the effect, the central part of the château appears to be a transparent arch of light, thanks to its huge glass doors and windows.

The viscountess is a keen gardener and enjoys experimenting in the less formal **Jardin à l'Anglaise** (English Garden), and in her late-flowering **Autumn Garden.** Visitors are allowed to wander at leisure, although few dare stray from the official footpath through the **animal reserve!** Note that those parts of the reserve containing the wilder beasts—deer, zebra, camels, hippos, bears, elephants, and lions—can be visited only by car.

The reserve hit the headlines when the first ever ligrons—a cross between a lion and a tiger—were born here a few years ago. These new-look beasts (bigger than either a lion or a tiger) are now into their second generation and can be seen from the safety of a raised footbridge in the **Tiger Park.** Nearby, as emus and flamingoes stalk in search of tidbits, there is a **children's play area** that features an Enchanted Burrow to wriggle through and a huge netted Cobweb to bounce around in.

Highlights of the château's interior include the **Grand Staircase,** with its 18th-century Gobelin tapestries, and the **Green and White Salons,** with their old, painted harpsichord, portraits, and tapestries. There is an authentic, homey, faintly faded charm to these rooms, especially when log fires crackle in their enormous hearths on damp afternoons.

The distinguished history of the Panouse family—a Comte César even fought in the American Revolutionary War—is retraced in the **Archive Museum,** where papal bulls, Napoleonic letters, and Chopin manuscripts (discovered in the attic in 1973) mingle with missives from Thomas Jefferson and Benjamin Franklin.

The château pantries house a **Museum of Gastronomy,** whose tempting display of *pièces montées*—virtuoso banquet showpieces—re-create the designs of ace 19th-century chef Antoine Carême. Early recipe books, engravings, and old copper pots are also displayed. *Admission: château 26 frs.; animal reserve plus gardens 69 frs. adults, 56 frs. children. Open weekdays 10–6, weekends 10–6:30 (10–5 winter).*

Time Out The **self-service restaurant** at Thoiry is housed in the converted 16th-century château stables. You can break here for a snack or an inexpensive set-menu lunch before attacking the ligrons and other wild beasts. *Open same hours as the château and animal reserve.*

From Thoiry, get onto D11 once again and follow the signs back to Paris.

Tour 2: North to St-Germain-en-Laye and Chantilly

Although this second Ile de France tour explores the north of the region, we suggest that you again leave Paris by the A13 (Rouen-bound) expressway from Porte d'Auteuil. A spectacular curving bridge soon whisks you across the Seine, past the chic suburb of **St-Cloud.** To the right are the steep streets of the

old town, pierced by a church spire; to the left, the rolling,
wooded St-Cloud Park, once the site of the favorite palace of
Napoleon's nephew, Napoleon III; it was burned down by invading Prussians in 1870. Only the ground plan of the former
buildings and the imposing, tiered waterfall known as the
Grande Cascade (designed by architect Jules Hardouin-Mansart, François Mansart's grand-nephew, in the 17th century),
now remain. The park commands fine views of Paris and, with
its grassy expanses and broad, wooded paths, is a delightful
place for walks. The château's history and architecture are retraced in the **Musée Historique** (Historical Museum) by the ceremonial gates (Grille d'Honneur) of the main entrance.
*Admission free. Grounds open daily 7 AM–9 PM. Museum open
Easter–mid-Nov., Wed., and weekends 2–6; mid-Nov.–Easter
2–5; closed Mon., Tues., Thurs., and Fri.*

Just after St-Cloud, A13 veers right through a depressingly
long, dirty tiled tunnel, emerging into a corridor of tall trees
that lasts several miles. Instead of continuing to Versailles,
take the N186 exit just beforehand, signposted to St-Germain-
en-Laye, 5 kilometers (3 miles) away.

24 The elegant town of **St-Germain-en-Laye**, perched on a hill
above the Seine and encircled by forest, has lost little of its
original cachet, despite the invasion of wealthy Parisians who
commute to work on the RER (the regional express train that
puts St-Germain just 30 minutes from the capital). Next to the
train station, at the heart of St-Germain, is the town's chief attraction—its stone-and-brick **château.**

Most of the defensive-looking château, with its dry moat and
intimidating circular towers, dates from the 16th and 17th centuries. Yet a royal palace has existed here since the early 12th
century, when Louis VI—known as *Le Gros* (The Fat)—ex-
ploited St-Germain's defensive potential in his bid to pacify the
Ile de France. A hundred years later, Louis IX (St-Louis)
added the elegant **Sainte-Chapelle,** which is the château's oldest remaining section. The figures on the tympanum (the inset
triangular area over the main door) are believed to be the first
known representations of French royalty, portraying Louis
with his mother, Blanche de Castille, and other members of his
family.

Charles V (1364–80) built a powerful defensive keep in the mid-
14th century, but from the 1540s, François I and his successors
transformed St-Germain into a palace of more domestic, and
less warlike, vocation. Until 1682—when the court moved to
Versailles—it remained the country's foremost royal residence
outside Paris. Since 1867, the château has housed a major **Musée des Antiquités Nationales** (Museum of Ancient History),
holding a trove of artifacts, figurines, brooches, and weapons
from the Stone Age through to the 8th century. *Admission: 15
frs. (8 frs. on Sun.). Open Wed.–Mon. 9:45–noon and 1:30–
5:15; closed Tues.*

Another place to visit in St-Germain is the tranquil **Musée du
Prieuré** (Priory Museum), some 600 yards from the château
(follow rue au Pain from the church). This museum is devoted to
the work of the artist Maurice Denis (1870–1943) and his fellow
Nabis—painters opposed to the naturalism of their 19th-cen-
tury Impressionist contemporaries. Denis found the calm of
the former Jesuit priory suited to his spiritual themes, which

he expressed in stained glass, ceramics, and mosaics, as well as oils. *2 bis rue Maurice-Denis. Admission: 20 frs. adults, 10 frs. children and senior citizens. Open Wed.–Fri. 10–5:30, weekends 10–6:30; closed Mon. and Tues.*

Six and a half kilometers (4 miles) north of St-Germain along the River Seine, via D157, is the town of **Maisons-Laffitte.** The early Baroque **château** of Maisons, constructed by architect François Mansart from 1642 to 1651, is one of the least known châteaus in the Ile de France. This was not always the case: Sun King Louis XIV came to the housewarming party, and Louis XV (1715–74), Louis XVI (Marie Antoinette's husband, 1774–93), the 18th-century writer Voltaire, and Napoleon all stayed here. The interior clearly met their exacting standards, thanks to the well-proportioned entrance vestibule with its rich sculpture; the winding **Escalier d'Honneur,** a majestic staircase adorned with paintings and statues; and the royal apartments, above, with their parquet floors and elegant wall paneling. *Admission: 22 frs. adults, 12 frs. students and senior citizens. Open daily 9–12 and 2–6 (7 Sun.).*

Cross the bridge that links Maisons-Laffitte to Sartrouville and take the first left along the banks of the Seine. Parts of this river road, particularly at the neighboring town of La Frette, retain surprising pastoral charm, given the proximity of the industrial suburbs. At Herblay, the road leaves the river; head up through the housing development to the main road and turn left for Conflans, a couple of miles away.

The town of **Conflans-Ste-Honorine,** 32 kilometers (20 miles) northwest of Paris, reflects the importance of waterways to the Ile de France region. Boats and barges arrive from as far afield as the ports of Le Havre and Dunkerque, on France's northern coast, and are often moored up to six-abreast along the mile-long quayside, near the *conflans* (confluence, and hence the town's name) of the rivers Seine and Oise. The **Musée de la Batellerie** (Boat Museum), next to an old church high above the river, explains the historic role of the barges and waterways with the help of its collection of pictures and scale models. *Admission: free. Open Easter–Oct., weekdays 9–noon and 1:30–6 (closed Tues. AM), weekends 3–6; Nov.–Easter, weekdays 9–noon (except Tues.) and 1:30–5, weekends 2–5.*

The road that crosses the Seine at Conflans continues 8 kilometers (5 miles) north toward **Pontoise,** a pleasant old town on the banks of the Oise. One of the town's most illustrious past residents was Impressionist painter Camille Pissarro (1830–1903). Pissarro is the hero of a small **museum** in rue du Château, close to the Hôtel de Ville (Town Hall) and 12th-century **Cathedral of St-Maclou** up in the old town. *Admission free. Open Wed.–Sun. 2–6; closed Mon. and Tues.*

The tranquil Oise Valley, which runs northeast from Pontoise, retains much of the charm that attracted Pissarro and other Impressionists to this area a century ago. Pissarro, Paul Cézanne, and Vincent van Gogh all worked at the town of **Auvers-sur-Oise,** 6½ kilometers (4 miles) from Pontoise along D4. Van Gogh—whose vibrant *Irises* sold for a record $49 million in 1987—eked out the last few penniless months of his life in Auvers before committing suicide in a nearby field in July 1890. He lived above what was then a café (at 52 rue du Général-de-Gaulle) and is buried, along with his devoted brother Theo, in the cemetery above the church he made famous in one of his most powerful paintings, *The Church at Auvers* (now at the Musée d'Orsay in Paris). Stop in at the Auvers tourist office, which is a mine of information on the activity of Van Gogh and other painters in the area. *Office de Tourisme, rue de la Sansonne, tel. 30–36–10–06. Open daily 10–noon and 2–6.*

Six and a half kilometers (4 miles) upstream from Auvers, across the bridge at Parmain, is residentially exclusive **L'Isle-Adam,** one of the most picturesque towns in the entire Ile de France. Paris lies just 25 miles south, but it could be 100 miles and as many years away. There is a sandy **beach** along one stretch of the River Oise and an unassuming local museum, the **Musée Louis Senlecq,** in the main street, which often stages painting exhibitions. *46 Grande-Rue. Admission free. Open Apr.–Nov., weekends and Mon. 2–5:30; closed Tues.–Sat.*

From L'Isle-Adam, take N322/D922 to the small hilltop town of **Beaumont-sur-Oise**—worth a quick peek if only for its attractive 12th–13th-century **church of St-Laurent,** transformed into a cathedral by 19th-century French writer Emile Zola as the setting for his romantic novel *Le Rêve (The Dream).* From Beaumont, take D922 to Viarmes, then turn left along D909 to the Cistercian Abbey of **Royaumont,** 2½ kilometers (1½ miles) away. The abbey was founded by the only canonized French King, Louis IX, known as St-Louis, in 1228; 5 of his 11 children are buried here. Only part of the abbey church still stands (the south transept), which can be visited, along with the ivy-clad cloisters, the refectory where St-Louis served the monks, and the vaulted kitchens. The monks' dormitories, chapter-house, and library are now part of an international cultural center and are rarely open to the public (tel. 30–35–88–90 for details of the concerts held here in summer). *Admission: 20 frs. Open Easter–Oct., Wed.–Mon. 10–noon and 2–5, closed Tues.; Nov.–Easter, Sun. only, 10–noon and 2–5.*

Ten kilometers (6 miles) northeast via D909 lies the town of **Chantilly,** with its haughty, spacious, golden-stoned **château,** sitting snugly behind an artificial, carp-stocked lake. Despite appearances, much of the current building is not old but is 19th-century Renaissance pastiche, rebuilt in the 1870s. The lavish interior contains the outstanding **Condé Collection** of illuminated medieval manuscripts, tapestries, furniture, and paintings. The most famous room, the **Santuario,** boasts two celebrated works by Italian painter Raphael (1483–1520)—the *Three Ages of Woman* and *The Orleans Virgin*—plus an exquisite ensemble of 15th-century miniatures by the most illustrious French painter of his time, Jean Fouquet (1420–81). Farther on, in the Cabinet des Livres, is the **Book of Hours** of the Duc de Berri, one of the finest medieval manuscripts.

Other highlights of this unusual museum are the **Galérie de Psyché,** with 16th-century stained glass and portrait drawings by Flemish artist Jean Clouet II; the **chapel,** with sculptures by Jean Goujon and Jacques Sarrazin; and the extensive **collection of paintings** by 19th-century French artists, headed by Jean Auguste Ingres. *Admission: 30 frs. adults, 7 frs. children; 12 frs. (park only). Open Easter–Oct., Wed.–Mon. 10–6; Nov.–Easter, 10:30–12:30 and 2–5; closed Tues.*

Behind the château is a large **park,** based on that familiar combination of formal bombast (neatly planned parterres and a mighty straight-banked canal) and romantic eccentricity (the Jardin Anglais [English Garden], with its waterfall, or the make-believe village that inspired Marie Antoinette's version at Versailles).

Across the lake from the château is the Chantilly racecourse, inaugurated in 1834 by the prestigious French Jockey Club. In one corner (to the right as you leave the château) are the majestic 18th-century stables (**Grandes Ecuries**), where up to 240 horses and 400 hounds for stag and boar hunts could be accommodated in straw-lined comfort. Today the stables host the **Musée du Cheval** (Horse Museum) and a glittering array of carriages. *Admission: 40 frs. adults, 35 frs. students and senior citizens, 30 frs. children. Open daily 10:30–5:30 (6 on weekends).*

Time Out As the château of Chantilly is a fair walk from the town's main street, it makes sense to have a quick lunch on the spot—at the self-service **Capitainerie restaurant** in the château's medieval basement (adorned with old kitchen utensils). The buffet is available nonstop from 10:30 through 6:30: mostly salads, cheeses, and desserts, complemented by the occasional hot dish. *Closed Tues.*

③③ Ten kilometers (6 miles) east of Chantilly, along the picturesque, gently turning D924, is **Senlis,** whose crooked, mazelike streets are dominated by the svelte soaring spire of the Gothic cathedral of **Notre-Dame.**

As we noticed at Chantilly, this is prime hunting country. On the grounds of the ruined royal castle opposite the west front of the cathedral is the **Musée de la Vénerie,** which claims to be Europe's only full-fledged hunting museum. Suitable artifacts, prints, and paintings rekindle the atmosphere of the kingly pursuit. *Château Royal. Admission: 15 frs. adults, 8 frs. children. Open for guided visits on the hour, Mon. 10–noon and 2–3, Tues. and Wed. 2–5, Thurs.–Sun. 10–noon and 2–5.*

Down the lane behind the cathedral is the former church of **St-Pierre,** with its Flamboyant facade, while across place Notre-Dame, the large square beside the cathedral, is the **Fondation Cziffra:** the former church of St-Frambourg, converted into an exhibition center by Hungarian-born pianist Gyorgy Cziffra in 1977, with a small adjoining museum devoted to regional architectural finds. *1 pl. St-Frambourg. Admission: 10 frs. adults, 6 frs. students. Open weekends only 3–6.*

Time Out Senlis is not the liveliest place for taking a quick drink or lunch, but if you head down rue du Châtel from the cathedral you'll find cafés and bars in **rue Apport-du-Pain** (no. 16), **rue Vieille de Paris** (no. 19), and **place de la Halle** (no. 37).

③④ Just off N330, some 11 kilometers (7 miles) southeast of Senlis, stand the ruins of the 18th-century abbey of **Chaalis,** built on the site of a 13th-century Cistercian abbey. The landscaped park has been restored to its 18th-century appearance, and the château, which dates from the same period, has an eclectic collection of Egyptian antiquities and medieval paintings, together with three rooms devoted to the 18th-century French philosopher and writer Jean-Jacques Rousseau, who died at nearby Ermenonville. *Admission: 15 frs. Open Wed. and Sat.*

1:30–6, Sun. 10–noon and 1:30–6; closed Mon., Tues., Thurs., and Fri.

To return to Paris, take D84 about 8 kilometers (5 miles) due south, then follow the signs for Paris on the fast A102.

Tour 3: South to Fontainebleau

Fontainebleau, which forms the hub of our final tour, can be reached from Paris (65 kilometers/40 miles away) in as little as half an hour via A6 and N37. But we urge you not to bypass nearby Vaux-le-Vicomte, best reached from Paris (Porte de Bercy) via N6, leaving this road at Melun and continuing to Vaux, 5 kilometers (3 miles) northeast, along N36 and D215.

35 The château of **Vaux-le-Vicomte** was built between 1656 and 1661 for court financier Nicolas Fouquet. The construction process was monstrous even for those days: Entire villages were razed, 18,000 workmen called in, and ace designers Louis Le Vau, Charles Le Brun, and esteemed landscape architect André Le Nôtre hired to prove that Fouquet's sense of aesthetics matched his business acumen. Unfortunately, his housewarming party was too lavish for the likings of star guest Louis XIV. King Louis threw a fit of jealousy, hurled the tactless Fouquet in jail, and promptly began building Versailles to prove just who was boss.

The high-roofed château, partially surrounded by a moat, is set well back from the roadside behind iron railings topped with sculpted heads. A cobbled avenue winds its way up to the entrance. Stone steps lead to the vestibule, which, given the noble scale of the exterior, seems small. There is no grand staircase, either—the stairs are tucked away in the left wing and lead to a set of rooms that could almost be described as pokey.

Painter Charles Le Brun's lush interior decoration partly compensates: His major achievement is the ceiling of the **Chambre du Roi** (Royal Bedchamber), depicting Time Bearing Truth Heavenwards, framed by stucco work by sculptors François Girardon and Legendre. Along the frieze you can make out small squirrels—known as *fouquets* in local dialect.

But the château's most impressive room is the **Grand Salon** on the ground floor. With its unusual oval form and 16 caryatid pillars symbolizing the months and seasons, it possesses harmony and style despite its unfinished state (the cupola remains depressingly blank).

An astute exhibition, complete with lifesize wax figures, explains the rise and fall of Nicolas Fouquet. The version is, not surprisingly, favorable to the château's founder—accused by Louis XIV and subsequent historians of megalomania and shady financial dealings, but apparently condemned on little evidence by a court anxious to please the jealous, irascible monarch. The exhibition continues in the basement, whose narrow corridors and stone vaults have, in parts, a suitably dungeonlike feel. The **kitchens** are also down here, a more cheerful sight, with their gleaming copperware and old menus.

Although the château's interior lacks majesty, there is no mistaking the grandeur of Le Nôtre's **gardens,** which have been carefully restored. Visit the **Musée des Equipages** (Carriage

Museum) in the stables and inspect a host of lovingly restored carriages and coaches. *Admission: 42 frs. adults, 34 frs. students and senior citizens. Gardens only: 20 frs. Open daily 10–6 (5 in winter). Candlelight visits 8:30–11PM Sat. May–Sept.; admission: 50 frs.*

Time Out To the right of the château entrance is an imposing barn that has been transformed into a self-serve **cafeteria.** Here, beneath the ancient rafters of a stout wood-beam roof, you can enjoy coffee, cheap pitchers of wine, and good steaks. Insist on *bien cuit* if you don't want your meat too bloodily rare.

From Vaux, return to Melun (take the beltway around the north of the town) and head along D132 (which becomes D64) to **36** **Barbizon,** 10 kilometers (6 miles) south. Barbizon stands on the western edge of the 42,000-acre Forest of Fontainebleau and retains the atmosphere of a small village, despite the intrusion of expensive art galleries, tacky souvenir shops, and weekending Parisians.

Barbizon owes its renown to the colony of landscape painters—Camille Corot, Jean-François Millet, and Théodore Rousseau, among others—who lived here from the 1830s on. Their innovative commitment to working outdoors paved the way for the Impressionists, as did their willingness to accept nature on its own terms rather than use it as an idealized base for carefully structured compositions.

After working hours, the Barbizon painters repaired to the **Auberge du Père Ganne.** The inn is still standing—it's now a museum—and you can soak up the arty mood here or at the houses of Millet and Rousseau farther along the single main street (Grande-Rue). *Musée Auberge du Père Ganne, 92 Grande-Rue. Admission free. Open Easter–Oct., Wed.–Mon. 10–5:30, closed Tues.; Nov.–Easter, Wed., Fri., and Sun. only, 10–5:30.*

Eight kilometers (5 miles) southeast of Barbizon (via the fast **37** N7) lies the town of **Fontainebleau.** Like Chambord in the Loire Valley or Compiègne to the north, Fontainebleau earned royal esteem as a hunting base. Indeed, a hunting lodge once stood on the site of the current château, along with a chapel built in 1169 and consecrated during exile by Thomas à Becket (1118–70), the now-canonized archbishop of Canterbury. Today's château was begun under the flamboyant Renaissance prince François I, the French contemporary of England's Henry VIII.

Although Sun King Louis XIV's architectural energies were concentrated on Versailles, he nonetheless commissioned architect François Mansart to design new pavilions at Fontainebleau, and had Le Nôtre replant the gardens. But it was Napoleon who spent lavishly to make a Versailles, as it were, out of Fontainebleau.

Numbers in the margin correspond with points of interest on the Fontainebleau map.

Walk past the parterres to the left of the Etang des Carpes **38** (Carp Pond) and turn left into an alley that leads to the **Cour Ovale**—a courtyard shaped like a flattened oval with, at the **39** straight end, the domed **Porte du Baptistère,** an imposing gateway designed by court architect Francesco Primaticcio (1504–70). The gateway's name commemorates the fact that the Dau-

Cour du Cheval-
Blanc, **41**

Cour des Offices, **40**

Cour Ovale, **38**

Galerie de Diane, **45**

Horseshoe
Staircase, **42**

Napoleon's
Apartments, **43**

Porte du
Baptistère, **39**

Salle de Bal, **46**

Throne Room/Queen's
Bedroom, **44**

phin—the male heir to the throne, later to become Louis XIII—was baptized under its arch in 1606. Opposite is the **40** **Cour des Offices,** a large, severe square built at the same time as the place des Vosges in Paris (1609).

The hedge-lined alley continues to the Jardin de Diane (Garden of Diana), with its peacocks and statue of the hunting goddess surrounded by mournful hounds. Cross this informal garden **41** and enter the palace's most majestic courtyard, the **Cour du** **42** **Cheval-Blanc,** dominated by the famous **horseshoe staircase** built by Jean Androuet du Cerceau in the early 17th century. Climb the steps to the château entrance.

43 In **Napoleon's apartments** on the second floor, you can ogle a lock of his hair, his Légion d'Honneur medal, his imperial uniform, the hat he wore on his return from Elba in 1815, and the bed in which he used to sleep.

44 There is also a **throne room**—one of Napoleon's foibles, since the kings themselves were content with the one at Versailles— and the **Queen's Bedroom,** known as the Room of the Six **45** Maries. The seemingly endless **Galerie de Diane,** built during the reign of Henri IV (1589–1610), was used as a library. Other salons boast 17th-century tapestries, marble reliefs by Jacquet de Grenoble, and paintings and frescoes by the versatile Italian Francesco Primaticcio (besides being court architect to François I, he was also a top-rate painter, sculptor, and interior designer).

Jewel of the interior, though, is the ceremonial ballroom—the **46** **Salle de Bal**—nearly 100 feet long, with wood paneling and a gleaming parquet floor whose pattern matches that of the ceiling.

If time permits, complete your visit with a stroll around the leafy **Jardin Anglais** (English Garden) to the right of the Etang des Carpes. *Admission: 23 frs. adults, 12 frs. children. Open Wed.–Mon. 9:30–12:30 and 2–5; closed Tues. Gardens open 9–dusk; admission free.*

Numbers in the margin correspond with points of interest on the Ile de France map.

47 Ten kilometers (six miles) southeast of Fontainebleau on N6, close to the confluence of the rivers Seine and Yonne, is the charming village of **Moret-sur-Loing,** immortalized by Impressionist painter Alfred Sisley, who lived here for 20 years at 19 rue Montmartre (not open to the public), around the corner from the church of Notre-Dame. Close by, across the river, is the thatched **house-museum** of another illustrious former inhabitant: truculent World War I leader Georges Clemenceau (1841–1929), known as The Tiger. His taste for Oriental art and his friendship with Impressionist Claude Monet are evoked. *Follow signs to the Grange Batelière. Guided tours only: 35 frs. Open Easter–Oct., weekends 2:30–6; closed Nov.–Easter.*

The best view of Moret is from the far banks of the Loing. Cross the narrow bridge (one of the oldest in France and invariably clogged with traffic) to gaze back at the walls, rooftops, and church tower. A good time to visit Moret is on a summer evening when locals stage *son-et-lumière* (sound-and-light) pageants illustrating the village's history.

48 After crossing the Loing, take N6 for 6½ kilometers (4 miles), then turn left along D403 (via Montereau) to the attractive town of **Provins,** another 37 kilometers (23 miles) away. Provins grew up on the hilltop site of a Roman camp before acquiring international renown as a rose-growing center. Under the medieval influence of the counts of Champagne, Provins became an important commercial center, the third most important town in France (after Paris and Rouen) during the Middle Ages. Neither historic, hilltop Provins nor the more recent township below is much of an economic dynamo these days, however. Upper Provins sleeps in the past, tucked in behind its defensive walls at the foot of the solid 12th-century Tour de César, a circular keep on a sturdy mound. Climb to the top for a view of the town. *Admission: 6 frs. Open Mar.–Nov., Mon.–Sat. 9:30–noon and 2–6, Sun. 2–6; Dec.–Feb. until 5.*

Beneath the tower is the 12th-century Gothic church of **St-Quirace,** with its incongruous 17th-century Classical dome. Close by is a pleasant garden, the **Jardin des Brébans.** From here, rue du Palais leads up to place du Châtel, a sloping square with restaurants at the far end. Veer left down rue de Jouy; on the first corner is the 13th-century tithe-barn, or **Grange aux Dîmes,** whose vaulted ground floor contains a collection of stone sculptures. *Admission: 6 frs. Open Easter–Oct., daily 10–noon and 2:30–5; Nov.–Easter until 4:30.*

Rue St-Jean leads to the Porte St-Jean gateway. Here you can survey some of the best-preserved **medieval city walls** in France.

N19 links Provins to Paris, 72 kilometers (45 miles) away.

What to See and Do with Children

Euro Disney, set to open 30 kilometers (20 miles) east of Paris in April 1992, is based closely on the American original(s), with lifesize Disney heroes frolicking in a Magic Kingdom divided into five imaginary realms: Fantasyland, Frontierland, Adventureland, Discoveryland, and Main Street USA. Attractions include horse-drawn wagons, steamboats (and trains), lakes, a shooting range, a haunted manor, an African jungle, Treasure Island, Sleeping Beauty's castle, and high-tech visits to the Grand Canyon and outer space. The site will also offer shops, more than 30 restaurants, five hotels, and (by 1994) new RER and TGV rail stations. *Access: Take A4 east from Paris and look for the Euro Disney turn-off (D231). P.O. Box 105, 94350 Villiers-sur-Marne; for information and reservations, tel. 49–30–78–00, fax 49–30–71–00. Opening hours and admission prices unavailable at press time.*

Opposite the abbey of Chaalis, 11 kilometers (7 miles) southeast of Senlis, is the **Mer de Sable playground**—a cheerful place for children to play in, with its miniature train, giant slide, small zoo, and curious natural "desert" of white sand. *Parc d'Attractions Jean-Richard, Forêt d'Ermenonville, off N330. Admission: 50 frs. Open Apr.–Oct., Tues.–Sat. and weekends 10:30–7, closed Mon. and Fri.; Nov.–Mar., Wed. and weekends only 11–6:30.*

The **Mirapolis Amusement Park** in Cergy, 40 kilometers (25 miles) northwest of Paris, is a Gallic answer to Disneyland, with all the fun of the fair and a determinedly French flavor. There's no Mickey Mouse or Donald Duck here, though, just characters from French fiction. The hefty entrance fee covers all the rides. *Rte. de Courdimanche, Cergy-Pontoise, RER–A Cergy St-Christophe. Admission: 75 frs. weekdays, 90 frs. weekends. Open Easter–Oct. only.*

The theme park known as **Parc Astérix** takes its cue from a French comic book figure whose adventures are set during the Roman invasion of France 2,000 years ago. Highlights include a mock Romano-Gallic village, a dolphin lake, and a giant roller coaster. *Just off A1 at Plailly, 32 km (20 miles) north of Paris. Admission: 120 frs. adults, 90 frs. children under 12. Open Easter–Oct., Sun.–Fri. 10–6, Sat. 10–10.*

Most children will enjoy a visit to the animal reserve and Tiger Park of the **Château de Thoiry** *(see* Tour 1, above).

Off the Beaten Track

Take a short literary pilgrimage down the Seine Valley one Sunday to the little town of **Médan,** where Emile Zola moved in 1877 after the runaway success of his novel *L'Assommoir.* Until recently, his house was used as an orphanage, but it is now open to the public once a week. *26 rue Pasteur. Admission: 25 frs. adults, 12 frs. students and senior citizens. Open Sun. only, 2–6.*

Ecouen, a woody suburb 19 kilometers (12 miles) north of Paris, is known for its château, home of a museum devoted to the Renaissance and particularly strong on 16th- and 17th-century tapestry and furniture from France, Italy, and Holland. *Musée* *de la Renaissance, Château d'Ecouen. Admission: 15 frs. (8 frs. Sun.). Open Wed.–Mon. 10–12:30 and 2–5:15; closed Tues.*

The Orge Valley southwest of Paris presents an attractive mixture of hills, fields, and forest, and two outstanding man-made attractions: an enormous, airy 13th-century church in the tiny village of **St-Sulpice de Favières** and the enticing château of **Le Marais,** with lake, extensive grounds, and a small museum devoted to onetime inhabitant Talleyrand (a romantic but unscrupulous 19th-century diplomat). A car is the only means of access to these two sites, though the RER-C trains from Paris stop at nearby St-Chéron, where taxis can be hired. *Le Marais: Admission: 24 frs. (park only: 16 frs.). Open Sun. only Apr.–Sept., 11–6.*

Students of urban planning and modern architecture will have a field day in the Ile de France. **La Défense,** just west of Paris, is renowned for its steel-and-glass, Manhattan-style skyline, but five bigger developments—in fact, whole **new towns** *(villes nouvelles)*—have been undertaken in the past 20 years: at St-Quentin-en-Yvelines, Cergy-Pontoise, Evry, Melun-Sénart, and Marne-la-Vallée. All can be reached by train or RER from Paris within 45 minutes.

Shopping

Most of the Ile de France's working population either commutes to Paris or plows farmland. There is little in the way of regional specialties, and, with Paris never more than an hour away, serious shopping—particularly for clothes—means heading back to the capital.

Food Items Versailles is perhaps the region's most commercial town. After visiting the château, you might want to stop in at **Aux Colonnes,** a highly rated *confiserie* with an astounding array of chocolates and candies (14 rue Hoche; closed Mon.). A huge choice of cheeses—including one of France's widest selection of goat cheeses—can be smelled, admired, and eventually purchased from **Eugène Le Gall** (13 rue Ducis; closed Sun. afternoon and Mon.). Stuffed olives, dried fruits, and more exotic spices and teas than you thought existed can be had from **Arts Populaires** (15 rue des Deux-Portes; closed Sun. afternoon and Mon. morning).

Antiques Anyone in the mood for antiques hunting should visit Versailles's passage de la Geôle, site of a good thrice-weekly flea market (10 rue Rameau; open Fri.–Sun. 9–7). Antiques shops in other major towns include **A La Cour Des Adieux** (3 pl. Denecourt, Fontainebleau); **Leroy** (9 rue Villevert, Senlis); **Susen Antiquités** (18 rue des Coches, St-Germain-en-Laye); and **Ambiance & Style** (17 rue des Changes, Chartres).

Souvenirs There are notably fine souvenir shops at Vaux-le-Vicomte, Giverny, and Thoiry (where you can sample cookies and jams made by the American viscountess herself).

Gift Items Stained glass being the key to Chartres's fame, enthusiasts may want to visit the **Galerie du Vitrail** (17 rue Cloître Notre-Dame), which specializes in the noble art. Pieces range from small plaques to entire windows, and there are books on the subject in English and French.

Sports and Fitness

Bicycling Biking is an enjoyable and healthy way to explore the area; you can rent bicycles from many local train stations, including those of Rambouillet and Fontainebleau. A booklet detailing 16 bike routes in the region can be obtained from the **SNCF** (tel. 42–61–50–50).

If you like to watch people pedaling more than you enjoy doing it yourself, be in the region on the last Sunday of July, when the **Tour de France** cycle race passes through en route to its Champs-Elysées climax.

Golf Golf is a new, expensive cult sport in France, but there are several clubs open to the general public: **Bougival** (tel. 39–18–43–81), **Chambourcy** (tel. 30–74–45–98), **Fontainebleau** (tel. 64–22–22–95), and **St-Germain-en-Laye** (tel. 34–51–75–90).

Hiking The great forests of Rambouillet, St-Germain, and Fontainebleau are much frequented by walkers; if you'd prefer to go with a group, the local tourist offices *(see* Essential Information, above) can furnish details of organized hikes.

Horseback Riding Get in touch with one of the following stables *(centre équestre):* 29 rue de l'Arbre-Sec, Fontainebleau, tel. 64–22–31–55; rte. Nogent-le-Phaye, Chartres, tel. 16/37–30–10–10; 23 rue Franklin, St-Germain-en-Laye, tel. 34–51–10–94; or Chemin du Roy, Senlis, tel. 16/44–53–55–13.

Rock Climbing The region boasts numerous routes, particularly in the Forest of Fontainebleau. For more information, contact the **Club Alpin Français** (24 av. Laumière, 75019 Paris, tel. 42–02–75–94).

Swimming You'll never be too far away from a public swimming pool. The following are just a few of the options: route de l'Ermitage, Fontainebleau, tel. 64–22–16–85; blvd. Courtille, Chartres, tel. 16/37–28–05–87; 3 rue Léon-Gatin, Versailles, tel. 39–50–65–71.

Dining and Lodging

Dining

With wealthy tourists and weekending Parisians providing the backbone of the region's seasonal clientele, the smarter restaurants of Ile de France can be just as pricey as their Parisian counterparts. But in smaller towns, and for those prepared to venture only marginally off the beaten tourist track, nourishing, good-value meals are not hard to find. The style of cuisine mirrors that of Paris: There is plenty of variety but few things that can be considered specifically regional. The "local delicacies" cited by earnest textbooks—navarin lamb stew, pâté pantin (pastry filled with meat, chicken, game, or fish), pig's trotters, or vegetable soup—tend to be either banal or obsolete. In season, sumptuous game and asparagus are found in the south of the region; the soft, creamy cheese of Brie hails from Meaux and Coulommiers to the east. More generally, the Ile de France is a prolific producer of vegetables, and at table or the market, you have a right to refuse all but the freshest produce.

Highly recommended restaurants are indicated by a star ★.

Category	Cost*
Very Expensive	over 350 francs
Expensive	200–350 francs
Moderate	100–200 francs
Inexpensive	under 100 francs

per person for a three-course meal, including tax (18.6%) and tip but not wine

Lodging

Remember two things: In summer, hotel rooms are at a premium and reservations are essential; relative lack of choice means that almost all accommodations in the swankier towns—Versailles, Rambouillet, and Fontainebleau—are on the costly side. Take nothing for granted. Picturesque Senlis, for instance, does not have a single hotel in its historic downtown area. Some of the smaller hotels in the region may not accept credit cards, although the Carte Bleue and its international equivalents (MasterCard and Visa) are widely recognized—unlike American Express, which is often refused in all but the plushest establishments.

Highly recommended hotels are indicated by a star ★.

Category	Cost*
Very Expensive	over 750 francs
Expensive	350–750 francs
Moderate	200–350 francs
Inexpensive	under 200 francs

All prices are for a standard double room for two, including tax (18.6%) and service charge.

Barbizon
Dining

Le Relais. Delicious country-French specialties are served here in large portions, and there is a good choice of fixed-price menus. The restaurant is spacious, with a big open fire, and paintings and hunting trophies decorate the walls. The owner is rightly proud of the large terrace where diners can eat in the shade of lime and chestnut trees. *2 av. Charles-de-Gaulle, tel. 60–66–40–28. Reservations required weekends. Jacket and tie advised. MC, V. Closed Tues., Wed., second half Aug., most of Jan. Moderate.*

Lodging
★

Auberge des Alouettes. This delightful family-run 19th-century inn is set in two acres of grounds (which the better rooms overlook). The interior has been redecorated in '30s style, but many rooms still have their original oak beams. The popular restaurant (reservations are essential), with its large open terrace, features light cuisine (no heavy sauces) and barbecued beef in summer. *4 rue Antoine-Barye, 77630, tel. 60–66–41–98. 23 rooms with bath. Jacket and tie required in restaurant. Facilities: tennis. AE, DC, MC, V. Moderate.*

Chantilly
Dining
★

Relais Condé. What is probably the classiest restaurant in Chantilly is pleasantly situated opposite the racecourse, in a building that originally served as an Anglican chapel. A reasonably priced menu makes it a suitable lunch spot. An extensive wine list and several filling recipes—*burbet* (freshwater cod) with peppers, veal kidneys in mustard sauce—warrant a lengthier (if more expensive) visit in the evening. *42 av. du Marechal-Joffre, tel. 16/44–57–05–75. Reservations required. Jacket and tie required for dinner. AE, DC, V. Closed Mon. and Sun. evening. Moderate.*

Relais du Coq Chantant. The discreet, upmarket style of this well-established restaurant attracts a classy clientele of golfers and horse fanciers. They may be willing to splash out à la carte, but we suggest that you opt for a set menu to sample a traditional meal based on fowl or rabbit. *21 rte. de Creil, tel. 16/44–57–01–28. Reservations advised. Jacket required. AE, DC, MC, V. Moderate.*

Lodging

Campanile. Well-run and functional, this modern motel is set in a quiet, relaxing location just outside Chantilly, on the edge of the forest. (The forest setting goes far to compensate for the lack of interior atmosphere.) There's a grillroom for straightforward, if unexciting, meals. *Les Huits Curés, on the N16 to Creil, tel. 16/44–57–39–24. 47 rooms, some with bath. Facilities: garden, terrace for outdoor dining. MC, V. Moderate.*

Etoile. This small, underwhelming hotel is conveniently placed on the avenue leading from the train station to the château. It's cheap and acceptable for a night's stopover, though your reception may be somewhat lacking in warmth. *3 av. du Marechal-Joffre, 60500, tel. 16/44–57–02–55. 10 rooms with bath. MC, V. Inexpensive.*

Chartres
Dining

La Vieille Maison. Occupying a pretty 14th-century building just 100 yards from the cathedral, this restaurant is a fine choice for either lunch or dinner. The decor is intimate, based around a flower-strewn patio. The menu changes regularly but invariably includes regional specialties—such as asparagus or pig's feet with truffles. The homemade foie gras is superb. Prices, though justified, can be steep, but the set menus are a good bet. *5 rue au Lait, tel. 16/37–34–10–67. Reservations required. Jacket and tie required. AE, DC, MC, V. Closed Mon., Sun. evening. Moderate–Expensive.*

Le Buisson Ardent. A wood-beamed, second-floor restaurant, Le Buisson Ardent offers filling, low-priced menus, imaginative nouvelle food, and a view of Chartres cathedral (it's just opposite the south portal). Service is gratifyingly attentive. Try the fruity Gamay de Touraine, an ideal wine for lunchtime. *10 rue au Lait, tel. 16/37–34–04–66. Reservations accepted. Dress: casual. AE, DC, V. Closed Sun. and Tues. evening, Wed. Inexpensive–Moderate.*

Dining and Lodging
★

Grand Monarque. The venerable 18th-century Monarque recently had a face-lift: 11 rooms were added, and the entrance hall was completely renovated. Guest rooms have the level of consistent comfort you expect from a member of two hotel chains (Best Western and Mapotel); the most atmospheric overlook a small garden or are tucked away in the attic of this former coaching inn. There's also a classy restaurant, renowned for its nouvelle interpretations of seasonal fare, fowl, and fish. *22 pl. des Epars, 28000, tel. 37–21–00–72. 54 rooms, 52 with* *bath. Facilities: terrace used for outdoor dining. AE, DC, MC, V. Moderate–Expensive.*

Dreux
Dining and Lodging

Auberge Normande. This is a modest country hotel, excellently situated on the historic square that links the church to the belfry; ask for a room with a view. A cozy restaurant, Le Beffroi, is situated a couple of doors farther along the square. *6 pl. Métézeau, 28100, tel. 16/37–50–14–51. 20 rooms, most with shower. DC, MC, V. Closed Christmas–New Year's. Inexpensive–Moderate.*

Ermenonville
Dining and Lodging
★

Croix d'Or. For lunch or an overnight stop in tiny Ermenonville (just a few miles outside Senlis), why not try the Croix d'Or? Its small rooms and homey restaurant have the welcoming feel of a village inn. *2 rue du Prince-Radziwill, 60950, tel. 16/44–54–00–04. 11 rooms, some with bath or shower. Facilities: garden. MC, V. Restaurant closed Mon. and (winter only) Sun. evening; hotel closed mid-Dec.–first week Feb. Inexpensive.*

Fontainebleau
Dining
★

Chinois de l'Ile de France. Cheap eating is not the easiest task for Bellifontains (as the town's inhabitants are known), so an address like that of this restaurant needs noting. Chinese cooking is served here, with a fine meat dip the specialty—along with a plethora of set-price menus, each under 100 francs. What the restaurant lacks in style, it makes up for in value: Its prices are modest by Fontainebleau standards (200 francs and up). The Chinois has 25 moderately priced guest rooms as well. *128 rue de France, tel. 64–22–15–33. Reservations accepted. Dress: casual. AE, DC, MC, V. Inexpensive.*

Le Dauphin. The homey, rustic Dauphin is located near the Hôtel de Ville (Town Hall), just a five-minute walk from the château. Prices are reasonable, and specialties include snails, *confit de canard* (conserve of duck), and a variety of homemade desserts. *24 rue Grande, tel. 64–22–27–04. Reservations advised, especially on Sun. Dress: casual. Closed Tues. dinner, Wed., Feb., and Sept. 1–8. Inexpensive.*

Lodging

Hôtel de Londres. The balconies of this tranquil, family-style hotel overlook the château and the Cour des Adieux, where Napoleon bid his troops a fond farewell; the austere 19th-century facade is preserved by government order. Inside, the decor is dominated by Louis XV-style gilt furniture. *1 pl. Général-de-Gaulle, 77300, tel. 64–22–20–21. 22 rooms, most with bath. Facilities: restaurant, bar, outdoor dining. AE, MC, V. Closed Dec. 20–Jan. 31. Moderate.*

Dining and Lodging
★

Aigle-Noir. This may be Fontainebleau's costliest hotel, but you can't go far wrong: Most rooms overlook either the garden or the château and have late 18th- or early 19th-century reproduction furniture to evoke a Napoleonic mood. A thorough modernization program was recently undertaken, affecting the grand hotel restaurant, the **Beauharnais**, as well. The cooking here has the herbal subtlety of nouvelle cuisine, but the portions show none of its traditional parsimony. The set menus are recommended. *27 pl. Napoléon-Bonaparte, 77300, tel. 64–22–32–65. Restaurant reservations required; jacket and tie required. 57 rooms with bath. Facilities: pool, outdoor dining in garden, conference hall. AE, DC, MC, V. Very Expensive.*

L'Isle-Adam
Dining and Lodging

Le Cabouillet. The riverside Cabouillet aptly reflects the quiet charm of L'Isle-Adam, thanks to its pretty views over the Oise. You can savor these from each of its eight rooms or from the chic restaurant, where the cooking can be inspired (if it's on the menu, go for the crawfish in Sauternes sauce). *5 quai de l'Oise, 95290, tel. 34–69–00–90. 8 rooms with bath. Restaurant reservations accepted. Dress: neat but casual. V. Hotel closed Christmas to early Feb. Restaurant closed Mon. dinner and Tues. Moderate.*

Maintenon
Dining and Lodging
★

Château d'Esclimont. Nineteen kilometers (12 miles) southeast of Maintenon (take D116 to the village of Gallardon, keep an eye out for its magnificent old church, and then turn left) is the restored Renaissance Château d'Esclimont. The château is well worth seeking out if you wish to eat (or slumber) like a king (or queen). Set in luxurious grounds, with lawns, a lake, and a huge driveway, this member of the Relais et Châteaux chain is a regular target for smooth-talking and -eating Parisian power brokers. The cuisine is sophisticated and varied: Quail, rabbit fricassee, and lobster top the menu. Guest rooms are luxuriously furnished, and there are two private tennis courts and a heated swimming pool. The 16th-century château makes an admirable base for visiting Rambouillet and Chartres (A11 runs close by), both about 24 kilometers (15 miles) away. *28700 St-Symphorien-le-Château, tel. 16/37–31–15–15. 48 rooms with bath. Hotel and dinner reservations advised. Facilities: restaurant, tennis, pool, fishing. MC, V. Expensive.*

Provins
Dining and Lodging

Vieux Ramparts. Old wood beams inside and a cheerful, leafy courtyard for outdoor eating in the summer help to create a charming atmosphere at the Vieux Ramparts, housed—along with 25 rooms—in an attractive old building in the Ville Haute. The nouvelle menus offer good value for the money, and meals are sustaining. *3 rue Couverte, tel. 64–00–02–89. 25 rooms, some with bath. Reservations accepted. Dress: casual. AE, V. Closed Tues. dinner and late Feb.–first week in Mar. Moderate.*

Rambouillet
Dining

La Poste. You can bank on traditional, unpretentious cooking at this former coaching inn right in the center of town. Until recently, it could seat only 36 diners, but a new room was opened upstairs, doubling the capacity. Service is good, as is the selection of fixed-price menus, weekends included. Game is a specialty in season. *101 rue du Général-de-Gaulle, tel. 34–83–03–01. Reservations advised. Jacket and tie required. AE, MC, V. Moderate.*

St-Germain-en-Laye
Dining

La Feuillantine. Friendly service and an imaginative, good-value fixed-price menu have rapidly made this restaurant a success with locals as well as tourists. Gizzard salad, salmon with endive, and pullet with herbs are among the specialties. *10 rue des Louviers, tel. 34–51–04–24. Reservations advised. Dress: casual. MC, V. Closed Christmas. Moderate.*

La Petite Auberge. The specialty here is farmhouse-style cooking from the Aveyron region of southwest France. Fresh meat is cooked over an open fire throughout the year, and cheerful red wine (Chinon, from the Loire Valley) is drawn straight from the barrel. Game is served in season. *119-bis rue L. Desnoyer, tel. 34–51–03–99. Reservations accepted. Jacket and tie required. V. Closed Tues. dinner, Wed., second half of Mar., and July. Moderate.*

Lodging
★

La Forestiere. St-Germain is no stopover point for the faint walleted. The town is obsessed with style, and this is its most stylish hotel, a member of the deluxe Relais et Châteaux chain. The forest setting, 18th-century-style furniture, and a fine, if pricey, restaurant, the Cazaudehore (serving fish-based cuisine from southwest France), contribute to a sense of well-being. *1 av. President-Kennedy, 78100, tel. 39–73–36–60. 24 rooms with bath. MC, V. Restaurant closed Mon. (except public holidays). Expensive.*

Senlis
Dining
★

Les Gourmandins. This cozy, two-floored, recently opened restaurant in old Senlis serves some interesting dishes—try the salad with duck and truffles—and offers a fine wine list. The fixed-price menu is a bargain for a weekday lunch; dining à la carte can nudge the very expensive range. *3 pl. de la Halle, tel. 16/44–60–94–01. Reservations advised. Dress: casual. MC, V. Moderate.*

Lodging

Hostellerie Porte-Bellon. This is the closest you'll get to spending a night in the historic center of Senlis. A modest yet efficient hotel, the Porte-Bellon is just a five-minute walk from the cathedral and is close to the bus station. *35 rue Bellon, 60300, tel. 16/44–53–03–05. 20 rooms, most with bath. Facilities: restaurant. V. Closed mid-Dec.–mid-Jan., Fri. (except in summer). Inexpensive.*

Thoiry
Dining and Lodging

Etoile. Handily situated for visitors to Thoiry château and safari park, the Etoile offers a special low-priced tourist menu, as well as a wide choice of à la carte dishes. A garden and a Ping-Pong table add to the hotel's homey appeal. *38 rue de la Porte St-Martin, tel. 34–87–40–21. 12 rooms with bath. AE, DC, MC, V. Closed Mon. and Jan. Inexpensive–Moderate.*

Vernon
Dining and Lodging
★

Château de Brécourt. This 17th-century stone-and-brick château, with its high-pitched roofs and imposing forecourt, is set in extensive grounds 10 kilometers (6 miles) south of Vernon along D533 near Douains. Inventive food in the august atmosphere of the tastefully reupholstered dining room makes it a popular spot with visitors to Giverny, just across the Seine from Vernon. And, as similar hotel-cum-châteaus go, guest rooms can represent a relatively good value. *Douains, 27120 Pacy-sur-Eure, tel. 16/32–52–40–50. 25 rooms with bath. AE, DC, MC, V. Expensive.*

Versailles
Dining
★

Trois Marches. The most famous restaurant in Versailles is also recognized as one of the best in the Ile de France, thanks to its subtle and creative nouvelle cuisine. Even the most sophisticated foodophiles salivate at the thought of Gérard Vié's bisque of lobster, salmon with fennel, or turbot *galette*, impeccably served in a magnificent *hôtel-particulier* (town-house) setting. *3 rue Colbert, tel. 39–50–13–21. Reservations required. Jacket and tie required. AE, DC, MC, V. Closed Sun. and Mon. Very Expensive.*

Potager du Roy. There is excellent value in this restaurant run by Philippe Letourneur, a protégé of Gérard Vié *(see* Trois Marches, above). The cuisine improves constantly, yet prices stay moderate. The bistro and its adjoining terrace become crowded in summer because visitors find the 115- and 160-franc menus hard to resist. *1 rue Maréchal-Joffre, tel. 39–50–35–34. Reservations required. Jacket and tie required. MC, V. Closed Sun., Mon. Moderate.*

Quai No 1. Fish and seafood rule supreme amid the sails, barometers, and model ships of this quaintly decked-out restaurant. Home-smoked salmon and sauerkraut with fish are specialties. Eating à la carte isn't too expensive, and there are lower-priced set menus. *1 av. de St-Cloud, tel. 39–50–42–26.*

Reservations advised. Dress: casual. MC, V. Closed Sun. lunch, Mon. Moderate.

Lodging **Le Versailles.** This unpretentious, modern hotel is ideally situated close to the château and warmly recommended if you plan to explore the town on foot (or can't afford the palatial prices of the Trianon, above). Guest rooms have comfort but no character. No restaurant. 7 rue Ste-Anne, 78000, tel. 39–50–64–65. 48 rooms with bath. AE, DC, MC, V. Moderate.

Home St-Louis. The small, recently modernized Home St-Louis is a good, cheap, quiet bet—close to the cathedral and not too far from the château. There's no restaurant. 28 rue St-Louis, 78000, tel. 39–50–23–55. 27 rooms, some with bath. MC, V. Inexpensive.

Dining and Lodging **Trianon Palace.** This deluxe hotel is set in its own huge garden close to the château park. It is a turn-of-the-century creation of imposing size whose once-faded charm was given a thorough overhaul in 1991 by its new Japanese owners, determined to turn it into one of Europe's most prestigious hotels. The restaurant offers an inventive cuisine, served in fine weather on the huge outdoor terrace. 1 blvd. Reine, 78000, tel. 39–50–34–12. 120 rooms with bath. Facilities: restaurant, terrace for outdoor dining, garden, pool. AE, DC, MC, V. Very Expensive.

The Arts and Nightlife

The Arts

With Paris so close, it seems pointless to detail the comparatively minor offerings of the towns of the Ile de France in the domains of theater, music, or cinema (see The Arts in Chapter 3). There are, however, a number of arts festivals staged in the Ile de France that have earned esteem in their own right. Of these, the largest is the **Festival de l'Ile de France** (mid-May–early July), famed for concerts held at châteaus themselves (for details, tel. 47–23–40–84). There are also music festivals in **Provins** (June), **St-Denis** (mid-May–June, with concerts in the basilica), and at the abbey of **Royaumont** (May–June, tel. 30–35–40–18).

An invaluable list of monthly regional events is the *Tourisme Loisirs* brochure produced by the **Comité Régional du Tourisme Ile-de-France** (73 rue Cambronne, 75015 Paris, tel. 45–67–89–41).

Nightlife

We recommend that anyone interested in painting the town red do so in Paris; there's precious little to choose from in the little towns of the Ile de France. (See Nightlife in Chapter 3.)

5 The Loire Valley

Introduction

The Loire is the longest river in France, rising deep in the heart of the southern Massif Central and winding its way north and then west for over 600 miles before reaching the Atlantic at Nantes. Halfway along, just outside the town of Orléans, the river makes a wide, westward bend, gliding languidly through low, rich country known as the Val de Loire—the Loire Valley. In this temperate, "garden" region—a 140-mile stretch between Orléans and Angers—hundreds of chateaus rise from the rocky banks of the Loire and its tributaries: the rivers Cher, Indre, Vienne, and Loir (with no *e*).

For centuries the Loire river provided the area's principal means of transportation and acted as an important barrier to invading armies. Cities rose at strategic bridgeheads, and fortresses—the earliest châteaus—appeared on towering hill slopes. The Loire Valley was hotly disputed by France and England during the Middle Ages, belonging to England (under the Anjou Plantagenet family) between 1154 and 1216 and again during the Hundred Years War (1337–1453). It took the example of Joan of Arc, the "Maid of Orléans" (scene of her most rousing military successes), for the French finally to expel the English.

The Loire Valley's golden age came under François I (1515–47), flamboyant contemporary of Henry VIII. He hired Renaissance craftsmen from Italy and hobnobbed with the aging Leonardo da Vinci, his guest at Amboise. His salamander emblem is to be seen in many chateaus, including Chambord, the mightiest of them, begun in 1519. And although the nation's power base shifted to Paris around 1600, aristocrats continued to erect luxurious palaces along the Loire until the end of the 18th century. Since that time, many châteaus—too expensive for even the wealthiest to maintain—have fallen to the care of state and local authorities and are now preserved as cultural and historical monuments.

In addition to its abundant châteaus, the Loire Valley offers visitors a host of opportunities for outdoor recreation. Horseback riding, fishing, canoeing, and swimming facilities abound. In the summer, tourists and natives alike flock to concerts, music festivals, fairs, and the celebrated *son-et-lumière* (sound-and-light) extravaganzas held on the grounds of many châteaus. Simply wandering the banks of the placid river and exploring her gentle hills, dotted with woods and castles, provides a welcome break for tired city dwellers.

Essential Information

Important Addresses and Numbers

Tourist Information The Loire region has two area tourist offices; both deal with written inquiries only. For Chinon and points east, the regional office is **Comité Régional du Tourisme du Centre-de-Loire** (8 rue Etienne-Dolet, 45050 Orléans). For Fontevraud and points west, contact **Comité Régional du Tourisme des Pays-de-Loire** (pl. du Commerce, 44000 Nantes).

The addresses of other tourist offices in major towns mentioned in this chapter are as follows: **Amboise** (quai Général-de-Gaulle,

tel. 47–57–09–28), **Angers** (pl. Kennedy, tel. 41–88–69–93),
Blois (3 av. Jean-Laigret, tel. 54–74–06–49), **Orléans** (pl. Albert-Ier, tel. 38–53–05–95), **Saumur** (pl. de la Bilange, tel. 41–
51–03–06), and **Tours** (pl. du Maréchal-Leclerc, tel. 47–05–
58–08).

Travel Agencies **American Express** (12 pl. du Martroi, Orléans, tel. 38–53–84–
54) and **Wagon-Lits** (9 rue Marceau, Tours, tel. 47–20–40–54).

Car Rental **Avis** (6 rue Jean Moulin, Blois, tel. 54–74–48–15; 13 rue
Sansonnieres, Orléans, tel. 33–62–27–04; and 39 bis blvd.
Heurteloup, Tours, tel. 47–20–53–27), **Hertz** (5 rue du Dr.-
Desfray, Blois, tel. 54–74–03–03; and 24 rue des Docks, Tours,
tel. 47–20–40–24), and **Europcar** (81 rue André-Dessaux, Fleu-
ry-les-Aubrais, near Orléans, tel. 33–73–00–40; and 76 rue
Bernard-Pellissy, Tours, tel. 47–64–47–76).

Arriving and Departing

By Plane The closest airports to the Loire Valley are Paris's Charles de
Gaulle and Orly.

By Train The Loire region is served by fast, regular trains from Paris
and other major cities. Trains run every two hours from Paris's
Gare d'Austerlitz to Orléans (you must usually change at Les
Aubrais) and Blois; from Gare Montparnasse, TGV trains leave
for Tours (change at St-Pierre-des-Corps) and Angers every
two hours.

By Car A10 runs from Paris to Orléans—a distance of 130 kilometers
(78 miles)—and on to Tours, with exits at Meung, Blois, and
Amboise. A11 links Paris to Angers.

Getting Around

By Car Slower but more scenic routes than A10 run from the western
Channel ports down through Normandy into the Loire region.
You can arrange to rent a car in all the large towns in the region
or at train stations in Orléans, Blois, Tours, or Angers.

By Train The Loire region has a good local network. The main line follows the Loire itself, running from Orléans through Blois,
Tours, Saumur, and Angers to Nantes.

By Bus Local bus services are extensive and reliable and are a link between train stations and scenic areas off the river. Inquire at
tourist offices for information about routes and timetables.

By Bicycle With its gentle hills and lovely vistas, the Loire Valley is ideal
for bicycling. For more information, *see* Sports and Fitness.

Guided Tours

Orientation **Accueil de France** in Angers (pl. Président Kennedy) and Blois
(pl. du Maréchal-Leclerc) organizes numerous tours of the
Loire Valley, including car and bus excursions, and even hot-air
balloon and boat trips. The office in Blois also offers equestrian, bike, and horse-drawn carriage tours of the Loire-et-Cher
region. **Reservations Loisirs Accueil** in Blois (11 pl. du Château,
tel. 54–78–55–50) also arranges guided visits to the region's
châteaus, as well as balloon and bicycle trips.

Special-Interest **Cointreau,** that heart-warming liqueur, comes from Angers,
and the factory welcomes visitors (rue Croix Blanche, 49124 St-

Barthelemy d'Anjou, tel. 41–43–25–21). The one-hour tour covers the museum and distillery and includes a tasting. Cost is 15 francs (10 frs. children). A mile downstream from Saumur, on the road to Gennes, the wine-making firms of **Ackerman** (19 rue M-Palustre, 49400 St-Hilaire, tel. 41–50–25–33) and **Veuve Amiot** (21 rue Jean-Ackerman, 49400 St-Hilaire, tel. 41–50–25–24) offer organized tours during which you can watch wine being made by the champagne method. The tours last about an hour and include a free tasting.

Anyone interested in mushrooms, a specialty of the region, will be intrigued by an unusual subterranean tour through fossil-filled caverns where edible fungi are grown; it's offered by **La Musée du Champignon** (Mushroom Museum, Flines, rte. de Gennes, tel. 41–50–31–55). Tours are available daily from mid-March through June 10 AM–noon and 2–6; July and August 10–6; and September through mid-November 10–noon and 2–6. The cost is 18 francs (12 francs children).

Personal Guides The tourist offices in **Tours** and **Angers** (*see* Tourist Information, above) arrange city and regional excursions with personal guides. English-speaking guides will conduct visitors around the historic city of **Blois** during a walk that starts from the château at 4; cost is about 30 francs.

Exploring the Loire Valley

Numbers in the margin correspond with points of interest on the Loire Valley map.

Orientation

For touring purposes, we've divided the Loire Valley into two regions: the western Loire, from Angers to Tours, and the eastern Loire, from Amboise to Orléans. If you will be relying on public transportation, it's a good idea to use one of the region's four major cities—Tours, Blois, Angers, or Orléans—or the town of Saumur, about midway between Tours and Angers, as your base.

Highlights for First-time Visitors

Amboise, Tour 2
Blois, Tour 2
Chambord, Tour 2
Château d'Ussé, Tour 1
Chenonceau, Tour 2
Chinon, Tour 1
Germigny, Tour 2
Saumur, Tour 1
The gardens at Villandry, Tour 1

Tour 1: The Western Loire Valley—Angers to Tours

❶ Angers, former capital of the Anjou region, lies on the banks of the River Maine, just north of the Loire, about 106 kilometers (66 miles) west of Tours and 210 kilometers (130 miles) from Orléans. In addition to a towering medieval fortress filled with extraordinary tapestries, the town has a fine Gothic cathedral, a choice of art galleries, and a network of pleasant, traffic-free

The Loire Valley

shopping streets. Well served by public transportation, Angers is the starting point for numerous bus, riverboat, hiking, biking, horseback, and ballooning excursions.

The town's principal sights all lie within a compact square formed by the three main boulevards and the River Maine. When you arrive, head for the castle, just off the river between boulevard De Gaulle and quai Ligny. Before you go in, stop at the **Maison du Vin** (5 bis pl. Kennedy), the organization that represents Anjou's wine producers. It can provide lots of leaflets about wines, suggestions about which vineyards to visit, and even a free sample or two.

The **Château,** a massive shale-and-limestone castle-fortress dating from the 13th century, glowers over the town from behind its turreted moats. The moats are now laid out as gardens, overrun with deer and blooming flowers. As you explore the grounds, note the startling contrast between the thick, defensive walls and the formal garden, with its delicate, white tufa-stone chapel, erected in the 16th century. For a sweeping view of the city and surrounding countryside, climb one of the castle towers.

A new gallery within the castle grounds houses the great **Tapestry of the Apocalypse,** completed in 1390. Measuring 16 feet high and 120 yards long, it shows a series of 70 horrifying and humorous scenes from the Book of Revelation. In one, mountains of fire fall from heaven while boats capsize and men struggle in the water; another shows an intriguing, seven-headed beast. *Pl. Kennedy. Admission: 24 frs. adults, 13 frs. students and senior citizens, 5 frs. children. Open July and Aug., daily 10–7; Sept.–June, 9:30–noon and 2–5:30.*

Just east of the château is the **Cathédrale St-Maurice** (pl. Freppel), a 12th- and 13th-century Gothic cathedral noted for its curious Romanesque facade and original stained-glass windows; you'll need binoculars to appreciate both fully. A few steps north, practically in the cathedral's shadow, lies Angers's large covered food market, **Les Halles** (pl. Mondain; open Tues.–Sun. 9–7). Treat it as a gourmet museum, or stop in for an exotic lunch. A modern shopping mall sits right above it.

Time Out If you're visiting Les Halles during summer, look out for an impromptu café set up by local fish merchant Jean Foucher. Here you can choose your own sole and have it cooked on the spot, indulge yourself with a platter of *fruits du mer* (shellfish), or enjoy a snack of oysters with a bottle of Anjou wine. Prices are reasonable, the atmosphere quaint and colorful.

Just south of the cathedral, in a house that once sheltered Cesare Borgia and Mary, Queen of Scots, is the **Musée des Beaux-Arts** picture gallery. Among the museum's attractions is an impressive collection of Old Masters from the 17th and 18th centuries, including paintings by Raphael, Watteau, Fragonard, and Boucher. *10 rue du Musée. Admission: 5 frs. Open Tues.–Sun. 10–noon and 2–6.*

Around the corner, in the refurbished Eglise Toussaint, is the **Musée David d'Angers,** housing a collection of dramatic sculptures by Jean-Pierre David (1788–1859), the city's favorite son. *33 rue Toussaint. Admission: 10 frs. adults, children free. Open Tues.–Sun. 10–noon and 2–6.*

② The château of **Plessis-Bourré** lies 20 kilometers (12 miles) north of Angers by N162 and D768. Built between 1468 and 1473 by Jean Bourré, one of Louis XI's top-ranking civil servants, the château looks like a traditional grim fortress: The bridge across its moat is nearly 50 yards long. Once you step into the central courtyard, however, the gentler mood of the Renaissance takes over.

What makes this place special is the painted wooden ceiling in the Salle des Gardes (Guard Room). Jean Bourré's hobby was alchemy—an ancient branch of chemistry with more than a touch of the occult—and the ceiling's 24 hexagonal panels are covered with scenes illustrating the craft. Some have overtones of the grotesque dreamworld of Renaissance Dutch painter Hieronymus Bosch (1450–1516), while others illustrate folk tales or proverbs. A few must have been painted just for the fun of it: A topless lady steers a land-yacht with wooden wheels (thought to be an allegory of spirit and matter); people urinate ceremoniously (ammonia was extracted from urine); an emaciated wolf takes a bite out of a startled lady (according to folk legend, the wolf's diet was faithful wives, apparently in short supply); and Thurberesque dogs gambol in between. You may want to ignore the guide's lecture on furniture and spend your time gazing upward. *Admission: 26 frs. adults, 19 frs. students, 14 frs. children. Open Sept.–Nov. and Apr.–June, Thurs.–Tues. 10–noon and 2–6; Dec.–Mar., Thurs.–Tues. 2–5; closed Wed.*

③ About 83 kilometers (52 miles) east of Angers by road, and accessible by train, **Saumur** is an excellent base for exploring the western Loire Valley. The town is known for its flourishing mushroom industry, which produces 100,000 tons per year. The same cool tunnels in which the mushrooms grow also provide an ideal storage place for the local *mousseux* (sparkling wines).

You will find an efficient tourist office on place Bilange. Just next door, at the **Maison du Vin de Saumur,** local wine producers show off their products and provide information about visits to local vineyards. *25 rue Beaurepaire. Open summer, Sun., Tues.–Fri. 9–noon and 2–5; closed Mon. and Sat.*

Towering high above town and river is Saumur's elegant, white 14th-century **château.** Though you can reach it by car, it's only a 10-minute walk from the tourist office. The route takes you through the pretty old town and place St-Pierre, with its lively Saturday market.

Time Out   When you get to the top of the hill, why not stop off for a picnic on the grass outside the château? If you've forgotten your picnic provisions, there's a café just beside the parking lot.

If the château looks familiar, it's probably because you've seen it in countless reproductions from the famous *Très Riches Heures* (*Book of Hours*) painted for the duc de Berri in 1416, now in the Musée Condé at Château de Chantilly *(see* Tour 2 in Chapter 4). Inside it's bright and cheerful, with its fairytale gateway and plentiful potted flowers. Two museums, the **Musée des Arts Décoratifs** and the **Musée du Cheval** (Horse Museum), are housed here. The former offers a fine collection of medieval objets d'art and 18th- and 19th-century porcelain, while the latter covers the history of the horse, with exhibits ranging from saddles to skeletons. Both are included in the guided tour. Afterward, climb the **Tour de Guet** (Watch-tower) for an impressive view. *Admission: 25 frs. adults, 15 frs. children and senior citizens. Open July–Sept., daily 9–6:30; Oct. and Apr.–June, daily 9–11:30 and 2–6; Nov.–Mar., Wed.–Mon. 9:30–11:30 and 2–5, closed Tues.*

At **Montreuil-Bellay,** about 17 kilometers (11 miles) south of Saumur on N147, you can visit a 15th-century **château** with majestic towers and pointed roofs. The interior is equally fascinating, offering a fine collection of rich furniture and tapestries, a fully fitted medieval kitchen, and a chapel adorned with frescoes of angelic musicians. For a memorable view, take a stroll in the private gardens; graceful white turrets tower high above the trees and rosebushes, and down below, the little River Thouet winds its lazy way to the Loire. *Pl. des Ormeaux. Admission: 24 frs. Open Apr.–Nov., Wed.–Mon. 10–6; closed Tues.*

Even if the château is closed, be sure to visit the **public gardens** beside the river. Cafés and little restaurants abound.

About 16 kilometers (10 miles) southeast of Saumur is the town ❹ of **Fontevraud,** famous for its large, medieval **abbey,** which was of central importance in the history of both England and France.

Founded in 1099, the abbey offered separate churches and living quarters for nuns, monks, lepers, "repentant" female sinners, and the sick. Between 1115 and the French Revolution in 1789, 39 different abbesses—among them a granddaughter of William the Conqueror—directed its operations. The abbey church contains the tombs of Henry II of England; his wife, Eleanor of Aquitaine; and their son, Richard Coeur de Lion—Richard the Lionhearted. Though their bones were scattered during the Revolution, the effigies remain. Napoleon turned the abbey church into a prison, and so it remained until 1963, when historical restoration work—still under way—was begun.

The great 12th-century abbey church is one of the most eclectic architectural structures in France. The medieval section is built of simple stone and topped with a series of domes; the chapter-house, with its collection of 16th-century religious wall paintings (prominent abbesses served as models), is unmistakably Renaissance; and the paving stones bear the salamander emblems of François I. Next to the long refectory, you will find the unusual octagonal kitchen, its tall spire, the **Tour d'Evrault,** serving as one of the abbey's 20 faceted stone chimneys. *Admission: 24 frs. adults, 15 frs. senior citizens, 5 frs. children. Open June–mid-Sept., daily 9–noon and 2–6:30; Sept.–Apr., daily 9:30–12:30 and 2–5.*

❺ **Chinon** lies in the fertile countryside between the Loire and the Vienne rivers, 29 kilometers (18 miles) southeast of Saumur, via Fontevraud. Several trains a day run from Tours, stopping at Azay-le-Rideau on the way. Bicycles can be rented at Chinon station.

The town—birthplace of author François Rabelais (1494–1553)—is dominated by the towering ruins of its medieval **fortress-castle,** perched high above the River Vienne. Though the main tourist office is in the town below, during the summer months a special annex operates from the castle grounds. Both the village and the château stand among steep, cobbled slopes, so wear comfortable walking shoes.

The vast fortress dates from the time of Henry II of England, who died here in 1189 and was buried at Fontevraud. Two centuries later, the castle witnessed an important historical moment: Joan of Arc's recognition of the disguised dauphin, later Charles VII. In the early 17th century, the castle was partially dismantled by its then-owner, Cardinal Richelieu (1585–1642), who used many of its stones to build a new palace 21 kilometers (13 miles) away. (That palace no longer exists.)

At Chinon, all but the royal chambers—which house a small museum—is open to the elements. For a fine view of the region, climb the **Coudray Tower,** where, in 1302, leading members of the crusading Knights Templar were imprisoned before being taken to Paris, tried, and burned at the stake. The **Tour de Horloge,** whose bell has been sounding the hours since 1399, houses a small **Joan of Arc museum.** *Admission: 20 frs. adults, 14 frs. students and senior citizens. Open Feb–mid-Mar., Wed.–Mon. 10–noon and 2–5, closed Tues.; mid-Mar.–May, daily 10–noon and 2–6; June–Sept., daily 10–6; Oct., Wed.–Mon. 10–noon and 2–5, closed Tues.; closed Nov.–Feb.*

Follow the signposted steps down into the old town, or drive your car to the River Vienne pathway. **Place de l'Hôtel**—the main square—is the best place to begin exploring. Stop by the tourist office and pick up a town plan to help you explore the town's fine medieval streets and alleys. While you are there, visit **Le Musée du Vin** (Wine Museum) in the vaulted cellars. This is a fascinating exhibit, full of information on vine growing and wine- and barrel-making. An English commentary is available, and the admission charge entitles you to a sample of the local product. *Admission: 16 frs. Open May–Oct., Fri.–Wed. 10–noon and 2–5.*

About 10 kilometers (6 miles) northeast of Chinon, set between the Forest of Chinon and the Loire, is the archetypal fairytale château of **Ussé,** with its astonishing array of delicate towers and turrets. Tourist literature describes it as the original Sleeping Beauty castle—the inspiration for Charles Perrault's beloved 17th-century story. Though parts of the castle date from the 1400s, most of it was completed two centuries later. It is a flamboyant mix of Gothic and Renaissance styles—stylish and romantic, built for fun, not fighting. Its history supports its playful image: It suffered no bloodbaths—no political conquests or conflicts. And a tablet in the chapel indicates that even the French Revolution passed it by.

After admiring the château's luxurious furnishings and 19th-century French fashion exhibit, climb the spiral stairway to the tower to view the River Indre through the battlements. Here you will also find a waxwork effigy of Sleeping Beauty herself. Before you leave, visit the 16th-century chapel in the garden; its door is decorated with pleasingly sinister skull-and-crossbone carvings. *Admission: 40 frs. Open mid-Mar.–Oct., daily 9–noon and 2–6.*

Continuing east about 11 kilometers (7 miles) from Ussé, you'll soon arrive at **Azay-le-Rideau.** Nestled in a sylvan setting on the banks of the River Indre, this white, 16th-century château was—like Ussé—a Renaissance pleasure palace rather than a serious fortress.

A financial scandal forced its builder, royal financier Gilles Berthelot, to flee France shortly after its construction in 1520. For centuries, it passed from one private owner to another and was finally bought by the state in 1905. Though the interior offers an interesting blend of furniture and artwork, you may wish to spend most of your time exploring the enchanting private park. During the summer, visitors can enjoy delightful *son-et-lumiere* shows on the castle grounds. *Admission: 24 frs. adults, 13 frs. senior citizens, 5 frs. children. Open Apr.– Sept., daily 9:30–noon and 2–6; Oct.–Mar., 9:30–noon and 2– 4:45.*

8 About 6 kilometers (4 miles) east of Azay-le-Rideau is the village of **Saché**, best known for its associations with novelist Honoré de Balzac. Though the town had a real castle during the Middle Ages, the present **château,** built between the 16th and 18th centuries, is more of a comfortable country house than a fortress. Balzac came here—to the home of his friends, the Marjonnes—during the 1830s, both to write and to escape his creditors. The château houses a substantial **Balzac museum,** with exhibits ranging from photographs to original manuscripts to the coffeepot he used to help keep him writing up to 16 hours a day. Those who have never read Balzac and don't understand spoken French may find little of interest in Saché; those who have, and do, will return to the novels with fresh enthusiasm and understanding. *Admission: 16 frs. Open Feb.– mid-Mar., Thurs.–Tues. 9–noon and 2–5; mid-Mar.–Sept., daily 9–noon and 2–6; Oct.–Nov., Thurs.–Tues. 9–noon and 2–5; closed Dec. and Jan.*

9 From Saché, it's worth making a brief detour to **Villaines-les-Rochers,** about 6 kilometers (4 miles) southwest, to see the village's interesting **wickerwork cooperative.** Local people have been producing *osier* (willow) products for centuries. In 1849, when the craft was threatened with extinction, the parish priest persuaded 65 small groups of basketweavers to form France's first agricultural workers' cooperative. Museum exhibits tell the story, and lots of handmade objects—from sofas to cat baskets to babies' rattles—are on sale. *Sociéte Cooperative de Vannerie. Admission free. Open most of the year, Mon.– Sat. 10–noon and 2–6, Sun. 10–noon and 2–7.*

10 After leaving Villaines-les-Rochers, head for **Villandry,** following D57 back through Azay-le-Rideau. The **Château de Villandry** stands on the south side of the Loire, about 19 kilometers (12 miles) southwest of Tours. Its extravagant, terraced gardens are well worth a visit.

Both the gardens and the château date from the 16th century, but, over the years, they fell into disrepair. In 1906, Spanish doctor Joachim Carvalla and his wife, American heiress Ann Coleman, bought the property and began a long process of restoration. The gardens were replanted according to a rigorous, geometrical design, with zigzagging hedges enclosing flower beds, vegetable plots, and gravel walks. The result is an aristocratic 16th-century *jardin à la française.* Below an avenue of 1,500 precisely pruned lime trees lies an ornamental lake, filled with swans: Not a ripple is out of place. The aromatic and medicinal garden, with plots neatly labeled in three languages, is especially appealing.

The château itself has a remarkable gilded ceiling—imported from Toledo, in Spain—and a collection of fine Spanish paintings. However, the garden is unquestionably the main attraction, and since it is usually open during the two-hour French lunch break, you can have it to yourself for a good part of the afternoon. *Admission: château and gardens, 32 frs. adults (26 frs. students and senior citizens); gardens only, 20 frs. adults (16 frs. students and senior citizens). Château open mid-Mar.– mid-Nov., daily 9–6; garden is open all year, daily 9–sunset (or 8, whichever is earlier).*

About 20 kilometers (12 miles) east of Villandry lies the city of **Tours,** an ideal center from which to tour the Loire Valley's attractions by public transportation. Trains from Tours run along the river in both directions, and regular bus services radiate from here; in addition, the city is the starting point for a variety of organized bus excursions (many with English-speaking guides). The town has mushroomed into a city of a quarter of a million inhabitants, with an ugly modern sprawl of factories, high-rise blocks, and overhead expressway junctions. Nevertheless, the town center remains pleasant and manageable. Travelers with cars may prefer to base themselves in any of a dozen smaller towns within a half hour's drive of Tours (Montbazon, in particular, 10 kilometers/6 miles south, is recommended for its hotels and restaurants—*see* Dining and Lodging, below) but should certainly explore the city during their stay.

Numbers in the margin correspond with points of interest on the Tours map.

Start your tour at place du Maréchal Leclerc, usually called the **place de la Gare.** Here you'll find the fine Belle Epoque train station, with its cast-iron curlicues, the bus station, and the tourist office. Many of the most convenient hotels are situated here or just around the corner.

The city plan is fairly simple. Turn left from place du Maréchal Leclerc, down boulevard Heurteloup, to reach place Jean-Jaurès; then turn right into rue Nationale. This street holds many of the city's major shops, and if you continue along it for just over a half mile, you'll reach the River Loire. Turning right near the river end, you'll soon reach the cathedral, the château, and the Musée des Beaux-Arts. If you turn left, you'll come to the place Plumereau and a quaint pedestrian precinct.

The **Cathédrale St-Gatien,** built between 1239 and 1484, reveals a mixture of architectural styles. Its majestic two-towered facade was cleaned and restored in 1990. The stained glass, in particular, deserves binoculars, and you will want to visit the little children's tomb with its kneeling angels, built in memory of the two children of Charles VIII and Anne of Brittany. *Rue Lavoisier. Closed noon–2.*

What is left of the château is of minor interest, but, within it, you will find the **Historial de la Touraine**—a group of more than 150 waxwork models representing historical figures, such as St. Martin and Joan of Arc, whose deeds helped shape this region over 15 centuries. There's also a small aquarium. *Quai d'Orléans. Admission: wax museum, 28 frs. adults, 24 frs. students, 18 frs. children; aquarium, 16 frs. adults, 8 frs. children. Open daily, mid-Sept.–mid-Nov. 9–noon and 2–7; mid-*

Cathédrale
St-Gatien, **13**

Historial de la
Touraine, **14**

Musée des
Beaux-Arts, **15**

Musée des Vins/
Musée du
Compagnonnage, **16**

Musée du Gemmail, **17**

Place de la Gare, **12**

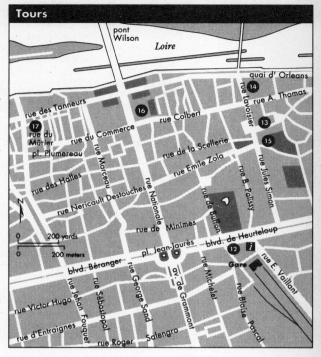

*Nov.–mid-Mar. 2–6; mid-Mar.–mid-June 9–noon and 2–7;
mid-June–mid-Sept. 9–7.*

Next door, in what was once the archbishop's palace, is the
⑮ Musée des Beaux-Arts (Fine Arts Museum). It houses an eclectic selection of treasures: works by Rubens, Rembrandt, Boucher, Degas, sculptor Alexander Calder—even Fritz the
Elephant, stuffed in 1902. *18 pl. François Sieard. Admission:
16 frs. adults, 8 frs. students, children and senior citizens free.
Open Wed.–Mon. 9–12:45 and 2–6; closed Tues.*

Two small museums stand at the river end of rue Nationale: the
⑯ Musée des Vins (Wine Museum) and the **Musée du Compagnonnage** (Guild Museum). You may wish to see the latter, at
least. *Compagnonnage* is a sort of apprenticeship-trade-union
system, and here you see the masterpieces of the candidates for
guild membership: virtuoso craftwork, some of it eccentric (an
Eiffel Tower made of slate, for instance, or a varnished-noodle
château). These stand as evidence of the devotion to craftsmanship that is still an important feature of French life. Both the
guild and the wine museums are set in and around the cloisters
of an old church—a pleasant setting, and you are free to visit
them at your own pace. *16 rue Nationale. Admission: 10 frs.
adults, 5 frs. students, children free. Open Wed.–Mon. 9–noon
and 2–6; closed Tues.*

From rue Nationale, narrow rue du Commerce leads you to the
oldest and most attractive part of Tours, the area around **place
Plumereau**. It's a great area for strolling, largely traffic-free,
and full of little squares, open-air cafés, and pricey antiques

shops. From place Plumereau, head one block along rue Briconnet, and take the first left into rue du Mûrier. The **Musée du Gemmail,** halfway down on the right in the imposing 19th-century Hôtel Raimbault, houses an unusual collection of three-dimensional colored-glass window panels. Depicting patterns, figures, and even portraits, the panels are both beautiful and intriguing, since most of the gemlike fragments of glass come from broken bottles. *7 rue du Mûrier. Admission: 14 frs. Open Apr.–mid-Oct., Tues.–Sun. 10–noon and 2:30–6.*

Tour 2: The Eastern Loire Valley— Amboise to Orléans

Numbers in the margin correspond with points of interest on the Loire Valley map.

On the south side of the Loire, about 26 kilometers (16 miles) due east of Tours, is **Amboise,** a picturesque little town with bustling markets, plentiful hotels and restaurants, and a historic **château.**

The history of Amboise is really the history of its château. A Stone Age fortress stood here, and an early bridge gave the stronghold strategic importance. In AD 503, Clovis, king of the Franks, met with Alaric, king of the Visigoths, on an island (now the site of an excellent campground). In the years that followed, the Normans attacked the fortress repeatedly. The 15th and 16th centuries were Amboise's golden age, and during this time, the château, enlarged and embellished, became a royal palace. Charles VII stayed here, as did the unfortunate Charles VIII, best remembered for banging his head on a low doorway (you will be shown it) and dying as a result. François I, whose long nose appears in so many château paintings, based his court here. In 1560, his son, young François II, settled here with his wife, Mary Stuart (otherwise known as Mary, Queen of Scots), and his mother, Catherine de' Medici. The castle was also the setting for the Amboise Conspiracy, an ill-fated Protestant plot organized against François II; visitors are shown where the corpses of 1,200 conspirators dangled from the castle walls. In later years, a decline set in, and demolition occurred both before and after the Revolution. Today only about a third of the original building remains standing.

The château's interior is partly furnished, though not with the original objects; these vanished when the building was converted to a barracks and then a button factory. The great round tower is reached by a spiral ramp rather than by a staircase; designed for horsemen, it is wide enough to accommodate a small car. You are free to explore the grounds at your own pace, including the little chapel of St-Hubert, with its carvings of the Virgin and Child, Charles VIII, and Anne of Brittany. There are frequent *son-et-lumière* pageants on summer evenings. *Admission: 26 frs. adults, 9 frs. children. Open Sept.–June, daily 9–noon and 2–5; July and Aug., daily 9–6:30.*

Up rue Victor-Hugo, five minutes from the château, is the **Clos Lucé,** a handsome Renaissance manor house. François I lent the house to Leonardo da Vinci, who spent the last four years of his life here, dying in 1519. You can wander from room to room at will. The basement houses an extraordinary exhibition: working models of some of Leonardo's inventions. Though impractical in his own time, perhaps, when technology was limited, they were built recently by engineers from IBM, using the detailed sketches contained in the artist's notebooks. Mechanisms on display include three-speed gearboxes, a military tank, a clockwork car, and even a flying machine. *At the eastern end of rue Victor-Hugo. Admission: 30 frs. adults, 20 frs. children and senior citizens. Open Sept.–June, daily 9–noon and 2–6; July and Aug., daily 9–7.*

Time Out After you've marveled at Leonardo's genius, you can explore the garden and grab a quick bite at the convenient snack bar.

⑲ About 10 kilometers (6 miles) south of Amboise lies the village of **Chenonceaux.** (For some reason, the village is spelled Chenonceaux and the château, Chenonceau.) You could happily spend the best part of a day here. From long-ago historical figures, such as Diane de Poitiers, Catherine de' Medici, and Mary, Queen of Scots, to a host of modern travel writers, many have called Chenonceau the "most exciting" and the "most romantic" of all the Loire châteaus. You are free to wander about (there are attendants to answer questions). For most of the year, the château is open—unlike many others—all day. The only drawback is its popularity: If you want to avoid a roomfull of English schoolchildren, take a stroll in the grounds and come back when they stop for lunch.

More pleasure palace than fortress, Chenonceau was built in 1520 by Thomas Bohier, a wealthy tax collector. When he went bankrupt, it passed to François I. Later, Henri II gave it to his mistress, Diane de Poitiers. After his death, Henri's not-so-understanding widow, Catherine de' Medici, expelled Diane to nearby Chaumont and took back the château. It is to Catherine that we owe the lovely gardens and the handsome three-story extension whose arches span the river.

Before you go inside, pick up an English leaflet at the gate. Then walk around to the right of the main building and admire the peaceful, delicate architecture; the formal garden; and the river gliding under the arches. The romantically inclined may want to rent a rowboat and spend an hour drifting. Inside the château are splendid ceilings, colossal fireplaces, and authentic furnishings. Paintings include works by Rubens, Andrea del Sarto, and Correggio. And as you tour the rooms, be sure to pay your respects to former-owner Madame Dupin, whose face is captured in Nattier's charming portrait. Thanks to the great affection Madame Dupin inspired among her proletarian neighbors, the château and its treasures survived the Revolution intact.

A waxwork exhibition (**Musée des Cires**), housed in one of the outbuildings, illustrates four centuries of French history. There are also excellent *son-et-lumière* shows throughout the summer. *Admission: château 30 frs. adults, 20 frs. children; wax museum 5 frs. Open mid-Feb.–mid-Nov., daily 9–5, 6, or 7, depending on the season; mid-Nov.–mid-Feb., daily 9–4:30.*

Time Out If you feel like spending the day at Chenonceau, refuel in the inexpensive, self-serve restaurant situated in the former stables.

⑳ About 18 kilometers (11 miles) due south of Chenonceaux lies the town of **Loches**, set on a rocky spur just beside the River

Indre. Like Chinon, Loches is a walled citadel dominating a small, medieval village. But although Chinon's citadel is a ruined shell, much of Loches's is well preserved and stands as a living part of the town.

As you approach the citadel, the first building you will come across is the church of **St-Ours:** Note its striking roof formed of octagonal pyramids, dating from the 12th century; the doorway sculpted with owls, monkeys, and mythical beasts; and the baptismal font converted from a Roman altar.

The **Logis Royaux**—the château—has a terrace that provides a fine view of the roofs and river below and the towers and swallows' nests above. Inside, keep an eye out for the vicious, two-man crossbow that could pierce an oak door at 200 yards. There are some interesting pictures, too, including a copy of the well-known portrait that shows an extremely disgruntled Charles VII and one of his mistresses, Agnes Sorel, poised as a virtuous Virgin Mary (though semitopless). Her alabaster image decorates her tomb, guarded by angels and lambs. Agnes died in 1450, at age 28, probably the result of poisoning by Charles's son, the future Louis XI. The little chapel was built by Charles VIII for his queen, Anne of Brittany, and is lavishly decorated with sculpted ermine tails, the lady's emblem.

After the tour, amble over to the *donjon*, or tower keep. One 11th-century tower, half-ruined and roofless, is open for individual exploration, though the others require guided supervision. These towers contain dungeons and will delight anyone who revels in prison cells and torture chambers. *Admission: 21 frs. adults, 14 frs. children, students, and senior citizens. Open Feb.–mid-Mar., Thurs.–Tues. 9–noon and 2–6, mid-Mar.–June, daily 9–noon and 2–6; July and Aug., daily 9–6; Sept. and Oct., Thurs.–Tues. 9–noon and 2–5; closed Nov.–Jan.*

㉑ The town of **Valençay,** with its pleasant château, lies just over 40 kilometers (25 miles) southeast of Chenonceaux and 48 kilometers (30 miles) east of Loches. Though it is some distance south of the Loire, it is well worth a visit.

A palace, rather than a castle, Valençay was started in the 16th century, though most of the surviving structure was added later. Talleyrand (1754–1838), the opportunistic statesman and diplomat, who managed to survive whatever the regime, left his mark here. A young but not very pious bishop under Louis XVI, Talleyrand played a leading role in the Revolution and was foreign minister under Napoleon. After Napoleon's fall he helped reshape Europe at the Congress of Vienna, supporting the return of the Bourbon monarchy. While serving as Napoleon's foreign minister, he was instructed to buy a suitable palace to impress visiting royalty and ambassadors: The result was Valençay. In these grandiose and seductive surroundings, he wove his political spells and enjoyed himself for a quarter of a century. The many rooms open to the public have luscious furnishings and decorations.

The grounds at Valençay include a formal French garden with statues, peacocks, and precisely cut hedges; a park where kangaroos and llamas roam; and the **Musée de l'Automobile Ancienne,** exhibiting more than 80 polished cars and motorcycles dating from 1898. *Admission: 26 frs. adults, 21 frs. senior citizens, 16 frs. children. Open mid.-Mar.–mid-Nov., daily 9–*

noon and 2–dusk or 8; mid-Nov.–mid-Mar., weekends and national holidays 9–noon and 1:30–4:30; château closed Nov.– Mar.

On your journey north, stop off for an afternoon at the village of **②** **Cour-Cheverny,** just over 20 kilometers (12 miles) outside Blois. The main attraction is the classical **château of Cheverny,** finished in 1634. The interior, with its painted and gilded rooms, splendid furniture, and rich tapestries depicting the labors of Hercules, is one of the grandest in the Loire region. American visitors will spot a bronze of George Washington in the gallery, alongside a document bearing his signature. Together, Louis XVI and Washington founded the Society of the Cincinnati, reserved for officers who fought in the War of Independence. Three of the present owner's ancestors were members of the group.

One of the chief delights of Cheverny is that you can wander freely at your own pace. Unfortunately, the gardens are off-limits, as is the Orangery, where the *Mona Lisa* and other masterpieces were hidden during World War II. But you are free to contemplate the antlers of 2,000 stags in a nearby Trophy Room. Hunting, called "venery" in the leaflets, continues vigorously here, red coats, bugles, and all. In the kennels next-door, dozens of hounds lounge about waiting for meals. Feeding times—*la soupe aux chiens*—are posted on a noticeboard, and visitors are welcome to watch the dogs gulp down their dinner. *Admission: 24 frs. adults, 16 frs. children and senior citizens. Open mid-June–mid-Sept., daily 9–6:30; mid-Sept.–mid-June, daily 9:30–noon and 2:30–5.*

② As you leave Cheverny, follow D765 north to **Blois,** a quaint yet convenient touring center off A10, about midway between Tours and Orléans. Perched on a steep hillside overlooking the Loire, its white facades, redbrick chimneys, and blue-slate roofs create a cheerful, tricolor effect. The town is also quite accessible, posing few traffic problems and offering direct train links to Paris and all the major towns along the Loire.

The **château** at Blois is among the valley's finest. Your ticket entitles you to a guided tour—in English when there are enough visitors who can't understand French—but you are more than welcome to roam around without a guide if you visit between mid-March and August. Before you enter the building, stand in the courtyard and admire four centuries of architecture. On one side stands the 13th-century hall and tower, the latter offering a stunning view of town and countryside. The Renaissance begins to flower in the Louis XII wing (built between 1498 and 1503), through which you enter, and comes to full bloom in the François I wing (1515–24). The masterpiece here is the openwork spiral staircase, painstakingly restored. The fourth side is the Classical Gaston d'Orléans wing (1635–38).

At the bottom of the staircase there's a *diaporama*, an audiovisual display tracing the château's history. Upstairs you'll find a series of enormous rooms with tremendous fireplaces, decorated with the gilded porcupine, emblem of Louis XII; the ermine of Anne of Brittany; and, of course, François I's salamander, breathing fire and surrounded by flickering flames. There are intricate ceilings, carved and gilded paneling, and a sad little picture of Mary, Queen of Scots. In the great council room, the duc de Guise was murdered on the orders of Henri III in 1588. Don't miss the **Musée des Beaux-Arts,** the art gallery, in the Louis XII wing. The miscellaneous collection of paintings from the 16th to the 19th centuries is interesting and often amusing. The château also offers a *son-et-lumière* display most summer evenings. *Admission: 24 frs. adults, 13 frs. children and senior citizens. Open Apr.–Aug., daily 9–6; Sept.–Mar., daily 9–noon and 2–5.*

24 The château of **Chambord** lies 18 kilometers (11 miles) east of Blois on D33, in the middle of a royal game forest. The largest of the Loire châteaus, Chambord is also one of the valley's two most popular touring destinations (Chenonceau being the other). But although everyone thinks Chenonceau is extravagantly beautiful, reactions are mixed as to the qualities of Chambord. Chambord is the kind of place William Randolph Hearst would have built if he had had more money: It's been described as "megalomaniac," "an enormous film-set extravaganza," and, in its favor, "the most outstanding experience of the Loire Valley."

A few facts set the tone: the facade is 420 feet long, there are 440 rooms and 365 chimneys, and a wall 32 kilometers (20 miles) long encloses the 13,000-acre forest (you can wander in 3,000 of these, the rest being reserved for wild boar and other game creatures). François I started building in 1519, a job that took 12 years and required 1,800 workmen. His original grandiose idea was to divert the Loire to form a moat, but someone (probably his adviser, Leonardo da Vinci) persuaded him to make do with the River Cosson. François used the château only for short stays; yet when he first arrived, 12,000 horses were required to transport his luggage, servants, and hangers-on! Later kings also used Chambord as an occasional retreat, and Sun King Louis XIV had Molière perform here. In the 18th century, Louis XV gave the château to Maréchal de Saxe as a reward for his victory over the English and Dutch at Fontenoy in 1745. When not besporting himself with wine, women, and song, the marshal stood on the roof overseeing the exercises of his own regiment of 1,000 cavalry.

Now, after long neglect—all the original furnishings vanished during the French Revolution—Chambord belongs to the state. Vast rooms are open to visitors (you can wander freely), and have been filled with a variety of exhibits—not all concerned with Chambord, but interesting nonetheless. Children will enjoy repeated trips up and down the enormous **double-helix staircase:** It looks like a single staircase, but an entire regiment could march up one spiral while a second came down the other, and they would never meet. Also be sure to visit the roof terrace, whose forest of towers, turrets, cupolas, gables, and chimneys was described by 19th-century novelist Henry James as "more like the spires of a city than the salient points of a single building."

Chambord also offers a short *son-et-lumière* show, in French, English, and German, successively, on many evenings from mid-May to mid-October. *Admission: 27 frs. adults, 15 frs. students and senior citizens, 6 frs. children. Open July and Aug., daily 9:30–6:30; Sept.–June, daily 9:30–11:45 and 2–4:30, 5:30, or 6:30 depending on season.*

The remainder of this last leg of our Loire Valley tour follows **(25)** the river itself. **Meung-sur-Loire** lies about 30 kilometers (20 miles) northeast, though you may want to backtrack to Blois and continue along the river road from there. The town's most famous citizen was Jehan de Meung, born in 1260 and author of the best-selling *Roman de la Rose*. (Later, Geoffrey Chaucer produced a well-known English translation.)

The **château** at Meung is part 12th-century fortress, part 18th-century residence. From the 12th century to the French Revolution, it served mainly as the official residence of the bishops of Orléans, although in 1429, Lord Salisbury used it as his headquarters during the seige of Orléans. (When he was killed in the fray, Lord Talbot took over, but could not prevent Joan of Arc from capturing the château.) It was sold after the French Revolution, and when its present owner, M. Tachon, bought it in 1970, it had stood empty and derelict for years. Tachon began a long process of restoring, furnishing it with a diverse collection of items ranging from 12th-century antiquities to souvenirs from his own life. The weapons room contains crossbows, World War II submachine guns, and military helmets from the Middle Ages to 1945.

The most unusual part of the château is underground, where the owner is in the process of exploring and reopening a network of tunnels, dungeons, and storehouses, with a chapel and torture chamber. *16 pl. Martroi. Admission: 20 frs. adults, 6 frs. children. Open mid-Mar.–mid-Nov., daily 8:30–5; mid-Nov.–mid-Mar., weekends and national holidays only, 9–5.*

Leaving Meung, follow N152 northeast about 18 kilometers (11 **(26)** miles) to **Orléans,** a thriving commercial city. Its strategic position as a natural bridgehead over the Loire has long made it the target of hostile confrontations and invasions. Julius Caesar slaughtered its inhabitants and burned it to the ground. Five centuries later, Atilla and his Huns did much the same. Next came the Normans; then the Valois kings turned it into a secondary capital. The story of the Hundred Years' War, Joan of Arc, and the siege of Orléans is widely known. During the Wars of Religion (1562–98), much of the cathedral was destroyed, and a century ago, ham-fisted town planners razed many of the city's fine old buildings. During World War II, both German and Allied bombs helped finish the job. Nevertheless, there is much of interest left, and, in recent years, dedicated and sensitive planners have done much to bring the city back to life.

Numbers in the margin correspond with points of interest on the Orléans map.

The tourist office is on boulevard de Verdun, just in front of the train station. From here, rue de la République takes you 400 yards south to the main square—the **place du Martroi,** with its statue of Joan of Arc. A block farther south, turn left for the cathedral, down rue Jeanne-d'Arc, or continue south down **rue Royale;** the latter is lined with excellent shops of all descriptions. Rue Royale brings you to the quai du Châtelet and the banks of the Loire. Make a left turn here to arrive at the **(27)** **Nouvelle Halle,** the covered market, with its tempting food displays. (Drivers would do best to park at the Campo Santo, by the cathedral, where there's a large underground parking lot.)

(28) **Cathédrale Ste-Croix** is a riot of pinnacles and gargoyles, both Gothic and pseudo-Gothic, the whole embellished with 18th-

Cathédrale
Ste-Croix, **28**
La Maison de Jeanne
d'Arc, **31**
Musée des
Beaux-Arts, **29**
Musée Historique, **30**
Nouvelle Halle, **27**

century wedding-cake towers. Novelist Marcel Proust (1871–1922) called it France's ugliest church, but most people find it impressive. Inside you'll see vast quantities of stained glass and 18th-century woodcarving, plus the modern **Chapel of Joan of Arc,** with plaques in memory of the British and American war dead. *Rue Jeanne-d' Arc. Open daily 8:30–noon and 2–7.*

29 The modern **Musée des Beaux-Arts** (the art gallery) is just across the street from the cathedral. Take the elevator to the top and work your way down, viewing works by such artists as Tintoretto, Velázquez, Watteau, Boucher, Rodin, and Gauguin. *1 rue Ferdinand Rabier. Admission: 12 frs. adults, 6 frs. students and senior citizens. Open Wed.–Mon. 10–noon and 2–6; closed Tues.*

30 Retrace your steps along the rue Jeanne-d'Arc and turn left into place Abbé Desnoyers for a visit to Orléans's **Musée Historique.** This Renaissance town house contains both "fine" and "popular" works of art connected with the town's history and a remarkable collection of pagan bronzes of animals and dancers. These last were hidden from zealous Christian missionaries in the 4th century and discovered in a sand pit near St-Benoît in 1861. *Hôtel Cabu, pl. Abbé Desnoyers. Admission: 8 frs. adults, 4 frs. students. Open Apr.–Sept., Wed.–Mon. 10–noon and 2–6; Oct.– Mar., 10–noon and 2–5; closed Tues.*

31 Another block west on rue Jeanne-d'Arc, in place du Général-deGaulle, is **La Maison de Jeanne-d'Arc.** Seventeen-year-old Joan stayed on the site during the 10-day siege of Orléans in 1429, in a house that underwent many changes before it was bombed flat in 1940. This reconstruction contains exhibits about her life, costumes of her time, and models of siege engines. *Pl. du Général-de-Gaulle. Admission: 8 frs. adults, 4 frs. students. Open May–Oct., Tues.–Sun. 10–noon and 2–6; Nov.–Apr., Tues.–Sun. 2–6; closed Mon.*

Number in the margin correspond with points of interest on the Loire Valley map.

About 25 kilometers (15 miles) east of Orléans, the leafy village of **Châteauneuf-sur-Loire** is a convenient base from which to explore the towns and countryside of the eastern Loire.

Though the **château** was destroyed in the French Revolution, its outbuildings and garden survive. Beyond them stretches a delightful public park, laid out *à l'anglaise*—in a "natural" way—with giant tulip trees, magnolias, weeping willows, and rhododendrons, especially beautiful in late May and early June. Little streams snake their way across the parkland, passing benches, shady copses, and scenic picnic spots on their way to the Loire.

You may also want to visit the **Musée de la Marine,** whose exhibits chronicle the history of navigation on the Loire. Paintings, photographs, documents, and model boats illustrate the boatman's life. *In the basement of the Mairie (town hall). Admission: 8 frs. adults, 4 frs. students. Open July and Aug., Wed.–Mon. 10–noon and 2–5:30, closed Tues.; June and Sept., Mon. and Wed.–Fri. 2–5:30, closed Tues.; Apr.–May, weekends only, 10–noon and 2–5:30. Other months by appointment.*

On the north bank of the Loire, just 5 kilometers (3 miles) southeast of Châteauneuf, is the little village of **Germigny-des-Prés.** Around AD 800, Theodulf, an abbot of St-Benoît, built a tiny **church** here, which is often cited as the oldest in France. A square Byzantine arrangement of rounded arches on square pillars, with indirect lighting filtering from smaller arches above the central square, it was carefully restored to its original condition during the last century. Though Theodulf himself brought most of the original mosaics from Italy, only one—covered in plaster and discovered in 1848—survives. Made of 130,000 cubes of colored glass, it shows the Ark of the Covenant transported by angels with golden halos. The Latin inscription asks us not to forget Theodulf in our prayers. *Open daily 9–noon and 2–5.*

The little town of **St-Benoît-sur-Loire** lies about 10 kilometers (6 miles) southeast of Chateâuneuf and 5½ kilometers (3½ miles) from Germigny. Its highlight is the ancient **Abbey of St-Benoît,** often hailed as the greatest Romanesque church in France; village signposts refer to it as *la Basilique.*

St-Benoît, or St. Benedict, was the founder of the Benedictine monastic order. In AD 650, a group of monks chose this safe and fertile spot for their new monastery, returning to Monte Cassino, Italy, to retrieve the bones of St. Benedict with which to bless the site. Despite protests from priests at the church at Monte Cassino, some of the relics remain here, in the 11th-century abbey church bearing his name. Following the Hundred Years' War of the 14th and 15th centuries, the monastery fell into a decline, and the Wars of Religion (1562–98) wrought further damage. During the French Revolution, the monks dispersed and the buildings

were destroyed, all except the abbey church itself, which became
the parish church. Monastic life here began anew in 1944, when
the monks rebuilt their monastery and regained the abbey church
for their own use. The pillars of the tower porch are noted for their
intricately carved capitals, and the choir floor is an amazing
patchwork of many-colored marble.

Gregorian chants can be heard daily, at mass or vespers, and Sunday services attract worshipers and music lovers from all around.
Visitors are welcome to explore the church crypt. *Mass and vespers Sun. 11 and 6:15 PM, Mon.–Sat. noon and 6:15 PM. Guided
English-language tours of the monastic buildings can be arranged; inquire at the monastery shop.*

What to See and Do with Children

Older children should enjoy visiting a handful of châteaus—especially **Chambord** (Tour 2), with its extravagant staircase and
wild parkland, and the eerie tunnels and dungeons at **Meung**
(Tour 2). Make-it-yourself cardboard models of the famous palaces—available in most gift shops—are also popular and help
enrich children's visits.

For a fun family outing, try the **Zoo de Doué,** a privately run zoo
in a garden setting surrounded by golden limestone quarries.
The deer, emu, monkeys—even the vultures—all look happy
and well cared for; the hefty admission charge goes to safe-
guard endangered species. *Rte. de Cholet, 49700 Doué-la-
Fontaine, about 16 km/10 mi west of Saumur, tel. 41–59–18–
58. Admission: 40 frs. Open May–Sept., daily 9–7:30; Oct.–
Apr., daily 10–noon and 2–6.*

Parc Floral de la Source, about 8 kilometers (5 miles) south of
Orléans, offers mighty trees, a minizoo, swings, acres of flowers and flowering plants, and a little train that comes in handy
when your feet give out. *Parc Floral, 45100 Orléans-la-Source,
tel. 38–63–33–17. Admission: 14 frs. (7 frs. winter). Open
May– Oct., daily 9–6; Nov.–Apr., daily 2–5.*

Off the Beaten Track

The 16th-century château of **Gué-Péan** is hidden in wooded
grounds near the village of Monthou-sur-Cher, about 10 kilometers (6 miles) from Montrichard. It's neither museum nor
showcase, but the ancestral home of the Marquis de Keguelin,
whose family still lives here. Inside you'll find a miscellany of
furniture, paintings, and interesting *objets.* To offset the cost
of maintaining the château, the Marquis also runs an excellent
bed-and-breakfast service; dinner, if wanted, is often taken in
his charming company. *Monthou-sur-Cher, 41400 Montrichard, tel. 54–71–43–01. Open mid-Mar.–Sept., daily 9–5; Oct.–
mid-Mar., daily 9–noon and 2–5.*

Thirty-two kilometers (20 miles) northwest of Blois via D957 is
the charming town of **Vendôme.** It's not on most tourists' itineraries, but its picturesque appeal amply merits the detour.
Vendôme's château is in ruins, but the **gardens** surrounding it
offer knockout views of the town center. From place du Château, head down to admire the Flamboyant Gothic abbey
church of **La Trinité,** with its unusual 12th-century clock tower
and fine stained glass. Take time to stroll through the narrow
streets of this enchanting little town.

The fortress-castle of **Châteaudun** lies 45 kilometers (28 miles) northeast of Vendôme via fast N10. Its austere facade is decidedly grim, but the internal courtyard is overlooked by buildings of a more welcoming aspect, thanks to 16th-century restoration work. The interior contains period furniture and tapestries, but the highlight is the **Sainte-Chapelle,** with its collection of 15th-century statues. *Admission: 24 frs. Open Easter–Sept., daily 8–11:45 and 2–6; Oct.–Easter, Sun. 10–11:45 and 2–6.*

Le Mans, 200 kilometers (125 miles) west of Paris, is close to—but not part of—four separate regions: Brittany, Normandy, Ile de France, and the Loire Valley. Le Mans is best known for its 24-hour automobile race. The hilltop city center and the cathedral are well worth a visit.

The sumptuous, moated **Château de Serrant** is only 16 kilometers (10 miles) southwest of Angers, near St-Georges-sur-Loire. Begun in 1546, and gaining additions during the 17th and 18th centuries, it contains lush interiors, paneled and hung with tapestries. The library, holding over 10,000 volumes, is magnificent. Like the château de Gué-Péan, the château is a private residence. *Admission: 25 frs. Open Easter–Oct., Wed.–Mon. 9–11:30 and 2–6; closed Tues.*

Champigny-sur-Veude is just 13 kilometers (8 miles) south of Chinon along D749, but visitors to its **Sainte-Chapelle** (holy chapel) are few. What many miss is some of the best Renaissance stained glass in the world. The chapel was originally part of a château built between 1508 and 1543 but razed a century later by order of jealous neighbor Cardinal Richelieu. Its 16th-century windows relate scenes from the Passion, Crucifixion, and life of 13th-century French King St-Louis; note the vividness and harmony of the colors, especially the purplish blues. *Admission: 25 frs. Open Apr.–Sept., daily 9–noon and 2–6.*

Five miles farther down D749 is the town of **Richelieu,** founded by Cardinal Richelieu in 1631, along with a huge château intended to be one of the most lavish in Christendom. All that's left of the latter are a few buildings and some parklands, though the town remains a rare example of rigid, symmetrical, and unspoiled Classical town planning, well worth seeing: Its bombastic scale and state of preservation are unique. The severe, straight streets have not changed for 350 years, give or take the occasional traffic sign.

Shopping

Wine The region's extra-special produce is Loire wine. It's not a practical buy for tourists—except for instant consumption—but if wine-tasting tours of vineyards inspire you, enterprising wine makers will arrange shipment to the United States; think in terms of hundreds rather than dozens. Try the **Maison du Vin** in Angers (pl. Président-Kennedy, next to the tourist office), and **Maison des Vins de Touraine** in Tours (4 bis blvd. Heurteloup).

Gift Ideas Loire food specialties include barley sugar *(sucre d'orge)* and prunes stuffed with marzipan *(pruneux fourrés);* both are widely available at food shops throughout the valley. A sweet-toothed specialty of the Orléans district is *cotignac*—an orangey-red molded jelly made from quinces. It, too, can be bought from most local patisseries and is produced almost exclusively by **Gilbert Jumeau** (1 rue Voisinas, St-Ay), 8 kilometers (5 miles) west of Orléans. For fine chocolates, try the **Chocolaterie Royale** in Orléans (53 rue Royale).

Antiques All major towns have high-quality antiques for sale. There are numerous antiques shops in **rue de la Scellerie** in Tours, and you can also pick up some fine pieces at **Au Vieux Tours** (91 rue Colbert). In Saumur, try **Galerie Beaurepaire** (7 rue Beaurepaire); in Fontevraud, **Christian Saulnier** (4 av. Rochechouart). Angers has an interesting **flea market** on Saturdays (pl. Imbach).

Arts and Crafts Gien, on the north bank of the Loire a few miles past Sully and St-Benoît, is a major earthenware center; the factory, **Faïenceries de Gien** (pl. de la Victoire, tel. 38–67–00–05), can be contacted for private visits. In addition to its wines, **La Maison de Touraine** in Tours (4 bis blvd. Heurteloup; closed Sun. and Mon. mornings) offers a wide selection of local products and crafts, including ceramics. For fine wickerwork, visit the shop at the **Société Coopérative de Vannerie** in Villaines-les-Rochers, near Saché.

Sports and Fitness

Bicycling The Loire region is excellent country for biking—not too hilly, not too flat. Bikes can be rented at most train stations and at dozens of other outlets (try **Au Col de Cygne,** 46 bis rue du Dr-Fournier, Tours; and **Leprovost,** 13 rue Carnot, Azay-le-Rideau). Loisirs Accueil offices in Blois and Orléans offer organized trips; these often include luggage transportation and camp or youth hostel accommodations. Ask at the nearest tourist office or contact **Loisirs Accueil** (3 rue de la Bretonnerie, Orléans, tel. 38–62–04–88; or 11 pl. du Château, Blois, tel. 54–78–55–50).

Fishing and Shooting The **Loisirs Accueil** office in Orléans (*see* above) organizes week-long and weekend fishing and shooting outings in the Forest of Orléans. Some include accommodations in two-star hotels.

Hiking Scenic footpaths abound. Long-distance walking paths *(sentiers de grande randonnée)* pass through the Loire Valley and are marked on Michelin maps with broken lines and route numbers. Tourist offices will supply sketch maps of interesting paths in their area.

Horseback Riding The region offers abundant facilities and activities, including pony-trekking trips and week-long equestrian tours. Try **La Poitevinere,** just north of Saumur on N147, tel. 41–52–55–08. You can also rent a horse at **Chambord,** from the former stables of the marshal of Saxe, and ride in the vast National Park surrounding the château (tel. 54–20–31–01).

Water sports Good facilities for canoeing, sailing, fishing, and windsurfing can be found at the **Centre Nautique du Lac de Maine** (tel. 41–48–12–47) in Angers and the **Lac de Loire** (tel. 54–78–82–05) near Blois. The Loire itself has swift and dangerous currents, so swim only at official beaches (signposted *plages*), which are safe and supervised. Package canoeing and kayaking trips can be arranged through local Loisirs Accueil offices (*see* above).

Dining and Lodging

Dining

The Loire region, known as the "garden of France," produces a cornucopia of farm-fresh products—from beef, poultry, game, and fish to butter, cream, wine, fruit, and vegetables. It sends its early crops to the best Parisian tables, yet keeps more than enough for local use. Loire wines can be extremely good—and varied. Among the best: Savennières, Cheverny (dry white); Coteaux du Layon (sweet white); Cabernet d'Anjou (rosé); Bourgueil, Chinon (red); and Saumur, Vouvray (white, still or sparkling).

Highly recommended restaurants are indicated by a star ★.

Category	Cost*
Very Expensive	over 350 francs
Expensive	200–350 francs
Moderate	100–200 francs
Inexpensive	under 100 francs

per person for a three-course meal, including tax (18.6%) and tip but not wine

Lodging

Even before the age of the train, the Loire Valley drew visitors from far and wide, anxious to see the great châteaus and sample the sweetness of rural life. Hundreds of hotels of all kinds have sprung up to accommodate today's travelers. At the higher end of the price scale is the **Relais et Châteaux** group; some of their best hotels are converted châteaus. **Chateaux-Hotels Independents** are usually somewhat less expensive, supervised by their live-in owners; though some are less efficient than ordinary hotels, they offer much individuality and charm. Two smaller groups, the **Château-Accueil** and **La Castellerie,** offer pleasant accommodations for a limited number of guests. Illustrated lists of these groups are available from French Government Tourist Offices abroad, as well as in France. At the lower end of the price scale are the **Logis de France** hotels. These small, traditional hotels are located in towns and villages throughout the region and usually offer terrific value for the money. The Logis de France handbook is available free from French Tourist Offices abroad and for about 50 frs. in French bookshops.

The Loire Valley is one of the country's most popular vacation destinations, so always make reservations well in advance.

Highly recommended hotels are indicated by a star ★.

Category	Cost*
Very Expensive	over 750 francs
Expensive	350–750 francs

Moderate	200–350 francs
Inexpensive	under 200 francs

All prices are for a standard double room for two, including tax (18.6%) and service charge.

Amboise
Dining

Manoir St-Thomas. Located between the château and the Clos Lucé, this restaurant occupies a fine Renaissance building with an adjacent garden. Chef François Le Coz serves elegantly traditional food. Try his stewed eels *(matelots d'anguilles)* or his stuffed guinea-fowl breast *(suprême de pintade farci)*. The list of Touraine wines is enticing. *Pl. Richelieu, tel. 47–57–22–52. Reservations advised. Jacket and tie required. AE, DC, MC, V. Closed Mon, first 2 weeks Nov., and mid-Jan.–mid-Feb. Expensive.*

Dining and Lodging

Choiseul. Amboise's top hotel also offers a superb restaurant. Choiseul sits on the banks of the Loire, just below the château. Though the guest rooms have recently been modernized, they retain an old and distinctive charm. *36 quai Charles Guinot, 37400, tel. 47–30–45–45. 35 rooms with bath. Facilities: restaurant, garden, pool. MC, V. Closed Jan.–mid-Mar. Expensive.*
Château de Pray. This real Louis XII château, with all the lordliness of a bygone era, is situated just outside Amboise on the south bank of the Loire, surrounded by a 25-acre park and a lovely garden. Inside you'll appreciate the cozy, hunting-lodge ambience. Sixteen elegantly appointed guest rooms are equipped with carved wooden furniture and modern conveniences. The restaurant is only adequate, but diners can enjoy a roaring fire and fine views of the Loire. *On D751, route de Chargé, 37530 Chargé, tel. 47–57–23–67. 16 rooms, 14 with bath. Facilities: restaurant, garden. AE, DC, MC, V. Closed Jan.–mid-Feb. Moderate–Expensive.*

Angers
Dining
★

Toussaint. Chef Michel Bignon dishes up nouvelle versions of traditional local dishes, plus fine wines and tasty desserts, in a cozy, 400-year-old dining room. Loire River fish with *beurre blanc* (white butter sauce) is a particular specialty. *7 pl. Kennedy, tel. 41–87–46–20. Reservations required. Jacket required. AE, DC, MC, V. Closed Sun. evening, Mon., part of Feb. Moderate–Expensive.*
Maître Kanter. This chain restaurant, located at Les Halles covered market, provides simple food and swift service. It's a convenient refueling spot, and the firm's own beer is available on tap. Try the steak and french fries, or the sauerkraut with sausages and ham. *Les Halles, tel. 41–87–93–30. No reservations. Dress: casual. V. Inexpensive.*

Dining and Lodging

Concorde. You won't find individuality in this standardized chain hotel, but, then again, you won't find problems either. The soundproof rooms are bright and modern, furnished with a copious amount of white Formica. There's a spacious lobby and a good brasserie restaurant. *18 blvd. Foch, 49000, tel. 41–87–37–20. 75 rooms with bath. Facilities: restaurant. AE, DC, MC, V. Expensive.*
Anjou. In business since 1850, Anjou has recently been redecorated in a vaguely 18th-century style. Each room is individually styled, though all are spacious and feature double-glazed windows. The restaurant, Salamandre, is an affordable place to sample local fare (try the duck with turnips), and has a fine

wine list. *1 blvd. Foch, 49000, tel. 41–88–24–82. 51 rooms with bath. Facilities: restaurant. AE, DC, MC, V. Moderate.*

Azay-le-Rideau
Dining and Lodging

Grand Monarque. Just yards from the château, this mildly eccentric, popular hotel draws hundreds of visitors. It has been in the same family for generations, playing host to celebrities, royals, and tourists alike. Guest rooms are tastefully, individually decorated. The restaurant serves good, traditional food, and the selection of Loire wines is extensive. *3 pl. de la République, 37190, tel. 47–45–40–08. 30 rooms, 28 with bath. AE, DC, MC, V. Facilities: restaurant. Restaurant closed mid-Nov.–mid-Mar. Moderate.*

Blois
Dining
★

La Bocca d'Or. Original dishes such as succulent pigeons and *chaud-froid* (cooked but served cold) of oysters and asparagus are the order of the day in this stylish, vaulted 14th-century cellar restaurant, presided over by chef Patrice Galland and his genial American wife, Francine. La Bocca d'Or is a small place with a growing reputation, so it's best to reserve a table. *15 rue Haute, tel. 54–78–04–74. Dress: casual. AE, MC, V. Closed Sun., Mon. lunch, and late Jan.–early Mar. Moderate–Expensive.*

La Péniche. This innovative restaurant is actually a luxurious barge moored along the banks of the Loire. Charming chef Germain Bosque serves up beautifully presented fresh seafood specialties (notably lobsters and oysters). *Promenade du Mail, tel. 57–74–37–23. Reservations advised. Dress: casual. AE, DC, MC, V. Moderate–Expensive.*

Lodging

Anne de Bretagne. A storybook-style French pension decked out with flowers, the Anne de Bretagne offers clean, simple rooms featuring bright bedspreads and curtains. It's a quaint and quiet place in which to spend a night *31 av.du Dr-Jean-Laigret, 41000, tel. 54–78–05–38. 29 rooms, most with bath. AE, DC, MC, V. Closed mid-Feb.–mid-Mar. Moderate.*

Chambord
Dining
★

Bernard Robin. Residents of Bracieux, 8 kilometers (5 miles) from Chambord, rate this as one of the country's best restaurants. From his gleaming kitchens, chef Bernard Robin produces fine nouvelle cuisine, but connoisseurs savor his simpler dishes: local carp, game in season, and salmon with beef marrow. The attentive staff bring delicious tidbits to keep you busy between courses. *1 av. de Chambord, Bracieux, tel. 54–46–41–22. Reservations required. Jacket and tie required. AE, MC, V. Closed Tues. dinner, Wed., and late Dec.–Feb. Expensive.*

Lodging

St-Michel. Guests enjoy simple and comfortable living in this revamped country house at the edge of the woods across from Chambord château. A few rooms boast spectacular views, and there's a pleasant café-terrace for contemplative drinks. *103 pl. St-Michel, 41250, tel. 54–20–31–31. 39 rooms, 31 with bath. Facilities: restaurant, tennis, terrace. MC, V. Closed mid-Nov.–Dec. 20. Inexpensive–Moderate.*

Chaumont-sur-Loire
Dining and Lodging
★

Domaine des Hauts de Loire. Three kilometers (2 miles) from Onzain, just over the bridge from Chaumont, this exquisite hotel occupies an 18th-century manor house set amid 180 acres of parkland. The turreted, vine-covered inn maintains high standards: Guest rooms are individually decorated in warm colors and feature antiques and heavy wooden furniture. Service is relaxed and not in the least pretentious. The restaurant is first-class. *Rte. d'Herbault, 41150 Onzain, tel. 54–20–72–57. 24* *rooms with bath. AE, DC, MC, V. Closed Dec.–Feb. Very Expensive.*

Pont d'Ouchet. This wonderfully inexpensive restaurant-hotel in Onzain is run by a hard-working professional couple, the Cochets. According to Louisette Cochet, her husband Antonin's *moules marinières* (mussels) are the best in France; take her advice on what to order. In addition to the terrific food, the inn offers 10 comfortable rooms. *50 Grande-Rue, 41150 Onzain, tel. 54–20–70–33. 10 rooms, some with bath. MC, V. Closed Nov.–Feb.; restaurant closed Sun. dinner and Mon. Inexpensive.*

Chenonceaux
Dining and Lodging

Bon Laboureur. In 1882, it won Henry James's praise as a simple, rustic inn. Since then, the Bon Laboureur has come up in the world: It's elegantly modern, with a few old oak beams surviving, and a pretty garden where you can eat in summer. The food—especially the fresh fish and the hotel's own garden vegetables—is commendable. *6 rue du Dr. Bretonneau, 37150, tel. 47–23–90–02. 26 rooms with bath. Facilities: restaurant, garden. AE, DC, MC, V. Closed Dec.–mid-Mar. Moderate.*

Chinon
Dining
★

Au Plaisir Gourmand. Gourmets from all around come here to celebrate, and lucky tourists will get a table only if they make reservations (the dining room in this charming old house seats only 30). Chef Jean-Claude Rigollet makes inventive use of fresh, local produce. For a real treat, try the Vienne River trout. Au Plaisir Gourmand gives top quality without frills and features exceptional local wines. *2 rue Parmentier, tel. 47–93–20–48. Reservations required. Jacket and tie required. MC, V. Closed Sun. dinner, Mon., last 3 weeks in Feb., and second half of Nov. Moderate–Expensive.*

Jeanne de France. Local families and swarms of young people patronize this lively little pizzeria in the town's main square. But it's a far cry from an American pizza joint: Here you can also buy jugfuls of local wine, steaks, and french fries. *12 pl. Général-de-Gaulle, tel. 47–93–20–12. Reservations accepted. Dress: casual. Closed Wed., Jan. Inexpensive.*

Lodging

Château de Marçay. Sophisticated luxury characterizes this 15th-century château, 6 kilometers (4 miles) south of Chinon by D49 and D116. Part of the Relais et Châteaux group, it's run with smooth efficiency. Some rooms are palatial (and cost well over 1,000 francs per night), but an annex contains smaller rooms that go for about half the price. In the original building, much care has been taken to blend modern conveniences with the old beamed and gabled structure. *37500 Marçay, tel. 47–93–03–47. 34 rooms with bath. Facilities: restaurant, gardens, pool, tennis. AE, MC, V. Closed Jan.–Feb. Expensive–Very Expensive.*

Dining and Lodging

Hostellerie Gargantua. In the 15th century, the building housing the Gargantua was a bailiff's palace. Today this small, quiet hotel offers an array of rooms in various sizes and styles. Simple good taste prevails throughout. The restaurant, with its charming old dining room and outside tables for summer, serves delicious local specialties. *73 rue Haute-St-Maurice, tel. 47–93–04–71. 10 rooms, most with bath. AE, DC, MC, V. Closed mid-Nov.–mid-Mar. Moderate–Expensive.*

Meung-sur-Loire
Dining and Lodging
★

St-Jacques. Located on Meung's busy main road, this inn is just a five-minute walk from the château and river. Its restaurant is one of the glories of France, a family-run affair where excellent fresh food is served without fuss at deliciously low prices. Even the cheapest menus are delightful, and the pike soufflé attracts gourmets from all around. The 12 guest rooms are clean and simple. *60 rue Général-de-Gaulle, tel. 38–44–30–39. Reservations advised. Dress: casual. AE, MC, V. Restaurant closed Mon.; hotel and restaurant closed last 2 weeks in Jan. Inexpensive.*

Montbazon
Dining and Lodging
★ **Château d'Artigny.** One of the most famous of the Relais et Châteaux group inns lies just outside town on D17. Built by the Coty perfume tycoon in 1912 as a vast pseudo-Louis XV house, it is now a suavely run palace-hotel. Ironically, the ambience recalls a perfume ad: Gilt, marble, and plush abound, creating a perfect backdrop for the frequent celebrity guests. The nouvelle restaurant is excellent, and you can jog away the calories in the 60-acre park. *Rte. d'Azay-le-Rideau, 37250 Montbazon, tel. 47–26–24–24. 46 rooms with bath. Facilities: restaurant, pool, tennis, gardens. MC, V. Closed Dec.–early Jan. Expensive.*

★ **Domaine de la Tortinière.** Although this charming little 19th-century château is more intimate and less expensive than the Château d'Artigny, it's hardly a country cousin. The Domaine's brand of elegance is simpler and subtler, but it still has everything you could want in a country hotel. Rooms in the main building exude a quiet, rustic luxury; those in the modern annex are less desirable. The hotel restaurant compares favorably with that of the Artigny. *10 rte. Ballan, Route des Monts, 37250 Veigné, tel. 47–26–00–19. 14 rooms with bath. Facilities: restaurant, pool, tennis, park. MC, V. Closed mid-Nov.–mid-Mar. Expensive.*

★ **Moulin Fleuri.** Located in a converted watermill 5 kilometers (3 miles) from town, this is really a restaurant with rooms. The Indre sweeps by the garden, and if you've brought a rod, you can fish without a license; if you catch something edible, chef Alain Chaplin may cook it for you. The delightful restaurant offers a tasty inexpensive menu, but it's wiser to budget for "moderate," since you may weaken to such specialties as roast pigeon with acacia honey. Guest rooms are simple but bright. *5 km (3 mi) from town by N10, D287, and D87, Route des Monts, 37250 Veigné, tel. 47–26–01–12. 12 rooms, 8 with bath. AE, MC, V. Restaurant closed Mon.; hotel closed last 2 weeks in Oct. and 3 weeks in Feb. Moderate.*

Orléans
Dining
★ **La Crémaillère.** Situated in a little street near the Maison de Jeanne d'Arc, Orléans's top restaurant is possibly the best in the valley for seafood of all kinds. Chef Claude Louboutin gets the pick of the daily catch from Brittany, from lobster to red mullet, "wild" salmon to turbot. Such dishes as *langoustines* (crayfish) in filo pastry with sweet-sour sauce reveal Louboutin's ability to innovate. *34 rue Notre-Dame-de-Recouvrance, tel. 38–53–49–17. Reservations advised. Jacket and tie required. AE, DC, MC, V. Closed Sun. evening and Aug. Expensive.*

L'Assiette. This is a brisk but comfortable place, right on place du Martroi (the main square). Choose your main course (simple grilled meats, mostly), and while it's cooking, help yourself to a wide variety of hors d'oeuvres and table wine from the barrel. You're entitled to as much of both as you want—and desserts are "free," too: The price of your meal depends on the main dish. *12 pl. du Martroi, tel. 39–53–46–69. Reservations advised. Dress: casual. AE, DC, MC, V. Inexpensive.*

Dining and Lodging **Le Rivage.** This small, white-walled hotel in Olivet makes a pleasant, affordable base for exploring Orléans 4 kilometers (3 miles) to the north. The dining room overlooks the River Loiret (ask for a room that does the same) and has a terrace for outdoor summer meals. *635 rue de la Reine-Blanche, 45160 Olivet, tel. 38–66–03–30. 20 rooms, some with bath. Facilities: restaurant with terrace, tennis court. AE, DC, MC, V. Closed Christmas–mid-Jan. Moderate.*

Saumur **Le Prieuré.** In a Renaissance manor 8 kilometers (5 miles) outside Saumur on D751, Le Prieuré offers elegant and gracious **Dining and Lodging** accommodations. The original structure dates from medieval times. Large guest rooms feature tasteful period decor; the nicest are in the main building, though the garden chalets are luxurious inside. Large windows overlook the Loire, while crystal and silver clink discreetly in the spacious dining room. The restaurant's chef, Jean-Noël Lumineau, prepares delicious nouvelle cuisine, blending imagination with fresh local ingredients. *Le Prieuré, 49350 Chênehutte, tel. 41–67–90–14. 33 rooms with bath. Facilities: restaurant, garden, tennis, pool. AE, MC, V. Closed early Jan.–early Mar. Expensive.*

Loire. For a more affordable stay in Saumur itself, cross the river to the Loire hotel. This member of the Best Western chain wins no prizes for charm or friendly service, but it is clean, spacious, and functional, and there is a stunning view of the château from the restaurant. *Rue de Vieux-Pont, 49400, tel. 41–67–22–42. 44 rooms with bath. AE, DC, MC, V. Moderate.*

Tours **Jean Bardet.** This restaurant is the brainchild and namesake of **Dining** Jean Bardet, one of France's top-20 chefs. Try the eight-course ★ *menu dégustation,* or from the *carte,* oysters poached in muscadet on a puree of watercress. Or why not a simple grilled lobster, some fine cheese, and a hot baked apple filled with cinnamon ice cream? Bardet was awarded a prize for the best wine list in France in 1988. The inn also has 15 luxurious guest rooms. *57 rue Groison, tel. 47–41–41–11. Reservations essential. Jacket and tie required. AE, DC, MC, V. Very Expensive.*

Les Tuffeaux. Though it has recently changed hands, this restaurant retains its place as one of Tours's best. Chef Gildas Marsollier has been winning customers with his delicious fennel-perfumed salmon and remarkable desserts. Gentle lighting and a warm, understated decor provide a soothing background. *19 rue Lavoisier, tel. 47–47–19–89. Reservations advised. Jacket required. MC, V. Closed Sun., Mon. lunch, and part of Jan. Moderate.*

Lodging **Univers.** Once a fine old coaching inn, the Univers, just off place de la Gare, has since been discreetly modernized. J. D. Rockefeller, William Randolph Hearst, Boris Karloff, Sugar Ray Robinson, and the Duke of Windsor have all stayed here; ask to see their entries in the hotel's "golden book." Despite its solemn appearance, the moderately priced restaurant, La Touraine, offers some fine, light dishes. *5 blvd. Heurteloup, 37000, tel. 47–05–37–12. 91 rooms with bath. Facilities: restaurant. AE, DC, MC, V. Restaurant closed Sat. Expensive–Moderate.*

Valençay **Chêne Vert.** If you want a reliable restaurant that serves good, **Dining** simple meals at rock-bottom prices, look no further. The Green Oak is a basic little tavern offering hearty regional specialties. The four-course meal will fill you up, and in fine weather, you can eat outside. *55 rue Nationale, tel. 54–00–06–54. Reservations accepted. Dress: casual. MC, V. Closed Sun. dinner, Sat.*

(except from July–mid-Sept.), and 3 weeks in June. Inexpensive.

Lodging ★ **Hôtel d'Espagne.** A recent addition to the Relais et Châteaux group, this intimate hotel retains the feel of an elegant provincial home. The Fourré family has run it for generations. A former coaching inn, it is built around a landscaped courtyard. Guest rooms are individually decorated, and many feature balconies. *9 rue du Château, 36600, tel. 54–00–00–02. 16 rooms with bath. Facilities: restaurant, garden, pool, tennis. AE, DC, MC, V. Closed Jan., Sun. and Mon. in winter. Expensive.*

Villandry
Dining and Lodging **Cheval Rouge.** This is a fine, old-fashioned hotel whose restaurant is popular with the locals. It boasts an excellent Loire wine list and surprisingly good food, considering its touristy location right next to the château. Good bets are the terrine of foie gras, the calf sweetbreads, and the wood-fired grills. The 20 guest rooms are tidy, and all have bath or shower. *37510 Villandry, tel. 47–50–02–07. Reservations advised. Dress: casual. MC, V. Closed Mon. out of season, and Nov.–mid-Mar. Moderate.*

The Arts and Nightlife

Son-et-Lumière The Loire Valley's favorite form of cultural entertainment is *son-et-lumière* (sound-and-light shows), a dramatic spectacle that takes place after dark on summer evenings on the grounds of major châteaus. Programs sometimes take the form of historical pageants, with huge casts of people in period costume and caparisoned horses, the whole floodlit and backed by music and commentary, often (as at **Amboise**) in English. They may also take the form of spectacular lighting and sound shows, with spoken commentary and dialogue but no visible figures, as at **Chenonceau.** The most magnificent *son-et-lumière* occurs at **Le Lude,** on the River Loir (not the Loire), 48 kilometers (29 miles) northeast of Saumur and 50 kilometers (30 miles) northwest of Tours. Here more than 100 performers present a pageant chronicling the history of the château and region from the Hundred Years' War on. The spectacle is enhanced by fountains and fireworks.

Open-Air Festivals For four weeks beginning in mid-June, the **Festival d'Anjou** enlivens the area around Anjou with music, theater, and dance. In July, the château grounds at **Loches** are the setting for a series of open-air concerts. And in the medieval **Grange du Meslay** near Tours, top-class international musicians gather in late June and July for the **Fêtes Musicales de Touraine.**

Nightclubs Though clubs and discos are not one of the Loire Valley's strong points, the larger cities offer several: In Tours, try **L'Excalibur** (35 rue Briçonnet) and **Pyms** (170 av. de Grammont); in Angers, **Le Boléro** (38 rue St-Laud) and **Lady L** (60 rue du Mail); in Orléans, **L'Empereur** (28 bis rue de l'Empereur).

6 Brittany

Introduction

Thanks to its proximity to Great Britain, its folklore, and its spectacular coastline, Brittany (Bretagne in French) is a favorite destination among English-speaking vacationers. The French love the area, too, but don't worry about hordes of tourists—Brittany's vast beaches aren't easily crowded.

Occupying the bulbous portion of western France that juts far out into the Atlantic, the stubborn, independent-minded Bretons have more in common—both historically and linguistically—with the Celts of Cornwall, Wales, and Ireland than with their French countrymen. Both Brittany and Cornwall claim Merlin, King Arthur, and the Druids as cult figures, while huge Stonehenge-like menhirs and dolmens (prehistoric standing stones) litter the Breton countryside. As in Wales, nationalistic fervor has been channeled into gaining official acceptance for the local language.

Brittany became part of France in 1532, but regional folklore is still very much alive. An annual village *pardon* (a religious festival) will give you a good idea of Breton traditions: Banners and saintly statues are borne in colorful parades, accompanied by hymns, and the whole event is rounded off by food of all kinds. The most famous *pardon* is held on the last Sunday of August at Ste-Anne-la-Palud, near Quimper. The surrounding Finistère (from *Finis Terrae*, or Land's End) département, Brittany's westernmost district, is renowned for the costumes worn on such occasions—notably the lace bonnets, or *coiffes*, which can tower 15 inches above the wearer's head.

Geographically, Brittany is divided in two: maritime Armor ("land of the sea") and hinterland Argoat ("land of the forest"). The north of Brittany tends to be wilder than the south, where the countryside becomes softer as it descends toward Nantes and the Loire. Wherever you go, the coast is close by; the frenzied, cliff-bashing Atlantic surf alternates with sprawling beaches and bustling harbors. Islands, many inhabited and within easy reach of the mainland, dot the coastal waters.

Although Brittany's towns took a mighty hammering from the retreating Nazis in 1944, most have been tastefully restored, the large concrete-cluttered naval base at Brest being an exception. Rennes, the only Breton city with more than 200,000 inhabitants, retains its traditional charm, as do the towns of Dinan, Quimper, and Vannes. Many ancient man-made delights are found in the region's villages, often in the form of *calvaries* (ornate burial chapels). Other architectural highlights include castles and cathedrals, the most outstanding examples being those of Fougères and Dol, respectively.

Essential Information

Important Addresses and Numbers

Tourist Information The principal regional tourist offices are at **Rennes** (Pont de Nemours, tel. 99–79–01–98), **Brest** (8 av. Georges-Clemenceau, tel. 98–44–24–96), and **Nantes** (pl. du Commerce, tel. 40–35–48–77).

The addresses of other tourist offices in towns mentioned on this tour are as follows: **Carnac** (74 av. des Druides, tel. 97–52–13–52), **Concarneau** (quai d'Aiguillon, tel. 98–70–01–44), **Dinan** (6 rue de l'Horloge, tel. 96–39–75–40), **Dinard** (2 blvd Féart, tel. 99–46–94–12), **Dol-de-Bretagne** (3 Grand Rue, tel. 99–48–15–37), **La Baule** (9 pl. de la Victoire, tel. 40–24–34–44), **Morlaix** (pl. des Otages, tel. 98–62–14–94), **Quiberon** (7 rue de Verdun, tel. 97–50–07–84), **Quimper** (rue de l'Amiral-de-la-Grandière, tel. 98–95–04–69), **St-Malo** (Esplanade St-Vincent, tel. 99–56–64–48), **Vannes** (1 rue Thiers, tel. 97–47–24–34), and **Vitré** (pl. St-Yves, tel. 99–75–04–46).

Travel Agencies   **Wagons-Lits** (22 rue du Calvaire, Nantes, tel. 40–08–29–18 and 2 rue Jules-Simon, Rennes, tel. 99–79–45–96).

Car Rental   **Avis** (pl. de la Gare, La Baule, tel. 40–60–36–28; 3 blvd. des Français-Libres, Brest, tel. 98–44–63–02; aéroport, Dinard, tel. 99–46–25–20; 18 blvd. de Stalingrad, Nantes, tel. 40–74–39–07; and 8 av. de la Gare, Quimper, tel. 98–90–31–34).

Arriving and Departing

By Plane   There are domestic airports at Rennes, Brest, Nantes, Morlaix, Dinard, Quimper, and Lorient.

By Car   Rennes, the gateway to Brittany, lies 368 kilometers (230 miles) west of Paris. It can be reached in about 4 hours, via Le Mans and the A81/A11 expressways (A11 continues from Le Mans to Nantes).

By Train   There are numerous services daily between Paris (Gare Montparnasse) and Rennes (2 hours). Nantes is on a direct TGV line from Paris (250 miles in 2 hours).

Getting Around

By Car   Rennes, a strategic base for penetrating Brittany, is linked by good roads to Morlaix and Brest (E50), Quimper (N24/N165), Vannes (N24/N166), Fougères (N12), and Dinan and St-Malo (N137).

By Train   Some trains from Paris stop at Vitré before forking at Rennes on their way to either Brest (via Morlaix) or Quimper (via Vannes). Change at Rennes for Dol and St-Malo; at Dol for Dinan and Dinard (bus link); at Morlaix for Roscoff; at Rosporden, 19 kilometers (12 miles) south of Quimper, for Concarneau; and at Auray for Quiberon. There is regular train service down the west coast from Nantes to La Rochelle and Bordeaux.

Guided Tours

France Tourisme (3 rue de'Alger, 75001 Paris, tel. 42–61–85–50) organizes seven-day bus tours of Brittany and a 10-day combined tour of Normandy and Brittany, plus a four-day trip to the Celtic Festival in Lorient. Prices are about 700 francs a day all-inclusive. Further details of organized tours of Brittany can be had from the **Maison de la Bretagne** in Paris (Centre Commercial Maine-Montparnasse, 17 rue de l'Arrivée, B.P. 1006, 75737 Paris cedex 15, tel. 45–38–73–15) or from the regional tourist offices in Brest (tel. 98–44–24–96) and Quimper (tel. 98–95–04–69).

Exploring Brittany

Numbers in the margin correspond with points of interest on the Brittany map.

Orientation

Our first tour is confined to northeastern Brittany, which stretches from Rennes to the fortified harbor of St-Malo. This region played a frontline role in Brittany's efforts to repel French invaders during the Middle Ages, as can be seen in the massive castles of Vitré, Fougères, and Dinan. Our second tour begins 144 kilometers (90 miles) farther west, at the Channel port of Roscoff, before swinging southeast down the Atlantic coast to the city of Nantes at the mouth of the River Loire. Though Nantes is officially part of the Pays de la Loire, it has historic ties with Brittany, embodied in the imposing Château des Ducs de Bretagne.

Highlights for First-time Visitors

Menhirs and dolmens at Carnac, Tour 2
Ville Close, Concarneau, Tour 2
Dinan (Old Town), Tour 1
Nantes, Tour 2
Rennes, Tour 1
Vitré (Old Town), Tour 1
St-Malo (ramparts), Tour 1

Tour 1: Northeast Brittany

1 Built high above the Vilaine Valley, **Vitré** (pronounced "vee-tray") is one of the age-old gateways to Brittany: There's still a feel of the Middle Ages about its dark, narrow alleys and tightly packed houses. The town's leading attraction is its formidable **castle**, shaped in an imposing triangle with fat, round towers. An 11th-century creation, it was first rebuilt in the 14th and 15th centuries to protect Brittany against invasion and was to prove one of the province's most successful fortresses: During the Hundred Years' War (1337–1453) the English repeatedly failed to take it, even though they occupied the rest of the town.

Time, not foreigners, came closest to ravaging the castle, which was heavily, though tastefully, restored during the past century. The town hall, however, is an unfortunate 1913 addition to the castle courtyard. You can visit the wing to the left of the entrance, beginning with the Tour St-Laurent and continuing along the walls via Tour de l'Argenterie, with its macabre collection of stuffed frogs and reptiles preserved in glass jars, to Tour de l'Oratoire. *Admission: 8 frs. Open Apr.–June, Wed.–Mon. 10–12 and 2:30–5:30, closed Tues; July–Sept., daily 10–12 and 1:30–6; Oct.–Mar., Wed.–Fri. 10–12 and 2–5:30, Mon. 2–5:30, closed Tues. and weekends.*

Vitré's castle makes a splendid sight, especially from a vantage point on rue de Fougères across the river valley below. The castle stands at the west end of town, facing the narrow, cobbled streets of the remarkably preserved old town. Rue Poterie, rue d'En-Bas, and rue Beaudrairie, originally the home of tanners

(the name comes from *baudoyers*—leather workers), make up a web of medieval streets as picturesque as any in Brittany; take time to stroll through them, soaking up the quaint atmosphere. Fragments of the town's medieval ramparts remain, including the 15th-century **Tour de la Bridolle** on place de la République, five blocks up from the castle. Built in the 15th and 16th centuries, **Notre-Dame** church has a fine, pinnacled south front, and dominates a large square of the same name (you'll have passed it on the left on your way to place de la République).

Thirty-two kilometers (20 miles) due north of Vitré via D178 and D798 is **Fougères**, a traditional cobbling and cider-making center. For many centuries, it was a frontier town, valiantly attempting to guard Brittany against attack. Perhaps one of the reasons for its conspicuous lack of success is the site of the **castle:** Instead of sitting high up on the hill, it spreads out down in the valley, though the sinuous River Nançon does make an admirable moat. The 13-towered castle covers over five acres, making it one of the largest in Europe. Although largely in ruins, it is impressive both inside and out. The thick walls—up to 20 feet across in places—were intended to resist 15th-century artillery fire, but the castle was to prove vulnerable to surprise attacks and sieges. A visit inside the castle walls reveals three lines of fortification, with the cosseted keep at their heart. There are charming views over Fougères from the Tour Mélusine and, in the Tour Raoul, a small shoe museum. The second and third stories of the Tour de Coigny were transformed into a chapel during the 16th century. *East end of town on pl. Raoul II. Admission: 12 frs. Open Apr.–Oct., daily 10–noon and 2–5; closed Nov.–Mar.*

The oldest streets of Fougères are alongside the castle, clustered around the elegant slate spire of **St-Sulpice** (rue de Lusignan), a Flamboyant Gothic church holding several fine altarpieces. A number of medieval houses line rue de la Pinterie, leading directly from the castle up to the undistinguished heart of town.

In the 1790s, Fougères was a center of Royalist resistance to the French Revolution. Much of the action in 19th-century novelist Honoré de Balzac's bloodcurdling novel *Les Chouans* takes place hereabouts; the novel's heroine, Marie de Verneuil, had rooms close to the church of **St-Léonard** (follow the river left from the castle), which overlooks the Nançon Valley. Both path and church, with its ornate facade and 17th-century tower, have changed little; the garden through which the path leads is known today as the **Jardin Public.**

Another man who was inspired by the scenery of Fougères was locally-born Emmanuel de La Villéon (1858–1944), a little-known Impressionist painter. His works are displayed in the **Musée La Villéon,** in one of the oldest surviving houses in hilltop Fougères; to reach it from the Jardin Public, head left past St-Léonard, and cross the square into the adjacent rue Nationale. The more than 100 paintings, pastels, watercolors, and drawings suggest serene, underestimated talent. The artist's work ranges from compassionate studies of toiling peasants to pretty landscapes in which soft shades of green melt into hazy blue horizons. *51 rue Nationale. Admission: 8 frs. Open Easter–mid-June, weekends only, 11–12:30 and 2:30–5; mid-June–mid-Sept., daily 10:30–12:30.*

③ Rennes (pronounced "wren"), lying 48 kilometers (30 miles) southwest, is the traditional capital of Brittany. It has a different flavor from other towns in the region, mainly because of a terrible fire in 1720, which lasted a week and destroyed half the city. The remaining cobbled streets and half-timbered, 15th-century houses make an interesting contrast with the Classical feel of Jacques Gabriel's disciplined granite buildings, broad avenues, and spacious squares.

Start at the west end of the old town, bordered by the River Rance. The **Cathédrale St-Pierre,** an early 19th-century building in Classical style, looms above rue de la Monnaie. Stop in to admire its richly decorated interior and outstanding 16th-century Flemish altarpiece. *Pl. St-Pierre. Open Sept.–June, daily 8:30–noon and 2–5; July–Aug., Mon.–Sat. 8:30–noon and 2–5, Sun. 8:30–noon.*

Time Out The swinging youths of Rennes have a nighttime rendezvous at the **Babylone Bar** (12 rue des Dames), next to the cathedral. This isn't a place to linger in, but try it for a tangy, premeal aperitif or end-of-evening, cream-and-brandy cocktail.

The surrounding streets are full of 15th- and 16th-century houses in both medieval and Renaissance styles. Many have been converted for use as shops, boutiques, restaurants, and pancake houses; a lively **street market** is held in and around place des Lices on Saturday morning.

The pedestrian rue Lafayette and rue Nationale lead to the **Palais de Justice** (Law Courts). This palatial building, originally home to the Breton Parliament, was designed in 1618 by Salomon de Brosse, architect of the Luxembourg Palace in Paris, and was the most important building in Rennes to escape the 1720 fire. After admiring its white stone-and-granite facade, venture inside to view the splendid interior. Among its various magnificent halls is the richly carved and painted **Grand' Chambre,** a former parliamentary chamber whose walls are covered with Gobelin tapestries that retrace the history of Brittany. *Pl. du Parlement. Admission: 15 frs. Open Wed.– Mon. 10–noon and 2–6; closed Tues.*

Head down from the Palais de Justice and left across quai Emile-Zola to the **Palais des Musées,** a huge building containing two museums—the **Musée des Beaux-Arts** and **Musée de Bretagne.** The Fine Arts Museum on the second floor houses one of the country's best collections of paintings outside Paris, featuring works by Georges de la Tour, Jean-Baptiste Chardin, Camille Corot, Paul Gauguin, and Maurice Utrillo, to name only a few. The ground-floor Museum of Brittany retraces the region's history, period by period, by way of costumes, models, porcelain, furniture, coins, statues, and shiny push-button visual displays. *20 quai Emile-Zola. Admission: joint ticket 18 frs. adults, 9 frs. children under 14.*

Northeast of the museum building, a five-minute walk via rue Gambetta and rue Victor-Hugo, is the **Jardin du Thabor,** a large, formal French garden with regimented rows of trees, shrubs, and flowers. Even the lawns are manicured—not often the case in France. There is a notable view of the church of **Notre-Dame-en-St-Mélaine** in one corner.

North of Rennes, the landscape is dotted with hefty castles and enticing châteaux. Twenty-four kilometers (15 miles) away via N137 and D27 is the castle of **Montmuran,** closely associated with Brittany's warrior-hero Bertrand du Guesclin; here, he was knighted in 1354 and married his second wife in 1372. An alley of oak and beech trees leads up to the main 18th-century building, which is surrounded by a moat and flanked by four towers, two built in the 12th century, two in the 14th. You can visit the towers and a small museum devoted to the castle's history. *Admission: 16 frs. Open Easter–Oct., daily 2–7; Nov.– Easter, weekends only, 2–6.*

⑤ Just 8 kilometers (5 miles) west is **Caradeuc,** a Classical château ambitiously dubbed the "Versailles of Brittany." Visitors can't go inside to check out this claim, unfortunately, but to compensate, explore the surrounding park—Brittany's largest—and admire its statues, flower beds, and leafy alleys. *Admission: 12 frs. Open Apr.–Oct., daily 9–noon and 1:30–8; Nov.–Mar., weekends only, 2–6.*

⑥ Take D20 to Tinténiac, then N137 north to **La Bourbansais**, a total of 19 kilometers (12 miles) from Caradeuc. This castle has remained in the same family since it was founded by local lord Jean de Breil in 1583. It, too, has extensive gardens, containing a small zoo and a pack of hunting hounds. The buildings were enlarged in the 18th century, and the majority of the interior furnishings date from that period. There are fine collections of porcelain and tapestries. *Admission: 32 frs. Castle open Apr.– Oct., daily 2–6; Nov.–Mar., weekends only, 2–6. Park open daily 10–noon and 2–7.*

⑦ **Combourg,** best known as the boyhood home of Romantic writer Viscount Chateaubriand (1768–1848), is 11 kilometers (7 miles) east along D75 and D794. The thick-walled, four-towered castle dates mainly from the 14th and 15th centuries and contains a roomful of Chateaubriand archives. You can visit the writer's austere bedroom in the Tour du Chat (Cat's Tower). The castle grounds—ponds, woods, and half-tended lawns— are suitably mournful and can seem positively desolate under leaden skies. *Admission: 22 frs., park only 11 frs. Castle open Mar.–Nov., Wed.–Mon. 2–5; closed Tues. Park open Mar.– Nov., Wed.–Mon. 9–noon and 2–5.*

⑧ Seventeen kilometers (10 miles) north via D795, the ancient town of **Dol-de-Bretagne** looks out from its 60-foot cliffs over Le Marais, a marshy plain stretching across to Mont St-Michel, 21 kilometers (13 miles) northeast. The **Promenade des Douves,** laid out along the northern part of the original ramparts, offers extensive views of Le Marais and Mont Dol, a 200-foot granite mound, 3 kilometers (2 miles) north, legendary scene of combat between St. Michael and the devil. Unfortunately, the stately trees that line the promenade suffered heavily in a 1987 hurricane.

At the end of the promenade, note the **Cathédrale St-Samson** (pl. de la Cathédrale), a damp, soaring, fortresslike bulk of granite dating mainly from the 12th to the 14th century. This mighty building shows just how influential the bishopric of Dol was in days gone by. The richly sculpted Great Porch, carved wooden choir stalls, and stained glass in the chancel all deserve close scrutiny.

Turn down rue des Ecoles to the small **Musée Historique d'Art Populaire**. During a short, cheerful guided tour, you'll see costumes, weapons, and a series of scale models retracing life in Dol since prehistoric times. The glory of the museum, though, is its assembly of colored wooden religious statues. *Rue des Ecoles. Admission: 14 frs. Open Apr.–Sept., Wed.–Mon. 10–5; closed Tues.*

Rue des Ecoles leads to Dol's picturesque main street, Grand-Rue des Stuarts, lined with medieval houses. The oldest, at no. 17, boasts a chunky row of Romanesque arches.

❾ From Dol, take N176 to **Dinan**, 24 kilometers (15 miles) southwest. Dinan has close links with Brittany's 14th-century anti-English warrior-hero Bertrand du Guesclin, whose name is commemorated in countless squares and hostelries across the province. Du Guesclin won a famous victory here in 1359 and promptly married a local girl, Tiphaine Raguenel. When he died in the siege of Auvergne (central France) in 1380, his body was dispatched home to Dinan. Owing to the great man's popularity, however, only his heart completed the journey—the rest of him having been confiscated by devoted followers in towns along the route.

Begin your stroll around the old town at the tourist office, housed in a charming 16th-century building in rue de l'Horloge. For a superb view of the town, climb to the top of the nearby belfry, the **Tour de l'Horloge**. *Admission: 5 frs. Open July–Aug., Mon.–Sat. 10–noon and 2–6.*

Turn left and head half a block along to admire the triangular-gabled wooden houses in **place des Merciers, rue de l'Apport,** and **rue de la Poissonnerie.** With their overhanging balconies and black-and-white half-timbered houses, these cobbled streets are so pretty you may think you've stumbled into a Hollywood movie set. Restore your faith with a visit to the nearby church, the **Basilique St-Sauveur** (turn right out of place des Merciers along rue Haute-Voie, then take the second left into the church square). The church is a mixture of styles, ranging from the Romanesque south front to the Flamboyant Gothic facade and Renaissance side chapels. Du Guesclin's heart lies in the north transept.

The **Jardin Anglais** (English Garden) is just behind the church; it's not really much of a garden, but its old trees nicely frame the east end of St-Sauveur. More spectacular views are found at the bottom of the garden, which looks down the plummeting Rance Valley to the river 250 feet below.

Leading down to the harbor, rue du Jerzual is a beautifully preserved medieval street, full of boutiques and crafts shops, divided halfway down by the town walls and massive Porte du Jerzual gateway.

Time Out Wool yarn by the yard and English cakes and scones by the dozen: That's the unlikely combination you'll find at this strange little American-run outfit, **La Toison d'Or** (Rue du Jerzual), long wooden benches add to the atmosphere, if not the comfort, as you settle down for a cup of coffee and a snack.

Dinan's harbor seems somewhat forlorn; although there are sailings in summer up the River Rance to Dinard and St-Malo, abandoned warehouses bear witness to vanished commercial activity, with only an occasional restaurant to brighten up the place.

Time Out   Just across the Vieux Pont, in what is officially the village of Lanvallay, is **Le Transfert** cocktail bar, whose cool-gray decor wouldn't be out of place in some trendy *quartier* of Paris. The cocktails are imaginative and inexpensive, and you can enjoy them in peace and quiet while drinking in the tranquil views over the River Rance and the old part of Dinan. *8 bis rue du Four, Lanvallay. Open 6 PM–2AM.*

Stagger back up the hill (it's steep) and turn right, well after the Porte du Jerzual, into rue de l'Ecole. This street leads down to another gateway, the Porte St-Malo, from which the leafy Promenade des Grands Fossés heads left on a tour of the best-preserved section of the town walls. Follow these walls around as far as the **castle.** Here you can visit the two-story Coëtquen Tower and 100-foot 14th-century keep, containing varied displays of medieval effigies and statues, Breton furniture, and local *coiffes* (bonnets). *Porte de Guichet. Admission: 14 frs. Open June–Aug., 9–noon and 2–7, Sept.–Oct. and Mar.–May, 9–noon and 2–6, Nov.–Feb., 2–5; closed Tues.*

🔟 **Dinard** is a stylish, slightly snobbish vacation resort, 22 kilometers (14 miles) north on D266, or farther away if you follow the picturesque meanderings of the Rance. The town may be fraying on the edges these days, but its picture-book setting on the Rance Estuary opposite St-Malo makes up for any shabbiness. Until the middle of the last century, Dinard was a minor fishing village. It became all the rage, thanks to propaganda from a rich American named Coppinger; avenues were baptized Edward VII and George V as English royalty jumped on the bandwagon. Grand hotels and luxurious villas are still plentiful.

It's not hard to see why uppercrust Edwardians loved the place, with its dramatic cliffs, lush vegetation, bracing coastal walks, and three sandy beaches. To make the most of Dinard's exhilarating setting, head down to the town's southern tip, the **Pointe de la Vicomté,** where cliffs offer panoramic views across the Baie du Prieuré and Rance Estuary. The **Plage du Prieuré,** named after a priory that once stood here, is a sandy beach ringed by yachts, dinghies, and motorboats. The **Clair de Lune Promenade** hugs the seacoast on its way toward the English Channel, passing in front of the small jetty used by boats crossing to St-Malo. Shortly after, the street reaches the **Musée de la Mer** (Marine Museum and Aquarium). Virtually every known species of Breton bird and sea creature is on display here, in two rooms and 24 pools. Another room is devoted to the polar expeditions of explorer Jean Charcot, one of the first men to chart the Antarctic; there are poignant souvenirs of his last voyage, in 1936, from which he never returned. *Claire de Lune Promenade. Admission: 10 frs. Open Pentecost Sun.–Sept., daily 10–noon and 2–6.*

The Clair de Lune Promenade, lined with luxuriant semitropical vegetation, really hits its stride as it rounds the Pointe du Moulinet to the Prieuré Beach. River meets sea in a foaming mass of rock-pounding surf, and caution is needed as you walk along the slippery path. Your reward: the calm and shelter of the **Plage de l'Ecluse,** an inviting sandy beach, bordered by a casino and numerous stylish hotels. The coastal path picks up again on the far side, ringing the Pointe de la Malouine and Pointe des Etêtés before arriving at Dinard's final beach, the **Plage de St-Enogat.**

Little more than a mile from Dinard by water, but 13 kilometers (8 miles) by road, is the ancient walled town of **St-Malo.** The stone ramparts of this onetime pirate base have stood firm against the Atlantic since the 13th century. The town itself has proved less resistant: A week-long fire in 1944, kindled by retreating Nazis, wiped out nearly all the old buildings. Restoration work was more painstaking than brilliant, but the narrow streets and granite houses of the old town, known as *Intra Muros* ("within the walls") have been satisfactorily recreated, enabling St-Malo to regain its role as a busy fishing port and seaside resort.

North American visitors can pay homage here to Jacques Cartier, who set sail from St-Malo in 1535 to discover the St. Lawrence River and found Quebec. Cartier's tomb is in the church of **St-Vincent** (off Grande-Rue), while his statue looks out over the town ramparts, four blocks away—along with that of swashbuckling corsair Robert Surcouf, hero of many daring 18th-century raids on the British Navy (he's the one pointing an accusing finger over the waves at *l'Angleterre*). The ramparts themselves date from the 12th century, but were considerably enlarged and modified in the 18th. They extend from the castle in St-Malo's northeast corner and ring the old town, with a total length of over a mile. The views from the ramparts are stupendous, especially at high tide. Five hundred yards offshore is the **Ile du Grand Bé,** a small island housing the somber military tomb of Viscount Chateaubriand, who was born in St-Malo. The islet can be reached by a causeway at low tide, as can the **Fort National,** a massive fortress with a dungeon constructed in 1689 by that military-engineering genius, Sébastien de Vauban. *By the castle. Admission: 8 frs. Open Apr.–Sept., daily 9:30–noon and 2:30–6.*

At the edge of the ramparts, overlooking the Fort National, is **St-Malo Castle,** whose great keep and watchtowers command an impressive view of the harbor and coastline. The castle houses two museums: the **Musée de la Ville,** devoted to local history, and the **Quic-en-Grogne,** a tower where various episodes and celebrities from St-Malo's past are recalled by way of waxwork reconstruction. *Porte St-Vincent. Admission: 10 frs. (Musée de la Ville), 15 frs. (Quic-en-Grogne). Open Apr.–Sept., daily 9:30–noon and 2–6:30; closed Tues. Oct.–Mar.*

Anyone who enjoys eating oysters should make the 13-kilometer (8-mile) trip east on D355 to **Cancale,** renowned for its oyster beds. You'll find lots of quayside restaurants in which to sample this delicacy. The town's delightful seaside setting is also an attraction.

Tour 2: Brittany's Western Coast

Our second tour begins at **Morlaix** (pronounced "Morley"), far to the west of St-Malo—144 kilometers (90 miles) by fast N12, considerably longer if you meander along the spectacular coastal road (D786 and D788) via Perros-Guirec and Lannion. Morlaix's town-spanning, 19th-century, two-tiered rail viaduct is an unforgettable sight—300 yards long and 200 feet high. Though there are no major sights in Morlaix, the old town is an attractive mix of half-timbered houses and low-fronted shops that rewards unhurried exploration. The pedestrian Grand' Rue is its commercial heart, lined with quaint 15th-century houses. The **Maison de la Reine Anne,** in adjacent rue du Mur, is a three-story 16th-century building adorned with statuettes of saints.

Just off rue d'Aiguillon, which runs parallel to Grand' Rue, is the town museum, known as the **Musée des Jacobins** because it is housed in the former Jacobin church; an early 15th-century rose window survives at one end as a reminder. The museum's eclectic display ranges from religious statues to archaeological findings and modern paintings. *Pl. des Jacobins. Admission: 10 frs. Open July–Aug., daily 10–noon and 2–6; Apr.–June and Sept.–Oct., Wed.–Mon. 10–noon and 2–6; Nov.–Mar., Wed.–Mon. 10–noon and 2–5.*

⑭ D73 hugs the riverbank north of Morlaix; branch left at Kerdanet and follow signs for **St-Pol-de-Léon,** 10 kilometers (6 miles) farther away. St-Pol is a lively market town dominated by three spires: Two belong to the cathedral, the highest to the Chapelle du Kreisker. The **Ancienne Cathédrale,** built between the 13th and 16th centuries, is pleasingly proportioned, and its finely carved 16th-century choir stalls are worth a trip inside. Rue du Général-Leclerc, with its large wood-framed houses, links the cathedral to the **Chapelle du Kreisker,** originally used for meetings by the town council. Its magnificent 250-foot 15th-century granite spire, flanked at each corner by tiny spirelets known as *fillettes* ("young girls"), is the prototype for countless Brittany bell towers. From the top there is a rewarding view across the Bay of Morlaix toward the English Channel. *Access to the tower mid-June–mid-Sept., daily 10–noon and 2–5. Admission: 5 frs.*

⑮ Just 5 kilometers (3 miles) north of St-Pol along D58 is the burgeoning port of Roscoff. From here, head 24 kilometers (15 miles) southwest toward Brest before turning right onto D30 and making for the nearby 15th-century château of **Kerjean.** With its vast park, ditch, and 40-foot-thick defensive walls, Kerjean at first looks like a fortress until you see the large windows, tall chimney stacks, and high-pitched roofs of its main buildings. The chapel, kitchens, and main apartments, full of regional furniture, can be visited. Temporary exhibitions are held in the stable wing. Notice the old well in the main courtyard. *Admission: 22 frs. Open Sept.–June, Wed.–Mon. 10–noon and 2–7; July–Aug., Wed.–Mon. 10–7.*

⑯ Sixteen kilometers (10 miles) west of Kerjean along D788 is **Le Folgoët** and its splendid **Notre-Dame basilica,** whose sturdy north tower, visible from afar, beckons pilgrims to the *pardon* (religious festival) held here in early September. On this occasion, many pilgrims drink at the Salaün fountain against the wall behind the church; its water comes from a spring beneath the altar, which can be reached through a sculpted porch. Inside the church is a rare, intricately worked, granite roodscreen separating the choir and nave.

⑰ Continue along D788 to the maritime city of **Brest,** 24 kilometers (15 miles) southwest. Brest's enormous, sheltered bay is strategically positioned close to the Atlantic and the English Channel. During World War II, Brest was used by the Germans as a naval base; it was liberated in 1944 by American forces, after a 43-day siege that left the city in ruins. Postwar reconstruction, resulting in long, straight streets of reinforced concrete, has left latter-day Brest with the unenviable reputation of being one of France's ugliest cities. Its waterfront, however, is worth visiting for the few old buildings and museums, as well as for dramatic views across the bay toward the Plougastel Peninsula.

Begin your visit at one of the town's oldest monuments, the **Tour Tanguy.** This bulky, round 14th-century tower, once used as a lookout post, is a majestic sight in its own right; the interior contains a museum of local history with scale models of the Brest of yore. *Admission free. Open Oct.–May, Thurs. and weekends 2–6; June and Sept., daily 2–7; July–Aug., daily 10–noon and 2–7.*

Next to the tower is the River Penfeld and, crossing it, the Pont de Recouvrance, at 95 yards Europe's longest lift-bridge. On the other side, Brest's medieval castle is home to the **Musée de la Marine** (Naval Museum), containing boat models, sculpture, pictures, and naval instruments. A section is devoted to the castle's 700-year history. The dungeons can also be visited. *Admission: 18 frs. adults, 9 frs. children under 12. Open Wed.–Mon. 9:15–noon and 2:20–6; closed Tues.*

A short walk inland leads to the **Musée Municipal** in rue Traverse. French, Flemish, and Italian paintings, spanning the 17th to the 20th century, make up the collection. *Rue Emile-Zola. Admission free. Open Wed.–Sat. and Mon. 10–11:45 and 2–6:45, Sun. 2–6:45; closed Tues.*

Farther east, overlooking the Moulin Blanc marina, is the brand-new, futuristic **Océanopolis** center. Maritime technology, fauna, and flora are the themes of its exhibits, but the biggest attraction is the aquarium—the largest in Europe. *Rue Alain-Colas. Admission: 40 frs. Open Tues.–Sun. 10–12 and 2–6.*

⓲ Southbound N165, which leaves Brest for Quimper, 104 kilometers (65 miles) away, soon passes through **Daoulas,** where you can stop off to admire the *Enclos Paroissial* (literally, "parish enclosure") and the 12th-century Romanesque abbey, with its cloisters and herbal garden. Keep on N165 to Port Launay, **⓳** then branch off southwest along scenic D7 to **Locronan,** a typical old weaving town with a magnificently preserved ensemble of houses, main square, and 15th-century church.

⓴ **Douarnenez,** 10 kilometers (6 miles) west of Locronan via D7, is a quaint old fishing town of quayside paths and narrow streets. Sailing enthusiasts will be interested in the town's biennial classic boat rally in mid-August (the next event will take place in 1992), when traditionally rigged sailing boats of every description ply the waters of the picturesque Bay of Douarnenez.

㉑ From Douarnenez, take D765 southeast to **Quimper.** This lively commercial town is the ancient capital of the Cornouaille province, founded, it is said, by King Gradlon 1,500 years ago. Quimper (pronounced "cam-pair") owes its strange-looking name to its site at the confluence *(kemper* in Breton) of the Odet and Steir rivers. The banks of the Odet make a charming place to stroll. Highlights of the old town include **rue Kéréon,** a lively shopping street, and the stately **Jardin de l'Evêché** (Bishop's Gardens) behind the cathedral in the center of the old town.

The **Cathédrale St-Corentin** is a masterpiece of Gothic architecture and the second-largest cathedral in Brittany (after that of Dol). Legendary King Gradlon is represented on horseback just below the base of the spires, harmonious mid-19th-century additions to the medieval ensemble. The luminous 15th-century stained glass is particularly striking. *Pl. St-Corentin.*

Two museums flank the cathedral. Works by major masters, such as Rubens, Corot, and Picasso, mingle with pretty landscapes from the local Gauguin-inspired Pont-Aven school in the **Musée des Beaux-Arts** (Fine Arts Museum; *admission 20 frs.; open Wed.–Mon. 9:30–noon and 1–5),* while local furniture, ceramics, and folklore top the bill in the **Musée Départemental** (Regional Museum) in adjacent rue du Roi-Gradlon (*admission 10 frs.; open mid-Sept.–Apr., Wed.–Sun. 9–noon and 2–5, May–mid-Sept., Wed.–Mon. 9–noon and 2–5).*

Quimper sprang to nationwide attention as an earthenware center in the mid-18th century, when it started producing second-rate imitations of the Rouen ceramics known as faïence, featuring blue Oriental motifs. Today's more-colorful designs, based on floral arrangements and marine fauna, are still often handpainted. There are guided visits to the main pottery, the **Faïencerie Henriot,** and its museum, situated on the banks of the Odet south of the old town. *Allée de Locmaria. Admission: 12 frs. Open Mon.–Thurs. 9:30–11 and 1:30–4:30; Fri. 9:30–11 and 1:30–3.*

② Pretty **Concarneau**, 21 kilometers (13 miles) from Quimper along D783, stands at the mouth of the Baie de la Forêt, facing south across the Atlantic toward the desolate Islands of Glénan. Concarneau is the third-largest fishing port in France. During its *criée,* an early morning auction held from Monday to Thursday, local fishwives can be heard in full cry as they sell off the recent catch.

The **Ville Close,** the fortified islet in the middle of the harbor, is Concarneau's main attraction. To reach it, you must cross a drawbridge. The islet's narrow streets and huge granite ramparts make for an enjoyable afternoon's roam, though rue Vauban—the main street—contains a lot of tacky souvenir shops; ignore them and concentrate on the fantastic views of the bay. From early medieval times, Concarneau was regarded as impregnable, and the fortifications were further strengthened by the English under John de Montfort during the War of Succession (1341–64). This enabled the English-controlled Concarneau to withstand two sieges by Breton hero Bertrand du Guesclin; the third siege was successful for the plucky du Guesclin, who drove out the English in 1373. Three hundred years later, Sébastien de Vauban remodeled the ramparts into what you see today: half a mile long and highly scenic, offering views across the two harbors on either side of the Ville Close. *Admission to ramparts: 5 frs. Open Easter–Sept., daily 9–7; winter 10–5.*

At the end of rue Vauban closest to the drawbridge is the **Musée de la Pêche** (Fishing Museum), occupying an enormous hall in the former arsenal. Here you will encounter historical explanations of fishing techniques from around the world, plus such displays as an antiwhale harpoon gun and a giant Japanese crab. Turtles and fish may be seen in the museum's many aquariums. *Admission: 25 frs. Open Sept.–June, daily 10–12:30 and 2–7; July–Aug., daily 10–8.*

If you're in Concarneau in the second half of August, you will be able to enjoy the Fête des Filets Bleus (Blue Net Festival) in the Ville Close. This festival used to involve simply blessing the nets before the fishing season, but it has now become a week-long folk celebration in which Bretons in costume swirl and dance to the wail of bagpipes.

N165 speeds down the coast, past the industrial port of Lorient, as far as Auray. Here, take D768 southwest toward Carnac at the northern end of the 10-mile-long Quiberon Peninsula, dangling off the Brittany coast. The Côte Sauvage (Wild Coast) on the west of the peninsula is a savage mix of crevices, coves, and rocky grottoes lashed by violent seas.

㉓ **Quiberon** itself is famed for more soothing waters: It is a spa town with fine, relaxing beaches.

Time Out In a country where gourmandism is virtually a cultural pursuit, **Henri Le Roux** (18 rue du Port-Maria) has taken the art of chocolateering to dizzying heights. Check out his delicious displays—created before your very eyes—at his shop near Quiberon harbor.

The cheerful harbor of Port-Maria is the base for boat trips to nearby Belle-Ile, at 11 miles long the largest of Brittany's islands. Because of the cost and inconvenience of reserving car-berths on the ferry, it's best to cross to Belle-Ile as a pedestrian and rent a car—or, better still, a bicycle—on the island.

㉔ Despite being a mere 45-minute boat trip from Quiberon, **Belle-Ile** is much less commercialized, and exhilarating scenery is its main appeal. Near Sauzon, the island's prettiest settlement, is a staggering view across to the Quiberon Peninsula and Gulf of Morbihan from the **Pointe des Poulains**, erstwhile home of the Belle Epoque's femme fatale, actress Sarah Bernhardt. The nearby **Grotte de l'Apothicairerie** is a grotto whose name derives from the local cormorants' nests, said to resemble pharmacy bottles. Farther south, near Port Goulphar, is another dramatic sight—the **Grand Phare** (lighthouse), built in 1835 and rising 275 feet above sea level. Its light is one of the most powerful in Europe, visible from 75 miles across the Atlantic. If the keeper is available, you may be able to climb to the top and admire the view.

㉕ Once back on the mainland, return to **Carnac** at the north end of Quiberon Bay. Carnac is famed for its beaches and, especially, its **megalithic monuments** dating from the Neolithic/Early Bronze Ages (3500–1800 BC). The whys and wherefores of their construction remain as obscure as those of their English contemporary, Stonehenge, although religious beliefs and astrology were doubtless an influence. The 2,395 menhirs that make up the three *Alignements* (Kermario, Kerlescan, and Ménec) are positioned with astounding astronomical accuracy in semicircles and parallel lines over half a mile long. There are also smaller-scale dolmen ensembles and three tumuli (mounds or barrows), including the 130-yard-long **Tumulus de St-Michel,** topped by a small chapel affording fine views of the rock-strewn countryside. *Guided tours of the tumulus daily Apr.–Sept. Cost: 5 frs.*

26 Just east of Carnac lies the yachtsman's paradise of **La Trinité-sur-Mer,** a resort town ringed by sandy beaches and oyster beds, and much favored by wealthy Parisians wanting a home-away-from-home vacation. From La Trinité, head up D781 and

27 D28 to Auray, then take N165 east to **Vannes** (pronounced "van"). Scene of the declaration of unity between France and Brittany in 1532, it's one of the few towns in Brittany to have been spared damage during World War II, so its authentic regional charm remains intact. Be sure to visit the **Cohue** (medieval market hall—now a temporary exhibition center) and the picturesque **place Henri IV** and browse in the small boutiques and antiques shops in the surrounding pedestrian streets. The ramparts, Promenade de la Garenne, and medieval wash-houses are all set against the backdrop of the much-restored **Cathédrale St-Pierre,** with its 1537 Renaissance chapel, Flamboyant Gothic transept portal, and treasury in the old chapterhouse. *Pl. du Cathédrale. Admission: 3 frs. Treasury open mid-June–mid-Sept., Mon.–Sat. 10–noon and 2–6.*

From Vannes, N165 goes to Muzillac, 19 kilometers (12 miles) away, from which D20 veers 43 kilometers (27 miles) east to the

28 little town of **Redon,** built at the junction of the River Vilaine and the Nantes–Brest canal. These days, Redon harbor is used exclusively by pleasure boats, but it was once a busy commercial port. A number of stylish 17th–19th-century mansions, with large windows and wrought-iron balconies, line the adjacent quays. Wood-framed medieval houses line the main street, Grande Rue, which is dominated by the slender spire and magnificent Romanesque tower of the church of **St-Sauveur,** all that remains of a once-powerful Benedictine abbey.

29 Head due south from Redon, via D114, to **Missillac,** at the edge of the **Grande Brière Regional Park.** This low-lying marshy area, crisscrossed by narrow canals, can be explored either by boat (trips are organized from St-Nazaire) or by car along D51 as you head southwest toward La Baule. Ever since a ducal edict of 1461, La Brière has been the common property of its inhabitants, who live in distinctive and picturesque white thatched cottages. Highlights include the panoramic view from the church tower at **St-Lyphard** and the curious **Kerbourg dolmen** 5 kilometers (3 miles) south, just off D47.

30 **La Baule,** 18 kilometers (11 miles) from St-Lyphard, is one of the most fashionable resorts in France. Like Le Touquet and Dinard, it is a 19th-century creation, founded in 1879 to make the most of the excellent sandy beaches that extend for 6 miles around the broad, sheltered bay between Pornichet and Le Pouliguen. A pine forest, planted in 1840, keeps the shifting local sand dunes firmly at bay.

An air of old-fashioned chic still pervades La Baule's palatial hotels, villas, and flowered gardens, but there's nothing old-fashioned about the prices: Hotels and restaurants should be chosen with care. Nightclubbers will be in their element here, while the resort's summer season buzzes with prestigious events, such as show jumping of horses, and classic car contests. The elegant promenade, overlooking the huge beach, is lined with luxury hotels and features a casino.

31 From La Baule head 72 kilometers (45 miles) east, past St-Nazaire and its struggling shipyard, to **Nantes,** a tranquil, prosperous city that seems to pursue its existence without too much concern for what's going on elsewhere in France. Although Nantes is not really part of Brittany—officially it belongs to the Pays de la Loire—the dukes of Brittany were in no doubt that Nantes belonged to their domain, and the castle they built is the city's principal tourist attraction.

Numbers in the margin correspond with points of interest on the Nantes map.

㉜ The **Château des Ducs de Bretagne** is a massive, well-preserved 15th-century fortress with a neatly grassed moat. The duke responsible for building most of it was François II, who led a hedonistic existence here, surrounded by ministers, chamberlains, and an army of servants. Numerous monarchs later stayed in the castle, where, in 1598, Henri IV signed the famous Edict of Nantes advocating religious tolerance.

Within the Harnachement—a separate building inside the castle walls—you'll find the **Musée des Salorges** (Naval Museum), devoted principally to the history of seafaring; a separate section outlines the triangular trade that involved transportation of African blacks to America to be sold as slaves. As you cross the courtyard to the Grand Gouvernement wing, home to the **Musée d'Art Populaire Régional** (Regional Folk Art Museum), look for the old well, where the ducal coat of arms is entwined in some magnificent wrought-iron decoration. The Musée d'Art Populaire features an array of armor, furniture, 19th-century Breton costumes, and reconstituted interiors illustrating the former life in the Vendée region to the south. *Just off rue du Château. Admission: 15 frs., free Sun. Castle and museums open Sept.–June, Wed.–Mon. 10–noon and 2–6, closed Tues.; July–Aug., daily 10–noon and 2–6.*

㉝ Opposite the castle is the **Cathédrale St-Pierre,** one of France's latest Gothic cathedrals; building began only in 1434, well after most other medieval cathedrals had been completed. The facade is ponderous and austere, in contrast to the light, wide, elegant interior, whose vaults rise higher (120 feet) than those of Notre-Dame in Paris. In the transept, notice Michel Colombe's early 16th-century tomb of François II and his wife, Marguerite de Foix, which is one of France's finest examples of funerary sculpture. *Pl. St-Pierre.*

㉞ Behind the cathedral, past the 15th-century Porte St-Pierre, is the **Musée des Beaux-Arts** (Fine Arts Museum), with a fine collection of paintings from the Renaissance on, featuring works by Jacopo Tintoretto, Georges de la Tour, Jean-Auguste Ingres, and Gustave Courbet. *10 rue G-Clemenceau. Admission: 10 frs., free Sun. Open Wed.–Mon. 10–noon and 2–5.*

The cobbled streets around the castle and cathedral make up the town's medieval sector. Across cours des 50 Otages, a broad boulevard, is the 19th-century city. From place Royale stroll and window-shop down busy rue Crébillon. Halfway down on
㉟ the left is the **Passage Pommeraye,** an elegant shopping gallery erected in 1843. At the far end of rue Crébillon is place Graslin
㊱ and its 1783 **Grand Théâtre.**

Time Out Miniature palm trees, gleaming woodwork, colorful enamel tiles, and painted ceilings have led to **La Cigale** (4 pl. Graslin) being officially recognized as a *monument historique.* You can savor its Belle Epoque ambience without spending a fortune: The 69- and 120-franc menus are just right for a quick lunch,

Cathédrale
St-Pierre, **33**

Château des Ducs de
Bretagne, **32**

Grand Theater, **36**

Manoir de la
Touche, **37**

Musée des
Beaux-Arts, **34**

Palais Dobrée, **38**

Passage
Pommeraye, **35**

although the banks of fresh oysters and the well-stacked dessert cart may tempt you to go for a leisurely meal à la carte.

Just along rue Voltaire from place Graslin is the 15th-century **Manoir de la Touche,** once home to the bishops of Nantes. Its medieval silhouette is offset by the mock-Romanesque **Palais Dobrée,** next door, built by arts connoisseur Thomas Dobrée during the last century. Among the treasures within are miniatures, tapestries, medieval manuscripts, and enamels, while one room is devoted to the Revolutionary Wars in Vendée. *Pl. Jean V. Admission: 10 frs., free Sun. Open Wed.–Mon. 10–noon and 2–5; closed Tues.*

What to See and Do with Children

Boat trips make entertaining excursions for old and young alike. Some of the most scenic include the tour of the Golfe du Morbihan (depart from Vannes), sea jaunts from Dinard or St-Malo to the Ile de Cézembre or along the rugged coast to Cap Fréhel, cruises up the River Rance from Dinard to Dinan, and the frequent 10-minute crossings between Dinard and St-Malo. (For information on trips to the numerous islands off the Brittany shore, *see* Off the Beaten Track, below.)

These other attractions are described in the Exploring section:

Château des Ducs de Bretagne, Nantes, Tour 2.
Fougères Castle, Tour 1.
Grand Phare (Lighthouse), Belle-Ile, Tour 2.

Musée de Bretagne, Rennes, Tour 1.
Musée de la Mer, Dinard, Tour 1.
Musée de la Pêche, Concarneau, Tour 2.
Océanopolis, Brest, Tour 2.
Vitré Castle, Tour 1.

Off the Beaten Track

You may enjoy visiting the inland countryside, particularly some of the spectacular castles north of Vannes. The first of these castles, set in a wooded park 19 kilometers (12 miles) from Vannes via N166, is the **Fortress of Largoët** near Elven. Its 170-foot 14th-century octagonal keep is the highest in France; its walls are up to 30 feet thick. Alongside is a faithfully restored 15th-century tower. Henry Tudor was held prisoner here before his return to England and the triumphant 1485 military campaign that led to his becoming Henry VII. *Admission: 13 frs. Open Apr.–Oct., daily 9–6.*

Continue along N166 past Brignac—a round 15th-century tower is all that remains of the fortress that once stood here—to La Chapelle. The elegant, nearby château of **Le Crêvy** houses a collection of costumes dating from 1730.

Sixteen kilometers (10 miles) northwest along D4 is **Josselin,** a picturesque medieval town. **Josselin Castle** has two faces. Overlooking the River Oust is a defensive stronghold with three stout turreted towers linked by austere, near-windowless walls. The landward facade, however, is a riot of intricate pinnacles, gables, and stone ornament, surrounded by gardens. You can visit the library, wood-paneled dining room, portrait gallery, and Grand Salon, with its ornate fireplace (only the ground floor is open to the public). *Admission: 21 frs. Open Apr.–May, Wed. and Sun. 2–6; June, daily 2–6; July–Aug., daily 10–noon and 2–6; Sept., daily 2–6.*

Another attraction in Josselin is the 500-strong collection of old dolls displayed in the former castle stables. Many are dressed in traditional costume; most date to the 18th century, and one to the 17th. *Admission: 22 frs. (separate from castle). Open May–Sept., Tues.–Sun. 10–noon and 2–6; Mar., Apr., and Oct.–mid-Nov., Wed. and weekends 10–noon and 2–6.*

The cheerful old town of **Rochefort-en-Terre,** 45 kilometers (28 miles) south of Josselin, boasts a cozy, ivory-clad 14th-century castle. The interior holds tapestries, armor, chests and old furniture, earthenware statuettes, and paintings by Alfred and Trafford Klots, American artists who lived here and restored the castle. *Admission: 12 frs. Open Apr.–May, weekends 10–12:30 and 2–6:30; June–Sept., daily 10–12:30 and 2–6:30.*

Apart from Belle-Ile (*see* Exploring, above), several other islands off the Brittany coast, none more than a few miles long, can also be visited. Take your pick from these:

Batz, with its tame landscape and sandy beaches. *Frequent daily crossings from Roscoff. Journey time: 15 minutes.*
Ouessant, whose melancholy scenery surrounds an ornithological research center for bird enthusiasts. *Crossings daily except Tues. from Brest. Journey time: 90 minutes.*
Molène, where relics of shipwrecks are on display at the old presbytery. *Crossings daily except Tues. from Brest. Journey time: 90 minutes.*

Sein, featuring narrow streets and a spectacular setting off the rugged Pointe de Raz. *Crossings daily except Wed. from Audierne.*

Glénan Archipelago, a string of eight uninhabited islands and dozens of rocks and islets. *Frequent crossings in summer from Concarneau.*

Groix, with its cliffs and sandy beaches. *Daily crossings from Lorient. Journey time: 45 minutes.*

Houat, highlighted by creeks, dunes, and beaches. *Daily crossings from Quiberon and Vannes. Journey time: 60 minutes.*

Hoëdic, a granite outcrop with just 126 inhabitants. *Daily crossings from Quiberon. Journey time: 90 minutes.*

Shopping

Folk Costumes and Textiles
When it comes to distinctive Breton folk costumes, **Quimper** is the best place to look. The streets around the cathedral (especially **rue du Parc)** are full of shops, several selling the woolen goods (notably thick marine sweaters) in which the region also specializes. Addresses for good textiles in **Rennes** are **Tidreiz** (pl. du Palais) and **Au Roy d'Ys** (29 blvd. de Magenta).

Gift Ideas
The commercial quarter of **Nantes** stretches from place Royale to place Graslin. For antiques, try **Cibot** (7 rue Voltaire). Don't miss chocolate specialist **Georges Gautier** (9 rue de la Fosse), with his *Muscadets Nantais*—grapes dipped in brandy and covered in chocolate. **Quimper** is best known for its faíence—hand-painted earthenware—which can be bought at the **Kéraluc Faiencerie** (14 rue de la Troménie on the Bénodet road) or at **Henriot** (12 pl. St-Corentin). Keep an eye out for such typical Breton products as woven or embroidered cloth, brass and wooden goods, puppets, dolls, and locally designed jewelry.

Markets
Among Brittany's most colorful markets are the ones held at Talensac in **Nantes** and in the streets of old **St-Malo** (Tuesday and Friday only). The most interesting street for arts and crafts is the cobbled, sloping **rue de Jerzual** in **Dinan,** whose medieval houses contain an assortment of wood-carvers, jewelers, leather-workers, glass specialists, and silk painters.

Sports and Fitness

Beaches and Water Sports
From St-Malo to Brest as far as the Côte d'Emeraude, then south to Nantes, the Brittany coast has any number of clean sandy **beaches**—the best are found at Dinard, Perros-Guirec, Trégastel-Plage, Douarnenez, Carnac, and Baule. Resorts offer numerous sports facilities, ranging from **underwater diving** and **spearfishing** to **canoeing** and **sand-sailing** (at St-Pierre Quiberon). To rent **sailboats,** try at St-Malo (tel. 99–82–00–78), Carnac (tel. 97–52–02–41), Douarnenez **(Iroise Nautique,** tel. 98–74–29–38), Dinard **(Yacht Club,** tel. 99–46–14–32), or Morlaix **(Loisirs 3000,** tel. 98–88–27–30).

Windsurfing possibilities include Carnac (boards can be rented from **De Petigny** at 90 rte. du Pô, tel. 97–52–02–41), the **Wishbone Club** in Dinard (Pont d'Emeraude), and the **Centre Nautique** in Brest (tel. 98–02–11–93). **Waterskiers** can try Concarneau (tel. 98–97–41–03). Among the region's **swimming pools** are those at Brest, Concarneau, Douarnenez, Morlaix, Quimper, Dinard, and St-Malo.

Bicycling Bikes can be rented at the train stations in Brest (tel. 98–44–21–55), Morlaix (tel. 98–88–60–47), and Quimper (tel. 98–80–50–50); in St-Malo, from **Diazo** (tel. 99–40–31–63); in Dol, from **Cycles Nicole** (tel. 99–48–03–20); or at Carnac (tel. 97–52–02–33) and Dinard (**Duval Cycles,** tel. 99–46–19–63).

Horseback Riding Riding stables include St-Malo (**Société Hippique,** tel. 99–81–20–34), Dinan (tel. 96–27–14–62), Carnac (**Centre Equestre des Menhirs,** tel. 97–55–73–45), and Dinard (**Centre Equestre de la Cote d'Emeraude,** tel. 99–46–23–57).

Dining and Lodging

Dining

Not surprisingly, Breton cuisine is dominated by fish and seafood. Shrimp, crayfish, crabs, oysters, and scallops are found throughout the region, but the linchpin of Breton menus is often lobster, prepared in sauce or cream or grilled. Popular meats include ham and lamb, frequently served with kidney beans. Fried eel is a traditional dish in the Nantes district. Brittany is particularly famous for its pancakes, served with both sweet and savory fillings. Accompanied by a glass of local cider, they make an ideal basis for a light, inexpensive meal.

Highly recommended restaurants are indicated by a star ★.

Category	Cost*
Very Expensive	over 350 francs
Expensive	200–350 francs
Moderate	100–200 francs
Inexpensive	under 100 francs

per person for a three-course meal, including tax (18.6%) and tip but not wine

Lodging

Brittany's economy is heavily dependent on the tourist industry, and its hotel infrastructure is correspondingly dense. English is more widely spoken here than in many French regions, but since Brittany pulls in visitors from the rest of France and much of northern Europe as well, it is essential to reserve ahead in summer. There are relatively few top-ranking deluxe hotels, however. Dinard, on the English Channel, and La Baule, on the Atlantic, are the two most exclusive resorts.

Highly recommended hotels are indicated by a star ★.

Category	Cost*
Very Expensive	over 750 francs
Expensive	350–750 francs

Moderate	200–350 francs
Inexpensive	under 200 francs

All prices are for a standard double room for two, including tax (18.6%) and service charge.

La Baule
Dining

La Marcaderie. This warm, yellow-walled restaurant has taken over from L'Espadon (now closed) as the best in town, helped by the cheerful welcome of Jean-Luc Girard and his wife. Potato and scampi tart or scallops in endive figure on the inventive menu. *5 av. d'Agen, tel. 40–24–03–12. Reservations required. Jacket and tie required. AE, MC, V. Closed Mon., Sun. evening, and Jan. Moderate–Expensive.*

La Pergola. The inventive finesse of its haute cuisine and the warmth of its welcome have given La Pergola a substantial reputation. The restaurant is conveniently situated in the center of La Baule, next to the casino and a stone's throw from the beach. Meat and fish are prepared with aplomb in a variety of subtle sauces. There is a set menu that's moderately priced, but you'll wind up in the expensive range if you eat à la carte. *147 av. des Lilas, tel. 40–24–57–61. Reservations advised. Jacket required. MC, V. Closed for lunch Mon., Wed., and Fri. Moderate.*

Lodging

Concorde. This establishment numbers among the least expensive good hotels in pricey La Baule. It's calm, comfortable, recently modernized, and close to the beach (ask for a room with a sea view). There's no restaurant. *1 av. de la Concorde, 44500, tel. 40–60–23–09. 47 rooms with bath or shower. Closed Oct.–Easter. Moderate.*

Belle-Ile
Dining

La Forge. A sure bet for lunch or dinner, La Forge specializes in traditional cuisine, based on seafood and fish, at affordable prices. Old wooden beams and remnants of the building's original purpose—blacksmithing—contribute to the pleasant, rustic atmosphere. *Rte. de Port-Goulphar, Bangor, tel. 91–31–51–76. Reservations required in summer. Dress: casual. AE, DC, MC, V. Closed Wed. and Jan.–Feb. Moderate.*

Cancale
Dining
★

Bricourt. The fishing village of Cancale, 13 kilometers (8 miles) east of St-Malo via D355, is the setting for this popular restaurant. The three intimate dining rooms are furnished in various styles: luxuriant Louis XV (mid-18th century); stylized, Classical-influenced French Empire (circa 1800); and homey, mid-19th-century English Victorian. Olivier Roellinger, the highly rated young chef, pays tribute to local seafaring tradition in his subtle preparations of seafood, fish, lamb, or veal with exotic spices. *1 rue Duguesclin, tel. 99–89–64–76. Reservations advised. Jacket required. AE, DC, MC, V. Closed Tues., Wed., and Jan.–Mar. Expensive.*

Concarneau
Dining

Le Galion. Flowers, wooden beams, silver candlesticks, old stones, and a roaring hearth form a pleasant backdrop to Henri Gaonach's marine *tours de force* at this, one of Concarneau's best fish restaurants. There are three set menus priced to suit those looking for an inexpensive meal as well as famished gourmets. *15 rue St-Guénolé, Ville-Close, tel. 98–97–30–16. AE, DC, MC, V. Closed Sun. evening and Mon. in winter and mid-Jan.–mid-Feb. Moderate–Expensive.*

Lodging

Sables Blancs. A great advantage of this old-fashioned hotel is that all guest rooms feature soul-satisfying views of the sea:

The name is derived from the hotel's location near the White Sands *(Sables Blancs)* Beach. The hotel restaurant is adequate, with menus at reasonable prices. *Plage des Sables Blancs, 29110 Concarneau, tel. 98–97–01–39. 48 rooms with bath. Facilities: restaurant. AE, DC, MC, V. Closed Nov.– mid-Mar. Inexpensive–Moderate.*

Dinan
Dining

Relais des Corsaires. The old hilltop town of Dinan is full of restaurants and pancake houses, but we suggest that you wander down to the old port on the banks of the Rance to dine at this spot, quaintly named after the pirates who apparently raided the wharves of Dinan. The mid-range *prix fixe* menu provides an ample four-course meal, with alternative menus at higher and lower prices. The costlier à la carte choices are not as good for the money. There are two separate, oak-beamed dining rooms; the lush main room with aquarium and attentive, rather unctuous service, communicates by way of a hatch with a smaller room with an impressively long bar, patrolled by Madame Ternisien, the attractive *patronne* who likes to give herself the airs and graces of a *grande dame. 7 rue du Quai, tel. 96–39–40– 17. Reservations accepted. Dress: casual. AE, DC, MC, V. Inexpensive.*

Dining and Lodging

D'Avagour. This hotel is splendidly situated opposite Dinan Castle's Tour du Connétable and has its own flower garden to boot; most of the cozy guest rooms look out onto either the garden or the castle. You can be sure of a warm welcome from the affable owner, Madame Quinton. The hotel attracts numerous foreign guests—American, English, and Italian, in particular. The restaurant offers traditional cuisine (shellfish, duck, apple tart) at reasonable prices (even considering that they go up dramatically from lunch to dinner), plus the chance to dine in the garden in warm weather. *1 pl. du Champ-Clos, 22100, tel. 96–39–07–49. 27 rooms with bath. Facilities: restaurant, garden. AE, DC, MC, V. Moderate.*

Dinard
Dining and Lodging

La Vallée. Prices at this traditional late-19th-century hotel vary according to the room. The best have a sea view: The Clair de Lune Promenade and Prieuré Beach are within shouting distance. The hotel itself is decorated in a stockily elegant *fin-de-siècle* style, with an authentic French feel. The restaurant's seafood comes on the moderate and expensive menus. *6 av. George-V, 35800, tel. 99–46–94–00. 26 rooms with bath. Facilities: restaurant. V. Closed mid-Nov.–mid-Dec., second half of Jan.; restaurant closed Tues. during Oct.–Apr. Moderate.*

Dol-de-Bretagne
Dining and Lodging

Logis de la Bresche Arthur. With its crisp outlines, white walls, and ample glass frontage, the hotel may not be quite as historic as it sounds, but it remains the coziest place in Dol in which to spend a night. Rooms are functional; local character is reserved for the restaurant, where smoked salmon, seafash, and home-prepared foie gras top the menu. *36 blvd. Deminiac, 35120, tel. 99–48–01–44. 24 rooms with bath. Facilities: restaurant. AE, DC, MC, V. Moderate.*

Morlaix
Dining and Lodging
★

Europe. Occupying an old building in the town center, the Europe is easily the best hotel in town, with simple, good-value, modernized guest rooms. Its restaurant (low-cost prix fixe menus, higher à la carte) provides an exuberant welcome, sumptuous many-mirrored decor, and some exciting recipes featuring lobster, warm oysters, and smoked salmon. *1 rue d'Aiguillon, 29210, tel. 98–62–11–99. 67 rooms, some with* bath. *Facilities: restaurant. AE, DC, MC, V. Inexpensive–Moderate.*

Nantes
Dining
★ **Colvert.** This small, modern bistro serves interesting dishes based on seafood or game, according to season. Chef Didier Macoin is an expert at original sauces (lentils and honey to accompany roast pigeon), and the charming waitresses are delighted to explain the intricate differences among the five prix fixe menus. The inexpensive lunchtime menu, including aperitif, is an excellent value. *14 rue Armand-Brossard, tel. 40–48–20–02. Reservations advised. Dress: casual. MC, V. Closed Sat. lunch, Sun., and Sept. Moderate.*

Mon Rêve. Fine food and a delectable parkland setting are offered at this cozy little restaurant about 8 kilometers (5 miles) east of town. Chef Gérard Ryngel concocts elegantly inventive regional fare (the duck or rabbit in muscadet are good choices), while his wife, Cécile, presides over the dining room with aplomb. *Rte. des Bords de Loire, Basse-Goulaine, tel. 40–03–55–50. Reservations advised. Dress: casual. AE, DC, MC, V. Closed 2 weeks in Feb., and Wed. during Oct.–Mar. Moderate.*

Lodging
Astoria. A conveniently central and unpretentious hotel in a quiet street near both the train station and the castle, the Astoria has prices that are as comfortable as its modern-looking rooms. There's no restaurant. *11 rue Richebourg, 44000, tel. 40–74–39–90. 45 rooms with bath or shower. MC, V. Closed Aug. Moderate.*

Pont-Aven
Dining
La Taupinière. Situated 16 kilometers (10 miles) from Concarneau along D783 on the outskirts of Pont-Aven, this roadside inn has an attractive garden. The food doesn't come cheap, but, then, chef Guy Guilloux doesn't dabble in mediocrity. Fish, crab, crayfish, and Breton ham (perhaps grilled over the large, open fire) are the bases of his inventions, while his wine cellar is renowned. *Rte. de Concarneau, tel. 98–06–03–12. Reservations required. Jacket required. MC, V. Closed Mon. dinner, Tues., and mid-Sept.–mid-Oct. Expensive.*

Rennes
Dining
★ **Palais.** The best, though not the most expensive, restaurant in Rennes must thank its highly inventive team of young chefs for its considerable reputation. Specialties include roast rabbit and, during winter, fried oysters in crab sauce. The lightish cuisine varies according to season and is offered via two menus. The decor is sharp-edged contemporary, the site conveniently central. *6 pl. du Parlement de Bretagne, tel. 99–79–45–01. Dinner reservations required. Jacket required. AE, DC, MC, V. Closed Sun. dinner, Mon., and Aug. Moderate.*

★ **Le Grain de Sable.** Situated at the bottom of rue des Dames leading to the cathedral is a thoroughly unusual restaurant. Plants, candelabra, faded photos, and a settee in the middle of the dining room create an ambience that escapes tackiness only by sheer eccentricity (a rocking horse sways in one corner). The cuisine is equally offbeat; expect garlic puree or endive with melted cheese to accompany the grilled meats that dominate the menu. Piped music warbles from opera to Louis Armstrong as the playful waitresses receive noisy reprimands from Hervé in the kitchen. *2 rue des Dames, tel. 99–30–78–18. Reservations advised. Dress: casual. MC, V. Closed Sun., Mon. dinner. Inexpensive.*

Lodging
Central. This stately, late 19th-century hotel lives up to its name and sits close to Rennes Cathedral. The individually dec-

orated guest rooms look out over the street or courtyard; ask for one of the latter, as they're quieter. English-speaking guests are frequent. There's no restaurant. *6 rue Lanjuinais, 35000, tel. 99–79–12–36. 43 rooms, most with bath. AE, DC, MC, V. Moderate.*

Angélina. This little charmer wins on sheer unpretentiousness: friendly welcome, clean rooms, robust breakfasts, and windows double-glazed to keep out the noise (it is on Rennes's principal boulevard, within a five-minute walk of the old town). Don't be put off by the fact that the hotel begins on the third floor of an ordinary-looking street block. *1 quai Lamennais, 35100, tel. 99–79–29–66. 26 rooms, with shower or bath. AE, DC, MC, V. Inexpensive.*

St-Malo   **Café de la Bourse.** Wherever you search for a restaurant in the
Dining   old town of St-Malo, you will feel you are being hemmed into an overcommercialized tourist trap. This restaurant, where prawns and oysters are downed by the shovel, is no exception. However, though its wooden seats and some tacky navigational paraphernalia—ships' wheels and posters of grizzled old sea dogs—are hardly artistic, the large, L-shaped dining room makes amends with genuinely friendly service and a seafood platter for two that includes at least three tanklike crabs, plus an army of cockles, whelks, and periwinkles. *1 rue de Dinan, tel. 99–56–47–17. Reservations accepted. Dress: casual. AE, V. Inexpensive–Moderate.*

Lodging   **La Digue.** Many of the rooms and the breakfast terrace at this hotel face the sea, offering magnificent views over St-Malo's long beach. The largest and most luxurious apartments are pricey, but many others are quite reasonably priced. A bar and *salon de thé* (tearoom) add to the hotel's attractions. *49 chaussée du Sillon, 35400, tel. 99–56–09–26. 53 rooms, some with bath. Facilities: bar, tearoom. AE, V. Closed mid-Nov.–mid-Mar. Moderate–Expensive.*

Jean-Bart. This clean, quiet hotel next to the ramparts, whose decor makes liberal use of cool blue, bears the stamp of diligent renovation: The beds are comfortable, the bathrooms shiny-modern, but the rooms are somewhat small. (Some offer sea views.) *12 rue de Chartres, 35400, tel. 99–40–33–88. 17 rooms, most with bath. MC, V. Closed mid-Nov.–mid-Feb. Moderate.*

Vannes   **Lys.** Intricate, nouvelle cuisine, based on fresh local produce,
Dining   makes this restaurant a pleasant dinner spot, close to the agreeable Promenade de la Garenne. The setting, in a late-18th-century Louis XVI style, is at its best by candlelight, with piano music in the background. *51 rue du Maréchal-Leclerc, tel. 97–47–29–30. Reservations required. Jacket and tie required. AE, DC, MC, V. Closed Mon., mid-Nov.–mid-Dec., and Sun. dinner. Moderate.*

Lodging   **Image Ste-Anne.** This charming hotel is housed in a suitably old, rustic building in the center of historic Vannes. The warm welcome and comfortable guest rooms make the price of a night here seem more than acceptable, as a varied foreign clientele has realized. Mussels, sole in cider, and duck are featured on the restaurant's menus; set menus are all very reasonably priced. *8 pl. de la Libération, 56000, tel. 97–63–27–36. 35 rooms with bath or shower. Facilities: restaurant. MC, V. Restaurant closed Sun. dinner, Nov.–Mar. Moderate.*

Vitré **Chêne Vert.** Vitré is badly placed in the hotel stakes, but since
Lodging this old town makes such a pleasant overnight stop we feel
obliged to suggest this establishment, which is conveniently
accessible from the road (D857, which links Rennes and Laval),
just opposite the train station and a 10-minute stroll through
cobbled streets from Vitré Castle. It is the epitome of a French
provincial hotel: creaky stairs, fraying carpets, oversoft mattresses, and less-than-enthusiastic service—all, including a copious dinner, for next to nothing. Look carefully, however, and
you will notice some intriguing touches—an enormous model
ship on the second floor, for example, or the zinc-plated walls
that submerge the dining room in art deco/ocean-liner pastiche. *2 pl. de la Gare, 35500, tel. 99–75–00–58. 22 rooms, a few
with bath. Closed mid-Sept.–mid-Oct.; restaurant closed Fri.
dinner and Sat., Oct.–May. Inexpensive.*

The Arts and Nightlife

The Arts

Pardons—the numerous traditional religious parades-cum-pil-
grimages that invariably showcase age-old local costumes—
are the backbone of Breton culture. There are further manifes-
tations of local folklore, often including dancers and folk singers, at the various Celtic festivals held in summer, of which the
Festival de Cornouaille in Quimper (late July) is the biggest.

Theater The region's principal theaters are the **Théâtre de la Ville** in
Rennes (pl. de la Mairie, tel. 99–28–55–87), the **Théâtre
Châteaubriand** in St-Malo (6 rue Groult-St-Georges, tel. 99–
40–98–05), and the **Théâtre Graslin** in Nantes (rue Scribe, tel.
40–69–77–18).

Concerts Of particular note is the **Festival de la Musique Sacrée** (sacred
music) held in St-Malo in August.

Nightlife

Bars and In Saint-Malo: **Le Faubourg** (7 rue St-Thomas), **La Selle** (24 rue
Nightclubs Ste-Barbe), or **La Belle Epoque** (11 rue de Dinan). In Rennes,
try **Le Pym's** (27 pl. du Colombier); in Nantes, the piano bar **Le
Tie Break** (1 rue des Petites-Ecuries); and in Brest, **Le Stendhal** (18 rue Colbert).

Jazz Clubs Two regional jazz venues are the **Cave du Louisiane** in St-Malo
(14 rue des Cordiers) and the **Pub Univers** in Nantes (16 rue J.J.
Rousseau).

Discos **Les Chandelles** in Carnac (av. de l'Atlantique) attracts a cosmopolitan crowd and enjoys a reputation as one of the country's
leading discos. You could also try **L'Escalier** in St-Malo (rue du
Tour-du-Bonheur) or **L'Espace** in Rennes (45 blvd. de la Tour
d'Auvergne).

Casinos There are casinos in **Dinard** (tel. 99–46–15–71), **Fréhel** (tel. 96–
41–49–05), **Perros-Guirec** (tel. 96–23–20–51), **Quiberon** (tel.
97–50–23–57), and **La Baule** (tel. 40–60–20–23).

For Singles **Le Batchi** in Rennes (34 rue Vasselot) and **L'Interdit** in Nantes
(14 rue Menou) cater to men only.

7 **Normandy**

Rouen to Mont-St-Michel

Introduction

Normandy (or Normandie, as the French spell it), the coastal region lying northwest of Paris, probably has more associations for English-speaking visitors than does any other part of France. William the Conqueror, Joan of Arc, the Bayeux Tapestry, and the D-Day landing beaches have become household names in English, just as they have in French.

Normandy is one of the country's finest gastronomic regions, producing excellent cheeses such as Camembert, and Calvados, a powerful apple brandy. The area has become popular with British vacationers not only because it's right across the Channel but also because of its charming countryside, from the wild, granite cliffs in the west to the long sandy beaches along the Channel coast, from the wooded valleys of the south to the lush green meadows and apple orchards in the center.

Historic buildings—castles, churches, and monuments—crown the Norman countryside as reminders of its rich and eventful past. Following the 1066 invasion of England by the Norman duke, William (the Conqueror), Normandy switched between English and French dominion for several centuries. In Rouen in 1431, Joan of Arc was burned at the stake, marking a turning point in the Hundred Years' War, the last major medieval conflict between the French and the English. The most celebrated building in Normandy is the abbey of Mont-St-Michel, erected on a 264-foot mound of granite cut off from the mainland at high tide; it's an architectural marvel and the most visited site in provincial France.

Normandy features 375 miles of coastline bordering the English Channel, four major ports—Le Havre, Rouen, Dieppe, and Cherbourg—and coastal towns with seafaring pasts, such as Honfleur, with its picturesque old harbor, and former fishing villages like Fécamp. Sandwiched between are the beaches of such fashionable resorts as Deauville, Cabourg, and Etretat, where visitors can be found reclining in deck chairs, gin and tonic in hand.

Essential Information

Important Addresses and Numbers

Tourist Information Each of Normandy's five *départements* has its own central tourist office: **Alençon** (Orne, 88 rue St-Blaise, tel. 33–28–88–71), **Caen** (Calvados, pl. du Canada, tel. 31–86–53–30), **Evreux** (Eure, 46 av. Mal-Foch, tel. 32–31–10–31), **Rouen** (Seine-Maritime, 2 bis rue du Petit-Salut, tel. 35–88–61–32), and **St-Lô** (Manche, Rondpoint de la Liberté, tel. 33–56–28–80).

Tourist offices of other major towns covered in this chapter are as follows: **Bayeux** (1 rue des Cuisiniers, tel. 31–92–16–26), **Dieppe** (1 blvd. du Général-de-Gaulle, tel. 35–84–11–77), **Fécamp** (pl. Bellet, tel. 35–28–20–51), **Le Havre** (1 pl. de l'Hôtel-de-Ville, tel. 35–21–22–88), and **Honfleur** (33 cours des Fossés, tel. 31–89–23–30).

Travel Agencies **American Express** (1–3 pl. Jacques-Lelieur, Rouen, tel. 35–98–19–80; 57 quai George V, Le Havre, tel. 35–42–59–11) and **Havas** (25 Grande-Rue, Alençon, tel. 33–32–88–88; 54 rue

St-Martin, Bayeux, tel. 31–92–14–46; 80 rue St-Jean, Caen, tel. 31–86–04–01; 14 blvd. Nationale, Dieppe, tel. 35–84–29–16).

Car Rental **Avis** (44 pl. de la Gare, Caen, tel. 31–87–31–84; 24 rue Malouet, Rouen, tel. 35–72–77–50). and **Europcar** (25 cours de la République, Le Havre, tel. 35–25–21–95).

Arriving and Departing

By Plane Paris's Charles de Gaulle (Roissy) and Orly airports will be American visitors' closest link with the region. From the United Kingdom, there are regular flights to Caen and Deauville (from London) and to Cherbourg (from Southampton and the Channel Islands).

By Boat Car ferries connect several Normandy ports with England and Ireland. There are crossings to Dieppe from Newhaven, to Le Havre from Portsmouth and Rosslare, and to Cherbourg from Portsmouth, Weymouth, and Rosslare.

By Car The A13 expressway from Paris spears its way to Rouen in 1½ hours and to Caen in 2¼ hours. A13/N13 takes you to Cherbourg via Bayeux in another two hours.

By Train From Paris's St-Lazare station, express trains stop at Rouen and Dieppe, Le Havre, or Fécamp, and at Caen and Cherbourg via Evreux and Lisieux. For Mont-St-Michel (nearest station: Pontorson), take the express from Paris's Montparnasse station to Rennes or Caen and switch to a local train.

Getting Around

By Plane Normandy's domestic airports are at Rouen, Le Havre, and Evreux.

By Car A13/N13 travels from Rouen to Cherbourg via Bayeux in two hours. Main roads also branch off from A13 to Le Havre (A15) and Dieppe (N27). To get to Mont-St-Michel, take A11 to Rennes, then N175 north.

Guided Tours

Bus and Car Excursions **Viking Voyages** (16 rue Général-Giraud, 14000 Caen, tel. 31–85–52–02) specializes in two-day packages by car, with overnight stays in private châteaus. Itineraries include "Normandy: From Rouen to Cherbourg"; "William the Conqueror's Route"; "Discovering the Manche," which includes a trip to Mont-St-Michel; a "D-Day Beaches" tour; and "From Lisieux to Suisse Normande." An all-inclusive tour, with car and English-speaking driver, is 1,795 francs. The **French Association of Travel Agents** offers a two-day tour of Mont-St-Michel and St-Malo, which includes a visit to Honfleur, the resorts of Deauville and Cabourg, the D-Day beaches, and Caen. The excursion, offered from April to October, costs 1,730 francs; contact **Clamageran Voyages** (4 rue Rollon, 76000 Rouen, tel. 35–07–39–07) for details.

Train Excursions Both **Paris-Vision** (214 rue de Rivoli, 75001 Paris, tel. 42–60–31–25) and **Cityrama** (4 pl. des Pyramides, 75001 Paris, tel. 42–60–30–14) organize one-day train excursions to Mont-St-Michel, with a two-day option that takes in the châteaus of the Loire on the second day. Costing 800 francs, the one-day trips leave Paris at 7:15 AM on Saturday, arriving in Mont-St-Michel in time for lunch (included in the cost). Following a guided tour of the mount and the abbey, you return to Paris—with a stop for dinner (also included in the cost) on the way—about 10:30 PM.

Special-Interest **Viking Voyages** in Caen *(see* above) organizes bike trips around the region, as well as a "Normandy Antiques" tour by car. A two-day bike tour, without guide, costs 995 francs, while a guided antiques excursion costs 1,795 francs. **Trans Canal** in Caen (22 rue de la Hève, 14780 Lion-sur-Mer, tel. 31–96–00–55) arranges two-hour cruises on Caen's canal.

Personal Guides A number of cities organize their own tours, including Bayeux, Rouen, Caen, and Le Havre. For details, contact the individual tourist offices *(see* Tourist Information, above).

Exploring Normandy

Numbers in the margin correspond with points of interest on the Normandy map.

Orientation

We've divided our Norman coverage into three separate tours. The first tour leads northwest from Paris to Rouen, the capital of Upper Normandy. From here, we meander west to the port town of Le Havre before heading up along the impressive coastline of chalky cliffs and pebble beaches known as the Alabaster Coast.

Lower Normandy covers a much larger area, and we explore its sights in two itineraries. The first starts in the market town of Lisieux before heading north to the coastal resort of Honfleur, then west through the region's swankiest resort towns along the Calvados Coast. From here, we turn inland, to Caen and Bayeux. This area saw some of the fiercest fighting after the D-Day landings, as many monuments and memorials testify. The last stop is at the fabled Mont-St-Michel, which lies at the western edge of Normandy.

Finally, there's a scenic drive along the River Orne south of Caen, through the hilly region called La Suisse Normande.

Highlights for First-time Visitors

Abbaye aux Hommes, Tour 2
Bayeux Tapestry, Musée de la Tapisserie, Bayeux, Tour 2
Cathédrale Notre-Dame and Old Town, Rouen, Tour 1
D-Day landing beaches, Tour 2
Deauville/Trouville, Tour 2
Honfleur, Tour 2
Musée des Beaux-Arts, Le Havre, Tour 1
Mont-St-Michel, Tour 2

Tour 1: Upper Normandy

Setting out from Paris, take the A13 expressway and branch off left, just after Bonnières-sur-Seine to **Evreux**, capital of the Eure *département*. From the 5th century on, the town was ravaged and burnt by a succession of armies—first the Vandals, then the Normans, the English, and various French kings.

World War II played its part as well. These days, the town has been well restored and is embellished by a number of gardens and overgrown footpaths by the banks of the River Iton.

Evreux's principal historic site is the **Cathédrale Notre-Dame,** (pl. Notre-Dame), in the heart of town just off rue Corbeau. Unfortunately, it was an easy victim for the many fires and raids that took place over the centuries; all that's left of the original 12th-century construction are the nave arcades. The lower parts of the chancel date from 1260, the chapels from the 14th century. Still, it's an outstanding example of Flamboyant Gothic inside and out. Don't miss the choir triforium and transept, the 14th-century stained-glass windows in the apse, or the entrance to the fourth chapel.

2 From Evreux, get on D316 heading for **Les Andelys,** 36 kilometers (21 miles) away on the north bank of the River Seine. The pretty little town is set against magnificent chalky cliffs in one of the most picturesque loops of the River Seine. Overlooking the town from the clifftops and affording spectacular views in both directions are the remains of the **Château de Gaillard,** a formidable fortress built by English king Richard the Lionhearted in 1196. Despite its solid defenses, the castle fell to the French in 1204. It had suffered considerable damage during the assault, and sections were later torn down at the end of the 16th century; only one of its five main towers remains intact. *Admission: 12 frs. Open Thurs.–Mon. 10–noon and 2–5, Wed. 2–5; closed Tues.*

Rather than take the most direct road from Les Andelys to Rouen (D126/D138), continue along D313 around the Seine for about 14 kilometers (9 miles), crossing it at St-Pierre du **3** Vauvry. You can then either stop at the busy town of **Louviers** on the Eure River to see its old houses and its Notre-Dame church or turn straight onto N15, the main road that passes just north of the town. Eight kilometers (5 miles) from Louviers, you'll cross the Pont de l'Arche, where the Eure and Seine rivers merge; from here, it's another 18 kilometers (11 miles) to Rouen. On the way, you'll pass through **Bonsecours,** now a suburb of the town and the site of the Basilique Notre-Dame, built in the early 1840s and one of the finest neo-Gothic churches in France.

4 The city of **Rouen** is a blend of ancient and modern, a large part having been destroyed during World War II. Even before its massive postwar reconstruction, the city had expanded outward during the 20th century with the development of industries spawned by its increasingly busy port, now the fifth largest in France. In its more distant past, Rouen gained celebrity when Joan of Arc was burned at the stake here in 1431.

Numbers in the margin correspond with points of interest on the Rouen map.

Rouen is known as the City of a Hundred Spires, and many of its important edifices are churches. Lording it over them all, in **5** place du Cathédrale, is the magnificent **Cathédrale Notre-Dame,** one of the masterpieces of French Gothic architecture. If you are familiar with the works of Impressionist Claude Monet, you will immediately recognize the cathedral's immense west facade, rendered in an increasingly misty, yet always beautiful, fashion in his series "Cathédrales de Rouen." The original 12th-century construction was replaced after a terri-

Normandy

0 —————— 20 miles
0 —————— 30 km

N

Baie de la Seine

Cherbourg

N13

Valognes

D2

Passage de la Déroute

La Haye-du-Puits D903 Isigny-sur-Mer

D900

St-Laurent-sur-Mer **Vierville-sur-Mer** **32** **31** Port-en-Bessin-Huppain **Arromanches** **30** **Cabourg**

D514

D516 D514

Colleville-sur-Mer

Bayeux **29** N13 Benouville D513

Coutances D972 **St-Lô** **33** N174 D572 **Caen** **28** Troarn

Entrée de la Déroute D971 D999 N175 D212 Orne Laize-la-Vil

Granville D973 N175 Villedieu-les-Poêles D577 **Thury-Harcourt** **35** D562 N158

Clécy **36** **Pont d'Ouilly** **37**

Vire Conde-S-Noireau **38** D909

Rabodanges

Putanges-Pont-Ecrepin **39**

Cancale

Mont-St-Michel **34**

Avranches N175

N176 **Bagnoles-de-l'Orne** **40**

Dol-de-Bretagne D19 D909

D795 D155 Antrain D998 D177 D918 N176

Combourg

D23

Pré-en-Pail

Fougeres

N12 Mayenne D35

Aître St-Maclou, **7**

Cathédrale
Notre-Dame, **5**

Eglise Jeanne
d'Arc, **12**

Eglise St-Maclou, **6**

Eglise St-Ouen, **8**

Gros-Horloge, **13**

Musée des
Beaux-Arts, **9**

Musée de la
Céramique, **10**

Musée de Ferronerie
Le Secq des
Tournelles, **11**

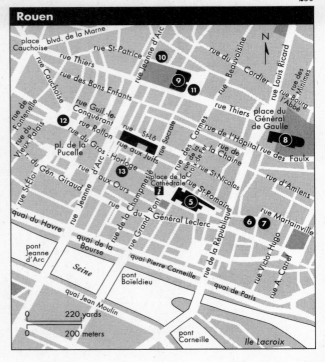

ble fire in 1200; only the left-hand spire, the Tour St-Romain,
survived the flames. The imposing 250-foot iron steeple on the
right, known as the "Butter Tower," was added in the 15th and
16th centuries and completed in the 17th, when a group of
wealthy citizens donated large sums of money—for the privilege of eating butter during Lent.

Interior highlights include the 13th-century choir, with its
pointed arcades; vibrant stained glass depicting the crucified
Christ (restored after heavy damage during World War II); and
massive stone columns topped by some intriguing carved faces.
The first flight of the famous Escalier de la Librairie (Booksell-
ers' Staircase) rises up from a tiny balcony just to the left of the
transept and is attributed to Guillaume Pontifs, who is also responsible for most of the 15th-century work seen in the cathedral. *Pl. de la Cathédrale.*

Leaving the cathedral, head right, and cross rue de la République to place St-Maclou, an attractive square surrounded by
picturesque half-timbered houses with steeply pointed roofs.
6 The square's neo-Gothic **Eglise St-Maclou** bears testimony to
the wild excesses of Flamboyant architecture; take time to examine the central and left-hand portals under the porchway on
the main facade, covered with little bronze lion heads and pagan engravings. Inside, note the 16th-century organ, with its
Renaissance woodcarving, and the fine marble columns. *Pl. St-
Maclou.*

7 To the right is the **Aître St-Maclou,** (184–186 rue Martainville),
a former ossuary that is one of the last reminders of the plague

that devastated Europe during the Middle Ages; these days, it holds Rouen's School of Art and Architecture. The ossuary (a charnel house used for the bodies of plague victims) is said to have inspired the French composer Camille Saint-Saëns (1835–1921) when he was working on his *Danse Macabre*. The building's massive double frieze is especially riveting, carved with some graphic skulls, bones, and grave diggers' tools.

8 Turn right up rue de la République to place du Général-de-Gaulle, site of the **Eglise St-Ouen,** a fine example of later Gothic architecture. The stained-glass windows, dating from the 14th to the 16th century, are the most spectacular features of the otherwise spare structure. The church's 19th-century pipe organs have few equals in France.

9 Walk west on rue Thiers to get to a cluster of Rouen's fine museums, the most important of which is the **Musée des Beaux-Arts** (Fine Arts Museum), on square Vedral. It contains a fine collection of French paintings from the 17th and 19th centuries, including works by Claude Monet, Alfred Sisley, and Auguste Renoir. An entire room is devoted to Rouen-born Théodore Gericault, and there are impressive works by Delacroix and Chassériau. The museum once showcased a superb collection of Norman ceramics, but these are now housed separately **10** in the **Musée de la Céramique** (Ceramic Museum), a few steps down the road. A single ticket will get you into both museums **11** and into the **Musée de Ferronerie Le Secq des Tournelles,** right behind the Musée des Beaux-Arts. This museum claims to possess the world's finest collection of wrought iron, with exhibits spanning the 3rd through the 19th century. Displays include a range of items used in daily life, accessories, and professional instruments used by surgeons, barbers, carpenters, clockmakers, and gardeners. *Admission: 12 frs. All three museums are open Thurs.–Mon. 10–noon and 2–6, Wed. 2–6; closed Tues.*

12 Continue down rue Thiers, then turn left onto rue Jeanne-d'Arc and head toward place du Vieux-Marché, dominated by the thoroughly modern **Eglise Jeanne d'Arc.** Dedicated to the saint, the church was built on the spot where she was burned to death in 1431. Not all is spanking new, however; the church is graced with some remarkable 16th-century glass windows taken from the former Eglise St-Vincent, destroyed in 1944.

13 Leading out of place du Vieux-Marché is Rouen's most popular attraction, the rue du Gros-Horloge. The name of this little pedestrian street comes from the **Gros-Horloge** itself, a giant Renaissance clock; in 1527, the Rouennais had a splendid arch built especially for it, and today its golden face looks out over the street (the ticket to the Musée des Beaux-Arts includes admission to the ornate belfry). Though the ancient thoroughfare is crammed with boutiques and fast-food joints, a few old houses, dating from the 16th century, remain. Wander through the surrounding old town, a warren of tiny streets lined with over 700 half-timbered houses. Instead of standing simply as monuments to the past, these cobbled streets have been successfully transformed into a lively pedestrian shopping precinct, and the old buildings now contain the most fashionable shops in the city.

Numbers in the margin correspond with points of interest on the Normandy map.

The Seine valley between Rouen and Le Havre is full of interesting sights, old and new, dotted amid some lovely scenery. Within 10 minutes of Rouen, along D982, is the 11th-century ⑭ abbey church of St-George in **St-Martin de Boscherville**. From here, follow D982 and D65 around the Seine for some 19 kilome- ⑮ ters (12 miles) to **Jumièges** to see the imposing ruins of its once-mighty Benedictine abbey, the **Abbaye de Jumièges,** founded in the 7th century and subsequently plundered by Vikings. The abbey was rebuilt in the 11th century and consecrated in 1067, but monks lived there until the French Revolution. It was then auctioned off to a timber merchant, who promptly demolished a large part of the building to sell the stones. *Admission: 15 frs. Open Mon.–Sat. 10–noon and 2–6.*

About 16 kilometers (10 miles) farther along the right bank of ⑯ the Seine, in **St.-Wandrille,** is another Benedictine abbey. The **Abbaye de St-Wandrille** survives as an active monastery to this day; like Jumièges, it was founded in the 7th century, sacked (by the Normans), and rebuilt in the 10th century. You can still hear the monks sing their Gregorian chants at morning Mass if you're there early in the day (9:25 weekdays and 10 Sunday and holidays). *Guided tour at 3 and 4 weekdays; cost: 14 frs. adults, children free.*

From St-Wandrille, it's only a couple of miles to the charming ⑰ little village of **Caudebec-en-Caux**; if the day is sunny, you should leave the car and walk along the banks of the Seine. The village's 15th-century Eglise Notre-Dame was described by French monarch Henri IV (1589–1610) as "the most beautiful chapel in the kingdom." A huge modern bridge, the Pont de Brotonne, spans the Seine at Caudebec. Instead of crossing it, however, drive west around the north bank of the Seine for a ⑱ couple of miles to **Villequier,** a peacefully situated riverside village dominated by its château. Villequier is famous as the place where 19th-century writer Victor Hugo lost his daughter, Léopoldine, and her husband, Charles Vacquerie, who drowned in the Seine's notorious seasonal tidal wave (these days it is held at bay by a dam). A museum, the **Musée Victor Hugo,** has been created in the couple's old house; exhibits include the manuscript of Hugo's poem *Contemplations,* a lament on their deaths. *Rue Ernet-Benet. Admission: 5 frs. Open Apr.–Sept., Wed.–Mon. 10–noon and 2–5:30, closed Tues.; Oct.–Mar., Wed.–Sun. 10–noon and 2–5:30, closed Mon. and Tues.*

Time Out   If the weather's fine when you are in Villequier, stop off for a light lunch at **Le Grand Sapin** (Rue Louis-Le-Graffic). The food is plain, traditional fare, but the riverside terrace is delightful.

⑲ The seaside port of **Le Havre** lies 53 kilometers (33 miles) west by D81 and N182. A bustling modern town, largely rebuilt after 1945, Le Havre is France's second-largest port (after Marseille). Le Havre was bombarded no less than 146 times during World War II, and reinforced concrete and bleak open spaces have not done much for the town's atmosphere. The old seafaring quarter of Ste-Adresse is worth a visit, however. From its fortress, you have panoramic views of the port and the Seine estuary.

At the opposite end of the seafront, at the tip of boulevard François-Ier, sits the metal-and-glass **Musée des Beaux-Arts.**

On the ground floor there's a remarkable collection of Raoul Dufy's work, including oils, watercolors, and sketches. Dufy (1877–1953) was born in Le Havre and devoted a lot of time to his native region: views of Norman beaches and of Le Havre itself. If you can't spend much time in Normandy, go upstairs to have a look at works by one of the forerunners of Impressionism—Eugène Boudin. Boudin's compelling beach scenes and Norman countrysides will give you a taste of what you're missing. *Blvd. Clemenceau. Admission: 15 frs. Open Wed.– Mon. 10–noon and 2–6; closed Tues.*

㉕ The first stop on the coast between Le Havre and Dieppe (a stretch known as the Alabaster Coast) is **Etretat**, about 30 kilometers (18 miles) away along D940. The town's white cliffs are almost as famous in France as Dover's are in England. Although the promenade running the length of Etretat's pebble beach has been spoiled by a proliferation of seedy cafés and french-fry stands, the town retains its vivacity and charm. Its landmarks are two arched cliff formations, the **Falaise d'Amont** and the **Falaise d'Aval,** which jut out over the sea on either side of the bay, and a 300-foot needle of rock, the **Aiguille,** which thrusts up from the sea near the Falaise d'Amont. Through the huge archways carved by the sea into the cliffs, you can walk to neighboring beaches at low tide. For a breathtaking view of the whole bay, take the path up to the Falaise d'Aval on the southern side, from which you can hike for miles across the Manneporte hills.

㉑ Seventeen kilometers (11 miles) from Etretat along D940 is **Fécamp,** an ancient fishing port that was Normandy's primary place of pilgrimage before Mont-St-Michel stole all the glory. Fécamp no longer has a commercial fishing fleet, but you will still see lots of boats in the private yachting marina. The magnificent **Eglise La Trinité** (just off blvd. de la République) bears witness to the town's religious past. The Benedictine abbey was founded by the duke of Normandy in the 11th century and became the home of the monastic order of the Précieux Sang et de la Trinité (referring to Christ's blood, which supposedly arrived here in the 7th century). Fécamp is also the home of the liqueur Benedictine. The **Musée de la Bénédictine,** seven blocks across town on rue Boufart, was rebuilt in 1892 in a florid mixture of neo-Gothic and Renaissance styles and remains one of Normandy's most popular attractions. *110 rue Alexandre-le-Grand. Admission: 23 frs. (including a tasting). Open Easter–mid-Nov., daily 9:30–12 and 2–6.*

From Fécamp it's about 65 kilometers (40 miles) to Dieppe; take D925 via Cany-Barville to St-Valéry-en-Caux and Veules-les-Roses, and then the scenic coast road, D68, the rest of the way. Just before reaching Dieppe, you'll pass through **Varengeville-sur-Mer.** Look for the tiny church perched on a hill: 20th-century painter Georges Braque—who, with Picasso, is credited with inventing Cubism—is buried in its graveyard.

㉒ **Dieppe** is a charming blend of a fishing and commercial port and a Norman seaside town. The boulevard du Maréchal-Foch, a seafront promenade, separates an immense lawn from an unspoiled pebble beach where, in 1942, many Canadian soldiers were killed during the so-called Jubilee raid. Overlooking the Channel, at the western end of the bay, stands the 15th-century **Château de Dieppe,** which dominates the town from its clifftop position. It contains the town museum, well known for its collection of ivories. In the 17th century, Dieppe imported vast quantities of elephant tusks from Africa and Asia, as many as 350 craftsmen settled here to work the ivory; their efforts can be seen in the form of ship models, nautical accessories, or, upstairs, in religious and day-to-day objects. The museum also has a room devoted to sketches by Georges Braque. *Sq. du Canada. Admission: 10 frs. Open mid-Sept.– mid-June, Wed.–Mon. 10–noon and 2–6; closed Tues.*

Tour 2: The Calvados Coast and Mont-St-Michel

㉓ Lisieux is the main market town of the prosperous Pays d'Auge, an agricultural region famous for cheeses named after such towns as Camembert, Pont l'Evêque, and Livarot. It is also a land of apple orchards from which the finest Calvados brandy comes. Lisieux emerged relatively unscathed from World War II, though it boasts few historical monuments beyond the **Cathédrale St-Pierre,** built in the 12th and 13th centuries. It is also famous for its patron saint, Ste-Thérèse, who was born and died in the last quarter of the 19th century, having spent the last 10 of her 25 years as a Carmelite nun. Thérèse was canonized in 1925, and in 1954 a basilica—one of the world's largest 20th-century churches—was dedicated to her; to get there from the cathedral, walk down avenue Victor-Hugo and branch left into avenue Ste-Thérèse.

㉔ From Lisieux, take D579 north to Pont l'Evêque and stay on that road when it forks right toward **Honfleur,** a distance of 32 kilometers (20 miles). This colorful port on the Seine estuary epitomizes Normandy for many people. It was once an important departure point for maritime expeditions, and the first voyages to Canada in the 15th and 16th centuries embarked from here. Its 17th-century harbor is fronted on one side by two-story stone houses with low, sloping roofs and on the other by tall, narrow houses whose wooden facades are topped by slate roofs. The whole town is a museum piece, full of half-timbered houses and cobbled streets.

Honfleur was colonized by French and foreign painters in the 19th century, and the group later known as the Impressionists used to meet in the **Ferme St-Siméon,** now a luxurious hotel (*see* Dining and Lodging, below). Honfleur has also inspired artists of other hues: Charles Baudelaire, the 19th-century poet and champion of Romanticism, wrote his poem *L'Invitation au Voyage* here, while the French composer Erik Satie was born in Honfleur in 1866.

Today Honfleur is one of the most popular vacation spots in northern France. During the summer, its hotels rarely have vacancies and its cafés and restaurants are always packed. Soak up the seafaring atmosphere by strolling around the old harbor, and pay a visit to the **Eglise Ste-Catherine,** which dominates the harbor's northern corner (rue des Logettes). The wooden church was built by townspeople to show their gratitude for the departure of the English at the end of the Hundred Years' War (1453), when masons and architects were occupied with national reconstruction.

㉕ ㉖ Leave Honfleur by D513 west and follow the coast for 14 kilometers (9 miles) until you arrive at the twin seaside resorts of **Trouville** and **Deauville,** separated only by the estuary of the River Touques. Although Trouville is now considered an overflow town for its more prestigious neighbor, it became one of France's first seaside resorts when Parisians began flocking here in the mid-19th century.

Deauville is a chic watering hole for the French bourgeoisie and would-be fashionable personalities from further afield, who are attracted by its racecourse, casino, marina and regattas, palaces and gardens, and, of course, its sandy beach. The **Promenade des Planches**—the boardwalk extending along the seafront and lined with deck chairs, bars, and striped cabanas—is the place for celebrity spotting. Nevertheless, if you are looking for authenticity rather than glamour, stay in Trouville. It, too, has a casino and boardwalk as well as a bustling fishing port and a native population that makes it a livelier place out of season than Deauville.

Time Out One of the most popular places in Trouville is **Les Vapeurs,** a friendly, animated brasserie with neon-lit '50s decor. It serves good, fresh food at any time, day or night, and both the famous and not-so-famous like to meet here after dark. *160 blvd. Fernand-Moureaux. Closed Tues. dinner and Wed.*

Continue west along D513, which takes you through a number of family seaside resorts, such as Houlgate and nearby Divessur-Mer, before reaching the larger and more elegant resort of **㉗ Cabourg,** just across the River Dives. Cabourg's streets fan out from a central hub near the seafront where the casino and the Grand Hôtel are situated. The early 20th-century novelist Marcel Proust, author of *Remembrance of Things Past*, was a great admirer of the town's pleasant seaside atmosphere, and spent much of his time here. One of the volumes in his epic paints a perfect picture of life in the resort, to which the town responded by naming its magnificent seafront promenade after him.

Leave Cabourg by D513, which veers inland and after 24 kilom-**㉘** eters (15 miles) brings you to **Caen,** the capital of Lower Normandy. Caen, with its abbeys and castle, presents a strong contrast to the somewhat uniform coastal resorts.

William of Normandy ruled from Caen in the 11th century before he conquered England. Nine hundred years later, the two-month Battle of Caen devastated the town in 1944. Much of the city burned in a fire that raged for 11 days, and the downtown area was almost entirely rebuilt after the war.

A good place to begin exploring is at the town's main tourist attraction, the **Abbaye aux Hommes,** a monastery built by William the Conqueror. "The Men's Abbey" was begun in Romanesque style in 1066 and was added to during the 18th century. Note the magnificent facade of the Eglise St-Etienne, whose spareness is enhanced by two 11th-century towers topped by Norman Gothic octagonal spires. Inside, what had been William the Conqueror's tomb was destroyed by 16th-century Huguenots during the Wars of Religion, but the choir still stands; it was the first to be built in Norman Gothic style, and many subsequent choirs were modeled after it. *Pl. Louis-Guillouard. Guided tours of the abbey cost 20 frs. morning, 24 frs. afternoon. Open daily 9–noon and 2–5.*

Head right up Fosses St-Julien to the Esplanade du Château. The ruins of William the Conqueror's **fortress,** built in 1060 and sensitively restored after the war, glower down on all who approach. The castle gardens are a perfect spot for strolling, and the ramparts afford good views of the city. Within the rampart walls lies the **Musée des Beaux-Arts,** a Fine Arts Museum whose impressive collection includes Rembrandts and Titians. Also within the castle are the **Musée de Normandie,** displaying regional arts, and the chapel of St-George. *Entrance by the Porte de Ville. Admission to each: 6 frs. Open Wed.–Mon. 10–1 and 2–5; closed Tues.*

Take rue des Chanoines right to the **Abbaye aux Dames,** the "Ladies' Abbey," built by William the Conqueror's wife, Matilda, in 1062. The abbey is now a hospital and not open to visitors, but you can visit its Église de la Trinité. This squat church is a good example of 11th-century Romanesque architecture, though its original spires were replaced by bulky balustrades in the early 18th century. The 11th-century crypt once held Matilda's tomb, which was destroyed during the French Revolution. Note the intricate carvings on columns and arches in the chapel. *Pl. Reine-Mathilde. Admission: free. Guided tours daily at 2:30 and 4.*

Head back down the rue des Chanoines, and continue on rue Montoir-Poissonnerie. Turning left onto place St-Pierre, you'll come face-to-face with the Caen Tourist Office. It merits a visit not only for its excellent information resources, but for its splendid site in the **Hôtel d'Escoville,** a 16th-century mansion built by a wealthy town merchant, Nicolas le Valois d'Escoville. The building was badly damaged during the war but has since been restored; the rather austere facade conceals an elaborate inner courtyard, reflecting the Italian influence on early Renaissance Norman architecture.

A good introduction to the Normandy landings of 1944 can be had at the **Mémorial,** a museum opened in the north of the city in 1988. Videos, photos, arms, paintings, and prints detail the Battle of Normandy and the French Liberation. *Esplanade Général-Eisenhower. Admission: 30 frs. adults, 15 frs. students. Open May–Sept., daily 9–6; Oct.–Apr., Tues.–Sun. 10–5.*

29 From Caen, N13 heads 28 kilometers (17 miles) northwest to **Bayeux,** an attractive city steeped in history and the first town to be liberated during the Battle of Normandy. Bayeux's long history stretches back many centuries before World War II, however, and we begin our tour at the **Musée de la Tapisserie,** located in an 18th-century building on rue de Nesmond and showcasing the world's most celebrated piece of needlework, the **Bayeux Tapestry.** The medieval work of art—stitched in 1067—is really a 225-foot-long embroidered scroll, which depicts, in 58 separate scenes, the epic story of William of Normandy's conquest of England in 1066, a watershed in European history. The tapestry's origins remain obscure, though it was probably commissioned from Saxon embroiderers by the count of Kent—also the bishop of Bayeux—to be displayed in his newly built cathedral. Despite its age, the tapestry is in remarkably good condition; the extremely detailed, often homey scenes provide an unequaled record of the clothes, weapons, ships, and lifestyles of the day. *Centre Culturel, rue de Nesmond. Admission: 20 frs. (5 frs. for a cassette translation). Open June–Sept., daily 9–7; opening times vary Oct.–May, so check locally.*

Your ticket also gains you entrance to the **Musée Baron Gérard.** Head up rue de Nesmond to rue Larchet, turning left into lovely place des Tribuneaux. The museum contains fine collections of Bayeux porcelain and lace, ceramics from Rouen, and 16th–19th-century furniture and paintings. *Pl. des Tribuneaux. Open daily, June–Aug., 9–7; Sept.–mid-Oct. and Mar.–May, 9:30–12:30 and 2–6:30; mid-Oct.–Mar., 10–12:30 and 2–6.*

Behind the museum, with an entrance on rue de Bienvenu, sits Bayeux's most important historic building, the **Cathédrale Notre-Dame.** The cathedral is a harmonious mixture of Norman and Gothic architecture. Note the portal on the south side of the transept, which depicts the assassination of English Archbishop Thomas à Becket in Canterbury Cathedral in 1170, following his opposition to King Henry II's attempts to control the church. Note the whimsical paintings in the nave.

Return to the 20th century by turning left, walking to the place au Blois, and continuing down rue St-Loup. Turn right on boulevard du Général-Fabian-Ware, site of the **Musée de la Bataille de Normandie,** whose detailed exhibits trace the story of the Battle of Normandy from June 7 to August 22, 1944. The ultramodern museum contains an impressive array of war paraphernalia, including uniforms, weapons, and equipment. *Blvd. Général-Fabian-Ware. Admission: 18 frs. Open June–Aug., daily 9–7; Sept.–Oct. and Mar.–May, daily 10–12:30 and 2–6:30; and Nov.–Feb., weekends 10:30–12:30 and 2–6:30.*

Operation Overlord, the code name for the Invasion of Normandy, called for five beachheads—dubbed Utah, Omaha, Gold, Juno, and Sword—to be established along the Calvados Coast, to either side of Arromanches. Preparations started in mid-1943, and British shipyards worked furiously through the following winter and spring building two artificial harbors (called Mulberries), boats, and landing equipment. The operation was originally scheduled to take place on June 5, but poor weather caused it to be postponed for a day.

The British troops that landed on Sword, Juno, and Gold quickly pushed inland and joined with parachute regiments that had been dropped behind the German lines. U.S. forces met with far tougher opposition on Omaha and Utah beaches, however, and it took them six days to secure their positions and meet the other Allied forces. From there, they pushed south and west, cutting off the Cotentin Peninsula on June 10 and taking Cherbourg on June 26. Meanwhile, British forces were encountering fierce resistance at Caen and did not take it until July 9. By then, U.S. forces were turning their attention southward, but it took two weeks of bitter fighting to dislodge the Germans from the area around St-Lô; the town was finally liberated on July 19.

After having boned up on the full story of the Normandy invasion, you'll want to go and see the area where it all took place. There's little point in visiting all five sites, since not much remains to mark the furious fighting waged hereabouts. In the bay of Arromanches, however, some elements of the floating harbor are still visible.

30 Head north from Bayeux along D516 to **Arromanches,** 10 kilometers (6 miles) away. Linger here a while, contemplating those seemingly insignificant hunks of concrete protruding from the water, and try to imagine the extraordinary technical feat involved in towing the two floating harbors across the Channel from England. (The other was moored at Omaha Beach but was destroyed on June 19, 1944, by an exceptionally violent storm.) If you're interested in yet more battle documentation, visit the **Musée du Débarquement,** right on the seafront, whose exhibits include models, mock-ups, and photographs depicting the invasion. *Admission: 15 frs. Open July and Aug. daily 9–7; Sept.– June, 9–11:30 and 2–5:30; closed most of Jan.*

From Arromanches, take D514 west.

Time Out About 10 kilometers (6 miles) along, you'll reach Port-en-Bessin-Huppain, a little fishing port that has a striking restaurant called **La Marine** (Quai Letourneur). The fish and seafood are fresh, and the upstairs dining room offers terrific views of the port.

Continue along D514 for another 8 kilometers (5 miles) to ③① **Colleville-sur-Mer**, then turn right to **Omaha Beach,** scene of a bloody battle in which nearly 10,000 American soldiers lost their lives. A little farther along D514, at St-Laurent-sur-Mer, turn right onto D517, which takes you back to the seafront at the site of the **Monument du Débarquement** (Monument to the Normandy Landings). You may want to park the car and stroll around the beaches and the grassy tops of the dunes overlooking them, from which you'll see sad remnants of the war—ruined bunkers, rows of trenches, and the remains of barbed-wire ③② defenses. Continue along the beachfront to **Vierville-sur-Mer,** which has a monument to the members of the U.S. National Guard who fought in both world wars.

Unless you decide to drive into the Cotentin Peninsula, past Utah Beach and on to Cherbourg, you can conclude your tour of the Calvados Coast either by returning to Bayeux via Isigny-sur-Mer, about 19 kilometers (12 miles) from Vierville, or con-③③ tinuing to **St-Lô,** 29 kilometers (18 miles) from Isigny. Given its sad sobriquet of the "capital of ruins," you won't be surprised that St-Lô played a strategic role in the Battle of Normandy and was almost completely destroyed in July 1944. The town was largely rebuilt after the war, and its only relic of the past is the ruined 13th–17th-century Eglise Notre-Dame.

From St-Lô, you'll be in striking distance of Normandy's most ③④ impressive monument, **Mont-St-Michel**, 72 kilometers (45 miles) southwest on the border of Normandy and Brittany.

Take D999, which joins with N175 at Villedieu-les-Poêles, and continue to Avranches; from here, follow the road around the bay to the Abbey of Mont-St-Michel. Before you visit this awe-inspiring monument, be warned that the sea that separates the rock from the mainland is extremely dangerous: It's subject to tidal movements that produce a difference of up to 45 feet between low and high tides, and because of the extremely flat bay bed, the water rushes in at an incredible speed. Also, there are nasty patches of quicksand, so tread with care!

The dramatic silhouette of Mont-St-Michel against the horizon may well be your most lasting image of Normandy. The wonder of the abbey stems not only from its rocky perch a few hundred yards off the coast (it's cut off from the mainland at high tide), but from its legendary origins in the 8th century and the sheer exploit of its construction, which took more than 500 years, from 1017 to 1521. The abbey stands at the top of a 264-foot mound of rock, and the granite used to build it was transported from the Isles of Chausey (just beyond Mont-St-Michel Bay) and Brittany and laboriously hauled up to the site.

Legend has it that the Archangel Michael appeared to Aubert, bishop of Avranches, inspiring him to build an oratory on what was then called Mont Tombe. The original church was completed in 1144, but new buildings were added in the 13th century to accommodate the monks, as well as the hordes of pilgrims who flocked here even during the Hundred Years' War, when the region was in English hands. The Romanesque choir was rebuilt in an ornate Gothic style during the 15th and 16th centuries. The abbey's monastic vocation was undermined during the 17th century, when the monks began to flout the strict rules and discipline of their order, a drift into decadence that culminated in the monks' dispersal and the abbey's conversion into a prison well before the French Revolution. In 1874, the former abbey was handed over to a governmental agency responsible for the preservation of historical monuments; only within the past 20 years have monks been able to live and work here once more.

A highlight of the abbey is the collection of 13th-century buildings on the north side of the mount. The exterior of the buildings is grimly fortresslike, but inside they are one of Normandy's best examples of the evolution of Gothic architecture, ranging from the sober Romanesque style of the lower halls to the masterly refinement of the cloisters and the elegance of the refectory.

A causeway—soon to be replaced by a bridge, thus allowing the bay waters to circulate freely—links Mont-St-Michel to the mainland. Leave your car in the parking lot at the foot of the mount, outside the main gateway.

The climb to the abbey is hard going, but it's worth it. Head first for the Grand Degré, the steep, narrow staircase on the north side. Once past the ramparts, you'll come to the pink-and-gray granite towers of the Châtelet and then to the Salle des Gardes, the central point of the abbey. Guided tours start from the Saut Gautier terrace (named after a prisoner who jumped to his death from it): You must join one of these groups if you want to see the beautifully wrought Escalier de Dentelle (Lace Staircase) inside the church. *Admission: 30 frs. Open mid-May–Sept., daily 9:30–11:30 and 1:30–6; Oct.–mid-May, Wed.–Mon. 9–11 and 1:30–4, closed Tues.*

The island village, with its steep, narrow streets, is best visited out of season, from September to May. The hordes of souvenir sellers and tourists can be stifling in summer months, but you can always take refuge in the abbey's gardens. The ramparts in general and the North Tower in particular offer dramatic views of the bay.

Tour 3: La Suisse Normande

Caen is the best starting point for a trip through La Suisse Normande, or Norman Switzerland, a rocky expanse of hills and gullies in the heart of Lower Normandy, containing lots of natural beauty and few man-made wonders. Striking as the scenery is, however, you'll need to exert all your powers of imagination to see much resemblance to the Swiss Alps! Taking D562 south for 45 kilometers (28 miles), you'll come to **Thury-Harcourt** on the Orne river, the gateway to La Suisse Normande. If you're not in a hurry and you enjoy twisting country roads, turn right off D562 at Laize-la-Ville, cross the Orne, and take the more scenic D212, which runs alongside the river and enters Thury-Harcourt from the opposite bank. This little country town is famous for the beautiful gardens of its ruined castle.

③⑥ Continue down D562, following the Orne, to **Clécy**, the area's main tourist center. It's a good base for visiting the sights of the Orne Valley; take the steep roads up to the clifftops overlooking the river, where there are lovely views of the woods on the other bank.

Time Out You'll find an open-air, riverbank café in Clécy, **La Potinière**, which is great for drinks or snacks. Pancakes top the bill, either sweet or with savory fillings such as ham and cheese, and there's a good selection of tarts and homemade ice cream. On Friday evening, you can enjoy a rowdy musical backdrop of jazz or rock. *On the river. Closed Oct.–Apr.*

From Clécy, continue for a couple of miles along D562 and then turn left at Le Fresne onto D1, which winds its way through ③⑦ the valley of the Noireau to another riverside resort, **Pont d'Ouilly**, situated at the point where the River Noireau flows into the Orne. Heading south along the Orne on D167, veer right at le Pont-des-Vers onto D43 and head into the most mountainous part of La Suisse Normande to the Roche d'Oëtre; from here, you'll get the most spectacular views of the craggy hills that give the region its name.

Continue along D301 for a few miles and then turn left across the Orne, joining D21 before turning almost immediately right ③⑧ along D239 to **Rabodanges**. Turn down any of the side roads leading to the riverside, where you'll be rewarded with a fine view of the river gorge (the Gorges de St-Aubert). A little farther upstream is the Rabodanges dam; from here, D121 skirts the eastern side of the lake. The road crosses the lake by the ③⑨ Ste-Croix bridge and brings you to **Putanges-Pont-Ecrépin**.

The Orne river now swings east to Argentan, a peaceful little town that was badly damaged during the last days of the Battle of Normandy. Rather than follow the river, however, it's more rewarding to head south from Putanges, along D909 and then ④⓪ D19 to **Bagnoles-de-l'Orne**, the most important spa town in the region. The town nestles in a beautiful setting overlooking a lake formed by the River Yée and is surrounded by forests and parkland that are well worth touring.

④① From Bagnoles-de-l'Orne, it's a fairly straight road to **Alençon**; follow D916 south, then turn left onto N176 to Pré-en-Pail and take N12 from there. The road runs through the middle of the Normandie-Maine Nature Park. Alençon lies on the eastern edge of the park, south of the Forest of Ecouves and west of the Forest of Perseigne. An attractive town with many historic buildings, Alençon has been a lace-making center since 1665; by the end of the century Alençon lace was de rigueur in all fashionable circles. The **Musée des Beaux-Arts et de la Dentelle** contains a sophisticated collection of lace from Italy, Flanders, and France, along with paintings from the French school that span the 17th to the 20th centuries. *Rue Julien. Admission: 10 frs. Open Tues.–Sun. 10–noon and 2–6.*

Turn right out of the museum and head right again at the corner. Seven blocks down, you'll come to the 14th–15th-century **Eglise Notre-Dame** (Rue St-Blaize), known for its highly ornate Gothic porch, erected around 1500.

What to See and Do with Children

The **Parc Zoologique de Clères,** 16 kilometers (10 miles) north of Rouen, is a wildlife park that's home to more than 750 species of birds, plus a motley assortment of free-roaming antelope, deer, kangaroos, and gibbons. Clères is a tiny village; you can't miss the park. *Admission: 30 frs. adults, 18 frs. children under 15. Open Mar.–May and Sept.–Nov., daily 9–noon and 3:30–sunset; June–Aug., daily 9–sunset.*

A **vintage car museum** is found at Le Bec-Hellouin, southwest of Rouen. Even those who are long past childhood will appreciate the 50 racing and touring automobiles from as early as 1920; the highlights must be the seven Bugattis. *Admission: 25 frs. Open 9–noon and 2–7.*

Most Norman resort beaches have supervised play areas where children can happily spend a half-day or so with their peers.

Off the Beaten Track

Connoisseurs of the apple brandy Calvados will be interested in a visit to the **Vallée d'Auge,** on the west side of the Pays d'Auge. This is the heart of Calvados country, between Troarn and Lisieux, through which the River Dives and its tributaries flow. You don't need a fixed itinerary; just follow your nose and look for local farmers offering Calvados for sale. However, there is a pretty, winding route to follow from Manerbe, north of Lisieux, which meanders west along D270, D117, and D85 to Beuvron-en-Auge, where you take D117 again across the River Dives to Troarn. Local Calvados producers will be delighted to let you taste their products, especially if you then buy a few bottles. They use traditional methods to distill the brandy, so you can be sure of finding something superior to the brands available in most shops.

Northwest of Evreux is **Le Bec-Hellouin,** near Brionne. Its famous Abbaye du Bec-Hellouin dates from the 11th century, but the monks were driven out during the French Revolution and the original abbey was demolished during the 19th century. Only the 15th-century St-Nicolas tower, part of the south transept, and the bases of some pillars remain, together with a 13th-century Gothic door and some statues from the 14th and 15th centuries. Next to the abbey is a vintage car museum. *(see* What to See and Do with Children, above). *Abbaye du Bec-Hellouin. Admission: 15 frs. Guided tours only, Wed.–Mon. June–Sept. at 10, 11, 3, 3:45, 4:30, and 5:15; Oct.–May at 11, 3:15, and 4:30.*

Shopping

Lace Handmade lace is a great rarity, and admirers will certainly think it's worth spending some time searching it out. Prices are high, but then, this kind of labor-intensive, high-quality creation never comes cheap. In Alençon, try the **Musée de la Dentelle** (31 rue du Pont-Neuf). In Bayeux, try the **Centre Normand de la Dentelle** on rue Leforestier.

Food Items Normandy is a food-lover's region, and some of the best buying is to be done in food markets and charcuteries. Gastronomes will want to drop by **La Ferme Normande** (pl. du Marché, Deauville) for regional delicacies, while those with a weakness for sweets should go straight to **Raten** (115 Grande-Rue, Dieppe).

Spirits It's true that you can buy Benedictine anywhere in the world, but if you've visited the **Musée de la Bénédictine** in Fécamp, the bottle you buy there will have a certain sentimental value (110 rue Alexandre-le-Grand). Calvados is harder to find outside France, and although it's generally available in wine shops around the country, you'll find a wider choice of good-quality Calvados in Normandy itself. If possible, buy Calvados that comes from the Vallée d'Auge, the area of Normandy reputed to produce the best (*see* Off the Beaten Track, above). In Lisieux, the **Distillerie du Père Jules** (rte. des Dives) offers first-rate Calvados.

Antiques Fairs and Markets If you enjoy the hunt as much as the prize, try the following: Caen hosts a bric-a-brac and antiques fair in June, while Cabourg has one in mid-August. Caen also has two morning flea markets: on Sunday in place Courtonne and on Friday in place St-Saveur.

Beaches

Wherever you go on the Normandy Coast, you'll look at the chilly waters of the English Channel: Those used to warmer climes may need all their resolve to take the plunge, even on hot, sunny days. The most fashionable Norman resorts lie along the Floral Coast, the eastern end of the Calvados Coast between Deauville/Trouville and Cabourg; it's virtually one long, sandy beach, with the different towns overlapping. The rest of the Calvados Coast is also a succession of seaside resorts, though the beaches that saw the Normandy landings have not been so developed as those farther east. While the resort towns of the western Calvados Coast don't lack for charm, they don't have the character of Honfleur or the unspoiled and rugged beauty of the pebbly Alabaster Coast, stretching from Le Havre to beyond Dieppe. The resorts here are more widely spaced, separated by craggy cliffs, and even in the summer months, beaches are relatively uncrowded. Perched on the clifftops are green fields and woodland where you can amble for hours, breathing the fresh sea air.

Sports and Fitness

Biking You can rent bicycles from train stations in Bayeux, Caen, Dieppe, and Le Tréport for about 35 francs per day. Or try **Family Home** in Bayeux (39 rue du Gal-de-Dais, tel. 31–92–15–22).

Golf The most spectacular golf course in Normandy is at **Le Vaudrueil,** in a park nestling between two branches of the River Eure; the course takes you past the ruins of a number of old castles. Other 18-hole courses are found in Cabourg, Deauville, Etretat, Dieppe, Le Havre, and Rouen; and nine-hole courses in Deauville, Houlgate, and Bagnoles-de-l'Orne.

Hiking There are 10 long-distance, signposted itineraries and count-less well-indicated footpaths for shorter walks; overnight hostels are found at many points. Contact the **Comité Départemental de la Randonnée Pedestre de Seine-Maritime** (B.P. 666, 76008 Rouen).

Horseback Riding Normandy is a leading horseracing and training region, with numerous stud farms, thoroughbred stables, and racecourses. The most important race of the year is the Grand Prix at Deau-ville, on the last Sunday in August. If you prefer riding to watching, contact Upper Normandy's center for equestrian tourism, the **Association Régionale de Tourisme Equestre** in Caen (Chambre d'Agriculture, 4 promenade Mme-de-Sévigné, 14039 Caen, tel. 31–84–47–19).

Rock Climbing There is good rock-climbing country in the Seine Valley and in the region of Suisse Normande; inquire at **C.A.F.** (13 rue Jacques-Durandes, 14000 Caen, tel. 31–93–07–23).

Water Sports With its miles of coastline, its rivers, and its lakes, Normandy offers a multitude of water-based activities. Many resorts have yachting marinas, where you can rent sailing dinghies and windsurfers as well as waterski. At the **Deauville Yacht Club** (quai de la Marine, tel. 31–88–38–19), a day in the smallest boat (16 feet) costs just 40 francs, while an 80-foot yacht will set you back about 300 francs. Similar prices are encountered at **Le Club Nautique de Trouville Hennequevelle** (Le Roches Noir, tel. 31–98–52–88). For swimmers, there are 60 outdoor and 20 in-door pools, in addition to the many safe bathing beaches; you can find public swimming pools in Bayeux, Cabourg, Caen, Deauville, Trouville, and Lisieux. The charming resort of Granville, 26 kilometers (16 miles) northwest of Avranches, is a center for aquatic sports; inquire about sailboat jaunts at the **Centre Regional de Nautisme de Granville** (Anse de Hérel, 50400 Granville, tel. 33–50–18–95). **Lepesqueux Voile** (3 rue Clément-Desmaisons, 50400 Granville, tel. 33–50–18–97) rents boats and yachts for vacation cruises.

Dining and Lodging

Dining

Normandy is the land of butter, cream cheese, and Calvados. The Normans are notoriously big eaters: In the old days, on festive occasions they wouldn't bat an eye at tucking into as many as 24 courses. Between the warm-up and the main course there was a *trou* (hole), often lasting several hours, during which lots of Calvados was downed, giving rise to the expres-sion *le trou normand*.

Many dishes are cooked with rich cream sauces; the description *à la normande* usually means "with a cream sauce." The rich-ness of the milk makes for excellent cheese: *Pont-l'Évêque* (known since the 13th century) is made in the Pays d'Auge with milk that is still warm and creamy, while *Livarot* (also pro-duced for centuries) uses milk that has stood for a while; don't be put off by its strong smell. Then there are the excellent *Pavé d'Auge* and the best known of them all, *Camembert*, a relative newcomer, invented by a farmer's wife in the late 18th century. Now so popular that it is produced all over France, the best

Camembert is still made in Normandy (known as *Camembert au lait cru*).

There are many local specialties. Rouen is famous for its *canard à la Rouennaise* (duck in blood sauce); Caen, for its *tripes à la mode de Caen* (tripe cooked with carrots in a seasoned cider stock); and Mont-St-Michel, for *omelette Mère Poulard* (hearty omelette made by a local hotel manager in the late 19th century for travelers to Mont-St-Michel). Then there are *sole dieppoise* (sole poached in a sauce with cream and mussels), excellent chicken from the Vallée d'Auge, and lamb from the salt marshes. Those who like *boudin noir* (blood sausage) have come to the right region, and for seafood lovers, the coast provides oysters, lobster, and shrimp.

Normandy is not a wine-growing area but produces excellent cider. The best comes from the Vallée d'Auge and is 100% apple juice; when poured into the glass, it should fizz a bit but not froth.

Highly recommended restaurants are indicated by a star ★.

Category	Cost*
Very Expensive	over 350 francs
Expensive	200–350 francs
Moderate	100–200 francs
Inexpensive	under 100 francs

*per person for a three-course meal, including tax (18.6%) and tip but not wine

Lodging

There are accommodations to suit every taste in Normandy. In the beach resorts, the season is very short, July and August only, but weekends are busy for much of the year; in June and September, accommodations are usually available at short notice.

Highly recommended hotels are indicated by a star ★.

Category	Cost*
Very Expensive	over 750 francs
Expensive	350–750 francs
Moderate	200–350 francs
Inexpensive	under 200 francs

*All prices are for a standard double room for two, including tax (18.6%) and service charge.

Bagnoles-de-l'Orne
Dining and Lodging
★

Le Manoir de Lys. Elegant guest rooms are decorated with flair at this magnificent Norman manor house, which lords it over a beautifully landscaped park on the edge of a forest. The restaurant has gained a considerable reputation for its cuisine *à la normande. Croix Gauthier, rte. de Juvigny (a mile from the casino), 61140, tel. 33–37–80–69. 12 rooms with bath. Facili-*

ties: restaurant, tennis. AE, MC, V. Closed Jan.–Feb.; restaurant closed Sun. dinner and Tues. Nov.–Mar. Expensive.

Bois Joli. A less-imposing Norman manor house, Bois Joli has been recently renovated, and its cozily stylish guest rooms will make you feel right at home; they're all individually decorated. Peace and quiet reign here, and the delightful terrace overlooks the hotel's gardens. A piano plays softly in the background while diners tuck into good regional fare in the elegant restaurant. *12 av. Philippe-du-Rozier (opposite the race course), 61140, tel. 33–37–92–77. 20 rooms, 15 with bath. Facilities: restaurant, terrace, garden. AE, DC, MC, V. Closed Jan.–Feb. Moderate.*

Bayeux
Dining and Lodging

Le Lion d'Or. The Lion d'Or is a handsome '30s creation, conveniently situated in the center of town. Palm trees arch over the garden courtyard, while flowers cascade from balcony window boxes. Rooms are comfortable and well furnished with pretty fabrics. Fine Norman cuisine is served in the chic wood-beamed restaurant, decorated in shades of apricot. Specialties include *andouille chaud Bovary,* no doubt Madame Bovary's own recipe for hot sausages, and fillet of sole in a creamy lobster sauce. *71 rue St-Jean, 14400, tel. 31–92–06–90. 22 rooms with bath. Facilities: restaurant. AE, DC, MC, V. Closed Christmas–mid-Jan. Moderate.*

Lodging

Churchill. This small, stylish, friendly hotel opened in the town center in 1986 and has already made a mark with foreign visitors. There are good-value menus, and solid breakfasts (ham and eggs available on request) are served in the airy veranda. *14 rue St-Jean, 14400, tel. 31–21–32–80. 32 rooms with bath or shower. AE, DC, MC, V. Closed mid-Nov.–Mar. Moderate.*

★ **Hôtel d'Argouges.** This lovely 18th-century hotel is an oasis of calm in the city center, and many rooms offer views of the well-tended flower garden. The rooms are superb, tastefully furnished in French provincial chic and featuring rustic beamed ceilings. There's no restaurant. *21 rue St-Patrice, 14400, tel. 31–92–88–86. 22 rooms with bath. Facilities: garden. AE, DC, MC, V. Moderate.*

Le Bec-Hellouin
Dining and Lodging
★

Auberge de l'Abbaye. You'll enjoy traditional Norman cooking in this rustic inn, which features beamed ceilings and stone walls hung with ornamental copper pans. Charming Madame Sergent has been in charge for over a quarter of a century; she also has eight delightfully old-fashioned bedrooms but says they are reserved for her diners (though you don't have to stay here to eat at the restaurant). According to one famous TV personality, this restaurant serves the best apple tart in France. *Pl. de l'Eglise, 27800, tel. 32–44–86–02. Reservations advised. Dress: casual. MC, V. Closed Mon. dinner, Tues., and mid-Jan.–Feb. Moderate.*

Bénouville
Dining
★

Le Manoir d'Hastings. One of Normandy's most celebrated restaurants is situated in a little village 10 kilometers (6 miles) north of Caen. The 17th-century building was originally a Norman priory. In addition to the main dining room, there are 11 private rooms for more intimate (and expensive) occasions. Aperitifs and coffee are served in the garden. The considerable reputation of owner-chef Claude Scaviner and his son is based mainly on their fish and seafood dishes. *18 av. de la Côte-de-Nacre, tel. 31–44–62–43. Reservations required. Jacket and tie required. AE, DC, MC, V. Closed Sun. dinner, Mon., and first half Feb. Expensive.*

Bonsecours
Dining
★

Auberge de la Butte. Master chef Pierre Hervé is renowned for his subtle way with fish and seafood; his best dishes include poached oysters wrapped in spinach leaves and fricasseed fillet of sole. The magnificent Norman dining room's half-timbered walls are adorned with paintings and shining copper pots and pans, and the ceiling features exposed beams as well. *69 rte. de Paris, tel. 35–80–43–11. Reservations advised. Jacket and tie required. AE, DC, MC, V. Closed Wed. dinner, Thurs., Sun. dinner, Dec. 22–Jan. 5, and Aug. Expensive.*

Cabourg
Lodging

Pullman Grand Hôtel. This luxurious, white-stucco hotel is set right on the seafront at the heart of town, and many guest rooms have balconies overlooking the sea. There's a lively piano bar during the summer season, and the hotel is connected to the casino. Its restaurant, Le Balbec, offers traditional French cuisine of a high standard but no great sophistication. *Promenade Marcel-Proust, 14390, tel. 31–91–01–79. 70 rooms with bath. Facilities: restaurant, bar. AE, DC, MC, V. Very Expensive.*

Caen
Dining
★

La Bourride. Normandy boasts a number of excellent restaurants; La Bourride is one of the best, situated close to the castle down one of Caen's oldest streets. Chef Michel Bruneau's inventive and delicate dishes are inspired mainly by local produce, but the cooking is essentially modern. The small dining room is typically Norman, with stone walls, beamed ceilings, and a large fireplace. *15 rue du Vaugueux, tel. 31–93–50–76. Reservations required. Jacket and tie required. AE, DC, MC, V. Closed Sun., Mon., first 3 weeks Jan. and second half Aug. Expensive.*

Dining and Lodging
★

Château d'Audrieu. Twenty-four kilometers (15 miles) west of Caen, on the road to Tilly-sur-Seulles, is a property that fulfills Hollywood's idea of a palatial château. A tree-lined avenue leads to an imposing, elegant 18th-century facade, which sets the tone for what lies within. The bedrooms and salons are the last word in Old World opulence, featuring wall sconces, overstuffed chairs, and antiques. The restaurant has an extensive wine list, and chef Alain Cornet uses produce from the château's own vegetable garden to create classic French dishes. *14250 Audrieu, tel. 31–80–21–52. 22 rooms with bath. Facilities: restaurant, bar, pool, park. MC, V. Closed Dec. 20–end Feb.; restaurant closed Wed., and Thurs. lunch. Very Expensive.*

Le Relais des Gourmets. One of the best hotels in town also has a terrific restaurant. The luxurious modern guest rooms are spacious and airy, and an Old World atmosphere reigns in the public rooms, which are dotted with some charming antiques. The plush restaurant offers a sophisticated level of service and classic local cuisine. The gratinéed lobster with crayfish and turbot with cèpe mushrooms are memorable. Meals are served in the garden during summer months. *15 rue de Geôle, 14000, tel. 31–86–06–01. 32 rooms with bath. Facilities: restaurant, garden. AE, DC, MC, V. Restaurant closed Sun. dinner. Expensive.*

★ **Le Dauphin.** Despite its downtown location—beware one-way streets as you arrive—Le Dauphin offers peace and quiet. The building is a former priory dating from the 12th century, though the smallish guest rooms are briskly modern. Those overlooking the street are soundproofed, while the rooms in back have views of the serene garden courtyard. The wood-beam breakfast room is a delightful place to start the day. The service is especially friendly and efficient, both in the hotel and in the excellent, though rather expensive, restaurant, which specializes in traditional Norman cooking. Fish is featured on the menu, though the veal sweetbreads in a mushroom sauce is a good choice as well. *29 rue Gémare, 14000, tel. 31–86–22–26. 21 rooms with bath. Facilities: restaurant, garden. AE, DC, MC, V. Closed mid-July–mid-Aug. Moderate.*

Deauville
Dining and Lodging

Normandy. The Normandy's exterior is a jet-set resort's idea of quaint: Gables and nooks create a sleek rendition of provincial style. Inside, the large guest rooms are rife with antiques and period-style furniture, and many overlook the sea. The restaurant extends into a Norman courtyard surrounded by apple trees. *38 rue Jean-Mermoz, 14800, tel. 31–98–66–22. 348 rooms, 290 with bath. Facilities: restaurant, garden. AE, DC, MC, V. Very Expensive.*

Le Royal. This gigantic five-star hotel, overlooking the sea and close to the casino, is stately and more than a trifle self-important. It has a range of guest rooms in various degrees of luxury and two restaurants: Le Royal, a sumptuous dining room in keeping with the establishment's general character, and L'Etrier, more intimate but still very plush, where the emphasis is on haute cuisine. *Blvd. Cornuché, 14800, tel. 31–98–66–33. 310 rooms, 281 with bath. Facilities: restaurants, pool, sauna, tennis. AE, DC, MC, V. Closed mid-Nov.–Easter. Very Expensive.*

Lodging

Le Continental. One of Deauville's oldest buildings is home to this provincial seaside hotel. The owner, Madame Perrot, is brisk and efficient, as is the service. The guest rooms are small and somewhat spartan—but this is Deauville, after all, and for the price you can't do much better. The Continental is handily placed between the port and the casino, but it doesn't have a restaurant. *1 rue Désiré-le-Hoc, 14800, tel. 31–88–21–06. 55 rooms, 36 with bath. AE, DC, MC, V. Closed mid-Nov.–mid-Mar. Inexpensive.*

Dieppe
Dining and Lodging

La Présidence. The modern Présidence overlooks the sea and offers airy, well-appointed guest rooms and an "English" bar, Le Verrazane. The delightful restaurant, Le Panoramic, is on the fourth floor, where classic, unpretentious, but tasty cooking predominates. *1 blvd. de Verdun, 76200, tel. 35–84–31–31. 88 rooms, 79 with bath. Facilities: restaurant. AE, DC, MC, V. Moderate.*

Duclair
Dining

Le Parc. Pierre Le Patezour, one of the region's most acclaimed chefs, has created an excellent restaurant in Duclair, about 20 kilometers (12 miles) west of Rouen, on the road to Caudebec-en-Caux. The dining room features plush, art-nouveau decor, and the menu offers such classic regional dishes as *canard à la Rouennaise* (duck in blood sauce). Le Patezour's subtle preparation of fillet of sole is an eye-opener. *721 av. du Président-Coty, tel. 35–37–50–31. Reservations advised. Jacket and tie required. AE, DC, MC, V. Closed Sun. dinner, Mon., and Dec. 20–Jan. 20. Expensive.*

Etretat
Dining

Les Roches Blanches. Expect a warm welcome at this cozily unpretentious family-run restaurant near the sea, which has three good-value menus. The house specialty is veal escalope with mushrooms, flambéed in Calvados, and there is a good range of fish and seafood dishes. *Rue Abbé-Cochet, tel. 35–27–07–34. Reservations advised, especially for Sun. lunch. Dress:*

casual. *MC, V. Closed Tues., Wed., and Thurs. (Wed. only July–early Sept.) and Jan. and Oct. Moderate.*

Lodging **Le Donjon.** This charming little château is set in a large park overlooking the resort and offers lovely bay views. The individually furnished guest rooms are huge, comfortable, and quiet. Reliable French cuisine is served with flair in the cozy restaurant. *Chemin de St-Clair, 76790, tel. 35–27–08–23. 7 rooms, 6 with bath. Facilities: restaurant, pool. AE, DC, V. Expensive.*
Dormy House. Thanks to its location halfway up the southern cliff, Dormy House provides dramatic views of the bay. Four buildings, dating from different periods and in a variety of architectural styles, make up the hotel. The large rooms are furnished in oak and sport cheerful floral drapes. Most guests stay on half-board; the restaurant specializes in fish and seafood. *Rte. du Havre, 76790, tel. 35–27–07–88. 32 rooms, 28 with bath. Facilities: restaurant. MC, V. Closed Jan.–end Mar. Moderate.*

Fécamp **Auberge de la Rouge.** The quaint Auberge de la Rouge is in a
Dining little hamlet a mile or so south of Fécamp. Its menu features a good mix of classic and modern dishes and includes many local specialties; the lobster is always a good bet. There are eight guest rooms, too. *Commune de St-Léonard, tel. 35–28–07–59. Reservations advised. Dress: casual. AE, DC, MC, V. Closed Sun. dinner and Mon. Moderate.*

★ **L'Escalier.** This delightfully simple little restaurant overlooks the harbor and serves traditional *cuisine à la Normande.* The several inexpensive fixed-price menus mainly offer fish and seafood. *101 quai Bérigny, tel. 35–28–26–79. Reservations essential in summer. Dress: casual. DC, MC, V. Closed Mon. and 2 weeks in Nov. Inexpensive.*

Honfleur **L'Absinthe.** The Absinthe's 17th-century dining room, with
Dining stone walls and beamed ceilings, is a magnificent setting in which to enjoy chef Antoine Ceffrey's masterly creations, though on sunny days you'll probably want to eat outside on the terrace. Ceffrey has a delicate way with fish and seafood; try the *burbet,* a freshwater cod, prepared with ginger. *10 quai de la Quarantaine, tel. 31–89–39–00. Reservations advised. Jacket and tie required. AE, DC, MC, V. Closed Mon. evening and Tues. Sept.–June. Expensive.*
L'Ancrage. Massive seafood platters top the bill at this delightful old restaurant, which occupies a two-story 17th-century building overlooking the harbor. The cuisine is authentically Norman—simple but good. If you want a change from fish and seafood, try the succulent calf sweetbreads. *16 rue Montpensier, tel. 31–89–00–70. Reservations advised, especially in summer. Dress: casual. MC, V. Closed Tues. dinner, Wed., and Jan. Moderate.*

Dining and Lodging **Ferme St-Siméon.** A 19th-century manor house—commonly
★ held to be the birthplace of Impressionism—is set in the park that inspired such 19th-century luminaries as Claude Monet and Alfred Sisley. The guest rooms are individually decorated in a style an ad-man might term "palatial provincial," and a few have Jacuzzis. Pastel colors and floral wallpaper create a gardenlike aura in some rooms, while antiques and period decor are featured in others. The sophisticated restaurant specializes in fish, and in good weather you can eat out on the terrace. Save room for the extensive cheese board. *Rue Adolphe-Marais, on D513 to Trouville, 14600 Honfleur, tel. 31–89–23–61. 38 rooms*

with bath. Facilities: restaurant, tennis, park. MC, V. Restaurant closed Wed. lunch Nov.–Mar. Very Expensive.

Auberge du Vieux Puits. Twenty kilometers (13 miles) southeast of Honfleur lies a quaint little cottage of a hotel, whose trellised and beamed exterior can't have changed much in the past 300 years. Early admirers included Gustave Flaubert, who gave the hotel a few lines in *Madame Bovary*. The guest rooms make use of heavy wooden furniture and pretty curtains and bedspreads to reflect the traditional feel of the architecture. The restaurant offers first-rate cuisine. *6 rue Notre-Dame-du-Pré, 27500 Pont-Audemer, tel. 32–41–01–48. 12 rooms, 6 with bath. MC, V. Closed Dec. 20–Jan. 22. Moderate-Expensive.*

Le Cheval Blanc. Occupying a renovated, 15th-century building on the harborfront, this hotel has one of the finest restaurants in town. All the guest rooms have recently been redecorated and offer views of the port across the main road through town. Chef Robert Samson prepares classic yet delicate cuisine that is served with panache in the beautiful Louis XIII–style dining room. Try the seafood and oyster mousse or the sliced turbot in a subtle cider-and-cream sauce. *2 quai des Passagers, 14600, tel. 31–89–13–49. 35 rooms, 14 with bath. Facilities: restaurant. MC, V. Closed last 3 weeks in Jan.; restaurant (tel. 31–89–39–87) closed Mon. and from mid-Nov.–Jan. 31. Moderate.*

Hostellerie Lechat. One of the best-known and -loved establishments in Honfleur stands in a pretty square just behind the harbor in a typical 18th-century Norman building. The spacious guest rooms have recently been renovated in pretty French-provincial decor that makes good use of cheerful prints and colors. Foreign guests are given a warm welcome, especially in The American bar. The rustic, beamed restaurant serves top-notch Norman cuisine; lobster features prominently on the menu. *3 pl. Ste-Catherine, 14600, tel. 31–89–23–85. 24 rooms with bath. Facilities: restaurant, bar. AE, DC, MC, V. Restaurant closed Jan., Wed., and Thurs. lunch mid-Sept.–May. Moderate.*

Houlgate
Dining and Lodging

Mon Castel. If you want to stay on the Calvados coast but don't fancy pricey Deauville or Cabourg, cheerful Houlgate is your best bet. The down-to-earth Mon Castel offers the best value in town, especially if you secure the large-windowed room 1 on the second floor. Seafood reigns in the old-fashioned dining room. *1 blvd. des Belges, 14510, tel. 31–91–34–75. 12 rooms, some with bath or shower. MC, V. Inexpensive.*

Mont-St-Michel
Dining and Lodging
★

Mère Poulard. The hotel of the most celebrated restaurant on the mount consists of adjoining houses whose cozy, newly modernized, second-floor rooms are both comfortable and quiet. The restaurant's reputation derives partly from Mère Poulard's famous omelette (a recipe that originated in the 19th century and requires slow cooking over an open wood fire) and partly from its dramatic location. Young chef Jean-Luc Wahl successfully combines traditional and nouvelle cuisine, adding his own inventions to the long-standing house specialties. *50116 Mont-St-Michel, tel. 33–60–14–01. Reservations required. Jacket and tie preferred. AE, DC, MC, V. Expensive.*

Terrasses Poulard. Monsieur Vannier bought this popular restaurant first, and later acquired its more prestigious sister establishment (above). The hotel is a recent addition, a result of buying up and renovating the neighboring houses to create an ensemble of buildings that exude great charm and character, clustered around a small garden in the middle of the mount. The large restaurant attracts hordes of tourists; if you don't mind being surrounded by fellow Americans, Canadians, and Britons, you'll no doubt enjoy the traditional cuisine. *On the main road opposite the parish church, 50116, tel. 33–60–14–09. 29 rooms with bath. Facilities: restaurant, library, billiards room. AE, DC, MC, V. Moderate.*

Rouen
Dining

Bertrand Warin. The most fashionable restaurant in Rouen occupies a 17th-century town house near the old market. Owner-chef Bertrand Warin has created an elegant dining room that contrasts half-timbered walls and Louis XIII chairs with sleek modern furnishings. The tables are widely spaced, and large windows look out onto an illuminated garden. *7 rue de la Pie, near the Vieux Marché, tel. 35–89–26–69. Reservations required. Jacket and tie required. AE, DC, MC, V. Closed Sun. evening, Mon., first half Jan., and last 2 weeks in Aug. Expensive.*

La Couronne. The dining room of this 15th-century Norman building features beamed ceilings, leather-upholstered chairs, wood-paneled walls, and a scattering of sculpture. The traditional Norman cuisine makes few concessions to modernism; specialties include crayfish salad with foie gras and caviar, duck with orange, and turbot in puff pastry. *31 pl. du Vieux-Marché, tel. 35–71–40–90. Reservations advised. Jacket and tie required. AE, DC, MC, V. Expensive.*

L'Entr'Acte. A friendly, bustling bistro, L'Entr'Acte is located just beside the market and Joan of Arc's memorial church. It has a motherly staff and a huge menu with some worthwhile specialties. This is the place for succulent oysters—there are five or six kinds on the menu—and delicious tripe cooked the local way. There are tables outside in summer. *2 pl. Vieux-Marché, tel. 35–15–14–24. Reservations advised. Dress: casual. AE, DC, V. Moderate.*

Dining and Lodging

Pullman Albane. This grandiose, modern (1976) hotel, just opposite the train station, has luxurious, comfortable rooms; the best feature '30s-style decor. There's an American bar, and the restaurant, Le Tournebroche, serves classic Norman cooking with creamy and cheesy sauces, as well as plain grilled and spit-roast dishes. *Rue Croix-de-Fer, 76000, tel. 35–52–69–52. 125 rooms with bath. Facilities: restaurant, bar. AE, DC, MC, V. Expensive.*

Hôtel de Dieppe. Dating from the late 19th century, the Dieppe remains fresh and up-to-date thanks to frequent redecoration. You can take your choice of rooms furnished in breezy modern style or those with antique furniture. The restaurant, Les Quatre Saisons, has a well-earned reputation and offers English-style roasts as well as such traditional French dishes as duck cooked in its blood (which tastes much nicer than it sounds). *Pl. Bernard-Tissot, 76000, tel. 35–71–96–00. 42 rooms with bath. Facilities: restaurant, breakfast room. AE, DC, MC, V. Moderate.*

Vernon
Dining and Lodging

Normandy. Good accommodation near Giverny has long been in short supply, so this hotel, opened in 1990, is good news. The service is friendly, the breakfasts substantial, and the rooms well equipped and calm (ask for one away from the street). *1 av. Mendès-France, 27200, tel. 32–51–97–97. 50 rooms with bath. Facilities: restaurant, bar. AE, MC, V. Moderate–Expensive.*

Trouville **Carmen.** This straightforward, unpretentious little hotel is
Lodging just around the corner from the casino. The rooms range from
the plain and inexpensive to the comfortable and moderate.
The restaurant offers good home cooking at value-for-the-money prices. *24 rue Carnot, tel. 31–88–35–43. 14 rooms, 12 with
bath. Facilities: restaurant. AE, DC, MC, V. Closed Jan., part
of May, and third week in Oct. Restaurant closed Mon. dinner
and Tues. Inexpensive–Moderate.*

The Arts and Nightlife

The Arts

Music Normandy's cultural activities revolve around music, both classical and modern. Many churches host evening concerts, with
organ recitals drawing an especially large number of enthusiasts. Particularly good programs are featured at the church of
St-Ouen in Rouen, **St-Etienne** in Caen, and **St-Pierre** in Lisieux
(get details from the tourist office). Rouen's **St-Maclou** hosts an
annual series of organ recitals in August; even the venerable
abbey of **Mont-St-Michel** gets into the act during July and August. Jazz aficionados will be interested in the **European Traditional Jazz Festival** held in mid-June at Luneray, 8 kilometers (5
miles) southwest of Dieppe. For those who like spectacle with
their music, the **Théâtre des Arts** (tel. 35–71–41–36) in Rouen
stages numerous operas.

Festivals A **Joan of Arc Commemoration** takes place in Rouen at the end
of May, featuring a variety of parades, street plays, concerts,
and exhibitions that recall the life—and death—of France's patron saint.

Film One of the biggest cultural events on the Norman calendar is
the **American Film Festival,** held in Deauville during the first
week of September.

Nightlife

The hot spots of Normandy nightlife are, predictably enough,
such resorts as Deauville, Trouville, and Cabourg, where
discos and clubs vie with casinos for space.

Casinos There are nearly 30 casinos dotted around the region, five
of which—**Deauville, Forges-les-Eaux, Trouville, Dieppe,** and
Bagnoles-de-l'Orne—rank among France's best, with floorshows and cabarets, as well as gaming rooms.

Bars and Try **Régine's** (rue Edmond-Blanc) in Deauville or Dieppe's **Ca-**
Nightclubs **sino** (3 blvd. de Verdun). Night owls will enjoy the smoky ambience of **Club Melody** in Deauville (13 rue Albert-Fracasse) and
the jiving crowd at **Le Loft** (29 blvd. des Belges) in Rouen.

8 Champagne and the North

Introduction

Too few people visit northern France. The crowd-following French head south each year in search of a suntan. The millions of foreign tourists who flock through the Channel ports of Calais, Boulogne, and Dunkerque make a beeline to Paris. The Channel Tunnel, perhaps the most ambitious engineering project of the late 20th century, could change this. It is due to open in 1993, and dynamic local tourist authorities are banking on an influx of British daytrippers and weekenders. The English are already busy buying homes in the region, many with an eye to commuting to London on the TGV.

Northern France was in the frontline of battle during the world wars and suffered heavily. The city of Reims was shelled incessantly during World War I, and such names as the Somme and Vimy Ridge evoke the bloody, deadlocked battles that raged from 1914 to 1918. Cemeteries and war memorials may not be the most cheerful items on a tourist's itinerary, but they do have a melancholy, thought-provoking beauty.

The Channel coast—mile upon mile of empty, sandy beaches— is featured in our first tour. It is unfortunate that Calais and Dunkerque, the first ports of call for many visitors to France, are among the country's ugliest towns. The old sectors of neighboring Boulogne are far more appealing, while, farther down the coast, there is a startling clash between the narrow streets of the ancient, rickety, walled town of Montreuil and the posh avenues of Le Touquet, a fashionable 19th-century resort.

The north of France is an industrial region, but ignore talk of slag heaps and pollution-spouting smokestacks; heavy industry is highly centralized. This is a green and pleasant land where wooded, restful landscapes predominate. To the east, the plains give way to hills. The grapes of Champagne flourish on the steep slopes of the Marne Valley and on the so-called Mountain of Reims. There are no mountains, of course, even though the mighty mound of Laon is known as the Crowned Mountain because of the bristling silhouette of its many-towered cathedral.

Reims is the only city in Champagne, and one of France's richest tourist venues. The kings of France were crowned in its cathedral until 1825, and every age since the Roman has left an architectural mark. The small nearby towns of Ay and Epernay play an equally important role in the thriving champagne business, which has conferred wealth and, sometimes, an arrogant reserve on the region's inhabitants. The down-to-earth folk of the north provide a warmer welcome.

Essential Information

Important Addresses and Numbers

Tourist Information The principal regional tourist offices are in **Lille** (pl. Rihour, tel. 20–30–81–00), **Reims** (2 rue Guillaume de Machault, tel. 26–47–25–69), and **Amiens** (20 pl. Notre-Dame, tel. 22–91–16–16).

The addresses of other tourist offices in towns mentioned on this tour are as follows: **Abbeville** (26 pl. de la Libération, tel. 22–24–27–92), **Arras** (place des Héros, tel. 21–51–26–95), **Boulogne** (Pont Marguet, tel. 21–31–68–38), **Calais** (12 blvd. Clemenceau, tel. 21–96–62–40), **Compiègne** (pl. de l'Hôtel-de-Ville, tel. 44–40–01–00), **Laon** (pl. du Parvis, tel. 23–20–28–62), **Montreuil-sur-Mer** (pl. Darnétal, tel. 21–06–04–27), **Le Touquet** (Palais de l'Europe, pl. de l'Hermitage, tel. 21–05–21–65), **Noyon** (pl. de l'Hôtel-de-Ville, tel. 44–44–21–88), **Pierrefonds** (pl. de l'Hôtel-de-Ville, tel. 44–42–81–44), and **St-Omer** (pl. du Pain-Levé, tel. 21–98–70–00).

Travel Agencies **Wagons Lits,** 1 rue Paul Bert (pl. de l'Hôtel-de-Ville, Calais, tel. 21–34–79–25; and 74 bis rue Nationale, Lille, tel. 20–57–72–45).

Car Rental **Avis** (36 pl. d'Armes, Calais, tel. 21–34–66–50; 18 blvd. du Maréchal-Joffre, Reims, tel. 26–47–10–08), **Europcar** (5 rue du Molinel, Lille, tel. 20–78–18–18), and **Hertz** (5 blvd. d'Alsace, Amiens, tel. 22–91–26–24; and 85 rue Victor-Hugo, Boulogne, tel. 21–31–53–14).

Arriving and Departing

By Plane American visitors should count on arriving at Paris's Charles de Gaulle or Orly airport; there are direct flights from London's Heathrow to Lille and from Gatwick to Beauvais.

By Car The A1 expressway from Paris passes close to Compiègne (N32 heads off to Noyon) and Arras before reaching Lille, where there are expressways to Brussels (E42) and Ghent (E3).

By Train Trains whistle from Paris to Lille (256 kilometers/160 miles) in just two hours, stopping at Arras. The Paris–Calais train chugs unhurriedly around the coast, taking nearly three hours to cover 300 kilometers (190 miles) and stopping at Amiens, Abbeville, Etaples (bus link to Le Touquet 4 miles away), Montreuil-sur-Mer, and Boulogne. There is frequent daily service from Paris to Compiègne and Noyon. The train from the Gare du Nord to Laon takes two leisurely hours to cover 140 kilometers (90 miles). Regular trains cover the 175 kilometers (110 miles) from Paris (Gare de l'Est) to Reims in 1½ hours, continuing to Luxembourg. The new TGV line to London should be operational in 1993 and will stop at Arras, Lille, and Calais.

Getting Around

By Plane Domestic airports are found at Le Touquet, Calais, and Reims.

By Car A26 heads inland from Calais and St-Omer to Arras (where it intersects with A1), Laon, and Reims, which is directly linked to Paris by A4. N1 follows the railroad around the coast from Belgium and Dunkerque through Calais, Boulogne, Montreuil-sur-Mer, Amiens, and Beauvais to Paris.

By Train The branch line between Lille and Calais stops at St-Omer. Trains run daily, though slowly, from Laon to Amiens and Reims.

Guided Tours

Bus Excursions The **Nord-Pas de Calais** tourist office in Lille (26 pl. Rihour, tel. 20–57–40–04) is a mine of information about companies that offer bus tours of northern France. **Loisirs-Accueil Nord** (15 rue du Nouveau-Siècle, Lille, tel. 20–57–00–61) offers bus trips to Boulogne and Flanders. In the Reims area, the **Comité Régional de Tourisme et des Loisirs Champagne-Ardennes** (5 rue de Jericho, Châlons-sur-Marne, tel. 26–64–35–92) has numerous bus excursions around the region, including tours within Reims, "nature" trips to the national parks and forest, and history tours to World War I sites. The cost per day is 200 francs.

Special-Interest   **Nuances** (26 pl. Rihour, Lille, tel. 20–40–02–57) offers archaeology and gastronomy tours, ranging from one to five days. One excursion focuses exclusively on the products of the region, including chocolate, cheese, foie gras, and medicinal plants. A two-day tour costs 500 francs. **Loisirs-Accueil Nord** (*see* above) specializes in outdoor pursuits and can arrange fishing and walking tours. It also provides beer-tasting tours.

Personal Guides   **Renaissance du Vieux Boulogne** (rue Bernet, Boulogne-sur-Mer, tel. 21–92–11–52) arranges trips to Boulogne's old town and port for groups up to four; the cost for two hours is 330 francs.

Exploring Champagne and the North

Numbers in the margin correspond with points of interest on the Champagne and the North map.

Orientation

We have divided the vast region covered in this chapter into two tours. The first covers the north of France proper, stretching from Beauvais up to the English Channel, Lille, and the Belgian frontier. The second covers the Champagne area northeast of Paris, with Reims at its heart.

Highlights for First-time Visitors

Cathédrale Notre Dame, Reims, Tour 2
Cathédrale St-Pierre, Beauvais, Tour 1
Cathedral and ramparts of Laon's old town, Tour 2
Wine towns of the Montagne de Reims, Tour 2
The resort town of Le Touquet, Tour 1
World War I battle sites near Arras, Tour 1
Musée Matisse (Le Cateau-Cambrésis), Off the Beaten Track

Tour 1: The North

❶ The gateway to the north is the cathedral town of **Beauvais,** 72 kilometers (45 miles) north of Paris on N1. Like Reims and Abbeville, Beauvais still bears the painful scars of two world wars. It was savagely bombed in June 1940, and the ramshackle streets of the old town have resurfaced as characterless modern blocks. One survivor is the beautiful old Bishop's Palace, now the **Musée des Beaux-Arts** (Fine Arts Museum). Within its chambered recesses, you'll find a varied collection of art, embracing painting, ceramics, and regional furniture. Highlights include an epic canvas of the French Revolution by 19th-century master Thomas Couture, complete with preparatory

sketches (all tastefully assembled in a large room once used as the district law court) and the charming attic under the sloping roofs, which qualifies as one of the loveliest rooms in all France. *Rue du Musée. Admission: 10 frs. Open Wed.–Mon. 10–noon and 2–6; closed Tues.*

The town's showpiece is unquestionably the **Cathédrale St-Pierre,** adjacent to the art museum. You may have an attack of vertigo just gazing up at its vaults, which, at 153 feet, are the highest in France. Such daring engineering was not without risk: The choir collapsed in 1284, shortly after completion. The transept, an outstanding example of Flamboyant Gothic, was not attempted until the 16th century. It was crowned by an improbable 450-foot spire that promptly came crashing down. With funds rapidly dwindling, the nave was never begun, delivering the final coup de grâce to Beauvais's ambition of becoming the largest church in Christendom. The 10th-century church, known as the **Basse Oeuvre** (closed to the public), juts out impertinently where the nave should have been. *Pl. St-Pierre.*

From 1664 to 1939, Beauvais was one of France's leading tapestry centers; it reached its zenith in the mid-18th century under the direction of renowned artist Jean-Baptiste Oudry. The **Galérie Nationale de la Tapisserie,** a modern museum next to the cathedral, has examples from all periods of the town's tapestry history. *24 rue Henri-Brispot. Admission: 15 frs. Open Mar.–Oct., Tues.–Sun. 9:30–11:30 and 2–6; Nov.–Feb., Tues.–Sun. 9:30–11:30 and 2 to 5.*

❷ **Amiens,** the capital of Picardy, lies 59 kilometers (37 miles) north of Beauvais via N1. Despite being a catastrophic example of postwar reconstruction, this stolid brick city has a couple of worthwhile attractions. By far the most important is the **Cathédrale Notre-Dame,** the largest church in France. Although it lacks the stained glass of Chartres or the sculpture of Reims, for architectural harmony, engineering proficiency, and sheer size, it has no peer. The soaring, asymmetrical facade boasts a notable Flamboyant Gothic rose window and dominates the nondescript surrounding brick streets. Inside, the overwhelming sensation of space is enhanced by the absence of pews in the nave, a return to medieval tradition. There is no stylistic disunity to mar the perspective: Construction took place between 1220 and 1264, a remarkably short period in cathedral-building terms. One of the highlights of your visit is hidden from the eye, at least until you lift up the choir stalls and admire the humorous, skillful misericord (seat) carvings executed between 1508 and 1518. *Pl. Notre-Dame. Open all day except noon–2.*

Turn left along rue Cormant and take the second right into rue Victor-Hugo. Midway down, you'll discover the **Hôtel de Berny,** *an elegant 1634 mansion full of period furniture and devoted to local art and regional history. 36 rue Victor-Hugo. Admission: 10 frs. Open Apr.–Oct., Tues.–Sun. 10–noon and 2–6; Nov.–Mar., Wed. and weekends 2–6.*

Amiens is the major city of the *département* of the Somme, a name forever etched into history as the site of one of the bloodiest battles of World War I. On July 1, 1916, whole regiments of Allied soldiers went "over the top" only to be mowed down by a

③ hail of German machine-gun fire. The major encounters took place northeast of Amiens near **Albert**.

④ To reach the former Somme battlefields, take D929 from Amiens to Albert, 24 kilometers (15 miles), then D151 north to the British War Memorial at **Thiepval**, 8 kilometers (5 miles) away. This brick memorial, shaped like a triumphal arch, dominates the Ancre Valley and bears the names of the 73,000 British soldiers who were killed nearby. A little over a mile northwest is the **Beaumont-Hamel** memorial park, where trenches, parapets, and barbed wire recall the fighting waged here by Newfoundland regiments in July 1916.

Time Out The white-painted, vine-covered exterior of **L'Escale** (22 Chaussée Léon-Blum), in the tiny village of Cappy, 16 kilometers (10 miles) southeast of Albert, marks it as a restaurant with a difference. The dining room, decorated with antiques and needlework tablecloths, has the feel of a country cottage, and the menu is illustrated with poems and old photos. The regional dishes (eel, duck, and black pudding) are chosen according to season and accompanied by subtle, refined sauces.

⑤ War cemeteries dot the countryside as you head north along D919 to **Arras**, 32 kilometers (20 miles) away. Capital of the historic Artois region between Flanders and Picardy, Arras has grown into something of a sprawling industrial town. Its historic core bears witness to the grandeur of another age, however, when the town enjoyed medieval importance as a trading and cloth-making center.

Grand' Place and **place des Héros,** separated by a short block, are the two main squares, harmonious examples of 17th- and 18th-century Flemish civil architecture. The gabled facades recall those in Belgium and Holland and are a reminder of the unifying influence of the Spanish colonizers of the "Low Lands" during the 17th century. The smaller, arcaded place des Héros is dominated by the richly worked—and much restored—**Hôtel de Ville,** capped by a 240-foot belfry.

Turn left out of the square, then right into rue Paul-Doumer. Walking a block along brings you to the imposing 18th-century premises of a former abbey, now the **Musée des Beaux-Arts.** The Fine Arts Museum houses a rich collection of porcelain and, especially, painting, with several major 19th-century French works. *22 rue Paul-Doumer. Admission: 10 frs. adults, 5 frs. children and senior citizens. Open Wed.–Mon. 10–noon and 2–5:30; closed Tues.*

The 19th-century **Cathédrale St-Vaast,** a short block farther on, is a white-stoned Classical building, every bit as vast as its name (pronounced "va") suggests. It replaced the previous Gothic cathedral destroyed in 1799; though it was half-razed during World War I, restoration was so skillfully done you'd never know.

At first glance you might not guess that Arras was badly mauled during World War I. Not far off, though, are parks and memorials recalling the fierce battles. Arras is a convenient base for visiting the area's numerous superbly cared-for cemeteries and memorials, which number among the most poignant sights in northern France.

6 Eight kilometers (5 miles) northwest of Arras via D341 lies the ruined abbey of **Mont St-Eloi.** Legend has it that this once-vast abbey is connected to Arras by an enormous underground tunnel. Ruined towers are all that remain of the abbey, which was destroyed during the French Revolution. They peer mournfully over the tiny village and surrounding countryside and are visible for miles around. Just 2 miles away, with gentle slopes lined with weeping willows, is the most beautiful and moving of all the French war cemeteries—**La Targette.**

7 From nearby Neuville-St-Vaast, D55 winds up to the Canadian War Memorial on top of **Vimy Ridge.** Thanks to its woods and lush grass, the Vimy memorial park has become a popular picnic spot, yet the preserved trenches and savagely undulating terrain are harsh reminders of the combat waged here in 1917. The simple, soaring, white-stone Canadian War Memorial, a cleft rectangular tower adorned with female figures in tearful lament, is highly effective. Its base is inscribed with thousands of names of the fallen.

Head back to Neuville and take D937 right shortly afterward, past the beautiful circular cemetery of the Cabaret Rouge and the village of **Souchez.** Turn left up to **Notre-Dame de Lorette,** a colossal cemetery standing on a windswept hill 500 feet above the plains of Artois. There is a mock-Byzantine church and a huge tower containing a small war museum; from the top of the tower, treat yourself to some superb views of the surrounding countryside.

8 Get onto southbound A26, branching off at N50 (follow signs for Douai). From Douai, it's just a 5-kilometer (3-mile) drive east on D943 to **Lewarde,** whose abandoned coal mine has been skillfully converted into a museum documenting the mining industry. You can admire the beefy mine machinery, stroll around an interesting photographic exhibit, and take a train ride through reconstructed coal galleries. *Admission: 30 frs. adults, 15 frs. children. Open daily 10–4.*

Time Out If you find yourself at the Mining Museum around lunchtime, make for the on-site brasserie, **Le Briquet.** The 100-franc menu is an excellent value: ham from the Ardennes, followed by trout with almonds, guinea fowl (or saddle of lamb), and cheese or dessert. *Closed Jan.–Feb. 8, and Mon. Oct. 10–Christmas.*

9 **Lille,** 40 kilometers (24 miles) north, is quickly reached via D943 and the A1 expressway. For a big city supposedly reeling beneath the problems of its main industry, textiles, Lille is a remarkably dynamic, attractive place. The city has had a checkered history, experiencing Flemish, Austrian, and Spanish rule before passing into French hands for good in 1667. Today it is thoroughly French, apart, perhaps, from its Belgianlike penchant for beer and french fries. Although the downtown area contains several narrow streets full of old buildings, Lille does not boast any outstanding tourist sights. Yet with its choice of shops, restaurants, and museums, it makes an enjoyable overnight rest stop.

Start your tour of the city at the **Hospice Comtesse,** in the northern sector of the old town. Founded by Jeanne de Constantinople, countess of Flanders, as a hospital in 1237, it was rebuilt in the 15th century after a fire destroyed most of the original building. Local artifacts from the 17th and 18th centuries form the backbone of the museum now housed here, but its star attraction is the Salle des Malades (Sick Room), featuring a majestic wooden ceiling. *32 rue de la Monnaie. Admission: 5 frs. adults, children free. Open Wed.–Mon. 10–12:30 and 2–6; closed Tues.*

Follow rue de la Monnaie as it curves right and branch off at rue de la Grand Chaussée. The Grand Place (or, to give it its full name, place du Général-de-Gaulle) is a fitting site for the **Vieille Bourse** (former stock exchange), one of the most charming buildings in central Lille. The quadrangle of elegant, richly worked buildings was erected by Julien Destrée in the 1650s as a commercial exchange to rival those already existing in Belgium and Holland. Just two short blocks down rue de Paris brings you to the sumptuous **Eglise St-Maurice** (on the right), a large, five-aisled church built between the 15th and 19th centuries.

A block farther along, turn right onto rue du Molinel and continue until you hit the frenzied traffic of boulevard de la Liberté, a vast street that roars through central Lille. Half a block down, on the left, is the **Musée des Beaux-Arts,** the largest fine arts museum in France outside of Paris, and extensively renovated in 1991. It houses a noteworthy collection of Dutch and Flemish painting (Anthony Van Dyck, Peter Paul Rubens, Flemish Primitives, and Dutch landscapists), as well as some charmingly understated still lifes by Chardin, works by the Impressionists, a few bombastic 19th-century French painters, and dramatic canvases by El Greco, Goya, Tintoretto, and Paolo Veronese. An extensive ceramics section displays some fine examples of Lille faïence, which uses opaque glazing techniques to achieve some remarkable effects. *Pl. de la République. Admission: 10 frs.; free Wed. and Sat. mornings; children free. Open Wed.–Mon. 9:30–12:30 and 2–6; closed Tues.*

Head left out of the art gallery, making for the gigantic **citadel,** which glowers down on the whole of the old town from its perch on the west end of the boulevard. Construction started shortly after that of the Vieille Bourse in the mid-17th century; of course that military marvel, Sébastien de Vauban, got the commission. Some 60 million bricks were used, and the result is a fortified town in its own right, with monumental towers and walls. These days, the citadel is used as a barracks. *Visits on Sun. during summer months.*

10 From Lille, take the A25 expressway toward Steenvorde, then N42 to St-Omer via Hazebrouck. **St-Omer** is a delightful small town, too often neglected by hasty motorists on their way south. It is not the archetypal northern industrial town; with its yellow-brick buildings, it even looks different from its neighbors, and a distinct air of 18th-century prosperity hovers about the place. Stroll through the narrow streets surrounding the Basilique Notre-Dame and, if time allows, visit the **Hôtel Sandelin** on rue Carnot (open Wed.–Sun. 10–noon and 2–5). Now the town museum, the 1777 mansion is furnished with 18th-century furniture and paintings and contains an exceptional collection of porcelain and faïence.

11 The port town of **Calais** lies 40 kilometers (25 miles) northeast of St-Omer via N43. Few vestiges remain of the old, once-pretty port that owed its wealth to the lace industry rather than to day-trippers (Calais lies just across the English Channel from Dover, 38 kilometers/24 miles away, so it's hardly surprising that nearly 8 million visitors flock to it via ferry each year). You won't want to stay here long, but there are a few sights to see before you dash off.

You don't need to be a sculpture fanatic to appreciate Auguste Rodin's bronze **Monument des Bourgeois de Calais,** which lords it over the east end of the Parc St-Pierre next to place Soldat-Inconnu. The bourgeois in question were townspeople who, in 1347, offered their lives to English king Edward III in a bid to save fellow citizens from merciless reprisals after Calais's abortive attempts to withstand an eight-month siege (Calais was an English possession until 1558 and was the last English toehold in France). Edward's queen, Philippa, intervened on their behalf and the courageous men were spared; Calais, on the other hand, remained in English hands for another 200 years.

Head up traffic-clogged boulevard Jacquard, turning right onto rue Richelieu. Three blocks along, at no. 25, is the **Musée des Beaux-Arts et de la Dentelle** (Fine Arts and Lace Museum, admission: 7 frs.; open Wed.–Mon. 10–noon and 2–5:30), which contains some fine 19th- and 20th-century pictures, local historical displays, and exhibits documenting the Calais lace industry. Turn left at the next block, making for the much-restored **Eglise Notre-Dame,** where Général de Gaulle was married in 1921. Take time to admire the simple, vertical elegance of the windows and the ornate fan vaulting inside.

D940, running from Calais to Boulogne, winds its picturesque way past vast sandy beaches, Sangatte (site of the French terminus for the Channel Tunnel, which, by 1993 should link France and Great Britain), and the cliffs of Cap Gris-Nez and Cap Blanc-Nez. It's worth making the short detour to **Cap Gris-Nez** for a bracing stroll along the cliff tops beneath the shadow of the lighthouse and the ominous outlines of a World War II concrete bunker.

⑬ Just before you arrive in **Boulogne** (another stomping ground for cross-Channel visitors), spin off left toward the **Colonne de la Grande Armée.** Work began on this 160-foot marble column in 1804 to commemorate Napoleon's soon-to-be abandoned plans to invade England, but it was finished 30 years later under Louis-Philippe. The 263 steps take you to the top and a wide-reaching panoramic view. If the weather is clear and you're blessed with Napoleonic vision, you may be able to make out the distant cliffs of Dover. *Admission free. Open daily 10–noon and 2–5.*

The contrast between the lower and upper sections of Boulogne is startling. The rebuilt concrete streets around the port are gruesome and sinister, but the Ville Haute—the old town on the hill—is a different world, and you can begin to understand why Napoleon chose Boulogne as his base while preparing to cross the channel. The Ville Haute is dominated by the formidable **Notre-Dame** basilica, its distinctive elongated dome visible from far out at sea. Surrounding the basilica are charming cobbled streets and tower-flanked ramparts, dating from the 13th century and offering excellent views. The four main streets of the old town intersect at place Bouillon, where you can see the 18th-century brick town hall, and the Hôtel Desandrouins, where Napoleon spent many long nights pondering how to invade Britain.

⑭ Le Touquet, 27 kilometers (17 miles) down the coast from Boulogne via D940, is a total contrast: a superb example of an elegant Victorian seaside resort that sprang out of nowhere in the 19th century, adopting the name Paris-Plage. Mainly because gambling laws were stricter in Victorian England than in France, Englishmen, not Parisians, were the town's mainstay. A cosmopolitan atmosphere remains, although many Frenchmen, attracted by the airy, elegant avenues and invigorating climate, have moved here for good. To one side lies a fine sandy beach; to the other, an artificial forest planted in the 1850s. A casino, golf courses, and racetrack cater to fashionable pleasure.

Time Out   The **Aqualud** waterpark has an unpretentious bar and restaurant, as well as numerous water-sports facilities; you can shoot the rapids, thunder down a toboggan run, or just relax in the sauna. *Blvd. Thierry-Sabine. Admission to waterpark: 50 frs.*

⑮ Despite its seaside-sounding name, **Montreuil-sur-Mer** lies 16 kilometers (10 miles) inland from Le Touquet along N39. This ancient town features majestic walls and ramparts, as well as faded, nostalgic charm to which various authors, notably Victor Hugo, have succumbed; an important episode of his epic work *Les Misérables* is set here.

Whenever citadels and city walls loom on the French horizon, it's a fair bet that Vauban had a hand in their construction. Montreuil is no exception. In about 1690, he supplemented the existing 16th-century towers of the **citadel** with an imposing wall, whose grassy banks and mossy flagstones can be explored at leisure. There are extensive views on all sides. *Admission: 7 frs. Open daily 10–noon and 2–5.*

The old cobbled streets of the town make equally agreeable places to stroll. The **Eglise St-Saulve** (just off rue Carnot; open summer only) boasts some fine paintings and a facade dating, in part, from the 11th century.

⑯ Forty-five kilometers (28 miles) south along N1 is another old town, **Abbeville,** heavily reconstructed after being reduced to rubble in 1940. It makes a fitting epilogue to a tour that began with the huge Gothic cathedrals of Beauvais and Amiens, just 48 kilometers (30 miles) down the Somme. **St-Vulfran's Abbeville,** begun in 1488, was one of the last cathedral-size churches to be constructed in the Gothic style. Its much-mauled facade, still undergoing renovation, is a riot of Flamboyant Gothic tracery and ornament. It was here that, according to 19th-century art historian John Ruskin, Gothic "lay down and died."

Tour 2: Champagne Country

⑰ One of the first stops for any visitor heading out of the Ile de France to the northeast is **Pierrefonds,** 88 kilometers (55 miles) from Paris and just 14 kilometers (9 miles) southeast of Compiègne. This attractive, lakeside village is dominated by its huge 12th-century **château,** comprehensively restored to imagined former glory by Viollet-le-Duc at the behest of upstart Emperor Napoleon III in the 1860s. What he left is a crenellated fortress with a fairy-tale silhouette. A visit takes in the chapel, barracks, and the majestic keep holding the lord's bedchamber and reception hall. *Admission: 24 frs. Guided tours only, Apr.–Oct., Wed.–Mon. 9:30–11:15 and 1:30–5:15; Nov.–Mar., until 4.*

⓲ Compiègne can be reached from Pierrefonds via D332. A bustling town of some 40,000 people, it stands at the northern limit of the Ile de France forest, on the edge of the misty plains of Picardy: prime hunting country, a sure sign that there's a former royal palace in the vicinity. The one here enjoyed its heyday in the mid-19th century under Napoleon III. But the town's place in history looks both farther back—Joan of Arc was held prisoner here—and farther forward: The World War I armistice was signed in Compiègne Forest on November 11, 1918.

The 18th-century **palace** was restored by Napoleon I and favored for wild weekends by his nephew Napoleon III, emperor from 1851 to 1870. The entrance ticket includes access to apartments, the Musée du Second Empire, Musée de la Voiture (Car Museum), and the attractive palace park. *Pl. du Palais. Admission: 23 frs. Open Wed.–Mon. 9:30–11:15 and 1:30–4:30; closed Tues.*

One of the central highlights of Compiègne is the late 15th-century town hall, or **Hôtel de Ville,** possessing an exceptional Flamboyant Gothic facade with fine statuary. Make time to visit the **Musée de la Figurine** for its amazing collection of 85,000 lead soldiers depicting military uniforms through the ages. *28 pl. de l'Hôtel de Ville. Admission: 10 frs. Open Apr.–Oct., Tues.–Sun. 9–12 and 2–6; Nov.–Mar. until 5.*

A short distance east of Compiègne, near Rethondes (take N31), is the **Clairière de l'Armistice,** where a railway car was run out on a spur line especially for the signing of the World War I Armistice of 1918, marking the Allied victory. In 1940, the Germans turned the tables on the French, who were made to sign their own surrender to the Nazis—accompanied by Hitler's famous jig for joy. The car you can visit these days is a replica of the original, which was destroyed by the Germans during the war. *Wagon du Maréchal Foch, Forêt de Compiègne. Admission: 7 frs. Open Apr.–Oct., daily 9–noon and 2–6:30; Nov.–Mar. until 5:30.*

⓳ Noyon, 26 kilometers (16 miles) northeast of Compiègne on N32, is a frequently overlooked cathedral town that owed its medieval importance to the cult of 7th-century saint Eloi, patron of blacksmiths and a former town bishop. The **Cathédrale St-Eloi** was constructed between 1150 and 1290, and its four-storied nave, intermittent use of rounded as well as pointed arches, and the thin, pointed lancet (as opposed to rose) windows in the austere facade all mark it as one of the earliest attempts at what was to become "The Gothic Cathedral." Despite the cathedral's size and architectural importance, Noyon itself is virtually unknown, so you can be sure of a peaceful, undisturbed visit.

From Noyon, take N32 and N44 54 kilometers (32 miles) due east to Laon. (Midway along, you'll see signs to St-Quentin, which has an excellent hotel/restaurant; *see* Dining and Lodging, below.)

⓴ Laon occupies a splendid hilltop site and is sometimes called the "crowned mountain"—a reference to the forest of towers sprouting from its ancient cathedral. The site, cathedral, and enchanting old town are worth seeing. Strangely, not many people do; few Parisians, for instance, have ever heard of the place.

In the middle of the old town, just off place Aubry, is **Cathédrale Notre-Dame,** constructed between 1160 and 1235 and a superb example of early Gothic. The recently cleaned, light interior gives the impression of order and immense length (120 yards in total). The flat east end, an English-inspired feature, is unusual in France. The upper galleries that extend around the building are typical of early Gothic; what isn't typical is that you can actually visit them (and the towers) with a guide from the tourist office on the cathedral square. The filigreed elegance of the five remaining towers is audacious by any standards and rare: Medieval architects preferred to concentrate on soaring interiors, with just two towers at the west end. Even those not usually affected by architecture will appreciate the sense of movement about Laon's majestic west front; compare it with the more placid, two-dimensional feel of Notre-Dame in Paris. Look, too, for the stone bulls protruding from the towers, a tribute to the stalwart, 12th-century beasts who carted up blocks of stone from quarries far below.

Time Out The **café** on place du Parvis is unremarkable in every respect but one: its location, just opposite the cathedral. What better place to drink in one of France's most exciting medieval facades with your morning coffee? *4 pl. du Parvis.*

The medieval **ramparts,** virtually undisturbed by passing traffic, provide a ready-made itinerary for a tour of old Laon. Panoramic views, sturdy gateways, and intriguing glimpses of the cathedral lurk around every bend. Another notable survivor from medieval times is the **Chapelle des Templiers,** a small, well-preserved octagonal 12th-century chapel on the grounds of the town museum. *Porte d'Ardon. Admission: 7 frs. Open Apr.– Oct., Wed.–Mon. 10–noon and 2–6; Nov.–Mar. until 5.*

Sixteen kilometers (10 miles) south of Laon via N2 lies the **Chemin des Dames,** a hilltop road separating the valleys of the Aisne and the Ailette. The French offensive launched here by Général Nivelle in April 1917 led to futile slaughter, mutiny, and Nivelle's eventual replacement by Marshal Pétain. Leave N2 a couple of miles after Chavignon and follow D18 to **Cerny-en-Laonnois,** where there is a French memorial. Continue to the **Caverne du Dragon,** which was used as an arsenal by the Germans and is now the site of an eerie, underground war museum (admission: 12 frs.). Just past Hurtebise, take D985 toward Corbeny; to the right is the **Plateau de Californie,** from whose terrace there is a panoramic view of the scenes of combat. N44 connects Corbeny to Reims, an additional 29 kilometers (18 miles) to the south.

㉑ Reims (48 kilometers/30 miles from Laon by A26) is the capital of the champagne industry. Several major producers are headquartered here, and you won't want to miss the chance to visit the chalky maze of cellars that tunnel under the city center.

Numbers in the margin correspond with points of interest on the Reims map.

Reims is renowned for its cathedral, one of the most famous in France and the age-old setting for the coronations of the French kings (Charles X's was the last, in 1825). The glory of the **Cathédrale Notre-Dame** is its facade: It's so skillfully proportioned that initially you have little idea of its monumental size. Above the north (left) door hovers the *Laughing Angel,* a delightful statue whose famous smile threatens to melt into an acid-rain scowl. Pollution has succeeded war as the ravager of the building's fabric. Restoration is an ongoing process; take a look in the postcard shops opposite to get an idea of the pounding the cathedral took between 1914 and 1918.

The high, solemn nave is at its best in summer when the plain lower walls are adorned by 16th-century tapestries relating the life of the Virgin. The east-end windows boast stained glass by Marc Chagall. Admire the vista toward the west end, with an interplay of narrow pointed arches of different sizes.

With the exception of the 15th-century towers, most of the original building went up in the 100 years after 1211. A stroll around the outside will reinforce the impression of harmony, discipline, and decorative richness. The east end presents an idyllic sight across well-tended lawns. There are spectacular light shows both inside (40 francs) and outside the cathedral (free) in July and August. *Pl. du Cardinal Luçon.*

Next door, the **Palais du Tau** (former archbishop's palace) houses an impressive display of tapestries and coronation robes, as well as several statues "rescued" from the cathedral facade. The second-floor views of Notre-Dame are terrific. *2 pl. du Cardinal-Luçon. Admission: 24 frs. adults, 13 frs. senior citizens, 6 frs. children. Open Tues.–Sun. 2–6.*

Time Out   Something out of the ordinary is always happening at the **Café du Palais** (14 pl. Myron-Herrick), just around the corner from the cathedral: a jazz quartet, a fashion-modeling session, or the screening of a silent movie. There's a piano, a veranda, and a choice of baguette sandwiches with such fillings as duck mousse or warm goat cheese.

Two blocks from the cathedral, on the right, is the **Musée St-Denis,** featuring an outstanding collection of paintings spearheaded by no fewer than 27 Corots and Jacques Louis David's celebrated portrait of Revolutionary leader Jean-Paul Marat, who was stabbed to death in his bath by a disillusioned female supporter. *8 rue Chanzy. Admission: 12 frs. Open Wed.–Mon. 10–noon and 2–6.*

As you leave the museum, turn right and continue along rue Chanzy and rue Gambetta to the 11th-century **Basilique St-Rémi,** honoring the 5th-century saint who gave his name to the city. St-Rémi is nearly as long as the cathedral, and its interior seems to stretch into the endless distance, an impression created by its relative murk and lowness. The airy, four-story Gothic choir contains some fine original 12th-century stained glass.

Several champagne producers organize visits to their cellars, combining video presentations with guided tours of their cavernous, chalk-hewn underground warehouses. **Taittinger** (9 pl. St-Nicaise; closed weekends Dec.–Feb.) has the most spectacular cellars. Few show much generosity when it comes to pouring

Basilique St-Rémi, **25**
Cathédrale
Notre-Dame, **22**
Mumm, **27**
Musée St-Denis, **24**
Palais du Tau, **23**
Porte Mars, **29**
Salle de Guerre, **28**
Taittinger, **26**

Reims

27 samples, though, so we recommend you double back across town to **Mumm,** which does. *34 rue du Champ-de-Mars. Open Mar.–Nov., Thurs.–Tues. 9:30–noon and 2–5:30; closed Wed.*

28 Head down rue du Champ-de-Mars toward the train station, turn right into avenue de Laon, then left into rue Franklin-Roosevelt. A short way along is the **Salle de Guerre,** where General Eisenhower established Allied headquarters at the end of World War II. It was here, in a well-preserved, map-covered room, that the German surrender was signed in May 1945. *12 rue Franklin-Roosevelt. Admission: 8 frs. adults, 4 frs. children. Open Wed.–Mon. 10–noon and 2–6; closed Tues.*

29 The **Porte Mars,** an unlikely but impressive Roman arch adorned by faded bas-reliefs depicting Jupiter, Romulus, and Remus, looms up just across from the train station.

Numbers in the margin correspond with points of interest on the Champagne and the North map.

Your first encounter with the champagne vineyards can be had 10 kilometers (6 miles) south of Reims via N51 on the **Montagne de Reims.** Despite its name, this is no mountain but a lofty, forest-topped plateau whose slopes are a tangle of vines. D26 winds around the eastern face of the plateau, through wine villages such as Chigny-les-Roses, Rilly-la-Montagne, Mailly-Champagne, and Verzy, each as pretty as its name. Pride of place goes to the unforgettable **Bouzy,** where a fashionable but overpriced still red wine is produced. South of Bouzy, D1 runs along the banks of the River Marne to Ay, once capital of the *ampagne* vineyards; Henry VIII was a keen tippler of its wines.

30 To understand why traditional still "wine" became exciting, sparkling "champagne," detour up D386 to nearby **Hautvillers,** a gem of a village and former home of Dom Pérignon (1638–1715), who invented champagne as we know it. This able monk, a cellar master whose blindness enhanced his tastebuds and sense of smell, is the supposed discoverer of the use of corks for stoppers, the blending of wines from different vineyards, and the systematic (rather than occasional) production of champagne bubbles. Dom Pérignon's simple tomb-slab, in the damp, forlorn village church (all that remains of the former abbey), is a modest memorial to the hero of one of the world's most lucrative drink industries.

31 Across the Marne lies **Epernay,** a town that, unlike Reims with its numerous treasures, appears to live for nothing other than champagne. Unfortunately, no relation exists between the fabulous wealth of Epernay's illustrious inhabitants and the drab, dreary appearance of the town as a whole. Most of the champagne houses are spaced out along the long, straight avenue de Champagne and, although their names may provoke sighs of wonder, their functional or overdressy facades are a disappointment.

The attractions are underground, in the cellars. Of the various houses open to the public, **Mercier** offers the best deal; its sculpted, labyrinthine caves contain one of the world's largest wooden barrels (with a capacity of over 200,000 bottles) and can be visited in the speed and comfort of a small train. A generous glass of champagne is your posttrip reward. *75 av. de Champagne. Admission free. Open 10–noon and 2–5.*

Time Out Champagne is not the only Epernay specialty. At **La Chocolaterie,** Monsieur Thibaut performs confectionary miracles before your eyes. If you feel the urge to indulge, take a seat in the adjoining Salon de Thé. *9 rue Gallice. Closed Sun. and Mon.*

32 Strangely enough, the official administrative center of the champagne industry is not Reims or Epernay but **Châlons-sur-Marne.** Yet this large town, 35 kilometers (22 miles) east of Epernay along D3, is of principal interest to fans of medieval architecture. The **Cathédrale St-Etienne** is a pure, harmonious 13th-century construction with large nave windows and tidy flying buttresses; the overall effect is marred only by the bulky 17th-century Baroque west front. Of equal merit is the church of **Notre-Dame des Vaux,** with its twin spires, Romanesque nave, and early Gothic choir and vaults. The small **museum** beside the excavated cloister contains outstanding medieval statuary. *Rue Nicolas-Durand. Admission: 15 frs. Open Tues.–Sun. 10–noon and 2–6.*

33 Another architectural treat lies in wait 8 kilometers (5 miles) east of Châlons along N3 at **L'Epine,** a tiny village dominated by the twin-towered Flamboyant Gothic basilica of **Notre-Dame de l'Epine.** The ornament here, weaving intricate patterns over the facade and spires, seems effortless, while the interior exudes elegance and restraint.

Head back to Epernay and take the north bank of the Marne
along D1, which twists its way high above the river valley, providing the most spectacular views of the entire champagne
vineyard. The vineyard continues almost to **Château-Thierry**,
51 kilometers (32 miles) from Epernay and birthplace of
French fable writer Jean de La Fontaine (1621–95). Pay a visit
to the ruined castle and old gateway, the Porte St-Pierre,
through which Joan of Arc passed in 1429 after delivering the
town from the English.

To return from Château-Thierry to Paris, 96 kilometers (60 miles) away, take the direct route along A4. Alternatively, you
can continue along the banks of the Marne to **Meaux**, site of another venerable medieval cathedral.

What to See and Do with Children

The earnest brick towns and soaring cathedrals that dominate
the landscape can make northern France seem a serious place.
The most obvious source of youthful amusement is found on the
seaside, along the huge, sandy **beaches** that stretch from Calais
to Le Touquet, home to a spectacular water-sports center,
Aqualud. Stop off at **Cap Gris Nez**, as well, for a walk along the
Channel cliffs. The **automated Métro** in Lille fascinates children
with its tiny cars and no driver.

The marshy Bay of the Somme has two attractions to entice
youthful visitors from nearby Abbeville. The first is the
Chemin de Fer de la Baie de Somme, a steam railway that runs
between Le Crotoy and Noyelles via St-Valéry-sur-Somme (tel.
22–26–96–96; tickets 50 frs. adults, 30 frs. children; operates
weekends in July–Aug., Sun. only May, June, and Sept.). Just
off D204 between St-Valmy and Cayeux is the **Maison de
l'Oiseau,** with its collection of 400 stuffed birds and video presentation of their local habitat. *Carrefour du Hourdel, tel. 22–
26–93–93. Open daily Mar.–Nov. 10–7.*

The following sights are described fully in the Exploring text.

Mini-train tour of the **Mercier** cellars, Epernay (Tour 2).
Mining Museum, Lewarde (Tour 1).
Musée de la Figurine (Toy Soldier Museum), Compiègne (Tour
2).

Off the Beaten Track

Midway between the two regions covered in our Exploring section is **Cambrai**, a name the French associate with minty candies known as *bêtises*. Cambrai would be a typical northern
French industrial town were it not for its white, chalky stone, a
total contrast with the red brick so prevalent elsewhere. Showcasing that stone are age-old town gateways, such as the 14th-
century Porte de Paris or the 17th-century Porte Notre-Dame,
and three bell towers—those of St-Géry, the cathedral, and the
former church of St-Martin. Above the sprawling main square
looms the town hall's strange-looking cupola, flanked by an exotic pair of beturbaned attendants who look as if they've just
arrived from India.

Twenty-four kilometers (15 miles) east of Cambrai along N43 is
Le Cateau-Cambrésis. Its most important building is the **Palais
Fénelon,** former home to the archbishops of Cambrai and today

a museum devoted to the artist Henri Matisse (1869–1954), born in Le Cateau. Along with a number of early oil paintings and sculptures, there is a superb collection of 50 drawings selected by Matisse himself and arranged in a carefully lit room on the second floor. The enthusiastic curator, Dominique Szymusiak, will show you around (her English is excellent). Reserve a guided tour by calling 27–84–13–15 at least a week before your visit. *Admission: 15 frs., children under 18 free. Open Wed.–Sun. 10–noon and 2–6 (5 in winter).*

Soissons lies 32 klometers (20 miles) southwest of Laon along the Paris-bound N2. Not to be outdone, it, too, possesses a sizable Gothic cathedral, nearly 130 yards long. The interior, with its pure lines and restrained ornament, creates a more harmonious impression than does the asymmetrical, one-towered facade. The most remarkable feature, however, is the rounded, two-story transept, a feature more frequently found in the German Rhineland than in France.

Shopping

Northern France and shopping are intimately associated in the minds of many visitors, especially the English. The cross-channel ferry trip to Calais and Boulogne has become something of an institution, with one rather ignoble aim: to stock up on as much tax-free wine and beer as is legally and physically possible. Supermarkets along the coast are admirably large and well stocked, though you may want to consider local juniper-based *genièvre* brandy, which is a more original choice. Boulogne, France's premier fishing port, is famous for its kippers (smoked herring).

Arts and Crafts Calais has long been renowned as a lace-making center. Lace shops still abound; try **La Dentellière** (30 blvd. de l'Egalite). Near Montreuil, the wickerwork tradition prevails at **Régis Quiénot** in Marles-sur-Canche. For individual paintings on silk, visit **Claudine Decq** at La Calotterie, again near Montreuil. Wooden puppets are a specialty at Amiens, and glazed earthenware is part of St-Omer's historical heritage.

Antiques Antiques dealers are legion; some of the best buys, though, can be made at the busy auction houses *(commissaires-priseurs)* at Douai, Lille, or Calais.

Champagne Reims owes its prestige to champagne, and a number of its central shops duly charge sky-high prices. You'll find the best buys at small producers in the villages along the Montagne de Reims between Reims and Epernay (not Bouzy, though).

Sports and Fitness

Beaches and Water Sports The northern French coast, from Calais to Le Touquet, is one long, sandy beach, known as the Côte d'Opale. The **Aqualud** complex on Le Touquet beach (blvd. Thierry-Sabine, tel. 21–05–63–59) has slides, toboggans, a wave machine, sauna, and solarium.

Apart from ocean swimming (backed up by indoor and outdoor pools throughout the region), you may care to try your hand at speed sailing or handling a sand buggy, those windsurf-boards on wheels that race along the sands at up to 70 mph. Known as *Char à Voile*, the sport can be practiced at Le Touquet, Hardelot, Dunkerque, Bray-Dunes, and Berck-sur-Mer. For details, contact amiable Claude Wantier at the **Drakkars** club in Hardelot, south of Boulogne (tel. 21–91–81–96); the cost is 60–80 francs per hour.

Biking　Bicycles can be rented from many train stations for around 40 francs a day. Get details of special circuits from the **Comité Départemental de Cyclotourisme** (75 rue Louis-Drouart, Les Ageux, 60700 Pont-Ste-Maxence). Mountain biking is also popular in the Noyon area; get in touch with **Patrick Drocourt** (48 rue du Maréchal-Joffre, 60150 Montmacq, tel. 44–76–40–49).

Golf　You'll find courses at Hardelot, Le Touquet (three courses), Wimereux, Lille, and Compiègne.

Horseback Riding　Horseback riding is possible in many places, including Hardelot (tel. 21–83–71–28) and St-Amand-les-Eaux (tel. 27–48–56–62).

Parachuting　Sky-diving thrills can be had at Hardelot (tel. 21–91–81–86).

Dining and Lodging

Dining

The cuisine of northern France is robust and hearty, like that of neighboring Belgium. Beer predominates and is often used as a base for sauces (notably for chicken). French fries and mussels are featured on most menus, and vans selling fries and hot dogs are common sights. Great quantities of fish, notably herring, are eaten along the coast, while inland delicacies include *andouillettes* (chitterling sausages), tripe, and pâté made from duck, partridge, or woodcock. Anyone with a sweet tooth will enjoy the region's ubiquitous macaroons and minty Cambrai *bêtises*. Ham, pigs' feet, gingerbread, and a champagne-based mustard are specialties of the Reims area, as is *ratafia*, a sweet aperitif made from grape juice and brandy. To the north, a glass of *genièvre* (a brandy made from juniper berries and sometimes added to black coffee to make a drink called a *bistoul)* is the typical way to conclude a good meal.

Highly recommended restaurants are indicated by a star ★.

Category	Cost*
Very Expensive	over 350 fancs
Expensive	200–350 francs
Moderate	100–200 francs
Inexpensive	under 100 francs

per person for a three-course meal, including tax (18.6%) and tip but not wine

Lodging

Northern France is overladen with old hotels, often rambling and simple, seldom pretentious. Good value is easier to come by than top quality, except in major cities (Amiens, Lille, and Reims) or at Le Touquet, whose Westminster Hotel numbers among the country's best.

Highly recommended hotels are indicated by a star ★.

Category	Cost*
Very Expensive	over 750 francs
Expensive	350–750 francs
Moderate	200–350 francs
Inexpensive	under 200 francs

All prices are for a standard double room for two, including tax (18.6%) and service charge.

Amiens
Dining

Joséphine. This unpretentious, good-value restaurant in central Amiens is a reliable choice. Solid fare, decent wines, and rustic decor (a bit on the stodgy side, like the sauces) pull in many foreign customers, notably the British. *20 rue Sire-Firmin-Leroux, tel. 22–91–47–38. Reservations advised in summer. Dress: casual. AE, MC, V. Closed Sun. evening, Mon., and 3rd week of Aug. Moderate.*

Mermoz. Nouvelle and traditional cuisine are skillfully blended here in a fresh, modern setting close to the train station. There are three menus, and the choice changes according to the season. *7 rue Jean-Mermoz, tel. 22–91–50–63. Reservations advised. Dress: casual. AE, V. Closed Sat., Sun., and mid-July–mid-Aug. Moderate.*

Lodging

Hôtel de la Paix. Near the Picardy Museum, the hotel is housed in a building reconstructed after World War II. Private parking and the view of a nearby church from some of the rooms offset a certain lack of personality, although the breakfast room tries valiantly to suggest an 18th-century Louis XV salon. Foreign visitors are frequent, and English is spoken. *8 rue de la République, 80000, tel. 22–91–39–21. 26 rooms, some with bath. No credit cards. Closed Sun. and mid-Dec.–mid-Jan. Inexpensive.*

Arras
Dining

Le Chanzy. Huge and popular, Le Chanzy offers three set menus and as many dining rooms. The restaurant specializes in standard brasserie fare (lunchtime only) and more ambitious gastronomy, based on the grills in which the chef is expert. There are more than 100,000 bottles in the cellar, and the main room is decked out in a luxuriously flashy '50s-style decor (renovation overdue). Le Chanzy also has 20 guest rooms. *8 rue Chanzy, tel. 21–71–02–02. Reservations advised. Dress: casual. AE, DC, MC, V. Moderate.*

L'Antoniolus. Large portions of fresh ingredients—showcased in a plethora of good-value menus—are dished out here, amid cheerful greenery that spills onto a veranda. *2 rue Eugène-Pottier, tel. 21–51–66–99. Reservations advised on weekends and in summer. Dress: casual. AE, MC, V. Inexpensive–Moderate.*

Lodging
★

Univers. This stylish hotel occupies a converted 18th-century monastery and has a pretty garden and a charming restaurant. Its central position and views of the courtyard and garden make it a favorite stopover with vacationers heading south. The interior has recently been modernized, but it retains its rustic provincial furniture. *5 pl. de la Croix-Rouge, 62000, tel. 21–71–34–01. 36 rooms, most with bath. Facilities: restaurant, garden. AE, MC, V. Restaurant closed Sun. in Aug. Moderate.*

Boulogne-sur-Mer
Dining
★

Brasserie Liégeoise. Good food spiced with delicious nouvelle touches helps this old, established restaurant remain at the forefront of the Boulogne eating scene. The decor is modern—an eccentric contrast of black and yellow—and so are the prices for both à la carte and set-menu meals. Chef Alain Delpierre justifies the expense with delicate sauces and interesting combinations, such as duck liver with mushrooms. *10 rue Monsigny, tel. 21–31–61–15. Reservations required on weekends. Jacket required. AE, DC, MC, V. Closed Wed., and Sun. dinner. Expensive.*

Lodging

Métropole. This small hotel is handy for ferry passengers but, like most of the Ville Basse (lower town), no great architectural shakes. While no exciting views are to be had from this rather faceless '50s building, the guest rooms are adequately furnished and individually decorated. There is no restaurant. *51 rue Thiers, 62200, tel. 21–31–54–30. 27 rooms, some with bath. Facilities: garden. AE, DC, MC, V. Closed Christmas and New Year's. Moderate.*

Dining and Lodging

Cléry. Eight kilometers (5 miles) inland from Boulogne, along N1, is the tiny village of Hesdin-l'Abbé, its 18th-century château now transformed into a stylish hotel. Extensive lawns, lined with tulips, rose beds, and an avenue of trees, create a favorable impression, enhanced by the entrance hall, with its old wooden staircase and wrought-iron banisters. As the vast price range indicates, each guest room is different; those in the former stables have been particularly well converted. The restaurant's nouvelle menu features dishes that are pretty rather than substantial, such as lobster with pink grapefruit butter. It was here at the château that Napoleon decided to abandon plans to invade England. As you bask in the peace and quiet of the beautiful grounds, you'll understand why. *62360 Hesdin-l'Abbé, tel. 21–83–19–83. 18 rooms with bath. Facilities: restaurant, tennis. AE, V. Moderate–Expensive.*

Calais
Dining

Sole Meunière. As its name ("sole fried in butter") suggests, the Sole Meunière is a temple of fish and seafood. Not that anything else could be expected from a restaurant next to Calais harbor! The good-value menus start at a very low price; the dining room's intimate decor is a medley of soft grays and pinks. *1 blvd. de la Résistance, tel. 21–34–43–01. Reservations advised. Dress: casual. AE, DC, MC, V. Closed Mon. and mid-Dec.–mid-Jan. Inexpensive–Moderate.*

Châlons-sur-Marne
Dining and Lodging

Angleterre. This stylish venue in central Châlons, close to the church of Notre-Dame-en-Vaux, has fully renovated rooms (most with marble bathrooms) and an airy, modern restaurant, where Jacky Michel uses champagne as a base for many of his sauces. *19 pl. Monseigneur-Tissier, 51000, tel. 26–68–21–51. 18 rooms with bath or shower. AE, DC, MC, V. Closed Sun., Christmas, and second half of July. Moderate–Expensive.*

Compiègne
Dining

Picotin. Its three inexpensive menus make the old-fashioned Picotin a good choice for lunch or dinner after you've visited the nearby château. The traditional cuisine (salads, steaks, and chocolate desserts) offers few surprises—or disappointments. *22 pl. de l'Hôtel-de-Ville, tel. 44–40–04–06. Reservations strongly advised. Dress: casual. V. Closed Tues. Inexpensive.*

L' Epine
Dining and Lodging

Aux Armes de Champagne. Just opposite the sumptuous facade of Notre-Dame de l' Epine, 10 kilometers (6 miles) east of Châlons, this cozy hotel, with solid, traditional furniture, is renowned for the imaginative cuisine of Patrick Michelon. Try his delicate rabbit terrine or fried mullet. *Pl. de la Basilique, 51460, tel. 26–66–96–79. 39 rooms with bath. MC, V. Closed Jan. and Sun., Mon. out of season. Moderate–Expensive.*

Laon
Dining

La Petite Auberge. Young chef Willy-Marc Zorn dishes up modern, imaginative cuisine at this 18th-century-style restaurant close to the train station in Laon's Ville Basse. Try his hare stew or salmon with pig's feet. The *recherché* 140-franc menu is a good bet. *45 blvd. Pierre-Brossolette, tel. 23–23–02–38. Reservations advised. Dress: casual. AE, DC, MC, V. Moderate.*

Dining and Lodging

Bannière de France. In business since 1685, the old-fashioned, uneven-floored Bannière de France is just five minutes' walk from Laon's picturesque cathedral and the medieval Ville Haute (upper town). Madame Lefèvre, the *patronne*, speaks fluent German and English. Guest rooms are cozy and quaintly decorated, and the restaurant's venerable dining room features sturdy cuisine (trout, guinea fowl) and good-value menus. *11 rue Franklin-Roosevelt, 02000, tel. 23–23–21–44. 18 rooms, a few with bath. Facilities: restaurant. AE, DC, MC, V. Closed Christmas and New Year's. Moderate.*

Lille
Dining
★

Devinière. Chef Willy Waterlot has created one of Lille's most fashionable eating places: The welcome is warm, the dining room embellished with cheerful flowers, and the produce fresh and changed according to the season. His nouvelle cuisine receives maximum attention, and the restaurant is frequently packed (with only 30 places, it's one of the city's smallest). *61 blvd. Louis-XIV, tel. 20–52–74–64. Reservations required. Jacket required. AE, DC, MC, V. Closed part of Aug. Moderate–Expensive.*

La Coquille. The wood-beamed, pink-brick decor of this venerable restaurant—the building dates from 1727–makes a delightful setting for a quiet, light, fish meal; the chocolate and caramel desserts are delicious. *60 rue St-Etienne, tel. 20–54–29–82. Reservations advised. Dress: casual. MC, V. Closed Sat. lunch, Sun., and Aug. Moderate.*

Lodging

Bellevue. This central, elegant hotel has many large, comfortable rooms and the sort of deferential service you can no longer take for granted. It's favored by British travelers and has a leather-lined *bar américain*. *5 rue Jean-Roisin, 59800, tel. 20–57–45–64. 80 rooms, most with bath. Facilities: bar. AE, MC, V. Moderate.*

Noyon
Lodging

St-Eloi. Handily situated in a turn-of-the-century building between the station and cathedral, St-Eloi was given a new modern annex in 1978 to help accommodate the flood of northern European visitors. Garden views and reassuring Louis XV-style furnishings are other attributes, as is the fine restaurant, none of whose four menus will strain your wallet. *81 blvd. Carnot, 60400, tel. 44–44–01–49. 30 rooms, 24 with bath. Facilities: restaurant, garden. MC, V. Closed Christmas; restaurant closed Sun. dinner. Moderate.*

Pierrefonds
Lodging

Etrangers. A small restaurant, serving game in season, and an attractive lakeside terrace make this an ideal halting place beneath the mighty castle of Pierrefonds. The three-story hotel was recently modernized, although it still lacks an elevator; American and Japanese visitors are frequent. *10 rue Beaudon, 60350, tel. 44–42–80–18. 32 rooms, many with bath. Facilities:*

restaurant. MC, V. Closed mid-Jan.–mid-Feb.; restaurant
closed Sun. dinner and Mon. Sept.–mid-Jan. Inexpensive.

Reims **Boyer–Les Crayères.** Gérard Boyer is one of the country's most
Dining highly rated chefs. Duck, foie gras in pastry, and truffles fig-
★ ure among his specialties and are complemented by an extensive wine list that pays homage to Reims's champagne
heritage. The setting, not far from the Basilique St-Rémi, is
magnificent, too: a 19th-century château surrounded by an extensive, well-tended park. The decor is opulent, typified by ornate chandeliers, towering ceilings, gilt mirrors, intricate
cornices, and glossy paneling. There are 22 luxurious suites as
well. *64 blvd. Henry-Vasnier, tel. 26–82–80–80. Reservations
required. Jacket and tie required. AE, DC, MC, V. Closed
Mon., Tues. lunch, and Christmas–New Year's. Very Expensive.*

Florence. This elegant, well-run restaurant occupies an old,
high-ceilinged mansion that has recently been given a
facelift—pictures and tapestries now festoon the walls. New
chef Jos Bergman serves wonderfully light versions of the classical French repertoire. Prices have risen accordingly, but the
weekday menu remains a good value. *43 blvd. Foch, tel. 26–47–
12–70. Reservations advised. Jacket required. AE, DC, MC,
V. Closed part of Feb., most of Aug., and Wed. and Sun. dinner. Expensive.*

★ **Le Vigneron.** This friendly little brasserie in a 17th-century
mansion is cozy and cheerful, with two tiny dining rooms that
display a jumble of champagne-related paraphernalia—from
old advertising posters to venerable barrels and tools of the
trade. The food is delightful as well: relatively cheap, distinctly
hearty, and prepared with finesse. Try the *andouillettes* (chitterling sausages), and be sure to slather on lots of Reims's delicious mustard made with champagne. *Pl. Paul-Jamot, tel. 26–
47–00–71. Reservations strongly advised. Dress: casual. MC,
V. Closed Sat. lunch, Sun., Christmas–New Year's, and most
of Aug. Moderate.*

Lodging **Hôtel de la Paix.** A modern, eight-story hotel, ten minutes'
walk from the cathedral, La Paix boasts admirably equipped,
stylish rooms, plus a pretty garden, swimming pool, and a rather incongruous chapel. Its brasserie-style restaurant, Drouet,
serves good, though not inexpensive, cuisine (mainly grilled
meats and seafood). The breakfasts are generous. *9 rue de
Buirette, 51000, tel. 26–40–04–08. 105 rooms with bath. Facilities: restaurant, pool, underground parking, patio-bar. AE,
DC, MC, V. Restaurant closed Sun. Moderate.*

Gambetta. The Gambetta experience is not what you'd call out
of this world, but, then, the prices are reassuringly down to
earth. A location close by Reims's venerable cathedral is the
hotel's main claim to fame. Guest rooms are small and somewhat featureless but clean and acceptable for the price. *9 rue
Gambetta, 51000, tel. 26–47–41–64. 14 rooms with bath. Facilities: restaurant. V. Restaurant closed Sun. dinner and Mon.
lunch. Inexpensive.*

St-Omer **Le Cygne.** Duck breast *(magret de canard)*, not swan, tops the
Dining menu at Le Cygne, in the old sector of St-Omer near the cathedral. There are two menus—one three-course, the other
four-course. Traditional, regional cooking holds sway. *8 rue
Caventou, tel. 21–98–20–52. Reservations accepted. Dress: ca-*

sual. *MC, V. Closed Tues., Sat. lunch, and Dec. 10–31. Moderate.*

Dining and Lodging
★

Moulin de Mombreux. Huge cogs and waterwheels, skillfully integrated into the decor of the open-fire reception area, reflect the 18th-century watermill origins of the Moulin de Mombreux, 5 kilometers (3 miles) west of St-Omer at Lumbres, close to the A26 expressway. Jean-Marc Gaudry has hoisted these old premises into the top league with his tasteful renovation and even tastier cuisine. Try his warm oysters in champagne, seafood (crayfish and crab), or salmon presented in a beautiful black-and-yellow sauce. There are three set menus, and their intricacy could do with an English translation. Silver candlesticks and original wooden beams lend the dining room atmosphere; piped music, plaster-covered walls, and slightly faded flowers take it away again. Six guest rooms occupy the second floor, and there are an additional 24 in a new annex across the grounds, where the discreet, if unoriginal, charm of the pastel-shaded rooms is outweighed by the spacious breakfast room, with its large windows and wicker chairs. *62380 Lumbres, tel. 21–39–62–44. 30 rooms with bath. Facilities: restaurant, garden. AE, DC, MC, V. Closed Christmas–New Year's. Expensive.*

St-Quentin
Dining and Lodging
★

Grand. After undergoing head-to-toe restoration, the Grand Hôtel hopes to underline its status as the best hotel in town. Its restaurant, Le Président, already has a reputation as one of the finest in northern France, with elegant decor and a highly rated new chef, Jean-Marc Le Guénnec, trained by the legendary Parisian Joël Robuchon. His gastronomic creations— roast pigeon with artichoke, for instance—don't come cheap, but there is also a less expensive menu available. *6 rue Dachery, 02100, tel. 23–62–69–77. 26 rooms with bath. DC, V. Closed Aug. and Christmas–New Year's. Restaurant closed Sun. dinner and Mon. Expensive.*

Le Touquet
Dining

Flavio. Fish and shellfish star at this elegant restaurant near the casino. Chef Guy Delmotte specializes in lobster and charges aficionados-only prices for his lobster menu. The other two menus will please most. Cut glass, chunky silverware, and original carpets add an appropriate note of chic. *2 av. du Verger, tel. 21–05–10–22. Reservations required except weekday lunch. Jacket and tie required. AE, DC, MC, V. Closed Jan.– Feb., and Wed. Very Expensive.*

Dining and Lodging
★

Westminster. The Westminster's mammoth redbrick facade looks as if it were built just a few years ago; in fact, it dates from the 1930s and, like the rest of the hotel, has been extensively restored by its new owners, the personable Flament brothers. The hotel offers a modestly priced coffee bar (serving lunch and dinner), a swanky dining room (classic but well-prepared French cuisine), and an "American bar" that serves cocktails for under 50 francs. Try the Westminster Special, a lethal concoction of vodka, blue curaçao, Grand Marnier, and orange juice. The enormous double rooms represent good value and the bridal suite is the last word in thick-carpeted extravagance. *Av. du Verger, 62520, tel. 21–05–48–48. 115 rooms with bath. Facilities: restaurants, bar, squash court, indoor pool, Jacuzzi, sauna, solarium. AE, DC, MC, V. Expensive.*

The Arts and Nightlife

The Arts

Lille is unquestionably the hub of cultural activity in northern France—a lively museum and concert center where exotic happenings can take place at any time (a recital of traditional music by Tibetan monks, for example). There are various local carnivals, notably the **Dunkerque Carnival** in February/March, the **Roses Festival** in Arras in May, and the **Kermesse de la Bêtise** festival in Cambrai in early September.

Theater   You are unlikely to encounter English-language productions in northern France. Lille's principal theater house is the **Opéra** (*see* below), while the **Théâtre d'Animation Picard** in Amiens (51 rue de Prague, tel. 22–46–29–09) partly overcomes the language barrier with its use of puppets.

Concerts   The **Orchestre National de Lille** is a well-respected symphony orchestra (3 pl. Mendès-France, tel. 20–54–67–00).

Opera   Lille boasts one of France's few regional opera houses, the **Opéra du Nord** (pl. du Théâtre, tel. 20–55–48–61).

Nightlife

Bars and   We suggest **Chez Marc** (92 rue d'Abbeville) or **Solitaire Club**
Nightclubs   (188 rue Riolan) in Amiens; **Cave du Vieux Lille** (55 rue Basse) in Lille; and **Le Palace** (114 rue Barbatre) in Reims.

Cabaret   Try **Harmonie-Jazz-Mélodie** (pl. Louise-de-Bettignies) in Lille, or **Croque-Notes** (24 rue Ernest-Renan) in Reims.

Casinos   Gamblers should head for the casinos at **Berck-Plage** (tel. 21–84–09–39), **Boulogne** (tel. 21–83–88–00), **Calais** (tel. 21–96–44–87), **Dunkerque** (tel. 28–59–18–23), and **Le Touquet** (tel. 21–05–16–99).

Discos   Good bets include **Penelope** (25 rue de l'Hôpital) in Epernay, **Cave du Roi** (97 rue Solferino) in Lille, or **L' Echiquier** (110 av. Jean-Jaures) in Reims.

9 Alsace-Lorraine

Strasbourg, Nancy

Introduction

Alsace-Lorraine, in the northeast corner of France, is often considered to have a single identity, but each of the two regions has its own traditions and economic, social, and geographic peculiarities.

Alsace has a heavy German influence: Regional dialect is still in extensive use; conversations between locals are incomprehensible even to most Frenchmen; town names in Alsace sound and look German; and the main daily paper is published in both French and German. The much-resented German occupation of 1870–1918 was limited to Alsace and just the eastern, German-speaking part of Lorraine.

Lorraine, pierced by the cheerful Moselle Valley, is an industrially depressed area whose richest days are past. Its towns and villages possess neither the self-confidence nor the picturesque appeal of those of Alsace, where the tourist industry booms and the economy thrives on excellent transportation links with neighboring Germany and Switzerland.

Strasbourg is the capital of Alsace and the unofficial "capital" of Europe, as it is home to European political institutions and a symbol of Franco-German reconciliation. It is a city of great cultural, historic, and architectural interest. The rest of Alsace is more than 100 miles long but seldom more than 30 miles wide, squeezed in between the Vosges Mountains and the River Rhine. Much of Alsace is a flat plain; the prettiest parts are the vineyards that nestle amid the Vosges foothills. The Route du Vin (Wine Road) weaves its way through any number of flower-strewn villages, which feature medieval towers, walls, and houses built in the unmistakable red sandstone of the Vosges. These mountains may not possess the craggy majesty of the Alps, but they are peppered with ski resorts and dramatic views of lakes and forests.

Noble storks flutter overhead; their distinctively large nests crown the spires of many church towers. Sauerkraut, foie gras, and, more unexpectedly, tobacco, number among the regional specialties. Although France's major breweries are situated here, Alsace is more famous for its white wine, named not by locality but by the variety of grapes. The best are elegant, dry Riesling; fragrant Muscat; fruity Tokay; and spicy Gewurtztraminer.

Grapes are scarcer in Lorraine; instead, plums are used to make Mirabelle brandy. At the region's heart is another city of great appeal: Nancy, former capital of the dukes of Lorraine and imbued with medieval and neoclassical elegance. The double-armed Cross of Lorraine was adopted by General de Gaulle's freedom fighters in World War II, but Lorraine has more potent links with World War I: The Battle of Verdun was the bitterest on the Western Front.

Nowhere in France is farther from the sea, so the climate in Alsace-Lorraine is continental: Winters can be extremely cold and summers mighty hot. The Vosges Mountains, which often act as a cloud buffer, ensure that rain is less frequent in Alsace than in Lorraine.

Essential Information

Important Addresses and Numbers

Tourist Information The principal regional tourist offices are to be found at **Strasbourg** (behind the cathedral, 9 rue du Dôme, tel. 88–22–01–02) and **Nancy** (14 pl. Stanislas, tel. 83–35–22–41). In **Strasbourg**, there is another tourist office, concerned more with the city than with the region (10 pl. Gutenberg, tel. 88–32–57–07).

The addresses of other tourist offices in towns mentioned in this chapter are as follows: **Colmar** (4 rue Unterlinden, tel. 89–41–02–29), **Guebwiller** (5 pl. St-Léger, tel. 89–76–10–63), **Metz** (pl. d'Armes, tel. 87–75–65–21), **Mulhouse** (9 av. du Maréchal-Foch, tel. 89–45–68–31), **Obernai** (Chapelle du Beffroi, pl. du Marche, tel. 88–95–64–13), **Saverne** (Château des Rohan, tel. 88–91–80–47), **Sélestat** (10 blvd. Leclerc, tel. 88–92–02–66), **Toul** (Parvis de la Cathédrale, tel. 83–64–11–69), and **Verdun** (pl. de la Nation, tel. 29–86–14–18).

Travel Agencies **Wagons-Lits** (30 pl. Kléber, Strasbourg, tel. 88–32–16–34; 2 rue Raymond-Poincaré, Nancy, tel. 83–35–06–97) and **Havas Voyages** (23 rue de la Haute-Montée, Stasbourg, tel. 88–32–99–77).

Car Rental In **Nancy**: Hertz (7 pl. Thiers, tel. 83–32–13–14) and Europcar (18 rue de Serre, tel. 83–37–57–24) In **Strasbourg**: Avis (Galerie Marchande, pl. de la Gare, tel. 88–32–30–44).

Arriving and Departing

By Plane Most international flights to Alsace land at Mulhouse-Basle airport on the Franco-Swiss border. There are also airports at Strasbourg, Metz, Nancy, and Mirecourt (Vittel/Epinal).

By Car The A4 expressway heads east from Paris to Strasbourg, via Verdun, Metz, and Saverne. It is met by A26, coming down from the English Channel, at Reims. A31 links Metz to Nancy, continuing south to Burgundy and Lyon.

By Train Mainline trains leave Paris (**Gare de l'Est**) every couple of hours for the four-hour, 504-kilometer (315-mile) journey to Strasbourg. Some stop at Toul and all stop at Nancy, where there are connections for Epinal, Gérardmer, and Vittel. Trains run three times daily from Paris to Verdun and more often to Metz (around three hours in each case). Mainline trains stop at Mulhouse (four to five hours) en route to Basle.

Getting Around

By Car N83, a fast, multilane highway that becomes the A35 expressway in parts, shoots through the Plain of Alsace, providing the quickest link between Strasbourg, Colmar, and Mulhouse.

By Train The local trains, which operate several times each day between Strasbourg and Mulhouse (en route to Dijon and Lyon), stop at Sélestat and Colmar.

Guided Tours

Bus Excursions **Horizons Européens** (France Tourisme, 3 rue d'Alger, 75001 Paris, tel. 42–60–31–25) organizes an excellent seven-day bus tour of Alsace-Lorraine, taking in Verdun, Nancy, Strasbourg, and Colmar, with an excursion to Germany and the Black Forest, for around 5,000 francs inclusive. It also offers three-day trips to Nancy, Strasbourg, and Colmar for 2,000 francs.

Aerial Tours You can take a 15-minute helicopter tour of Nancy with **Tecnavia** (tel. 83–21–09–75) or a plane ride over Strasbourg from the **Aérodrome du Polygone** (tel. 88–34–00–98).

Orientation Tours **Strasbourg Port Authority** (25 rue de la Nuée-Bleue, tel. 88–32–49–15) organizes 75-minute boat tours along the River Ill, which encircles Old Strasbourg; the commentary, though trite, is at least audible, and the views are superb. The fare is 30 francs for adults, 16 francs for children under 16. Departures (every half hour beginning at 9:30 in summer, less frequently in spring and fall) are from the quay on rue de Rohan, just down from place de Château.

Landlubbers might be interested in the 50-minute tour of the old city of Strasbourg by **minitrain,** which leaves place de Château from April to October, daily every half hour beginning at 9:30. The fare is 22 francs for adults, 13 francs for children under 12.

Exploring Alsace-Lorraine

Numbers in the margin correspond with points of interest on the Alsace and Strasbourg maps.

Orientation

Our tour of Alsace-Lorraine begins in Strasbourg, a city of such historic and cultural importance that it is well worth exploring in detail. From here, our second tour takes you through the rest of Alsace, south through the charming villages along the Route du Vin (Wine Road) to Thann, and north again via a 72-kilometer (45-mile) scenic drive past lakes, valleys, and forests along the Route des Crêtes (Crest Road). The third tour covers the region of Lorraine, with a thorough look at the artistic town of Nancy.

Highlights for First-time Visitors

Cathédrale Notre-Dame, Strasbourg, Tour 1
Main Street, Riquewihr, Tour 1
Château des Rohan, Strasbourg, Tour 1
Haut-Koenigsbourg, Tour 2
Issenheim Altarpiece, Musée d'Unterlinden, Colmar, Tour 2
Cathédrale, Metz, Tour 3
Mont Ste-Odile, Tour 2
Nancy, Tour 3
Toul, Tour 3

Tour 1: Strasbourg

① **Strasbourg** is perhaps the most interesting and attractive French city after Paris—an irresistible mixture of old houses, waterways, museums, the European Parliament, and, looming above them all, the colossal single spire of the cathedral.

Alsace

The Romans knew Strasbourg as Argentoratum. After a spell as part of the Holy Roman Empire, the city was united with France in 1681, but retained independence regarding legislation, education, and religion under the honorific title Free Royal City. Since World War II, Strasbourg has become a symbol city, embodying Franco-German reconciliation and the wider idea of a united Europe. It plays host to the European Parliament and Council of Europe and acts as a neutral stomping ground for such controversial political figures as Yasser Arafat, leader of the Palestinian Liberation Organization.

At the hub of Strasbourg, on place de la Cathédrale, is the **②** **Cathédrale Notre-Dame,** with its splendid openwork spire. Pink masonry covers the facade. Not content with the outlines of the walls themselves, medieval builders stuck huge, slender, rodlike shafts of stone everywhere: You feel as if you can reach up and snap one off. The spire, finished in 1439, looks absurdly fragile as it tapers skyward like some elongated, 466-foot wedding cake; only the 528-foot spire of Ulm, in West Germany, climbs higher.

The interior presents a stark contrast to the facade. For a start, it is older, virtually finished by 1275. Then, at 105 feet, the nave does not create the same impression of soaring height: Its broad windows emphasize the horizontal rather than the vertical. In the nave, note Hans Hammer's ornately sculpted pulpit (1484–86), with its 50 statuettes, and the richly painted 14th–15th-century organ loft that rises from pillar to ceiling.

Another contrast is apparent within—that between the choir and the nave. The choir is not ablaze with stained glass but is framed by chunky masonry. The original brickwork of the cupola is visible, as if no one had ever gotten around to decorating it. The fact that the choir is raised above the level of the rest of the church heightens the contrast and reinforces an aura of murky mystical sanctity.

The elaborate 16th-century **Chapelle St-Laurent,** to the left of the choir, merits a visit, but most visitors turn to the right to admire the **Angels' Column,** an intricate pillar dating from 1230, formed by clustering, tubelike colonnettes harboring three tiers of delicate statues. Nearby, the daring Renaissance machinery of the 16th-century **Astronomical Clock** whirs into action at 12:30 PM daily: Macabre clockwork figures—including a skeletal Father Time and the screeching rooster that reminds the Apostle Peter of his broken promise—enact the story of Christ's Passion. *Admission to clock: 7 frs.*

There is a *son-et-lumière* (sound-and-light) performance in the cathedral every evening from April through the end of September. The text is in French or German, but virtuoso lighting effects translate into any language. *Admission: 25 frs. adults, 13 frs. children under 18. Performances at 8:15 and 9:15PM.*

3 A worthy complement to the cathedral is the **Musée de l'Oeuvre Notre-Dame,** opposite the south front. There is more to this museum than the usual assembly of dilapidated statues rescued from the local cathedral before they fell off. A conscious effort has been made to create a church atmosphere and provide an appropriate setting for the works of art. Part of one room evokes a narrow, low-roofed cloister. A dimly lit, high-walled chamber, reached through a creaky wooden door, is ringed by stone screens with pinnacles and pointed gables. Soon you'll find yourself in the stonemasons' workshop. A polished wooden staircase leads to a suite of small passages and large rooms, with drawings, stained glass, and gold objects. All the architectural elements of the Renaissance—pediments, spiral pillars, and cornices—can be found on the bulky wardrobes and cupboards produced by local cabinetmakers. There are some fine Old Master paintings as well. *Pl. du Château. Admission: 12 frs. adults, 6 frs. students and children. Open Apr.–Sept., Wed.–Mon. 10–noon and 2–6; Oct.–Mar., Wed.–Sat., Mon. 2–6, Sun. 10–noon; closed Tues.*

4 Alongside the Musée de l'Oeuvre Notre-Dame, between the cathedral and the river, is the **Château des Rohan,** onetime palace of the powerful Rohans, a dynasty of prince-bishops who

Strasbourg

Ancienne Douane, **6**
Cathédrale
Notre-Dame, **2**
Château des Rohan, **4**
Cour du Courbeau, **7**
Musée Alsacien, **8**
Musée Historique, **5**
Musée de l'Oeuvre
Notre-Dame, **3**
Orangerie, **19**
Palais de l'Europe, **18**

Palais de
l'Université, **17**
Place Broglie, **14**
Place Kléber, **13**
Place de la
République, **15**
Ponts Couverts, **10**
St-Paul, **16**
St-Pierre-le-Jeune, **12**
St-Pierre-le-Vieux, **11**
St-Thomas, **9**

place de
Bordeaux

rue Lauth

blvd. Jacques-Preiss

rue Oberlin

av. de la Paix

rue Schwilgué

rue Erwin

allée de la Robertsau

avenue de l'Europe

18

19

Orangerie

rue Trubner

rue Schubert

rue de Verdun

rue Schweighauser

15

16

av. de la Forê Noire

av. de la Marseillaise

17

Jardin
Botanique

rue de l'Observatoire

frères

blvd. de la Victoire

rue de l'Académie

rue de G. Zimmer

es Bateliers

rue René Descartes

rue Blaise Pascal

av. du G. de Gaulle

rue de Londres

N

0   300 yards

0   300 meters

held both political and spiritual sway over the city and region. The exterior of Robert de Cotte's neoclassical building (1732–42) is starkly austere. The glamour is inside, in Robert le Lorrain's magnificent ground-floor rooms, led by the great **Salon d'Assemblée** (Assembly Room) and the book- and tapestry-lined **Bibliothèque des Cardinaux** (Cardinals' Library).

The library leads to a series of less august rooms that house the **Musée des Arts Décoratifs** (Decorative Arts Museum) and its elaborate display of ceramics. Works by Hannong, a porcelain manufacturer active in Strasbourg from 1721 to 1782, are comprehensively represented; dinner services by other local kilns reveal the influence of Chinese porcelain in their delicate patterns. Equally interesting are the dishes and terrines in animal form (turkeys and hogs' heads), or table decorations imitating plums and cauliflowers—of doubtful taste but technical tours de force. Furniture, tapestries, and silver-gilt complete the collection. *Pl. du Château. Admission: 16 frs. adults, 8 frs. students and children. Open Apr.–Sept., Wed.–Mon. 10–noon and 2–6; Oct.–Mar., Wed.–Sat., Mon. 2–6, Sun. 10–noon; closed Tues.*

About 50 yards north of the cathedral, and running parallel to it, is rue des Hallebardes, Strasbourg's most stylish pedestrian-only shopping street. It leads to **place Gutenberg,** dominated by an elegant three-story building with large windows, constructed between 1582 and 1585, now used as the Chamber of Commerce and city tourist office. Johannes Gutenberg (1400–68), after whom the square is named, invented the printing press in Strasbourg in 1434. On one side of his statue, executed in 1840 by sculptor David d'Angers, is a plaque bearing the U.S. Declaration of Independence, in acknowledgment of its influence on French revolutionary soldiers from Alsace.

⑤ The **Musée Historique** (Local History Museum) stands between place Gutenberg and the river. Wooden floors and beam roofs create a suitably historic atmosphere in which to admire maps, armor, arms, bells, uniforms, printing paraphernalia, cardboard toy soldiers, and two huge relief models of Strasbourg, one made in 1727, the other in 1836. *3 rue de la Grande-Boucherie. Admission: 18 frs. adults, 9 frs. students and senior citizens. Open Oct.–Mar., Wed.–Mon. 2–6; Apr.–Sept., Wed.–Mon. 10–noon and 2–6; closed Tues.*

⑥ The **Ancienne Douane,** opposite, was constructed in 1358 to serve as a customs house. It now houses a brasserie and temporary exhibitions. *Admission: 20 frs. adults, 10 frs. students and children. Open Wed.–Mon. 11–6; closed Tues.*

Time Out Apart from the usual cafés, Alsace is filled with down-to-earth wine bars, known as *winstubs*, serving snacks, local specialties (sauerkraut, sausages, and snails), and wine by the jug. The long, wood-paneled, large-window *winstub* just up from rue du Maroquin and place de la Grande-Boucherie, between the cathedral and the river, makes a cool, seldom-crowded place to pause from museums and monuments.

⑦ Across the river is the **cour du Courbeau,** a ramshackle 14th-century courtyard whose hostelry once welcomed kings and
⑧ emperors. Facing the Ancienne Douane is the **Musée Alsacien.** If you want a glimpse of how Alsace families used to live, this is the place to visit. Local interiors—kitchens, bedrooms, and

sitting rooms (the latter two often combined)—have been faithfully reconstituted. The diverse activities of blacksmiths, clog makers, saddlers, and makers of artificial flowers are explained with the help of old-time artisans' tools and equipment. *23 quai St-Nicolas. Admission: 12 frs. adults, 6 frs. students and children. Open Oct.–Mar., Wed.–Sat., Mon. 2–6, Sun. 10–noon and 2–6; Apr.–Sept., Wed.–Mon. 10–noon and 2–6; closed Tues.*

9 Cross the river two bridges farther down to admire the church of **St-Thomas** (quai Finkwiller), particularly the mausoleum of Marshal Maurice of Saxony (1696–1750), a key figure in the 1740–48 War of Austrian Succession. Follow the banks of the River Ill toward the picturesque quarter of **La Petite France,** lined with richly carved, half-timbered Renaissance houses and cobbled streets. The Ill, which branches into several canals, is spanned by the **Ponts Couverts,** three connected 14th-century covered bridges, each with its tall, stern, stone tower.

10

11 Quai Turckheim leads to the church of **St-Pierre-le-Vieux,** whose choir is decorated with scenes from the Passion (circa 1500) by local painter Henri Lutzelmann. Follow the quay
12 around to **St-Pierre-le-Jeune,** consecrated in 1320, to admire its painted rood screen, immense choir, and 14th-century frescoes.

13 Alsace provided the French Revolution with 64 generals and marshals. One of the most famous was Jean-Baptiste Kléber (1753–1800), assassinated in Cairo after being left in charge of Egypt by Napoleon in 1799. Kléber's statue lords it over Strasbourg's busiest square, **place Kléber,** situated up rue des Grandes-Arcades from St-Pierre-le-Jeune.

Time Out Rue des Orfèvres, one of the lively pedestrian streets leading off from rue des Hallebardes, is connected to the noisy, commercial rue des Grandes-Arcades by a cobbled, leafy square—the **place du Marché-Neuf**—seldom discovered by visitors. This peaceful oasis is a fine place to stop for a drink, and its two open-air cafés are open till late at night.

---

14 Rue de l'Outre heads down to another large square, **place Broglie,** home of the city hall, the 18th-century Municipal Theater, and the Banque de France. The bank occupies the site of the house where the *Marseillaise* (composed by Rouget de Lisle, and originally entitled *Battlesong of the Rhine Army)* was sung for the first time in 1792.

15 The spacious layout and ponderous architecture of **place de la République** have nothing in common with the old town across the river, except the local red sandstone. A different hand was at work here—that of occupying Germans, who erected the former Ministry (1902); the Academy of Music (1882–92), ex-Regional Parliament; and the Palais du Rhin (1883–88), destined to be the German imperial palace.

16 **17** Much of northern Strasbourg bears the German stamp. Head right out of place de la République, past the neo-Gothic church of **St-Paul,** to the pseudo-Renaissance **Palais de l'Université**—constructed between 1875 and 1885 (though Strasbourg University itself dates from 1621). Heavy, turn-of-the-century houses, some betraying the whimsical curves of the art-nouveau style, frame allée de la Robertsau, a tree-lined boulevard

that would not look out of place in Berlin; follow its length to
18 reach the modern **Palais de l'Europe,** designed by Paris architect Henri Bernard in 1977. The Palais houses the European
Court of Human Rights and the Council of Europe, founded in
1949 and independent of the European Community (founded in
1957), whose 12 members are joined here by representatives
from the traditionally nonaligned countries—Austria, Norway, Sweden, and Switzerland—plus Cyprus, Iceland, Liechtenstein, Malta, and Turkey. The European flag that flutters in
front of the Palais—a circle of 12 gold stars on a blue background—was created for the Council of Europe in 1955 and
adopted by the European Community in 1986. *Av. de l'Europe.
Visits weekdays at 9, 10, 3, 4 and 5.*

Just across the street from the Palais de l'Europe, the
19 **Orangerie** is a delightful park laden with flowers and punctuated by imperious copper beeches. It contains a lake and, close
by, a small reserve of rare birds, including flamingoes and
noisy local storks.

Tour 2: Alsace

Leaving **Strasbourg,** take the fast A4 40 kilometers (24 miles)
20 northwest to **Saverne,** gateway to the northern Vosges. Its
18th-century **Château des Rohan,** built in red sandstone, is renowned for its majestic north facade, lined by fluted pilasters
and a Corinthian colonnade. The right wing houses an interesting museum devoted to archaeology, religious statuary, and local history. *Admission: 12 frs. Open mid-June–mid-Sept.,
Mon., Wed.–Sat. 2:30–5:30, Sun. 10–noon and 2:30–5:30;
closed Tues.*

Head south from Saverne along N4 to **Marlenheim** and the start
of the great Alsace **Route du Vin** (Wine Road), which forms the
backbone of this tour. Regular signs marked *Route du Vin* will
help you keep your bearings on the way due south to Thann,
some 60 miles as the crow flies but considerably more on the
twisty Wine Road. Nearly all the villages along the route are
beautifully maintained, with red geraniums flowing from balconies and carefully preserved old wells.

21 D422 connects Marlenheim with **Rosheim,** a pleasant village
with medieval ramparts, gateways, and a sturdy Romanesque
church with an octagonal tower. The two-story, stone **Heidehuss** is reputedly the oldest house in Alsace (circa 1170).

22 **Boersch,** 3 kilometers (2 miles) from Rosheim on D35, conserves three medieval gateways and the 16th-century Hôtel de
Ville (Town Hall). Just south of Boersch lies the **Château de la
Léonardsau,** surrounded by formal and botanical gardens
adorned with fountains, statues, and a wide variety of trees.
Since 1985, the château has hosted the **Musée du Cheval et de
l'Attelage** (Horse and Harness Museum), complete with magnificent 18th- and 19th-century carriages, a blacksmith, and a
collection of swords and other arms from the Royal Works at
nearby Klingenthal. *Admission: 15 frs. Open Easter–Oct.,
Tues.–Sun. 2–6, closed Mon.; Nov.–Easter, weekends 2–6,
closed weekdays.*

23 **Obernai,** one of Alsace's most attractive towns, can be reached
from Boersch via D322 (about 6 kilometers/4 miles). At its
heart is the medieval place du Marché, dominated by the stout,

square 13th-century **Kappellturm Beffroi** (Belfry), topped by a pointed steeple flanked at each corner by frilly openwork turrets added in 1597. The nearby **Puits à Six-Seaux,** constructed in the 1570s, is an elaborate Renaissance well whose name recalls the six buckets suspended from its metal chains. Just behind the belfry is Obernai's **Hôtel de Ville,** rebuilt in 1848 but incorporating much of the original Renaissance building, notably its richly carved balcony.

North of the town hall, the twin spires of the parish church of **St-Pierre-et-St-Paul** compete with the belfry for skyline preeminence. They date, like the rest of the church, from the 1860s, although the 1504 Holy Sepulcher altarpiece in the north transept is a survivor from the previous church, along with some 15th-century stained glass.

㉔ D426 from Obernai heads back west to cross the Route du Vin at Ottrott, renowned for its red wine. From Ottrott, D109 winds its way 6 kilometers (4 miles) up to the **Mont Ste-Odile,** a 2,500-foot mound that has been an important religious and military site for 3,000 years. An eerie 6-mile-long pagan wall, up to 12 feet high and, in parts, several feet thick, rings the summit; its mysterious origins and purpose still baffle archaeologists. The Romans established a settlement here, and at the start of the 8th century, Odile, daughter of Duke Etichon of Obernai, founded a monastery on the same spot after recovering her sight while being baptized (she had been born blind). Odile—venerated as the patron saint of Alsace—died here in AD 720; her sarcophagus rests in the chapel.

The **monastery** still remains, rescued by the bishop of Strasbourg in 1853, after repeated plunder, military vandalism, and the expulsion of its monks in the French Revolution. The bishop's restoration has left us with the current tidy ensemble of buildings. One of its principal attractions is the splendid view from the clifftop terrace, over the Plain of Alsace toward Strasbourg and the Black Forest over the German border.

㉕ D854 tumbles down the hillside to **Barr,** another 6 kilometers (4 miles) farther, a thriving little town surrounded by vines, with some charming narrow streets (notably rue des Cigognes, rue Neuve, and the tiny rue de l'Essieu) and the cheerful Hôtel de Ville. Most buildings in Barr date from after a catastrophic fire of 1678; the only medieval survivor is the Romanesque tower of the Protestant church, St-Martin.

The **Musée de la Folie Marco,** up rue du Dr. Sultzer from the town hall, is housed in a steep-tiled mansion built by local magistrate Félix Marco in 1763. Despite its name, this is no architectural folly, though jealous villagers may have considered its three large reception rooms to embody a certain crazy extravagance. You can admire lots of original furniture here, plus local porcelain, earthenware, and pewter. One section of the museum explains the traditional process of *schlittage:* Sleds, bearing bundles of freshly sawn tree trunks, used to be slid down forest slopes along a "corduroy road" made of logs. *Rue du Dr. Sultzer. Admission: 8 frs. Open July–Sept., Wed.–Mon. 10–noon and 2–6; June and Oct., weekends 10–noon and 2–6.*

Time Out If you're feeling hungry, stop at the **winstub** on the central square, adjacent to the flower-trimmed town hall. You can enjoy an outdoor meal on the veranda, with hefty salads (radish, carrots, egg, and celery), a more than adequate substitute for the usual *choucroûte* (sauerkraut) or charcuterie. *4 pl. de la Mairie. Closed Tues.*

26 A small road leads from Barr through the vineyards and the tiny village of Mittelbergheim to **Andlau,** 3 kilometers (2 miles) away. The abbey church of **St-Pierre St-Paul** was built in the mid-12th century after fire had destroyed most of the 11th-century building constructed by Pope Leo IX's niece, Mathilda. The spire above the octagonal bell tower was finished only in 1737, but the abbey's chief glories date to the 11th century: The west front boasts the richest ensemble of Romanesque sculpture in Alsace. Sculpted vines wind their way around the doorway as a reminder of the time-honored importance of wine to the local economy.

The 15th-century abbey choir stalls are adorned with the coats of arms of the princess abbesses. A statue of a female bear, the mascot of the abbey—bears used to roam local forests and were bred at the abbey until the 16th century—can be seen in the north transept. Legend has it that Queen Richarde founded the abbey in 887 after being enjoined by an angel to construct a church on the spot where a female bear would appear to her.

27 Take D253 from Andlau, past the parish church, to the junction with D35. From here, you can enjoy a splendid view down the valley toward Andlau. A mile later, bear left through the overcute village of Itterswiller (its many restaurants are outrageously expensive) before setting off right toward **Dambach-la-Ville,** a fortified medieval town protected by ramparts and three powerful 13th-century gateways. Dambach is particularly rich in half-timbered, high-roofed houses from the 17th and 18th centuries, mainly clustered around place du Marché and its 16th-century Hôtel de Ville.

28 D35 continues to Châtenois, from which it's just a 3-kilometer (2-mile) detour along N59 to **Sélestat,** a busy town with two impressive churches. **St-Foy** dates from between 1155 and 1190; its Romanesque facade remains largely intact (the spires were added in the 19th century), as does the 140-foot octagonal tower over the crossing. Sadly, the interior was mangled during the centuries, chiefly by the Jesuits; their most inspired legacy is the Baroque pulpit of 1733 illustrating the life of the founder of their movement, St. Francis Xavier. Note the Romanesque bas-relief next to the baptistery, originally the lid of a sarcophagus. *Just off rue du Marché Vert.*

Take rue de Babil one block south to the later, Gothic church of **St-Georges.** It, too, has a fine tower, built in 1490 and some 200 feet tall. There is medieval stained glass in the rose window above the south door and in the windows of the choir, telling the tales of saints Catherine, Helen, and Agnes.

Head left down rue du Sel to the **Bibliothèque Humaniste,** a major library founded in 1452 and installed in the former Halle aux Blés. Among the precious manuscripts on display are a 7th-century lectionary and a 12th-century Book of Miracles. Altarpieces, jewelry, sculpture, and earthenware are also exhibited. *1 rue de la Bibliothèque. Admission: 7 frs. Open weekdays 9–noon and 2–5, Sat. 9–noon.*

29 D159 now makes the steep, twisting climb to **Haut-Koenigsbourg.** This romantic, crag-top castle looks just as a kaiser thought it should: In 1901, German emperor Wilhelm II was presented with the 13th-century ruins by the town of Sélestat (or Schelestadt, the German name was used then) and restored them with some diligence and no lack of imagination—squaring the main tower's original circle, for instance. Today Haut-Koenigsbourg is besieged by tourists and should be avoided on sunny summer days. At other times, the site, panorama, drawbridge, and amply furnished imperial chambers merit a visit. *Admission: 30 frs. Open Apr.–Oct., daily 10–noon and 2–6; Nov.–Dec., Feb.–Mar., daily 10–noon and 2–5; closed Jan.*

Head south from Haut-Koenigsbourg, via Ribeauvillé, to Riquewhir—stop here to amble up the enchanting, steep cobbled main street—then continue to the proud merchant city of **Colmar.** The heart of Colmar remains intact: A web of pedestrian streets fans out from the beefy-towered church of **St-Martin.** To the east lies Grand'Rue, with its 15th-century **Ancienne Douane** (Customs House) and twin-turreted **Maison aux Arcades** (1609). To the south is the pretty, water-crossed district known as **Petite Venise.**

Alongside St. Martin's, on rue Mercière (no. 11), is the **Maison Pfister** (1537), which, with its decorative frescoes and medallions, counts as one of the most impressive dwellings in town. On the other side of rue des Marchands is the **Musée Bartholdi,** former home of Frédéric Auguste Bartholdi (1834–1904), the local sculptor who designed the Statue of Liberty. *30 rue des Marchands. Admission: 10 frs. Open Apr.–Oct., daily 10–noon and 2–6; Nov.–Mar., weekends 10–noon and 2–5; closed weekdays.*

In the nearby **Dominican Church** (pl. des Dominicains) can be seen the Flemish-influenced *Madonna of the Rosebush* (1473) by Martin Schongauer (1445–91), a talented engraver as well as a painter. This work, stolen from St. Martin's in 1972 and later recovered and hung here, has almost certainly been reduced in size from its original state. Realistic birds, buds, thorns, and flowers add life to the gold-background solemnity. *Admission: 8 frs.*

Take rue des Têtes past the Maison des Têtes (1608)—so called because of the carved heads proliferating on its facade—to the **Musée d'Unterlinden,** France's best-attended provincial museum. The star attraction of this former medieval convent is the **Issenheim Altarpiece** (1512–16) by Martin Grünewald, majestically displayed in the convent's Gothic chapel. The altarpiece was originally painted for the Antoine convent at Issenheim, 32 kilometers (20 miles) south of Colmar, and was believed to have miraculous healing powers over ergot, a widespread disease in the Middle Ages caused by poisonous fungus found in moldy grain. The altarpiece's emotional drama moves away from the stilted restraint of earlier paintings toward the humanistic realism of the Renaissance: The blanched despair of the Virgin, clutched by a weeping St. John, is balanced, on the other side of the cross, by the grave expression of John the Baptist. The blood of the crucified Christ gushes forth, while his face is racked with pain. A dark, simple background heightens the composition's stark grandeur.

The altarpiece was closed and folded according to the religious calendar and contains several other scenes apart from the *Crucifixion:* The *Incarnation* features angelic musicians playing celestial melodies as a white-bearded God, the Father, patrols the heavens; to the left, an incredulous Mary receives the Angel Gabriel; to the right, Christ rises from his tomb amid a bold halo of orange and blue. The third arrangement portrays, to the left, St. Anthony in conversation with St. Paul in a wild, overgrown landscape, while to the right, nightmarish beasts, reminiscent of Hieronymous Bosch, make up the torturous *Temptation of St. Anthony.*

Modern art, stone sculpture, and local crafts cluster around the 13th-century cloisters to complete Unterlinden's folksy charm. *Pl. de la Sinn. Admission: 22 frs. adults, 11 frs. students. Open Apr.–Oct., daily 9–noon and 2–6; Nov.–Mar., Wed.–Mon. 9–noon and 2–5; closed Tues.*

31 Twenty-five kilometers (15 miles) south on N83 is the **Guebwiller** exit. The town's **Eglise St-Leger** (1180–1280) is one of the most harmonious Romanesque churches in Alsace, though its original choir was replaced by the current Gothic one in 1336. The bare, solemn interior is of less interest than the three-towered exterior. The towers of the facade match—almost: The one on the left has small turrets at the base of its steeple, whereas the one on the right is ringed by triangular gables. The octagonal tower over the crossing looms above them both, topped by a seldom-visited stork's nest.

The surrounding square, home to a lively weekly market, faces rue de la République, Guebwiller's main street. Head left upon leaving the church: One hundred yards down the road is the Renaissance **Hôtel de Ville,** with its small spire and crenellated oriel (or bay) window, built by wealthy draper Marquart Hesser. Continue down the main street before turning left into rue de l'Hôpital. The **Dominican Church** is unmistakable, thanks to the thin, lacy lantern that sticks out of its roof like an effeminate chimney. Its large, early 14th-century nave is adorned with frescoes and contains a fine rood-screen.

Rue de la République continues to Guebwiller's third and largest church, **Notre-Dame** (1762–85). The church possesses a Baroque grandeur that would not be out of keeping in a chic district of Paris—a reflection of the wealth of the Benedictine abbey at nearby Murbach, whose worldly friars, fed up with country life, opted for the bright lights of Guebwiller in the mid-18th century. The monks—who needed a noble pedigree of at least four generations to take the cloth—outmaneuvered church authorities by pretending to take temporary exile in Guebwiller while "modernizing" Murbach Abbey, thus circumnavigating the papal permission normally required before abbeys could move. As a token gesture, the crafty clerics smashed the nave of Murbach Abbey but failed to replace it and refused to budge from their "temporary" home. Instead, they commissioned Louis Beuque to design a new church in Guebwiller—Notre-Dame.

The church's facade, with its double layer of cornice-bearing columns, is devoid of ornament except for the statues halfway up. The interior is majestic but not overbearing, thanks to the cheerful pale pink of the stone and the survival of much of the original decoration. The gold-and-marble high altar fits in better, perhaps, than does the trick 3-D–effect stucco *Assumption,* which puffs its way out of a half-open coffin behind the altar before erupting over the walls and balcony and making for the roof, an example of Baroque craftsmanship at its most outlandish. *Rue de la République.*

The **Musée du Florival,** on one side of the church square, is housed in one of the 18th-century canon's houses. It has a fine collection of ceramics designed by Théodore Deck (1823–91), a native of Guebwiller and director of the renowned porcelain factory at Sèvres near Paris. *1 rue du 4 Février. Admission: 8 frs. Open May–Oct., weekends 10–noon and 2–6, Mon., Wed.–Fri. 2–6; closed Tues.; Nov.–Apr., weekends only, 10–noon and 2–5:30.*

D430 now heads up the valley toward Lautenbach; at Buhl, take the exit to **Murbach.** This road is a dead end, so it's all the more surprising to discover a vast rump of a church towering above the hillside. Only the east end remains of the **Eglise St-Léger,** once part of the most powerful abbey in Alsace. Roofs and towers create a geometric interplay of squares and triangles, lent rhythm and variety by those round-arched windows and arcades so loved by Romanesque architects. Note the tympanum above the door to the south transept: Its elongated lions, seen in profile, resemble stone images found more commonly in the Middle East.

Time Out A few miles from Murbach, a small *route forestière* (forest road) heads from Lautenbach up the 2,800-foot col de Boenlesgrab. At the summit, the **Auberge de Boenlesgrab** commands splendid views down the valley toward Wasserbourg. In an unpretentious setting of wooden benches and checkered tablecloths you'll find a solid, filling *Menu Marcaire*, featuring pies, potatoes, and game in season.

Make your way back to Guebwiller and take the Ensisheim road, passing over N83, as far as **Ungersheim,** home of the **Ecomusée de Haute-Alsace.** This "open-air museum," a small village created from scratch in 1980, includes 35 historic peasant houses typical of the region, which have been transferred here lock, stock, and barrel (or more precisely, stable, barn, and pigeon loft) to escape demolition. Storks, another example of the local heritage, are nurtured here in a reserve. *Maisons Paysannes d'Alsace. Admission: 30 frs. adults, 12 frs. students, 9 frs. children under 12. Open June–Aug., daily 10–8; Sept.–Nov., Mar.–May., daily 11–6; Dec.–Feb., daily 11–4.*

From the old town of Ensisheim, D20 spears south to **Mulhouse,** 16 kilometers (10 miles) away. Mulhouse, a pleasant if unremarkable industrial town, is worth visiting for its museums. Dutch and Flemish masters of the 17th to 18th centuries top the bill at the **Musée des Beaux-Arts** (Fine Arts Museum, 14 pl. Guillaume Tell; closed Tues). But it is cars and trains that attract most visitors. Some 500 vintage and modern cars, dating from the steam-powered Jacquot of 1878 and spanning 100 different makes, are featured in the **Musée National de l'Automobile.** The highlights are the two Bugatti Royales. Only a handful of these stately cars was ever made; one was auctioned in 1987 for $8 million. *192 av. de Colmar. Admission: 30 frs. adults, 20 frs. students. Open Wed.–Mon. 10–6.*

A reconstructed Stephenson locomotive of 1846 sets the wheels rolling at the **Musée Français du Chemin de Fer** (National Train Museum), a 10-minute walk west down rue J.-Hofer. Rolling stock is spread over 12 tracks, including a vast array of steam trains and the BB 9004 electric train that held the rail speed record of 207 mph from 1955 to 1981. A section of the museum also houses a display of firefighters' equipment. *2 rue de Glenn. Admission: 30 frs. adults, 20 frs. students. Open Apr.–Sept., daily 9–6; Oct.–Mar., daily 10–5.*

West of Mulhouse, 16 kilometers (10 miles) along N66, is **Thann.** A local ditty has it that "Strasbourg's spire is the highest, Freiburg's the biggest, and Thann's the finest." The spire of the church of **St-Thiébaut** in Thann is certainly elegant and delicate but, at 254 feet, little over half the height of Strasbourg Cathedral's. St-Thiébaut's square tower was built in 1350, the octagonal spire in 1516; the colored tiles of the roof date only from the 1890s. The Flamboyant Gothic north door and the portals of the facade, still under restoration after the damage inflicted during World War II, boast more than 500 sculpted figures.

The interior is relatively high and narrow, with a choir as long as the nave. The 15th–16th-century oak choir stalls, carved with whimsical figures and topped by decorative pinnacles, are the most important in Alsace. Apart from the small Chapelle de la Vierge (Chapel of the Virgin) in the south aisle (1629–31), take a look at the amusing late 15th-century statue of the Virgin and an infant Jesus who chuckles to himself while clutching a bunch of grapes (the statue was donated by local vintners).

D35 wends its way east through the last of the Alsace vineyards to Cernay and the start of the **Route des Crêtes,** the historic Crest Road sliced along the wooded Vosges hilltops during World War I. The road is known successively as D431, D430, D61, and D148 on its spectacular 45-mile path north, accompanied by plummeting views of lake, valley, and forest, from Cernay to the 3,000-foot pass at col du Bonhomme. From here, take D48, then N59 to Bertrimoutier, and turn right up N159 as far as Provenchères and right again onto D23. Just past Lubine, fork left onto D214, which winds its way up the Vosges for 16 kilometers (10 miles) into the Champ du Feu (the Field of Fire). This name is appropriately hellish, given that our next and final stopping point is the concentration camp built by the Nazis at **Le Struthof,** 8 kilometers (5 miles) west along D130. Its barbed wire and modest huts, spread over several levels, remain intact and appear strangely peaceful; a stark, white marble monument recalls their appalling past and purpose. (Admission: 6 frs. Open daily 10–noon and 2–5). Farther down D130 is the innocuous-looking farmhouse that was used as a gas chamber.

Tour 3: Lorraine

Numbers in the margin correspond with points of interest on the Lorraine map.

Our tour of Lorraine begins in its northwest corner, 3 kilometers (2 miles) from the Belgian frontier, at **Avioth.** If you're coming from Paris, leave the A4 expressway (which continues to Verdun and Metz; *see* below) at Reims, then take the old Luxembourg road (D980/D947 via Vouziers) to nearby Montmédy. Coming from Alsace, turn off the A4 at Verdun and take D905 north.

Lorraine

A sumptuous **basilica** unexpectedly rises above the lowly rooftops of the tiny village of Avioth (population 103). A miraculous statue of the Virgin was discovered here in the 11th century, and the faithful poured in for the next 300 years, which explains the church's surprising richness. Construction of the church lasted from the late 13th to the early 15th century, finishing amid the elaborate stone lace of the Flamboyant Gothic style. The interior contains a 14th-century altar, and recent restoration has revealed medieval frescoes on the choir vaults.

38 N43 continues east to Longuyon, 34 kilometers (21 miles) from Avioth, from which D17A heads 5 kilometers (3 miles) northeast to the fort of **Fermont,** an imposing memorial to the famous, if ineffective, Maginot Line, built after World War I to defend France's eastern frontier. Although observation posts and concrete bunkers armed with machine guns protrude aboveground to stave off would-be aggressors, the main interest of Fermont lies 100 feet under the surface in the galleries once manned by crews 600 strong. Kitchens, dormitories, showers, a soldiers' mess, and sewage and ventilation systems make up a sizable underground town. There is also a museum devoted to the history of the Maginot Line, complete with guns and howitzers. Outside, the ground is still pockmarked with the craters caused by the German shell attack of June 1940. *Admission: 20 frs. adults, 10 frs. children under 14. Open May–Sept., daily 1:30–5; Apr. and Oct., 1:30–4.*

39 From Longuyon, head south along N18, D66, D65, and D905 to **Verdun,** 43 kilometers (27 miles) away. A key strategic site along the Meuse Valley, Verdun was besieged by the Prussians in 1792 and 1870, but is famous, above all, for the 18-month battle waged between the French and the Germans from February 1916 to August 1917, which left over 700,000 dead. Much as the Battle of Stalingrad came to assume symbolic importance during World War II, so Verdun proved to be the turning point of World War I. To this day, the scenes of battle are scarred by undulating terrain and stunted vegetation. Circuits of the major war sites extend on either side of the River Meuse, with the leading memorial—a huge chapel and ossuary surrounded by an endless cemetery—at Douaumont, 10 kilometers (6 miles) to the north.

Verdun itself, however, is far from the ruined, battered, hastily rebuilt place one might expect. As one of three medieval bishoprics (along with Toul and Metz), it enjoyed much prestige: Verdun's bishops were untitled princes of the Holy Roman Empire. The **Bishop's Palace,** built in the 18th century by Robert de Cotte, is opulent in the extreme, with a vast semicircular Court of Honor to intimidate the unworthy. The adjacent **cathedral,** perched at the highest point of the town, dates from the 1130s, although the Gothic nave was restyled in Classical taste (round, not pointed arches) during the 18th century. The three-sided cloisters that nestle along the south side are mainly Flamboyant Gothic.

Other old buildings in Verdun include the **Hôtel de Ville** (Town Hall, 1623), the **Hôtel de la Princerie** (16th century), Vauban's late 17th-century **citadel,** and two crenellated, neighboring gateways: the **Porte Chaussée** (14th century) and the **Porte Châtel** (13th-century). A soldier-topped pyramid, above a steep-stepped terrace, provides an imposing war memorial, the **Monument de la Victoire;** a register kept in the crypt contains the names of all who fought at the Battle of Verdun.

40 The A4 expressway offers a fast, 72-kilometer (45-mile) link between Verdun and **Metz,** the largest town of northern Lorraine. Despite its industrial background, Metz is officially classed as one of France's greenest cities: Parks, gardens, and leafy squares crop up everywhere. At its heart, towering above the Hôtel de Ville (Town Hall) and the 18th-century place d'Armes, is the **Cathédrale St-Etienne.**

At 137 feet from floor to roof, Metz Cathedral is one of the highest in France. It is also one of the lightest, thanks to nearly 1½ acres of window space. The narrow, 13th–14th-century nave channels the eye toward the dramatically raised 16th-century choir, whose walls have given way to huge sheets of gemlike glass by masters old and modern, including Russian-born artist Marc Chagall (1887–1985). A pair of symmetrical 290-foot towers flank the nave, marking the medieval division between two churches that were merged to form the cathedral. The tower with a fussy 15th-century pinnacle houses **Dame Mutte,** an enormous bell cast in 1605 and tolled on momentous occasions. The Grand Portal beneath the large rose window was reconstructed by the Germans at the turn of the century. The statues of the prophets include, on the right, *Daniel* sycophantically sculpted to resemble Kaiser Wilhelm II (his unmistakable upturned mustachios were shaved off in 1940). *Pl. d'Armes.*

Close by, in a 17th-century former convent, is the **Musée d'Art et d'Histoire** (Art and History Museum); turn left out of the cathedral and take rue des Jardins. The museum's wide-ranging collections encompass French and German paintings from the 18th century on, military arms and uniforms, and archaeology; local finds evoke the city's Gallo-Roman, Carolingian, and medieval past. Religious works of art are stored in the **Grenier de Chèvremont,** a granary built in 1457, with a many-windowed facade and stone-arcade decoration. *2 rue du Haut-Poirier. Admission: 14 frs., free Wed. Open Wed.–Mon. 10–noon and 2–5; closed Tues.*

Now walk back past the cathedral, continuing for another two blocks. At one end of the **Esplanade,** an agreeable terraced park overlooking the Moselle, is the 18th-century **Palais de Justice,** noted for the sculpted bas-reliefs in the courtyard (the one on the right portrays the 1783 Peace Treaty between France, England, Holland, and the United States) and its ceremonial staircase with wrought-iron banisters. Farther down the Esplanade is the small, heavily restored church of **St-Pierre-aux-Nonnains** (rue Poncelet). Parts are thought to date from the 4th century, making it the oldest church in France. Neighboring 13th-century **Chapelle des Templiers** (blvd. Poincaré) is also rare: It's the only octagonal church in Lorraine.

㊶ Leave Metz by D952, which speeds 55 kilometers (33 miles) south along the River Moselle to the charming old town of **Toul,** nestling behind mossy, star-shaped ramparts. The ramshackle streets of central Toul can't have changed much for centuries— not since the embroidered, twin-towered facade, a Flamboyant Gothic masterpiece, was woven onto the **cathedral** in the second half of the 15th century. The cathedral's interior, begun in 1204, is long (321 feet), airy (105 feet high), and more restrained than the exuberant facade. The tall, slender windows of the unusually shallow choir sparkle in the morning sunshine.

The cathedral is flanked on one side by 14th-century **cloisters** and on the other by a pleasant garden behind the **Hôtel de Ville** (Town Hall), built in 1740 as the Bishop's Palace. Continue down rue de Rigny, turn right onto rue Michâtel, and then take a second right onto rue de Ménin, which winds its way down to the Porte de Metz. Veer left at the gateway, then left again onto rue Gouvion St-Cyr; at no. 25 is the **Musée Municipal** (Town Museum), housed in a former medieval hospital. The museum's well-preserved Salle des Malades (Patients' Ward) dates from the 13th century and displays archaeological finds, ceramics, tapestries, and medieval sculpture. *25 rue Gouvion St-Cyr. Admission: 12 frs. adults, 6 frs. children. Open Wed.– Mon. 10–noon and 2–6; closed Tues. and mornings in winter.*

Fork right onto rue de la Boucherie, which, over a 300-yard stretch lined with old houses, becomes successively rue du Collège, rue Pont de Vaux, and rue Gengoult. Eventually rue Sonaire leads off (right) to the attractive church of **St-Gengoult,** whose choir boasts some of the finest 13th-century stained glass in eastern France. The Flamboyant Gothic cloisters are later than those of the cathedral but equally picturesque. Owing to vandalism, St-Gengoult is open at certain times only. Inquire at the tourist office (next to the cathedral) for details.

㊷ **Nancy,** 23 kilometers (14 miles) east of Toul via A31, is one of France's richest cities in architectural terms. Medieval ornament, 18th-century grandeur, and Belle Epoque fluidity rub shoulders in a town center that combines commercial bustle with stately elegance.

Numbers in the margin correspond with points of interest on the Nancy map.

The symbolic heart of Nancy is **place Stanislas.** The severe, gleaming-white Classical facades of this stylish square are given a touch of rococo jollity by fancifully wrought gilt-iron railings. King Stanislas had a bit of a rococo history himself. He was offered the throne of Lorraine by his French son-in-law Louis XV, after managing to lose the crown of Poland—twice (once in 1709 and again in 1736).

43 44 One side of place Stanislas is occupied by the **Hôtel de Ville** (Town Hall); another houses the **Musée des Beaux-Arts** (Fine Arts Museum). On the ground floor, 19th- and 20th-century pictures by Claude Monet, Edouard Manet, Maurice Utrillo, and the Italian painter Amedeo Modigliani rub shoulders with 150 works in glass and crystal by local Art Nouveau master Antonin Daum. A hefty *Transfiguration* by Rubens adorns the staircase that leads to the second floor and its wealth of Old Masters from the Italian, Dutch, Flemish, and French schools. *Pl. Stanislas. Admission: 14 frs. adults, 9 frs. children; free Wed. for children and students. Open Wed.–Sun. 10:15–12:30 and 1:30–5:45 and Mon. 1:30–5:45; closed Tues.*

45 Before leaving place Stanislas, take a look down rue Maurice-Barrès (to the left of the Hôtel de Ville) at the twin towers of the **cathedral.** This vast, frigid edifice was built in the 1740s in a chunky Baroque style that has none of the ease and grace of the 18th-century place Stanislas. Its most notable interior feature is a murky 19th-century fresco in the dome; restoration is promised and sorely needed.

46 47 From place Stanislas, the tree-lined place de la Carrière leads down to the colonnaded facade of the **Palais du Gouvernement,** former home to the governors of Lorraine. To the right are some spacious formal gardens known as **La Pépinière;** to the left is the 275-foot spire of **St-Epvre,** a splendid neo-Gothic church rebuilt in the 1860s. Thanks to the efforts of Monsignor Trouillet, an entrepreneurial builder-priest, St-Epvre embodies craftsmanship of a cosmopolitan kind. Most of the 2,800 square yards of stained glass were created by the Geyling workshop in Vienna, Austria; the chandeliers were made in Liège, Belgium; many carvings are the work of Margraff of Munich, Germany; the heaviest of the eight bells was cast in Budapest, Hungary; and the organ, though manufactured by Merklin of Paris, was inaugurated in 1869 by Austrian composer Anton Bruckner.

Opposite St-Epvre is Nancy's principal medieval thoroughfare, Grande-Rue. Note the equestrian statue of Duke Antoine (1512) above the elaborate doorway of the Palais Ducal (Ducal Palace) to the right. The main entrance to the palace, and the Lorraine History Museum, which it now houses, is 80 yards farther down the street.

48 The **Musée Historique Lorrain** has a delightfully far-flung assembly of exhibits. Your visit begins in a low terracelike building across the palace lawn, with several showcases of archaeological finds ranging from Stone Age implements and ancient pottery to Roman coins and sculpture. Across the

Avenue Foch, **59**

Boulevard
Charles-V, **51**

Cathedral, **45**

Cours Léopold, **52**

Eglise des
Cordeliers, **50**

Hôtel de Ville, **43**

Musée des Arts
et Traditions
Populaires, **49**

Musée des
Beaux-Arts, **44**

Musée de l'Ecole de
Nancy, **43**

Musée Historique
Lorrain, **48**

Palais du
Gouvernement, **46**

Rue Bénit, **55**

Rue Chanzy, **56**

Rue Henri-
Poincaré, **57**

Rue Louis-
Majorelle, **60**

Rue Mazagran, **58**

Rue Raugraff, **54**

Rue St-Dizier, **53**

St-Epvre, **47**

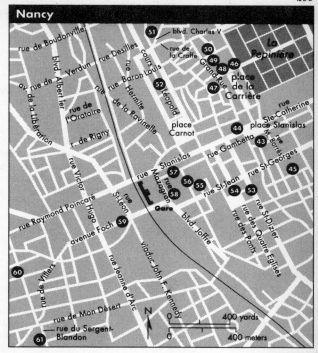

courtyard is the poorly indicated entrance to the main building, which welcomes visitors into a long, narrow room lined with medieval statues.

A spiral stone staircase leads up to the palace's most impressive room, the **Galerie des Cerfs;** exhibits here (including pictures, armor, and books) recapture the Renaissance mood of the 16th and 17th centuries—one of elegance and jollity, though not devoid of stern morality, as an elaborate series of huge tapestries, *La Condemnation du Banquet,* expound on the evils of drink and gluttony with their allegorical sermon.

The rest of the museum is taken up mainly with paintings, furniture, and an extensive display of porcelain and earthenware. In a series of attic rooms, posters, proclamations, and the inevitable *tricolor* banners retrace local history from Napoleon up to World War I. *64 Grande-Rue. Admission: 18 frs. adults, 12 frs. children. Open mid-June–Sept., Wed.–Mon. 10–noon and 2–6; Oct.–mid-June, Wed.–Mon. 10–noon and 2–5; closed Tues.*

Continue along Grande-Rue to the Couvent des Cordeliers, a former convent that contains the **Musée des Arts et Traditions Populaires.** Its treatment of local preindustrial society is based on reconstituted rural interiors equipped with domestic tools and implements. The dukes of Lorraine are buried in the crypt of the adjoining **Eglise des Cordeliers,** a Flamboyant Gothic church; the intricately sculpted limestone tombs of René II and his wife Philippa de Gueldra are impressive. The octagonal Ducal Chapel was begun in 1607 in the Classical style, modeled on the Chapel of the Medicis in Florence. *Grande-Rue. Admission to chapel: 12 frs. adults, 8 frs. children. Open Easter–Oct., Tues.–Sun. 10–noon and 2–6; Nov.–Easter, Tues.–Sun. 10–noon and 2–5; closed Mon.*

From the medieval to the modern, head down rue de la Craffe to begin an **Art Nouveau tour** of Nancy. Art Nouveau caught fire here at the end of the 19th century, representing a breakaway from decorative stereotype toward an innovative, fluid style of design based on motifs taken from nature.

51 Around the corner from rue de la Craffe, at 1 **boulevard Charles-V,** is a house by Lucien Weisenburger (1904) whose windows, by Jacques Gruber, include one in the form of the **52** double-armed cross of Lorraine. The adjacent **cours Léopold** has another Weissenburger creation (1905) at no. 52, and you'll see more Gruber windows at no. 40.

Continue to the end of cours Léopold, cross place Carnot, turn **53** left onto rue Stanislas, then take a second right onto **rue St-Dizier.** At no. 42 is a bank designed in 1903 by French architects Biet and Vallin; its interior can be inspected during working hours (9–5 weekdays). Make the next left onto rue St-Jean, **54** then a left onto **rue Raugraff.** At no. 86 is a house by Vallin **55** (1906). Return to rue St-Jean and continue to **Rue Bénit.** At no. 2 is the first building in Nancy with a metallic structure: not just iron girders, either, but intricately wrought metal pillars, the work of Schertzer to the design of Gutton. There is more stained glass by Gruber, while the exterior decoration tells us that the building began life as a seed shop. The next street **56** along, parallel to rue Bénit, is **rue Chanzy;** at no. 9 is another bank, designed by Emile André, with interior furnishings by Majorelle and yet more Gruber windows.

57 At no. 40 **rue Henri-Poincaré,** a street running parallel to rue Stanislas, is a commercial building of 1908 by Toussaint and Marchal, with metal structure by Schertzer, glass by Gruber, and wrought iron by Majorelle. The facade is adorned with the Lorraine thistle, while hops—used to make beer—symbolize **58** local breweries. **Rue Mazagran** greets you at the far end of the street with, at no. 5, the Excelsior Brasserie; its rhythmic facade, severe by Art Nouveau standards, is illuminated at night.

59 At the far end of rue Mazagran is **avenue Foch,** a busy boulevard that heads past the train station into a district lined with solid, serious mansions clearly built for Nancy's affluent 19th-century middle class. At no. 41, more ironwork by Majorelle can be admired; yet another architect, Paul Charbonnier, was responsible for the overall design in 1905. At no. 69, the occasional pinnacle suggests Gothic influence on a house built in 1902 by Emile André, who designed the neighboring no. 71 two years later.

60 On the right, past rue de Villers, is **rue Louis-Majorelle.** At no. 1 stands a villa built in 1902 by Paris architect Henri Sauvage for Majorelle himself. Sinuous metal supports seem to sneak up on the unsuspecting balcony like swaying cobras, scrutinizing the spacious windows and reckoning them to be yet further productions of that in-demand glazier Jacques Gruber.

61 End your Art Nouveau survey at the **Musée de l'Ecole de Nancy,** at 36 rue du Sergent-Blandan. This airy, turn-of-the-century town house was built by Eugène Corbin, an early patron of the School of Nancy. His personal collection forms the basis of this, the only museum in France devoted to Art Nouveau, and underlines the fact that architecture was not the only vehicle for the expression of Art Nouveau: Lamps, chairs, beds, stained glass, paintings, tables, and silverware are arrayed over two creaky stories. *36 rue Sergent-Blandon. Admission: 12 frs. adults, 8 frs. children. Open Nov.–Mar., Wed.–Mon. 10–noon and 2–6; Apr.–Oct. until 5; closed Tues.*

62 If you've any appetite left for exploring churches, make the quick trip (20 kilometers/12 miles; *see* Lorraine map) southeast to **St-Nicolas-de-Port,** a small industrial town saved from mediocrity by its colossal **basilica** (1495–1555). Legend has it that a finger of St-Nicholas was brought here during the 11th-century Crusades, and the church was rapidly besieged by pilgrims. Architecture buffs will recognize—in the absence of a triforium (an arcaded story between the nave arches and domed clerestory), the simplified column capitals, and the elaborate rib vaulting—a shining example of Flamboyant Gothic, which here enjoys a final fling before the gathering impetus of the Renaissance movement. But you don't need to have specialized knowledge to sense the excitement of the 280-foot oniondomed towers, almost symmetrical but, as was the Gothic wont, not quite. There's excitement inside, too: Daylight floods in through vast windows and cascades around the recently cleaned, honeycolored walls. The slender, free-standing 90-foot pillars in the transept (the "arm" of the church's cruciform shape) are the highest in France.

What to See and Do with Children

Children should be delighted by the **Big Bang Schtroumpf** theme park, featuring the cuddly blue dwarves known in English as Smurfs. *Voie Romaine, 57300 Hagondange, just off A31 north of Metz. Admission: 100 frs. adults, 80 frs. children under 12. Open Easter–Oct., weekdays 10–6, Sat. 10–midnight, Sun. 10–8.*

All items listed below are described in the Exploring section.
Astronomical Clock, Strasbourg Cathedral, Tour 1
Automobile and Train Museums, Mulhouse, Tour 2
Fort of Fermont, Tour 3
Haut-Koenigsbourg, Tour 2
Horse and Harness Museum, Château de la Léonardsau, near Boersch, Tour 2
Musée Alsacien, Strasbourg, Tour 1
Ungersheim Ecomusée, Tour 2

Off the Beaten Track

Anyone with an interest in glassblowing may be glad to make an excursion to the tiny town of **Passavant-la-Rochère,** 100 kilometers (62 miles) south of Nancy. The **Verrerie de la Rochère** has been in operation since 1475, making it one of the oldest glassworks in France. Next to a roaring furnace, glassblowers respect time-honored techniques and dexterously wield their long metal reeds. A wide selection of glassware is sold in an adjoining 17th-century building with a majestic wooden roof. In a modern gallery, contemporary pictures, sculpture, and tapestries can be admired and purchased. *Admission free. Open May–Sept., daily 2:30–5:30. No glassblowing Sun. or in Aug.*

Alsace makes a handy base for a day across the Rhine in **Germany.** Between the elegant spa town of Baden Baden and the historic university center of Freiburg lie the valleys, lakes, and wooded mountains of the Black Forest.

To the south of Alsace-Lorraine is the **Jura-Franche-Comté** region. Better known to Europeans than Americans, the Jura Mountains form a natural border some 150 miles long that curves between France and Switzerland and provide a winter sports alternative to the Alps. The birthplace of Louis Pasteur and Victor Hugo, and home to the celebrated aperitif Pernod, the Jura is dotted with picturesque little towns where local craftsmen still make wooden toys, clocks, and pipes. The area is renowned for its wines and cheese, and a cuisine that draws on the plentiful local lake and river fish—especially trout. There is much here to reward the traveler willing to meander a bit on a drive from Alsace-Lorraine south to Lyon, or southwest to Dijon. Whether you venture any farther into the Jura, go to **Ronchamp,** some 25 miles south of Mulhouse, to see one of the most famous 20th-century buildings in Europe, the chapel of **Notre-Dame du Haut de Ronchamp.** The Swiss-born French architect Le Corbusier designed this beautiful and original building to replace the chapel here that was destroyed during World War II (previous chapels on this site have also been destroyed by war). With its rounded corners, austere white exterior, rolled-back roof and "sun-breaker" windows, this 1955 chapel resembles nothing so much as a ship. Southeast of Ronchamp, in **Belfort,** is a work of art of an altogether different sort, the superb statue of the **Lion of Belfort.** Carved in sandstone by Frédéric Bartholdi—who also made the Statue of Liberty in New York—this 72-foot-long by 35-foot-high sculpture symbolizes the townspeople's heroism during the Prussian seige in 1870.

Shopping

Gift Ideas Among the specialties of Alscace are the handwoven checkered napkins and tablecloths known as **kelches** and the hand-painted **earthenware molds** for *Kouglof* bread. These goods can be found throughout this tourist-oriented province, where every pretty village has a souvenir shop of greater or lesser standing. In Obernai, try **Dietrich** (place du Marché) for useful and beautifully crafted household goods.

Glass Glass and crystal are produced by skilled artisans at **Passavant-la-Rochère** (*see* Off the Beaten Track, above) and especially at **Baccarat** (60 kilometers/37 miles east of Nancy on N59), whose town center is dominated by attractive crystal shops.

Shopping Districts The lively city centers of Strasbourg and Colmar are crammed with specialized shops and boutiques. **Rue des Hallebardes** next to the cathedral, adjacent **rue des Grandes Arcades** (with its shopping mall), and **place Kléber** form the commercial heart of Strasbourg; chocolate shops and delicatessens selling local foie gras are delicious places for browsing. Nancy has less regional cachet for shoppers, though the streets next to the cathedral are full of life.

Wine In Nancy, at 9, place Stanislas, is the Dickensian **La Cave du Roy**. Old wines, champagne, and spirits are arranged in endearing confusion, while mustachioed Monsieur Henné chuckles his way around with Gallic courtesy. His rare red Côtes de Toul is highly recommended.

Sports and Fitness

Bicycling A guide for biking in Lorraine is available from the **Comité Départemental de Cyclotourisme** (33 rue de la République, 54950 Laronxe). Bikes can be rented at many local train stations.

Hiking Hiking in the Vosges foothills is a rewarding pastime; for a list of signposted trails, contact the **Sélestat** tourist office (*see* Essential Information, above).

Horseback Riding There are many possibilities, notably at Kintzheim (tel. 88–82–30–33) and Ensisheim (tel. 89–81–10–10). For further details, contact the **Association Départemental de Tourisme Equestre** (4 rue des Violettes, 67200 Eckbolsheim, tel. 88–77–39–64).

Skiing Both downhill and cross-country skiing are possible in winter at Le Bonhomme (altitude 3,300 feet), Gérardmer (3,800 feet), Valley of Munster (up to 4,300 feet), Champ du Feu (3,600 feet), and Le Hohwald (2,800 feet).

Dining and Lodging

Dining

Alsatian cooking is distinctive in its marriage of German and French tastes. It tends to be heavy: *Choucroute* (sauerkraut), served with ham and sausages, or *Baeckoffe* (a type of potato pie), washed down with a mug of local beer or a pitcher of wine, is a filling means of combating the cold of winter or fueling up during long walks through the Vosges. But there is some sophistication, too. The local foie gras is admirably accompanied by a glass of Gewurztraminer, preferably late-harvested *(vendanges tardives)* for extra sweetness. Riesling, the classic wine of Alsace, is often used to make a sauce that goes exceptionally well with trout or chicken. Snails and seasonal game (pheasant, partridge, hare, venison, and boar) are other favorites, as are Muenster cheese, salty *Bretzel* loaves, and flaky, briochelike *Kouglof* bread.

Salmon, pike, eel, and trout can be found in rivers throughout Alsace and Lorraine. Carp fried in breadcrumbs is a specialty of southern Alsace. Lorraine, renowned for its famous quiches, is also known for its dumplings, Madeleines, almond candies *(dragées)*, and macaroons. Lorraine shares the Alsatian love of pastry and fruit tarts, often made with mirabelle plums, but only in German-influenced Alsace will you find *winstubs* (inns serving wine and snacks or meals, with a passing resemblance to English pubs). Restaurant prices tend to be lower in Lorraine than in Alsace.

Highly recommended restaurants are indicated by a star ★ .

Category	Cost*
Very Expensive	over 350 francs
Expensive	200–350 francs
Moderate	100–200 francs
Inexpensive	under 100 francs

per person for a three-course meal, including tax (18.6%) and tip but not wine

Lodging

Hotel accommodations are easier to find in Lorraine than in Alsace, where advance reservations are essential during summer months (especially in Strasbourg and Colmar). Alsace is rich in *gîtes*, or rented country houses, which provide excellent value for families or small groups. Local tourist offices or the regional office in Strasbourg (9 rue du Dôme, tel. 88–22–01–02) can provide full details.

Highly recommended hotels are indicated by a star ★ .

Category	Cost*
Very Expensive	over 750 francs
Expensive	350–750 francs
Moderate	200–350 francs
Inexpensive	under 200 francs

All prices are for a standard double room for two, including tax (18.6%) and service charge.

Colmar
Dining

Schillinger. Genial Jean Schillinger lords it over one of the smoothest-run restaurants in Alsace. Impeccable service, velvet upholstery, and gleaming silver cutlery complement an exhaustive wine list and the meticulously prepared fish, veal, and salt-cooked pigeon. *16 rue Stanislas, tel. 89–41–43–17. Reservations required. Jacket and tie required. AE, DC, V. Closed Sun. dinner, Mon. Expensive.*

★ **Buffet de la Gare.** Not all train-station buffets can claim gastronomic fame, but hungry travelers will enjoy this one. With its stained-glass windows, Buffet de la Gare looks more like a church than a station. And the waiters exude pastoral concern rather than ticket-collecting officiousness: They will happily advise you how best to connect between platters of crayfish or pâté *en croute* (in pastry) and duck in red-wine sauce. *Pl. de la Gare, tel. 89–41–21–26. Reservations accepted. Dress: casual. Inexpensive–Moderate.*

Lodging
★

Hostellerie Le Maréchal. A maze of corridors connects the three Renaissance town houses that make up this charming hotel near the River Lauch. Some of the rooms are small and are decorated predominantly in light, cheerful colors. Some are endearingly rustic, with exposed beams and curvy walls and floors, while those in back have good river views. *4–6 pl. des Six-Montagnes-Noires, 68000, tel. 89–41–60–32. 40 rooms with bath. Facilities: restaurant, garden. AE, MC, V. Closed Jan. and Feb. Moderate–Expensive.*

Colbert. The convenient location is a plus here, halfway be-

tween the train station and the ancient town center. Ask for
one of the quieter rooms along rue des Taillandiers. Guest
rooms are well equipped and air-conditioned, though the decor
is a little loud. *2 rue des Trois-Epis, 68000, tel. 89–41–31–05.
50 rooms with bath or shower. Facilities: bar. MC, V. Inexpensive.*

Hirtzbach
Dining and Lodging
★

Ottié-Baur. Explorers of the Sundgau region, south of Mulhouse, are rewarded here with far more *carpe frite* (fried carp)
than they can possibly eat. This local specialty is no delicacy,
but it is unusual, especially when the traditional breadcrumb
batter is replaced by fine semolina. Snails, salmon-trout, and
crayfish salad are other mainstays, and a bottle of Riesling will
accompany them nicely. Try to reserve a table on the veranda
overlooking the garden; the varisectioned dining room has too
much phony dark wood for its own good. Thirteen inexpensive
guest rooms are available for overnight stays. *9 rue de Lattre
de Tassigny, 68118 Hirtzbach, 20 km (13 mi) south of Mulhouse
on D432, tel. 89–40–93–22. 13 rooms. Reservations advised.
MC, V. Closed Mon. dinner, Tues., Christmas–New Year's,
and late June–mid-July. Moderate.*

Longuyon
Dining and Lodging

Buffet de la Gare. The train station at Longuyon—an undistinguished town in the heart of industrial north Lorraine—is an
unexpected focus of attention for marauding gourmets from
neighboring Belgium and Luxembourg. At the station itself, in
the Buffet de la Gare, chubby-cheeked Roland Reinalter,
known locally as "Napo," acts the emperor as far as seasonal
dishes and succulent roasts are concerned. Eight guest rooms
are available for overnight stays. *Rue de la Gare, 54260, tel.
82–26–50–85. 8 rooms. Reservations advised. Dress: casual.
AE, DC, MC, V. Closed Fri. dinner, last 2 weeks Sept., and
first 2 weeks Mar. Moderate.*

★

Le Mas. Next to Buffet de la Gare is the distinguished, wood-
beamed dining room of Le Mas run by Gérard Tisserant, a former winner of France's coveted Best *Sommelier* (wine waiter)
award. Crayfish in flaky pastry, scallops with asparagus, and
lightly peppered Scottish salmon rank among the high spots of
his gastronomic menu; there's also a good, reasonably priced
set menu during the week. Note that while rooms are available
on either side of the station square, those at Le Mas are only
marginally more expensive and possess greater style. *Pl. de la
Gare, 54260, tel. 82–26–50–07. 15 rooms. Reservations required. Dress: neat but casual. AE, DC, MC, V. Closed Jan.;
restaurant closed Mon. out of season. Moderate.*

Metz
Dining

La Dinanderie. Chef Claude Piegiorgi serves clever cuisine—
salmon cooked in mustard and chives or kiwi with lime and ba-
nana sorbet—for modest prices at this intimate restaurant,
just across the River Moselle from the Metz Cathedral. *2 rue de
Paris, tel. 87–30–14–40. Reservations advised. Dress: casual.
AE, MC, V. Closed Sun., Mon., Christmas–New Year's, mid-
Feb., and last 3 weeks Aug. Moderate–Expensive.*

A La Ville de Lyon. Just behind the cathedral is this new venture in a venerable vaulted setting, well worth checking out for
its fabulous wine list (30,000 bottles in stock) and inventive
menu. Dishes range from fowl to curried fish. *7 rue des Piques,
tel. 87–36–07–01. Reservations advised. Dress: casual. AE,
DC, MC, V. Closed Sun. dinner, Mon., end of July and most of
Aug. Moderate.*

Lodging **Royal Concorde.** The fully modernized Royal Concorde occu-
★ pies a sumptuous Belle Epoque building not far from the train
station and provides a choice of style (old-fashioned luxury versus simpler modernity). All rooms are soundproofed. There are
two hotel restaurants: a good-value brasserie, Le Caveau, and
a higher-class dining room. *23 av. Foch, 57000, tel. 87–66–81–
11. 75 rooms with bath. Facilities: 2 restaurants, bar. AE, DC,
MC, V. Expensive.*

Nancy **Capucin Gourmand.** A sinuous, art-nouveau decor and faultless
Dining service set the tone at Capucin Gourmand, one of Nancy's fin-
★ est restaurants. Chef Gérard Veissière's menu includes such regional specialties as foie gras, game *en casserole,* and an
excellent rendition of the classic quiche Lorraine. Local Toul
wines make an admirable accompaniment to your meal. *31 rue
Gambetta, tel. 83–35–26–98. Reservations required. Jacket
and tie required. AE, MC, V. Closed Sun., Mon., and first 3
weeks Aug. Expensive.*

Petit Gastrolâtre. Admirers of nouvelle cuisine shouldn't pass
up a visit to Nancy's most famous purveyor of the art, under the
direction of chef Patrick Tanesy. Recommended dishes include
salmon—try it any way it's offered—and a delectable fricassee
of snails. *7 rue des Maréchaux, tel. 83–35–51–94. Reservations
required. Jacket and tie required. No credit cards. Closed
Sun., Mon., Christmas–New Year's, May, and first half Sept.
Moderate.*

L' Entracte. New owners have toned down the former razzma-
tazz (this used to be called the Manhattan Grill!) to concentrate
on earnest French country cooking (quiche, steaks, salads).
Ask for a table in the atmospheric candlelit cellar. *123 Grande-
Rue, tel. 83–36–62–71. Reservations accepted. Dress: casual.
V. Inexpensive–Moderate.*

Lodging **Grand Hôtel de la Reine.** This hotel is every bit as swanky as the
★ place Stanislas on which it stands; the magnificent 18th-centu-
ry building it occupies is officially classified as a historic monument. The guest rooms are decorated in a suitably grand Louis
XV style, and the most luxurious look out onto the square. The
classic-nouvelle restaurant, Le Stanislas, is costly, although
there is a good-value set menu at weekday lunch. Try the
briochelike *kouglof,* a local delicacy made with mirabelle
plums. *2 pl. Stanislas, 54000, tel. 83–35–03–01. 51 rooms with
bath. Facilities: restaurant, bar, TV. Restaurant reservations
required. Jacket and tie required. AE, DC, MC, V. Expensive.*

Central. Located next to the train station, the Central makes a
less expensive but equally convenient alternative to the Grand
Hôtel de la Reine. It is fully modernized, with double glazing to
keep out the noise, and has a charming courtyard garden.
There's no restaurant. *6 rue Raymond-Poincaré, 54000, tel.
83–32–21–24. 68 rooms with bath. AE, MC, V. Inexpensive.*

Ottrott **L'Ami Fritz.** Standing in the hilly village of Ottrott near
Dining Obernai, L'Ami Fritz has the stolid heaviness of many an Alsa-
★ tian *winstub.* No coincidence, perhaps, since owner Fritz uses
this restaurant to showcase his own wine—the famous local
Rouge d'Ottrott, a fruity red. Homemade terrine is the highlight of a menu that ranges from steaks and hams to an ice
cream crescendo. *8 rue du Château, tel. 88–95–80–81. Reservations advised. Dress: casual. AE, DC, MC, V. Closed Wed.
and Jan. Inexpensive.*

Strasbourg
Dining

Crocodile. Chef Emile Jung is celebrated throughout the region for his Alsatian dishes prepared with a delicate nouvelle flair. The restaurant's opulent Old World decor makes a sophisticated backdrop to such dishes as pressed duck and frogs' legs, though if it's on the menu you won't regret choosing the beef Wellington (known to the French as *boeuf en croûte*). *10 rue de l'Outre, tel. 88–32–13–02. Reservations advised. Jacket and tie required. AE, DC, MC, V. Closed Sun., Mon., first week July–first week Aug., and Christmas–New Year's. Very Expensive.*

Buerehiesel. The setting can't be bettered—a 17th-century mansion in Strasbourg's leafy Orangerie—but it's the inventive nouvelle cuisine of top French chef Antoine Westermann that really pulls in the customers. His fish cooked in onion and dry Reisling wine is exceptional, as is the poached lobster. Your meal will be pricey, but the fine views over the park come gratis. *4 parc de l'Orangerie, tel. 88–61–62–24. Reservations required. Jacket and tie required. AE, DC, MC, V. Closed Tues. dinner, Wed., most of Feb., July–early Aug., and Christmas–New Year's. Expensive.*

★ **Kammerzell.** This restaurant glories in its richly carved, woodframed, 15th-century building—probably the most familiar house in Strasbourg, given its position on the corner of the cathedral square. The shortish menu is served on four stories: Fight your way through the tourist hordes on the terrace and ground floor to one of the atmospheric rooms above, with their gleaming wooden furniture and stained-glass windows. Foie gras and *choucroûte* are best bets, while oysters head the seafood that dominates the menu. *16 pl. de la Cathédrale, tel. 88–32–42–14. Reservations advised. Jacket required. AE, DC, MC, V. Expensive.*

★ **Au Gourmet Sans Chiqué.** A cheerful welcome can be expected at this intimate, *sans chiqué* (unpretentious) bistro down one of Old Strasbourg's many narrow streets, where herbs and spices are tellingly used by young chef Daniel Klein. The set menu represents fine value and is best accompanied by a bottle of the house Gewürztraminer. *15 rue Sainte-Barbe, tel. 88–32–04–07. Reservations advised. Dress: casual. AE, DC, MC, V. Closed Mon., part of Jan., and most of Aug. Moderate.*

Lodging

★ **Le Régent Contades.** This sleek, modern hotel has only recently opened its doors; it's located in a revamped mansion near the old town in a residential turn-of-the-century district close to the River Ill (ask for a room with a view of St-Paul's). First-class amenities add to the appeal of the spacious rooms. There's no restaurant. *8 av. de la Liberté, 67000, tel. 88–36–26–26. 30 rooms with bath. Facilities: sauna, bar, solarium. AE, DC, MC, V. Closed Christmas–New Year's. Expensive.*

Gutenberg. A 200-year-old mansion is the setting of this charming hotel, just off place Gutenberg and only a few hundred yards from the cathedral. Several rooms, and the reception and breakfast area, have kept their original furniture, underlining a picturesque appeal that once enjoyed the dubious favors of Hitler's Wehrmacht. There's no restaurant. *31 rue des Serruriers, 67000, tel. 88–32–17–15. 50 rooms, some with bath. MC, V. Closed first week Jan. Inexpensive–Moderate.*

Toul
Dining

Le Dauphin. The large, flower-laden dining room was once a G.I. canteen, and the setting (in an industrial sector three miles from the town center) has little of the ambience of historic Toul. Yet Christophe Vohmann entices gourmets with cooking

of great finesse—chicken with foie gras or scallops with urchins—for prices that start at 130 francs but soon attain heady
heights (300 francs or more) for his most ambitious creations.
*Rte. de Villey-St-Etienne, 54200, tel. 83–43–13–46. Reserva-
tions advised. Jacket and tie required. MC, V. Closed Sun. dinner and Mon., Feb., and first half of Nov. Expensive.*

Verdun
Dining and Lodging

Coq Hardi. On the banks of the Meuse is this large, steep-
roofed hotel furnished in solid regional style. A family-style
welcome pervades here and in the large, comfortable restaurant, where lamb and local Ardennes ham figure on the menu. *8
av. de la Victoire, 55100, tel. 29–86–36–36. 42 rooms, most
with bath. AE, DC, MC, V. Closed Jan. Restaurant closed
Wed. Moderate–Expensive.*

The Arts and Nightlife

The Arts

Many regional towns and villages, especially the wine villages
of Alsace, stage festivals in summer. Note the spectacular, pa-
gan-inspired burning of the three pine trees at **Thann** (late
June) and the Flower Carnival at **Sélestat** (mid-August). The
major regional wine fair is held at **Colmar** (first half of August);
organization is chaotic. There are impressive *son-et-lumière*
performances at the château of **Saverne** and the cathedral of
Strasbourg (check dates and times locally). A monthly handbook, *Strasbourg Actualités,* is a mine of information on local
cultural events.

Theater
Leading regional venues are **Strasbourg**—Théâtre National
(Salle Hubert Gignoux, av. de la Marseillaise, tel. 88–35–44–
52) and Théâtre Municipal (19 pl. Broglie, tel. 88–36–71–12);
Nancy—Théâtre de la Manufacture (6 rue du Baron-Louis, tel.
83–30–23–32) and Théâtre de Nancy (rue Ste-Catherine, tel.
83–37–65–01); **Metz**—Théâtre Municipal (pl. de la Comédie,
tel. 87–75–40–50) **Colmar**—Théâtre Municipal (3 rue Unterlinden, tel. 89–41–29–82); and **Mulhouse** (39 rue Sinne, tel. 89–
45–26–96).

Concerts
The annual Festival de Musique is held in **Strasbourg** from June
to early July at the modern Palais des Congrès and at the cathe-
dral (tel. 88–32–43–10 for details). There is a rock festival in
June, organized by Strasbourg's Centre Culturel (13 pl. André
Maurois), and the city offers summer concerts at the Pavillon
Joséphine in the Orangerie. Tuesday evening concerts are held
at **Colmar** Collegiate Church in summer. Permanent regional
venues and orchestras include Salle Poirel (tel. 83–32–31–25)
and Nancy Orchestre Symphonique & Lyrique (pl. Colonel
Driant, tel. 83–36–69–93) in **Nancy;** Strasbourg Philharmonic
Orchestra (Palais des Congrès, tel. 88–37–67–77) in **Strasbourg;** and Orchestre Philharmonie de Lorraine (rue Cham-
bière, tel. 87–32–66–30) in **Metz.**

Opera
Opéra du Rhin (19 pl. Broglie, tel. 88–75–48–35) in **Strasbourg;**
and Opéra de Lorraine (rue Ste-Catherine, tel. 83–32–04–43)
in **Nancy.**

Nightlife

Cabaret   In **Nancy:** Cabaret Eve (63 rue Jeanne d'Arc). In **Metz:** Le Palladium (1 en Nexirue). In **Strasbourg:** L'Aiglon (27 rue Vieux Marché aux Vins).

Bars and Nightclubs   In **Nancy:** Le Whisky Club (12 av. Foch), L'Isba (126 rue Jeanne d'Arc), or Le Chalet (10 pl. des Vosges). In **Strasbourg:** Charlie's (24 pl. des Halles). In **Mulhouse:** Sarway Piano Bar (20 rue du Capitaine Alfred-Dreyfus).

Jazz Clubs   In **Nancy:** Les Bacchanales (16 rue de la Primatiale; doubles as restaurant). The Nancy Jazz Festival takes place each October at the Parc de la Pepinière. In **Strasbourg:** Le Funambule (3 rue Klein).

Discos   There is a good choice in **Nancy:** Metro (1 ter rue du Gal-Hoche); Pussy Cat (7 rue St-Julien); Club 1900 (19 rue Stanislas); or Tarif de Nuit (3 rue Lafayette). Two of the best bets in **Strasbourg** are the Blue Hawaï (19 rue du Marais-Vert) and Le Chalet (376 rte. de la Wantzeneau). There's a cozy village atmosphere at the Pop Corn disco in **Guebwiller** (169 rue de la République).

10 Burgundy

over the surrounding countryside; cost: 700 francs for an hour-long flight, including champagne.

Exploring Burgundy

Numbers in the margin correspond with points of interest on the Burgundy map.

Orientation

Our first tour covers northern Burgundy, stretching from Sens in the north to Autun in the south and the River Loire in the west, with a rewarding detour to the interesting town of Troyes. Our second tour of Burgundy's wine country begins at Dijon before heading south to Mâcon through some of the world's most distinguished and picturesque vineyards.

Highlights for First-time Visitors

Beaune (and wine-tasting at the Marché aux Vins), Tour 2

Cathédrale St-Etienne, Sens, Tour 1

Fontenay Abbey, Tour 1

A meal at L'Espérance, Vézelay, Tour 2

Morvan Forest, Tour 1

Palais des Ducs (Ducal Palace), Dijon, Tour 2

Ruins of Cluny Abbey, Tour 2

Troyes, Tour 1

Vézelay (village and basilica), Tour 1

Tour 1: Northern and Western Burgundy

❶ It makes sense for **Sens** to be your first stop on the way down to Burgundy, since it lies just 112 kilometers (70 miles) from Paris on N6, a fast road that hugs the pretty Yonne Valley south of Fontainebleau.

Sens was for centuries the ecclesiastical center of France and is still dominated by the **Cathédrale St-Etienne,** begun around 1140. You can see the cathedral's 240-foot south tower from far off; the main Paris–Auxerre road forges straight past it. The pompous 19th-century buildings that line this road can give a false impression to visitors in a hurry: The streets leading off it near the cathedral (notably rue Abelard and rue Jean-Cousin) are full of half-timbered medieval houses, and within their midst sits the 13th-century church of **St-Pierre-le-Rond** with its unusual wooden roof and 16th-century stained glass.

The cathedral's sturdy facade used to have two towers; one was destroyed in the 19th century, and the other was topped in 1532 by an elegant, though somewhat incongruous, Renaissance campanile that contains two monster bells. The statue gallery, starring former archbishops of Sens, is a 19th-century addition, but the statue of St. Stephen, between the twin doors of the central portal, is thought to date from the late 12th century.

The vast, harmonious interior is justly renowned for its stained-glass windows. The oldest (circa 1200) are in the north choir; those in the south transept were manufactured in 1500 at nearby Troyes and include a much-admired *Tree of Jesse.* The cathedral treasury (access near the sacristy to the south of the choir) is one of the richest in France. It contains a collection of miters, ivories, and gold plates, together with the richly woven gold-and-silver robes of the archbishops of Sens. Robes belonging to Thomas à Becket are here as well. Becket fled to Sens from England to escape the wrath of Henry II before returning to his cathedral in Canterbury where, in 1170, he was murdered. Stained-glass windows in the north of the chancel retrace his story. *Pl. de la République.*

The 13th-century **Palais Synodal,** alongside the cathedral, provides a first encounter with Burgundy's multicolored tiled roofs: From its courtyard, there is a fine view of the cathedral's Flamboyant Gothic south transept, constructed by master stonemason Martin Chambiges at the start of the 16th century. (Rose windows were his specialty, as you can appreciate here.) The Palais Synodal houses a museum with statues, mosaics, and tapestries, but its six grand windows and the vaulted Synodal Hall are outstanding features. *Admission: 12 frs. Open Apr.–Nov. 10–noon and 2–5; closed Wed. Apr.–May and Oct.–Nov.*

2 The inhabitants of **Troyes** would be seriously insulted if you mistook them for Burgundians. This old town, 64 kilometers (40 miles) from Sens along N60, is the capital of southern Champagne; as if to prove the point, its historic town center is shaped like a champagne cork. Visitors will be struck by the town's phenomenal number of old buildings, magnificent churches, and fine museums: Few, if any, French town centers contain so much to see and do. A wide choice of restaurants and a web of enchanting pedestrian streets with timber-framed houses add even more to Troyes's appeal.

Numbers in the margin correspond with points of interest on the Troyes map.

The center of Troyes is divided in two by quai Dampierre, a broad, busy boulevard. A good place to begin exploring is **place de la Libération,** where quai Dampierre meets the rectangular artificial lake known as the Bassin de la Préfecture. Although Troyes stands on the Seine, it is the capital of the département named after the River Aube, administered from the elegant **3** **Préfecture** that gazes across both the lake and place de la Libération from behind its gleaming gilt-iron railings.

But the most charming view from place de la Libération is undoubtedly that of the cathedral, whose 200-foot tower peeps through the trees above the statue and old lamps of the square's **4** central flower garden. The **Cathédrale St-Pierre St-Paul** is just a five-minute walk, in a tumbledown square that, like the narrow surrounding streets, has not changed for centuries.

Perhaps the first thing to strike you about the cathedral will be its resemblance to that of Sens. You'll see this in the incomplete one-towered facade; the small Renaissance campaniles on top of the tower; and the artistry of Martin Chambiges, who worked on Troyes's facade (note the large rose window) around the same time he did the transept of Sens. Try to see the facade at

Basilique St-Urbain, **8**

Cathédrale St-Pierre
St-Paul, **4**

Hôtel-Dieu, **7**

Hôtel de Ville, **9**

Maison de l'Outil, **12**

Musée d'Art
Moderne, **5**

Musée
Historique/Musée de la
Bonneterie, **14**

Musée St-Loup, **6**

Préfecture, **3**

Ste-Madeleine, **11**

St-Jean, **10**

St-Nicolas, **15**

St-Pantaléon, **13**

Troyes

night, when its floodlit features are thrown into dramatic relief.

The cathedral's vast five-aisled interior, refreshingly light thanks to large windows and the near-whiteness of the local stone, dates mainly from the 13th century. Like Sens, it has renowned stained glass—fine examples of primitive 13th-century glass in the choir and richly colored 16th-century glass in the nave and facade rose window. Note the arcaded triforium above the pillars of the choir: It was one of the first in France to be glazed rather than filled with stone. *Pl. St-Pierre. Open daily 10–noon and 2–6. Son-et-lumière (sound-and-light) shows are held in the cathedral on Tues., Fri., and Sat. at 10:30 PM, late June–mid-Sept. Admission: 30 frs. adults, 15 frs. children under 16.*

⑤ To the right of the cathedral is the **Musée d'Art Moderne** (Modern Art Museum), housed in the 16th–17th-century former Bishop's Palace. Its magnificent interior, with huge fireplaces, carved wood-beamed roofs, and a Renaissance staircase, plays host to the Levy Collection of modern art, featuring drawings, sculpture, and nearly 400 paintings. The assembly of Fauve works—a short-lived style that succeeded Impressionism at the start of the 20th century—is exceptional, notably the frenzied, hotly colored canvases by Maurice de Vlaminck, Georges Braque, and André Derain. *Pl. St-Pierre. Joint ticket covering all town museums: 15 frs. Open Wed.–Mon. 10–5; closed Tues.*

On the other side of the cathedral square are the former abbey
⑥ buildings of the **Musée St-Loup,** containing two museums. The

ground-floor display is devoted to natural history, with impressive collections of birds and meteorites; the Musée des Beaux-Arts et Archéologie (Fine Arts and Archaeology Museum) is confusingly spread over two floors. In the former abbey cellars are local archaeological finds, especially gold-mounted 5th-century jewelry and a Gallo-Roman bronze statue of Apollo. There is also a section devoted to medieval statuary and gargoyles. Paintings from the 15th to the 19th centuries are exhibited on the second floor and include works by Rubens, Anthony Van Dyck, Antoine Watteau, François Louis Boucher, and Jacques Louis David. *21 rue Chrétien de Troyes. Joint ticket: 15 frs. Open Wed.–Mon. 10–noon and 2–6; closed Tues.*

From the Musée St-Loup, the rue de la Cité, packed with restaurants, leads back to quai Dampierre, passing in front of the **7** superb wrought-iron gates of the 18th-century **Hôtel-Dieu** (hospital), topped with the blue-and-gold fleurs-de-lis emblems of the French monarchy. Around the corner is the entrance to the **Pharmacie**, the only part of the Hôtel-Dieu open to visitors. Take time to inspect the former medical laboratory, with its quaint assortment of pewter dishes and jugs, earthenware jars, and painted wooden boxes designed to contain herbs and medicines. *Quai Dampierre. Joint ticket: 15 frs. Open Wed.–Mon. 10–noon and 2–6; closed Tues.*

The cathedral sector north of quai Dampierre seems quiet and drowsy compared with the more upbeat, commercial southern part of Troyes. Cross over from the Hôtel-Dieu and continue **8** down rue Clemenceau to the **Basilique St-Urbain,** built between 1262 and 1286 by Pope Urban IV, who was born in Troyes. St-Urbain is one of the most remarkable churches in France, a perfect culmination of Gothic's quest to replace stone walls with stained glass. Huge windows, containing much of their original glass, ring the church, while the exterior bristles with the thrust-bearing flying buttresses that made this daring structure possible.

Follow rue Urbain-IV down to **place du Maréchal-Foch,** the main square of central Troyes, flanked by cafés, shops, and the **9** delightful early 17th-century facade of the **Hôtel de Ville** (Town Hall). In summer, the square throbs from morning to night as residents and tourists swarm in to drink coffee or eat pancakes in the various cheap restaurants that spill into the rue Champeaux, Troyes's liveliest pedestrian street. Rue **10** Champeaux runs parallel to **St-Jean,** a lengthy church where England's warrior king, Henry V, married Catherine of France in 1420. The church's tall 16th-century choir contrasts with the low earlier nave; the clock tower is an unmistakable landmark of downtown Troyes.

A little farther along rue Champeaux, the **ruelle des Chats** wanders off toward the church of Ste-Madeleine. The *ruelle*, or alley, is the town's narrowest thoroughfare: Its overhanging dwellings practically bump attics. Halfway down is the tastefully restored cour du Mortier d'Or, a tiny medieval courtyard.

Time Out   A good place to settle into the medieval ambience of Troyes is the friendly, unpretentious **Bouchon Champenois.** This restaurant serves both light lunches and plentiful, inexpensive evening meals in a wood-beamed dining room whose large mirrors reflect the striped timbered patterns of the cour du Mortier d'Or. *Closed Mon.*

⓫ The church of **Ste-Madeleine** (Rue de Général-de-Gaulle), the oldest in Troyes, is best known for its elaborate triple-arched stone rood screen separating the nave and the choir. Only six other such screens still remain in France—most were dismantled during the French Revolution—and this one was carved with panache by Jean Gailde between 1508 and 1517. The church's west tower and main door also date from the early 16th century.

Take rue des Quinze-Vingts, which runs parallel to the ruelle des Chats, as far as rue Emile-Zola. Turn right, then second **⓬** left, into rue de la Trinité. The museum known as **Maison de l'Outil** stands at no. 7 in the 16th-century Hôtel de Mauroy. Upstairs is a collection of pictures, models, and tools relevant to such traditional wood-related trades as carpentry, clog making, and barrel making. *7 rue de la Trinité. Joint ticket: 15 frs. Open daily 10–noon and 2–6.*

⓭ Close to the Maison de l'Outil, via rue Bordet, is another 16th-century building: the church of **St-Pantaléon.** A number of fine stone statues, surmounted by canopies, cluster around its pillars. The tall, narrow walls are topped not by stone vaults but by a wooden roof, unusual for such a late church. Just as unexpected are the red-and-white streamers and *Solidarnosc* (Solidarity) banners sometimes found next to the altar: St-Pantaléon is used for services by the Polish community. *Rue de Turenne. Open 10–noon and 2–6 in summer months only; at other times apply to the tourist office.*

The Renaissance Hôtel de Vauluisant, opposite, houses two **⓮** museums. The **Musée Historique** (History Museum) traces the development of Troyes and southern Champagne, with a section devoted to religious art. The **Musée de la Bonneterie** (Textile Museum) outlines the history and manufacturing process of the town's traditional bonnet-making industry; some of the bonnets on display are over 200 years old. *Rue de Turenne. Joint ticket: 15 frs. Open daily 12–noon and 2–6.*

⓯ Close by, beyond place Jean-Jaurès, is yet another church: that of **St-Nicolas.** You may not be tempted by its grimy exterior, but undaunted souls will be rewarded by the chance to scale a wide stone staircase up to an exuberantly decorated chapel and an unexpected view over the nave. Notice the funny little spiral staircase on the left of the nave that appears to vanish into mid-wall.

Numbers in the margin correspond with points of interest on the Burgundy map.

Leaving Troyes—by far the largest town in this tour—you will soon be plunged back into rural tranquillity as you drive southwest along the Auxerre-bound N77. Don't let your sense of **⓰** well-being fog your curiosity, however. **Pontigny,** just 21 kilometers (13 miles) short of Auxerre, can be easily mistaken for another drowsy, dusty village, but its once-proud **abbey** is as large as many cathedrals; in the 12th and 13th centuries, it sheltered three archbishops of Canterbury, including St. Thomas à Becket.

The abbey was founded in 1114, but the current church was begun in 1150. The monks belonged to the Cistercian order, which, frowning on the opulence of the rival House of Cluny, fostered buildings of intense sobriety. Small, even-spaced windows render the abbey's silhouette monotonous: The single tower, that of the facade, scrambles almost apologetically to roof level. The austere, 330-foot interior is divided in two by a wooden screen. The only ornament is provided by the late 17th-century wooden choir stalls, carved with garlands and angels.

⑰ Auxerre is a small, peaceful town dominated by its **Cathédrale St-Etienne,** perched on a steep hill overlooking the River Yonne. The 13th-century choir, the oldest part of the edifice, contains its original stained glass, dominated by dazzling reds and blues. Beneath the choir is the frescoed 11th-century Romanesque crypt; alongside is the Treasury, featuring medieval enamels, manuscripts, and miniatures. *Pl. St-Etienne. Admission to crypt and treasury: 5 frs. each. Open daily 10–noon and 2–5.*

Fanning out from Auxerre's main square, place des Cordeliers (just up from the cathedral), are a number of venerable streets lined by 16th-century houses. Explore these before heading north toward the town's most interesting church, the former abbey of **St-Germain,** which stands parallel to the cathedral some 300 yards away. The church's earliest section aboveground is the 11th-century Romanesque bell tower, but the extensive underground crypt dates to the 9th century and preserves its original frescoes, some of the oldest in France. *Pl. St-Germain. Admission: 10 frs. (free Wed.). Guided tours of the crypt, Wed.–Mon. 9–11:30 and 2–5:30; closed Tues.*

⑱ Chablis, famous for its white wine, lies just 16 kilometers (10 miles) east of Auxerre along N65 and D965. A pretty village, it nestles on the banks of the River Serein ("serene") and is protected by the massive, round, turreted towers of the Porte Noël gateway. Much less welcoming are the inflated prices charged for local wines by the plentiful village tourist shops! You can ferret out a better deal at a local producer, and at the same time scour the surrounding vineyards for dramatic views, as their towering slopes contrast with the region's characteristic rolling hills.

⑲ Continue along D965 from Chablis to the village of **Tonnerre,** 16 kilometers (10 miles) away. The Armançon Valley and 16th-century houses can be surveyed from the terrace of the church of St-Pierre, rebuilt, like most of the town, after a devastating fire in 1556. Tonnerre's chief attraction, the high-roofed **Ancien Hôpital,** was built in 1293 and has survived the passing centuries—flames and all—largely intact. The main room, the Grande Salle, is 250 feet long and retains its oak ceiling; it was conceived as the hospital ward and after 1650 served as the parish church. The original hospital church leads off from the Grande Salle; in the adjoining Chapelle du Revestière is a dramatic 15th-century stone group representing the *Burial of Christ. Rue du Part. Admission: 10 frs. Open Wed.–Mon. 10–noon and 2–5; closed Tues.*

⑳ Ten kilometers (6 miles) east of Tonnerre lies the château of **Tanlay,** built around 1550 and betraying the classical influence of the Renaissance. The vestibule, framed by wrought-iron railings, leads to a wood-paneled salon and dining room filled with period furniture. A graceful staircase leads to the second floor; notice the frescoed gallery and ornate fireplaces. A small room in the tower above was used as a secret meeting place by Huguenot Protestants during the 1562–98 Wars of Religion; its cupola boasts a fresco of scantily clad 16th-century religious personalities. *Admission: 25 frs. Open Apr.–Nov. 11, Wed.– Mon. 10–noon and 2–5; closed Tues.*

Continue along D965 to Pimelles, then turn right onto D12. Eleven kilometers (7 miles) south is another, slightly earlier château, **Ancy-le-Franc.** The Renaissance styling here has an Italian flavor: The château was built to the designs of Sebastiano Serlio with interior decor by Primaticcio, both of whom worked at the court of French king François I (1515–47). The plain, majestic exterior contrasts with the sumptuous rooms and apartments, many—particularly the magnificent Chambre des Arts—with carved or painted walls and ceilings and their original furniture. Such grandeur won the approval of Sun King Louis XIV, no less, who once stayed in the Salon Bleu. Adjoining the château is a small Musée Automobile featuring vintage cars. *Admission: 25 frs. Open Apr.–Nov. 11, daily 10–noon and 2–5.*

Twenty-nine kilometers (18 miles) southeast along D905 (take D32 at Marmagne, just past Montbard) is the Cistercian abbey of **Fontenay,** founded by St-Bernard in 1118. The same Cistercian criteria applied to Fontenay as to Pontigny: no-frills architecture and an isolated site. By the end of the 12th century, the church and other buildings comprising the monastery were finished. The abbey's community grew to some 300 monks and prospered until the 16th century, when religious wars and administrative mayhem hastened its decline. The abbey was dissolved during the French Revolution and used as a paper factory until 1906. Fortunately the historic buildings emerged unscathed from their industrial use, and, with the help of original plans, Fontenay has since been restored to its former glory.

The abbey is surrounded by extensive gardens dotted with the fountains that gave it its name. The church and cloister are the most important buildings to survive. The church's solemn interior is lit by windows in the facade and by a double row of three narrow windows, representing the Trinity, in the choir. A staircase in the south transept leads to the wood-roofed dormitory (spare a thought for the bleary-eyed monks who were frequently obliged to stagger down for services in the dead of night). The chapter house, flanked by a majestic arcade, and the scriptorium, where monks worked on their manuscripts, lead off from the adjoining cloisters. *Admission: 30 frs. Guided visits daily 10–11:30 and 2–4.*

Head back to Montbard and take D980 south—via the picturesque old town of Semur-en-Auxois—to **Saulieu,** 48 kilometers (30 miles) away. The reputation of Saulieu belies its size: It is renowned for good food (Rabelais, that roly-poly 16th-century man of letters, extolled its Gargantuan hospitality) and Christmas trees (a million are packed off from the area each year). The basilica of **St-Andoche** is almost as old as that of Vézelay, though less imposing and much restored. The adjoining **town museum** contains a room devoted to François Pompon (1855–1933), an animal-bronze sculptor whose smooth, stylized creations seem contemporary but predate World War II. *Rue Salli-*

er. Admission: 7 frs. Open Wed.–Mon., 10–noon and 2–5; closed Tues.

24 On your way south through the brooding Morvan Forest toward Autun, detour to the Renaissance château of **Sully.** Take N6 to Arnay-le-Duc, then D36, turning right for Sully after the village of Vellerot. The turreted château stands in a stately park and is surrounded by a moat, while a monumental staircase leads to the north front and a broad terrace. Marshal Mac-Mahon, president of France from 1873 to 1879, was born here in 1808. *Admission: 7 frs. Visits to the grounds only, Apr.–Nov., daily 10–noon and 2–5.*

25 D326 links Sully to D973 and, 9 kilometers (6 miles) later, **Autun**—an important town since Roman times, as you can detect at the well-preserved archways, Porte St-André and Porte d'Arroux, and at the Théâtre Romain, once the largest arena in Gaul. Julius Caesar even referred to Autun as the "sister and rival of Rome itself." Another famous warrior, Napoleon, studied here in 1779 at the military academy (now the Lycée Bonaparte).

Autun's principal monument, however, is its **cathedral,** built from 1120 to 1146 to house the relics of St. Lazarus; the main tower, spire, and upper reaches of the chancel were added in the late 15th century. The influx of medieval pilgrims accounts for the building's size (35 yards wide and nearly 80 yards long). Lazarus's tomb was dismantled in 1766 by canons who were believers in the rationalist credo of the Enlightenment. These clergy did their best to transform the Romanesque-Gothic cathedral into a Classical temple at the same time, adding pilasters and classical ornament willy-nilly. Fortunately, some of the best medieval stonework, including the nave capitals and the tympanum above the main door—a *Last Judgment* sculpted by Gislebertus in the 1130s—emerged unscathed. Jean Auguste Ingres's painting depicting the *Martyrdom of St-Symphorien* has been relegated to a dingy chapel in the north aisle of the nave. *Pl. St-Louis.*

Across from the cathedral, the **Musée Rolin** boasts several fine paintings from the Middle Ages and good examples of Burgundian sculpture, including another Gislebertus masterpiece, the *Temptation of Eve,* which originally topped one of the side doors of the cathedral. *Pl. St-Louis. Admission: 8 frs. Open Wed.–Sat., Mon. 10–noon and 2–5, Sun. 10–noon; closed Tues.*

26 Our next port of call, **Château-Chinon,** lies 37 kilometers (23 miles) west of Autun along D978. This small town has been in the news during recent years thanks to its former mayor, François Mitterrand, now the French president. One of Mitterrand's legacies is the brash, colorful, and controversial fountain by Niki de St-Phalle, which is in front of the town hall. Another is the **Musée du Septennat,** housing an astonishing variety of gifts received by Mitterrand as president. The museum (admission free) can be found at the top of the hill as you leave the town.

Château-Chinon is capital of the Morvan, and a fine view of the town and forest can be had from the Panorama du Calvaire near square d'Aligre. The costumes and traditions of the Morvan are the subject of the **Musée du Folklore.** *Rue St-Cristophe. Ad-*

mission: 12 frs. Open Easter–Nov., Wed. and weekends only, 10–noon and 2–5.

From Château-Chinon you can either cut north across the Morvan Forest to Clamecy or continue to **Nevers,** 64 kilometers (40 miles) away—Burgundy's western outpost on the banks of the Loire. Nevers is renowned for its ceramics; earthenware has been produced here since the late 16th century, promoted initially by Italian craftsmen. The French Revolution prompted a slowdown in activity, but three traditional manufacturers still remain. An extensive selection of Nevers earthenware, retracing its stylistic development, can be admired at the **Musée Municipal.** *Rue St-Genest. Admission: 4 frs. Open Wed.–Mon. 10–noon and 2–5; closed Tues.*

Part of the medieval walls extend behind the museum, culminating in the intimidating gateway known as the **Porte du Croux** (built in 1393), which, thanks to its turrets and huge, sloping roof, resembles a small castle. The nearby **Cathédrale St-Cyr-Ste-Juliette,** with its 160-foot square tower, is another sizable building, constructed over several periods of the Middle Ages.

Beyond the cathedral, the **Palais Ducal** has a sumptuous, large-windowed Renaissance facade; unfortunately, its interior is closed to the public. A few hundred yards north, across a park that can be entered from place Carnot, is **St-Gildard's convent,** where Ste-Bernadette of Lourdes (1844–79) spent the last 13 years of her life. A small museum contains mementos and outlines her life story (Bernadette claimed to have seen the Virgin several times in 1858 and was canonized in 1933). *Admission free. Open daily 10–5.*

Unlike those of Pontigny and Fontenay, the abbey church of **La Charité-sur-Loire,** 24 kilometers (15 miles) downstream from Nevers, was dependent on Cluny; it was also the country's second-largest church after Cluny when consecrated by Pope Pascal II in 1107. Fire and neglect have taken their toll on the massive original edifice, and these days the church is cut in two, with the single-towered facade separated from the imposing choir and transept by the pretty place Ste-Croix (which occupies the former site of the nave). A fine view of the church's exterior can be had from square des Bénédictins, just off the main street (Grande-Rue).

From La Charité, head northeast to **Clamecy,** 51 kilometers (32 miles) away. Slow-moving Clamecy is not on many tourist itineraries, but its tumbling alleyways and untouched, ancient houses epitomize *La France Profonde.* Clamecy's multishaped roofs, dominated by the majestic square tower of St-Martin's collegiate church, are best viewed from the banks of the Yonne. The river played a crucial role in Clamecy's development; trees from the nearby Morvan Forest were chopped down and floated in huge convoys to Paris. The history of this form of transport *(flottage),* which lasted until 1923, is detailed in the **town museum.** *Rue Bourgeoise. Admission: 5 frs. Open Easter–Oct., 10–noon and 2–5; closed Tues.*

Time Out In homage to the logs that used to be floated downriver from Clamecy to Paris, a log-shaped, sugared-almond candy has long been chewed by Clamecycois, as the local inhabitants are known. You can find your *bûchettes* at the **Avignon** (22 rue de la

Monnaie) pastry shop (which doubles as a tearoom), close to the steps leading up to the church square.

30 The picturesque old town of **Vézelay** lies 24 kilometers (15 miles) east of Clamecy along D951. In the 11th and 12th centuries, its celebrated **basilica,** perched at the top of a rocky crag, was one of the focal points of Christendom. Pilgrims poured in to gasp at the relics of St. Mary Magdalene before setting off on the great medieval trek to the shrine of St. James at Santiago de Compostela in northwest Spain.

By the mid-13th century, the authenticity of St. Mary's relics was in doubt; others had been discovered in Provence. The decline continued until the French Revolution, when the basilica and adjoining monastery buildings were sold by the state. Only the basilica escaped demolition and was itself falling into ruin when ace restorer Viollet-le-Duc rode to the rescue in 1840 (he also restored the cathedrals of Laon and Amiens, and Paris's Notre-Dame).

Today the basilica at Vézelay has recaptured its onetime glory and is considered France's most prestigious Romanesque showcase. Nowhere is this more evident than in the nave, whose carved column capitals are imaginatively designed and superbly executed, representing miniature medieval men in all manner of situations—working in the fields, wielding battle swords, or undergoing the tortures of hell.

The basilica's exterior is best seen from the leafy terrace to the right of the facade. Opposite is a vast, verdant panorama encompassing lush valleys and rolling hills. In the forefront is the Flamboyant Gothic spire of St-Père-sous-Vézelay, a tiny village a couple miles away, with an excellent restaurant (*see* Dining, below).

31 Another 13 kilometers (8 miles) east via D957 lies **Avallon,** spectacularly situated on a promontory jutting over the Cousin Valley. The town's old streets and ramparts are pleasant places to stroll, before or after viewing the works of medieval stone carvers whose imaginations ran riot on the portals of the venerable church of St-Lazarus.

The A6 expressway passes close to Avallon and can whisk you north to Paris or south to Dijon and the famous Burgundy vineyards that are part of our second tour. If you have time, however, we suggest that you make an excursion from Avallon to the northern part of the **Morvan Regional Park,** whose photogenic lakes, hills, and forest may be viewed around every twisty corner. **32** Take D10 to **Quarré-les-Tombes,** so called because of the empty prehistoric stone tombs discovered locally and eerily arrayed in a ring around the church. The **Rocher de la Pérouse,** 8 kilometers (5 miles) south of Quarré-les-Tombes, is a mighty outcrop worth scrambling up for a view of the Morvan and the Cure Valley.

Tour 2: Wine Country

33 **Dijon,** linked to Paris 314 kilometers (195 miles) away by expressway (A6/A38) and TGV train, is the age-old capital of Burgundy. Throughout the Middle Ages, Burgundy was a duchy that led a separate existence from the rest of France, culminating in the rule of the four "Grand Dukes of the West" between

1364 and 1477. A number of monuments date from this period, such as the Palais des Ducs (Ducal Palace), now largely converted into an art museum.

Dijon's fame and fortune outlasted its dukes, and the city continued to flourish under French rule from the 17th century on. It has remained the major city of Burgundy—the only one, in fact, with more than 100,000 inhabitants. Its site, on the major European north–south trade route and within striking distance of the Swiss and German borders, has helped maintain its economic importance. The same can be said of its numerous gastronomic specialties: snails, mustard, and cassis (a blackcurrant liqueur often mixed with white wine—preferably Burgundy Aligoté—to make Kir, one of France's most popular aperitifs).

Numbers in the margin correspond with points of interest on the Dijon map.

❸❹ The **Palais des Ducs** is Dijon's leading testimony to bygone splendor. These days, it's home to one of France's major arts museums, the **Musée des Beaux-Arts,** where tombs of two of the aforementioned dukes—Philip the Bold and John the Fearless—spearhead a rich collection of medieval objects and Renaissance furniture. Among the paintings are works by Italian Old Masters, and French 19th-century artists, such as Théodore Géricault and Gustave Courbet, and their Impressionist successors, notably Édouard Manet and Claude Monet. The **ducal kitchens** (circa 1435) with their six huge fireplaces, and the 14th-century chapter house catch the eye, as does the 15th-century **Salle des Gardes** (Guard Room), with its richly carved and colored tombs and late 14th-century altarpieces. The elegant, Classical exterior of the former palace can best be admired from place de la Libération and cour d'Honneur. *Pl. de la Libération. Admission: 20 frs. (free Sun.), ticket valid for all town museums. Open 10–6; closed Tues.*

Further links with Dijon's medieval past are found west of the town center, just off the avenue Albert Ier beyond the train station. Keep an eye out for the exuberant 15th-century gateway to the Chartreuse de Champmol—all that remains of a former charterhouse—and the adjoining **Puits de Moïse,** the so-called Well of Moses, with six large, compellingly realistic medieval statues on a hexagonal base (1395–1405).

❸❺ Among the city's outstanding old churches is **Notre-Dame** (rue de la Préfécture), with its elegant towers, delicate nave stonework, 13th-century stained glass, and soaring chancel. The **❸❻** church of **St-Michel** (rue Rameau) takes us forward 300 years **❸❼** with its chunky Renaissance facade. **Cathédrale Ste-Bénigne** (off rue Mariotte) is comparatively austere; its chief glory is the 10th-century crypt—a forest of pillars surmounted by a rotunda.

Dijon is rich in museums, which all can be visited on a single **❸❽** 20-franc ticket. The **Musée Archéologique** (Archaeological Museum), housed in the former abbey buildings of Ste-Bénigne, traces the history of the region through archaeological discoveries (*5 rue du Docteur-Maret. Open Wed.–Mon. 9–noon and* **❸❾** *2–6; closed Tues.).* The **Musée Magnin** is a 17th-century mansion showcasing original furnishings and a variety of paintings from the 16th to the 19th centuries (*4 rue des Bons-Enfants.* **❹❶** *Open Sun.–Fri. 9–noon and 2–6; closed Sat.).* The **Musée**

Dijon

rue Diderot

rue Jeannin

rue Berbier

blvd. Carnot

rue J.J. Rousseau

330 yards
300 meters

 36

rue Chabot-Charny

34

35

rue des Bon-Enfants

39

place de la Libération

rue de la Préfecture

rue des Forges

rue Admiral Roussin

rue Pasteur

place des Cordeliers

rue Musette

rue du Bourg

rue Ste-Anne

40

rue de la Liberté

rue Bossuet

rue Berbisy

pl. Bossuet

rue Michelet

place Emile Zola

rue Monge

38
37

rue Condorcet

place St-Bénigne

rue Mariotte

blvd de Brosses

rue de l'Arquebuse

rue de l'Arquebuse

av. Albert Ier

rue du Fg. Raines

41

Cathédrale
Ste-Bénigne, **37**
Musée
Archéologique, **38**
Musée d'Art Sacré, **40**
Musée d'Histoire
Naturelle et Jardin
Botanique, **41**

Musée Magnin, **39**
Notre-Dame, **35**
Palais des Ducs, **34**
St-Michel, **36**

d'Art Sacré, devoted to religious art, has a collection of sculpture and altarpieces in the appropriate setting of a former church *(17 rue Ste-Anne. Open Sun.–Fri. 9–noon and 2–6; closed Sat.).* The **Musée d'Histoire Naturelle et Jardin Botanique** encompasses a natural-history museum and impressive botanical gardens, with a wide variety of trees and tropical flowers *(1 av. Albert Ier. Museum open Wed.–Mon. 2–5; closed Tues.).*

Time Out   Place Darcy has more to recommend it than the Dijon tourist office in one corner. Gastronomically speaking, this square caters to all tastes and budgets. In addition to the famed **Jean-Pierre Billoux's** restaurant, a mecca for serious gourmets *(see Dining and Lodging, below),* you can choose from the bustling **Concorde** brasserie, the quiet bar of the **Hôtel de la Cloche,** the underground **Caveau de la Porte Guillaume** wine-and-snack bar, or—for those with a sweet tooth—the **Pâtisserie Darcy.**

Numbers in the margin correspond with points of interest on the Burgundy map.

A31 connects Dijon to Beaune, 40 kilometers (25 miles) south, but you may prefer a leisurely route through the vineyards to racing down the expressway. Chug along D122, past Gevrey-Chambertin, Chambolle-Musigny, and Morey-St-Denis, to **Clos de Vougeot.** The **Château du Clos de Vougeot** was constructed by Cistercian monks in the 12th century and completed during the Renaissance; it's famous as the seat of Burgundy's elite company of wine lovers, the *Confrérie des Chevaliers du Tastevin,* who gather here in November at the start of an annual three-day festival, *Les Trois Glorieuses.* You can admire the château's cellars, where ceremonies are held, and ogle the huge grape presses. *Admission: 18 frs. Guided visits daily 10–noon and 2–4:30; closed Christmas–New Year's.*

Wine has been made in nearby **Nuits-St-Georges** since Roman times; its "dry, tonic, and generous qualities" were recommended to Louis XIV for medicinal use. It is appropriate, then, that some of the region's finest vineyards should be owned by the **Hospices de Beaune,** founded in 1443 as a hospital, which carried on its medical activities until 1971, its nurses still sporting their strange medieval uniform. A visit to the Hospices is one of the highlights of a stay in **Beaune.** The hospital's medical history is retraced in a museum whose wide-ranging collections feature some of the weird and wonderful instruments used by doctors back in the 15th century. You can also see Roger Van der Weyden's medieval Flemish masterpiece, *The Last Judgment,* plus a collection of tapestries (though a better series from the late 15th century, relating the life of the Virgin, can be admired in Beaune's main church, the 12th-century **Collégiale Notre-Dame,** just off avenue de la République). Each year, as part of the Trois Glorieuses, an auction of its wines is held at the Hospices on the third Sunday of November, attended by international connoisseurs and dealers. *Rue Deslandes. Museum admission: 20 frs. Open daily 10–noon and 2–5.*

Despite the hordes of tourists, Beaune remains one of the most charming and attractive French provincial towns. There are few more delightful experiences than a visit to the candle-lit cellars of the **Marché aux Vins** (rue Nicolas Rolin). Here you can taste as many of the regional wines as you wish—beginning with whites and fruity Beaujolais and ending with big reds like Gevrey-Chambertin—for around 40 francs.

Time Out A good place to find refreshment in the center of Beaune—and to drink something other than wine—is the **Bouché** tearoom opposite the old belfry. Pastries and homemade ice cream are specialties. *1 pl. Monge.*

From Beaune, another scenic route cuts through the vineyards on the way south to Chalon-sur-Saône. Take D973 from Beaune, which soon passes through Pommard, Volnay, and Meursault before continuing to Auxey-Duresses, La Rochepot and its pretty château, and Nolay. From Nolay, N6 scissors through another vineyard, Chassagne-Montrachet, on its way to Chagny. D981 runs south to Rully, past the Mercurey vineyard and the start of the Côte Chalonnaise, which links the vineyards of Burgundy and Beaujolais to Germolles and Givry, where you take D69 to Chalon.

44 **Chalon-sur-Saône** has its medieval heart near the **Eglise St-Vincent**—a former cathedral displaying a jumble of styles—close to the banks of the River Saône. Chalon is the birthplace of Nicéphore Niepce (1765–1833), whose early experiments, developed further by Jacques Daguerre, qualify him as the father of photography. The **Musée Nicéphore Niepce,** a fine museum occupying an 18th-century house overlooking the Saône, retraces the early history of photography and motion pictures with the help of some pioneering equipment. It also includes a selection of contemporary photographic work and a lunar camera used during the U.S. Apollo program. But the star of the museum must be the primitive camera used to take the first photographs in 1816. *Hôtel des Messageries, quai Gambetta. Admission: 10 frs. Open 10–noon and 2–5; closed Tues.*

45 N6 continues down the Saône Valley to **Tournus**, (24 kilometers/ 15 miles away), a town that retains much of the charm of the Middle Ages and the Renaissance. One of Burgundy's most spectacular and best-preserved Romanesque buildings is the **abbey of St-Philibert.** Despite its massiveness—the nave is supported by unadorned cylindrical pillars over four feet thick—it is spacious and light. No effort was made to decorate or embellish the interior, whose sole hint of frivolity is the alternating red and white stones in the nave arches. The crypt and former abbey buildings, including the cloister and magnificent 12th-century refectory, can also be visited.

Head west from Tournus along picturesque D14 to the fortified hilltop town of Brancion, with its old castle and soaring keep.
46 Shortly after, turn left along D146 to **Cluny**, another 19 kilometers (12 miles) away. The **Abbey of Cluny,** founded in the 10th century, was the biggest church in Europe until the 16th century, when Michelangelo built St. Peter's in Rome. Cluny's medieval abbots were as powerful as popes. In 1098, Pope Urban II (himself a Cluniac) assured the head of his old abbey that Cluny was the "light of the world." That assertion, of dubious religious validity, has not stood the test of time, and today Cluny stands in ruins—a reminder of the limits of human grandeur.

The ruins nonetheless suggest the size and glory of Cluny Abbey at its zenith. Only the Clocher de l'Eau-Bénite (a majestic bell tower) and the right arms of the two transepts, climbing 100 feet aboveground, remain. The 13th-century *farinier* (flour mill), with its fine chestnut roof and collection of statues, can also be seen. The gardens contain an ancient lime tree, several hundred years old, named Abélard after the controversial philosopher who sought shelter at the abbey in 1142. No one is sure the tree is quite that old, though! *Admission: 23 frs. (16 frs. Nov.–Easter). Guided visits Easter–Oct., daily 9–noon and 2–5; late morning/early afternoon only the rest of the year.*

Mâcon is a mere 25 kilometers (16 miles) along N79 southeast of Cluny. Stop just outside the town to admire the giant rocky outcrop of **Solutré** on your right, towering above the vineyard of Pouilly-Fuissé, renowned for its white wine. Excavations around the Rock of Solutré have revealed the presence of prehistoric man—and prehistoric horse (so many horses, in fact, that one school of thought asserts that the poor beasts were driven over the top of the cliff to crash to a horrific death below).

47 **Mâcon** is a bustling town, best known for its wine fair in May and for its pesky stone bridge across the Saône, whose low arches are a headache for the pilots of large river barges. The two octagonal towers of the ruined cathedral of St-Vincent loom over the wide quays along the river. The Romantic poet Alphonse de Lamartine (1790–1869) was born in Mâcon.

What to See and Do with Children

Burgundy is a quiet, mainly rural region that lends itself to peaceful pursuits—walks and picnics in the **Morvan Forest** (maybe along the shores of one of its small lakes) or more energetic hikes up the imposing **Rock of Solutré** (Tour 2).

In Troyes (Tour 1), youngsters may be curious to see the yard-wide, overhanging **ruelle des Chats** (alleyway) in the heart of a town whose medieval atmosphere has few peers.

Medieval architecture may be viewed in a new light by means of a visit to the spectacular **son-et-lumière** (sound-and-light) show at Troyes Cathedral on a summer evening, if the 10:30 starting time isn't too late for your schedule.

The beautifully restored **abbey of Fontenay** (Tour 1) brings history alive by showing how and where monks lived as well as worshiped.

Musée Nicéphore Niepce, in Chalons-sur-Sâone (Tour 2) will interest children of all ages with its collection of antique camera equipment.

Off the Beaten Track

Burgundy is a convenient launching place for a trip to **Bourges,** just 51 kilometers (32 miles) from La Charité-sur-Loire along N151. The towers of its 13th-century cathedral can be seen on the horizon as you draw near, though, ironically, **Cathédrale St-Etienne** is less easy to spot once you've arrived in the town itself; its asymmetrical facade is hidden away down a narrow street and is impossible to photograph. The central portal is a masterpiece of medieval sculpture: Cherubim, angels, saints, and prophets cluster in the archway above the tympanum, which contains an elaborate representation of the *Last Judgment.*

The interior is unlike that of any other Gothic cathedral. The forest of tall, slender pillars rising from floor to vaults is remarkable enough, but the unique feature is the height of the side aisles flanking the nave: 65 feet, high enough to allow windows to be pierced above the level of the second side aisle. The cathedral contains some exquisite stained glass, some dating to its construction. *Off rue du Guichet.*

The center of Bourges, downhill from the cathedral, has been restored to medieval glory. Rue Mirebeau and rue Coursalon, pedestrian-only streets full of timber-framed houses, are charming places for browsing and shopping. At one end of rue Coursalon, over rue Moyenne—Bourges's busy but less-distinguished main street—is the **Palais Jacques-Coeur,** one of the most sumptuous Gothic dwellings in France. Interior highlights are the vaulted chapel, wooden ceilings covered with original paintings, and the dining room with its wall tapestries and massive fireplace. *Rue Jacques-Coeur. Admission: 16 frs. Open Apr.–Oct., Wed.–Mon. 9–11 and 2–5, Nov.–Mar. 10–11 and 2–4; closed Tues.*

Shopping

Antiques
The auction houses at Semur-en-Auxois and Dijon are good places to prospect for antiques and works of art; the streets of Tournus are riddled with antiques shops.

Clothes
If there is an ideal place for a shopping spree, it's Troyes. Numerous clothing manufacturers are established just outside the town, with the result that clothes prices in stores can be up to 50% cheaper than elsewhere in France. Rue des Bas-Trévois, rue Bégand (leather goods also), and rue Cartalon are good places to look; the best buys on jeans can be had at the **Jeans Shop** (64 rue Emile-Zola).

Food Items
Shopping is not one of life's major activities in sleepy Burgundy, where eating and drinking are most important. Mustard, snails, and all manner of candies (including chocolate snails—*Escargots de Bourgogne)* may be found without difficulty, especially in the commercial heart of Dijon, with its numerous pedestrian streets. You can get the famous Burgundy wine at a good price if you buy it from an individual producer. Local blackcurrant liqueur (cassis) can be found easily enough anywhere in France for much the same price.

Sports and Fitness

Bicycling and Hiking
Popular, simple sports in Burgundy start with walking and cycling. Keen hikers should consult the **Comité Départmental de la Randonnée Pédestre** (B.P.1601, 21000 Dijon cedex, tel. 80–73–81–81) for information on paths and circuits. Cycle tours are organized by **La Peurtantaine** (Accueil Morvan Environment, Ecole du Bourg, 71550 Anost, tel. 85–82–77–74). Most tourist offices will be able to give details about recommended routes and where to rent bikes (train stations are a good bet).

Horseback Riding
Among the numerous establishments that provide lessons or from which you can rent horses are **Locacheval** (Martine Richard, 21540 Turcey, tel. 80–33–21–13), **Les Grilles** (89710 St-

Fargeau, tel. 86–74–12–11), and the **Ecuries de la Sarial** (71260
La Salle, tel. 85–37–52–44). Horses can be taken out for about
80 francs an hour.

Dining and Lodging

Dining

The Burgundians are hearty eaters; whatever the class of restaurant, you are unlikely to go hungry. Dijon ranks with Lyon
as one of the unofficial gastronomic capitals of France. Wealthy
Parisian gourmets think nothing of the three-hour drive
needed to sample the cuisine of Dijon's Jean-Pierre Billoux or
that of Marc Meneau at Vézelay. Game, freshwater trout, ham,
goat cheese, coq au vin, snails, mustard, and mushrooms number among the region's specialties. Meat is often served in rich,
wine-based sauces. There is wine of all types and prices; whites
range from cheapish Aligoté to classy Chablis and legendary
Meursault and reds, from unpretentious Mâcon to indescriba-
ble Gevrey-Chambertin and Romanée-Conti.

Highly recommended restaurants are indicated by a ★.

Category	Cost*
Very Expensive	over 350 francs
Expensive	200-350 francs
Moderate	100-200 francs
Inexpensive	under 100 francs

*per person for a three-course meal, including tax (18.6%) and
tip, but not wine*

Lodging

For all its charms, Burgundy is seldom deluged by tourists, and
finding accommodations is not hard. But there are few towns
with so many hotels that you can be sure to find something, so
always make advance reservations, especially in the "wine
country" (from Dijon to Beaune). If you intend to visit Beaune
for the Trois Glorieuses wine festival in November, make your
hotel reservation several months in advance. Note that nearly
all country hotels have restaurants, and you are usually expected to eat in them.

Highly recommended hotels are indicated by a star ★.

Category	Cost*
Very Expensive	over 750 francs
Expensive	350-750 francs
Moderate	200-350 francs
Inexpensive	under 200 francs

*All prices are for a standard double room for two, including
tax (18.6%) and service charge.*

Arnay-le-Duc
Dining and Lodging

Chez Camille. Small, quiet, and friendly are words to sum up this hotel on N6 between Saulieu and Beaune. The original 16th-century house has been tastefully renovated and features period furniture and original wooden beams in many rooms. The light, airy restaurant has a glass roof. Traditional Burgundian fare—duck and boar are specialties—figures high on the menu, and there is a thoughtful choice of regional wines. *1 pl. Edouard-Herriot, 21230, tel. 80–90–01–38. 11 rooms with bath. AE, DC, MC, V. Moderate.*

Autun
Dining

Chalet Bleu. Recently opened in the center of Autun, this restaurant serves solid traditional French cuisine. The setting, complemented by spruce white furniture, is fresh and green and resembles a converted conservatory. Foie gras and beef with shallots are trustworthy choices. *3 rue Jeannin, tel. 85–86–27–30. Reservations advised. Dress: casual. AE, DC, MC, V. Closed Mon. dinner and Tues. Inexpensive–Moderate.*

Lodging

St-Louis. This comfortable hotel dates from the 17th century; legend has it that Napoleon once slept here. Guest rooms are cozily decorated and have a slightly faded charm. The hotel boasts a pleasant patio-garden and its own restaurant, La Rotonde. *6 rue de l'Arbalète, 71400, tel. 85–52–21–03. 52 rooms, some with bath. Facilities: restaurant, garden. AE, DC, MC, V. Closed Dec. 20–Feb 2. Inexpensive.*

Auxerre
Dining

Jardin Gourmand. As its name implies, this restaurant features a pretty garden where you can eat *en terrasse* during summer months; the interior, dominated by light-colored oak, is equally congenial. The cuisine is innovative—try the ravioli and foie gras or the duck with blackcurrants—and the service is discreet. *56 blvd. Vauban, tel. 86–51–53–52. Reservations advised. Dress: neat but casual. MC, V. Closed part of Feb. and first 3 weeks of Nov.; Sun. dinner Nov.–Mar., and Mon. Moderate.*

Lodging

Le Maxime. This slightly old-fashioned, family-run hotel on the banks of the Yonne is a good bet for anyone who likes the personal touch. The guest rooms are pleasantly decorated, and many offer fine river views. The restaurant is quaintly rustic, with exposed beams and the inevitable row of gleaming copper pots and pans. *2–5 quai de la Marine, 89000, tel. 86–52–14–19. 25 rooms with bath. Facilities: restaurant, garden. AE, DC, MC, V. Restaurant closed Sat. and part of Feb. Moderate.*

Le Normandie. The picturesque, vine-covered Normandie occupies a grand-looking building conveniently set in the center of Auxerre, a short walk from the cathedral. The guest rooms are unpretentious but of good value and are spanking clean. You can relax in the charming garden, but there is no restaurant on the premises. *41 blvd. Vauban, 89000, tel. 86–52–57–80. 48 rooms, with bath or shower. Facilities: garden, garage, sauna, gym, bar. AE, DC, MC, V. Moderate.*

Avallon
Dining

Morvan. Solid, filling dishes are offered at this folksy eatery just outside town; fish terrine, rabbit, and chocolate cake number among the menu's best. There is an adjoining rock garden. *7 rte. de Paris, tel. 86–34–18–20. Reservations accepted. Dress: casual. DC, V. Closed Sun. evening, Mon., Jan., and second half of Nov. Moderate.*

Lodging

Château de Vault-de-Lugny. This 16th-century château (3 miles east of Avallon via D957), with its own moat and extensive grounds that include a 13th-century keep, has been harmoniously renovated; most rooms have four-poster or canopy beds, period-style furniture, and spacious, gleaming tile bathrooms. Tranquility is assured; meals are served to residents only. *Pontaubert, 89200 Avallon, tel. 86–34–07–86. 11 rooms with bath. Facilities: tennis, trout-fishing. MC, V. Very Expensive.*

Dining and Lodging
★

Les Capucins. This intimate hotel offers rooms in a wide range of prices, but is better known for its restaurant, which features four set menus dominated by regional cooking. Dishes of especially good value are the duck and the trout in flaky pastry. The desserts are excellent. *6 av. Paul-Doumer, 89200, tel. 86–34–06–52. 8 rooms with bath. MC, V. Restaurant closed Wed., Tues. dinner out of season (Nov.–Mar.). Hotel closed 3rd week in Oct. and Christmas–late Jan. Moderate.*

Moulin des Ruats. Part of the prestigious Relais et Châteaux group, the Moulin des Ruats is housed in an old flour mill just southwest of Avallon along D427. The guest rooms are decorated with a pretty country-French decor, and many have balconies. Most overlook the River Cousin (in the summer you can eat on the riverbank). Dishes served up in the wood-paneled restaurant are honest and copious: Try the coq au vin cooked in local Burgundy wine. *Vallée du Cousin, 89200, tel. 86–34–07–14. 24 rooms, most with bath. Facilities: restaurant, garden. AE, DC, MC, V. Closed Nov.–Feb. Moderate.*

Beaune
Dining

Auberge St-Vincent. Perhaps the best thing about this restaurant is its admirable setting opposite the Hospices de Beaune. Not surprisingly, it pulls in plenty of tourists, and, consequently, the cuisine and ambience can seem bland. Service, though, is attentive, and the wine list is appropriately lengthy. Prices are reasonable, with kidneys and marinated mullet among the top attractions. *Pl. Fleury, tel. 80–22–42–34. Reservations advised. Dress: casual. AE, DC, MC, V. Closed Dec. and Sun. evening in winter. Moderate.*

L'Ecusson. Don't be put off by its unprepossessing exterior. This is a comfortable, friendly, thick-carpeted restaurant whose four variously priced menus offer outstanding value. Rabbit terrine with tarragon followed by leg of duck in oxtail sauce, cheese, and dessert is a typical offering. *2 rue du Lieutenant-Dupuis, tel. 80–22–83–08. Reservations advised. Dress casual. AE, DC, MC, V. Closed Wed. and mid-Feb.–mid-Mar. Moderate.*

Lodging

La Poste. The front rooms of this traditional French provincial hotel look out over the ramparts and the rear ones over nearby vineyards; not a bad combination! The service is charming; the hotel is tastefully renovated; and the long, narrow restaurant, with its gleaming silverware, smacks of tradition. The setting compensates somewhat for the uninventive cuisine, as does the fabulous wine list. *1 blvd. Clemenceau, 21200, tel. 80–22–08–11. 21 rooms with bath. Facilities: restaurant, terrace. AE, DC, MC, V. Closed Winter. Expensive.*

Central. A well-run establishment with several enlarged and modernized rooms, the Central lives up to its name: It's just around the corner from the Hôtel-Dieu in downtown Beaune. The stone-walled restaurant is cozy—some might say cramped—and the cuisine is reliable. The service is efficient, if a little hurried. The evening meal is obligatory in season (July and August). *2 rue Victor-Millot, 21200, tel. 80–24–77–24. 20 rooms, most with bath. Facilities: restaurant. V, MC. Closed mid-Nov.–Apr. Restaurant closed Wed. Nov.–June. Moderate.*

Chagny
Dining and Lodging
★

Château de Bellecroix. Located in Chagny, a little town on N6 16 kilometers (10 miles) south of Beaune, the Bellecroix is just what you expect a château to be. It bristles with turrets, is draped in creepers, and is set in its own park. Some of the buildings date from 1199, and the huge dining room, with its majestic fireplace, conjures up the atmosphere of medieval feasts. Salmon with fennel and chocolate cake number among the latter-day specialties. Four of the bedrooms are round, set in the towers, and are reached by a picturesque spiral staircase. *71150 Chagny, tel. 85–87–13–86. 19 rooms with bath. Facilities: restaurant, park. AE, DC, MC, V. Closed Wed. and Dec. 20–Jan. Moderate.*

Chalon-sur-Saône
Dining and Lodging

St-Georges. Situated close to the train station, a few hundred yards from the town center, the friendly, white-walled St-Georges hotel has been tastefully modernized and possesses many spacious rooms. Its cozy restaurant is known locally for its efficient service and menus of outstanding value. You can't go wrong with the duck in white pepper, foie gras with truffles, or roast pigeon. *32 av. Jean-Jaurès, 71100, tel. 85–48–27–05. 48 rooms, most with bath. AE, DC, MC, V. Moderate.*

Clamecy
Dining

L' Angélus. The cuisine in this newly opened restaurant is as charming as the setting—opposite the collegiate church, in a wood-beamed, listed medieval building. When young chef Pascal Choppin escapes from the conservative eye of *patronne* Mafoy Danjean, the *grande dame* of Clamecy cuisine, he lets loose with creations such as perch in orange sauce or duck-and-chicken salad in raspberry vinegar. *11 pl. St-Jean, tel. 86–27–23–25. Reservations advised. Dress: elegant casual. AE, DC, MC, V. Closed Wed. evening and Thurs. Moderate.*

Dining and Lodging

Boule d'Or. This down-to-earth country hotel (not particularly comfortable but oh-so-cheap) boasts a delightful setting by the River Yonne. Ask for a room facing the river—there are lovely views of Old Clamecy. The restaurant is housed in a former medieval chapel, which, together with absurdly cheap menus, more than compensates for the often apathetic service. *Pl. Bethléem, 58500, tel. 86–27–11–55. 12 rooms, most with bath. Closed Nov.–Mar. Inexpensive.*

Cluny
Dining and Lodging
★

Bourgogne. There's no better place to get into Cluny's medieval mood than the Bourgogne. What remains of the famous abbey is just next door, and the old-fashioned hotel building, which dates from 1817, stands where other parts of the abbey used to be. There is a small garden and a splendid restaurant with sober pink decor and refined cuisine: foie gras, snails, and the more exotic fish with ginger. The evening meal is compulsory in July and August. *Pl. de l'Abbaye, 71250, tel. 85–59–00–58. 14 rooms with bath. AE, DC, V. Closed Dec. and Jan. Restaurant closed for lunch Tues. and Wed., except during July and Aug. Moderate–Expensive.*

Moderne. Guest rooms at this friendly, unpretentious little hotel are clean and airy, but the Moderne is better known for its peaceful, traditional waterside restaurant, serving nouvelle cuisine as well as rich Burgundian dishes (fish, saddle of lamb, fillet of beef). You must take dinner at the hotel if you reserve a room between June and October. *Pont-de-l'Etang, 71250, tel. 85–59–05–65. 15 rooms, most with bath. AE, DC, V. Restaurant closed mid–Nov.–mid–Feb. Inexpensive–Moderate.*

Dijon
Dining

Jean-Pierre Billoux. Chef Jean-Pierre Billoux has created a restaurant that is outstanding in this most gastronomic of French cities. The stone-vaulted restaurant is magnificently situated in a spacious, restored town house, complete with garden, bar, and chintz-curtained dining room. Service is refined and charming. Specialties include frogs' legs steamed and served with watercress pancakes and guinea fowl with foie gras. *14 pl. Darcy, tel. 80–30–11–00. Reservations required. Jacket and tie required. MC, V. Closed Mon., and mid-Feb.– mid-Mar. Very Expensive.*

★ **Thibert.** Like Jean-Pierre Billoux, chef Jean-Paul Thibert has no need to give his restaurant a fancy name. The severely art-deco setting is less appealing than that of Billoux, but the cuisine is nearly as refined and imaginative. The menu changes regularly. Cabbage stuffed with snails and prawns with peas and truffles figure among the *tours de force;* sorbets encased in black-and-white mixed chocolate will tempt you to indulge in dessert. Compared to Billoux, Thibert also represents remarkable value for the money—for the moment at least. *10 pl. Wilson, tel. 80–67–74–64. Reservations required. Jacket and tie required. AE, MC, V. Closed Sun., Mon. lunch, and 2 weeks in both Feb. and Aug. Moderate–Expensive.*

Pré aux Clercs & Trois Faisans. Situated on the pretty, semicircular square opposite the ducal palace, this venerable eating institution has recently been salvaged after years of indifference. The all-too-classic cuisine (sometimes heavy and dull) is offset by an extensive wine cellar, deferential service, and the wood-beamed, stone-walled setting. According to local legend, it was here that Canon Kir invented his famous aperitif (Kir), made with cassis (blackcurrant liqueur) and white (Burgundy Aligoté) wine. *13 pl. de la Libération, tel. 80–67–11–33. Reservations required. Jacket required. AE, DC, MC, V. Moderate.*

★ **Toison d'Or.** A collection of superbly restored 16th-century buildings belonging to the Burgundian Company of Wine-tasters forms the backdrop to this fine restaurant, which features a small wine museum in the cellar. Toison d'Or is lavishly furnished and quaint (candlelight *de rigueur* in the evening). The food is increasingly sophisticated. Try the langoustines with ginger and the nougat and honey dessert. *18 rue Ste-Anne, tel. 80–30–73–52. Reservations accepted. Jacket required. AE, DC, MC, V. Closed Sat. lunch, Sun., part of Feb., most of Aug., and public holidays. Moderate.*

Dining and Lodging

Chapeau Rouge. The thick, venerable stone walls of the Chapeau Rouge near Dijon Cathedral encase both a hotel (quiet, well-appointed rooms) and a newly redecorated restaurant, renowned as a haven of classic regional cuisine. Snails cooked in basil and stuffed pigeon provide the menu's robust highlights. *5 rue Michelet, 21000, tel. 80–30–28–10. 30 rooms with bath. Facilities: restaurant, bar. AE, DC, MC, V. Reservations required for the restaurant. Expensive.*

Urbis–Central. This central, old-established hotel has benefited from recent modernization: Its sound-proofed, air-conditioned rooms offer a degree of comfort in excess of their price. The adjoining grill room, the Central Grill Rôtisserie, offers a good alternative to the gastronomic sophistication that is difficult to avoid elsewhere in Dijon. *3 pl. Grangier, 21000, tel. 80–30–44–00. 90 rooms, most with bath. AE, DC, MC, V. Restaurant closed Sun. Moderate.*

Sens
Dining and Lodging

Paris & Poste. The newly modernized Paris & Poste is a convenient and pleasant stopping point on the drive down to Burgundy from Paris. The guest rooms are clean, bright, and airy, in line with the hotel's Mapotel connections. The restaurant's helpful service and sumptuous breakfasts confirm the sense of well-being created by the robust evening meal (duck, steak, and snails are high on the various set menus) served in the large, solemn restaurant. *97 rue de la République, 89100, tel. 86–65–17–43. 30 rooms with bath. Facilities: restaurant, garden. AE, DC, MC, V. Moderate–Expensive.*

Croix Blanche. A five-minute walk from the cathedral will bring you to this calm, straightforward hotel. Its two-room restaurant (plus veranda) provides three good-value menus, headed by turbot in crayfish sauce, salmon with sorrel, and beef with Roquefort (cheese) sauce. *9 rue Victor-Guichard, 89100, tel. 86–64–00–02. 25 rooms with bath or shower. V. Inexpensive.*

Troyes
Dining

Valentino. Although the restaurant is housed in an old, half-timbered building on a pedestrian street next to the Hôtel de Ville, its flowery interior makes a bold effort to rejoin the 20th century by mimicking art-deco chic. Tables are set outside in summer, and oysters are served in winter as a complement to the menu's fish specialties. There is a fine choice of wines to accompany the gastronomic menus. *27 rue Paillot-de-Montabert, tel. 25–73–14–14. Reservations advised. Jacket and tie required. AE, DC, MC, V. Closed Sun. dinner, Mon., and mid-Aug.–Sept. 10. Expensive.*

Lodging

Relais St-Jean. This calm, stylish hotel, opened in 1990 in the heart of the old town near the Eglise St-Jean, has rooms that are fully equipped and air-conditioned. *Rue Paillot-de-Montabert, 10000, tel. 25–73–89–90. 22 rooms with bath. Facilities: bar, parking lot. AE, DC, MC, V. Expensive.*

Le Marigny. Churches, pancakes, and pizzas dominate the cobbled, half-timbered core of Troyes. Le Marigny sits in their midst, in a quiet street adjacent to the narrow ruelle des Chats. With its tottering gables and uncertain wooden strips, the hotel looks pretty shaky from the outside; creaking floorboards confirm that it's shaky inside, too. The guest rooms are few, small, and faintly run-down. Prices are suitably old-fashioned. There is no restaurant. *3 rue Charbonnet, 10000, tel. 25–73–10–67. 15 rooms, 5 with bath. V. Inexpensive.*

Vézelay
Dining
★

L'Espérance. In the small neighboring village of St-Père-sous-Vézelay, this elegant spot is one of France's premier restaurants. Chef Marc Meneau is renowned for the subtlety and originality of his cuisine and, as he is constantly inventing new combinations, it is difficult to recommend particular dishes; some of his most reputed successes have been with liver of veal, pigeon, and lobster. Madame Meneau is a charming, attentive hostess, and the setting—by a park and stream with Vézelay's hill and basilica in the background—is delightful. One word of warning, though: The restaurant sells bottles of wine to take out at prices lower than for those served on the premises; make sure to distinguish between the take-out wine list and the restaurant wine list. L'Espérance also has 17 luxurious guest rooms and four 1,800-franc suites. *89450 Vézelay, tel. 86–33–20–45. Reservations required. Jacket and tie required. AE, DC, MC, V. Closed Jan., and Tues. and Wed. lunch. Very Expensive.*

Lodging **Relais du Morvan.** With its delightful setting, Vézelay makes a
great place to stay. But it is, after all, a mere village (500 inhabitants) and contains just two hotels. Don't opt for the large, un-
friendly, and astronomically expensive Lion d'Or; try instead
to reserve a room at the cozy, good-value Relais du Morvan.
There is a choice of three very affordable menus in the restaurant. The welcome is cheerful, the rooms functional and unpretentious. *89450 Vézelay, tel. 86–33–25–33. 9 rooms, most with
bath. V. Closed mid-Jan.–Feb. Inexpensive.*

The Arts and Nightlife

The Arts

It is perhaps true to say that Burgundy is hotter on folklore
than it is on the performing arts. Dijon alone stages a **Festival
International de Folklore** (September), a **Bell-Ringing Festival**
(mid-August), and an **International Fair of Gastronomy** (November). The Trois Glorieuses in mid-November represent
merrymaking for a privileged wine elite.

Cultural activity is best represented by music. The august ruined abbey of Cluny forms the backdrop to the **Grandes Heures
de Cluny** in August (tel. 85–59–05–34 for details). Autun Cathedral is the main venue for the **Musique en Morvan** festival in
the second half of July, and Nevers the base for **Musique en Ni-
vernais** during September and October. Dijon stages its own
Eté Musical in June and July. Check local tourist offices for details of the programs.

Nightlife

Nightlife to most Burgundians means staying up late to finish
yet another big meal. Since the province's one and only city,
Dijon, is one of the most serious eating venues on earth, it is not
surprising that nightclubbers can expect a lean time. For a
more sedate ambience, try **L' Iceberg** (47 rue Devosge) or the
Bahia Brazil piano bar (39 rue des Godrans). **Le Messire** (3 rue
Jules-Mercier) and **L'An Fer** (8 rue Pierre-Marceau) cater to a
slightly younger clientele.

11 Lyon and the Alps

Introduction

Even state authorities find it difficult to pin a name on this part of central-eastern France. Their solution, "Lyon-Rhône-Alpes," is hardly poetic, but at least it sums up the major features—the grand city of Lyon, the broad valley of the Rhône, and the towering Alpine mountain range on the frontier with Switzerland and Italy. Although the region is pierced by expressways and high-speed train lines, the pace of life is far from frenzied. Tiny medieval towns dot the landscape, while the only city apart from Lyon is Grenoble, in a majestic setting in the foothills of the Alps.

Lyon is often neglected by drivers pelting down from Paris en route to the Riviera. What they miss is one of the country's most appealing cities, renowned for its historic buildings, quaint *traboules* (passageways), and outstanding setting on the banks of the Saône and Rhône rivers. Lyon is also a major gastronomic center, with more good restaurants to the square mile than any other European city except Paris.

Before reaching Lyon, the Saône flows between the lush hillside of the Beaujolais vineyards and the flat marshland of the Dombes. The Rhône, the great river of southern France, actually trickles to life high up in the Swiss mountains, but it's only at Lyon, where it merges with the Saône, that it truly comes into its own, plummeting due south in search of the Mediterranean. The river's progress south from Lyon is often spectacular, as steep-climbing vineyards conjure up vistas that are more readily associated with the river's Germanic cousin, the Rhine. All along the way, you'll find an abundance of small-town vintners inviting you to sample their wine, without obliging you to buy a crateful. Be warned, though: Rhône wine and the noonday sun make a heady combination.

Roman towns like Vienne and Valence reflect the Rhône's age-old importance as a trading route. To the west lies the Ardèche, a rugged, rustic area where time has stood still; away to the east, the skiing industry has hurtled once-inaccessible Alpine villages into the 20th century.

Essential Information

Important Addresses and Numbers

Tourist Information Contact the **Comité Régional du Tourisme de la Vallée du Rhône** (5 pl. de la Baleine, 69005 Lyon, tel. 78–42–50–04) for information on the Rhône Valley and Lyon, **Maison du Tourisme** (14 rue de la République, B.P. 227, 38019 Grenoble cedex, tel. 76–54–34–36) for the Isère *département* and the area around Grenoble, and the **Comité Régional du Tourisme de Savoie–Mont-Blanc** (9 blvd. Wilson, 73100 Aix-les-Bains, tel. 79–88–23–41) for the Alps and the Savoie and Haute-Savoie *départements*.

Local tourist offices in major towns covered in this chapter are **Annecy** (Clos Bonlieu, 1 rue Jean-Jaurès, tel. 50–45–00–33), **Bourg-en-Bresse** (6 av. d'Alsace-Lorraine, tel. 74–22–49–40), **Chambéry** (24 blvd. de la Colonne, tel. 79–33–42–47), **Grenoble** (14 rue de la République, tel. 76–54–34–36), **Lyon** (pl. Bellecour, tel. 78–42–25–75, and pl. Carnot, next to the train station, tel. 78–42–22–07), **Montélimar** (av. Rochemaure, tel.

75–01–00–20), **Privas** (3 rue Elie-Reynier, tel. 75–64–33–35), **Valence** (blvd. Maurice-Clerc, tel. 75–43–04–88), and **Vienne** (cours Brillier, tel. 74–85–12–62).

Travel Agencies **American Express** (6 rue Childebert, Lyon, tel. 78–37–40–69) and **Wagons-Lits** (Park Hôtel, 10 pl. Paul-Mistral, 38027 Grenoble cedex, tel. 76–87–15–54; and 48 blvd. Vauban, 26000 Valence, tel. 75–42–02–04).

Car Rental **Avis** (av. du Docteur-Desfrançois, Chambéry, tel. 79–33–58–54; and Airport de Satolas, Lyon, tel. 78–22–75–25); and **Hertz** (8 rue Emile-Gueymard, Grenoble, tel. 76–43–12–92; and 11 rue Pasteur, Valence, tel. 75–44–39–45).

Arriving and Departing

By Plane The international airport at **Satolas,** 26 kilometers (16 miles) from Lyon, is one of France's busiest (for flight information, call 72–22–75–05).

Between the Airport and Downtown Buses leave for the center of Lyon every 20 minutes between 5 AM and 9 PM, and for the train station every 20 minutes between 6 AM and 11 PM; journey time is 35 minutes, and the fare is 36 francs adults, 18 francs children. There's also a bus from Satolas to Grenoble; journey time is just over an hour, and the fare is 100 francs.

By Train The TGV high-speed train to Lyon leaves from Paris's Gare de Lyon station hourly and arrives in just two hours.

By Car A6 speeds south to Lyon from Paris (463 kilometers/287 miles away), but be warned that the Tunnel de Fourvière, which cuts through Lyon, is a classic vacationers' hazard, and at peak times you may have to sit for hours.

Getting Around

By Plane There are domestic airports at Grenoble, Valence, Annecy, Chambéry, and Aix-les-Bains.

By Train Major rail junctions include Grenoble, Annecy, Valence, Chambéry, and Lyon.

By Car Regional roads are fast and well maintained, though smaller mountainous routes can be difficult to navigate in winter, if not impassable.

Guided Tours

Orientation **Lyon Ballade** (8 rue Perrod, 69004 Lyon, tel. 78–27–08–42) offers three-hour minibus tours of the city, with a commentary by tape cassette. Buses leave from place Bellecour, in front of the tourist office, daily at 9:30 and 3; call to reserve your seat. The **French Travel Agents' Association** offers a "Weekend Contract in Lyon," including a tour of the old city, cooking demonstrations, and hotel accommodations. The cost per person in a single room is 2,600 francs; per person in a double room, 2,300 francs. Contact **Sorotour Voyages** (18 rue de Sèze, 69006 Lyon, tel. 78–52–85–38) for reservations.

Special-Interest The Rhône Valley and the Alps offer a variety of special-interest tours, the most relaxing of which are by boat or barge along the region's waterways. **Navig-Inter** (13 bis quai Rambaud, 69002 Lyon, tel. 78–42–96–81) offers daily boat trips on the

Saône and Rhône, leaving from quai des Célestins. If you prefer to survey Lyon and Beaujolais from a plane, contact the **Aero-Club du Rhône et du Sud-Est** (Aeroport de Lyon-Bron, 69500 Bron, tel. 78–26–83–97).

Walking Tours The **Office du Tourisme** in Lyon (pl. Bellecour, tel. 78–42–25–75) offers guided walks of the city's sights; take your choice of a taped commentary or an English-speaking guide.

Exploring Lyon and the Alps

Numbers in the margin correspond with points of interest on the Lyon and the Alps and Lyon maps.

Orientation

Our exploring tours use Lyon as a base and concentrate on three points of the compass: north toward Burgundy, south down the Rhône Valley, and east into the Alps. The highlights of the relatively inaccessible Auvergne region, to the west, are presented in Off the Beaten Track (*see* below).

Our first tour concentrates on Lyon itself before heading north into the hilly Beaujolais vineyards, then crossing the Saône to the marshy Dombes area between Bourg-en-Bresse and Lyon. Our second tour heads south from Lyon toward the venerable Rhône towns of Vienne, Valence, and Montélimar and includes an excursion into the dramatic country of the Ardèche, to the west of the river. Last, we move east from Lyon to Grenoble and the Alps, taking in Europe's highest cable car (at Chamonix), Europe's highest mountain (Mont Blanc), and Europe's highest road pass (Col de l'Iseran).

Highlights for First-time Visitors

Cable car ascent from Chamonix, Tour 3
Grenoble, Tour 3
Route de l'Iseran, Tour 3
"Trabouling" in Lyon, Tour 1
Medieval village of Pérouges, Tour 1
Route Panoramique from Tournon, Tour 2
Vienne, Tour 2

Tour 1: Lyon, Beaujolais, and La Dombes

❶ **Lyon** and Marseille both like to claim they are France's "second city." In terms of size and commercial importance, Marseille probably grabs that title. But when it comes to tourist appeal, Lyon's a clear winner.

Lyon's development owes much to the city's exceptional site: halfway between Paris and the Mediterranean and within striking distance of Switzerland, Italy, and the Alps. The site is physically impressive, with steep cliffs dominating the River Saône, which flows parallel to the Rhône before the two converge south of the city center.

Because Lyon has never really had to endure hard times, a mood of untroubled complacency, rather than big-city bustle, prevails. The Lyonnais bask in the knowledge that their city has been important for over 2,000 years, ever since the Romans made it the capital of the occupied province of Gaul, shortly after founding the city in 43 BC. Even the name sounds appropriately proud—until you learn that it derives from the Roman Lugdunum, or "Hill of the Crow."

Few, if any, crows, rooks, or ravens are found these days on **place Bellecour,** where we begin our tour. This imposing tree-shaded square, midway between the Saône and the Rhône, is one of the largest in France, lent architectural distinction by the Classical facades erected along its narrower sides in 1800. The large bronze statue of Louis XIV on horseback is the work of local sculptor Jean Lemot, installed in 1828 to replace the original, which failed to survive the French Revolution.

The city's main tourist office is located in an isolated pavilion in the southeast corner; stop in for a city map, information leaflets, and a 30-franc day-pass, which enables you to visit all the city's museums. Then cross the square and head 500 yards north along lively rue du Président-Herriot before turning left into rue Grenette. Take the Pont du Maréchal-Juin over the Saône to the old town at the foot of Fourvière Hill, crowned by the imposing silhouette of **Notre-Dame** basilica.

On the right bank of the Saône lies **Vieux Lyon** (Old Lyon), an atmospheric warren of streets and alleys. Turn right after the bridge, then take the first left down a little alley to **place de la Baleine,** a small square lined with 17th-century houses.

Time Out   At one corner of place de la Baleine is a cozy lunch spot, **Aux Trois Maries** (1 rue des Trois-Maries). The curious name comes from the carved stone niche on the wall of no. 7, holding statuettes of the Virgin Mary, Mary of Bethany, and Mary Magdalene.

At the far end of place de la Baleine lies **rue St-Jean,** one of the many streets that weave their way around the banks of the Saône. Many of the area's elegant houses were built for the town's most illustrious denizens—bankers and silk merchants—during the French Renaissance under the 16th-century king François I. Originally, they had four stories; the upper floors were added in the last century. Look for the intricate old iron signs hanging over the shop doorways, many of which gave the streets their names.

A peculiarity of the streets of old Lyon are the *traboules*, quaint little passageways that cut under the houses from one street to another. Don't hesitate to venture in; they aren't private. There's a fine example at 24 rue St-Jean, just off place de Baleine (to the left), which leads through to rue du Boeuf via an airy, restored courtyard.

Rue St-Jean was old Lyon's major thoroughfare. Stop in the elegant courtyard of no. 27 on your way north from place de la Baleine to place du Change, where money changers would operate during Lyon's medieval trade fairs. The **Loge du Change** church, on one side of the square, was built by Germain Soufflot (best known as architect of the Panthéon in Paris) in 1747.

Take rue Soufflot to one side of the church and turn left into rue de Gadagne, where the largest Renaissance ensemble in Lyon

Lyon and the Alps

SWITZERLAND

Montreux

Lausanne

Mont Blanc

Chamonix 51

Bourg-St-Maurice
Les Arcs
53
54

Evian-
les-Bains
50

Thonon-
les-Bains
49

Lac Leman

Morzine

Ayoriaz

Megève

Albertville
52

Geneva

Annemasse

Bonneville

Cluses

La Clusaz

Menthon St-Bernard
48
Talloires
46
Duingt
47

Annecy
45

Lac d'Annecy

Aix-les-Bains
44

Chambéry

St-Laurent-en-
Grandvaux

Mijoux

St-Cloud

Frangy

Seyssel

Belley

Moresel

La Tour-
du-Pin

Lons-le-Saunier

Cuiseaux

Nantua

Ambérieu-en-
Bugey

Lagnieu

Louhans

Bourg-en-
Bresse
30

Villars-les-Dombes

32

Pérouges

Bourgoin-
Jallieu

St-Trivier-
de-Courtes

Châtillon-sur-
Chalaronne
31

Tournus

Pont de
Veyle

Macon

Villefranche-
sur-Saône

23

Cormatin

Cluny

St-Amour

Juliénas 29
Chénas 28
Fleurie 27
Chiroubles 26
Villié 25
Morgon
Odenas 24

Lac du Bourget

Lyon
1 — 22

Hôtel Paterin, **13**

Hôtel de Ville, **19**

Jardin
Archéologique, **7**

Jardin des
Chartreux, **15**

Jardin des Plantes, **16**

Loge du Change, **4**

Maison des Canuts, **18**

Maison du Crible, **6**

Musée des Arts
Décoratifs, **21**

Musée des
Beaux-Arts, **20**

Musée de la
Civilisation Gallo-
Romaine, **10**

Musée Historique de
Lyon/Musée de la
Marionnette, **5**

Musée Historique des
Tissus, **22**

Notre-Dame-de-
Fourvière, **11**

Place de la Baleine, **3**

Place Bellecour, **2**

Primatiale St-Jean, **8**

St-Paul, **14**

St-Polycarpe, **17**

Théâtres Romains, **9**

Tour Métallique, **12**

is located: the Hôtel de Gadagne, built between the 14th and
the 16th centuries and now home to the **Musée Historique de
Lyon.** The first floor of this history museum contains medieval
sculpture from long-gone local churches and abbeys, while other floors showcase local furniture, pottery, paintings, engravings, and antique playing cards. On the second floor is the
Musée de la Marionnette (Puppet Museum), which traces the
history of marionnettes from Guignol and Madelon (Lyon's local equivalent of Punch and Judy, created by Laurent
Mourguet in 1795) through to contemporary hand and string
puppets from across the globe. *10 rue de Gadagne. Admission
to both museums free. Open Wed.–Mon. 10:45–6; closed Tues.*

Continue through tiny place du Petit-Collège to rue du Boeuf.

Time Out The **Cour des Loges** (6 rue du Boeuf) is actually four Renaissance mansions transformed into a luxury hotel. Stop in for a snack at the informal **tapas bar,** and admire the original stone spiral staircase, gigantic roof beams, and ancient sculpted faces that decorate the walls.

One of old Lyon's finest mansions lies farther down rue du Boeuf, at no. 16: the 17th-century **Maison du Crible,** now a high-class restaurant (Tour Rose, *see* Dining and Lodging, below). Venture into its courtyard to glimpse the Tour Rose itself—an elegant, pink-washed tower—and the charming terraced garden. Close by, at the corner of place Neuve St-Jean, is one of the most famous hanging signs in old Lyon, the work of Giambologna (1529–1608), a renowned French sculptor who honed his skills in Renaissance Italy; the sign portrays the bull for which rue du Boeuf is named. Head down place Neuve and turn right into rue St-Jean. A hundred yards farther, turn right into rue de la Bombarde, which leads to the peaceful **Jardin Archéologique** (Archaeological Gardens), with its excavated remains of the four churches that succeeded one another on the spot.

Alongside is one church that has withstood the onslaught of time: the **Primatiale St-Jean,** Lyon's somewhat disappointing cathedral. You won't find any soaring roof or lofty spires here. Instead, a stumpy facade is stuck almost bashfully onto the nave, while the interior mishmash has its moments—the 13th-century stained-glass windows in the choir or the variety of window tracery and vaulting in the side chapels—but lacks drama and a sense of harmony. The cathedral dates from the 12th century, and the chancel is Romanesque, but construction continued over three centuries and most of the building is Gothic (note the high pointed windows). Pope John XXII was consecrated here in 1316, and Henri IV married Marie de' Medici here in 1600. The 14th-century astronomical clock, in the north transept, chimes a hymn to St-Jean (St. John) on the hour from noon to 3 PM as a screeching rooster and other automatons enact the Annunciation.

To the right of the cathedral facade stands the venerable 12th-century **Manécanterie** (choir school); upstairs you'll find a small Treasury museum housing medieval Limoges enamels, fine ivories, and embroidered robes. *70 rue St-Jean. Admission: 10 frs. Open weekdays 7:30–noon and 2–7:30; weekends 2–5.*

To the left of the cathedral as you leave is the **Gare St-Jean;** to continue our tour, take the *ficelle* (funicular railway) that leaves from here on its way to the top of Fourvière Hill. At the top, head along the Montée de Fourvière to the Roman ruins **(Théâtres Romains)** nearby. There are two semicircular theaters here: the **Grand Théâtre,** the oldest Roman theater in France, built in 15 BC to seat 10,000 spectators, and the smaller **Odéon,** with its geometric-patterned tiled flooring. The best time to appreciate the theaters is September, when they are used to stage events during the Lyon International Arts Festival. *Fourvière Hill. Admission free. Open Easter–Oct., weekdays 8–noon and 2–6, Sat. 9–noon and 3–6, Sun. 3–6; Nov.– Easter, weekdays 8–noon and 2–5, Sat. 9–noon and 3–5, Sun. 3–5.*

Since 1933, systematic excavations have unearthed many vestiges of the opulent Roman city of Lugdunum. These remains

⑩ can be viewed in the **Musée de la Civilisation Gallo-Romaine** (Gallo-Roman Museum), which overlooks the theaters. The museum's semisubterranean open-plan design is an unusual showcase for the collection of statues, mosaics, vases, coins, and tombstones. One of the museum's highlights is a large bronze plaque, the **Table Claudienne,** upon which is inscribed part of Emperor Claudius's speech to the Roman Senate in AD 48, conferring senatorial rights on the Roman citizens of Gaul. *Rue Radisson. Admission: 20 frs. adults, 15 frs. students and senior citizens, children free. Open Wed.–Sun. 9:30–noon and 2–6; closed Mon. and Tues.*

Head back to the spot where the *ficelle* dropped you off. You won't be able to miss the pompous, late 19th-century basilica of **⑪** **Notre-Dame-de-Fourvière,** which has unfortunately become one of the symbols of Lyon. In terms of its mock-Byzantine architecture and hilltop site, it's a close cousin of Paris's Sacré-Coeur. Both were built for a similar reason: to underline the might of the Roman Catholic Church after the Prussian defeat of France in 1870 gave rise to the birth of the anticlerical Third Republic. The riot of interior decoration—an overkill of gilt, marble, and colorful mosaics—reveals that the Church had mind-boggling wealth to compensate for its waning political clout. *Fourvière Hill. Open daily 8–noon and 2–6.*

One of the few places in Lyon from which you can't see the Fourvière basilica is the terrace alongside it. The plummeting panorama reveals the city laid out on either side of the Saône and Rhône rivers, with the St-Jean cathedral facade in the foreground and the huge glass towers of the reconstructed Part-Dieu business complex glistening behind. For an even more sweeping view—encompassing the surrounding hills—climb the 287 steps of the basilica's **observatory.** *Admission: 6 frs. Open Easter–Oct., daily 10–noon and 2–6; Nov.–Easter, weekends 10–noon and 2–5.*

⑫ Looming beyond the basilica is a skeletal metal tower, **Tour Métallique,** built in 1893 and now used as a television transmitter. Take the stone staircase, **Montée Nicolas-de-Lange,** at the foot of the tower, which sneaks back down to old Lyon, emerging alongside the St-Paul train station at place St-Paul. **⑬** Venture briefly into rue Juiverie, to the right; the **Hôtel Paterin** at no. 4 is a splendid Renaissance mansion, and the Hôtel Bullioud (no. 8) has a courtyard with an ingenious gallery constructed in 1536 by Philibert Delorme, one of France's earliest and most accomplished exponents of Classical architecture (he worked at the châteaus of Fontainebleau and Chenonceau in the Loire Valley).

⑭ To the left of place St-Paul is the 12th-century church of **St-Paul,** whose octagonal lantern, frieze of animal heads in the chancel, and Flamboyant Gothic chapel are all worth a look. Head around the church, take the St-Vincent footbridge over the Saône, and turn left along quai St-Vincent. Two hundred **⑮** yards along, to the right, is the **Jardin des Chartreux,** a small, leafy park. Cut through the park up to cours du GénéralGiraud, then turn right into place Rouville, pausing to admire the splendid view of the river and Fourvière Hill.

⑯ Rue de l'Annonciade leads from place Rouville to the **Jardin des Plantes,** 250 yards away, a haven of peace in this otherwise busy quarter. These luxurious botanical gardens contain remportals on the 15th-century facade are carved with Old Testament scenes. The cathedral was built between the 12th and 16th centuries, with later interior additions, such as the splendid 18th-century mausoleum to the right of the altar, which contains the tombs of two of Vienne's archbishops. The entrance to the vaulted passage that once led to the cloisters, but now opens onto place St-Paul, is adorned with a frieze of the zodiac.

Place St-Paul and rue Clémentine bring you to place du Palais and the remains of the **Temple d'Auguste et de Livie** (Temple of Augutus and Livia), thought to date, in part, to the earliest Roman settlements in Vienne (1st century BC). The slender Corinthian columns that ring the temple were filled in with a wall during the 11th century, when the temple was used as a church; today, however, the temple has been restored to its original appearance.

Take rue Brenier to rue Chantelouve, site of a **Roman gateway** decorated with delicate friezes (the last vestige of the city's sizable Roman baths), then continue to rue de la Charité and the **Théâtre Romain.** This was one of the largest Roman theaters in Gaul (143 yards in diameter) and is only slightly smaller than Rome's famed Theater of Marcellus. Vienne's theater was buried under tons of rubble until 1922, but since then, the 46 rows of seating and parts of the marble flooring and frieze on the original stage have been excavated and renovated. Shows and concerts are staged here on summer evenings. *Admission: 12 frs. Open Apr.–mid-Oct., Wed.–Mon. 9–noon and 2–5:30; mid-Oct.–Mar., Wed.–Sat. 10–noon and 2–5, Sun. 1:30–5:30.*

Take rue de la Charité back down to rue des Orfèvres, lined with Renaissance facades, and continue on to the church of **St-André-le-Bas,** once part of a powerful abbey. Extensive restoration is in progress, but, if possible, venture inside to see the finely sculpted 12th-century capitals and the 17th-century wooden statue of St. Andrew. The adjacent cloisters are at their best during the summer music festival held here (and at the cathedral) from June to August.

Take the nearby bridge across the Rhône to inspect the excavated Cité Gallo-Romaine, where the Romans built most of their sumptuous private villas. *Admission: 12 frs. Open Apr.–Sept., daily 9–12:30 and 2:30–9; Oct.–Apr., daily 9–noon and 2–5.*

34 Stay on this bank of the Rhône and take N86 south 32 kilometers (20 miles) to the little town of **Serrières,** a traditional stopping point for Rhône river craft. You can see the valley boatmen's way of life from the exhibits at the **Musée des Mariniers du Rhône** (Boatmen's Museum) in the wooden-roofed Gothic chapel of St-Sornin. *Admission: 12 frs. Open Apr.–Oct., weekends 3–6.*

Nearly 10 kilometers (6 miles) south of Serrières along N82, just beyond Peaugres, is the 200-acre **Haut Vivarais Safari Park.** Some 800 animals (including lions, bears, buffalo, bison, tigers, wolves, and camels) can be encountered here—from the safety of your car, with the windows firmly rolled up. Stroll along the separate pedestrian trail to admire tamer beasts such as giraffes and ostriches and check out the snakes, crocodiles, and lizards lounging inside their vivarium. The park also has its own bars, cafeteria, souvenir shops, and playground, making it a great place to spend an afternoon if you're traveling with children. *Admission: 60 frs. adults, 40 frs. children. Open Apr.–Oct., daily 9:30–7; Nov.–Mar., daily 11–5.*

35 N82 shortly reaches **Annonay,** a prosperous town that grew up around the leather industry. It's best known, though, as home to the Montgolfier brothers, Joseph and Etienne, who, in 1783, invented the hot-air balloon (known in French as *une montgolfière*). The first flight took place at Annonay on June 4, 1783; it lasted half an hour, and the balloon soared to 6,500 feet. The brothers' exploit is commemorated by an obelisk on avenue Marc-Seguin, although the actual balloon launch took place from place des Cordeliers (close to the tourist office).

The narrow streets and passageways of central Annonay are full of character. Local history and folklore are evoked at the **Musée Vivarais César Filhol,** between the Mairie (Town Hall) and Notre-Dame church. *15 rue Béchetoille. Admission: 8 frs. Open June–Aug., Tues.–Sun. 2–6; Sept.–May, Wed. and weekends 2–6.*

36 D578/D532 head southeast to **Tournon,** 37 kilometers (23 miles) away on the banks of the Rhône at the foot of some impressive granite hills. Tournon's chief attraction is its hefty 15th–16th-century **château.** From the chateau's two terraces, there are sumptuous views of the old town, river, and—towering above the village of Tain-l'Hermitage across the Rhône—the steep-climbing vineyards that produce Hermitage wine, one of the Rhône Valley's most refined (and costly) reds. The château houses a museum of local history, the **Musée Rhodanien,** which features an account of the life of Annonay-born Marc Seguin (1786–1875), the engineer who built the first suspension bridge over the Rhône at Tournon in 1825 (the bridge was demolished in 1965). *Admission: 10 frs. adults, 5 frs. children. Open June–Aug., Wed.–Mon. 10–noon and 2–6; Apr.–May and Sept.–Oct., Wed.–Mon. 2–6; closed Tues.*

From Tournon's main square (place Jean-Jaurès), slightly inland from the château, take the signposted "Route Panoram-**37** ique" in the direction of **St-Romain-de-Lerps.** There are breathtaking views at every turn along this narrow, twisting, clambering road. At the old village of St-Romain, you are rewarded with an immense panorama that, in fine weather, takes in no fewer than 13 *départements* and extends to Mont-Blanc in the east and the whalelike bulk of arid Mont Ventoux to the south.

D287 winds its way down from St-Romain to St-Péray. Looming 650 feet above the plain is the Montagne de Crussol, a white cliff topped by the 12th-century ruins of Crussol Castle. The **38** largish town of **Valence** lies just a couple of miles away along N532. Valence is capital of the Drôme *département* and is the principal fruit-and-vegetable market for the surrounding region. Steep-curbed alleyways—known as *côtes*—extend from the banks of the Rhône to the heart of the old town around the cathedral of **St-Apollinaire.** Although the cathedral was begun in the 12th century in the Romanesque style, it's not altogether as old as it looks: Parts were rebuilt in the 17th century, and the belfry in the 19th. Alongside the cathedral, in the former 18th-century Bishops' Palace, is the **Musée des Beaux-Arts** (Fine Arts Museum), featuring local sculpture and furniture and a collection of 96 red-chalk drawings by deft landscapist Hubert

Robert (1733–1808), a master of the picturesque. *Just off rue Sauniere. Admission: 10 frs. adults, children free. Open daily 2–6; also 9–noon on Wed., Sat., and Sun.*

Turn left out of the museum and cross hectic avenue Gambetta to the Champ-de-Mars, a broad terraced garden overlooking the Rhône, where there are fine views across to Crussol Castle. Just below the Champ-de-Mars is the **Parc Jouvet,** with 14 acres of pool and gardens.

Continue 16 kilometers (10 miles) south from Valence along N86 and turn right into D120 just before La Voulte. This attractive road follows the Eyrieux Valley as far as Les Ollières-sur-Eyrieux, where you should turn south along D2, under the shade of horse-chestnut trees, toward **Privas,** capital of the spectacular Ardèche *département*, renowned for its rocky gorges and stalagmite-bearing caves.

Privas was a Protestant stronghold during the 16th-century Wars of Religion. In 1629, it was razed by the army of Louis XIII after a siege lasting 16 days. The **Pont Louis XIII** over the River Ouvèze celebrates the king's reconciliation with Privas, which rose from the dust to become a peaceful administrative town, best known for the production of that delicious French delicacy the *marron glacé* (candied chestnut).

Privas makes a good base for exploring the Ardèche, and the tourist office just off place Charles-de-Gaulle, in the center of town, will provide details of the region's beauty spots. Our tour, meanwhile, continues to another town of sweet-toothed fame: **Montélimar,** the home of the *nougat,* a white or pink candy that usually contains chopped almonds and cherries.

Montélimar, 35 kilometers (22 miles) southeast of Privas (via D2) on the other side of the Rhône, is named after the 12th-century fortress of **Mont-Adhémar.** This château, enlarged in the 14th century, stands in a park surveying the town and valley. *Admission: 10 frs. adults, 5 frs. children. Open Wed. 2–7, Thurs.–Mon. 10–noon and 2–7; closed Tues.*

You can buy nougat in virtually every shop in town; it makes for a mighty chew, a good idea if you want to keep the children quiet.

Tour 3: Grenoble and the Alps

Whatever the season, the Alpine mountain range is captivating. In winter, the dramatic, snow-carpeted slopes offer some of the best skiing in the world; in summer, chic spas, shimmering lakes, and breathtaking hilltop trails come into their own. The Savoie and Haute-Savoie *départements* occupy the most impressive Alpine territory, but our tour begins in the Dauphiné, with the area's only city: Grenoble.

Grenoble, 104 kilometers (65 miles) southeast of Lyon via A48, is a large, cosmopolitan city whose skyscrapers and forbidding gray buildings may seem intimidating by homey French standards. Along with the city's nuclear research plant, they bear witness to Grenoble's fierce desire to move with the times.

A cable car starting at quai St-Stéphane-Jay whisks you up to the hilltop and its **Fort de la Bastille** (open Apr.–Oct., 9–midnight, Nov.–Dec. and Feb.–Mar., 10–7:30), offering splendid views of the city and River Isère. Walk down rue Maurice-

Gignoux, past gardens, cafés, and stone mansions, to the **Musée Dauphinois,** a lively regional museum in a 17th-century convent, featuring displays of local folk arts and crafts. *30 rue Maurice-Gignoux. Admission: 10 frs. Open Wed.–Mon. 9–noon and 2–6; closed Tues.*

Heading left from the museum, make for the church of **St-Laurent,** which contains an atmospherically murky 6th-century crypt (one of the country's oldest Christian monuments) supported by a row of formidable marble pillars. *Rue St-Laurent. Open June–Sept., Wed.–Mon. 10–noon and 2:30–6:30; Oct.–May, by appointment only; closed Tues.*

Art buffs will want to cross the river and pick up rue Bayard, which runs four blocks down to the **Musée de Peinture et de Sculpture** (Painting and Sculpture Museum). The museum showcases an excellent series of 17th-century French and Spanish paintings, plus one of the most exciting modern collections outside Paris, starring Paul Gauguin, Henri Matisse, Amedeo Modigliani, and Pablo Picasso. *Pl. Verdun. Admission: 10 frs. Open Wed.–Mon. 10–noon and 2–6.*

Time Out   Leave place Verdun by rue Blanchard and follow it five blocks to **place Grenette,** a lively, flower-strewn pedestrian mall lined with a plethora of sidewalk cafés. It makes a great place to relax and enjoy a *pastis*—an anise-flavored aperitif—while admiring the city's majestic mountain setting.

Take D512 north from Grenoble through the Chartreuse mountain range. Seventeen kilometers (11 miles) from Grenoble, fork left off D512 and follow the small D57-D as far as you can (only a few miles) before leaving your car and making the 30-minute climb to the top of the 6,000-foot Charmant Som peak. Your reward: a stimulating view over the **Grande Chartreuse** monastery, 10 kilometers (6 miles) north. The monastery's 12-acre setting, enclosed by wooded heights and limestone crags, is both austere and serene.

Return to D512 and continue north, forking left 8 kilometers (5 miles) along D520-B, just before **St-Pierre-de-Chartreuse;** the Grande Chartreuse is set well back to the right a mile along this road. The monastery, which was to spawn 24 similar charterhouses throughout Europe, was founded by St-Bruno in 1084 according to the ascetic principles of the Benedictine order. It was burned down and rebuilt several times, then finally stripped of its possessions during the French Revolution, when the monks were expelled. The monks were allowed to return several years later and concoct their sweet Chartreuse liqueur, which soon became a main source of the monastery's income; today "Green" and "Yellow" Chartreuse are marketed worldwide, though their ingredients are known only to three monks. You can't visit the monastery itself, but stop in at **La Correrie,** close by, to see exhibits on monastic life. You'll also be able to purchase some of the monks' famous brew. *Admission: 12 frs. adults, 6 frs. children. Open Easter–Oct., daily 9–noon and 2–6.*

Chartreuse is now produced in nearby **Voiron,** where you can visit cellar and distillery for free (open daily except winter weekends, 8–11:30 and 2–5:30).

Return to St-Pierre-de-Chartreuse and continue north along the windy D512 and D912 roads to the elegant old town of **(43)** **Chambéry,** 40 kilometers (25 miles) away. Stop for coffee on the pedestrian **place St-Léger** before heading two blocks to visit the 14th-century **Château des Ducs de Savoie.** The château's Gothic Sainte-Chapelle contains some good stained glass and houses a replica of the notorious Turin Shroud, once thought to have been used to wrap up the crucified Christ (but probably, according to recent scientific analysis, a medieval hoax). *Rue Basse du Château. Admission: 15 frs. Guided tours daily at 2:15, Sept.–June, four times daily, July and Aug.*

(44) N201 propels you 14 kilometers (9 miles) north to the gracious spa town of **Aix-les-Bains,** on the eastern shore of Lac du Bourget. Although swimming in the lake is not advised (it's freezing cold), you can sail, fish, play golf and tennis, or picnic on the 25 acres of parkland that stretches along the lakefront. Visit the ruins of the original Roman baths, under the present **Thermes Nationaux** (Thermal Baths), built in 1934 (guided tours only; Apr.–Oct., Mon.–Sat. at 3 PM; Nov.–Mar., Wed. at 3 PM). The Roman Temple of Diana (2nd–3rd century AD) now houses an **archaeology museum** (entrance via the tourist office on place Mollard).

There are half-hour boat trips from Aix-les-Bains across Lac du Bourget to the **Abbaye de Hautecombe,** where mass is celebrated with Gregorian chant. *Cost: 35 frs. Departures from the Grand Pont, Mar.–June and Sept.–Oct., daily at 2:30; July–Aug. at 9:30, 2, 2:30, 3, 3:30, and 4:30.*

Leaving Aix-les-Bains, follow the striking D911 some 24 kilometers (15 miles) to La Charniaz, then turn left along D912, which snakes 24 kilometers (15 miles) farther north alongside **(45)** the Montagne du Semnoz to **Annecy.**

Annecy stands on the shores of a crystal-clear mountain lake— the Lac d'Annecy—and is surrounded by rugged snow-tipped peaks. The canals, flower-covered bridges, and cobbled pedestrian streets of old Annecy are at their liveliest on market days, Tuesday and Friday, though the town park and the tree-lined boulevard have tranquil, invigorating appeal any day of the week.

There are views over the lake from the towers of the 12th-century **castle,** set high on a hill above the town. Allow a morning or afternoon to make the 40-kilometer (25-mile) drive around the **(46)** lake, stopping at the picturesque village of **Talloires** and the **(47)** **(48)** medieval châteaus at **Duingt** and **Menthon-St-Bernard** (tours every afternoon in July and Aug.; open Thurs. and weekend afternoons only in May, June, and Sept.).

Take N201 north from Annecy and turn off after 18 kilometers (11 miles) into D14, which follows a winding course along Mont Salève to Annemasse 34 kilometers (21 miles) away. From Annemasse, Geneva is just a few minutes away over the Swiss **(49)** border, but we follow N206/D903 north to **Thonon-les-Bains,** on the banks of Lake Geneva (Lac Léman in French). Thonon and **(50)** its neighboring sister-spa, **Evian-les-Bains,** have all the trappings (restful parks and lakefront promenades) of chic spa towns. From Evian there are daily excursions across Lake Geneva to the Swiss town of Lausanne.

Many of the leading Alpine ski resorts lie south of Thonon. A river road (D902) runs 32 kilometers (20 miles) from Thonon to **Morzine. Avoriaz,** renowned for its annual Fantasy Film Festival in January, is reached from Morzine via D338 or by cable car. D902 continues down to Cluses, where the N205 heads left

51 along the Arve Valley to the largish town of **Chamonix** (about 64 kilometers/40 miles from Morzine), the oldest and biggest French winter-sports resort and site of the first Winter Olympics in 1924. The world's highest cable car soars 12,000 feet from Chamonix up the Aiguille du Midi, from which there are staggering views of Europe's loftiest peak, the 15,700-foot **Mont-Blanc** (open May–Sept. daily 8–4:45, Oct.–Apr. 8–3:45; 120 frs. round-trip).

N205/D909 leads back down the valley to **Megève,** another major ski resort. From there N212 spears 32 kilometers (20 miles)

52 south through the Arly Valley to **Albertville,** base for the 1992 Winter Olympics. Stop off at the suburb of **Conflans,** a well-preserved military town perched precariously on a rocky crag.

Another spectacular road, D925 (becoming D902), heads 61 ki-

53 lometers (38 miles) east from Albertville to **Bourg-St-Maurice,** a cheerful base for summer vacations, with winter sports ca-

54 55 tered to at the nearby complexes of **Les Arcs** or **Tignes** (24 kilometers/15 miles south via D902). Tignes features an extensive network of chair lifts and cable cars, which connect it with small resorts such as La Daille, Les Boisses, and Les Brévières, as well as with the resort of **Val d'Isère,** a favorite among the rich and famous.

The **Route de l'Iséran** (D902) runs from Val d'Isère to Bonneval-sur-Arc, at 9,084 feet the country's highest mountain pass; it's accessible only between July and late October. Along the Iseran Way, a succession of magnificent views unfurl beneath your eyes.

What to See and Do with Children

Lyon is home to an amusing puppet museum, but if your children would like to see the puppets in action, take them to the **Théâtre du Guignol.** *Nouveau Guignol de Lyon, Palais du Conservatoire, rue Louis-Carrand. Children's shows at 3 PM Wed; general performances at 8:30 PM Tues., Thurs., and Fri., and 3 PM Sun.*

The 300-acre **Parc de la Tête d'Or,** on the banks of the Rhône in the north of Lyon, contains a lake, botanical gardens, and a small zoo, as well as facilities for rowing, miniature golf, pony rides, and go-carting. *Take the métro from Perrache train station to Masséna. Admission free. Open dawn to dusk.*

The following are described in our exploring text:

Chair lift at Chamonix, Tour 3
Haut Vivarais Safari Park, Tour 2
Maison des Canuts, Lyon, Tour 1
Musée de la Marionette (Puppet Museum), Lyon, Tour 1
Parc des Oiseaux, Villars-les-Dombes, Tour 1

Off the Beaten Track

Hauterives, 40 kilometers (25 miles) south of Vienne (D538), would be just another quaint village if it weren't for the **Palais**

Idéal, one of the weirdest constructions in western Europe. This make-believe palace, constructed entirely of stones and pebbles, was built single-handedly by a local postman, Ferdinand Cheval (1836–1924). Although Cheval was haunted by visions of faraway mosques and temples, the result is pure fantasy. It came to be Cheval's lifework: One of the many wall inscriptions reads "1892–1912: 10,000 days, 93,000 hours, 33 years of toil." *Admission 18 frs. adults, 9 frs. children. Open daily 8–8 (closed dusk in winter).*

For a tour of the Auvergne, start at **Le Puy,** 120 kilometers (75 miles) from Privas via N104 and N102, set on a high plateau broken by giant cores of sheer solidified lava, called *puys.* Le Puy's four cores are crowned with man-made monuments: on the lowest, a statue of St. Joseph and the Infant Jesus; on the highest, the 11th-century chapel of St-Michel; on another, a huge statue of the Virgin. Most spectacular is the Romanesque cathedral, **Notre-Dame-du-Puy,** which balances at the top of the fourth narrow pinnacle, approachable only by a long flight of steps. Built of polychrome lava, the cathedral is reminiscent of an Islamic mosque; interior highlights include the statue of the Black Virgin and the Carolingian *Bible of Théodulfe.*

Some 40 kilometers (25 miles) north via N102 and D906 lies the abbey of **Chaise-Dieu,** famous for its splendid red-and-black frescoes of the *Danse Macabre* (Death dancing with the nobility, bourgeoisie, and peasants). The abbey also features 16th-century Brussels and Arras tapestries and 144 carved oak choir stalls.

West of Chaise-Dieu (about 40 kilometers/25 miles via D588) is the town of **Brioude,** whose **St-Julien** basilica is the largest Romanesque church in the Auvergne. Go inside to see the intricately carved column capitals and medieval wall paintings.

The ancient town of **Clermont-Ferrand,** the threshold of the Puy-de-Dôme, Auvergne's volcanic region, lies about 100 kilometers (60 miles) north of Brioude via N102 and N9. If you have time for only one excursion in the Auvergne, make it a drive—or walk—to the top of the nearby **Puy-de-Dome volcano,** from whose lofty heights you can take in an extraordinary panorama; extinct volcanoes—these days, harmless green mounds with hollow, craterlike summits—roll far into the horizon.

Shopping

Clothing and Gift Ideas

Lyon, France's second-largest city, makes for the region's best shopping for chic clothing; try the stores on **rue du Président Edouard-Herriot** and **rue de la République** in the center of town. Lyon has maintained its reputation as the French silks-and-textile capital, and all the big-name French and international designers have shops here; Lyonnais designer **Clémentine** (18 rue Emile-Zola) is a good bet for well-cut clothes, or, for trendy outfits for youngsters, try **Etincelle** (34 rue St-Jean) in the old town. If it's antiques you're after, wander down **rue Auguste-Comte** (from place Bellecour to Perrache); you'll find superb engravings at **Image en Cours** (26 rue du Boeuf) and authentic Lyonnais puppets on **place du Change,** both in the old town.

Food Items

Two excellent Lyon charcuteries are **Reynon** (13 rue des Archers) and **Vital Pignol** (17 rue Emile-Zola). For chocolates and patisserie, try **Bernachon** (42 cours Franklin-Roosevelt). In the Drôme region, the town of **Montélimar** has more nougat shops than cafés; **Chabert et Guillot** (1 rue André-Ducatez) is one of the best.

Arts and Crafts The tiny Ardèche villages of **Thines** and **Les Yans** are popular crafts centers, with several showrooms set up by the **Compagnons de Gerboul**, an association of craftsmen. The medieval village of **Châteauneuf-de-Mazenc** (Drôme) has a particularly pretty arts-and-crafts shop with a range of handmade jewelry and trinkets.

Sports and Fitness

Golf Golf clubs are found at **Aix-les-Bains** (av. du Golf), **Annecy** (85 rue du Val Vert), **Chamonix** (rte. de Tines, Les Praz de Chamonix), **Villars-les-Dombes** (Le Clou), **Montélimar** (Château Le Monard, Montboucher-sur-Labron), and St-Didier de Charpey, near **Valence.**

Horseback Riding This is a wonderful region for exploring on horseback. Try the *centres equestres* (stables) at **Aix-les-Bains** (Hippodrome Marlioz), **Chambéry** (rue Sainte-Rose); **Montélimar** (Ile Montmélian), and **Vienne** (Ecuries du Couzon, La Petite Rente).

Skiing The ski season begins in December and lasts through April. The region's most famous ski venue is **Chamonix** (6,063 feet). Most of the slopes are for experienced skiers, but there are plenty of other things to do here: hiking, visiting the casino, or simply admiring the incredible scenery via cable cars. **Val d'Isère** (6,068 feet) ranks as one of Europe's swankiest resorts, with lots of cross-country runs as well as downhill slopes. Nearby **Tignes** is the highest of the Savoie resorts (6,930 feet), with a range of slopes for both beginners and more daring skiers. Family groups should try **Morzine** (3,280 feet), a popular small resort whose gentle slopes are geared to the inexperienced. Chic, expensive **Megève** (3,650 feet) offers a lively night life by way of casino, nightclubs, and restaurants; it also features a particularly impressive network of *téléfériques* (cable cars) and helicopter services. **Courchevel** (6,068 feet) is renowned for its après-ski, while across the mountain, fashionable **Meribel** (5,428 feet) boasts lots of difficult runs; late spring skiing is possible.

Swimming The Alpine lakes are pretty chilly for swimming at any time of year, but you'll find warmer water at the following public swimming pools: **Aix-les-Bains** (pl. Daniel Rops), **Albertville** (av. des Chaussures Alpins), **Annecy** (29 rte. Marquisats), **Chambéry** (Nautiparc, rue Eugène-Ducretet), **Evian** (Centre Nautique, alongside the lake), **Grenoble** (rue Lazère-Carnot), **Lyon** (221 rue Garibaldi), and **Valence** (av. Valensolles).

Dining and Lodging

Dining

Lyon is a renowned capital of good cuisine. Both gourmets and gourmands will enjoy the robust local specialties, such as *saveloy* (sausage), and *quenelles* (poached fish dumplings). More refined fare is provided by the surrounding regions. The Dombes, extending northeast from Lyon toward Bresse, is rich in game and fowl; chicken, cooked in any number of ways, usually with cream, is a firm favorite. Thrush, partridge, and hare feature prominently on menus as you head south along the Rhône; the marrons glacés of Privas and the nougats of Montélimar cater to the sweet tooth. The rivers and lakes of the Alps teem with pike and trout, while the hills are a riot of wild raspberries and blackcurrants during summer months. *Raclette* is a warming Alpine winter specialty: melted cheese served with salami, ham, and boiled potatoes. Mountain herbs form the basis of traditional drinks—try a tangy, dark **Suédois** or a bitter sweet **Suze** (made from gentian), and round off your meal with a green Chartreuse.

Highly recommended restaurants are indicated by a star ★.

Category	Cost*
Very Expensive	over 350 francs
Expensive	200–350 francs
Moderate	100–200 francs
Inexpensive	under 100 francs

per person for a three-course meal, including tax (18.6%) and tip but not wine

Lodging

The area covered in our exploring text is too vast for you to make Lyon a central base. But the region is filled with hotels and country inns; at many, you'll be expected to take your evening meal (especially in summer), but this tends to be more a pleasure than an obligation. The Alpine region has an extensive hotel infrastructure—geared primarily to winter visitors, who are invariably expected to take *demi-pension* or *pension complète* (room with some or all meals).

Highly recommended restaurants are indicated by a star ★.

Category	Cost*
Very Expensive	over 750 francs
Expensive	350–750 francs
Moderate	200–350 francs
Inexpensive	under 200 francs

All prices are for a standard double room for two, including tax (18.6%) and service charge.

Chamonix
Dining and Lodging

Albert I & Milan. The welcoming chalet-style Albert I & Milan is the best-value quality hotel in Chamonix. Many guest rooms have balconies, and all are furnished with elegant period reproductions. The dining room offers stupendous views of Mont Blanc, while the cuisine scales heights of invention and enthusiasm; try the oysters fried with asparagus. *119 impasse du Montenvers, 74400, tel. 50–53–05–09. 30 rooms with bath. Facilities: restaurant, pool, tennis, sauna, Jacuzzi. AE, DC, MC, V. Closed middle 2 weeks of May and Oct. 23–Dec. 9; restaurant closed Wed. lunch. Moderate–Expensive.*

Bourg-en-Bresse
Dining

L'Auberge Bressane. The beauty of this restaurant's location—the terrace looks out on the elegant Brou church—makes up for the rather chilly welcome you'll receive inside. The rustic dining room is an excellent setting in which to enjoy the academic rigor of Jean-Pierre Vullin's cooking. The wine list offers more than 300 vintages. Frogs' legs and succulent Bresse chicken with morel mushroom cream sauce are house specialties. *116 blvd. de Brou, tel. 74–22–22–68. Reservations required. Jacket and tie required. AE, DC, MC, V. Closed Mon. dinner, and Tues., mid-Nov.–mid-Dec. Expensive.*

Jacques Guy. The softly lit pastels of the decor and the neoclassical-style furniture lend this restaurant an appealing ambience. The regional cuisine varies with the seasons; poached Bresse chicken with tarragon or bass with red butter sauce both make fine choices. *19 pl. Bernard, tel. 74–45–29–11. Reservations advised. Dress: neat but casual. AE, DC, MC, V. Closed Sun. dinner, Mon. Moderate–Expensive.*

★ **La Petite Auberge.** This cozily informal flower-bedecked inn is set in the countryside just on the outskirts of town. Motherly Madame Bertrand is a kindly hostess and even provides games for children on the summer terrace. Inside, you'll appreciate chef Philippe Garnier's subtle way with mullet (he grills it in saffron butter) and Bresse chicken (browned in tangy cider vinegar). *St-Just, Ceyzeriat, tel. 74–22–30–04. Reservations accepted. Dress: casual. MC, V. Closed Mon. dinner and Jan. Moderate–Expensive.*

Lodging

Terminus. The best hotel in town is a converted mansion close to the train station. The guest rooms have been renovated with considerable taste and feature traditional French decor; the best room in the house is the two-room suite. The flower garden makes a fine place in which to relax and sip *pastis* (an anise-flavored drink). You'll be given a hearty meal *(saveloy—*sausage—and seasonal game birds) in the unpretentious restaurant; in fine weather, you can dine outdoors on the terrace. *19 rue Alphonse-Baudin, 01000 Bourg-en-Bresse, tel. 74–21–01–21. 50 rooms with bath. Facilities: restaurant, garden. AE, DC, MC, V. Moderate.*

Hauterives
Dining and Lodging

Le Relais. The local tourist wonder, the Palais Idéal, is just a stone's throw from this comfortable, rustic inn. The reasonably sized guest rooms feature an unpretentious country look, with chunky wooden desks and headboards, and wicker-seated chairs. The same warm, golden color scheme dominates the cozy restaurant, where you can enjoy such specialties as roasted partridge or delicately seasoned frogs' legs. Half-board is mandatory during summer months. *Pl. de l'Eglise, 26390 Hauterives, tel. 75–68–81–12. 13 rooms with bath. Facilities: restaurant. AE, DC, V. Closed Sun. dinner, Mon., and Jan.–Feb. Moderate.*

Lyon
Dining
★

Paul Bocuse. One of the country's most celebrated gourmet temples lies 12 kilometers (7 miles) north of town in Collonges-au-Mont-d'Or. The dining room's grand decor is a fitting backdrop for the culinary expertise of larger-than-life chef Paul Bocuse. Bocuse is often away on the lecture-tour trail, but his restaurant continues to please its elegantly dressed diners, who feast on such house specialties as truffle soup and succulent sea bass. The restaurant's reputation means you'll have to reserve a table long in advance; this won't be an impromptu meal. *50 quai de la Plage, tel. 78–22–01–40. Reservations re-*

quired. *Jacket and tie required. AE, DC, MC, V. Very Expensive.*

Tour Rose. Romantics look no farther. Le Tour Rose is set in one of the most distinctive 17th-century residences of old Lyon, inside a mellow pink tower. The dining-room decor is sumptuous and sophisticated, with gleaming cutlery and crisp linen cloths. Chef Philippe Chavent's nouvelle dishes are served with style in an intimate, candlelit setting. Chavent is a master of seafood; try the lightly cooked salmon or the sea urchin bisque. *16 rue du Boeuf, tel. 78–37–25–90. Reservations required. Jacket and tie required. AE, DC, MC, V. Closed Sun. and Aug. Very Expensive.*

★ **Léon de Lyon.** A mixture of regional tradition (dumplings, hot sausages) and eye-opening innovation keep this restaurant at the forefront of the city's gastronomic scene. The restaurant occupies two floors in an old house full of alcoves and wood paneling (there is a room for nonsmokers). The blue-aproned waiters blend in with the old-fashioned decor, and such dishes as fillet of veal with celery or leg of lamb with fava beans will linger in your memory. *1 rue Pléney, tel. 78–28–11–33. Reservations required. Jacket and tie required. MC, V. Closed Sun., Mon. lunch, most of Aug., and Dec. 24–Jan. 6. Expensive.*

★ **Café des Federations.** For the past 80 years, this sawdust-strewn café has reigned as one of the city's friendliest eating spots; expect to be treated like one of the gang. Jocular Raymond Fulchiron not only serves up such deftly prepared Lyonnaise classics as hearty *boudin blanc* (white-meat sausage), but he also comes out to chat with guests and make sure everyone feels at home. The decor is a homey mix of red-checked tablecloths, wood paneling, and old-fashioned bench seating. *8 rue du Major-Martin, tel. 78–28–26–00. Reservations advised. Dress: casual. AE, DC, MC, V. Closed weekends, and Aug. Moderate.*

Chez Sylvain. The old-fashioned decor of Chez Sylvain is a delightful reminder of its days as a favorite neighborhood beanery. Little has changed since, and the huge wooden counter, turn-of-the-century wall decorations, and original spiral staircase are the ideal backdrop for Sylvain's robust Lyonnaise cuisine; the tripe and *andouillettes* (chitterling sausages) are especially good. *4 rue Tupin, tel. 78–42–11–98. Reservations accepted. Dress: casual. V. Closed Sun., Mon., and Aug. Inexpensive.*

Lodging **La Cour des Loges.** A team of young Lyonnais architects and
★ Italian interior designers worked for three years to transform four Renaissance mansions into the most stylish hotel in Lyon. Four stories of sand-colored stone, an immense courtyard, spiral stone staircases, and exposed roof beams lend a courtly ambience, while guest rooms are furnished with the best in modern furniture design and effects. In the cellar there's an exclusive wine club, while an informal little *tapas* bar provides an array of appetizer-size snacks. Service throughout is impeccable. *6 rue du Boeuf, 69005, tel. 78–42–75–75. 63 rooms with bath. Facilities: air-conditioning, bar, pool, Jacuzzi, sauna, health club, wine cellar, boutiques. AE, DC, MC, V. Very Expensive.*

Grand Hôtel des Beaux-Arts. An explosion of columns, seashells, and swags covers the walls of this downtown hotel, conveniently situated next to place Bellecour and the downtown pedestrian area. The authentic Old European mood is further bolstered by an abundance of old leather armchairs. Guest rooms, while on the small side, retain the opulent Belle Epoque atmosphere of the public areas, and most have air-conditioning. There's no restaurant. *74 rue du Président Edouard-Herriot, 69002, tel. 78–38–09–50. 79 rooms with bath. AE, DC, MC, V. Expensive.*

★ **Morand.** This quiet and delightfully idiosyncratic hotel is located in a residential area of the city. Flowers abound on the pretty inner courtyard that doubles as a breakfast veranda, and the smiles at reception foster a mood of good cheer and friendliness. Guest rooms are on the small side but feature lots of homey knickknacks. There's no restaurant. *99 rue de Créqui, 69006, tel. 78–52–29–96. 33 rooms, 27 with bath. AE. Inexpensive.*

Montélimar **Les Hospitaliers.** This tastefully designed modern hotel is in
Lodging the center of the tiny hilltop town of Poët-Laval, 22 kilometers (14 miles) east of Montélimar along D540. With its stone walls and red-tile roof, the hotel blends perfectly into the medieval surroundings; there are sweeping views of the valley and mountains from the terrace. In cold weather, you can escape from the tacky '70s decor of the large guest rooms to warm yourself by the immense stone hearth in the sitting room. Local specialties are served in the airy restaurant; thrush pâté with truffles is always a good bet. *Le Vieux Village, Poët-Laval, 26160 La Bégude de Mazenc, tel. 75–46–22–32. 20 rooms with bath. Facilities: restaurant, pool. AE, DC, MC, V. Closed mid-Nov.–Feb. Expensive.*

★ **Relais de l'Empéreur.** Sure enough, Napoleon spent a night here, on April 24, 1814, after his return from exile on the Mediterranean island of Elba—sufficient reason for the hotel to have carved a niche in the hearts of many visitors. The grandiose Empire decor of the guest rooms does its bit as well. There's a stylish, if costly, restaurant, where the Napoleonic heartstrings are tugged to the breaking point (guinea fowl *à la Joséphine*, "imperial" thrush pâté). *1 pl. Marx-Dormoy, 26000, tel. 75–01–29–00. 40 rooms, most with bath. AE, DC, MC, V. Closed mid-Nov.–Christmas. Moderate–Expensive.*

Pérouges **Ostellerie du Vieux Pérouges.** This historic Bresson inn is an ex-
Dining and Lodging traordinary place even by French standards. Antiques are
★ scattered throughout, and the venerable rustic tone is heightened by glossy wood floors and tables, as well as gigantic stone hearths. You'll be served your meal on chunky pewter plates, by waitresses decked out in colorful folk costume; the crayfish is particularly good. Reserve a room in the geranium-clad 15th-century manor, rather than in the modern annex; those in the former are more spacious, with marble bathrooms and period furniture. *Pl. des Tilleuls, 01800, tel. 74–61–00–88. 25 rooms with bath. Facilities: restaurant. Restaurant closed Thurs. lunch and Wed., during Nov.–Mar. Expensive.*

Privas **Lous Esclos.** In the countryside, just 5 kilometers (3 miles)
Dining southwest of Privas on D2, is a striking modern restaurant with more windows than walls—all looking out over the wild Ardèche landscape. Monsieur Costechareyre serves succulent French cuisine—including goose and snail *feuilleté* (in a flaky pastry)—at a price that's almost too good to be true. *Quartier Rabagnol, 07210 Alissas, tel. 75–65–12–73. Reservations accepted. Dress: casual. AE, V. Closed last week Dec.–Jan. 10. Inexpensive.*

Serrières
Dining and Lodging

Chez Schaeffer. In a sophisticated setting of white wood trim, halfway between Vienne and Tournon, Chef Bernard Mathé dishes up inventive variants of traditional French dishes: smoked duck cutlet in lentil stew and curried lamb cutlet with morel mushrooms. Don't skimp on dessert; the choice is somewhat overwhelming, but the pistachio cake with bitter chocolate is a clear winner. There are 12 contemporary guest rooms as well. *Quai J.-Roche, 07340, tel. 75–34–00–07. 12 rooms with bath. Reservations required. Jacket and tie required. AE, DC, V. Closed Jan. and 3rd week in Oct. Moderate–Expensive.*

Talloire
Dining and Lodging

Le Père Bise. This deluxe *auberge* (inn) on the banks of Lake Annecy has a leafy veranda, marvelous views—be they from hotel rooms or restaurant—and a classy menu, where truffles and foie gras fight for star billing. *Rte. du Port, 74290, tel. 50–60–72–01. 35 rooms with bath. Facilities: restaurant, garden. AE, DC, MC, V. Closed Dec.–Mar. Very Expensive.*

Tournon
Dining

Jean-Marc Reynaud. Tain l'Hermitage, just across the river from Tournon, is the setting for this fine restaurant, which boasts a magnificent view over the Rhône and a comfortable, atmospheric dining room. Brilliantly prepared traditional cuisine is served in the traditionally styled dining room; house specialties include poached egg with foie gras and pigeon fillet in a blackcurrant sauce. *82 av. du Président Roosevelt, 26600, tel. 75–07–22–10. Reservations advised. Dress: casual. AE, DC, MC, V. Closed Sun. dinner, Mon., Jan. and 1 week in Aug. Moderate.*

Dining and Lodging

Michel Chabran. This sophisticated hotel/restaurant is decidedly modern; it's on the east bank of the Rhône at Pont de l'Isère, 10 kilometers (6 miles) south of Tournon via N7. The guest rooms, lounge, and dining rooms feature slick Danish-style furniture, elaborate floral displays, and airy plate-glass windows opening onto the private garden. Chabran's cuisine is equally light and imaginative; try his grilled salmon in creamed butter sauce. *29 av. du 45e Parallele, 26600 Pont de l'Isère, tel. 75–84–60–09. 12 rooms with bath. Facilities: restaurant. MC, V. Closed Sun. evening and Mon. in winter. Expensive.*

Valence
Dining and Lodging
★

Pic. The Pic family are the undisputed kings among Drôme restaurateurs, with subtle and original recipes to please the most demanding gourmets; try the truffle or bass with caviar. Comfortable, embroidered armchairs; flowering plants on all the tables; wall-to-wall carpeting; and the smiling service of Madame Pic lend a cozy warmth to the peach-colored dining room. In summer you can eat outside on the terrace. Two elegantly furnished guest rooms and two even more opulent suites are available, but you'll have to reserve long in advance. *285 av. Victor-Hugo, 26000, tel. 75–44–15–32. Reservations required. Jacket and tie required. AE, DC, V. Closed Sun. dinner, Wed., most of Aug., and 2 weeks in Feb. Very Expensive.*

Vienne
Dining

Le Bec Fin. An inexpensive weekday menu makes the Bec Fin a good lunch spot, and it's a serious dinner venue as well. The well-run, unpretentious eatery is just opposite the cathedral; its main dishes—steak and freshwater fish—seldom disappoint and occasionally display a deft touch (*burbot,* or cod, cooked with saffron). The gray-and-white dining room has an understated elegance. *7 pl. St-Maurice, tel. 74–85–76–72. Reservations accepted. Jacket required. MC, V. Closed Sun. dinner and Mon. Moderate.*

Vonnas
Dining and Lodging
★

Georges Blanc. It's worth making the 19-kilometer (12-mile) trip from Bourg-en-Bresse west to Vonnas (via D936, D45, and D96) because Georges Blanc must rank as one of the world's best chefs. The simple 19th-century country inn has been embellished with flowers, rugs, grandfather clocks, and antique country furniture, and makes a fine setting in which to appreciate Blanc's constantly updated menu. Try the frogs' legs any way he offers them. The wine list is extensive, the desserts superb, and there is a separate room for nonsmokers. There are also 30 guest rooms, ranging from (relatively) simple to downright luxurious. Make your reservations well in advance. *01540 Vonnas, tel. 74–50–00–10. 30 rooms with bath. Facilities: restaurant, pool, tennis, golf, helipad. AE, DC, MC, V. Closed Jan.–mid-Feb.; restaurant closed Wed. and Thurs. (except for dinner June–mid-Sept.). Very Expensive.*

The Arts and Nightlife

The Arts

Lyon is the region's liveliest arts center; *Lyon-Poche*, a weekly guide published on Wednesdays and sold at any newsstand, will give details of the week's cultural events. In Grenoble, pick up the monthly *Grenoble-Spectacles*.

Festivals September in Lyon sees the internationally renowned **Festival Berlioz** (odd years) and the **Biennale de la Danse** (even years), as well as the **International Puppet Festival.** October brings the **Festival Bach** (tel. 78–72–75–31) and the Contemporary Arts Festival, **Octobre des Arts** (tel. 78–30–50–66). During the second week of October, Lyon stages a pottery fair, **Foire aux Tuppiniers** (tel. 78–37–00–68), while in November, there's a **Music Festival** in Vieux Lyon (tel. 78–28–53–48).

Jazz enthusiasts will want to catch Grenoble's popular **Cinq Jours de Jazz** (Five Days of Jazz) in February or March, and those with classical tastes are catered to during the **Session Internationale de Grenoble-Isère** in June and July. Vienne's cathedral and church host a **Summer Music Festival** throughout June, July, and August.

Theater The café-theater, a Lyonnais specialty, fuses art with café society: **Espace Gerson** (1 pl. Gerson, tel. 78–27–96–99) or **Café-Théâtre Accessoire** (26 rue de L'Annonciande, tel. 78–27–84–84). More conventional Lyon theaters include **Théâtre Tête d'Or** (24 rue Dunoir, tel. 78–62–96–73); **Théâtre de Lyon** (7 rue des Aqueducs, tel. 78–36–67–67); and **Théâtre des Ateliers** (5 rue du Petit David, tel. 78–37–46–30). And in Grenoble: **Hexagon** (rue des Ayjinards, in the suburb of Meylan, tel. 76–90–00–45) and **Théâtre Municipale** (2 rue Hector-Berlioz, tel. 76–40–06–94).

Music Lyon's Société de Musique de Chambre (Chamber Music Society) performs at **Salle Molière** (18 quai Bondy, tel. 78–28–03–11).

Nightlife

Lyon is your best bet for nighttime entertainment, with dozens of discos, piano bars, and nightclubs; for a full list of what's available, pick up a copy of the weekly guide *Lyon-Poche*.

Discos and Nightclubs Laser beams and video screens make **L'Aquarius** (43 quai Pierre-Scize) a frenetic place for dancing the night away in Lyon. **Comoëdia** (4 rue Charles-Dullin) is more low-key, with a downstairs disco and an old-fashioned piano bar upstairs. Expect anything from the tango to rock and roll at **Place Mobile** (2 rue Rene-Leynaud). Caribbean and African music are featured at **Le Club des Iles** (1 grande rue des Feuillants).

Bars and Pubs Lyon's **Hot Club** (26 rue Lanterne) has been going strong for 40 years in a vaulted stone basement that features live jazz. **Le Melhor** (20 quai Dr-Gailleton) is a more restrained cocktail bar catering to the city's intellectual set. If you'd like a casual game of darts and a pint of bitter, head to the **Albion Public House** (12 rue Ste-Catherine). The **Bouchon aux Vins** wine bar (62 rue Mercière) has over 30 vintages for you to choose from; for a more romantic evening, make it a champagne toast in the intimate, wood-paneled **Metroclub** (2 rue Stella). Fifties fans should try the **Navire Bar** (3 rue Terme).

12 Provence

Introduction

As you approach Provence, there is a magical moment when the north is finally left behind: Cypresses and red-tiled roofs appear; you hear the screech of the cicadas and catch the scent of wild thyme and lavender. Even on the modern highway, oleanders flower on the central strip against a backdrop of harsh, brightly lit landscapes that inspired the paintings of Paul Cézanne and Vincent Van Gogh.

Provence lies in the south of France, bordered by Italy to the east and the blue waters of the Mediterranean. The Romans called it Provincia—The Province—for it was the first part of Gaul they occupied. Roman remains litter the ground in well-preserved profusion. The theater and triumphal arch at Orange, the amphitheater at Nîmes, the aqueduct at Pont-du-Gard, and the mausoleum at St-Rémy-de-Provence are considered the best of their kind in existence.

Provençal life continues at an old-fashioned pace. Hot afternoons tend to mean siestas, with signs of life discernible only as the shadows under the *platanes* (plane trees) start to lengthen and lethargic locals saunter out to play *boules* (the French version of bocce) and drink long, cooling *pastis*, an anise-based aperitif.

Provence means dazzling light and rugged, rocky countryside, interspersed with vineyards, fields of lavender, and olive groves. Any Provençal market provides a glimpse of the bewildering variety of olives and herbs cultivated, and the local cuisine is pungently spiced with thyme, rosemary, basil, and garlic.

The famous *mistral*—a fierce, cold wind that races through the Rhône Valley—is another feature of Provence. It's claimed that the extensive network of expressways has lessened the mistral's effect, but you may have trouble believing this as the wind whistles around your ears. Thankfully, clear blue skies usually follow in its wake.

The Rhône, the great river of southern France, splits in two at Arles, 15 miles before reaching the Mediterranean: The Petit Rhône crosses the region known as the Camargue on its way to Saintes-Maries-de-la-Mer, while the Grand Rhône heads off to Fos, an industrial port just along the coast from Marseille.

A number of towns have grown up along the Rhône Valley owing to its historical importance as a communications artery. The biggest is dowdy, bustling Marseille; Orange, Avignon, Tarascon, and Arles have more picturesque charm. The Camargue, on the other hand, is the realm of birds and beasts; pink flamingoes and wild horses feel more at home among its marshy wastes than people ever could.

North of Marseille lies Aix-en-Provence, whose old-time elegance reflects its former role as regional capital. We have extended Provence's traditional boundaries westward slightly into Languedoc, to include historic Nîmes and the dynamic university town of Montpellier. The Riviera, meanwhile, is part of Provence—but so full of interest that we devote an entire chapter to it.

Essential Information

Important Addresses and Numbers

Tourist Information
Provence's two regional tourist offices accept written inquiries only. **Comité Régional du Tourisme du Languedoc-Roussillon** (20 rue de la République, 34000 Montpellier, tel. 67–92–67–92) will provide information on all towns west of the River Rhône, while the remainder of towns covered in this chapter are handled by the **Comité Régional du Tourisme de Provence-Alpes–Côte d'Azur** (Immeuble C.M.C.E., 2 rue Henri-Barbusse, 13241 Marseille, tel. 91–39–38–00).

Local tourist offices for major towns covered in this chapter are as follows: **Aix-en-Provence** (2 pl. du Général-de-Gaulle, tel. 42–26–02–93), **Arles** (35 pl. de la République, tel. 90–93–49–11), **Avignon** (41 cours Jean-Jaurès, tel. 90–82–65–11), **Marseille** (4 La Canebière, tel. 91–54–91–11), **Montpellier** (Esplanade Charles-de-Gaulle, tel. 67–79–15–15), **Nîmes** (6 rue Auguste, tel. 66–67–29–11), and **Toulon** (8 av. Colbert, tel. 94–22–08–22).

Travel Agencies
Wagons-Lits (10 rue Portail Boquier, Avignon, tel. 90–82–20–56; 67 La Canebière, Marseille, tel. 91–90–12–46; Midi-Libre Voyages, 20 blvd. de l'Amiral-Courbet, Nîmes, tel. 66–67–45–34; 2 pl. Jeanne d'Arc, Aix-en-Provence, tel. 42–27–86–35).

Car Rental
Avis (11 cours Gambetta, Aix-en-Provence, tel. 42–21–64–16; 267 blvd. National, Marseille, tel. 91–50–70–11; and 92 blvd. Rabatau, Marseille, tel. 91–80–12–00), **Europcar** (2 bis av. Victor-Hugo, Arles, tel. 90–93–23–24; 27 av. St-Ruf, Avignon, tel. 90–82–49–85), and **Hertz** (Parking des Gares, 18 rue Jules-Ferry, Montpellier, tel. 67–58–65–18; 39 blvd. Gambetta, Nîmes, tel. 66–76–25–91).

Arriving and Departing

By Plane
The airports at Marseille and Montpellier are served by frequent flights from Paris and London, and there are daily flights from Paris to the smaller airport at Nîmes. Nice (*see* Chapter 13) is only 160 kilometers (100 miles) from Aix-en-Provence, and there are direct flights from the United States. If you are going to rent a car on arrival, the airports of Marseille and Montpellier are equally easy to get away from without driving into either town.

By Car
The A6/A7 expressway (toll road) from Paris is known as the Autoroute du Soleil—the Expressway of the Sun—and takes you straight to Provence, whereupon it divides at Orange.

By Train
Avignon is less than four hours from Paris by high-speed train (TGV); trains depart from Paris's Gare de Lyon station.

Getting Around

By Car
After the A7 divides at Orange, the A9 heads west to Nîmes and Montpellier (765 kilometers/475 miles from Paris), extending into the Pyrenees and across the Spanish border. A7 continues southeast from Orange to Marseille on the coast (1,100 kilometers/680 miles from Paris), while A8 goes to Aix-en-Provence (with a spur to Toulon), and then to the Riviera and Italy.

By Train After the main line divides at Avignon, the westbound link heads to Nîmes, Montpellier (fewer than five hours from Paris by TGV), and points west. The southeast-bound link takes in Marseille (also fewer than five hours from Paris by TGV), Toulon, and the Riviera.

By Bus A moderately good network of bus services links places not served, or badly served, by the railway. If you plan to explore Provence by bus, Avignon is the best base. The town is well served by local buses, and excursion buses and boat trips down the Rhône start from here.

Guided Tours

The regional tourist offices' "52 Week" program pools 52 tours offered by various agencies, allowing visitors to choose from a myriad of tours throughout the year, touching on wine tasting, sailing, hang gliding, golfing, gastronomy, and cultural exploration. Contact **GIE**, Loisirs-Acceuil (Domaine de Vergon, 13370 Mallemort, tel. 90–59–18–05) for details. In addition, local tourist offices can arrange many tours, ranging from one-hour guided walks to excursions taking a week or longer by bus, bicycle, on horseback, or on foot.

Bus Tours The **Comité Départemental du Tourisme** (6 rte. Jeune-Anacharsis, 13006 Marseille, tel. 91–54–92–66) offers a five-day bus tour called "Découverte de la Provence," which includes full board in two-star hotels and entry to all places of interest. The tour starts in Marseille, continues to Cassis (from which there is a boat trip in the fjordlike waterways known as *calanques*), and includes a day in the Camargue and visits to Aix-en-Provence, Les Baux, and Arles; the cost is 1,800 francs per person. **Capodano Voyages** (110 blvd. des Dames, 13002 Marseille, tel. 91–91–10–91) offers a "Bouillabaisse Weekend" in Marseille, taking in a trip to the harbor, the Château d'If, and Les Iles de Frioul; the cost is 2,650 francs per person. The **Arles Tourist Office** (35 pl. de la République, tel. 90–93–49–11) employs 15 guide-lecturers to run excursions of the town and region.

Horseback Tours The **Office Municipal de Tourisme** in Marseille features a six-day guided tour on horseback, during which you can stay in simple houses or tents. Beginning near Marseille in the hills of the Massif de la Sainte-Beaune, the tour continues through some wild but picturesque countryside, including Cézanne's mountain, La Sainte-Victoire; the cost, including insurance, is 2,650 francs per person. Twenty-seven kilometers (17 miles) from Aix-en-Provence lies **Ranch Lou Maze** (13680 Lançon de Provence, tel. 90–57–74–17), which offers horseback excursions of the Camargue; the cost ranges from 250 to 400 francs a day.

Special-Interest Tours **Capodano Voyages** offers a two-day "Wines of the Sun and Gastronomy" tour that includes Avignon, a trip to the "Wine University" at Suze-la-Rousse, and stops at Orange and Villeneuve-les-Avignon. The price for one person is 1,250 francs, though it is lower for groups of two or more.

Exploring Provence

*Numbers in the margin correspond with points of interest on
the Provence and Nîmes maps.*

Orientation

We have divided Provence into three exploring tours; each follows directly from the other. The marshy Camargue forms the
heart of our first tour, which ventures briefly into the Languedoc region to visit the fine old towns of Nîmes and Montpellier
before wheeling back across the Camargue to examine the Roman remains at Arles and St-Rémy. The tour finishes at
Tarascon on the Rhône. The second tour begins farther up the
river valley at Avignon, with its papal palace. This tour falls
neatly within the boundaries of the Vaucluse *département*,
ranging from Avignon in the south to the Roman towns of Orange and Vaison-la-Romaine to the north; the main natural feature is Mont Ventoux, towering above surrounding plains. The
third tour begins in Aix, the historic capital of Provence, then
heads south to Marseille and east along the spectacular Mediterranean coast to Toulon.

Highlights for First-time Visitors

Aix-en-Provence, Tour 3
Roman remains at Arles, Tour 1
Palais des Papes (Papal palace), Avignon, Tour 2
Roman remains at Nîmes, Tour 1
Pont du Gard, Tour 1
St-Remy-de-Provence, Tour 1
Théâtre Antique, Orange, Tour 2
Les Baux-de-Provence, Tour 1

Tour 1: Nîmes and the Camargue

The first tour starts with a bridge, symbolically linking the
20th century to the Roman grandeur that haunts Provence: the
❶ **Pont du Gard,** midway between Avignon and Nîmes off the N86
highway (take D981 at Remoulins; if you arrive by the A9 expressway, take the Remoulins exit).

The Pont du Gard is a huge, three-tiered aqueduct, erected
2,000 years ago as part of a 30-mile canal supplying water to
Roman Nîmes. It is astonishingly well preserved. Its setting,
spanning a rocky gorge 150 feet above the River Gardon, is
nothing less than spectacular. There is no entry fee or guide,
and at certain times you can have it all to yourself: Early morning is best, when the honey-colored stone gleams in the sun-
light. The best way to gauge the full majesty of the Pont du
Gard is to walk right along the top.

Time Out   In the enchanting little medieval town of Uzès, 14 kilometers (9
miles) northwest via D981, the **Alexandry** restaurant is a good
choice for an inexpensive bite to eat. *6 blvd. Gambetta.*

❷ **Nîmes** lies 20 kilometers (13 miles) southwest of the Pont du
Gard (via N86) and 24 kilometers (15 miles) south of Uzès (via
D979). Few towns have preserved such visible links with their
Roman past: Nemausus, as the town was then known, grew to

CitéFoulc. Admission: 16 frs. adults, 9 frs. children, valid for all museums; joint ticket as above. Open daily 9–noon and 1:30–6.

Return to the Arènes and head right, along boulevard de la Libération, which soon becomes boulevard de l'Amiral-Courbet.
5 A hundred and fifty yards down on the left is the **Musée Archéologique et d'Histoire Naturelle,** rich in local archaeological finds, mainly statues, busts, friezes, tools, glass, and pottery. It also houses an extensive collection of Greek, Roman, and medieval coins. *Blvd. de l'Amiral-Courbet. Admission: 16 frs. adults, 9 frs. children, valid for all museums; joint ticket as above. Open Mon.–Sat. 9–noon and 1:30–6, Sun. 1:30–6.*

Turn right into Grand' Rue behind the museum, then take the
6 second left up toward the **cathedral.** This uninspired 19th-century reconstruction is of less interest than either the sur-
7 rounding pedestrian streets or the **Musée du Vieux Nîmes** (Museum of Old Nîmes), housed opposite the cathedral in the 17th-century Bishop's Palace. Embroidered garments and woolen shawls fill the rooms in an exotic and vibrant display. Nîmes used to be a cloth-manufacturing center and lent its name to what has become one of the world's most popular fabrics—denim (*de Nîmes*—from Nîmes). Two rooms contain colorful, sometimes grisly, exhibits on the regional sport of bullfighting. *Pl. aux Herbes. Admission: 16 frs. adults, 9 frs. children, valid for all museums; joint ticket as above. Open daily 10–6.*

Head right from the cathedral along rue des Halles, then left
8 down rue du Général-Perrier, to reach the **Maison Carrée.** Despite its name (the "square house"), this is an oblong Roman temple, dating from the 1st century AD. Transformed down the ages into a stable, a private dwelling, a town hall, and a church, today the building is a museum that contains an imposing statue of Apollo and other antiquities. The exquisite carvings along the cornice and on the Corinthian capitals rank as some of the finest in Roman architecture. Thomas Jefferson admired the Maison Carrée's chaste lines of columns so much that he had them copied for the Virginia state capitol at Richmond. *Blvd. Victor-Hugo. Admission: 13 frs. adults, 8 frs. children; joint ticket as above. Open mid-June–mid-Sept., daily 9–7; mid-Sept.–Oct. and Apr.–mid-June, daily 9–noon and 2–6; Nov.–Mar., daily 9–noon and 2–5.*

Rue Molière and rue Boissier lead from the Maison Carrée to
9 the **Jardin de la Fontaine.** This elaborate, formal garden was landscaped on the site of the Roman baths in the 18th century, when the Source de Nemausus, a once-sacred spring, was channeled into pools and a canal. Close by, you'll see the shattered
10 remnant of a Roman ruin, known as the **Temple of Diana.** At the
11 far end of the jardin is the **Tour Magne**—a stumpy tower that was probably used as a lookout post, which, despite having lost 30 feet in the course of time, still provides fine views of Nîmes for anyone who is energetic enough to climb the 140 steps to the top. *Quai de la Fontaine. Admission to Tour Magne: 13 frs. adults, 8 frs. children; joint ticket as above. Open mid-June–mid-Sept., daily 9–7; mid-Sept.–Oct. and Apr.–mid-June, daily 9–noon and 2–6; Nov.–Mar., daily 9–noon and 2–5.*

12 Both N113 and the A9 expressway link Nîmes to **Montpellier,** 50 kilometers (30 miles) southwest. Montpellier is a comparatively young town, a mere 1,000 years old; no Romans settled here. Ever since medieval times, Montpellier's reputation has been linked to its university, which was founded in the 14th century. Its medical school, in particular, was so highly esteemed that François Rabelais, one of France's top 16th-century writers, left his native Loire Valley to take his doctorate here. Montpellier remains one of France's premier universities, and a student population of 20,000 peps things up during the school year.

The 17th-century town center has been improved by an imaginative urban planning program, and several streets and squares are now banned to cars. The heart of Montpellier is place de la Comédie, a wide square now freed of traffic jams, much to the benefit of the cafés and terraces laid out before the handsome 19th-century facade of the civic theater.

Boulevard Sarrail leads from the far end of the square, past the leafy Esplanade with its rows of plane trees, to the **Musée Fabre.** The museum's collection of art highlights important works by Gustave Courbet (notably *Bonjour Monsieur Courbet*) and Eugène Delacroix *(Femmes d'Alger)*, as well as paintings by Frédéric Bazille (1841–70)—whose death during the Franco-Prussian War deprived Impressionism of one of its earliest exponents. Older standouts of the museum's varied collection include pictures from the English (Joshua Reynolds), Italian (Raphael), Flemish (David Teniers) and Spanish (Jusepe de Ribera) schools. *Blvd. Sarrail. Admission: 15 frs. (free Wed.). Open Tues.–Sat. 9–12:30 and 1:30–5:30.*

Follow rue Montpelliéret, alongside the museum, into the heart of old Montpellier—a maze of crooked, bustling streets ideal for shopping and strolling. Rue Foch strikes a more disciplined note, slicing straight through to the pride of Montpellier, the **Promenade du Peyrou.** With its wrought-iron railings and majestic flights of steps, this long, broad, tree-shaded terrace has great style. An equestrian statue of Louis XIV rides triumphant and at the far end carved friezes and columns mask a water tower. Water used to arrive along the **St-Clément aqueduct,** an imposing two-tiered structure 70 feet high and nearly 1,000 yards long. Locals still cluster beneath the aqueduct's arches to drink pastis and play boules.

Just down boulevard Henri IV from the Promenade du Peyrou is France's oldest **botanical garden,** planted by order of Henri IV in 1593. Horticulture buffs will admire the exceptional range of plants, flowers, and trees that grow here, and even nongardeners will appreciate this oasis of peace, where water lilies float among the lotus flowers. *Admission: free. Gardens open daily 9–noon and 2–5. Greenhouses open weekdays 9–noon and 2–5, Sat. 9–noon.*

The arid, rocky Midi landscape begins to change as you head southeast from Montpellier along D21, past pools and lagoons, ⓭ to **La Grande Motte,** the most lavish of a string of new resorts built along the Languedoc coast. The mosquitoes that once infested this watery area have finally been vanquished, and tourists have taken their place. La Grande Motte was only a glint in an architect's eye back in the late '60s; since then, its arresting pyramid-shape apartment blocks have influenced several French resorts. They host thousands of vacationers each year.

Time Out Thousands of tons of oysters are cultivated in the nearby Etang (lagoon) de Thau; many end up featured on the menu of the elegant **Alexandre-Amirauté.** You can eat your oysters amid impressive Louis XV surroundings while gazing out over the clear blue waters of the Mediterranean. *345 esplanade Maurice-Justin.*

---

⑭ Thirteen kilometers (8 miles) farther east is **Aigues-Mortes,** an astonishing relic of medieval town planning, created at the behest of Louis IX (St-Louis) in the 13th century. Medieval streets are usually crooked and higgledy-piggledy; at Aigues-Mortes, however, a grid plan was adopted, hemmed in by sturdy walls sprouting towers at regular intervals. Aigues-Mortes was originally a port, and Louis used it as a base for his Crusades to the Holy Land. The sea has long since receded, though, and Aigues-Mortes's size and importance have decreased with it.

Unlike most of the medieval buildings, the **fortifications** remain intact. Walk along the top of the city walls and admire some remarkable views across the town and salt marshes. You can also explore the powerful **Tour de Constance,** originally designed as a fortress-keep, and used in the 18th century as a prison for Protestants who refused to convert to official state Catholicism. One such unfortunate, Marie Durand, languished here for 38 years. Abraham Mazel was luckier. He spent 10 months chiseling a hole in the wall, while his companions sang psalms to distract the jailers. The ruse worked: Mazel and 16 others escaped. *Admission: 24 frs. adults, 13 frs. students and senior citizens, 5 frs. children. Tower and ramparts open Apr.–Oct., daily 9–7; Nov.–Mar. 9:30–noon and 2–5:30.*

Head east on D58 across the haunting, desolate **Camargue:** a marshy wilderness of endless horizons, vast pools, low flat plains, and, overhead, innumerable species of migrating birds. The Camargue is formed by the sprawling Rhône delta and extends over 300 square miles. Much of it is untouched by man; this is a land of black bulls and sturdy, free-roaming gray horses. There are just two towns worthy of the name: Aigues-Mortes and, 32 kilometers (20 miles) southeast via D58/D570, Saintes-Maries-de-la-Mer.

⑮ **Stes-Maries-de-la-Mer** is a commercialized resort, mainly frequented by British tourists in search of the Camargue's principal sandy beach. Its tiny, dark fortress-church houses caskets containing relics of the "Holy Maries" after whom the town is named. Legend has it that Mary Jacobi (the sister of the Virgin), Mary Magdalene, Mary Salome (mother of the apostles James and John), and their black servant Sarah were washed up here around AD 40 after being abandoned at sea—why, no one knows. Their adopted town rapidly became a site of pilgrimage, particularly among gypsies. Sarah was adopted as their patron saint, and to this day, gypsies stage colorful pilgrimages to Stes-Maries in late May and late October, while guitar-strumming pseudogypsies serenade rich-looking tourists throughout the summer.

Take D85-A north from Stes-Maries through the 30-acre **Parc Ornithologique,** itself part of the vast Réserve Nationale centered on the Etang (lagoon) de Vaccarès. The Parc Ornithologique offers a protected environment to vegetation and wildlife: Birds from northern Europe and Siberia spend the winter here, while pink flamingoes flock in during the summer months. *Admission: 22 frs. Open Mar.–Oct., daily 8–dusk.*

Continue along D85-A until it rejoins D570, then keep north on this road for 25 kilometers (16 miles) until you reach **Arles.** The first inhabitants of Arles were probably the Greeks, who arrived from Marseille in the 6th century BC. The Romans, however, left a stronger mark, constructing the theater and amphitheater (Arènes) that remain Arles's biggest tourist attractions. Arles used to be a thriving port before the Mediterranean receded over what is now the marshy Camargue. It was also the site of the southernmost bridge over the Rhône, and became a commercial crossroads; merchants from as far afield as Arabia, Assyria, and Africa would linger here to do business on their way from Rome to Spain or northern Europe.

Firebrand Dutchman Vincent Van Gogh produced much of his best work—and chopped off his ear—in Arles during a frenzied 15-month spell (1888–90) just before his suicide at 37. Unfortunately, the houses he lived in are no longer standing—they were destroyed during World War II—but one of his most famous subjects remains: the **Pont de Trinquetaille** across the Rhône. Van Gogh's rendering of the bridge, painted in 1888, was auctioned a century later for $20 million.

Local art museums such as the **Musée Réattu,** 300 yards from the bridge along quai Marx-Dormoy, can't compete with that type of bidding—which is one reason none of Van Gogh's works are displayed there. Another is that Arles failed to appreciate Van Gogh; he was jeered at and eventually packed off to the nearest lunatic asylum. To add insult to injury, Jacques Réattu, after whom the museum is named, was a local painter of dazzling mediocrity. His works fill three rooms, but of much greater interest is the collection of modern drawings and paintings by Pablo Picasso, Fernand Léger, and Maurice de Vlaminck, as well as the photography section containing images by some of the field's leading names. *Rue du Grand-Prieuré. Admission: 15 frs.; joint ticket to all monuments and museums: 40 frs. adults, 28 frs. students and senior citizens, children free. Open June–Sept., daily 9:30–7; Nov.–Mar., daily 10–12:30 and 2–5; Apr.–May and Oct., daily 9:30–12:30 and 2–6.*

The museum facade, facing the Rhône, dates from the Middle Ages and formed part of a 15th-century priory. Beside it are the ruins of the **Palais Constantin** (same opening times as above), site of Provence's largest Roman baths, the **Thèrmes de la Trouille** (entrance on rue Dominique-Maisto; admission: 12 francs; joint ticket as above).

Most of the significant sights and museums in Arles are set well away from the Rhône. The most notable is the 26,000-capacity **Arènes,** built in the 1st century AD to showcase circuses and fight-to-the-death gladiator combats. The amphitheater is 150 yards long and as wide as a football field, with each of its two stories composed of 60 arches; the original top tier has long since crumbled, and the three square towers were added in the Middle Ages. Climb to the upper story for some satisfying views across the town and countryside. Despite its venerable age, the amphitheater still sees a lot of action, mainly Sunday afternoon bullfights. *Rond Point des Arènes. Admission: 15 frs.; joint ticket as above. Open June–Sept., daily 8:30–7; Nov.–Mar., daily 9–*

noon and 2–4:30; Apr.–May and Oct., daily 9–12:30 and 2–6:30.

Just 100 yards from the Arènes are the scanty remains of Arles's **Théâtre Antique** (Roman theater); the bits of marble column scattered around the grassy enclosure hint poignantly at the theater's onetime grandeur. The capacity may have shrunk from 7,000 to a few hundred, but the orchestra pit and a few tiers of seats are still used for the city's Music and Drama festival each July. *Rue du Cloître, tel. 90–96–93–30 for ticket information. Admission: free. Open June–Sept., daily 8:30–7; Nov.–Mar., daily 9–noon and 2–4:30; Apr.–May and Oct., daily 9–12:30 and 2–6:30.*

Follow rue de la Calade to place de la République. To the left is the church of **St-Trophime,** dating mainly from the 11th and 12th centuries; subsequent additions have not spoiled its architectural harmony. Take time to admire the accomplished 12th-century sculptures flanking the main portal, featuring the Last Judgment, the apostles, the Nativity, and various saints. There are other well-crafted sculptures in the cloisters. *Rue de l'Hôtel-de-Ville. Admission to cloisters: 15 frs.; joint ticket as above. Open June–Sept., daily 8:30–7; Nov.–Mar., daily 9–noon and 2–4:30; Apr.–May and Oct., daily 9–12:30 and 2–6:30.*

Opposite St-Trophime is the **Musée d'Art Païen** (Museum of Pagan Art), housed in a former church next to the 17th-century Hôtel de Ville (Town Hall). The "pagan art" displays encompass Roman statues, busts, mosaics, and a white marble sarcophagus. You'll also see a copy of the famous statue the *Venus of Arles;* Sun King Louis XIV waltzed off to the Louvre with the original. *Pl. de la République. Admission: 12 frs.; joint ticket as above. Open June–Sept., daily 8:30–7; Nov.–Mar., daily 9–noon and 2–4:30; Apr.–May and Oct., 9–12:30 and 2–6:30.*

Turn left alongside the Hôtel de Ville into plan de la Cour. A hundred yards down, in a former 17th-century Jesuit chapel, is the **Musée d'Art Chrétien** (Museum of Christian Art). One of the highlights is a magnificent collection of sculpted marble sarcophagi, second only to the Vatican's, that date from the 4th century on. Downstairs, you can explore a vast double gallery built in the 1st century BC as a grain store and see part of the great Roman sewer built two centuries later. *Rue Balze. Admission: 12 frs.; joint ticket as above. Open June–Sept., daily 8:30–7; Nov.–Mar., daily 9–noon and 2–4:30; Apr.–May and Oct., daily 9–12:30 and 2–6:30.*

The **Museon Arlaten,** an old-fashioned folklore museum, is housed next door in a 16th-century mansion. The charming displays include costumes and headdresses, puppets, and waxworks, lovingly assembled by that great 19th-century Provençal poet, Frédéric Mistral. *Rue de la République. Admission: 12 frs.; joint ticket as above. Open June–Sept., daily 8:30–7; Nov.–Mar., Tues.–Sun. 9–noon and 2–4:30; Apr.–May and Oct., Tues.–Sun. 9–12:30 and 2–6:30.*

Head down rue du Président-Wilson opposite the museum to the **boulevard des Luces,** a broad, leafy avenue flanked by trendy shops and sidewalk cafés. Locals favor it for leisurely strolls and aperitifs.

At the east end of the boulevard is the **Jardin d'Hiver,** a public garden whose fountains figure in several of Van Gogh's paintings. Cross the gardens to rue Fassin and head left to place de la Croisière and the start of the allée des Sarcophages, which leads to the **Alyscamps,** a Provençal term meaning "mythical burial ground." This was a prestigious burial site from Roman times through the Middle Ages. A host of important finds have been excavated here, many of which are exhibited in the town's museums. Empty tombs and sarcophagi line the allée des Sarcophages, creating a powerfully gloomy atmosphere in dull weather.

⑰ Leave Arles on Avignon-bound N570, and almost immediately turn right along D17 to the striking village of **Fontvieille,** 10 kilometers (6 miles) away and home of the **Moulin de Daudet.** Nineteenth-century author Alphonse Daudet dreamed up his short stories, *Lettres de Mon Moulin,* in this well-preserved, charmingly situated windmill just up D33 on the outskirts of the village. Inside there's a small museum devoted to Daudet, and you can walk upstairs to see the original grain-grinding system. *Admission: 7 frs. adults, 4 frs. children. Open Apr.– Oct., daily 9–noon and 2–7; Nov.–Dec. and Feb.–Mar., daily 10–noon and 2–5; Jan., Sun. only, 10–noon and 2–5.*

⑱ From Fontvieille, take D17 and then D78-A to **Les Baux-de-Provence,** 8 kilometers (5 miles) farther. Les Baux-de-Provence is an amazing place, perched on a mighty spur of rock high above the surrounding countryside of vines, olive trees, and quarries. The mineral bauxite was discovered here in 1821. Half of Les Baux is composed of tiny climbing streets and ancient stone houses inhabited, for the most part, by local craftsmen selling pottery, carvings, and assorted knickknacks. The other half, the Ville Morte (Dead Town), is a mass of medieval ruins, vestiges of Les Baux's glorious past, when the town boasted 6,000 inhabitants and the defensive impregnability of its rocky site far outweighed its isolation and poor access.

Cars must be left in the parking lot at the entrance to the village. Close to the 12th-century church of St-Vincent (where local shepherds continue an age-old tradition by herding their lambs to midnight mass at Christmas) is the 16th-century **Hôtel des Porcelets,** featuring some 18th-century frescoes and a small but choice collection of contemporary art. *Pl. St-Vincent. Admission: 18 frs. (joint ticket with Musée Lapidaire and Ville Morte). Open Easter–Oct., daily 9–noon and 2–6.*

Rue Neuve leads around to the **Ville Morte.** Enter through the 14th-century Tour-de-Brau, which houses the Musée Lapidaire, displaying locally excavated sculptures and ceramics. You can wander at will amid the rocks and ruins of the Dead Town. A 13th-century castle stands at one end of the clifftop, and, at the other, the Tour Paravelle and the Monument Charloun Rieu. From here, you can enjoy a magnificent view of Arles and the Camargue as far as Stes-Maries-de-la-Mer. *Ville Morte. Admission: 18 frs. (joint ticket with museums). Open daily 9–noon and 2–6.*

Half a mile north of Les Baux, off D27, is the **Cathédrale d'Images,** where the majestic setting of the old Baux quarries, with their towering rock faces and stone pillars, is used as a colossal screen for nature-based film shows (Jacques Cousteau gets frequent billing). *Rte. de Maillane. Admission: 45 frs. adults, 22 frs. children. Open Mar.–Oct., daily 10–7.*

⑲ Hilly D5 heads 8 kilometers (5 miles) north from Les Baux to the small town of **St-Rémy de Provence,** founded in the 6th century BC and known as Glanum to the Romans. St-Rémy is renowned for its outstanding Roman remains: Temples, baths, forum, and houses have been excavated, while the Mausoleum and Arc Municipal (Triumphal Arch) welcome visitors as they enter the town.

The **Roman Mausoleum** was erected around AD 100 to the memory of Caius and Lucius Caesar, grandsons of the Emperor Augustus; the four bas-reliefs around its base, depicting ancient battle scenes, are stunningly preserved. The Mausoleum is composed of four archways topped by a circular colonnade. The nearby **Arc Municipal** is a few decades older and has suffered heavily; the upper half has crumbled away, although you can still make out some of the stone carvings.

Excavations since 1921 have uncovered about a tenth of the site of the adjacent Roman town. Many of the finds—statues, pottery, and jewelry—can be examined at the town museum, **Le Musée Archéologique,** in the center of St-Rémy. *Hôtel de Sade, rue Parage. Admission: 12 frs. adults, 6 frs. children. Open June–Oct., daily 9–noon and 2–6; Apr.–May and Oct., weekends 10–noon, weekdays 3–6; closed Nov.–Mar.*

Opposite the Hôtel de Sade, in a grand 16th-century mansion, is the **Musée des Alpilles.** It boasts a fine collection of minerals found in the nearby hills (the Alpilles), plus items of regional folklore: costumes, furniture, and figurines. Exhibits also touch on the 16th-century astrologer, Nostradamus, who was born in St-Rémy (his house can be seen on the other side of the church, on rue Hoche, but it's not open to the public). *Pl. Favier. Admission: 12 frs. Open Apr.–Oct., Wed.–Mon. 10–noon and 2–6; Mar. and Nov., weekends 10–noon and 2–4; closed Dec.–Feb.*

⑳ Take D99 16 kilometers (10 miles) west from St-Rémy to **Tarascon,** home of the mythical Tarasque, a monster that would emerge from the Rhône to gobble children and cattle. Luckily St. Martha, washed up with the three Maries at Stes-Maries-de-la-Mer, allegedly tamed the beast with a sprinkle of holy water, after which the inhabitants clobbered it senseless and slashed it to pieces. This dramatic event is celebrated on the last Sunday in June with a colorful parade.

Ever since the 12th century, Tarascon has possessed a formidable **castle** to protect it from any beast or man that might be tempted to emulate the Tarasque's fiendish deeds. The castle's massive stone walls, towering 150 feet above the rocky banks of the Rhône, are among the most daunting in France, so it's not surprising that the castle was used as a prison for centuries. Since 1926, however, the chapels, vaulted royal apartments, and stone carvings of the interior have been restored to less-intimidating glory. *Admission: 22 frs. adults, frs. senior citizens, 5 frs. children. Open July and Wed.–Mon. 9–7; Sept.–June guided tours only 9–11 (last tour at 5 in Apr. and May; at 4, Oct.–May Tues.*

It's just 24 kilometers (15 miles) from Tarascon to Avignon and the start of our second tour.

Tour 2: The Vaucluse

㉑ A warren of medieval alleys nestling behind a protective ring of chunky towers, **Avignon** is possibly best known for its Pont St-Bénezet, the Avignon bridge that many will remember singing about during their nursery-rhyme days. No one dances across the bridge these days, however; it's amputated in midstream, and has been ever since the 17th century, when a cataclysmic storm washed half of it away. Still, Avignon has lots to offer, starting with the Palais des Papes (Papal Palace), where seven exiled popes camped between 1309 and 1377 after fleeing from the corruption of Rome. Avignon remained papal property until 1791, and elegant mansions and a population of 80,000 bear witness to the town's 18th-century prosperity.

Numbers in the margin correspond with points of interest on the Avignon map.

㉒ Avignon's main street, rue de la République, leads from the tourist office (41 cours Jean-Jaurès) past shops and cafés to place de l'Horloge and place du Palais, site of the colossal **Palais des Papes.**This "palace" creates a disconcertingly fortresslike impression, underlined by the austerity of its interior decor; most of the furnishings were dispersed during the French Revolution. Some imagination is required to picture it in medieval splendor, awash with color and worldly clerics enjoying what the 14th-century Italian poet Petrarch called "licentious banquets."

On close inspection, two different styles of building emerge: the severe **Palais Vieux** (Old Palace), built between 1334 and 1342 by Pope Benedict XII, a member of the Cistercian order, which frowned on frivolity, and the more decorative **Palais Nouveau** (New Palace), built in the following decade by the arty, lavish-living Pope Clement VI. The Great Court, where visitors arrive, forms a link between the two.

The main rooms of the Palais Vieux are the consistory (council hall), decorated with some excellent 14th-century frescoes by Simone Martini; the Chapelle St-Jean (original frescoes by Matteo Giovanetti); the Grand Tinel, or Salle des Festins, with a majestic vaulted roof and a series of 18th-century Gobelin tapestries; the Chapelle St-Martial (more Matteo frescoes); the Chambre du Cerf, with a richly decorated ceiling, murals featuring a stag hunt, and a delightful view of Avignon; the Chambre de Parement (papal antechamber); and the Chambre à Coucher (papal bedchamber).

The principal attractions of the Palais Nouveau are the Grande Audience, a magnificent two-naved hall on the ground floor, and, upstairs, the Chapelle Clémentine, where the college of ̲ls gathered to elect the new pope. *Pl. du Palais des ̲ Admission: 27 frs. adults, 15 frs. students, popes and ̲n free. Guided tours only Mar.–Oct. Open Easter– daily 9–12:15 and 2–5:15; July–Sept., daily 9–6; Oct.– r, daily 9–11:15 and 2–4:15.*

̲2th-century **cathedral** nearby contains the Gothic tomb of ̲ John XII. Beyond is the **Rocher des Doms,** a large, attract- ̲arden offering fine views of Avignon, the Rhône, and the

The 70-foot arch, the third-highest Roman arch still standing, towered over the old Via Agrippa between Arles and Lyon and was probably built around AD 25 in honor of the Gallic Wars. The carvings on the north side, depict the legionaries' battles with the Gauls and Caesar's naval showdown with the ships of Marseille. Today the arch presides over a busy traffic circle.

③① The D975 heads 27 kilometers (17 miles) northeast from Orange to **Vaison-la-Romaine.** As its name suggests, Vaison was also a Roman town. The remains here are more extensive though less spectacular than those at Orange; they can be explored on either side of the avenue du Général-de-Gaulle. The floors and walls of houses, villas, a basilica, and a theater have been unearthed, and the Roman street plan is partly discernible. Statues and objects are housed in a small museum near the theater. With its lush lawns and colorful flower beds, the entire site suggests a well-tended historical garden. *Admission to remains and museum: 26 frs. adults, 15 frs. students and senior citizens. Open Apr.–Oct., daily 9–7; Nov.–Mar., daily 9–5.*

③② Before leaving Vaison, pause to admire the 2,000-year-old Roman bridge over the River Ouvèze and venture briefly into the medieval town across the river. Then head 10 kilometers (6 miles) south along D938 to **Malaucène,** at the foot of **Mont Ventoux**—a huge mountain that looms incongruously above the surrounding plains. Weather conditions on this sprawling, whalelike bulk—known reverentially as "Le" Ventoux—can vary dramatically. In summer, few places in France experience such scorching heat; in winter, the Ventoux's snow-topped peak recalls the Alps. Its arid heights sometimes provide a grueling setting for the Tour de France cycling race; British bicyclist Tommy Simpson collapsed and died under the Ventoux's pitiless sun in 1967.

③③ D974 winds its way from Malaucène up to the summit, 6,250 feet above sea level. Stay on D974 as it doubles back around the southern slopes of the Ventoux, then follow it southwest from Bédoin toward Carpentras. From here, take D938 south to **L'Isle-sur-la-Sorgue,** 18 kilometers (11 miles) away, where the River Sorgue splits into a number of channels and once turned the waterwheels of the town's silk factories. Silk worms were cultivated locally, one reason for the profusion of mulberry trees in Provence (mulberry leaves being a silkworm's favorite food). Some of the waterwheels are still in place, and you can admire them as you stroll along the banks of the river that encircles the town. The richly decorated 17th-century church is also of interest.

Time Out A good place for lunch is **Le Pescador,** an inexpensive restaurant whose shaded terrace overlooks the arms of the Sorgue. There is a wide choice and an excellent-value menu during the week. *Le Partage des Eaux. Closed Mon.*

---

③④ Tiny D25 leads east from L'Isle-sur-la-Sorgue to **Fontaine-de-Vaucluse,** 8 kilometers (5 miles) away. The "fountain" in question is the site of the River Sorgue's emergence from underground imprisonment: Water shoots up from a cavern as the emerald-green river sprays and cascades at the foot of steep cliffs. This is the picture in springtime or after heavy rains; in the drought of summer, the scene may be less spectacular and infested with tourists.

It's just 6 kilometers (4 miles) from Fontaine-de-Vaucluse to
③⑤ Gordes as the crow flies, but drivers have to wind their way
south, east, and then north for 16 kilometers (10 miles) on
D100-A, D100, D2, and D15 to skirt the impassable hillside.
The golden-stoned village of Gordes is perched dramatically on
its own hill. At the summit sits a Renaissance **château** with a
collection of mind-stretching, geometric-patterned paintings
by 20th-century Hungarian-French artist Victor Vasarely. *Admission: 16 frs. adults, 10 frs. students and senior citizens,
children free. Open Wed.–Mon. 10–noon and 2–6; closed Tues.*

In a wild valley some 4 kilometers (2 miles) north of Gordes (via
D177) stands the beautiful 12th-century **Abbey of Sénanque.** In
1969, its Cistercian monks moved to the island of St-Honorat
(*see* Chapter 13), off the shore of Cannes, and the admirably
preserved buildings here are now a cultural center that presents concerts and exhibitions. The dormitory, refectory,
church, and chapter house can be visited, along with an odd
museum devoted to the Sahara's Tuareg nomads. *Admission:
15 frs. Open July and Aug., Mon.–Sat. 10–7, Sun. 2–7; Sept.–
June, Mon.–Sat. 10–noon and 2–5, Sun. 2–5.*

Return to Gordes and strike 10 kilometers (6 miles) east along
③⑥ D2/D102 to another hilltop village, **Roussillon,** whose houses
are built with a distinctive orange-and-pink-colored stone. This
is ocher country, and local quarrying has slashed cliffs into bi-
③⑦ zarre shapes. **Bonnieux,** 11 kilometers (7 miles) south of
Roussillon (D149), is equally picturesque. Climb to the terrace
of the old church (not to be confused with the big 19th-century
one lower down) for a sweeping view north that takes in
Gordes, Roussillon, and the nearby château of Lacoste, now in
ruins but once home to that notorious aristocrat, the Marquis
de Sade.

Time Out The setting of the **Prieuré**—a charming old priory in the pretty
hilltop village of Bonnieux—is its main appeal. The simple Provençal dishes are made memorable by the accompanying panoramic views. *Closed Tues. and Thurs. lunch.*

Aix-en-Provence, starting point for our third tour, lies 48 kilometers (29 miles) southeast.

Tour 3: The Marseille Area

Many villages, but few towns, are as well preserved as the tra-
③⑧ ditional capital of Provence: elegant **Aix-en-Provence**. The Romans were drawn here by the presence of thermal springs; the
name Aix originates from *Aquae Sextiae* (the waters of
Sextius) in honor of the consul who reputedly founded the town
in 122 BC. Twenty years later, a vast army of Germanic barbari-
ans invaded the region but were defeated by General Marius at
a neighboring mountain, known ever since as the Montagne
Sainte-Victoire. Marius remains a popular local first name to
this day.

Aix-en-Provence numbers two of France's most creative geniuses among its sons: Impressionist Paul Cézanne (1839–
1906), many of whose paintings feature the nearby countryside, especially Montagne Sainte-Victoire (though Cézanne
would not recognize it now, after the forest fire that ravaged its
slopes in 1990), and novelist Emile Zola (1840–1902), who, in

several of his works, described Aix (as "Plassans") and his boyhood friendship with Cézanne.

The celebrated **cours Mirabeau,** flanked by intertwining plane trees, is the town's nerve center, a gracious, lively avenue with the feel of a toned-down, intimate Champs-Elysées. It divides old Aix into two, with narrow medieval streets to the north and sophisticated, haughty 18th-century mansions to the south. Begin your visit at the west end of cours Mirabeau (the tourist office is close by at 2 place de la Libération). Halfway down is the **Fontaine des Neuf Canons** (Fountain of the Nine Cannons), dating from 1691, and farther along is the **Fontaine d'Eau Thermale** (Thermal Water), built in 1734.

Any route through the quaint pedestrian streets of the old town, north of cours Mirabeau, is rewarding. Wend your way up to the **Cathédrale St-Sauveur.** Its mishmash of styles lacks harmony, and the interior feels gloomy and dilapidated, but you may want to inspect the remarkable 15th-century triptych by Nicolas Froment, entitled *Tryptique du Buisson Ardent (Burning Bush),* depicting King René (duke of Anjou, Count of Provence, and titular king of Sicily) and Queen Joan kneeling beside the Virgin. Ask the sacristan to spotlight it for you (he'll expect a tip) and to remove the protective shutters from the ornate 16th-century carvings on the cathedral portals. Afterward, wander into the tranquil Romanesque cloisters next door to admire the carved pillars and slender colonnades.

The adjacent Archbishop's Palace is home to the **Musée des Tapisseries** (Tapestry Museum). Its highlight is a magnificent suite of 17 tapestries made in Beauvais that date, like the palace itself, from the 17th and 18th centuries. Nine woven panels illustrate the adventures of the bumbling Don Quixote. *28 pl. des Martyrs de la Résistance. Admission: 20 frs. Open Wed.–Mon. 9:30–noon and 2–6, Tues. 2–6.*

Return past the cathedral and take rue de la Roque up to the broad, leafy boulevard that encircles Old Aix. Head up avenue Pasteur, opposite, then turn right into avenue Paul-Cézanne, which leads to the **Musée-Atelier de Paul Cézanne** (Cézanne's studio). Cézanne's pioneering work, with its interest in angular forms, paved the way for the Cubist style of the early 20th century. No major pictures are on display here, but his studio remains as he left it at the time of his death in 1906, scattered with the great man's pipe, clothing, and other personal possessions, many of which he painted in his still lifes. *19 av. Paul-Cézanne. Admission: 10 frs. adults, 5 frs. senior citizens and children. Open Wed.–Mon. 10–noon and 2:30–6; closed Tues.*

Time Out   Good addresses for picnic provisions are the **Olivier** *charcuterie* (rue Jacques-de-la-Roque near the cathedral) and the **Brémond** *patisserie* (36 cours Mirabeau, on the corner of rue du Quatre-Septembre).

Make your way back to cours Mirabeau and cross into the southern half of Aix. The streets here are straight and rationally planned, flanked by symmetrical mansions imbued with classical elegance. Rue du Quatre-Septembre, three-quarters of the way down cours Mirabeau, leads to the splendid **Fontaine des Quatre Dauphins,** where sculpted dolphins play in a fountain erected in 1667. Turn left along rue Cardinale to the **Musée Granet,** named after another of Aix's artistic sons: François

Granet (1775–1849), whose works are good examples of the formal, at times sentimental, style of art popular during the first half of the 19th century. Granet's paintings show none of the fervor of Cézanne, who is represented here with several oils and watercolors. An impressive collection of European paintings from the 16th to the 19th century, plus archaeological finds from Egypt, Greece, and the Roman Empire, complete the museum's collections. *13 rue Cardinale. Admission: 12 frs. Open Apr.–Oct., Wed.–Mon. 10–noon and 2–6; Nov.–Mar., Wed.–Mon. 2–6; closed Tues.*

The quickest, most effective route by car between Aix and Marseille is the toll-free A51 expressway, provided you avoid the heavy morning and evening rush-hour traffic.

39 **Marseille** is not crowded with tourist goodies, nor is its reputation as a big dirty city entirely unjustified, but it still has more going for it than many realize: a craggy mountain hinterland that provides a spectacular backdrop, superb coastal views of nearby islands, and the sights and smells of a Mediterranean melting pot where different peoples have mingled for centuries—ever since the Phocaean Greeks invaded around 600 BC. The most recent immigrants come from North Africa.

Numbers in the margin correspond with points of interest on the Marseille map.

Marseille is the Mediterranean's largest port. The sizable, ugly industrial docks virtually rub shoulders with the intimate, pic-
40 turesque old harbor, the **Vieux Port,** packed with fishing boats and pleasure craft: This is the heart of Marseille, with the Canebière avenue leading down to the water's edge.

Pick up your leaflets and town plan at the tourist office (4 La Canebière) and peruse them on a café terrace overlooking the Vieux Port. Until the mid-19th century, this was the center of maritime activity in Marseille. These days, a forest of yacht and fishing-boat masts creates an impression of colorful bustle. Restaurants line the quays, and fishwives spout incomprehensible Provençal insults as they serve gleaming fresh sardines each morning. The Marseillais can be an irascible lot: Louis XIV built the Fort St-Nicolas, at the entry of the Vieux Port, with the guns facing inland to keep the citizens in order.

A short way down the right quay (as you look out to sea) is the elegant 17th-century Hôtel de Ville (Town Hall). Just behind, in rue de la Prison, is the Maison Diamantée, a 16th-century mansion with an elaborate interior staircase. The mansion now houses the **Musée de Vieux Marseille,** whose displays of costumes, pictures, and figurines depict old Marseille. *Rue de la Prison. Admission: 10 frs. adults, 5 frs. students and senior citizens, children free. Open daily 10–5.*

41 Marseille's pompous, striped neo-Byzantine **cathedral** stands around the corner, but it is of considerably less interest than
42 the **Basilique St-Victor** across the water, in the shadow of the
43 **Fort St-Nicolas** (which can't be visited). With its powerful tower and thick-set walls, the basilica resembles a fortress and boasts one of southern France's oldest doorways (circa 1140), a 13th-century nave, and a 14th-century chancel and transept. Downstairs, you'll find the murky 5th-century underground crypt, with its collection of ancient sarcophagi. *Rue Sainte.*

Basilique St-Victor, **42**
Cathedral, **41**
Château d'If, **47**
Fort St-Nicholas, **43**
Musée des
Beaux-Arts, **46**
Musée de la
Marine, **45**
Beaux-Arts, **46**
Notre-Dame de la
Garde, **44**
Vieux Port, **40**

Marseille

Time Out Just up the street from the basilica is the **Four des Navettes**—a bakery that has been producing slender, orange-spiced, shuttle-shaped *navette* loaves for over 200 years. Since the navettes can last for up to a year, they make good take-home presents as well as on-the-spot snacks. *136 rue Sainte.*

A brisk half-mile walk up boulevard Tellène, followed by a trudge up a steep flight of steps, will bring you to the foot of **Notre-Dame de la Garde.** This church, a flashy 19th-century cousin of the Sacré-Coeur in Paris and Fourvière in Lyon, features a similar hilltop location. The expansive view, clearest in early morning (especially if the mistral is blowing), stretches from the hinterland mountains to the sea via the Cité Radieuse, a controversial '50s housing project by Swiss-born architect Le Corbusier. The church's interior is generously endowed with bombastic murals, mosaics, and marble, while, at the top of the tower, the great gilded statue of the Virgin stands sentinel over the old port, 500 feet below. *Blvd. A. Aune.*

Return to the Vieux Port and venture along the legendary **La Canebière**—the "Can O' Beer" to prewar sailors—where stately mansions recall faded glory. La Canebière has been on the decline in recent years, but cafés and restaurants continue to provide an upbeat pulse. A hundred yards down on the left is the big white Palais de la Bourse (stock exchange) and, inside, the **Musée de la Marine** (Nautical Museum), with a rundown on the history of the port and an interesting display of model ships. *Admission: 10 frs. Open Wed.–Mon. 9–noon and 2–6.*

Behind the bourse is the **Jardin des Vestiges,** a public garden that holds the remains of Roman foundations. Here you will find the little **Musée de l'Histoire de Marseille** (Town Museum), featuring exhibits related to the town's history. One of the highlights is the 60-foot Roman boat. *Cours Belsunce. Admission: 10 frs. adults, 5 frs. senior citizens and children. Open Tues.–Sat. 10–4:45.*

Continue past such busy shopping streets as rue Paradis, rue St-Ferréol, and rue de Rome, and turn right into boulevard Garibaldi to reach **cours Julien,** a traffic-free street lined with sidewalk cafés, restaurants, bookshops, and boutiques. The atmosphere is that of a scaled-down St-Germain-des-Prés wafted from Paris to the Mediterranean.

Return to La Canebière and, when you reach the undistinguished church of St-Vincent de Paul, fork left along cours Jeanne-Thierry (which becomes boulevard Longchamp) to the imposing **Palais Longchamp,** built in 1860 by the same architect who built Notre-Dame de la Garde, Henri Espérandieu (1829–74). The palais is home to the **Musée des Beaux-Arts** (Fine Arts Museum); its collection of paintings and sculptures includes works by 18th-century Italian artist Giovanni Battista Tiepolo, Rubens, and French caricaturist and painter Honoré Daumier. *Admission: 10 frs. adults, 5 frs. students and senior citizens. Open daily 10–5.*

Marseille is no seaside resort, but a scenic 5-kilometer (3-mile) coast road (Corniche du Président J. F. Kennedy) links the Vieux-Port to the newly created Prado beaches in the swanky parts of southern Marseille. There are breathtaking views across the sea toward the rocky Frioul Islands, which can be visited by boat. Ninety-minute trips leave the Vieux-Port hourly in summer and frequently in winter to visit the **Château d'If,** a castle in which various political prisoners were held captive down the ages. Alexandre Dumas condemned his fictional hero, the count of Monte Cristo, to be shut up in a cell here, before the wily count made his celebrated escape through a hole in the wall. *Admission included in the boat fare (35 frs.). Open June–Sept., daily 8:30–noon and 1:30–6:30; Oct.–May, daily 8:30–noon and 1:30–4.*

Numbers in the margin correspond with points of interest on the Provence map.

Head east from Marseille along D2 to **Aubagne,** 16 kilometers (10 miles) away. The headquarters of the French Foreign Legion is situated along D44A (turn left off D2 just before you reach Aubagne). The legion was created in 1831 and accepts recruits from all nations, no questions asked. The discipline and camaraderie instilled among its motley team of adventurers, criminals, and mercenaries has helped the legion forge a reputation for exceptional valor—a reputation romanticized by songs and films in which sweaty deeds of heroism are performed under the desert sun. The **Musée du Képi Blanc,** named after the *légionnaires'* distinctive white caps, does its best to polish the image by way of medals, uniforms, weapons, and photographs. *Caserne Viénot. Admission: free. Open June–Sept., Tues.–Sun. 9–noon and 2–5; Oct.–May, Wed. and weekends only, 9–noon.*

Head south from Aubagne via D559/D1 to the fishing village of **Cassis,** 11 kilometers (7 miles) away. Cafés, restaurants, and seafood shops cluster around its harbor and three beaches, at the foot of Europe's highest cliff, the 1,300-foot Cap Canaille. Boats leave the harbor from quai St-Pierre to visit the neighboring *calanques*—long creeks that weave their way between towering white-stone cliffs. The farthest of the hree *calanques* visited by boat, **En-Vau**, is the most intimidating; you may want to walk back from here along the scenic footpath.

From Cassis, a daring clifftop road runs along the top of Cap Canaille to the shipbuilding base of La Ciotat, 13 kilometers (8 miles) away. Stay on D559 for another 19 kilometers (12 miles), **⑩** through Bandol, to **Sanary**, whose old streets and charming seafront invite discovery. At neighboring Six-Fours-les-Plages, spin right on D616, around the Cap Sicié peninsula, in search of more fine panoramas and a colossal view across the Bay of Toulon.

⑪ **Toulon** is France's leading Mediterranean naval base. Leave your car in the underground parking lot at place de la Liberté, head along boulevard de Strasbourg, and turn right after the theater into rue Berthelot. This street leads into the pedestrian streets that constitute the heart of old Toulon. Shops and colorful stalls make it an attractive area by day, but avoid it at night.

Time Out   Good-value menus and a cozy setting make **La Ferme**, situated on a small square at the harbor end of cours Lafayette, a sensible choice for a filling lunch. *6 pl. Louis-Blanc. Closed Sun. and Aug.*

Avenue de la République, an ugly array of concrete apartment blocks, runs parallel to the waterfront, where yachts and pleasure boats—some available for trips to the Iles d'Hyères or around the bay—add bright splashes of color. At the western edge of the quay is the **Musée Naval**, with large models of old and new ships, figureheads, paintings, and other items related to Toulon's maritime history. *Pl. Monsenergue. Admission: 20 frs. adults, 10 frs. children. Open Wed.–Mon. 9–noon and 2–5; closed Tues.*

Leading up from the quayside is the Cours Lafayette; on weekdays it turns into a colorful street market selling glistening fish and masses of fruit.

Mighty hills surround Toulon. **Mont-Faron,** towering 1,600 feet above sea level, is the highest of all; its steep slopes veer up just outside the town. You can drive to the top, taking the circular route du Faron in either direction, or make the six-minute ascent by cable car from boulevard de l'Amiral Jean-Vence (operates 9:15–noon and 2:15–6, closed Mon., Sept.–May; call 94–92–68–25 to check operating times in winter or bad weather).

⑫   Head east from Toulon along D559 to Hyères-Plage, then turn right along D97 to **La Tour-Fondue** at the tip of the narrow Giens peninsula. Boats leave here frequently (every half hour in July and August) for the nearby island of Porquerolles. *Crossing time 20 min.; round-trip fare 60 frs.*

⑬   At five miles long, **Ile de Porquerolles** is the largest of the Iles d'Hyères, an archipelago spanning some 20 miles. Although the village of Porquerolles has several small hotels and restaurants, the main reason for coming here is simply to escape from the hustle of the modern world. Filmmakers love the island and use it as a handy base for shooting tropical or South Sea Island-type scenery. You can stroll across the island from the harbor to the lighthouse *(le phare)* in about 90 minutes, or head east among luxuriant flowers and thick woods.

Boats for two of the other islands in the archipelago leave from Hyères-Plages and, farther around the coast, from Port-de-Miramar and Le Lavandou. The smaller of the two, **Ile de Port-Cros,** is classed as a national park and offers delightful, well-marked nature trails. The **Ile du Levant** is long and rocky, and much less interesting; the French navy has grabbed part of it, and much of the rest is occupied by the Heliopolis nudist camp.

What to See and Do with Children

The Wild West has invaded Provence at the **O.K. Corral,** a huge amusement park that piles on the thrills by way of roller coasters, Ferris wheels, and rootin' tootin' cowboy shows. Roy Rogers might do a double take at the less-than-authentic flavor—more Gallic than "Gunsmoke"—but children love it nonetheless. *11 km (7 mi) west of Aubagne on N8, just beyond Cuges-les-Pins, tel. 42–73–80–05. Admission: 60 frs. adults, 45 frs. children. Open June, daily 10:30–6:30; July–Aug., daily 10:30–7:30; Apr.–May and Sept., weekends 10:30–6:30; Mar. and Oct., Sun. 10:30–6:30.*

Just outside Stes-Maires-de-la-Mer is the **Musée de Cire** (also known as the **Musée du Boumian**), which provides an entertaining overview of local life by way of 18 scenes composed of wax-work figures. *Quartier Boumian. Admission: 16 frs. Open Apr.–Oct., daily 10–noon and 2–7.*

The following attractions are covered in the Exploring text:
Boat tour of the calanques by Cassis, *see* Tour 3
Cathédrale d'Images, near Les Baux-de-Provence, *see* Tour 1
Moulin de Daudet, Fontvieille, *see* Tour 1
Museon Arlaten, Arles, *see* Tour 1
Parc Ornithologique, north of Stes-Maries-de-la-Mer, *see* Tour 1
Children might also enjoy the raucous flavor of the Marseille fish market, *see* Tour 3 (also, *see* Shopping, below).

Off the Beaten Track

Our exploring tour bypasses Six-Fours-les-Plages on its way from the pretty harbor of Sanary to the dramatic Cap Scié peninsula. While Six-Fours is a sprawling town of limited interest, three nearby sites deserve a visit. The first is at Six-Fours itself, or, really, above it. The **Fort of Six-Fours,** at the top of a steep hill that has seemed even more rugged since fire destroyed its pine forest in 1987, can be seen for miles around. Although the fort is a private military base that can't be visited, the views across the Bay of Toulon are stupendous. Nearby is the former parish church of **St-Pierre,** featuring a Romanesque nave and a rich medieval altarpiece by Louis Bréa. Archaeological finds to the right of the entrance have revealed Roman walls built on the site.

Just north of Six-Fours (take D63 and turn left following signs marked *Monument Historique)* is the small stone chapel of **Notre-Dame de Pépiole,** hemmed in by pines and cypresses. While the chapel doesn't seem particularly interesting from a distance, it is, in fact, one of the oldest Christian buildings in France, dating from the 5th century. The simple interior has survived the years in remarkably good shape, although the colorful stained glass that fills the tiny windows is modern—composed mainly of broken bottles! *Chapel open most afternoons.*

Continue 5 kilometers (3 miles) north (via D11) to Ollioules and take N8 (direction Le Beausset) through the spectacular **Gorge d'Ollioules;** the 3-mile route twists its scenic way beneath awesome chalky rock faces. Turn right along D462 to pay a visit to the village of **Evenos,** a patchwork of inhabited and ruined houses dominated by an abandoned clifftop castle.

Shopping

Gift Ideas
Santons, colorful painted clay figures traditionally placed around a Christmas crib, make excellent gifts or souvenirs. There are literally hundreds of characters from which to choose, ranging from Mary, Joseph, and the Wise Men to fictional characters and notable personalities, both historic and contemporary. While santons can be found throughout the region (especially at Aubagne), the best places to purchase them are **Paul Fouque** (65 cours Gambetta, Aix-en-Provence) or **Atelier Ferriol** (2 chemin de Barriol, Arles).

Two specialties of Aix-en-Provence are deliciously fragrant soaps with natural floral scents and *calissons d'Aix*, ingeniously sculpted high-quality marzipan made of almonds and eggs. At **La Provence Gourmande** (66 rue Boulagon) you'll find a vast selection of soaps, as well as herbs, spices, and calissons d'Aix, while **À La Reine Jeanne** (32 cours Mirabeau) specializes in marzipan. Delicately patterned Provençal print fabrics made by Souleiado are beautiful and can be bought in lengths or already fashioned into dresses, scarves, tea cosies, and other accessories. You can find the prints in better-quality shops throughout the region, though Arles and Aix-en-Provence seem to have cornered most of the market.

Markets
Aix-en-Provence has several markets that are a delight to explore: the flower market on Tuesday, Thursday, and Saturday mornings at place de l'Hôtel-de-Ville; the fruit and vegetable market every morning at place Richelme; and the fruit, vegetable, and herb market on Tuesday, Thursday, and Saturday mornings at place des Prêcheurs. There is also an antiques market on Tuesday, Thursday, and Saturday mornings at place de Verdun. At **Arles,** fruit, vegetables, and household goods are sold on Wednesday and Saturday mornings in the boulevard de Lices, while **Marseille's** famous fish market is held on Monday through Saturday mornings at the Vieux Port. The flower market at **Nîmes** is open Monday mornings at boulevard J-Jaurès, and you can purchase fruit, herbs, honey, and truffles at **Orange** on Thursday mornings in cours Aristide-Briand. Finally, in **Toulon,** there's a celebrated fish, fruit, and household-goods market from Monday to Saturday mornings on rue LaFayette near the harbor.

Sports and Fitness

Biking
Bikes can be rented from train stations at Aix-en-Provence, Arles, Avignon, Marseille, Montpellier, Nîmes, and Orange; the cost is about 40 francs per day. Contact the **Comité**

Départemental de Federation Française de Cyclo (2 rue La-voisier, Avignon) for a list of the area's more scenic bike paths.

Bullfighting Provence's most popular spectator sport is bullfighting, both Spanish-style or the kinder *courses libres*, where the bulls have star billing and are often regarded as local heroes (they always live to fight another day). There are Spanish-style spectacles in the Roman arenas at Rond-Point des Arènes in **Arles** and at place des Arènes in **Nîmes.** Courses libres are also held at Nîmes, and in nearly all the surrounding little villages throughout the summer.

Golf Golf is still considered a pastime for the rich, and you will find many more golf courses on the Riviera. However, Provence has an excellent course at La Grande Motte (tel. 67–56–05–00) and another near Aix-en-Provence (**Golf International du Château de l'Arc,** Rousset, tel. 42–53–28–38). Eighteen kilometers (11 miles) east of Hyères is **Golf de Valcros** (Valcros, La Londe, tel. 94–66–81–02).

Hiking This has become newly popular in France, and you'll find blazed trails (discreet paint marks on rocks) on the best routes. Contact the **Comité Départemental** (63 av. C-Franck, Avignon) for a detailed list of trails and outfitters.

Horseback Riding Practically every locality in Provence has stables where horses can be rented. **Cheval Nomade** (col du Pointu, Bonnieux, tel. 90–74–40–48) specializes in tours on horseback (also, *see* Guided Tours under Essential Information, above). In Avignon, **Barthelasse** (Chemin du Mont Blanc, tel. 90–85–83–48) offers lessons for children at **Le Pony Club,** a children's riding school, in addition to renting horses to more experienced equestrians.

Water Sports You can windsurf and sail at La Grande Motte, Stes-Maries-de-la-Mer, Carry-le Rouet and Martigues (near Marseille), Cassis, Hyères-Plage, and the island of Porquerolles, where equipment and sailboats can be rented. In Hyères, the **Wanako School of Windsurf and Sunboards** (5 Centre de Nautisme, tel. 94–57–77–20) rents sailboats from 300 francs for the day, while a windsurfer costs from 320 francs.

Dining and Lodging

Dining

Provence has more than its share of France's top restaurants. Thank tourism for this: Nature didn't intend Provence to be a gastronomic paradise. There are no deep, damp pastures for cattle and no chill rivers for salmon. In the old days, cooking was based on olive oil, fruit, and vegetables grown in valleys where summer irrigation is possible; salt cod was another staple, while the heady scent and flavor of garlic and wild herbs from stony, sun-baked hills improved the scant meat dishes. The current gastronomic scene is a far cry from this frugality: Wealthy tourists demand caviar and champagne, and Parisian chefs have created internationally renowned restaurants to satisfy them. Still, there's a lot to be said for simple Provençal food on a vine-shaded terrace. Have a *pastis*, that pale green, anise-based aperitif, accompanied by black olives, or try the *tapenade*, a delicious paste of capers, anchovies, olives, oil, and lemon juice, best smeared on chunks of garlic-rubbed bread. Follow it up with *crudités* (raw vegetables served with *aïoli*, a garlicky mayonnaise), and a simple dish of grilled lamb or beef, accompanied by a bottle of chilled rosé. Locals like to end their meal with a round of goat cheese and fruit.

The Provençal image comes through in a love of color; bell peppers, eggplant, zucchini, saffron, and tomatoes crop up everywhere. Fish is very trendy these days. A trip to the fish market at Marseille will reveal the astronomical price of the fresh local catch; in the Mediterranean there are too few fish chased by too many boats. Steer clear of the multitude of cheap Marseille fish restaurants, many with brisk ladies out front who deliver throaty sales pitches; any inexpensive fish menu must use frozen imports. The Marseille specialty of *bouillabaisse* is a case in point: Once a fisherman's cheap stew of spanking-fresh specimens too small or bony to put on sale, it has now become a celebration dish, with such heretical additions as lobster. The high-priced versions can be delicious, but avoid the cheaper ones, undoubtedly concocted with canned, frozen, and even powdered ingredients.

Highly recommended restaurants are indicated by a star ★.

Category	Cost*
Very Expensive	over 350 francs
Expensive	200–350 francs
Moderate	100–200 francs
Inexpensive	under 100 francs

*per person for a three-course meal, including tax (18.6%) and tip but not wine

Lodging

Accommodations are varied in this much-visited part of France, ranging from luxurious *mas* (converted farmhouses) to modest downtown hotels convenient for sightseeing. Service is often less than prompt, a casualty of the sweltering summer heat. Reservations are essential for much of the year, and many hotels are closed during winter.

Highly recommended hotels are indicated by a star ★.

Category	Cost*
Very Expensive	over 750 france
Expensive	350–750 francs
Moderate	200–350 francs
Inexpensive	under 200 francs

*All prices are for a standard double room for two, including tax (18.6%) and service charge.

Aix-en-Provence
Dining
★

Le Clos de la Violette. Aix's best restaurant lies in a residential district north of the old town. You can eat under the chestnut trees or in the charming, airy dining room. Chef Jean-Marc Banzo uses only fresh, local ingredients in his nouvelle and traditional recipes. Try the *saumon vapeur,* an aromatic steamed salmon. The weekday lunch menu is moderately priced and well worth the trek uptown. *10 av. de la Violette, tel. 42–23–30–71. Reservations advised. Jacket required. AE, MC, V. Closed Sun., Mon. lunch, most of Nov., and late Feb.–early Mar. Expensive.*

Brasserie Royale. This noisy, bustling eatery on cours Mirabeau serves up hearty Provençal dishes amid a background din of banging pots, vociferous waiters, and tumultuous cries for more wine. The best place to eat is in the glassed-in patio out front, so you can soak up the Champs-Elysées-style atmosphere of the leafy boulevard while enjoying your meal. *17 cours Mirabeau, tel. 42–26–01–63. Reservations advised. Dress: casual. AE, V. Inexpensive.*

Lodging
★
Mercure-Paul Cézanne. Georges Delorme runs this stately town-house hotel, and his taste for antiques and ornate furnishings has made it a civilized and sophisticated place. Each guest room is individually decorated with lots of marble, gilt, and period furniture. There's no restaurant. *40 av. Victor-Hugo, 13100, tel. 42–26–34–73. 56 rooms with bath. AE, MC, V. Expensive.*

Nègre-Coste. A cours Mirabeau location makes this hotel both a convenient and an atmospheric choice; it's extremely popular, so make reservations long in advance. The elegant 18th-century town house has been completely modernized but features a luxurious Old World decor that extends to the guest rooms as well as the public areas. The views from the front rooms are worth the extra bit of noise. There's no restaurant. *33 cours Mirabeau, 13100, tel. 42–27–74–22. 37 rooms with bath. AE, DC, MC, V. Moderate–Expensive.*

Anduze
Dining and Lodging
Les Demeures du Ranquet. A hilly, wooded setting, an outdoor pool, a piano bar, and 10 stylish, spacious, air-conditioned rooms justify the 32-kilometer (20-mile) detour to Les Demeures du Ranquet, northwest of Nîmes. Annie Majourel is one of France's few top-ranking female chefs; her menus (two are moderately priced) change every two months. *Rte. de St-Hippolyte du Fort, Tornac, 30140 Anduze, tel. 66–77–51–63. 10 rooms with bath. Facilities: restaurant, piano bar, pool. AE, DC, MC, V. Closed Tues. and Wed. out of season; mid-Nov.–Christmas; Feb.–mid-Mar. Expensive.*

Arles
Dining
Le Vaccarès. In an upstairs restaurant overlooking place du Forum, chef Bernard Dumas serves classical Provençal dishes with a touch of invention and some particularly good fish creations. Try his mussels dressed in herbs and garlic. The dining-room decor is as elegant as the cuisine. *Pl. du Forum, tel. 90–96–06–17. Reservations advised. Dress: casual. MC, V. Closed end of Dec.–end of Jan., Sun. dinner, and Mon. Moderate–Expensive.*

Lodging
Arlatan. Follow the signposts from place du Forum to the picturesque street holding this 15th-century house, former home of the counts of Arlatan and built on the site of a 4th-century basilica (tiled flooring dating from this period is visible below glass casing). The hotel was renovated in 1989, and antiques, pretty fabrics, and lots of tapestries and elegant furniture lend it a gracious atmosphere. There's no restaurant, but there's an attractive garden and a private bar. *26 rue du Sauvage, 13200, tel. 90–93–56–66. 51 rooms with bath. Facilities: garden. AE, DC, MC, V. Expensive.*

Dining and Lodging
★

Jules César. This elegant hotel was originally a Carmelite convent, and many guest rooms overlook the attractive 17th-century cloisters. Rooms are tastefully decorated with antiques, and the garden is an oasis of tranquillity. The restaurant, Lou Marquès, is the most fashionable eating place in Arles, thanks to new chef Pascal Renaud, who pleases his international clientele with nouvelle cuisine and traditional Provençal dishes. Try his cod with lentils and fresh cream. *Blvd. des Lices, 13200, tel. 90–93–43–20. 55 rooms with bath. Facilities: restaurant, garden, pool. AE, DC, MC, V. Closed Nov.–Dec. 23. Expensive.*

★

Mas de la Chapelle. A 16th-century farmhouse surrounded by pretty gardens and outbuildings is the setting of this fine hotel-restaurant, reader-recommended for an overnight stay or to use as a base from which to explore the area. It features an ancient chapel that has been skillfully converted into a cozy–though sometimes stifling–restaurant, decorated with Aubusson tapestries and original 18th-century stained glass. The menu varies; the seasonal game dishes are a good bet, or try the *coquilles St.-Jacques.* There is one slight drawback, however: the nearby whoosh of high-speed trains. *Petite Route de Tarascon, 13200, tel. 90–93–23–15. 13 rooms with bath. Facilities: restaurant, riding, tennis, pool, park. AE, DC, MC, V. Moderate–Expensive.*

Avignon
Dining
★

Hiély-Lucullus. According to most authorities, this establishment numbers among the top-50 restaurants in France. The upstairs dining room has a quiet, dignified charm and is run with aplomb by Madame Hiély. Husband Pierre's greater delights include crayfish tails in scrambled eggs hidden inside a puff-pastry case. Save room for the extensive cheese board. *5 rue de la République, tel. 90–86–17–07. Reservations required. Dress: neat but casual. AE, V. Closed most of Jan., last 2 weeks in June, Mon. (except July–mid-Aug.) and Tues. Moderate–Expensive.*

Dining and Lodging

Europe. This noble 16th-century town house became a hotel in Napoleonic times. In fact, the great man himself was one of the very first customers; since then, everyone from crowned heads of state to Robert and Elizabeth Browning has stayed here. Lovers of gracious living find it an excellent value; the guest rooms are spacious, filled with period furniture, and feature lavishly appointed modern bathrooms. Make reservations well ahead. The restaurant, La Vieille Fontaine, features respectable regional cuisine, and you can eat outside in the stone courtyard. Gourmands will want to try the chicken with wild mushrooms or the duck liver. *12 pl. Crillon, 84000, tel. 90–82–66–92. 50 rooms with bath. Facilities: restaurant. AE, DC, MC, V. Expensive.*

★

Les Frênes. The thumbnail-size town of Montfavet, 5 kilometers (3 miles) outside Avignon, is the setting for this luxurious hotel-restaurant. The country house features gardens to ramble in, splashing fountains, and individually decorated guest rooms; style ranges from subtle modern to art deco. Whatever the period of decor, each room is distinctive and equipped with every modern convenience. The excellent restaurant specializes in stylish country cuisine; the pigeon with black truffles in a puff-pastry case is always a good bet. *645 av. Vertes Rives, 84000 Montfavet, tel. 90–31–17–93. 25 rooms with bath. Facilities: garden, pool, restaurant, tennis, sauna, golf. AE, DC, MC, V. Closed end of Dec.–early Mar. Expensive.*

Les Baux-de-Provence
Dining and Lodging
★

L'Oustaù de Baumanière. An idyllic setting under chalky-white cliffs, sumptuous guest rooms, and exquisite food make this a place of pilgrimage for lovers of the good life. The top-ranking restaurant occupies an old Provençal farmhouse; you'll be served your meal in a cavernous room decked out with ornate furniture and resembling a luxurious crypt. Try a plump pigeon stuffed with foie gras or some simple local thyme-fed lamb. The guest rooms are fit for a monarch—Queen Elizabeth II has slept here. *13520 Les Baux-de-Provence, tel. 90–54–33–07. 25 rooms with bath. Facilities: restaurant, tennis, pool, riding. Restaurant reservations required. AE, DC, MC, V. Closed late Jan.–early Mar.; restaurant closed Wed., Thurs. lunch Sept.–June. Very Expensive.*

Gordes
Dining
★

Comptour du Victuailler. You'll find only 10 tables at this tiny restaurant in the village center, which serves elegantly simple meals using only the freshest local ingredients: capon, guinea fowl, asparagus, artichokes, truffles . . . The fruit sorbets are a revelation, and there is an admirable choice of little-known Rhône wines. *Place du Château, tel. 90–72–01–31. Reservations required. Dress: neat but casual. AE, DC, MC, V. Closed mid-Nov.–mid-Dec., mid-Jan.–mid-Mar., and Tues. and Wed. Sept.–May. Moderate–Expensive.*

Dining and Lodging
★

Domaine de l'Enclos. Small, private stone cottages make up this charming hotel just outside Gordes; they have deceptively simple exteriors, but inside you'll find them luxurious in a quaint, countrified way. The restaurant serves remarkably good nouvelle dishes; the menu varies with the seasons, but if it's offered, try the excellent aromatic duck. *Rte. de Sénanque, 84220 Gordes, tel. 90–72–08–22. 14 rooms with bath. Facilities: restaurant, pool, tennis. AE, MC, V. Very Expensive.*

Ile de Porquerolles
Dining and Lodging
★

Mas du Langoustier. This luxurious hideout lies amid some stunningly lush terrain at the westernmost point of the island, 3 kilometers (2 miles) from the harbor. Anchor your yacht, and Madame Le Ber will pick you up in a handy launch; arrive by ferry, and she'll send a car to meet you. The rooms are delightful, the views superb. Hotel guests must eat their meals here (no hardship), but the restaurant is open to nonresidents, too. Chef Jean-Louis Vosgien uses a delicate nouvelle touch with his seafood dishes; try the fresh sardines in ginger, or the grilled red mullet or lobster. *83400 Ile de Porquerolles, tel. 94–58–30–09. 60 rooms with bath. Facilities: restaurant, tennis, private beach. AE, DC, MC, V. Closed mid-Nov.–mid-Mar. Expensive.*

Marseille
Dining
★

Chez Fonfon. The Marseillais come here for the best bouillabaisse in the world, and past diners lured by the top-quality seafood have included John Wayne and Nikita Khrushchev. "Fonfon" is the chef, sometimes known as Alphonse Mounier; he's thinking of retiring, but a successor is being trained to his rigorous standards. The restaurant is located on the corniche J. F. Kennedy, which twists its scenic path around the edges of the Mediterranean; the great sea views come gratis. *140 Vallon des Auffes, tel. 91–52–14–38. Reservations strongly advised. Jacket and tie required. AE, DC, MC, V. Closed Oct., Christmas–New Year's, Sat. and Sun. Expensive.*

Chez Madie. Every morning Madie Minassian, the colorful *patronne*, bustles along the quayside to trade insults with the fishwives at the far end of the Vieux Port—and scour their catch for the freshest ingredients, which swiftly end up in her bouillabaisse, fish soup, *favouilles* sauce (made from tiny local crabs), and other dishes you'll savor from the good-value menus at her restaurant. *138 quai du Port, tel. 91–90–40–87. Reservations advised. Dress: casual. AE, DC, MC, V. Closed Mon., Sun. dinner, and most of Aug. Moderate.*

Dar Djerba. This is perhaps the best of the North African restaurants that are scattered throughout Marseille. The cozy, white-walled Dar Djerba on bustling Cours Julien specializes in couscous of all kinds (with lamb, chicken or even quail) as well as in Arab coffees and pastries. The Moorish tile patterns and exotic aromas will waft you away on a Saharan breeze. *15 cours Julien, tel. 91–48–55–36. Reservations advised in summer. Dress: casual. DC, MC, V. Closed Tues. Moderate.*

Dining and Lodging
★ **Sofitel.** The Sofitel possesses more appeal than most modern chain hotels, mainly because of the idyllic views across the old fort to the Vieux Port. Rooms with a balcony are more expensive, but the pleasure of an outdoor breakfast in the morning sunshine—possible most of the year—is worth a splurge. The top-floor restaurant, Les Trois Forts, boasts stunning panoramic views and delicious Provençal fare; the red mullet, flavored with pepper, is superb. *36 blvd. Charles-Livon, 13007, tel. 91–52–90–19. 127 rooms with bath. Facilities: pool, restaurant. AE, DC, MC, V. Expensive.*

Lodging
★ **Pullman Beauvau.** Right on the Vieux Port, a few steps from the end of the Canebière, the Beauvau is the ideal town hotel. The 200-year-old former coaching inn was totally modernized in 1986, and its charming, Old World opulence is enhanced by wood paneling, designer fabrics, fine paintings, genuine antique furniture—and exceptional service. The best rooms look out onto the Vieux Port. There's no restaurant, but you can start your day in the cozy breakfast room. *4 rue Beauvau, 13001, tel. 91–54–91–00 (to make reservations toll-free from the U.S. call 800/223–9868; in the U.K., 071/621–1962). 71 rooms with bath. Facilities: bar, breakfast room. AE, DC, MC, V. Expensive.*

Lutétia. There's nothing remarkable about this small hotel, but its rooms are quiet, airy, modernized, and a good value for the money, given the handy setting between La Canebière and St-Charles rail station. *38 allée Léon-Gambetta, 13001, tel. 91–50–81–78. 29 rooms with bath or shower. DC, MC, V. Moderate.*

Montpellier
Dining
Le Chandelier. The only complaints here concern the prices à la carte; service is impeccable, the trendy pink decor is more than acceptable, and the inventive cuisine is delicious. Try the lobster in lasagne or the pigeon. There's a sound wine list, and the cinnamon-honey ice cream makes a fine end to your meal. *3 rue Leenhardt, tel. 67–92–61–62. Reservations advised. Dress: casual. AE, DC, MC, V. Closed part of Feb., first 2 weeks Aug., Sun., and Mon. lunch. Moderate–Expensive.*

★ **Hôtel Montpelliérian des Vins du Languedoc.** The local wine producers run this little restaurant, which occupies a stone-vaulted cellar. The food is simple—you can have a plate of mixed charcuterie or just bread and cheese—but the choice of wines to drink with your meal runs the gamut of Languedoc vintages. *7 rue Jacques-Coeur, tel. 67–60–42–41. No reservations. Dress: casual. No credit cards. Closed Sun., Mon. Inexpensive.*

Nîmes
Dining
★

Nicolas. Locals have long known about this homey place, which is always packed; you'll hear the noise before you open the door. A friendly, frazzled staff serves up delicious *bourride* (a garlicky fish soup) and other local specialties—all at unbelievably low prices. *1 rue Poise, tel. 66–67–50–47. Reservations strongly advised. Dress: casual. MC, V. Closed Mon., first 2 weeks July, and mid-Dec.–first week Jan. Inexpensive.*

Dining and Lodging
★

Impérator. This little palace-hotel, just a few minutes' walk from the Jardin de La Fontaine, has been totally modernized in excellent taste. Most guest rooms retain a quaint Provençal feel, and all are cozy but spacious. If this hotel were suddenly whisked to the Riviera, you would expect to pay twice as much for the pleasure of staying here. The fine restaurant, L'Enclos de la Fontaine, is Nîmes's most fashionable eating place, where chef Jean-Michel Nigon provides such inventive dishes as iced, dill-perfumed *langoustine* (crayfish) soup, and calves' liver with blackcurrant sauce and Calvados-soaked apples. The moderately priced set menus are bargains, but you can easily order your way into the expensive level. *Quai de la Fontaine, 30000, tel. 66–21–90–30. 59 rooms with bath. Facilities: restaurant. AE, DC, MC, V. Restaurant closed Sat. lunch. Moderate–Expensive.*

★

Louvre. Occupying a 17th-century house on a leafy square near the Roman arena, the Louvre is the best sort of carefully run provincial hotel. The guest rooms are spacious and have high ceilings, and they manage to retain the feel of a private house; ask for one that faces the courtyard. The restaurant serves well-prepared traditional cuisine. The most tempting dishes are at the moderate level, though the inexpensive menu is a remarkably good deal. Seafood addicts will enjoy the lobster or the mussels in a flaky pastry crust. *2 sq. de la Couronne, 30000, tel. 66–67–22–75. 33 rooms with bath. Facilities: restaurant. AE, DC, MC, V. Moderate.*

Orange
Dining
★

Le Pigraillet. One of Orange's best lunch spots is Le Pigraillet, on the Chemin Colline St-Eutrope at the far end of the gardens. You may want to eat in the garden, but most diners seek shelter from the mistral in the glassed-in terrace. The modern cuisine includes crab ravioli, foie gras in port, and duck breast in the muscat wine of nearby Beaumes-de-Venise. *Colline St-Eutrope, tel. 90–34–44–25. Reservations advised. Jacket required. AE, DC. Closed Dec.–Feb., Sun. dinner, and Mon. Moderate–Expensive.*

Le Bec Fin. While hardly elegant, Le Bec Fin is a perfect example of a small-town restaurant, serving local specialties to tourists and locals alike. Try the rabbit with mustard for a real taste of Provençal cooking at its best. *14 rue Segond-Wéber, tel. 90–34–14–76. Reservations accepted. Dress: casual. No credit cards. Closed Thurs., Fri., and Nov. Inexpensive.*

St-Rémy-de-Provence
Lodging

Château des Alpilles. This lavishly appointed, 19th-century château lords it over a fine park. In its heyday, it counted statesmen and aristocrats among its guests. The crowd these days is almost as sophisticated, and the guest rooms offer the best in classic luxury. Decorators have gone wild with plush carpeting and wood furniture to enhance the elegant ambience. Many rooms are equipped with kitchenettes. *Ancienne route des Grès, 13210 St-Rémy-de-Provence, tel. 90–92–03–33. 15 rooms with bath. AE, DC, MC, V. Facilities: pool, tennis, sauna, gardens. Closed mid-Nov.–mid-Mar. Expensive.*

★ **Château de Roussan.** A manicured 15-acre park makes a lush setting for this 18th-century mansion, a mile outside town on the road to Tarascon. Originally a country retreat for the Roussan family, the château was converted into a hotel just after World War II. Today it seems so well preserved that it's almost spooky. The interior is quiet and gracious and appears virtually unaltered, save for the newly renovated bathrooms. The guest rooms are large and comfortable, and many feature pleasant parkland views. *Rte. de Tarascon, 13210 St-Rémy-de-Provence, tel. 90–92–11–63. 20 rooms with bath. Facilities: restaurant, park. AE, MC, V. Closed mid-Nov.–Jan. Moderate–Expensive.*

The Arts and Nightlife

The Arts

Theater and Music The summer music and drama festivals at Aix-en-Provence, Arles, Avignon, and Orange attract top performers. At Aix, the **International Arts and Music Festival,** with first-class opera, symphonic concerts, and chamber music, flourishes from mid-July to mid-August; its principal venue is the Théâtre de l'Archevêché in the courtyard of the Archbishop's Palace (pl. des Martyrs de la Résistance). At Arles, the **Music and Drama Festival** takes place in July in the Théâtre Antique (rue de la Calade/rue du Cloître). Avignon's prestigious **International Music and Drama Festival,** held during the last three weeks of July, is centered on the Grand Courtyard of the Palais des Papes (pl. du Palais, tel. 90–86–33–84). The **International Opera Festival** in Orange, during the last two weeks of July, takes place in the best-preserved Roman theater in existence, the Théâtre Antique (pl. des Frerès-Mounet).

Opera and concerts are performed throughout the year in Aix-en-Provence's 18th-century Théâtre Municipal (rue de l'Opéra, tel. 42–38–07–39), while Montpellier presents similar spectacles at the 19th-century Théâtre des Treize Vents (pl. de la Comédie, tel. 67–52–77–17).

Nightlife

Provence is a disappointing provincial backwater as far as razzle-dazzle nightlife goes; if you've come to the south of France hoping to paint the place red—keep heading east to the Riviera. Your best bets for clubs and discos are those towns that have a major student population—such as Aix-en-Provence, Marseille, and Montpellier—or the seaside resorts of La Grande Motte and Stes-Maries-de-la-Mer. Most night spots open and close with alarming frequency, but at press time, Marseille's two cabaret-nightclubs were still going strong: **Au Son des Guitares** (18 rue Corneille) and **Cabaret Star** (9 rue Thubaneau). In Montpellier, we suggest **Le Rimmel** (4 bis rue de Baussairolles); in La Grande Motte, **Copacabana** (Grand Travers, rte. des Plages). Aix has a noteworthy jazz club, **Scat Club** (11 rue de la Verrerie), while one of Marseille's more exciting dance venues is the **Roll's Club** (76 corniche J. F. Kennedy). Finally, for those who thrive on roulette and blackjack, go to **The Casino,** open from 3 PM to 2 AM (2 bis av. Napoléone-Bonaparte, Aix-en-Provence).

13 The Riviera

St-Tropez to Monaco

Introduction

It's important to begin with a realistic sense of Riviera life so you won't spend your holiday nursing wounded expectations. The Riviera conjures up images of fabulous yachts and villas, movie stars and palaces, and budding starlets sunning themselves on ribbons of golden sand. The truth is that most beaches, at least east of Cannes, are small and pebbly. In summer, hordes of visitors are stuffed into concrete high rises or roadside campsites—on weekends it can take two hours to drive the last six miles into St-Tropez. Yes, the film stars are here—but in their private villas. When the merely wealthy come, they come off-season, in the spring and fall—the best time for you to visit, too.

That said, we can still recommend the Riviera, even in summer, as long as you're selective about the places you choose to visit. A few miles inland are fortified medieval towns perched on mountaintops, high above the sea. The light that Renoir and Matisse came to capture is as magical here as ever. Fields of roses and lavender still send their heady perfume up to these fortified towns, where craftspeople make and sell their wares, as their predecessors did in the Middle Ages. Some resorts are as exclusive as ever, and no one will argue that the chefs hereabouts have lost their touch.

It's impossible to be bored along the Riviera. You can try a different beach or restaurant every day. When you've had enough of the sun, you can visit pottery towns like Vallauris, where Picasso worked, or perfumeries at Grasse, where three-quarters of the world's essences are produced. You can drive along dizzying gorges, one almost as deep as the Grand Canyon. You can disco or gamble the night away in Monte Carlo and shop for the best Paris has to offer, right in Cannes or Nice. Only minutes from the beaches are some of the world's most famous museums of modern art, featuring the works of Fernand Léger, Henri Matisse, Pablo Picasso, Pierre Auguste Renoir, Jean Cocteau—all the artists who were captivated by the light and color of the Côte d'Azur.

Essential Information

Important Addresses and Numbers

Tourist Information The Riviera's regional tourist office is the **Comité Régional du Tourisme de Riviera–Côte d'Azur** (55 Promenade des Anglais, 06000 Nice; written inquiries only). Local tourist offices in major towns covered in this chapter are as follows: **Antibes** (11 pl. Général-de-Gaulle, tel. 93–33–95–64), **Cannes** (Palais des Festivals, 1 La Croisette, tel. 93–39–24–53), **Juan-les-Pins** (5 blvd. Guillaumont, tel. 93–61–04–98), **La Napoule** (272 av. Henri-Clews, tel. 93–49–95–31), **Menton** (Palais de l'Europe, av. Boyer, tel. 93–57–57–00), **Monte Carlo** (2-A blvd. des Moulins, tel. 93–30–87–01), **Nice** (av. Thiers, tel. 93–87–07–07), and **St-Tropez** (quai Jean-Jaurès, tel. 94–97–45–21).

Travel Agencies **American Express** (8 rue des Belges, Cannes, tel. 93–38–15–87; 11 Promenade des Anglais, Nice, tel. 93–87–29–82; and 26 av. du Général-Leclerc, St-Tropez, tel. 94–97–20–66) and **Wagons-Lits** (2 av. Monte Carlo, Monte Carlo, tel. 93–25–01–05).

Car Rental Avis (9 av. d'Ostende, Monte Carlo, tel. 93–30–17–53; and 13 blvd. Louis Blanc, St-Tropez, tel. 94–97–03–10), **Europcar** (9 av. Thiers, Menton, tel. 93–28–21–80), and **Hertz** (147 rue d'Antibes, Cannes, tel. 93–99–04–20; and 12 av. du Suede, Nice, tel. 93–87–11–87).

Arriving and Departing

By Plane The area's only international airport is at Nice; for information and reservations, call 93–21–30–12.

By Train Mainline trains from the French capital stop at most of the major resorts; the trip to Nice takes about seven hours.

By Car If you're traveling from Paris by car, you can avoid a lengthy drive by taking the overnight motorail *(train-auto-couchette)* service to Nice, which departs from Paris's Gare de Bercy, five minutes from the Gare de Lyon. Otherwise, leave Paris by A6 (becoming A7 after Lyon), which continues down to Avignon. Here A8 branches off east toward Italy, with convenient exit/entry points for all major towns (except St-Tropez).

Getting Around

By Train The train is a practical and inexpensive way of getting around the Riviera and stops at dozens of stations.

By Car If you prefer to avoid the slower, albeit spectacularly scenic, coastal roads, opt for the Italy-bound A8.

By Bus Local buses cover a network of routes along the Riviera and stop at many out-of-the-way places that can't be reached by train. Timetables are available from tourist offices, train stations, and the local bus depots *(gare routières)*.

Guided Tours

Bus Tours Two of the largest companies offering 1½-day tours are **Santa Azur** (11 av. Jean-Médecin, 06000 Nice, tel. 93–85–46–81) and **CTM** (Compagnie des Transports Méditerranéens, 5 sq. Mérimée, 06100 Cannes, tel. 93–39–07–68). CTM has a day trip to St-Tropez on Thursday (about 125 francs), as well as a half-day excursion to St-Raphäel and Lac de St-Cassien (about 90 francs); buses leave on Tuesday and Thursday at 8 AM. Santa Azur's one-day tour destinations include Nice (Monday, Wednesday, and Friday; 90 francs), Monaco, and the hill town of Eze (Monday, Wednesday, Friday, and Sunday; 100 francs).

Boat Tours **Gallus Excursions 80** (24 quai Lunel, 06000 Nice, tel. 93–55–33–33) offers an enjoyable day-long jaunt to the Iles de Lérins; cost is about 120 francs.

Special-Interest Any tourist office will produce a sheaf of suggestions on gourmandizing, golfing, and walking tours, among others. **Novatour** (9 rue de Lille, 06400 Cannes, tel. 93–69–47–47) offers tailor-made packages for its clients, though museum tours are a specialty; a three-day/two-night museum tour of Vence and Antibes, including half-board, costs about 2,800 francs.

Exploring the Riviera

Numbers in the margin correspond with points of interest on the Riviera maps.

Orientation

Our Riviera text covers the 75 miles between St-Tropez and the Italian border. The first tour concentrates on the Mediterranean coast from St-Tropez to Cannes and Antibes. The second begins with the inland towns of Grasse, Vence, and St-Paul-de-Vence, then rejoins the Mediterranean at Cagnes and continues to Nice and Monaco.

Highlights for First-time Visitors

Sunning on the beach at St-Tropez, Tour 1
A stroll down La Croisette, Cannes, Tour 1
Picasso Museum in the Château Grimaldi, Antibes, Tour 1
A walk along the Cap d'Antibes peninsula, Tour 1
St-Paul-de-Vence, Tour 2
Fondation Maeght, La Gardette, Tour 2
Old Town, Nice, Tour 2
Musée Ephrussi de Rothschild, St-Jean-Cap-Ferrat, Tour 2
The hill village of Peillon, Tour 2
Casino at Monte Carlo, Tour 2

Tour 1. St-Tropez to Antibes

❶ Old money never came to **St-Tropez,** but Brigitte Bardot did. Bardot came with her director Roger Vadim in 1956 to film *And God Created Woman,* and the resort has never been the same. Actually, the village was first "discovered" by the writer Guy de Maupassant (1850–93) and again, later, by the French painter Paul Signac (1863–1935), who came in 1892 and brought his friends—Matisse, Pierre Bonnard, and others. What attracted them was the pure, radiant light and the serenity and colors of the landscape. The writer Colette moved into a villa here between the two world wars and contributed to its notoriety. When the movie people staked their claim in the 1950s, St-Tropez became St-Trop *(trop* in French means "too much").

Anything associated with the distant past almost seems absurd in St-Tropez. Still, the place has a history that predates the invention of the string bikini, and people have been finding reasons to come here for centuries. First, in AD 68 there was a Roman soldier from Pisa named Torpes who was beheaded for professing his Christian faith in the presence of the Emperor Nero. The headless body was put in a boat between a dog and a cock and sent drifting out to sea. The body eventually floated ashore, perfectly preserved, still watched over by the two animals. The buried remains became a place of pilgrimage, which by the 4th century was called St-Tropez. In the late 15th century, under the Genovese, St-Tropez became a small independent republic.

Since then, people have come for the sun and the sea, and, starting in the 1950s, the celebrities. But whatever celebrities there are here stay hidden away in villas, and the people you'll see are mere mortals–lots of them. In summer, the population swells

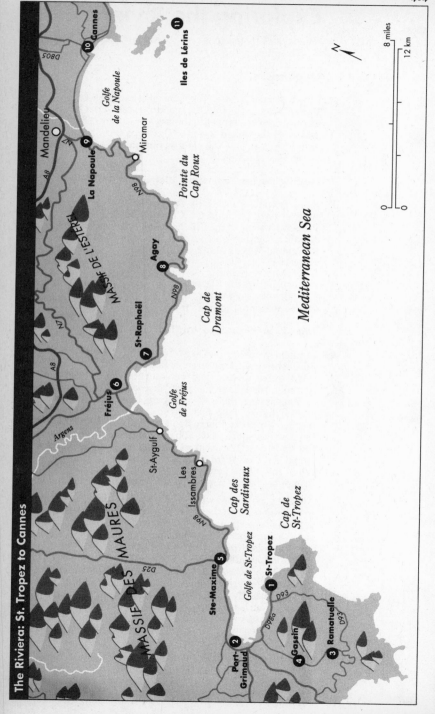

The Riviera: St. Tropez to Cannes

404

Cannes
Iles de Lérins
Golfe de la Napoule
Mandelieu
La Napoule
Miramar
Pointe du Cap Roux
MASSIF DE L'ESTEREL
Agay
St-Raphaël
Cap de Dramont
Fréjus
Golfe de Fréjus
Argens
St-Aygulf
MASSIF DES MAURES
Les Issambres
Cap des Sardinaux
Ste-Maxime
Golfe de St-Tropez
St-Tropez
Cap de St-Tropez
Port-Grimaud
Gassin
Ramatuelle

Mediterranean Sea

N

8 miles
12 km

The Riviera: Cannes to Menton

405

Mediterranean Sea

Baie des Anges

Golfe Juan

Sospel

Castillon

St-Agnès

l'Escarène

Peillon **42**

St-Martin-du-Var

Castagniers

Menton

55

Roquebrune 53

Cap-Martin 54

Monte-Carlo

Monaco 44 — 52

Èze 43

Beaulieu

Golfe de St-Hospice

St-Jean-Cap-Ferrat 41

Villefranche-sur-Mer 40

39

Nice 22 — 38

St-Jeannet

Vence 18

St-Paul-de-Vence 19

Cagnes-sur-Mer 20

21

Tourette-sur-Loup 17

Villeneuve-Loubet 15

Biot

Antibes 13

Cap d'Antibes 14

Gourdon

Grasse 16

Roquefort-les-Pins

Mouans-Sartoux

Mougins

Vallauris 12

Cannes 10

Golfe Juan

Iles de Lérins 11

8 miles

12 km

from 7,000 to 64,000 and the beaches are filled with every imaginable type of human animal, each displaying the best (or at least the most) of his or her youth, beauty, or wealth.

Off-season is the time to come, but even in summer there are reasons to stay. The soft, sandy beaches are the best on the coast. Take an early morning stroll along the harbor or down the narrow medieval streets—the rest of the town will still be sleeping off the Night Before—and you'll see just how pretty St-Tropez is, with its tiny squares and rich, pastel-colored houses bathed in light. There's a weekend's worth of trendy boutiques to explore—to be delighted or shocked by—and many cute cafés, where you can sit under colored awnings sipping wine and feel very French. Five minutes from town, you'll be in a green world of vineyards and fields, where you'll see nothing more lascivious than a butterfly fluttering around some chestnut leaves or a grapevine clinging to a farmhouse wall. Above the fertile fields are mountains crowned with medieval villages, where you can come at dusk for wild-strawberry tarts and fabulous views. Perhaps it's the soft light, perhaps the rich fields and faded pastels, but nowhere else along the coast will you experience so completely the magic of Provence.

Two cafés on the harbor provide dress-circle seats for admiring the St-Tropez scene: **Le Gorille,** on quai Suffren, and **Sénéquier's,** the café with the big terrace on quai Jean-Juarès, beyond the tourist office. Walk along the harbor, filled with pleasure boats, and along the breakwater (the Môle), and continue to the **Musée de l'Annonciade,** a church converted into a major art museum. The collection of Impressionist paintings is filled with views of St-Tropez by Matisse, Bonnard, Paul Signac, Maurice Vlaminck, and others. *Quai de l'Epi. Admission: 20 frs. adults, 8 frs. children. Open Wed.–Mon. 10–noon and 3–6; closed Tues.*

Rue de la Citadelle leads inland from the tourist office to the **Citadel,** a 16th-century fortress with commanding views from St-Tropez across the bay to Ste-Maxime. In the keep is the **Musée de la Marine,** stocked with marine paintings and ship models, including a Greek galley. *Admission: 14 frs. Open Nov.–Easter, Fri.–Wed. 10–5; Easter–Oct., 10–6; closed Thurs.*

Stroll down Montée Ringrave to **place Carnot,** site of a twice-weekly market (Saturday/Tuesday) and daily games of *boules.* Trendy boutiques are on **rue Sibilli.**

Time Out Food at the **Café des Arts** may be ordinary, but the café is a popular place in which to sit and feel as if you're part of the in-crowd. *Pl. Carnot. Closed Oct.–Mar.*

Beaches close to town—**Plage des Greniers** and the **Bouillabaisse**—are great for families, but holiday people snub them, preferring a 6-mile sandy crescent at **Les Salins** and **Pampellone.** These beaches are about 3 kilometers (2 miles) from town, so it helps to have a car, motorbike, or bicycle.

❷ Visitors seem to enjoy a trip through **Port-Grimaud,** a modern architect's idea of a Provençal fishing village-cum-Venice, built out into the gulf for the yachting crowd—each house with its own mooring. Particularly appealing are the harmonious pastel colors, which have weathered nicely, and the graceful bridges over the canals.

❸ From St-Tropez, take D93 south 11 kilometers (7 miles) to the old Provençal market town of **Ramatuelle.** The ancient houses are huddled together on the slope of a rocky spur 440 feet above the sea. The central square has a 17th-century church and a huge 300-year-old elm. Surrounding the square are narrow, twisting streets with medieval archways and vaulted passages.

❹ From Ramatuelle, follow signs to the old village of **Gassin,** which is less than 3 kilometers (2 miles) away. The ride through vineyards and woods is lovely, and takes you over the highest point of the peninsula (1,070 feet), where you can stop and enjoy a splendid view. The perched village of Gassin, with its venerable old houses and 12th-century Romanesque church, has somehow managed to maintain its medieval appearance.

❺ D98a runs 6 kilometers (4 miles) west from St-Tropez, joining the major coastal highway, the N98, which proceeds eastward 8 kilometers (5 miles) to **Ste-Maxime**—a family resort with a fine sandy beach.

❻ The coastline between Ste-Maxime and Cannes consists of a succession of bays and beaches. Minor resorts have sprung up wherever nature permits—curious mixtures of lush villas, campsites, and fast-food stands. **Fréjus,** 19 kilometers (12 miles) farther along N98, was founded by Julius Caesar as Forum Julii in 49 BC, and it is thought that the Roman city grew to 40,000 people—10,000 more than the population today. The Roman remains are unspectacular, if varied, and consist of part of the theater, an arena, an aqueduct, and city walls.

Fréjus Cathedral dates to the 10th century, although the richly worked choir stalls belong to the 15th century. The baptistry alongside it, square on the outside and octagonal inside, is thought to date from AD 400, making it one of France's oldest buildings. The adjacent cloisters feature an unusual contrast between round and pointed arches.

❼ **St-Raphaël,** next door to Fréjus, is another family resort with holiday camps, best known to tourists as the railway stop to St-Tropez. It was here that the Allied forces landed in their offensive against the Germans in August 1944.

The rugged Massif de l'Estérel, between Fréjus and Cannes, is a hiker's joy, made up of volcanic rocks (porphyry) carved by the sea into dreamlike shapes. The harshness of the landscape is softened by patches of lavender, cane apple, and gorse. The deep gorges with sculpted, parasol pines could have inspired Tang- and Sung-Dynasty landscape painters. Drivers can take N7, the mountain route to the north or, as we propose, stay on the N98 coast road past tiny rust-colored beaches and sheer rock faces plunging into the sea.

❽ Some 10 kilometers (6 miles) from St-Raphaël is the resort of **Agay,** whose deep bay was once used by traders from ancient Greece. Agay has the best-protected anchorage along the coast. It was here that writer Antoine de Saint-Exupéry *(The Little Prince)* was shot down in July 1944, having just flown ❾ over his family castle on his last mission. **La Napoule,** 24 kilometers (15 miles) from Agay, forms a unit with the older, inland village of **Mandelieu.** The village explodes with color during the Fête du Mimosa in February and boasts extensive modern sports facilities (swimming, boating, waterskiing, deep-sea diving, fishing, golf, tennis, horseback riding, and parachuting).

Art lovers will want to stop in La Napoule at the **Château de la Napoule Art Foundation** to see the eccentric work of the American sculptor Henry Clews. A cynic and sadist, Clews had, as one critic remarked, a knowledge of anatomy worthy of Michelangelo and the bizarre imagination of Edgar Allan Poe. *Av. Henry-Clews. Admission: 25 frs. Guided visits Mar.–Nov., Wed.–Mon., at 3, 4, and 5.*

Cosmopolitan, sophisticated, smart—these are words that describe the most lively and flourishing city on the Riviera, 6 kilometers (4 miles) farther up the coast. **Cannes** is a resort town—unlike Nice, which is a city—that exists only for the pleasure of its guests. It's a tasteful and expensive breeding ground for the upscale (and those who are already "up"), a sybaritic heaven for those who believe that life is short and that sin has something to do with the absence of a tan.

Alongside the long, narrow beach is a broad, elegant promenade called La Croisette, bordered by palm trees and flowers. At one end of the promenade is the modern Festival Hall, a summer casino, and an old harbor where pleasure boats are moored. At the other end is a winter casino and a modern harbor for some of the most luxurious yachts in the world. All along the promenade are cafés, boutiques, and luxury hotels like the Carlton and the Majestic. Speedboats and waterskiers glide by; little waves lick the beach, lined with prostrate bodies. Behind the promenade lies the town, filled with shops, restaurants, and hotels, and behind the town are the hills with the villas of the very rich.

The first thing to do is stroll along **La Croisette,** stopping at cafés and boutiques along the way. Near the eastern end (turning left as you face the water), before you reach the new port, is the **Parc de la Roserie,** where some 14,000 roses nod their heads in the wind. Walking west takes you past the **Palais des Festivals** (Festival Hall), where the famous film festival is held each May. Just past the hall is **Place du Général-de-Gaulle,** while on your left is the **old port.** If you continue straight beyond the port on **Allés de la Liberte,** you'll reach a tree-shaded area, where flowers are sold in the morning, *boules* is played in the afternoon, and a flea market is held on Saturday. If instead of continuing straight from the square you turn inland, you'll quickly come to rue Meynadier. Turn left. This is the old main street, which has many 18th-century houses—now boutiques and specialty food shops, where you can buy exotic foods and ship them.

You may want to visit the peaceful **Iles de Lérins** (Lerin Islands) to escape the crowds. The ferry leaves from Cannes harbor (near the Palais des Festivals), and takes 15 minutes to **Ste-Marguerite,** 30 to **St-Honorat** (tel. 93–39–11–82 for information).

Ste-Marguerite, the larger of the two, is an island of wooded hills, with a tiny main street lined with fishermen's houses. Visitors enjoy peaceful walks through a forest of enormous eucalyptus trees and parasol pines. Paths wind through a dense undergrowth of tree heathers, rosemary, and thyme. The main attraction is the dank cell in **Fort Royal,** where the Man in the Iron Mask was imprisoned (1687–98) before going to the Bastille, where he died in 1703. The mask, which he always wore, was in fact made of velvet. Was he the illegitimate brother of Louis XIV or Louis XIII's son-in-law? No one knows.

St-Honorat is less tamed but more tranquil than its sister island. It was named for a hermit-monk who came here to escape his followers; but when the hermit founded a monastery here in AD 410, his disciples followed and the monastery became one of the most powerful in all Christendom. It's worth taking the two-hour walk around the island to the **old fortified monastery,** where noble Gothic arcades are arranged around a central courtyard. Next door to the "new" 19th-century monastery (open on request) is a shop where the monks sell handicrafts, lavender scent, and a home-brewed liqueur called Lerina. *Monastère de Lérins. Admission free. Open May–Oct., daily 9:45–4:30; Nov.–Apr. 10:45–3:30. High Mass at the abbey 10:45 Sun.*

⑫ From Cannes, take D803 northeast to the pottery-making center of **Vallauris,** 5 kilometers (3 miles) away. Pottery is on sale throughout the village, and several workshops can be visited. Picasso spurred a resurgence of activity when he settled here in 1947 and created some whimsically beautiful ceramics. He also decorated the tunnel-like medieval chapel of the former priory with a fresco entitled *War and Peace. Pl. de la Mairie. Admission: 12 frs. Open Wed.–Mon. 10–noon and 2–6; closed Tues.*

⑬ From Vallauris, continue east to **Antibes,** founded as a Greek trading port in the 4th century BC and now a center for fishing and rose growing. Avenue de l'Amiral Grasse runs along the seafront from the harbor to the **market place,** a colorful sight most mornings, and to the church of the **Immaculate Conception,** with intricately carved portals (dating from 1710) and a 1515 altarpiece by Nice artist Louis Bréa (c. 1455–1523).

The **Château Grimaldi,** built in the 12th century by the ruling family of Monaco and extensively rebuilt in the 16th century, is reached by nearby steps. Tear yourself away from the sun-baked terrace overlooking the sea to go inside to the Picasso Museum. There are stone Roman remains on show, but the works of Picasso—who occupied the château during his most cheerful and energetic period—hold center stage; they include an array of paintings, pottery, and lithographs inspired by the sea and Greek mythology. *Pl. du Château. Admission: 20 frs. adults, 10 frs. students and senior citizens. Open Dec.–Oct., Wed.–Mon. 10–noon and 2–6; closed Tues.*

Continue down avenue de l'Amiral Grasse to the St-André Bastion, constructed by Sébastien de Vauban in the late 17th century and home to the **Musée Archéologique.** Here 4,000 years of local history are illustrated by continually expanding displays. *Bastion St-André. Admission: 14 frs. adults, 7 frs. children and senior citizens. Open Dec.–Oct., Wed.–Mon. 10–noon and 2–6; closed Tues.*

Antibes officially forms one town (dubbed "Juantibes") with the more recent resort of **Juan-les-Pins** to the south, where beach- and nightlife attract a younger and less affluent crowd than in Cannes. In the summer, the mood is especially frenetic.

⑭ The **Cap d'Antibes** peninsula is rich and residential, with beaches, views, and large villas hidden in luxurious vegetation.

Barely two miles long by a mile wide, it offers a perfect day's outing. An ideal walk is along the **Sentier des Douaniers,** the customs officers' path.

From Pointe Bacon, there is a striking view over the Baie des Anges (Bay of Angels) toward Nice; climb up to the nearby Plateau de la Garoupe for a sweeping view inland over the Esterel massif and the Alps. The **Sanctuaire de la Garoupe** (sailors' chapel) has a 14th-century icon, a statue of Our Lady of Safe Homecoming, and numerous frescoes and votive offerings. The lighthouse alongside, which can be visited, has a powerful beam that carries over 40 miles out to sea. *Admission free. Open Nov.–Mar., daily 10:30–12:30 and 2:30–7:30; Apr.–Oct., daily 10:30–12:30 and 2–5.*

Nearby is the **Jardin Thuret,** established by botanist Gustave Thuret (1817–75) in 1856 as France's first garden for subtropical plants and trees. The garden, now run by the Ministry of Agriculture, remains a haven for rare, exotic plants. *Blvd. du Cap. Admission free. Open weekdays 8–12:30 and 2–5:30.*

At the southwest tip of the peninsula, opposite the luxurious Grand Hôtel du Cap d'Antibes (*see* Dining and Lodging, below), is the **Musée Naval & Napoléonien,** a former battery, where you can spend an interesting hour scanning Napoleonic proclamations and viewing scale models of ocean-going ships. *Batterie du Grillon, blvd. du Maréchal-Juin. Admission: 10 frs. adults, 5 frs. children and senior citizens. Open Oct.–Apr., Wed.–Mon. 10–noon and 3–7; Dec.–Mar., Wed.–Mon. 10–noon and 2–5; closed Tues.*

Marineland, Europe's first aquatic zoo, is only a short distance from Antibes. Take N7 north and then head left at La Brague onto D4; Marineland is on the right. Performing dolphins leap into action every afternoon, abetted by a supporting cast of seals, penguins, and sea lions. There is also an amusement park. *309 rue Mozart. Admission: 80 frs. adults, 60 frs. children. Open Apr.–Oct. daily 10–9; Nov.–Mar. 11–6; first performance at 2:30.*

15 Mimosa and roses for the cut-flower market are grown at the charming old village of **Biot,** 4 kilometers (2½ miles) up D4. The glassworks at the edge of the village welcomes visitors to observe its glassblowers, but it is wise to call first to check opening times, which vary. *Verrerie de Biot, chemin Combes, tel. 93–65–03–00.*

Artist Fernand Léger (1881–1955) lived in Biot, and hundreds of his paintings, ceramics, and tapestries are on display at the museum here. Léger's stylistic evolution is traced from his early flirtation with Cubism to his ultimate preference for flat expanses of primary color and shades of gray, separated by thick black lines. *Chemin du Val de Pome. Admission: 18 frs. adults, 9 frs. senior citizens, children free. Open Apr.–Oct., Tues.–Sun. 10–noon and 2–7; Nov.–Mar., 10–noon and 2–6.*

Tour 2: Grasse to Menton

16 Our tour of the eastern Riviera begins a dozen miles inland at **Grasse.** If you are coming from Cannes or Antibes, stop off en route to admire the dramatic hilltop setting of **Mougins,** a quaint, fortified town just north of Cannes.

If touring a perfume factory in a tacky modern town is your idea of pleasure, by all means visit Grasse. If you had visited four centuries ago, when the town specialized in leather work, you would have come for gloves. In the 16th century, when scented gloves became the rage, the town began cultivating flowers and distilling essences. That was the beginning of the perfume industry. Today some three-fourths of the world's essences are made here from wild lavender, jasmine, violets, daffodils, and other sweet-smelling flowers. Five thousand producers supply some 20 factories and six cooperatives. If you've ever wondered why perfume is so expensive, consider that it takes 10,000 flowers to produce 2.2 pounds of jasmine petals and that nearly one ton of jasmine is needed—nearly 7 million flowers—to distill 1½ quarts of essence. Sophisticated Parisian perfumers mix Grasse essences into their own secret formulas; perfumes made and sold in Grasse are considerably less subtle. You can, of course, buy Parisian perfumes in Grasse—at Parisian prices.

Several perfume houses welcome visitors for a whiff of their products and an explanation of how they're made: Galimard (73 rte. de Cannes, tel. 93–09–20–00); Molinard (60 blvd. Victor-Hugo, tel. 93–36–01–62); and Fragonard (20 blvd. Fragonard, tel. 93–36–44–65), which is conveniently central and has its own museum. All perfume houses invite you to purchase their products. *Admission to perfume houses free. Open daily 9–noon and 2–6.*

A new perfume museum, the **Musée International de la Parfumerie,** was opened in early 1989, and explains the history and manufacturing process of perfume. Old machinery, pots, and flasks can be admired; toiletry, cosmetics, and makeup accessories are on display; and there is a section devoted to perfume's sophisticated marketing aids, with examples of packaging and advertising posters. *8 pl. du Cours. Admission: 12 frs. adults, 6 frs. children and senior citizens. Joint ticket for all Grasse museums: 22 frs. adults, 11 frs. children and senior citizens. Open Wed.–Mon. 10–6; closed Tues.*

The artist Jean-Honoré Fragonard (1732–1806) was born in Grasse, and many of his pictures, etchings, drawings, and sketches—plus others by his son Alexandre-Evariste and his grandson Théophile—are hung in the 17th-century Villa Fragonard, situated close to the perfumerie of the same name. *23 blvd. Fragonard, tel. 93–36–01–61. Admission: 12 frs. adults, 6 frs. children and senior citizens. Joint ticket for all Grasse museums: 22 frs. adults, 11 frs. children and senior citizens. Open weekdays 10–noon and 2–5 and the first and last Sun. of each month.*

The **Musée d'Art et d'Histoire de Provence,** around the corner on rue Mirabeau, is in an 18th-century mansion. It houses a collection of Provençal furniture, folk art, tools and implements, and china. *2 rue Mirabeau. Admission: 12 frs. adults, 6 frs. children and senior citizens. Joint ticket for all Grasse museums: 22 frs. adults, 11 frs. children and senior citizens. Open Apr.–Oct., Mon.–Sat. 10–noon and 2–6; Dec.–Mar., 10–noon and 2–5.*

From Grasse, strike east along D2085/D2210 toward Vence, 25 kilometers (16 miles) away. About 5 kilometers (3 miles) before you reach Vence is **Tourette-sur-Loup,** whose outer houses form a rampart on a rocky plateau, 1,300 feet above a valley full of violets. The town is much less commercialized than many others in the area; its shops are filled not with postcards and scented soaps but with the work of dedicated artisans. A rough stone path takes you on a circular route around the rim of the town, past the shops of engravers, weavers, potters, and painters. Ask any artisan for a map of the town that locates each of the shops. Also worth visiting is a single-nave 14th-century church that has a notable wooden altarpiece.

⑱ When you arrive in **Vence**, leave your car on avenue Foch and climb up to the medieval town (Vieille Ville). The Romans were the first to settle on the 1,000-foot hill; the **cathedral** (built between the 11th and 18th century), rising above the medieval ramparts and traffic-free streets, was erected on the site of a temple to Mars. Of special note are a mosaic by Marc Chagall of Moses in the bullrushes and the ornate 15th-century wooden choir stalls.

At the foot of the hill, on the outskirts of Vence, is the **Chapelle du Rosaire,** a small chapel decorated with beguiling simplicity and clarity by Matisse between 1947 and 1951. The walls, floor, and ceiling are gleaming white and are pierced by small stained-glass windows in cool greens and blues. "Despite its imperfections I think it is my masterpiece . . . the result of a lifetime devoted to the search for truth," wrote Matisse, who designed and dedicated the chapel when he was in his eighties and nearly blind. *Av. Henri-Matisse. Admission free. Open Tues. and Thur. 10–11:30 and 2:30–5:30.*

⑲ A few miles south along D2 is **St-Paul-de-Vence,** a gem of a town whose medieval atmosphere has been perfectly preserved. Not even the hordes of tourists—to which the village now caters—can destroy its ancient charm. You can walk the narrow, cobbled streets in perhaps 15 minutes, but you'll need another hour to explore the shops—mostly galleries selling second-rate landscape paintings, but also a few serious studios and gift shops offering everything from candles to dolls, dresses, and hand-dipped chocolate strawberries. Your best bet is to visit in the late afternoon, when the tour buses are gone, and enjoy a drink among the Klees and Picassos in the Colombe d'Or (*see* Dining and Lodging, below). Be sure to visit the remarkable 12th-century Gothic church; you'll want to light a candle to relieve its wonderful gloom. The treasury is rich in 12th–15th-century pieces, including processional crosses, reliquaries, and an enamel Virgin and Child.

At La Gardette, just northwest of the village, is the **Fondation Maeght,** one of the world's most famous small museums of modern art. Monumental sculptures are scattered around its pinetree park, and a courtyard full of Alberto Giacometti's elongated creations separates the two museum buildings. The rooms inside showcase the works of Joan Miró, Georges Braque, Wassily Kandinsky, Bonnard, Matisse and others. Few museums blend form and content so tastefully and imaginatively. There is also a library, cinema, and auditorium. *Admission: 40 frs. adults, 26 frs. children. Open Apr.–Oct., daily 10–12:30 and 3–7; Nov.–Mar., daily 10–12:30 and 2:30–6.*

⑳ Return to D2 and continue 6 kilometers (4 miles) south to **Cagnes-sur-Mer.** An attractive **château,** once a medieval fortress, is perched high above the modern seaside resort within the walls of Haut-de-Cagnes, the old town. Much of the château's Renaissance decoration—frescoes, plasterwork, and fireplaces—remains intact, and the third floor hosts an art gallery devoted to Mediterranean artists, including Chagall and Raoul Dufy. There's an exciting panorama from the top of the tower. *Pl. du Château. Admission: 6 frs. adults, 3 frs. students. Open Easter–mid-Oct., daily 10–noon and 2:30–7; mid-Nov.–Easter, Wed.–Mon. 10–noon and 2–5, closed Tues.*

The painter Auguste Renoir (1841–1919) spent the last years of his life at Cagnes. His home at Les Collettes has been preserved, and you can see his studio, as well as some of his work. A bronze statue of Venus nestles amid the fruit trees in the colorful garden. *Av. des Collettes. Admission: 20 frs. adults, 10 frs. children. Open Apr.–Oct., daily 2:30–6:30; Nov.–Mar., Wed.–Mon. 2–5.*

㉑ A mile west of Cagnes is the tiny village of **Villeneuve-Loubet,** worth visiting for its **Fondation Escoffier:** a gourmet shrine that can be fitted in between meals because there's nothing to eat. As kitchen overlord at the London Carlton and the Paris Ritz, Auguste Escoffier (1846–1935) carved out a reputation as Europe's top chef. One of his inventions is Peach Melba. This museum, in the house where he was born, displays some elaborate *pièces montées* in sugar and marzipan, and boasts a lip-smacking collection of 15,000 menus. *3 rue Escoffier. Admission: 12 frs. adults, 6 frs. students. Open Dec.–Oct., Tues.–Sun. 2:15–6.*

The congested N7 from Cagnes to Nice is enough to put you off the Riviera for life. Tedious concrete constructions assault the eye; the railroad, on one side, and the stony shore, on the other, offer scant respite. Soon, however, you'll arrive at the Queen of **㉒** the Riviera—**Nice.**

Nice is less glamorous, less sophisticated, and less expensive than Cannes. It's also older—weathered-old and faded-old—like a wealthy dowager who has seen better days but who still maintains a demeanor of dignity and poise. Nice is a big, sprawling city of 350,000 people—five times as many as Cannes—and has a life and vitality that survive when tourists pack their bags and go home.

Nice is worth a visit, but should you stay here? On the negative side, its beaches are cramped and pebbly. Many of its hotels are either rundown or being refurbished for the convention crowd. On the positive side, Nice is likely to have hotel space, at prices you can afford, when all other towns are full. It's also a convenient base from which to explore Monte Carlo and the medieval towns in the interior. It does have its share of first-class restaurants and boutiques, and an evening stroll through the old town or along the Promenade des Anglais is something to savor.

Numbers in the margin correspond with points of interest on the Nice map.

We suggest that you divide your visit of Nice into three
㉓ minitours, with arcaded **place Masséna,** the city's main square, as a common starting point. First, head west through the foun-
㉔ ㉕ tains and gardens of the **Jardin Albert I** to the **Promenade des Anglais,** built, as the name indicates, by the English community in 1824. Traffic on this multilane highway can be heavy, but once you have crossed to the seafront, there are fine views, across private beaches, of the Baie des Anges.

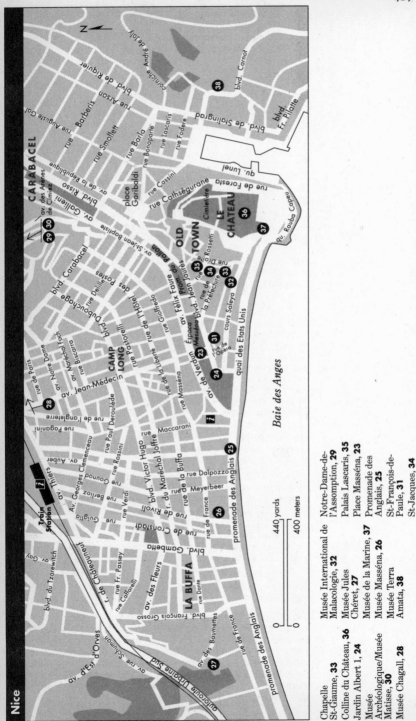

Time Out Walk as far as the Neptune Plage (beach) and cross over to the **Hôtel Negresco.** If you can't afford to stay here, spend a few dollars on a cup of coffee and think of it as an admission charge to this palatial hotel. *37 Promenade des Anglais.*

②⑥ Just up rue de Rivoli from the Hôtel Negresco is the **Musée Masséna,** concerned principally with the Napoleonic era and, in particular, with the life of local-born general André Masséna (1756–1817). Bonaparte rewarded the general for his heroic exploits during the Italian campaign with the sonorous sobriquet *l'Enfant chéri de la victoire* (the Cherished Child of Victory). Sections of the museum evoke the history of Nice and its cherished carnival; there are also some fine Renaissance paintings and objects. *67 rue de France. Admission free. Open Tues.–Sun. 10–noon and 2–5; closed 2 weeks in Nov. or Dec.*

②⑦ Head left along rue de France, then turn right up avenue des Baumettes to the **Musée Jules Chéret,** Nice's fine-arts museum, built in 1878 as a palatial mansion for a Russian princess. The rich collection of paintings includes works by Auguste Renoir, Edgar Degas, Claude Monet, Raoul Dufy, Oriental prints, sculptures by Auguste Rodin, and ceramics by Picasso. Jules Chéret (1836–1932) is best known for his Belle Epoque posters; several of his oils, pastels, and tapestries can be admired here. *33 av. des Baumettes. Admission free. Open May–Sept., Tues.–Sun. 10–noon and 3–6; Oct. and Dec.–Apr., Tues.–Sun. 10–noon and 2–5.*

②⑧ Nice's main shopping street, avenue Jean-Médecin, runs inland from place Masséna; all needs and most tastes are catered to in its big department stores (Nouvelles Galeries, Prisunic, and the split-level Etoile mall). Continue past the train station, on avenue Thiers, then take the first right down to the **Musée Chagall**—built to show off the paintings of Marc Chagall (1887–1985) in natural light. The Old Testament is the primary subject of the works, which include 17 huge canvases covering a period of 13 years, together with 195 preliminary sketches, several sculptures, and nearly 40 gouaches. In summertime, you can buy snacks and drinks in the garden. *Av. du Dr-Ménard. Admission: 16 frs. adults, 8 frs. children and senior citizens; free Wed. Open July–Sept., Wed.–Mon. 10–7; Oct.–July, Wed.–Mon. 10–12:30 and 2–5.30.*

②⑨ Boulevard de Cimiez heads to the residential quarter of Nice—the hilltop site of **Cimiez,** occupied by the Romans 2,000 years ago. The foundations of the Roman town can be seen, along with vestiges of the arena, less spectacular than those at Arles or Nîmes but still in use (notably for a summer jazz festival). Close by is the Franciscan monastery of **Notre-Dame-de-l'Assomption,** with some outstanding late-medieval religious pictures; guided tours include the small museum and an audiovisual show on the life and work of the Franciscans. *Admission free. Open weekdays 10–noon and 3–6.*

③⓪ A 17th-century Italian villa amid the Roman remains contains two museums: the **Musée Archéologique,** with a plethora of ancient objects, and the **Musée Matisse,** with paintings and bronzes by Henri Matisse (1869–1954), illustrating the different stages of his career. The Matisse Museum is scheduled to reopen in 1992 after a four-year renovation program. *164 av. des Arènes-de-Cimiez, tel. 93–53–17–70. Admission free.*

Open May–Sept., 10–noon and 2:30–6:30; Oct.–Apr., 10–noon and 2–5.

The **old town** of Nice is one of the delights of the Riviera. Cars are forbidden on streets that are so narrow that their buildings crowd out the sky. The winding alleyways are lined with faded 17th- and 18th-century buildings, where families sell their wares. Flowers cascade from window boxes on soft pastel-colored walls. You wander down cobbled streets, proceeding with the logic of dreams, or sit in an outdoor café on a Venetian-looking square, basking in the purest, most transparent light.

To explore the old town, head south from place Masséna along rue de l'Opéra, and turn left into rue St-François-de-Paule. ③① You'll soon come to the 18th-century church of **St-François-de-Paule**, renowned for its ornate Baroque interior and sculpted decoration.

Time Out Shop for the best crystallized fruits in Nice at **Henri Auer** (7 rue St-François-de-Paule) and have an ice cream and pastry in his cozy tea room.

Rue St-François-de-Paule becomes the pedestrian-only cours Saleya, with its colorful morning market selling seafood, flowers, and orange trees in tubs. Toward the far end of cours ③② Saleya is the **Musée International de Malacologie,** with a collection of seashells from all over the world (some for sale) and a small aquarium of Mediterranean sea life. *3 cours Saleya. Admission free. Open Dec.–Oct., Tues.–Sat. 10:30–1 and 2–6.*

Next, stroll left up rue la Poissonnerie and pop into the ③③ **Chapelle St-Giaume** to admire its gleaming Baroque interior and grand altarpieces. Continue to rue de Jésus; at one end is ③④ the church of **St-Jacques,** featuring an explosion of painted an- ③⑤ gels on the ceiling. Walk along rue Droite to the elegant **Palais Lascaris,** built in the mid-17th century and decorated with paintings and tapestries. The palace boasts a particularly grand staircase and a reconstructed 18th-century pharmacy. *15 rue Droite. Admission free. Open Dec.–Oct., Tues.–Sun. 9:30–noon and 2–6.*

③⑥ Old Nice is dominated by the **Colline du Château** (Castle Hill), a romantic cliff fortified many centuries before Christ. The ruins of a 6th-century castle can be explored and the views from the ③⑦ surrounding garden admired. A small naval museum, the **Musée de la Marine,** is situated in the 16th-century tower known as the **Tour Bellanda,** with models, instruments, and documents charting the history of the port of Nice. *Rue du Château, tel. 93–80–47–61. Admission free. Open Apr.–Sept., Wed.–Mon. 10–noon and 2–7; Oct.–Mar., Wed.–Mon. 10–noon and 2–5, closed Tues.*

The elevator between Tour Bellanda and the quayside operates daily 9 until 7 in summer and 2 until 7 in winter. The back of Castle Hill overlooks the harbor. On the other side, along boul- ③⑧ evard Carnot, is the **Musée Terra Amata,** containing relics of a local settlement that was active 400,000 years ago. There are recorded commentaries in English and films explaining the life style of prehistoric dwellers. *25 blvd. Carnot, tel. 93–55– 59– 93. Admission free. Open Tues.–Sun. 9–noon and 2–6; closed second half Sept.*

There are three scenic roads at various heights above the coast between Nice and Monte Carlo, a distance of about 19 kilometers (12 miles). All are called "corniches"—literally, a projecting molding along the top of a building or wall. The **Basse** (lower) **Corniche** is the busiest and slowest route because it passes through all the coastal towns. The **Moyenne** (middle) **Corniche** is high enough for views and close enough for details. It passes the perched village of Eze. The **Grande** (upper) **Corniche** winds some 1,300 to 1,600 feet above the sea, offering sweeping views of the coast. The Grande Corniche follows the Via Aurelia, the great Roman military road that brought Roman legions from Italy to Gaul (France). In 1806, Napoleon rebuilt the road and sent Gallic troops into Italy. The best advice is to take the Moyenne Corniche one way and the Grande Corniche the other. The view from the upper route is best in the early morning or evening.

Numbers in the margin correspond with points of interest on the Riviera maps.

(39) Boulevard Carnot becomes the popular, pretty Basse Corniche (N98), which crawls along the coast from Nice to **Villefranche-sur-Mer,** 4 kilometers (2½ miles) east. The harbor town is a miniature version of old Marseille, with steep narrow streets—one, **rue Obscure,** an actual tunnel—winding down to the sea. The town is a stage set of brightly colored houses—orange buildings with lime-green shutters, yellow buildings with ice-blue shutters—the sort of place where *Fanny* could have been filmed. If you're staying in Nice, include Villefranche on a tour of Cap Ferrat. To see the Cocteau Chapel you'll need to arrive by 4 PM. If you skip the chapel, your best bet is to come at sundown (for dinner, perhaps) and enjoy an hour's walk around the harbor, when the sun turns the soft pastels to gold.

The 17th-century **St-Michel** church has a strikingly realistic Christ, carved of boxwood by an unknown convict. The chapel of St-Pierre-des-Pêcheurs, known as the **Cocteau Chapel,** is a small Romanesque chapel once used for storing fishing nets, which the French writer and painter Jean Cocteau decorated in 1957. Visitors walk through the flames of the Apocalypse (represented by staring eyes on either side of the door) and enter a room filled with frescoes of St. Peter, gypsies, and the women of Villefranche. *Admission: 10 frs. Open May–Oct., daily 9–noon and 2–4:30; Nov.–Apr. 9–noon and 2:30–7.*

(40) **Beaulieu** is just next door to Villefranche, a place for high society at the turn of the century. Stop and walk along the promenade, sometimes called Petite Afrique (Little Africa) because of its magnificent palm trees, to get a flavor of how things used to be.

The one thing to do in Beaulieu is visit the **Villa Kérylos.** In the early part of the century, a rich amateur archaeologist named Theodore Reinach asked an Italian architect to build an authentic Greek house for him. The villa, now open to the public, is a faithful reproduction, made from cool Carrara marble, alabaster, and rare fruitwoods. The furniture, made of wood inlaid with ivory, bronze, and leather, is copied from drawings of Greek interiors found on ancient vases and mosaics. *Admission: 18 frs. adults, 10 frs. children and senior citizens. Open July–Aug., daily 3–7; Sept.–June, Tues.–Sun. 2–6.*

41 From Beaulieu, make a detour along D25 around the lush peninsula of **St-Jean-Cap-Ferrat** and visit the 17-acre gardens and richly varied art collection of the **Musée Ephrussi de Rothschild.** The museum reflects the sensibilities of its former owner, Madame Ephrussi de Rothschild, sister of Baron Edouard de Rothschild. An insatiable collector, she surrounded herself with an eclectic but tasteful collection of Impressionist paintings, Louis XIII furniture, rare Sèvres porcelain, and objets d'art from the Far East. *Villa Ile-de-France, tel. 93–01–33–09. Admission: 28 frs. adults, 16 frs. students, children free. Guided tours only. Open Dec.–Oct., Tues.–Sat. 10–noon and 2–6, Sun. 2–6.*

42 The perched village of **Peillon** is about 10 kilometers (6 miles) inland from Nice. Take D2204, turn right on D21, and turn right again, up the mountain. Of all the perched villages along the Riviera, Peillon is the most spectacular and the least spoiled, a fortified medieval town situated on a craggy mountaintop more than 1,000 feet above the sea. Unchanged since the Middle Ages, the village has only a few narrow streets and many steps and covered alleys. There's really nothing to do here but look—which is why the tour buses stay away, leaving Peillon uncommercialized for the 50 families who live there—including professionals summering away from Paris and artists who want to escape the craziness of the world below. Visit the **Chapel of the White Penitents** (key available at the Auberge); spend a half hour exploring the ancient streets, then head back down the mountain to Nice.

Time Out Stay for lunch or dinner at the charming **Auberge de la Madame,** a short walk from the chapel.

43 Almost every tour from Nice to Monaco includes a visit to the medieval hill town of **Eze,** perched on a rocky spur near the Middle Corniche, some 1,300 feet above the sea. (Don't confuse Eze with the beach town of **Eze-sur-Mer,** which is down by the water.) Be warned that because of its accessibility the town is also crowded and commercial: Eze has its share of serious craftspeople, but most of its vendors make their living selling perfumed soaps and postcards to the package-tour trade.

Enter through a fortified 14th-century gate and wander down narrow, cobbled streets with vaulted passageways and stairs. The church is 18th century, but the small Chapel of the White Penitents dates to 1306 and contains a 13th-century gilded wooden Spanish Christ and some notable 16th-century paintings. Tourist and crafts shops line the streets leading to the ruins of a castle, which has a scenic belvedere. Some of the most tasteful crafts shops are in the hotel/restaurant **Chèvre d'Or.**

Near the top of the village is a garden with exotic flowers and cacti. It's worth the admission price, but if you have time for only one exotic garden, visit the one in Monte Carlo.

If you're not going to Grasse, the perfume capital of the world (*see* above), consider visiting a branch of a Grasse perfumerie called **La Perfumerie Fragonard,** located in front of the public gardens.

44 From Eze it's just a short—albeit spectacular—drive up the coast to **Monaco.** The Principality of Monaco covers just 473 acres and would fit comfortably inside New York's Central Park or a family farm in Iowa. Its 5,000 citizens would fill only a small fraction of the seats in Yankee Stadium. The country is so tiny that residents have to go to another country to play golf.

The present ruler, Rainier III, traces his ancestry to Otto Canella, who was born in 1070. The Grimaldi dynasty began with Otto's great-great-great-grandson, Francesco Grimaldi, also known as Frank the Rogue. Expelled from Genoa, Frank and his cronies disguised themselves as monks and seized the fortified medieval town known today as the Rock in 1297. Except for a short break under Napoleon, the Grimaldis have been here ever since, which makes them the oldest reigning family in Europe. On the Grimaldi coat of arms are two monks holding swords (look up and you'll see them above the main door as you enter the palace).

Back in the 1850s, a Grimaldi named Charles III made a decision that turned the Rock into a giant blue chip. Needing revenues but not wanting to impose additional taxes on his subjects, he contracted with a company to open a gambling facility. The first spin of the roulette wheel was on December 14, 1856. There was no easy way to reach Monaco then—no carriage roads or railroads—so no one came. Between March 15 and March 20, 1857, one person entered the casino—and won two francs. In 1868, however, the railroad reached Monaco, filled with wheezing Englishmen who came to escape the London fog. The effects were immediate. Profits were so great that Charles eventually abolished all direct taxes.

Almost overnight, a threadbare principality became an elegant watering hole for European society. Dukes (and their mistresses) and duchesses (and their gigolos) danced and dined their way through a world of spinning roulette wheels and bubbling champagne—preening themselves for nights at the opera, where such artists as Vaslav Nijinsky, Sarah Bernhardt, and Enrico Caruso came to perform.

Monte Carlo—the modern gambling town with elegant shops, man-made beaches, high-rise hotels, and a few Belle Epoque hotels—is actually only one of four parts of Monaco. The second is the medieval town on the Rock ("Old Monaco"), 200 feet above the sea. It's here that Prince Rainier lives.

The third area is **La Condamine,** the commercial harbor area with apartments and businesses. The fourth is **Fontvieille,** the industrial district situated on 20 acres of reclaimed land.

Numbers in the margin correspond with points of interest on the Monaco map.

Start at the Monte Carlo tourist office just north of the casino gardens (ask for the useful English booklet *Getting Around in the Principality*). The **Casino** is a must-see, even if you don't bet a cent. You may find it fun to count the Jaguars and Rolls-Royces parked outside and breathe on the windows of shops selling Saint-Laurent dresses and fabulous jewels. Within the gold-leaf splendor of the casino, where fortunes have been won and shirts have been lost, the hopeful traipse in from tour buses to tempt fate at the slot machines beneath the gilt-edged Rococo ceiling.

The main gambling hall, once called the European Room, has been renamed the American Room and fitted with 150 one-armed bandits from Chicago. Adjoining it is the Pink Salon,

Casino, **45**
Cathedral, **49**
Jardin Exotique, **51**
Loew's Casino, **46**
Musée Nationale, **47**
Musée
Océanographique, **50**
Museum of Prehistoric
Anthropology, **52**
Palace, **48**

now a bar where unclad nymphs float about on the ceiling smoking cigarillos. The Salles Privées (private rooms) are for high rollers. The stakes are higher here, so the mood is more sober, and well-wishers are herded farther back from the tables.

On July 17, 1924, black came up 17 times in a row on Table 5. This was the longest run ever. A dollar left on black would have grown to $131,072. On August 7, 1913, the number 36 came up three times in a row. In those days, if a gambler went broke, the casino bought him a ticket home.

The casino opens at 10 AM and continues until the last die is thrown. Ties and jackets are required in the back rooms, which open at 4 PM. Bring your passport.

Place du Casino is the center of Monte Carlo, and, in the true spirit of this place, it seems that the **Opera House,** with its 18-ton gilt bronze chandelier, is part of the casino complex. The designer, Charles Garnier, also built the Paris Opera.

46 The serious gamblers, some say, play at **Loew's Casino,** nearby. It opens weekdays at 4 PM and weekends at 1 PM. You may want to try parking here, as parking near the old casino is next to impossible in season.

From place des Moulins there is an escalator down to the Larvotto beach complex, artfully created with imported sand,
47 and the **Musée National,** housed in a Garnier villa within a rose garden. This museum has a beguiling collection of 18th- and 19th-century dolls and mechanical automatons, most in working order. *17 av. Princesse Grace, tel. 93–30–91–26. Admission: 23 frs. adults, 12 frs. children. Open 10–12:15 and 2:30–6:30; closed holidays.*

Prince Rainier spends much of the year in his grand Italianate
48 **Palace** on the Rock. The changing of the guard takes place here each morning at 11:55, and the State Apartments can be visited in summer. *Admission: 22 frs. adults, 11 frs. children. Joint ticket with Musée Napoléon: 30 frs. adults, 15 frs. children. Open June–Oct., daily 9:30–6:30.*

One wing of the palace, open throughout the year, is taken up by a museum full of Napoleonic souvenirs and documents related to Monaco's history. *Admission: 18 frs. adults, 9 frs. children. Joint ticket with palace apartments: 30 frs. adults, 15 frs. children. Open Tues.–Sun. 9:30–6:30.*

From here, a stroll through the medieval alleyways takes you
49 past the **cathedral,** a neo-Romanesque monstrosity (1875–84), with several important paintings of the Nice school. Continue
50 to one of Monaco's most outstanding showpieces, the **Musée Océanographique**—also an important research institute headed by celebrated underwater explorer and filmmaker Jacques Cousteau. Prince Rainier's great-grandfather Albert I (1848–1922), an accomplished marine biologist, founded the institute, which now boasts two exploration ships, laboratories, and a staff of 60 scientists. Nonscientific visitors may wish to make straight for the well-arranged and generously stocked aquarium in the basement. Other floors are devoted to Prince Albert's collection of seashells and whale skeletons, and to Cousteau's diving equipment. *Av. St-Martin, tel. 93–30–15–14. Admission: 48 frs. adults, 24 frs. children. Open daily, July–Aug., 9–9, Sept.–June, 9:30–7.*

Time Out | Take the museum's elevator to the roof terrace for a fine view and a restorative drink.

A brisk half-hour walk back past the palace brings you to the
51 **Jardin Exotique** (Tropical Gardens), where 600 varieties of
52 cacti and succulents cling to a sheer rock face. The **Museum of Prehistoric Anthropology,** on the grounds, contains bones, tools, and other artifacts. Shapes of the stalactites and stalagmites in the cavernous grotto resemble the cacti outside. *Blvd. du Jardin Exotique. Admission: 29 frs. adults, 19 frs. senior citizens, 14 frs. children. Open daily 9–7 (dusk in winter).*

*Numbers in the margin correspond with points of interest on
the Riviera maps.*

Five kilometers (3 miles) northeast of Monaco is the engaging
53 hilltop village of **Roquebrune,** with its steps and narrow
54 streets. The adjacent **Cap-Martin** peninsula is colonized by
wealthy villa dwellers. Near the tip, on avenue Winston-
Churchill, is the start of a coastal path—promenade Le Corbusier—that leads hardy ramblers to Monte Carlo in 1½ hours.

55 Next door to Roquebrune is **Menton,** a comparatively quiet all-
year resort with the warmest climate on the Riviera. Lemon
trees flourish here, as do senior citizens, enticed by a long
strand of beaches. Menton likes to call itself the Pearl of the
Riviera—beautiful, respectable, and not grossly expensive.

Walk eastward from the casino along promenade du Soleil to
the harbor. There is a small 17th-century fort here, where
writer, artist, and filmmaker Jean Cocteau (1889–1963) once
worked. The fort now houses the **Cocteau Museum** of fantasti-
cal paintings, drawings, stage sets and a large mosaic. *Bastion
du Port, 111 quai Napoléon III. Admission free. Open Apr.–
Oct., Wed–Sun. 10–noon and 2–6; Nov.–Mar., Wed.–Sun. 10–
noon and 3–6; closed Mon. and Tues.*

The quaint old town above the jetty has an Italian feel to it. Visit the church of **St-Michel** for its ornate Baroque interior and
altarpiece of St. Michael slaying a dragon. Concerts of chamber
music are held on the square on summer nights.

Higher still is the **Vieux Cimetière** (old cemetery), with a magnificent view of the old town and coast. Here lie Victorian foreigners—Russians, Germans, English—who hoped (in vain, as
the dates on the tombstones reveal) that Menton's balmy climate would reverse the ravages of tuberculosis.

Return to the center and the pedestrian rue St-Michel. On avenue de la République, which runs parallel, is the **Hôtel de Ville**
(Town Hall). The room where civil marriage ceremonies are
conducted has vibrant allegorical frescoes by Cocteau; a tape in
English helps to interpret them. *17 rue de la République. Admission free. Open weekdays 8:30–noon and 1:30– 5:45.*

Two other places of interest lie at opposite ends of Menton. To
the west is the **Palais Carnolès,** an 18th-century villa once used
as a summer retreat by the princes of Monaco. The gardens are
beautiful, and the collection of European paintings (13th- to
18th-century) is extensive. *3 av. Madone. Admission free.
Open Wed.–Sun. 10–noon and 2–6; closed holidays.*

At the other end of Menton, above the Garavan harbor, lie the
Colombières Gardens, where follies and statues lurk among 15
acres of hedges, yew trees, and Mediterranean flowers.
*Chemin de Valleya. Admission: 16 frs. Open Feb.–Sept., daily
9–noon and 3–8 (or sunset if earlier).*

The Italian frontier is just a mile away, and the first Italian
town, **Ventimiglia** (Vintimille in French), 10 kilometers (6
miles) beyond.

What to See and Do with Children

The **Jungle des Papillons,** opposite Marineland in Antibes,
hosts a fluttering "Butterfly Ballet" that must be seen to be be-

lieved. Visitors are requested to wear colored clothing, as this apparently stimulates the butterflies into a wing-flapping frenzy. *309 av. de Mozart, tel. 93–33–55–77. Admission 25 frs. Open daily, Easter–Oct., 10–noon and 2–5.*

The following attractions are described in our Exploring section:

Automatons at the Musée Nationale, Monte-Carlo, Tour 2
Glassblowers at Biot, Tour 1
Marineland, near Antibes, Tour 1
Musée Océanographique (Museum of Oceanography), Monte Carlo, Tour 2

Off the Beaten Track

Consider a visit to the Italian towns of Ventimiglia and San Remo by train, bus, or car; bring your passport. **Ventimiglia** lies just 10 kilometers (6 miles) over the border and is best known for its colorful Friday flower market, which draws huge crowds (mostly French). If you decide to visit on market day, take the train or bus; there will be no place to park. The elegant town of **San Remo,** just 6 kilometers (4 miles) farther down the coast, still maintains some of the glamour of its late 19th-century heyday; compare its casino with that of Monte Carlo. From October to June, you can visit Italy's most important flower market, the Mercato dei Fiori. The old town is an atmospheric warren of alleyways leading up to the piazza Castello, which features a splendid view of the old town.

Costumes, furniture, buildings, and even entire towns often evoke the stuff of heroes. Occasionally, so do roads—and one of the most famous roads in France is the **Route Napoléon,** taken by Napoleon Bonaparte in 1815 after his escape from imprisonment on the Mediterranean island of Elba. Napoleon landed at Golfe-Juan, near Cannes, on March 1 and forged northwest to Grasse and through dramatic, hilly countryside to Castellane, Digne, and Sisteron. In Napoleon's day, most of this "road" was little more than a winding dirt track, but now N85 allows drivers to mix history with scenery. Commemorative plaques bearing the imperial eagle stud the route, inspired by Napoleon's remark that "The eagle will fly from steeple to steeple until it reaches the towers of Notre-Dame." That prediction came true. Napoleon covered the 110 miles from the coast to Sisteron in just four days, romped north through Grenoble and Burgundy, and entered Paris in triumph on May 20.

One of the most spectacular roads in France is the **Corniche Sublime** (D71), which runs along the south side of the **Gorges du Verdon** (Verdon River Gorge), France's answer to the Grand Canyon. To reach the gorge, take the Route Napoléon (N85) from Grasse; turn left after 43 kilometers (27 miles) along D21, which becomes D71 at Comps-sur-Artuby. This is not a road for anyone who is afraid of heights. The narrow lane—just wide enough for two cars to scrape by—snakes its way for 25 miles along the cliffside, 3,000 feet above the tiny River Verdon. At times the river disappears from view beneath the sheer rock face. At the far end of the gorge you'll arrive at the sparkling blue Lac de Ste-Croix.

Shopping

Clothes Cannes is one of the Riviera's top spots for chic clothing. Some of the most exclusive shops are **Chanel** (5 La Croisette); **Alexandra Scherra** (rond-Point Duboys d'Angers); **Cacharel** (16 rue des Belges); **Révillon** (45 La Croisette); and **St-Laurent** (21 rue d'Antibes). For well-cut menswear, try **Cerruti 1881** (15 rue des Serbes) and **Christian Dior** and **Francesco Smalto** (both at the Hôtel Gray Albion, 38 rue des Serbes).

Food Items Crystallized fruit is a Nice specialty; there's a terrific selection at **Henri Auer** (7 rue St-François-de-Paule). Locals and visitors alike buy olive oil by the gallon from tiny **Alziari**, just down the street at no. 14; the cans sport colorful, old-fashioned labels, and you can also pick up lots of Provençal herbs and spices. For cheese, try **l'Etable** (1 rue Sade) in Antibes. **Georget** (11 rue Allard), in St-Tropez, sells delicious handmade chocolates.

Markets St-Tropez's **place des Lices** has a clothing and antiques market on Tuesday and Saturday mornings. In addition to plants, Nice's famous flower market at **cours Saleya** also features mounds of fish, shellfish, and a host of other food items; on Monday, there's a flea market at the same spot. In Cannes, a market selling everything from strings of garlic to secondhand gravy boats is held on Saturday on **allées de la Liberté**.

Sports and Fitness

La Napoule is the best place for active sportspeople. As well as facilities for boating, golf, horseback riding, and tennis, there are eight beaches with facilities for waterskiing and jet-skiing (there's a school on the plage du Sweet), and a deep-sea diving club (Club Nautique de L'Esterel) that gives lessons to anyone over age eight.

Biking Bikes can be rented from train stations at **Antibes, Cannes, Juan-les-Pins,** and **Nice.** Two especially scenic trips on fairly level ground are from Nice to the area around Cap d'Antibes, and around Cap Ferrat from Cannes. Bikes are ideal at St-Tropez, since the beach is a few miles from town.

Golf There are 18-hole courses at **Cannes, La Napoule, Menton,** and **Monte Carlo** (the last is spectacularly sited on the slopes of Mont Angel).

Horseback Riding Just a couple of miles inland from Mandelieu-La Napoule on N7 is the **Poney Club** (Domaine de Barbossi); children will enjoy the small zoo, as well as the pony rides, while adults can rent horses and, if they like, receive lessons.

Water Sports If you want to get in some sailing while on the Riviera, try **Sportmer** (8 pl. Blanqui) in St-Tropez, and **Yacht Club de Cannes** (Palm Beach Port) and **Camper & Nicholson's** (Port Canto) in Cannes. This is a great area for windsurfing; you can rent equipment from **La Club Nautique La Croisette** (plage Jardin Pierre-Longue, Cannes), **Centre Nautique Municipal** (9 rue Esprit-Violet, Cannes), and **Sillages** (av. Henry-Clews, Mandelieu-La Napoule).

Beaches

If you like your beaches sandy, stick to those between St-Tropez and Antibes; most of the others are pebbly, though

Menton and Monaco have imported vast tons of sand to spread around their shores. Private beaches are everywhere. You'll have to pay to use them (between 70 and 120 francs a day), but you get value for money—a café or restaurant, cabanas and showers, mattresses and umbrellas, and the pleasure of watching the perpetual parade of stylish swimwear and languid egos.

St-Tropez's best beaches are scattered along a 3-mile stretch reached by the Routes des Plages; the most fashionable are **Moorea, Tahiti Plage,** and **Club 55.** You'll see lots of topless bathers, and some beaches allow total nudity. If you're traveling with children, try the family beaches at **Ste-Maxime** and **St-Raphaël. La Napoule** has no less than eight beaches, offering facilities for waterskiing, windsurfing, diving, and snorkeling, or you can just swim or stretch out on a lounge chair. One of Cannes's most fashionable beaches, which belongs to the **Carlton Hotel,** and is open from March to October, has a glassed-in terrace and heating to offset out-of-season chills. Nice's beaches extend along the Baie des Anges (the Bay of Angels); **Ruhl Plage** is one of the most popular, with a good restaurant and facilities for waterskiing, windsurfing, and children's swimming lessons. Not to be outdone, **Neptune Plage** has all that plus a sauna.

Dining and Lodging

Dining

Though prices often scale Parisian heights, the Riviera shares its cuisine with Provence, enjoying the same vegetable and fish dishes prepared with vivid seasonings. The most famous is *bouillabaisse,* a fish stew from around Marseille. Genuine bouillabaisse combines *rascasse* (scorpion fish), eel, and half a dozen other types of seafood; crab and lobster are optional. Local fish is scarce, however, so dishes like *loup flambé* (sea bass with fennel and anise liqueur), braised tuna, and even fresh sardines are priced accordingly.

With Italy so close, it's no surprise that many menus feature such specialties as ravioli and potato gnocchi. Try vegetable *soupe au pistou,* an aromatic brew seasoned with basil, garlic, olive oil, and Parmesan cheese; or *pissaladière,* a pastry-based version of pizza, topped with tomato, olives, anchovy, and plenty of onion. Nice claims its own specialties: *pan bagna* (salad in a bun) and *poulpe à la niçoise* (octopus in a tomato sauce). Of the various vegetable dishes, the best is *ratatouille,* a stew of tomatoes, onions, eggplant, and zucchini.

Anise-flavored *pastis* is the Riviera's number-one drink.

Highly recommended restaurants are indicated by a star ★ .

Category	Cost*
Very Expensive	over 450 francs
Expensive	250–450 francs

Moderate	150–250 francs
Inexpensive	under 150 francs

per person for a three-course meal, including tax (18.6%) and tip but not wine

Lodging

Hotels on the Riviera can push opulence to the sublime—or the ridiculous. Pastel colors, gilt, and plush are the decorators' staple tools in the resort hotels catering to *le beau monde*. The glamour comes hand in hand with hefty price tags, however, and while inexpensive hotels do exist, they're found mainly on the duller outskirts of the big centers and in less fashionable "family" resorts.

Highly recommended hotels are indicated by a star ★ .

Category	Cost*
Very Expensive	over 1,000 francs
Expensive	500–1,000 francs
Moderate	250–500 francs
Inexpensive	under 250 francs

All prices are for a standard double room for two, including tax (18.6%) and service charge.

Antibes Juan-les-Pins Dining ★

Bacon. This is the Riviera's top spot for bouillabaisse or any other dish that depends on prime fish, simply and perfectly cooked. The Sordello brothers have run Bacon for over 40 years and don't regard a fish as fresh unless it's still twitching—count on eating only the pick of the local catch. Eat outside on the airy terrace overlooking the port. *Blvd. de Bacon, Cap d'Antibes, tel. 93–61–50–02. Reservations required. Jacket and tie required. AE, DC, MC, V. Closed Sun. dinner, Mon., and mid-Nov.–Jan. Expensive.*

La Bonne Auberge. Chef Jo Rostang and his son Philippe rarely disappoint, with such specialties as lobster ravioli, salads of red mullet, and airy soufflés. The dining room is a flower-filled haven of exposed beams, dim lantern lighting, and rose-colored walls; huge glass windows allow diners a view of the inspired work going on in the kitchen. *Quartier de la Brague, Antibes, tel. 93–33–36–65. Reservations strongly advised. Jacket and tie required. AE, MC, V. Closed Mon. (except for dinner mid-Apr.–Sept.), and mid-Nov.–mid-Dec. Expensive.*

Auberge de l'Esterel. The affable Denis Latouche runs the best moderately priced restaurant in Juan-les-Pins, lending a nouvelle twist to local dishes; try the monkfish, and, for dessert, the lemon tart. The secluded garden is a romantic setting for dinner under the stars. There are 15 bedrooms in the small attached hotel. *21 rue des Iles, Juan-les-Pins, tel. 93–61–86–55. Reservations advised. Dress: neat but casual. MC, V. Closed mid-Nov.–mid-Dec., part of Feb., Sun. dinner, and Mon. Moderate–Expensive.*

Dining and Lodging

Grand Hôtel du Cap. Crystal chandeliers, gilt mirrors, gleaming antique furniture, and lots of marble make the Cap d'Antibes a glorious testimony to the opulence of another age.

Guest rooms are enormous and feature the same impressive decor as the public rooms. The glass-fronted Pavillon Eden Roc is the place for lobster thermidor, accompanied by vintage champagne. *Blvd. Kennedy, 06600 Antibes, tel. 93–61–39–01. 130 rooms with bath. Facilities: restaurant, tennis, pool. Closed Nov.–Apr. No credit cards. Very Expensive.*

Juana. This luxuriously renovated '30s hotel sits opposite the casino, just a couple of blocks from the beach. Towering pine trees overhang the grounds and the white marble pool. The restaurant, La Terrasse, is one of the best on the Côte d'Azur; chef Christian Morisset wins praise for his fine seafood creations. Eat outside on the terrace, overlooking the palm trees in the landscaped garden. All the guest rooms are large and individually decorated. *Av. Gallice, 06160 Juan-les-Pins, tel. 93–61–08–70. 45 rooms with bath. Facilities: restaurant, bar, pool. No credit cards. Closed late Oct.–mid-Apr. Very Expensive.*

Le Mas Djoliba. There are only 14 rooms at this converted Provençal farmhouse, all with a country-house feel. The salon features an airy bamboo-shoot motif, while the guest rooms, painted in a range of pastel shades, have antique furnishings. Choose between views of the park or the sea. The restaurant is open for dinner only. *29 av. de Provence, 06600 Antibes, tel. 93–34–02–48. 14 rooms with bath. Facilities: restaurant, garden, pool. AE, DC, MC, V. Closed Jan.; restaurant closed Oct.–Mar. Moderate.*

Cannes
Dining
★

La Mère Besson. Mix with the locals at this boisterous family eatery that features a range of authentic Provençal fare. Go on Friday for the *aïoli,* a heaped platter of fish, seafood, and boiled vegetables in a thick garlic mayonnaise. Decor borders on the frumpy, but the food is what counts here. *13 rue des Frères-Pradignac, tel. 93–39–59–24. Reservations advised. Dress: casual. AE, DC, MC, V. Closed Sun.; dinner only, July–Aug. Expensive.*

Villa Dionysos. Thanks to chef Claude Verger's culinary talents, an exceptionally accommodating staff, and the dining room's tongue-in-cheek Italianate decor, Villa Dionysos has forged a substantial reputation in the few years since it opened. Dine in the 18th-century Venetian-style dining room or outside on the spectacular terrace. Try the fillet of duck with tarragon sauce or the roast pigeon. *7 rue Marceau, tel. 93–38–79–73. Reservations advised. Dress: neat but casual. AE, MC, V. Moderate.*

Au Bec Fin. A devoted band of regulars will attest to the quality of this family-run restaurant near the train station. Don't look for a carefully staged decor: It's the spirited local clientele and the homey food that distinguish this cheerful bistro. The fixed-price menus are a fantastic value at 75 or 95 francs; try the fish cooked with fennel or the *salade niçoise. 12 rue du 24-Août, tel. 93–38–35–86. Reservations advised. Dress: casual. AE, DC, MC, V. Closed Sat. dinner, Sun., and Christmas-late Jan. Inexpensive.*

Lodging
★

Le Fouquet's. If you're looking for a central and comfortable base from which to explore the beach, the shops, the bistros, and the nightclubs, this is the place, located in a quiet residential area of town. The hotel ambience is welcoming—from the entrance, with its brightly lit archway, plants, and mirrors, to the rooms, decorated in warm shades and decked out with lots of French flounces. All the guest rooms are large and feature covered loggias. There's no restaurant. *2 rond-point Duboys-*

d'Angers, 06400, tel. 93–38–75–81. 10 rooms with bath. AE, DC, MC, V. Closed Nov.–Dec. Expensive.

Mondial. A three-minute walk from the beach takes you to this six-story hotel, a haven for the traveler seeking solid, unpretentious lodging in a town that leans more to tinsel. Many guest rooms offer sea views. There's no restaurant. 77 rue d'Antibes, 06400, tel. 93–68–70–00. No credit cards. Closed Nov. Moderate.

Roches Fleuries. Escape from the crowds at this pistachio-hued '30s villa, perched on a hillside high above town in the Le Suquet district. Guest rooms are small and unexciting, but the friendly welcome from the English-speaking proprietors and the vine-draped garden help to compensate. There's no restaurant. 92 rue Georges-Clemenceau, 06400, tel. 93–39–28–78. 24 rooms, 15 with bath. No credit cards. Closed mid-Nov.–Dec. Inexpensive.

Dining and Lodging **Carlton.** Cannes's most elegantly old-fashioned hotel is the gleaming white Carlton, built at the turn of the century right on the seafront. The opulent public rooms feature marble floors, chandeliers, floral bouquets, and glittering mirrors. Service, though, is not what it was, and some rooms are cramped. Those in the west wing are best; they're quieter and have terrific views. There are two restaurants: La Côte serves haute cuisine in an imposingly formal atmosphere; the Grill Room is simpler but still impressive. The bar is one of *the* places to mingle with the Riviera's Beautiful People. 58 La Croisette, 06400, tel. 93–68–91–68. 325 rooms with bath. Facilities: restaurants, bar, terrace, health center, private beach. Main restaurant closed Nov.–Christmas. AE, DC, MC, V. Very Expensive.

Gray d'Albion. This striking contemporary hotel is the last word in state-of-the-art luxury. Its white facade is austere; inside, the atmosphere is ultrasophisticated, with gray and cream walls, and plenty of leather, metal, and mirrors. Guest rooms are fitted out with slick, modern accessories. There's a number of restaurants; the Royal Gray is one of Cannes's most fashionable. 38 rue des Serbes, 06400, tel. 93–68–54–54. 174 rooms with bath. Facilities: 3 restaurants, disco, private beach. AE, DC, MC, V. Restaurant closed Feb., Sun., and Mon. Very Expensive.

★ **Martinez.** While many of the luxury palace-hotels that cosseted kings and heads of state have receded into history, the Martinez still manages to retain that sybaritic atmosphere of indulgence, despite the fact it wasn't built until the 1920s—a little late for classic status. The Concorde group bought it in 1982 and revamped it in '30s style, while a gentle renovation in 1989 redid 100 bedrooms in cool blue and salmon shades, with wooden furniture and large marble bathrooms. One of the hotel's biggest assets is the Palme d'Or restaurant, whose chef, Christian Willer, draws lavish praise for his choice line of modern cuisine. 73 La Croisette, 06400, tel. 92–98–30–18. 425 rooms with bath. Facilities: restaurants, tennis, pool, beach, bar. Restaurants closed mid-Nov.–mid-Jan., Feb., and Mon. and Tues. lunch. Very Expensive.

Eze
Dining and Lodging
★ **Château de la Chèvre d'Or.** Located above Monte Carlo in the medieval hilltop village of Eze, the Chèvre d'Or is comprised of a number of ancient houses whose mellow stone walls are set off by terracotta pots brimming with geraniums. The guest rooms, while small, are individually decorated and feature an-

tique furnishings and attractive fabrics and wallpapers; ask for room no. 9. The views of Cap Ferrat from the poolside terrace are sensational. The restaurant is dignified, a far cry from some of the Riviera's flashier dining rooms; try the grilled mullet. *Rue du Barri, 06360, tel. 93–41–12–12. 15 rooms with bath. Facilities: restaurant, café, bar, terrace, pool. AE, DC, MC, V. Closed Dec.–Feb. Very Expensive.*

Grasse
Lodging

Panorama. This tidy modern hotel has a pleasant, helpful staff and well-appointed, soundproof, air-conditioned rooms, where snacks can be served on request. *2 pl. Cours, 06130, tel. 93–36–80–80. 36 rooms with bath. MC, V. Moderate.*

Menton
Dining and Lodging

Auberge des Santons. Sea views and a peaceful setting on a hill near l'Annonciade Monastery are the lures of this tiny hotel. The spacious white villa has studio apartments for longer stays. The British owners have studied the art of Oriental cooking, so restaurant specials range from a traditional Chinese banquet to mince pie to Provençal dishes. *Colline de l'Annonciade, 06500, tel. 93–35–94–10. 9 rooms with bath. Facilities: restaurant. AE, MC, V. Moderate.*

Londres. This small, central hotel, close to the beach and casino, has its own restaurant, serving solid, traditional French cuisine, and a small garden for outdoor summer dining. *15 av. Carnot, 06500, tel. 93–35–74–62. 26 rooms with shower or bath. Facilities: restaurant (closed Wed.), bar, ping-pong. AE, MC, V. Inexpensive.*

Monte Carlo
Dining

Port. Harbor views from the terrace and top-notch Italian food make the Port a good choice. A large, varied menu includes shrimp, pastas, lasagna, fettuccine, fish risotto, and veal with ham and cheese. *Quai Albert 1er, tel. 93–50–77–21. Reservations advised. Dress: casual. AE, DC, MC, V. Closed Mon. and Nov. Moderate–Expensive.*

★ **Polpetta.** This popular little trattoria is close enough to the Italian border to pass for the real McCoy and is excellent value for the money. If it's on the menu, go for the vegetable *soupe au pistou. 2 rue Paradis, tel. 93–50–67–84. Reservations required in summer. Dress: casual. V. Closed Tues. and Sat. lunch and Feb. Inexpensive.*

Lodging

Alexandra. Shades of the Belle Epoque linger on in this comfortable hotel's spacious lobby and airy guest rooms. Tan and rose colors dominate the newer rooms. If you're willing to do without a private bath, this place sneaks into the Inexpensive category. The friendly proprietress, Madame Larouquie, makes foreign visitors feel right at home. *35 blvd. Princesse-Charlotte, 98000, tel. 93–50–63–13. 55 rooms, 46 with bath. AE, DC, MC, V. Moderate.*

Dining and Lodging

★ **Hôtel de Paris.** Though discreetly modernized, the Hôtel de Paris still exudes the gold-plated splendor of an era in which kings and granddukes stayed here. The restaurant, The Louis XV, stuns you with such royal decor that you might be distracted from the food; but make the effort to give it your attention, since Alain Ducasse is one of Europe's most celebrated chefs. Try his ravioli de foie gras. *Pl. du Casino, 98000, tel. 93–50–80–80. 255 rooms with bath. Restaurant closed Tues., Wed. (except dinner July–Aug.), late Feb.–early Mar., and Nov.–Dec. Very Expensive.*

Loews. Big, brash, and more than a touch vulgar, Loews has a plush extravagance on a scale Donald Trump would envy.

Fountains splash, contemporary rooms are decorated in ice-cream shades, and celebrities mix with sheikhs in the bars, casino, and restaurants. Die-hard football fans can watch the Super Bowl by satellite; those in search of live entertainment should head for the Folie Russe, boasting lines of scantily clad showgirls and mountains of caviar. *12 av. des Spélugues, 98000, tel. 93–50–65–00. 650 rooms with bath. Facilities: restaurants, pool, health spa, casino, Jacuzzi. AE, DC, MC, V. Very Expensive.*

Mougins
Dining and Lodging
★

Moulin de Mougins. A 16th-century olive mill houses one of the country's top 20 restaurants. Chef Roger Vergé has an ever-changing repertoire, and creates new dishes every season. Some of them capitalize on traditional regional cuisine, others are innovative concoctions using lobster, caviar, and other ingredients that many crave but few can afford. The intimate beamed dining rooms, with oil paintings, plants, and porcelain tableware, are the perfect setting for world-class fare. Dine outside in summer, under the awnings. There are five elegantly rustic guest rooms as well. *Notre-Dame-de-Vie, 06250, tel. 93–75–78–24. Reservations required. Jacket and tie required. AE, DC, MC, V. Closed Feb.–Mar., Mon. (except summer), and Thurs. lunch (times are variable). Very Expensive.*

La Napoule
Lodging

Le Domaine d'Olival. There's not the slightest hint of mass production at this charming hotel, whose rooms have been individually designed by the architect-owner. It's small, so make reservations long in advance. All the guest rooms are air-conditioned and have balconies, as well as tiny kitchens. Some suites sleep six, which brings the price per couple down to Moderate. *778 av. de la Mer, 06210, tel. 93–49–31–00. 18 rooms with bath. AE, DC, MC, V. Closed Nov.–mid-Jan. Expensive.*

Dining and Lodging

Loews. Weighing in at just over 200 rooms, this is a pocket edition of the Loews at Monte Carlo, with plenty of marble, plush, and gilt. Guest rooms have sea views and balconies and are decorated in pink and blue, with blond wooden furniture and large bathrooms. Diners at the moderately priced restaurant, Chez Loulou, can gaze out over a flood-lit swimming pool and deliberate between such textbook delicacies as caviar, lobster, and vintage champagne; try the grilled fish. *Blvd. Henry-Clews, 06210, tel. 93–49–90–00. 211 rooms with bath. Facilities: pool, casino, restaurants, cabaret, bars, shops, bank, travel agency, tennis. AE, DC, MC, V. Very Expensive.*

Nice
Dining
★

Ane Rouge. The Vidalots run a tight ship. Their tiny restaurant, perched right by the harbor, is always crowded and has been famous for generations as the place to go to for Nice's best fish and seafood. The best bets are the sea bass braised in champagne and the stuffed mussels. *7 quai des Deux-Emmanuel, tel. 93–89–49–63. Reservations advised. Dress: neat but casual. MC, V. Closed Sat., Sun., and mid-July–Sept. Expensive.*

Barale. This is one of Nice's most fashionable restaurants, and eating here is almost like attending a theatrical performance. The tempestuous proprietress and chef, Hélène Barale, displays her varied menu on a blackboard hanging in the extraordinary dining room, a warehouse of artifacts and unusual odds and ends. The food blends elements of French cuisine with Italian; try the salade Niçoise or the stuffed poached veal. Madame Barale often makes appearances in the dining room and is known to sing to her guests. It sounds a bit hokey, but go in the right mood and you may love it. *39 rue Beaumont, tel. 93–89–17–94. Reservations essential. Dress: neat but casual. No credit cards. Closed Sun., Mon., and Aug. Moderate.*

★ **La Mérenda.** This noisy bistro lies in the heart of the old town, and its down-to-earth Italo-Provençal food is tremendously good value. The Giustis, who run it, refuse to install a telephone, so go early to be sure of getting a table. House specials include pasta with *pistou* (a garlic-and-basil sauce) and succulent tripe. *4 rue de la Terrasse. No resrvations. Dress: casual. No credit cards. Closed Sat., Sun., Mon., Feb., and Aug. Moderate.*

Lodging **Little Palace.** Monsieur and Madame Loridan run the closest thing to a country-house hotel in Nice. The old-fashioned decor, the jumble of bric-a-brac, and the heavy wooden furniture lend an Old World air; some may say it's like stepping onto a film set. *9 av. Baquis, 06000, tel. 93–88–70–49. 36 rooms, 31 with bath. MC, V. Closed Nov. Inexpensive.*

La Mer. This small hotel is handily situated on place Masséna, close to the old town and seafront. Rooms are spartan (and carpets sometimes frayed), but all have a minibar and represent good value. Ask for a room away from the square to be sure of a quiet night. *4 pl. Masséna, 06000, tel. 93–92–09–10. 12 rooms with bath or shower. No credit cards. Inexpensive.*

Dining and Lodging **Elysée Palace.** This glass-fronted addition to the Nice hotel scene lies close to the seafront; all guest rooms feature views of the Mediterranean. The interior is spacious and ultramodern, with plenty of marble in evidence. The large restaurant is a sound bet for nouvelle cuisine, enjoyed amid surroundings of contemporary works of art. *59 Promenade des Anglais, 06000, tel. 93–86–06–06. 150 rooms with bath. Facilities: restaurant, pool, sauna, health club, bar, AE, DC, MC, V. Very Expensive.*

★ **Negresco.** Henri Negresco wanted to out-Ritz all the Ritzes when he built this place. There were eight kings at the opening ceremony in 1912, grouped on the 560,000-franc gold Aubusson carpet (the world's largest, naturally) beneath the one-ton crystal chandelier in the great oval salon. No two rooms are the same (except for the bathroom fittings), though all feature antique furniture and classical decor, evocative of various periods from the 16th through the 19th century. New chef Dominique le Stanc forged a name for himself in Monte Carlo and should cement the Chantecler restaurant's reputation as one of France's finest dining rooms. *37 Promenade des Anglais, 06000, tel. 93–88–39–51. 130 rooms with bath. Facilities: 2 restaurants, bar, private beach. Very Expensive.*

★ **Beau Rivage.** Occupying an imposing late 19th-century town house near the cours Saleya, the Beau Rivage is run by the same hotel group (Clef d'Or) as the Elysée Palace (*see* above). While rooms are decorated in a similar modern style, the overall effect is more intimate and personal. Renowned chef Roger Vergé oversees a catering school on the premises; his nouvelle touch can be appreciated in the hotel's fine restaurant. *24 rue St-François-de-Paule, 06000, tel. 93–80–80–70. 110 rooms with bath. Facilities: restaurant, private beach. AE, DC, MC, V. Expensive–Very Expensive.*

St-Paul-de-Vence **Colombe d'Or.** Anyone who likes the ambience of a country inn
Dining and Lodging will feel right at home here. You'll be paying for your room or
★ meal with cash or credit cards; Picasso, Klee, Dufy, Utrillo—

all friends of the former owner—paid with the paintings that now decorate the walls. The restaurant has a very good reputation. The Colombe d'Or is certainly on the tourist trail, but many of the tourists who stay here are rich and famous—if that's any consolation. *06570 St-Paul-de-Vence, tel. 93–32–80–02. 24 rooms with bath. Facilities: restaurant, pool. AE, DC, MC, V. Closed mid-Nov.–late Dec., part of Jan. Expensive.*

St-Tropez
Dining

Bistrot des Lices. You'll find a mix of celebrities and locals at this popular bistro, a hot spot for interesting food, served by a staff as fashionable as the clientele. Bronzed men and glamorous women lounge in the garden or eat inside in the pastel interior. The barman is renowned for his way with a cocktail shaker, high praise in a town where cocktails are a way of life. *3 pl. des Lices, tel. 94–97–29–00. Reservations advised. Dress: neat but casual. MC, V. Closed for lunch July–Aug.; closed Wed. out of season and Jan.–Feb. Moderate.*

Le Girelier. Fish enthusiasts—especially those with a taste for garlic—will enjoy the hearty, heavily spiced dishes at this bustling restaurant, located right on the quai. The fish soup and the giant shrimp are local favorites. *Quai Jean-Jaurès, tel. 94–97–03–87. Reservations accepted. Dress: casual. AE, DC, MC, V. Closed mid-Jan.–early Mar. Moderate.*

Lodging

Ermitage. This is the ideal town hotel, featuring an old-fashioned charm rarely found in modern-day St-Tropez. The guest rooms' white walls are offset by coordinated patterns of strong primary colors on the beds and at the windows. There's no restaurant. *Av. Paul-Signac, 83990, tel. 94–97–52–33. 27 rooms with bath. AE, DC, MC, V. Expensive.*

Lou Cagnard. This is one of the few inexpensive hotels in St-Tropez, just two minutes' walk from place des Lices, so book well ahead. Don't expect great style or comfort, but the rooms are clean and not too cramped. *18 av. Paul-Roussel, 83990, tel. 94–97–04–24. 19 rooms, most with bath or shower. No credit cards. Closed Nov.–Christmas. Inexpensive.*

Dining and Lodging

Byblos. The Byblos is the Côte d'Azur's sophisticated answer to Disneyland. Designed with ingenuity, taste, and humor, the complex resembles a Provençal village, with cottagelike suites grouped around courtyards paved with Picasso-inspired tiles and shaded by olive trees and magnolias. Inside, the atmosphere is distinctly New York Casbah, with lots of heavy damask and hammered brass, a leopard-skin bar, and Persian carpets on the dining-room ceiling. If you can't afford to stay here, at least go to use the pool (for a steep fee). The restaurant, Le Chabichou, is lucky to have the talented Michel Rochedy as chef; his grilled sardines are memorable. *Av. Paul Signac, 83990, tel. 94–97–00–04. 106 rooms with bath. Facilities: restaurant, pool, nightclub. AE, DC, MC, V. Closed Nov.–Feb.; restaurant closed early Oct.–early May. Very Expensive.*

Le Mas de Chastelas. In an old farmhouse that was once a silkworm farm, guests can enjoy a happy marriage of traditional and modern surroundings. The pink-toned facade, offset by white shutters, is half hidden behind trees and flowering shrubbery. Inside, white walls, modern furniture, and sculptures by the owner's sister combine to create a cool retreat from the blazing Mediterranean sun. The restaurant is usually filled with a congenial melange of celebrities and well-heeled travelers attracted by the subtle cuisine (asparagus with sea urchins, for example) of chef Michel Gaudin. *Rte. de Gassin, 83990, tel. 94–56–09–11. 30 rooms with bath. Facilities: restaurant, pool. AE, DC, MC, V. Closed Oct.–Mar. Very Expensive.*

Vence
Dining and Lodging
★

Château St-Martin. The secluded, elite St-Martin stands on the site of a crusader castle, surrounded by tall, shady trees and set within spacious grounds. Guest rooms are exquisitely decorated with antiques, needlepoint, and brocade; those in the tower are smaller and less expensive but feature the same loving attention to detail. There's an excellent restaurant serving Provençal-inspired dishes. *Rte. de Coursegoules, 06140, tel. 93–58–02–02. 25 rooms with bath. Facilities: restaurant, garden, pool, tennis, helicopter landing pad. AE, DC, MC, V. Closed mid-Nov.–mid.-Mar. Very Expensive.*

Le Roseraie. While there's no rose garden here, a giant magnolia spreads its venerable branches over the terrace. Chef Maurice Ganier hails from the southwest, as do the ducks that form the basis of his cooking. Polished service and sophisticated menus prove you don't have to be rich to enjoy life in this part of France. There are 12 guest rooms and a swimming pool. *Av. Henri-Giraud, 06140, tel. 93–58–02–20. 12 rooms with bath. Facilities: restaurant, pool. AE, MC, V. Closed Jan.; restaurant closed Tues. lunch and Wed. Moderate.*

The Arts and Nightlife

The Arts

Festivals
The Riviera's cultural calendar is splashy and star-studded, and never more so than during the region's world-famous festivals. The biggest and most celebrated is the **Cannes Film Festival** in May, rivaled by Monte Carlo's arts festival, **Printemps des Arts** (late March through late April). Antibes and Nice both host **jazz festivals** during July, drawing international performers. Menton has a **chamber music festival** in August and a **September music festival** at the Palais d'Europe.

Music and Ballet
Monte Carlo's primary venue for jazz and rock is **Le Chapiteau de Fontvieille** (tel. 93–25–18–68); the **Salle Garnier** (Casino de Monaco, tel. 93–50–76–54) offers both classical music and ballet, as does Nice's **L'Acropolis** (Palais des Arts et de Congrès de Tourisme, Esplanade de Lattre de Tassigny, tel. 93–32–82–82). St-Tropez's major concert hall is the **Salle de la Renaissance** (pl. des Lices, tel. 94–97–48–16). There are frequent jazz and pop concerts at Nice's **Théâtre de Verdure** (Jardin Albert 1er, tel. 93–82–38–68), which relocates to the **Arènes de Cimiez** during summer months.

Opera
The Nice **Opéra** (4 rue St-François-de-Paul, tel. 93–85–67–31) has a season that extends from September to June. In Monte Carlo, the **Salle Garnier** (*see* above) hosts operatic performances, most frequently during the spring arts festival.

Theater
In Nice try the **Théâtre Municipal du Vieux-Nice** (4 rue St-Joseph, tel. 93–62–00–03) or the **Café-Théâtre de Nice** (12 av. St-Jean-Baptiste, tel. 93–85–40–28). In Monte Carlo, the **Théâtre Princesse Grace** (12 av. d'Ostende, tel. 93–25–32–27) stages a number of plays during the spring festival; off-season, there's usually a new show each week.

Nightlife

There's no need to go to bed before dawn in any of the Riviera's major resorts, the most fashionable of which are St-Tropez, Cannes, Juan-les-Pins, Nice, and Monte Carlo. Juan-les-Pins draws a young crowd, St-Tropez has gay appeal, and clubs in Cannes, Nice, and Monte Carlo are expensive and sophisticated. Note that to get into many of the Riviera's night spots, you'll have to dress the part—or risk being brushed aside by the burly doormen.

Discos and Nightclubs   **La Siesta** (rte. du Bord de Mer, Antibes) is an enormous setup, with seven dance floors, roulette, bars, and supper places—all dramatically lit by torches; it's open during the summer season only. The top spot in Cannes is the **Studio-Circus** (52 blvd. de la République), which admits celebrities, stars, and starlets, but not necessarily everyone else. The cabaret shows are legendary, accompanied by lasers and deafening noise. Top-class cabaret is offered at Menton's **Club 06,** at the casino (Promenade de Soleil). In Monte Carlo, head to **Jimmy'z;** it operates from place du Casino from September to June, then moves to premises on avenue Princesse-Grace. The location may be different, but the disco remains expensive and chic, and the clientele is drawn from the elite. The **Navy Club** (plage du Larvotto) is a friendly place whose devotees dance from 11:30 PM to dawn all year (closed Mon.). In the avenue des Spélugues, you'll find **The Living Room** (at no. 7) and **Tiffany's** (at no. 3); both are popular, crowded, and open year-round. **The Camargue** (6 pl. Charles-Félix, on the cours Saleya) is Nice's trendiest spot, but you'll have to dress sharp to get past the doorman. If you don't make it, try the young, lively **Centre Ville Discothèque** (1 pl. Masséna). The hottest place in St-Tropez is **Les Caves du Roy** (Byblos Hotel, av. Signac); the decor is stunningly vulgar, but the *très chic* clientele don't seem to mind. It's large but always crowded, so look your best if you want to get in.

Casinos   There are casinos in **Cannes** (pl. Franklin-Roosevelt), **Nice** (Promenade des Anglais), and **Menton** (Promenade de Soleil), but the Riviera's most famous gambling venue is at **Monte Carlo** (pl. du Casino).

14 Corsica

Introduction

The island of Corsica lies in the heart of the Mediterranean, only 50 miles west of the Italian mainland and just 7 miles north of the island of Sardinia; Menton, on France's border with Italy, lies about 120 miles northeast. The ancient Greeks called Corsica Kallisté, "The Most Beautiful," while less-effusive English invaders nicknamed it the Scented Isle. But it was that most famous Corsican, Napoleon Bonaparte, who paid the island its greatest compliment: "I would recognize Corsica with my eyes closed," he declared, referring to the heady scent of myrtle, honeysuckle, lavender, eucalyptus, cyclamen, and wild mint that carries far out to sea.

Aside from the island's natural perfume, the first thing that strikes visitors, whether they arrive by air or sea, is the dramatic backbone of mountain ranges, which rise abruptly from the coastal shelf to loom high over beaches and bays. The approach by air is superb: Ajaccio, the island's capital, resembles an amphitheater, with the port occupying the stage and the houses perched where the seats would be. The island's sprawling sandy beaches are fringed with palm trees, ancient buildings, and cafés; Genoese watchtowers stud the coast, and houses and boats alike glitter with wild, bright hues of red, green, yellow, and blue.

Corsica seems more Italian than French. Over the centuries, it has served as a meeting point for myriad civilizations and was a hotly contested prize for successive waves of hostile invaders. In 1077, the Pisans took control; in the 15th century, Genoa established supremacy. In 1769, Genoa sold her rights in Corsica to France, and the island has been a French *département* ever since.

Corsica's main appeal is its scenery, a wild, rugged landscape covered with jagged, forested mountains. Perched in the foothills and nestled in the valleys are tiny villages that haven't changed since the Middle Ages, give or take the occasional traffic light. Many of the smaller bays are inaccessible except by boat.

The best way to appreciate the island is to drive along the entire coastal circuit, venturing inland to admire the remote rural regions and picturesque villages, with their stone fortresslike houses topped by heavy slate roofs and pierced by narrow windows; tiny alleys masquerade as village streets, better suited to donkeys and goats than to four-wheeled traffic. Though the main roads are full of hairpin curves and daredevil drivers, breathtaking views reward the effort.

Late spring and early fall are favorite times to visit, when the moderate temperature (61°–68°F) is ideal for exploring both inland and coastal areas. Corsica enjoys the longest beach season in France—from early May to November. Visitors flock here during the celebrated "white spring," from mid-April to mid-June, when the island's ubiquitous white heather is in full bloom. Avoid visiting in July and August, when Corsica is overrun with tourists and there are no hotel vacancies.

Essential Information

Important Addresses and Numbers

Tourist Information
The **Agence Régionale du Tourisme et des Loisirs** (ARTL, 22 cours Grandval, Ajaccio, tel. 95–51–15–23) can provide information about all areas of the island. Local tourist offices are as follows: **Ajaccio** (Hôtel de Ville, pl. Foch, tel. 95–21–40–87), **Bastia** (pl. St-Nicholas, tel. 95–31–00–89), **Bonifacio** (rue des Deux Moulins, tel. 95–73–11–88), **Calvi** (Port de Plaisance, tel. 95–65–16–67), and **Sartène** (rue Borgo, tel. 95–77–15–40).

Travel Agencies
Havas (1 av. du 1er-Consul, Ajaccio, tel. 95–21–49–66) and **Ollandini** (40 blvd. Paoli, Bastia, tel. 95–31–11–71).

Car Rental
Avis (77 quai Comparetti, Bonifacio, tel. 95–73–01–28), **Europcar** (1 rue du Nouveau Port, Bastia, tel. 95–31–59–29) and **Hertz** (8 cours Grandval, Ajaccio, tel. 95–21–70–94; and 2 rue du Maréchal-Joffre, Calvi, tel. 95–65–06–64).

Arriving and Departing

By Plane
Corsica has four major airports, in Ajaccio, Bastia, Calvi, and Figari. **Air France** (tel. 45–35–61–61 Paris; 95–21–00–61 Ajaccio) and **Air Inter** (tel. 45–39–25–29 Paris; 95–21–63–06 Ajaccio) offer daily service between Paris and Ajaccio, Bastia, and Calvi. In addition, **TAT** (Transport Aérian Transrégional, tel. 46–87–35–53 Paris; 95–71–01–20 Figari) flies to Figari from Paris.

Between the Airports and Downtown
The airports at Ajaccio and Bastia run regular *navette* (shuttle) bus services to and from town. At Figari, a bus meets all incoming flights and will take passengers as far as Bonifacio and Porto-Vecchio for 36 francs. If you arrive at Calvi, take a taxi into the town center.

By Ferry
SNCM (Société Nationale Maritime Corse Méditérranée, tel. 91–56–80–20 in Marseille) runs a regular ferry service (twice daily in the low season; more frequently during peak summer months) from Marseille, Nice, and Toulon to Ajaccio, Bastia, Calvi, L'Ile-Rousse, and Propriano; crossings take from 5 to 10 hours.

Getting Around

By Plane
Air Corse (tel. 95–20–61–30), **Air Transport Méditérranée** (tel. 95–76–04–99), and **Kyrnair** (tel. 95–20–52–29) offer interisland flights throughout the year.

By Car
While driving is undoubtedly the best way to explore the island's scenic stretches, note that winding, mountainous roads and uneven surfaces can as much as double your expected travel time.

By Train
Corsica's simple train network consists of one main route and two branch lines. The main line runs from Ajaccio, in the west, to Corte, in the central valley, then divides at Ponte Leccia. From here, one line continues to L'Ile-Rousse and Calvi in the north and the other to Bastia, in the northeast. Another daily service runs directly between Ajaccio and Bastia, the island's two largest cities. During the summer months, a train-tram service connects Calvi and L'Ile-Rousse, stopping at numerous

beaches and resorts (for information, call 95–32–60–06 in Bastia or 95–65–00–61 in Calvi).

By Bus The local bus network is geared to residents, who use it in the morning and evening to get to and from school and work; afternoon buses are few and far between.

Guided Tours

Orientation Tours **Ollandini** (3 pl. de Gaulle, Ajaccio, tel. 95–21–72–20) is one of Corsica's largest bus tour companies, with branches all over the island. Typical half-day bus excursions from Ajaccio visit the prehistoric site at Filitosa, taking in the Col de Bellavelle, Pila-Canale, Taravo Valley, Pietrosella, Isobella, and Porticcio. The most attractive whole-day excursion includes a trek along the breathtaking Scala di Santa Regina, Calacuccia, the forest of Valdoniello, and a lunch break at the Col de Vergio.

Boat Tours Much of Corsica's most spectacular scenery is best viewed from the water. Boats leave regularly from Ajaccio for the Iles Sanguinaires ("Bloody Islands"—named for the red hue of the rocks in the setting sun), which lie just off the tip of the peninsula. The three-hour trip starts twice daily (at 9 and 2), leaving from the Bar du Golfe, below place Foch (for information, call 95–21–06–95). From Bonifacio, you can visit the Dragon Grottoes and Venus's Bath (boats that make one-hour trips set out every 15 minutes during July and August) and the Lanezzi Islands (boats leave from outside the Hôtel La Caravelle, tel. 95–75–05–43). Whole-day tours leave from Calvi and visit Girolata, Scandola, and the Golfe de Porto. Boats depart at 9 AM, mid-May through September, and return at about 4:30 (contact **Autocars Mariani** in Calvi, tel. 95–65–02–55).

Aerial Tours **Corse Aero Service** (Figari Airport, tel. 95–23–21–42) offers a series of sightseeing flights that cover the southern half of the island; an hour's flight costs 600 francs. **Bastia Aeroclub** (tel. 95–36–24–85) features tours over the island's central region.

Exploring Corsica

Numbers in the margin correspond with points of interest on the Corsica map.

Orientation

Our tour begins in the bustling port of Bastia, on the northeastern coast, and moves west, creeping inland to the Balagne region before reaching the popular resort town of Calvi. Our second tour actually describes two alternate, but equally dramatic, routes. Both veer inland to start; one branches off to reach Ajaccio by the coastal road and the other snakes down through the center of the island. Our final circuit explores the southern tip before swinging north to Alèria on the eastern coast.

Highlights for First-time Visitors

Ajaccio, Tour 2
The Asco Valley, Tour 2
Hill towns of the Balagne, Tour 1
Bonifacio, Tour 3

Calvi, Tour 1
Menhir statues at Filitosa, Tour 3
Scala di Santa Regina (D84), Tour 2

Tour 1: The Northern Coast

❶ We begin our tour in **Bastia,** whose name derives from *bastaglia,* or fortress. The Genoese built a prodigious one here in the 14th century as a stronghold against pugnacious inland natives and other potential invaders from across the Tuscan Straits. Today, as the island's commercial nerve center and largest town, the city has fallen to a new strain of invaders; a full 50% of Corsica's visitors, as well as over half its maritime traffic, pass through each year. Despite its reputation as the island's industrial center, with sprawling suburbs, modern tower blocks, and laundry-decked tenements, the city retains much of the color and flavor of a bustling Mediterranean port.

Start your tour in the atmospheric **Terra-Vecchia** (Old Town), at place St-Nicholas, bounded on one side by cafés and shops and on the other by the sea. Head right, along the waterfront, until you reach quai du Premier Bataillon de Choc. Most of the quayside buildings date from the 17th and 18th centuries, but their once-impressive facades are badly in need of restoration. To the right is the **place de l'Hôtel de Ville,** enlivened each morning by a bustling outdoor market where black-swathed grandmothers haggle over the price of fish and fruit.

A few hundred yards up boulevard Général-de-Gaulle, to the right, stands the **Chapelle de l'Immaculée Conception,** occupying a pebble-studded square. Step inside to admire the church's ornate 18th-century interior: The walls are covered with a riot of woodcarvings, gold, and marble, and the ceiling is vibrantly frescoed. A copy of the *Immaculate Conception,* by 17th-century Spanish painter Bartolomé Murillo, adorns the altar, while the sacristy houses numerous relics used by Corsican religious cults between the 15th and 19th century. *Blvd. Général-de-Gaulle.*

Walking left from the Chapelle de l'Immaculée Conception and around the old port brings you to the city's **Terra-Nova** (New Town), dominated by its 16th-century **citadel.** If it's a clear day, climb to the top for a sweeping view of the islands of Capraja, Elba, Pianosa, and Monte-Cristo; in the distance, you'll be able to make out Italy's Tuscan hills.

While you are at place de la Citadelle, stop in at the **Genoese Governors' Palace,** whose vaulted, colonnaded galleries today house the **Musée d'Ethnographie Corse,** with collections detailing Corsican daily life and history. There are also archaeological, botanical, and anthropological exhibits, and a lifelike mock-up of a shepherd's hut. One of the museum's major attractions is an 18th-century rebel flag bearing the elaborate national coat of arms: a Moor's head in profile, bound by a white band enclosed in a crowned shield, supported by a pair of winged, cloven-hoofed giants. Outside, the palace's courtyard is the setting for local festivities and colorful historical pageants. Behind the ancient defense tower, a tiny flight of steps leads to the governors' private hanging gardens, an intimate green oasis offering a superb view over the old port to the towers of St-Jean-Baptiste. *Pl. du Donjon la Citadelle. Admission: 6 frs. Open*

Corsica

MARSEILLE
TOULON

NICE

MARSEILLE
TOULON

NICE

Centuri
Rogliano
D80
Pino
D180
*Cap Corse
Peninsula*
Canari
Monte Stello
GENOA
LIVORNO
Canelle
Nonza
D80
Erbalunga
Patrimonio
2
St-Florent
3
Bastia
1
Oletta
D81
D82
N193

L'Ile-Rousse
4
N197
5
Corbara
N197
Calvi
8
6
Montemaggiore
D151
Cassano
Casamozza
Mariana
N193
7
Calenzana
Asco
9
Ponte Leccia
Golo
D506
Piedicroce
Partinello
Calacuccia
D84
N193
D71
*Golfe de
Porto*
Evisa
10
Corte
Porto
11
D81
D84
Monte d'Oro
12
Piana
D81
SARDINIA
D70
Vico
Vivario
N200
N98
Cargese
Sagone
26
Aléria
Tiuccia
Ghisoni
*Golfe de
Sagone*
N193
D69
Ghisonaccia
D343
Ajaccio
13 — 20
N196
Gravona
D8
Cauro
Solenzara
*Iles
Sanguinaires*
*Golfe
d'Ajaccio*
Porticcio
D69
D268
NICE
TOULON
MARSEILLE
Petreto-
Bicchisano
N198
Filitosa
21
Zonza
*Capo di
Muro*
Olmeto
Propriano
Golfe de Porto-Vecchio
Cauria
23
22
Sartène
25
N196
Porto-Vecchio
*Mediterranean
Sea*
D859
Figari
N196
N198
*Tyrrhenian
Sea*
N

0   40 miles
0   60 km
Bonifacio
24
Iles Lavezzi
SARDINIA

Apr.–Oct., Mon.–Sat. 9–noon and 2– 6; Nov.–Apr., Mon.–Sat. 9–noon and 2–5.

Opposite the museum, a network of cobbled alleyways rambles across the citadel to the 15th-century church of **Ste-Marie** (rue Notre-Dame). Inside, textbook Baroque abounds in an explosion of gilt decoration. The church's 18th-century silver sculpture depicting the Assumption is paraded through the streets of the Terra-Vecchia each August 15, at the head of a solemn religious procession. Just behind Ste-Marie stands the **Chapelle Sainte-Croix;** with its sumptuous Baroque interior, it looks more theater than church. The chapel owes its name to its major attraction, the "Christ of Miracles," a blackened oak crucifix discovered in 1428 and venerated to this day by Bastia's fishing community. *Just off pl. Guasco.*

As you set off west by car along D81, you'll have dramatic views of mountains looming to the north, which form the backbone of the wild **Cap Corse peninsula** *(see* Off the Beaten Track, below). Before turning toward St-Florent, 23 kilometers (14 miles) **2** from Bastia, stop in the little town of **Patrimonio,** lying among acres of vineyards that stretch into the distance, a centuries-old source of some of Corsica's best red, white, and rosé wines. You'll find lots of local producers happy to sell you a bottle or two.

3 The resort town of **St-Florent** nestles in the crook of the Golfe de St-Florent, between the rich Nebbio Valley and the Desert des Agriates, an expanse of barren rocks sloping into the sea. The 13th-century limestone church of **Santa Maria Assunta** stands in isolated splendor among the vines, less than a mile from town. The church is one of only two Pisan cathedrals remaining on the island; though its bell tower crumbled in the 19th century, Santa Maria Assunta ranks as one of the most interesting Romanesque monuments Corsica has to offer. The facade and interior columns feature sculpted capitals depicting human masks, snakes, snail shells, and mythical animals with flowing manes and fierce-looking teeth. In the apse, notice the gilt statue of St-Flor, a martyred Roman soldier; his relics are displayed in a glass case nearby.

4 D81 snakes about 20 kilometers (12 miles) west from St-Florent to the small resort town of **L'Ile-Rousse.**

Time Out **Napoléon Bonaparte** (3 pl. Paoli) is a rambling 18th-century palace-hotel, whose dining room, La Piscine, serves simple, satisfying meals against a backdrop of green foliage and starched white tablecloths.

From L'Ile-Rousse, pick up N197 and drive about 10 kilometers (6 miles) south into the ancient Roman region of **Balagne.** This western *Terre des Seigneurs* (Land of Lords) remained a feudal society right up to the French Revolution, and even today its population remains more insular than other Corsican folk.

Balagne long boasted a higher standard of living than other regions in Corsica, thanks, in part, to the area's rich agricultural resources. Oil, olives, barley, cheese, and grapes made more than a few fortunes for the Balagne gentry; the region is dotted with hill villages whose crumbling mansions hint at the wealth of former denizens.

⑤ D151 boasts a number of postcard-perfect towns. In **Corbara,** the first major village south of L'Ile-Rousse, sinister passageways and shady alleys recall Hollywood images of southern Spain. In the villages of Montemaggiore, Cassano, Calenzana, Aregno, and Lumio you'll find myriad churches, many built by wealthy nobles when the island was under Pisan rule (1077–1284). **⑥** The chapel at **Montemaggiore** has its own legend. The steps beside it are a monument to Miguel Manara, better known as Don Juan. Born in Seville to Corsican parents in 1627, the womanizing Miguel returned to Corsica at the height of his infamy to seduce his half sister, Vannina. Vannina's screams of protest awakened the family, and the frustrated rake was forced to flee the village, escaping down these very steps.

The 11th-century church of **Ste-Restitute,** half a mile from **⑦ Calenzana,** is particularly interesting. The church's white marble, granite-topped 4th-century altar is backed by two 13th-century frescoes depicting Ste-Restitute's life. Legend has it that the saint was martyred here, and when the people of Calenzana began building a church on another site, the stone blocks were moved each night by two huge white bulls, to be discovered here the next morning. Apparently, this happened several times before the Calenzanais finally got the divine message and changed building sites.

⑧ Continue northwest along D151 until you reach **Calvi,** one of Corsica's most sophisticated resort towns and the port closest to mainland France. Like that of Bastia, Calvi's location has long made it a strategic spot for warriors and tourists alike. The Middle Ages saw numerous struggles between local clans, while during the 18th century, Calvi endured assaults from Corsican nationalists, the most prominent being the celebrated patriot Pasquale Paoli.

Today's Calvi sees an annual summertime invasion of French and Italian visitors, drawn by the resort's four miles of white sand beaches flanked with graceful umbrella pines, a perfectly carved bay, and a busy marina.

Calvi's major attraction is the **Genoese citadel,** perched on a rocky promontory at the tip of the bay; the citadel's ramparts are the natural place to begin your tour of the city. As you cross the drawbridge, notice the plaque above; the inscription— *Civitas Calvi semper fidelis* (Calvi always faithful)—reflects the town's unswerving allegiance to Genoa. Calvi remained Genoese for centuries, even after the rest of the island had declared independence.

Next to the citadel is the **Oratoire de la Confrérie St-Antoine,** a 15th-century chapel showcasing Calvi's religious art. The wide collection of sacred objects spans the period from the 16th through the 19th centuries, and many items were discovered in recent excavations. *Admission: 6 frs. Open July–mid-Sept., Mon.–Sat. 10–noon and 3–6.*

Time Out Stop at **Chez Tao,** (Pl. de la Citadelle), in the former Bishops' Palace at the citadel, to wine, dine, or just listen to the music that fills the ocher-colored 16th-century vaults from 7 PM till 3 AM.

Stroll down the elegant quai Landry, lined with attractive bayside cafés and restaurants. Rue Clemenceau and boulevard

Wilson, just behind, are major shopping streets. As you explore the narrow, winding streets of the old town, stop at the 13th-century church of **St-Jean-Baptiste** on place d'Armes, which contains an interesting marble baptismal font dating from the Renaissance. Look up at the dome to see the rows of seats screened by grillwork; the chaste women of Calvi's upper classes would sit here saying their prayers, protected from the hot glances of any lusty young peasant who might happen to look up.

Tour 2: Two Scenic Routes to Ajaccio

The route south from Calvi takes in a feast of varied scenery. Head east along N197 about 8 kilometers (5 miles); then follow the road south to the village of **Ponte Leccia,** standing between the spectacular regions of the Gorges de l'Asco and the Castigniccia. The **Asco Valley** runs west to an awe-inspiring barrier of mountains whose colors vary from a red-mauve to a dark purple-gray, depending on the time of day. As you travel, the maquis-covered valley gives way to deep, granite gorges hung with sweet-smelling juniper. The Asco region's foothills are studded with beehives, and honey and cheese abound in the village shops. This is a land of tradition, where shepherds and goatherds practice the age-old winter ritual of transhumance, taking their flocks to graze in the pastures of Balagne or on the rocks of Agriates and remaining with them until the summer heat signals them back to the mountains.

We offer two alternative routes from the island's center to Ajaccio. The first, and fastest, option is to follow N193 through Corte to Ajaccio. **Corte,** the biggest inland city in Corsica, has long been associated with the island's struggle for independence against the Genoese. The city's old town proves more austere than picturesque, however, and only hard-core history buffs should plan to linger here for a look at the 15th-century citadel. N193 runs 80 kilometers (50 miles) through the center of the island along the Vecchio Valley and over the Col de Vizzavona. In places, the junglelike chestnut, beech, and pine forests transform the road into little more than a thin green tunnel burrowing through the undergrowth. Along the way, stop for a superb view of the majestic Monte d'Oro, whose purple bulk looms against the skyline. As you enter the Gravona Valley, an unending chain of ridges alters the landscape at every turn.

Time Out Stop off in the village of Vivario, whose relaxed **Café-Restaurant des Amis** is the perfect place for a light lunch or mid-afternoon snack. The menu features local produce. *About 12 km (7 mi) south of Corte.*

For a less efficient but even more dramatic route, pick up D84 just before you reach Corte and head west for the coastal towns of Porto and Piana, about 80 kilometers (50 miles) away. Known as the **Scala di Santa Regina** (Staircase of the Sainted Queen), the road is one of the most spectacular on the island; it's also one of the wildest and most difficult to navigate, particularly in winter. The route follows the twisty path of the River Goli, which has carved its way through layers of red granite, forming dramatic gorges and waterfalls; jagged needles of rock rise threateningly on all sides. Local legend has it that the Santa Regina mountains were the setting for the desperate struggle between St. Martin and the devil—good versus evil—the theme of many traditional Corsican songs and poems. The road passes through two forests, the Forêt de Valdo-Niello and the Forêt d'Aitone, before descending to the Golfe de Porto. Porto and Piana lie on either side of the deep blue gulf, separated by an enormous red *calanche*, or jagged rock outcropping, that counts as one of the most extraordinary natural sites in France.

⑪ **Porto** is somewhat garish and self-consciously spruced, with an abundance of neon-lit hotels and restaurants; the village of ⑫ **Piana,** about 8 kilometers (5 miles) away, is much more welcoming. In addition to offering a series of breathtaking views of the Golfe de Porto, Piana serves as an excellent base for scenic walks. Visit the old fortress at the top of Capo Rosso to admire the craggy rocks that jut up from the bay.

Leaving Piana, pick up D81 and follow it about 35 kilometers ⑬ (21 miles) south along the coast to **Ajaccio,** which sits snugly on a protected bay surrounded by green mountains and rocky crags. High-rise buildings and overpasses loom as you approach this booming commercial city—Napoleon's birthplace and Corsica's modern capital.

Numbers in the margin correspond with points of interest on the Ajaccio map.

⑭ Begin your tour at **place Maréchal-Foch,** the city's main square ⑮ planted firmly on the waterfront. Stop in at the **Hôtel de Ville** (Town Hall), whose Empire-style Grand Salon is hung with portraits of a long line of Bonapartes. Exhibits include a fine bust of Letizia, Napoleon's formidable mother, and a bronze death mask of the emperor himself; the frescoed ceiling portrays Napoleon's meteoric rise to fame. The Salle des Medailles (Medal Room) displays a handsome collection of coins and medals. *Pl. Maréchal-Foch. Admission: 5 frs. Open Apr.–Oct., Mon.–Sat. 9–noon and 2:30–5:30; Nov.–Mar., Mon.–Sat. 9–noon and 2–5.*

⑯ Walk across the square and turn down rue Bonaparte. The **Maison Bonaparte** (the Bonaparte House) is a small, intimate museum in a modest 18th-century row house in rue St-Charles, overlooking place Letizia; Napoleon was born here on August 15, 1769. The museum features original Louis XV and XVI interiors, decorated by Letizia Bonaparte herself. In addition, glass cases display mementoes belonging to Napoleon and his father, Carlo; another room contains portraits and cameos of the Bonaparte clan. Other highlights include the two family trees, one spanning nearly 200 years (1769–1959), the other a tiny 19th-century plaque over the chimney, woven out of human hair. *Rue St-Charles. Admission: 16 frs. Open Apr.–Oct., Tues.–Sat. 9–noon and 2–6, Mon. 2–6, Sun. 9–noon; Nov.–Mar., Tues.–Sat. 10–noon and 2–5, Sun. 10–noon, Mon. 2–5.*

Turn left outside the Maison Bonaparte and continue two ⑰ blocks to the 16th-century **cathedral,** where Napoleon was baptized. Inside you'll see Eugène Delacroix's famous painting *Virgin of the Sacré Coeur,* while the marble statue of *Notre-Dame-de-la-Miséricorde,* Ajaccio's patron saint, has a place of honor opposite. *Rue Forcioli-Conti.*

A Bandera, **20**
Cathedral, **17**
Chapelle Impériale, **18**
Hôtel de Ville, **15**
Maison Bonaparte, **16**
Musée Fesch, **19**
Place Maréchal-
Foch, **14**

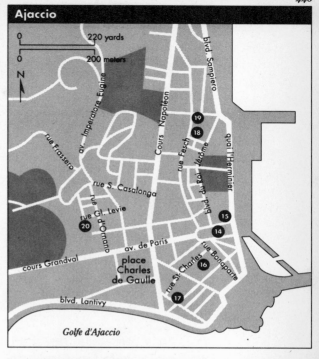

Ajaccio

Golfe d'Ajaccio

Time Out   After visiting the cathedral, make your way down the **Plage St-François** and stop at one of the many cafés, restaurants, or ice-cream parlors lining the quayside.

Before leaving Ajaccio, work your way back through the narrow streets to place Maréchal-Foch. Four blocks up rue Fesch is the Renaissance-style **Chapelle Impériale**, built in 1857 by Napoleon's nephew, Napoleon III, to accommodate the tombs of the Bonaparte family. (The great man himself isn't buried here, however; his pretentious tomb is housed in Paris's Hôtel des Invalides.) A Coptic crucifix, taken from Egypt during the general's 1798 campaign, hangs over the chapel's main altar. Opposite is one of the island's finest museums, the **Musée Fesch,** showcasing a superb collection of early Italian paintings. *Admission: 15 frs. Open Wed.–Mon. 10–noon and 2–6. Rue Fesch, tel. 95–21–48–17.*

If you're interested in Corsican military history, make a trip to **A Bandera,** a tiny museum in rue Général-Levie. To get there from the Musée Fesch, walk back down rue Fesch, turn right toward cours Napoleon, then take the first left and first right, finally turning left into rue d'Ornano. The museum has a collection of documents, maps, uniforms, and armaments that illustrate the island's long and important history as a Mediterranean military station. *1 rue Général-Levie. Admission: 15 frs. Open June–Sept., Mon.–Sat. 10–noon and 3–7; Oct.–May, Mon.–Sat. 10–noon and 2–6.*

Tour 3: Ajaccio to Alèria

Numbers in the margin correspond with points of interest on the Corsica map.

Leaving Ajaccio, follow N196 20 kilometers (12 miles) south-east to **Filitosa,** site of Corsica's largest collection of megalithic menhir statues. Bizarre, life-size stone figures rise up almost menacingly from the undulating terrain, many with human faces that have been eroded and flattened with time. A small museum on the site houses a variety of fascinating archaeological specimens, including the figure of Scalsa Murta, whose delicately carved spine and rib cage make it difficult to believe the statue dates from some 3,000 years before the birth of Christ. During the peak summer season (June through August), English-speaking guides are on hand to show visitors around. *Filitosa, tel. 95–74–00–91. Admission: 40 frs. Open Easter–mid-Oct., daily 8–noon and 3–7. Phone for information about winter hours.*

Time Out | Stop at the pleasant museum **café** and soak up the prehistoric ambience over a light lunch or snack.

Following N196 about 16 kilometers (10 miles) southeast from Filitosa, you'll arrive at the hillside town of **Sartène.** Founded by the Genoese in the 16th century, Sartène has survived raids by Barbary pirates and internal feuding among the town's leading families. Centuries of fighting have left the town with an almost spooky atmosphere; as you draw near, a line of tall, 18th-century granite houses rises in surly greeting.

The most interesting part of town is the **Vieux Sartène** (Old Town), just behind the ancient ruined ramparts. Start at place de la Libération, which is flanked by palms, elms, and intimate cafés. Locals traditionally gather here at night, and, more often than not, you'll find them engaged in heated—and incomprehensible—political discussions. To one side of the square is the Hôtel de Ville (Town Hall), the former Genoese Governors' Palace, whose facade is decorated with an ornate coat of arms. For a taste of the Middle Ages, follow the vaulted passageway through the building to place du Maggiu and the old quarter of **Santa Anna,** an eerie warren of narrow, cobbled streets lined with granite houses. Scarcely 100 yards from the Town Hall, down a steep and winding street, a 12th-century watchtower stands out in stark contrast to the modern apartment blocks behind.

For a look at some prehistoric relics, venture farther afield to the **Musée Archéologique Départemental de Préhistoire Corse** (Archaeology Museum), a short distance outside town in Sartène's former prison. Sartène is the center for research on the island's prehistory, and the museum offers a fine collection of artifacts. *Admission: 10 frs. Open mid-June–mid-Sept., Mon.–Sat. 10–noon and 2–6; mid-Sept.–mid-June, Mon.–Sat. 10–noon and 2–4.*

About 10 kilometers (6 miles) southwest of Sartène lies the Cauria Plateau, a region that is rich in megalithic statues and formations. Follow N196 south along the River Loreto, then turn off onto tiny D48 to arrive at **Cauria.** Leave your car here and set off on foot along the paths through the maquis, where grazing goats share the countryside with spectacular remains.

One of the best-preserved ruins is the **Dolmen Fontanaccia funeral chamber,** discovered in 1840.

Backtracking to N196, continue south toward Bonifacio. As you pass Roccapino, you'll probably see parked cars lining the cliffs, their passengers taking in the spectacular **Rocher du Lion** (Lion Rock), a glowing pink granite formation at the top of a promontory. About 11 kilometers (7 miles) farther is another rock formation, perched precariously among the mountains— **Omo di Cagna** (The Cagna Man).

About 16 kilometers (10 miles) south of the N196 exit to Figari looms the ancient fortress-town of **Bonifacio,** the southernmost town in France. At its feet lies a handsome, fjordlike harbor carved from the limestone cliffs. The city is just 8 miles from Sardinia, and local speech is heavily influenced by the accent and idiom of the neighboring Italian island. Don't be surprised if you find the inhabitants difficult to understand—many Corsicans do.

Established in the 12th century as Genoa's first Corsican stronghold against the Moors, Bonifacio remained Genoese through centuries of battles and sieges; these days, the town contains many reminders of past military conflicts. As you explore the area, think of Homer's *Odyssey;* it was here, in the bottleneck harbor at Bonifacio, that Ulysses's fleet was supposedly bombarded by the vicious Laestrygonians.

From the port-side village hamlet in the center of town, follow the broad cobbled ramp up to the fortified **citadel** and the **Vieille Ville** (Old Town). The citadel, which overlooks the harbor and the Straits of Bonifacio, has long been the city's main defensive post, and from 1963 to 1983 served as the main garrison of the French Foreign Legion. Wander down to the tip of the promontory for a look at the ruins of the Franciscan monastery. As you walk about, note the circular silos that were used to hoard food and supplies, testimony to the plight of a city constantly under siege. *Pl. de la Citadelle. Admission: 6 frs. Open June–mid-Sept., daily 9–7.*

Finding hotel accommodations in Bonifacio during the peak season can be difficult, since the sheltered, sandy beaches of southeastern Corsica draw thousands of summer visitors. You're more likely to find lodging at the large tourist resort of **Porto-Vecchio,** about 27 kilometers (17 miles) north on N198. Though the town itself is of limited interest, the **Golfe de Porto-Vecchio** is lined with beautiful beaches and backs onto Corsica's largest cork-oak forest. The walled old town features a network of medieval streets, now given over to bistros, boutiques, and cafés.

Time Out   While in Porto-Vecchio, it's worth making a special detour to one of the island's most famous hotels, **Grand Hôtel de Cala Rossa,** at the northernmost tip of the gulf *(see* Dining and Lodging, below). Even if you can't afford to stay here, stop in for lunch; the food is light and refined, and you can eat your meal on a shady terrace among the fragrant pines overlooking the bay. *8 kilometers (5 miles) outside town; Lecci de Porto-Vecchio.*

Leaving Porto-Vecchio, follow N198 60 kilometers (36 miles) north, skirting the marshy eastern plain, to the Roman city of

26 **Aléria,** whose chief attraction is its rich archaeological heritage. Just outside town, on a pine-tree-studded plateau, is the 16th-century **Fort de Matra.** On the ground floor is the **Musée d'Aléria,** housing a fascinating collection of relics from Classical times, including some well-preserved Etruscan *rhytons,* or drinking cups, discovered in a 5th-century tomb nearby. Detailed exhibits chronicle daily life in Roman Aléria. One rather grisly display is the skeleton of an unfortunate prisoner who died around 50 BC; he was discovered curled in his tomb with his ankles still locked in heavy cuffs and chains. *Fort de Matra. Admission: 9 frs. Open Apr.–Oct., daily 8–noon and 2–7; Nov.–Mar., Mon.–Sat. 8–noon and 2–5.*

What to See and Do with Children

Corsica's **beaches** provide the best island entertainment for children *(see* Beaches, below). Or take them to the **Acqua Cyrné Gliss** water park in Porticcio, just south of Ajaccio, which offers water slides, swimming pools, and plenty of organized aquatic games. *Stagnola Rotolo, RD 55, 20128 Porticcio. Admission: 75 frs. Open mid-June–mid-Sept., daily 10:30–7.*

Many children are fascinated by the megalithic menhir statues at **Filitosa,** Tour 3.

Off the Beaten Track

The rugged **Cap Corse peninsula** points like an accusing finger toward France's south coast, and its wild scenery and atmospheric villages make a rewarding day's exploration. A scenic coastal road (D80) runs right around the peninsula, skirting either side of a mountain range that culminates at the Monte Stello, soaring skyward near the tiny port of **Erbalunga** on the east coast. Erbalunga is one of the cap's prettiest villages, and its tiny houses tumble to the water's edge. Going north, the scenery grows wilder as the maquis covers the slopes. The road cuts across the tip of the peninsula from the fishing port of Macinaggio to its hinterland counterpart, **Rogliano.** A tiny road (D353) on the other side of the peninsula leads down to the picturesque 18th-century port of **Centuri,** an excellent spot for underwater diving.

The only other road that crosses the peninsula (D180) climbs to the Col de Sante Lucie pass and the **Tour de Sénèque,** a tower to which the luckless Seneca was supposedly exiled after having seduced Roman Emperor Claudius's niece. The west coast of the Cap Corse peninsula offers several pretty villages, notably **Pino, Canari,** and **Cannelle. Nonza** is the largest of the west-coast villages; its location is particularly appealing, overlooking the sea and a stretch of blue-gray beaches on one side and an expanse of terraced vineyards on the other.

Shopping

Arts and Crafts Corsica's rich forests have led to the development of healthy arts and crafts and cottage industries. Many craftsmen are still hidden away on Cap Corse *(see* Off the Beaten Track, above) or in inland mountain villages, producing beautifully carved pipes, letter openers, and other decorative objects using the wood of the surrounding chestnut and juniper trees. If the sweet scent of the maquis appeals to you, why not take some home, sewn up in attractive little bags; stop in at any of the tiny shops set back off the Corsican roads advertising "Essences du Maquis." As you wander up to the citadel in Bonifacio, you'll pass lots of small shops that sell a wide range of objects, hand-carved from sweet-smelling juniper wood—anything from miniature cars to smooth pebble shapes intended to keep moths out of the laundry cupboard; **Pierres de Cade** offers an especially good selection.

The villages of the Balagne region are also good hunting grounds for local crafts. **Casa di l'Artigiani** at Pigna, 8 kilometers (5 miles) from L'Ile-Rousse, offers a wide range of items, from local honey and jams to hand-knitted sweaters, silk scarves, local pottery, and watercolors. The **Poterie d'Olette** at Nebbio, between St-Florent and Oletta, sells a variety of handsome clay designs; choose from pots, dinner services, or painted lampstands.

Sports and Fitness

Bicycling Rental shops include **Locacycles** (40 rue César-Campinchi, Bastia) and **Avis** (Hôtel Marina Viva, Porticcio).

Hiking While the opportunities for scenic strolls are many and varied, the island's forests are not well maintained, and you may find yourself beating down the undergrowth even on well-marked trails. Leaflets covering walking paths are available from most tourist offices; ask for *Da Paese a Paese* ("From Village to Village") maps and brochures. The **Associu di Muntagnoli Corsi** (quartier Pentaniedda, 20122 Quenza) offers two- and three-day guided hikes through the mountain and lake areas.

Horseback Riding Corsican equestrian trails are actually former mule paths. There are numerous stables, including **Poney-Club d'Ajaccio** (Centre de Randonnées Equestres, rte. de Sartène, Campo dell' Oro), **La Jument Pie** (rte. de Calvi, 20260 Lumio), and **Société Hippique Urbaine de Bastia La Marana** (Plaine de Montesoro, 20200 Bastia).

Water Sports Corsica is an ideal place for water-sports enthusiasts because it offers 16 "Sub-Aqua" clubs for underwater diving, swimming, and fishing. In Ajaccio, try the **Club des Calanques** (Hôtel des Calanques, rte. des Sanguinaires) or, in Bonifacio, the **Club Atoll** (to contact the manager, M. Ferrari, call 95–73–02–83). If you'd like to get in some sailing, contact the **Tahiti Nautic Club d'Ajaccio** (plage du Ricanto) or, in Bastia, the **Rugby Club Bastiais** (Cala Biancah, 20290 Borgo). Canoeing, kayaking, and rafting are popular pastimes on inland mountain rivers; for details, write the **Association Municipale de Ponte-Leccia** (20218 Ponte Leccia).

Beaches

The island's coastline offers astonishing variety: from the long, white stretches of sand along the eastern plain to the steep, rocky creeks of the rugged west coast; from the wild, undeveloped beaches of Cap Corse to the commercial tourist beaches near Calvi or Propriano. The most unusual and attractive beaches back onto the maquis and the forest; when the wind is offshore, the heady scent of juniper and pine is sensational. Even in July and August, when the popular beaches of seaside resorts (Calvi, L'Ile Rousse, St-Florent, Propriano, Porto

Vecchio) are swarming with tourists, you can always find privacy in one of the numerous little creeks on the west coast or north of Porto-Vecchio on the east coast.

Dining and Lodging

Dining

Corsica isn't known for luxurious restaurants or haute cuisine, but local food is tasty and the helpings more than lavish. Seafood is abundant and delicious, whether grilled, baked, broiled, or fried. Oysters, crayfish, and sardines are island staples, and local fishermen's wives produce a rich bouillabaisse called *aziminu*.

The island also offers a variety of local cheeses and *charcuterie*. The best-known cheese is *brocciù* (pronounced "brucho"), used in both sweet and savory dishes; others to look for are the mild *basteliccacis* and the *bleu de Corse*. Notable *charcuterie* products include *figatelli* (small, dry pork sausages), salami sausages, and pork *lonzu* (fillet) or *coppa* (shoulder). Traditional stews of pork, lamb, or blackbird feature prominently on menus and are often accompanied by a *pebronata* sauce of bell peppers, garlic, and tomatoes. Other island specialties include kid drenched in herbs and wild, chestnut-fed boar. Visitors with sweet tooths will appreciate the local fritters, tarts, and cookies, which have such enticing names as *pisticcine*, *canestrone*, *rappi*, and *pane biscottu*.

Highly recommended restaurants are indicated by a star ★.

Category	Cost*
Very Expensive	over 350 francs
Expensive	200–350 francs
Moderate	100–200 francs
Inexpensive	under 100 francs

*per person for a three-course meal, including tax (18.6%) and tip but not wine

Lodging

Corsican hotels are generally clean and modern, though service may be haphazard. Prices are high—marginally less than the Côte d'Azur and the Riviera—though few hotels can be classed as "deluxe." Most close for half the year (October or November through Easter). During the peak season (July and August), most insist on half-board or even full-board terms. Many will provide a convenient packed lunch for guests who venture into remote areas of the countryside, where restaurants are few; it's a good idea to take advantage of the service, but check your hotel bill for every item.

Highly recommended hotels are indicated by a star ★.

Category	Cost*
Very Expensive	over 750 francs
Expensive	350–750 francs
Moderate	200–350 francs
Inexpensive	under 200 francs

All prices are for a standard double room for two, including tax (18.6%) and service charge.

Ajaccio
Dining

Auberge de Prunelli. Pisciatello, about 11 kilometers (7 miles) from Ajaccio, is the setting for this authentic Corsican inn on the banks of the Prunelli River. Hosts Santa and Mathea serve a range of homey Corsican meals, including *omelette au brocciù* (a ewe- or goat-milk cheese) and delicious roast kid. The atmosphere is cheerful, especially if the fire's blazing in the hearth. *Pisciatello, tel. 95–20–02–75. Reservations required. Dress: casual. No credit cards. Closed Mar. and Oct.–Nov. Moderate.*

Côte d'Azur. Don't be disappointed if there's no space in the oak-beamed ground-floor dining room; there are two other dining rooms upstairs. The crayfish salad, fish "sausages," and lobster stews all are fine choices. *12 cours Napoléon, tel. 95–21–50–24. Reservations required. Dress: casual. AE, DC, MC, V. Closed Sun. and mid-June–mid-July. Moderate.*

Lodging

Eden Roc. Ajaccio's best four-star hotel is in the city's most exclusive suburb, 8 kilometers (5 miles) from the center of town. The hotel overlooks the gulf of Ajaccio and the islands at the tip of the peninsula; extraordinary sunsets are guaranteed. Large guest rooms and sumptuous suites abound, all facing south and decorated with chic simplicity. *Rte. des Iles Sanguinaires, 20000, tel. 95–52–01–47. 42 rooms with bath. Facilities: restaurant, piano bar, garden, pool, health spa, sauna, Jacuzzi. AE, DC, MC, V. Expensive–Very Expensive.*

Bastia
Dining

Lavezzi. Diners will enjoy a view over Bastia's old port as they make their choice of a host of fish and seafood specials. Wall-to-wall carpeting and white, rough-cast plaster walls enhance Lavezzi's charm. The cuisine is traditional Corsican; try the devilfish in mint or sardines in *brocciù* cheese. *8 rue St-Jean, tel. 95–31–05–73. Reservations required. Jacket and tie required. AE, DC, MC, V. Closed Sun. and Feb.–Mar. Expensive.*

★ **Le Canari.** Corsican and Mediterranean specialties—lots of seafood salads and grilled fish—are served in this brick-vaulted former chapel, once part of a Genoese private mansion. If the baked rabbit is on the menu, go for it. *4 pl. de la Fontaine Neuve, tel. 95–31–53–73. Reservations required. Dress: neat but casual. AE, DC, MC, V. Closed Sun. dinner and Jan.–Feb. Moderate.*

Lodging

L'Alivi. A striking contemporary hotel, L'Alivi, is less than a mile north of town, in Pietra Nera. The guest rooms are stylishly furnished with plenty of chrome and glass; those nearest the beach feature vast sliding windows and balconies overlooking the sea. On clear days, you can see the Italian islands and Tuscany. There's no restaurant. *Palagaccio, 20200, tel. 95–31–61–85. 35 rooms with bath. V. Expensive.*

Posta Vecchia. An old building overlooking the port was renovated and transformed into the Posta Vecchia hotel in 1978. The unpretentious guest rooms are decorated with floral wallpaper and print bedspreads, while the wood-beamed ceilings add a rustic touch. Some rooms are small; the best are in the main house, facing the port. There's no restaurant. *Quai des Martyrs, 20200, tel. 95–32–32–38. 49 rooms with bath. AE, DC, MC, V. Moderate.*

Calvi
Dining
★

Ile de Beauté. One of Calvi's most celebrated restaurants, Ile de Beauté has been pulling in the crowds since 1929; it's on the quayside, right next to the port. The original wood paneling lends the dining room a classical ambience, while the terrace catches Calvi's festive atmosphere. The menu features a range of fish specials, including lobster fricassee; meat eaters should try the beef *feuilleté* (in a pastry case) stuffed with *cèpe* mushrooms. *Quai Landry, tel. 95–65–00–46. Reservations strongly advised. Jacket and tie required. AE, DC, MC, V. Closed Wed. lunch (except July and Aug.) and Oct.–Apr. Expensive.*

★ **Abri Côtier.** This place is as refreshing by day as it is romantic by night. At lunchtime or on warm summer evenings, you can eat on the covered terrace overlooking the port. When the weather gets cooler, dine indoors in the large dining room, where apricot linen and chunky silver cutlery set the tone. For a light lunch, order the salmon rolls. House specials include fish dishes of all sorts, grilled, baked, or covered in refined sauces. Save room for the homemade desserts. *2 rue du Mal-Joffre, 95–65–12–76. Reservations advised. Dress: neat but casual. AE, DC, MC, V. Closed Oct.–Apr. Moderate.*

La Voute. Jolly patronne Pastourette came here from her native Nîmes in 1988. When she spotted this tiny, medieval vaulted restaurant, she opted to pursue a long-standing family tradition and become a chef, drawing inspiration from a 19th-century recipe book penned in obscure Provençal dialect by her great-grandmother. Salads are Pastourette's lunchtime mainstay, while evening fare is more sophisticated, ranging from lamb with fresh mint cooked in peach wine, to fish in flaky pastry with a champagne sauce. Desserts include chestnuts and prunes in brandy and apple tart with honey and pine nuts. *Rue St-François, tel. 95–65–12–83. Reservations advised. Dress: casual. V. Moderate.*

Lodging

Balanéa. The best feature of the modern Balanéa is its portside setting, from which you can watch the fishing boats chug in and out of the harbor. The stark modern decor lacks character, but the guest rooms are air-conditioned and some are spacious. It's worth the extra cost to have a room with a bay view; try to reserve one of the penthouse rooms. There's no restaurant, but breakfast is served on a balcony overlooking the port. *6 rue Clemenceau, 20260, tel. 95–65–00–45. 37 rooms with bath. Facilities: bar. AE, DC, MC, V. Moderate–Expensive.*

Dining and Lodging
★

Magnolia. Massive floral bouquets decorate the cream-colored lobby, and stained-glass windows cast shimmering pools of light onto the central, banistered staircase of this elegant, turn-of-the-century hotel. Outside there's a pleasant garden-patio, shaded by fragrant magnolias and pines. Each guest room has a different monochromatic decorative scheme, though all feature built-in closets and beds framed by niches. There's no restaurant. *Pl. du Marché, 20260, tel. 95–65–19–16. 13 rooms, 10 with bath. Facilities: bar, garden. AE, DC, MC, V. Expensive.*

Le Signoria. This rustic country inn occupies a park some 5 kilometers (3 miles) outside town. The 17th-century homestead has been fitted out with bedrooms, large bathrooms, and a swimming pool that is directly accessible from the ground-floor rooms. Le Signoria also boasts a fine restaurant, decorated in rosy stucco; specialties include lobster and other seafood. *Rte. de l'Aéroport, 20260, tel. 95–65–23–73. 10 rooms with bath. Facilities: restaurant, pool, garden. AE, MC, V. Closed Oct.–Easter. Expensive.*

Centuri
Dining and Lodging
★

Le Vieux Moulin. If you're after Old World charm and an authentic Corsican flavor, Le Vieux Moulin is the place to try. The main house was built in 1870 as a private residence; the eight-room annex is more recent, but no less inviting, with bougainvillea cascading from its balconies. The friendly staff will arrange boat rides and fishing trips around the coast of the wildly dramatic Cap Corse peninsula, and there's a tennis court and small golf course nearby. The restaurant specializes in seafood; try the bouillabaisse. *Centuri Port, 20238, tel. 95–35–60–15. 14 rooms with bath. Facilities: restaurant. AE, DC, MC, V. Closed Nov.–Mar. Moderate.*

Corte
Dining and Lodging
★

Auberge de la Restonica. This Swiss chalet à la Corse lies in the heart of a remote, wooded valley, hemmed in by rocky peaks. The lobby/living room is reminiscent of a hunting lodge, with red-tiled floors, stone walls, and chunky wooden furniture arranged around a massive hearth; the dining-room terrace looks out over a cascading stream. The restaurant offers a good-value set menu, with such specials as fresh river trout and herb tart. *Rte. de la Restonica, 20250, tel. 95–46–09–58. 10 rooms with bath. AE, MC, V. Closed Nov.–Feb. Inexpensive–Moderate.*

Piana
Dining and Lodging

Capo Rosso. The four-star Capo Rosso sits high in the hills overlooking the Golfe de Porto, just yards from the famous rocky outcropping. The views—whether seen from your room, the outdoor pool, or the restaurant's terrace—are mind-bogglingly dramatic. Unfortunately, the modern guest rooms are functional rather than charming. *20115 Piana, tel. 95–27–82–40. 70 rooms with bath. Facilities: restaurant. AE, DC, MC, V. Closed Oct. Moderate–Expensive.*

Les Roches Rouges. On the hillside just below the Capo Russo, this rambling old mansion caters to an essentially British clientele. Don't be misled by the crumbling facade; the current owners took over only a few years ago and are still renovating. Most guest rooms are sparse and monastic, but the irrepressible owner, Mady, the eccentric British atmosphere, and the hotel's stunning location, make Les Roches Rouges a definite winner. The vast Imperial-style restaurant is classified as a historical monument; go for the fish soup or the grilled lobster. *Route de Porto, 20115 Piana, tel. 95–27–81–81. 20 rooms with bath. Facilities: restaurant. AE, DC, MC, V. Closed Nov.–Mar. Moderate.*

Porticcio
Dining and Lodging
★

Le Maquis. The evocatively named Maquis ranks as one of the island's finest *hôtels de charme*. The quaint, ivy-covered building reaches down to its own private beach, and sea-level rooms open directly onto arch-covered patios. West-facing rooms and terraces capture the stunning sunsets over the hills beyond Ajaccio. The candlelit restaurant features hand-hewn beams and white plaster walls, decorated with an ornate gilt mirror; tile floors and wicker chairs add to the rustic elegance. The food is a blend of traditional and nouvelle: fish tartare, scrambled eggs with truffles, *coquilles St-Jacques*, or fresh *tagliatelles* all make fine choices. *CD55, 20166 Porticcio, tel. 95–*

25–05–55. 27 rooms with bath. Facilities: restaurant, pool, tennis, private beach, solarium. AE, DC, MC, V. Expensive–Very Expensive.

Sofitel. In such a superb setting overlooking the Gulf of Ajaccio, it's a shame that this hotel has such a plain, functional appearance. If you're looking for straight relaxation and excellent service, however, you'll excuse the hotel's leaden architecture and overplush decor. Candlelight dinners on the terrace of the vast Le Caroubier restaurant—offering French cuisine and Corsican specialties—help compensate as well. *20166 Porticcio, tel. 95–25–00–34. 100 rooms with bath. Facilities: restaurant, pool, tennis, piano bar, disco, solarium, thalassotherapy, water sports. AE, DC, MC, V. Restaurant closed Dec. Expensive–Very Expensive.*

Porto-Vecchio
Dining and Lodging
★

Grand Hôtel de Cala Rossa. This mansion-hotel is one of the island's finest, showcasing modern design at its best. Nothing jars, from the curves of the heavy white walls to the choice of contemporary paintings lining the corridors. Rooms vary greatly in price but are all luxurious. An early morning breakfast outside under the trees, just yards from the beach, will make you forget your sightseeing plans. Corsican-style nouvelle dishes are featured in the restaurant; you can't go wrong with the roast kid or the fresh-mint omelet. *8 km (5 mi) north of town, 20137 Lecci, tel. 95–71–61–51. 50 rooms with bath. Facilities: restaurant, terrace, tennis. AE, DC, MC, V. Closed Nov.–Apr. Moderate–Very Expensive.*

Hôtel du Roi Théodore. This modern hotel is run with smooth efficiency. From the covered balconies—each room has its own—views extend over the ocean and sandy beaches. The guest rooms, reception, and bars are decorated in a Moorish-influenced style, with white walls and furnishings and dark wood trim. The restaurant serves Corsican and international specialties. *Rte. de Bastia, 20137, tel. 95–70–14–94. 40 rooms with bath. Facilities: restaurant, pools, tennis, Ping-Pong. AE, DC, MC, V. Closed mid-Oct.–Mar. Moderate–Expensive.*

Moby Dick. The scheme here is sophisticated simplicity: white stucco walls, white marble lamps, and blue comb-painted doors. The modern hotel 8 kilometers (5 miles) south of Porto-Vecchio is virtually surrounded by water and sandy beaches, and the guest rooms offer views of the sea and mountains. The restaurant serves a good-value buffet lunch and both a "normal" and *gastronomique* (gargantuan) menu at dinner. The crayfish is delicious. *Baie de Santa Giulia, 20137 Porto Vecchio, tel. 95–70–21–18. 44 rooms with bath. Facilities: restaurant. AE, DC, MC, V. Closed Oct.–Apr. Moderate–Expensive.*

The Arts and Nightlife

The Arts

Music and Festivals

Singing plays an important role in both traditional and daily island life. You'll doubtless come across impromptu café gatherings where the locals are singing their hearts out, giving impressive renderings of a traditional *paghiella* (a three-voice harmony), a *voceru* (funeral chant), or a *chjiama e rispondi* duel (in which two singers rival each other in a lyrical Ping-Pong match, throwing questions and answers in an attempt to outdo each other by the wit, beauty, or rhyme of their invention).

The island has two major **carnivals,** one in Bastia in April and the other in Ajaccio in May, when the towns come alive with song, costumed processions, and outdoor theater. Both towns feature similar festivities throughout the summer, reaching a climax on August 15, when Ajaccio celebrates Napoleon's birthday. Other island festivals include an **Italian Film Festival** in Bastia in February; a **Jazz Festival** in Calvi in June; **pop concerts** in Porto-Vecchio in July and August; a classical **International Music Meeting** in Ajaccio in July; and an **International Music Festival** in Bastia in late August/early September, when the music varies from classical to jazz.

Nightlife

Cabaret For traditional Corsican cabarets, try **Le Pavillon Bleu** (54 cours Grandval) and **Le Lido** (plage St-François, blvd. Lantivy) in Ajaccio and in Bastia, **U'Rataghiu** (rue Carnot) and **U'Fanale** (Le Vieux Port).

Piano Bars In Ajaccio, we recommend the **Premier Consul** (9 pl. Foch), **Le Palm Beach** (rte. des Sanguinaires), and **Le Santa Lina** (Espace Santa Lina). In Bastia, try **L'Alba** (22 quai des Martyrs); in Calvi, **Chez Tao** (pl. de la Citadelle).

15 Toulouse and the Midi-Pyrénées

Introduction

Midi-Pyrénées is France's largest region, stretching 28,500 square miles from the Massif Central in the north to the Spanish border in the south. Mountains, plains, lakes, rivers, verdant hills, and arid limestone plateaus lend the region extreme natural variety. This is the perfect vacation spot for nature lovers and sports enthusiasts; walking, hiking, climbing, horseback-riding, sailing, canoeing, skiing, windsurfing, and rafting are all possible.

The Pyrenees, western Europe's highest mountain range after the Alps, give birth to the Garonne, the great river of Toulouse and Bordeaux. The Garonne is joined by the Aveyron, Lot, and Tarn rivers, which cross the region from east to west, carving out steep gorges and wide green valleys. The Pyrenean foothills are riddled with streams, lakes, and spas established in Roman times. Armagnac brandy has its home among the gently undulating hills of the Gers, while, farther north, hearty red wine has been produced in the rugged country around Cahors for over 2,000 years.

The region has few large towns. Chief among them is Toulouse, an upbeat university center whose energetic nightlife smacks more of Spain (less than two hours' drive away) than of the drowsy French provinces. Toulouse, known as the Ville Rose because of its soft pink brick, is an elegant old city. The Canal du Midi, built in the 17th century, passes through Toulouse and continues east, near the medieval walls of Carcassonne, on its way from the Atlantic to the Mediterranean.

Other highlights range from the picturesque hilltop villages of Cordes and Rocamadour to the fortified medieval bridge at Cahors and the Romanesque basilica perched precariously above the valley at Conques. The religious mecca of Lourdes is here as well, but its football-stadium-like appearance may come as a bit of a disappointment. There are two outstanding art museums, however: the Musée Ingres at Montauban, devoted to one of France's most accomplished pre-Impressionist painters, and the Musée Toulouse-Lautrec at Albi, with its racy testimony to the leading observer of Belle Epoque cabaret. Albi also holds the most impressive monument in the Midi-Pyrénées: the redbrick cathedral of Ste-Cécile, with slits for windows and walls like cliffs.

Essential Information

Important Addresses and Numbers

Tourist Information The regional tourist office for the Midi-Pyrénées (written inquiries only) is the **Comité Régional du Tourisme** (CRT, 12 rue Salambo, 31200 Toulouse, tel. 61–47–11–12). Local tourist offices in other towns covered in this chapter are as follows: **Albi** (pl. Ste-Cécile, tel. 63–54–22–30), **Auch** (1 rue Dessoles, tel. 62–05–22–89), **Cahors** (pl. Aristide-Briand, tel. 65–35–09–56), **Lourdes** (pl. du Champ-Commun, tel. 62–94–15–64), **Montauban** (2 rue du Collège, tel. 63–63–60–60), **Pau** (pl. Royale, tel. 59–27–27–08), **Rodez** (pl. du Mal-Foch, tel. 65–68–02–27), and **Toulouse** (Donjon du Capitole, pl. Charles-de-Gaulle, tel. 61–23–32–00).

Travel Agencies **American Express** (Office Catholique De Voyages, 14 chaussée du Bourg, Lourdes, tel. 62–94–40–84), **Havas** (73 rue d'Alsace Lorraine, Toulouse, tel. 61–23–16–35), and **Wagons-Lits** (Voyages Dépêche, 42 bis rue d'Alsace-Lorraine, Toulouse, 61–23–40–15).

Car Rental **Avis** (pl. de la Gare, Lourdes, tel. 62–34–26–76; Blagnac Airport, Toulouse, tel. 61–30–04–94), **Hertz** (pl. Lagarrasic, Auch, tel. 62–05–26–26; 5 av. Chamier, Montauban, tel. 63–20–29–00).

Arriving and Departing

By Plane All international flights arrive at Toulouse's **Blagnac Airport,** a few minutes' drive from the center of town. Regular **Air France** flights link Toulouse to most European capitals, while **Air Inter** runs as many as 30 flights a day during the week between Paris and Toulouse (for reservations, call 45–39–25–25 in Paris or 61–71–11–10 in Toulouse). **TAT** (Transport Aérien Transregional) offers direct flights from Paris's Orly Airport to Rodez (for reservations, call 42–79–05–05 in Paris or 65–42–20–30 in Rodez).

Between the Airport and Downtown Buses run regularly (every half hour between 8:15 AM and 8:45 PM) from the airport to the bus station in Toulouse; single fare is 20 francs. Three later buses are available, too—at 9:20, 10, and 10:45. From Toulouse bus station to the airport, buses leave at 5:30 AM, 6, 7, 7:30, and then every half hour until 8:30 PM.

By Train Trains for the southwest leave from Gare d'Austerlitz in Paris. There are direct trains to Toulouse (six to seven hours), Cahors (five to six hours), Carcassonne (seven to eight hours), and Montauban (six hours). For Rodez (seven to eight hours), change in Brive, and for Auch (over eight hours), in Toulouse. Note that at least one TGV train per day leaves Paris for Toulouse—from Gare Montparnasse. Journey time is five hours.

By Car The fastest route from Paris to Toulouse is via Bordeaux (on A10), then switch to A62; journey time is about nine hours.

Getting Around

By Plane From Toulouse's Blagnac Airport, you can pick up an **Air Inter** flight to Tarbes, near Lourdes (for information, call tel. 61–71–11–10).

By Train The French rail network in the southwest provides regular services to all towns.

By Car The A62 expressway slices through the region on its way to the coast at Narbonne. At Toulouse, various highways fan out in all directions: N117 to Pau, N20 to Montauban and Cahors, and N88 to Albi and Rodez.

Guided Tours

The **Comité Régional du Tourisme** *(see* Tourist Information, above) publishes a detailed brochure, *Mille et Une Evasions en Midi-Pyrénées* ("1,000 and One Ways to Escape in the Midi-Pyrénées"), which provides a host of suggestions for weekends and short organized package vacations throughout the region. The tourist office in **Toulouse** offers a wide range of guided tours in and around the city; guides are knowledgeable and multilingual.

Orientation From July to September, a tour of Toulouse's monuments and historical houses leaves Monday to Saturday from the tourist office at 10 AM; cost is 30 francs. A "Toulouse: Past and Present" bus tour, also leaving from the tourist office, departs at 3 PM and costs 40 francs. A walking tour that takes in the Jacobins church and the private mansions of the St-Rome quarter leaves from the tourist office at 3 PM; cost is 30 francs, plus 6 francs entrance fee to the church's cloister. On Wednesday, a walking tour of the Musée des Augustins and the rue Croix-Baragnon leaves at 5 PM from the museum's main entrance; cost is 30 francs, plus 6 francs for admission to the museum.

Sightseeing Tours Day-long regional circuits run from May through September, departing from the Toulouse tourist office and costing 125 francs; stops include Rocamadour, Conques, and Cordes, as well as Moissac Abbey, the Ingres museum at Montauban, and the Toulouse-Lautrec museum at Albi.

Exploring Toulouse and the Midi-Pyrénées

Numbers in the margin correspond with points of interest on the Midi-Pyrénées and Toulouse maps.

Orientation

We have divided this region into four tours. The first takes in southwest France's only city: Toulouse, a lively center imbued with culture and history. Toulouse can be the base for our three other tours. The most important of these, heading north, caters to many tastes. Nature lovers will savor the rugged Causses plateau and the dramatic Tarn and Lot valleys. Architecture buffs can admire the bravura of Cahors's tower-bridge and Albi's fortress-cathedral. Art enthusiasts will feast on the works of local-born geniuses Jean Auguste Dominique Ingres (in Montauban) and Henri de Toulouse-Lautrec (in Albi). For those with an eye for the picturesque, we'll visit the daringly sited medieval villages of Conques, Cordes, and Rocamadour.

Our third tour moves west from Toulouse into the verdant, once-grand region of Gascony, known more prosaically these days as the Gers *département*, and home of Armagnac brandy. The final tour plunges south to the Pyrenees, taking in snow-capped peaks, mountain passes, thermal spas, and the holy site at Lourdes.

Highlights for First-time Visitors

Cordes, Tour 2
Grande Cascade, Tour 4
Lourdes, Tour 4
Musée Ingres, Montauban, Tour 2
Palais de la Berbie (Toulouse-Lautrec Museum), Albi, Tour 2
Rocamadour, Tour 2
Ste-Cécile, Albi, Tour 2
Ste-Foy, Conques, Tour 2

Tour 1: Toulouse

❶ The ebullient, pink-brick city of **Toulouse** lies just 60-odd miles from the border with Spain, and its flavor is more Spanish than French. The city's downtown sidewalks and restaurants are thronged way past midnight as foreign tourists mingle with immigrant workers, college students, and technicians from the giant Airbus aviation complex headquartered outside the city.

Place du Capitole, a vast, open square lined with shops and cafés in the city center, is the best spot for getting your bearings. One side of the square is occupied by the 18th-century fa-
❷ cade of the **Capitole** itself, home of the Hôtel de Ville (Town Hall) and the city's highly regarded opera company. The coats of arms of the Capitouls, the former rulers of Toulouse, can be seen on the balconies in the Capitole's courtyard, and the building's vast reception rooms are open to visitors when not in use for official functions. Halfway up the Grand Escalier (Grand Staircase) hangs a large painting of the *Jeux Floraux*, or Floral Games, organized by the Compagnie du Gai-Savoir—a literary society created in 1324 to promote the local language, Langue d'Oc. The festival continues to this day: Poets give public readings here each May, the best receiving silver- and gold-plated flowers as prizes. The pompous Salle des Illustres, with its late 19th-century paintings, is used for official receptions and uppercrust wedding ceremonies. Weddings are also held in the Salle Gervaise, beneath a series of paintings inspired by the theme of Love at ages 20, 40, and 60; while the men age, the women stay young forever.

Four more giant paintings in the Salle Henri-Martin, named after the artist (1860–1943), show how important the River Garonne has always been to the region. Look out for Jean Jaurès, one of France's greatest Socialists (1859–1914), in *Les Rêveurs (The Dreamers)*; he's the one who's wearing a boater and a beige-colored coat. *Pl. du Capitole. Tel. 61– 22–29–22 (ext. 3412) to check opening times. Admission free. Closed Tues. and weekends.*

Head north from place du Capitole along rue du Taur, lined with tiny shops. Half a block up, the 14th-century church of
❸ **Notre-Dame du Taur** was built on the spot where St-Saturnin (or Sernin), the martyred bishop of Toulouse, was dragged to his death in AD 257 by a rampaging bull. The church is famous for its *cloche-mur*, or wall tower; the wall looks more like an extension of the facade than a tower or steeple and has inspired many similar versions throughout the Toulouse region.

❹ The basilica of **St-Sernin,** Toulouse's most famous landmark, lies at the far end of rue du Taur. The basilica once belonged to a Benedictine abbey, built in the 11th century to house pilgrims on their way to Santiago de Compostela in Spain. When illuminated at night, St-Sernin's five-tiered octagonal tower glows red against the sky, dominating the city. Not all the tiers are the same: The first three, with their rounded windows, are Romanesque; the upper two, with their pointed Gothic windows, were added around 1300.

The size of the basilica—particularly the width of the transept, more than 68 feet—is striking. It's worth paying the token entry fee to the crypt and ambulatory to admire the tomb of St-Sernin and seven exquisitely preserved marble bas-reliefs of Christ and his apostles, dating from the end of the 11th century. *Rue du Taur. Admission to crypt: 8 frs. Open daily 10–11:30 and 2:30–5:30.*

⑤ Opposite the basilica is the **Musée St-Raymond,** the city's archaeological museum. The ground floor has an extensive collection of imperial Roman busts, while the second floor is devoted to the applied arts, featuring ancient and medieval coins, lamps, vases, and jewelry. *Pl. St-Sernin. Admission: 15 frs. adults, children free. Open Wed.–Mon. 8–noon and 2–6; closed Sun. morning and Tues.*

Retrace your steps down rue du Taur, turn right at place du

⑥ Capitole and then left into rue Lakanal to arrive at the **Jacobins church,** built in the 1230s for the Dominicans; the name "Jacobins" was given to the Dominicans in 1217 when they set up their Paris base at the Porte St-Jacques. The church was harmoniously restored in the 1970s, its interior retaining the original orange-ocher tones. The two rows of columns running the length of the nave—to separate the monks from their congregation—is a feature of Dominican churches, though this one is special, since the column standing the farthest from the entrance is said to be the world's finest example of palm-tree vaulting. The original refectory is used for temporary art exhibitions, while the cloisters provide an atmospheric setting for the city's summer music festival.

⑦ Around the corner, in rue Gambetta, stands the **Hôtel de Bernuy,** built during the 16th century, when Toulouse was at its most prosperous. Merchant Jean de Bernuy made his fortune exporting pastel, a blue dye made from the leaves of a plant cultivated around Toulouse and Albi and used to color cloth, especially bed linen. Merchant wealth is reflected in the mansion's use of stone, a costly material in this region of brick, and by the octagonal stair tower, the highest in the city. Building such towers was a rarely bestowed privilege, and this one makes its opulent point by rising above the ceiling of the top floor. The Hôtel de Bernuy is now part of a school, but you may wander freely around its courtyard.

Walk down rue Jean-Suau to place de la Daurade and the 18th-

⑧ century church of **Notre-Dame de la Daurade,** overlooking the River Garonne. The name "Daurade" comes from *doré* (gilt), referring to the golden reflection given off by the mosaics decorating the 5th-century temple to the Virgin that once stood on this site. The flowers presented to the winners of the Floral Games are blessed here.

Take time to saunter along quai de la Daurade, beside the

⑨ church, and admire the view from **Pont Neuf** across to the left bank. Then head east along rue de Metz. A hundred yards

⑩ down, on the left, is the **Hôtel d'Assézat,** built in 1555 by Toulouse's top Renaissance architect, Nicolas Bachelier. The facade is particularly striking: Superimposed classical orders frame alternating arcades and rectangular windows, with ornately carved doorways lurking below. Climb to the top of the tower for splendid views over the city rooftops. *Rue de Metz. Admission free. Open daily 10–noon and 2–6.*

Continue along rue de Metz. The second road on the left (rue des Changes, which becomes rue St-Rome) was once part of the

Midi-Pyrénées

Bordeaux

Bergerac

Dordogne

Garonne

Marmande

Lot

Agen

N113

A62

Moissac

23

N133

D95t

Mont-de-Marsan

Barbotan

Condom

28

Lectoure

27

Moissac

D931

Cassaigne

29

D7

Fleurance

26

Eauze

N124

N21

Auch

25

24

N124

Gimont

N21

Baïse

Gers

N21

Pau

30

N117

Tarbes

Garonne

D940

Lourdes

31

N21

D935

Pic du Midi
de Bigorre

St-Bertrand
de Comminges

39

N125

D920

D921

Arreau

Cauterets

32

34

35

D918

36

Barèges

Luz-
St-Sauveur

D618

D125

Gavarnie

33

Superbagnères

37

Bagnères
de Luchon

38

SPAIN

MALADETA

Capitole, **2**

Hôtel d'Assézat, **10**

Hôtel de Bernuy, **7**

Jacobins church, **6**

Musée des Augustins, **11**

Musée St-Raymond, **5**

Museum d'Histoire Naturelle, **13**

Notre-Dame de la Daurade, **8**

Notre-Dame du Taur, **3**

Pont Neuf, **9**

St-Etienne, **12**

St-Sernin, **4**

Toulouse

Roman road that sliced through Toulouse from north to south; today it's a chic pedestrian shopping area. Running parallel is the swinging rue d'Alsace-Lorraine, a center of nightlife, luxury boutiques, and department stores. On the corner of rue d'Alsace-Lorraine and rue de Metz, just beyond busy place Esquirol, is the largest museum in Toulouse: the **Musée des Augustins,** housed in a medieval Augustinian convent whose sacristy, chapter house, and cloisters provide an attractive setting for an outstanding array of Romanesque sculpture and religious paintings by such renowned artists as Spain's Bartolomé Esteban Murillo (1618–82) and Flemish maestro Peter Paul Rubens (1577–1640). *21 rue de Metz. Admission: 7 frs., free Sun. Open Wed.–Mon. 10–noon and 2–6.*

Time Out Around the corner from the Musée des Augustins, on place St-Georges—a delightful little square—is the intimate **Le Père Bacchus** (20 pl. St-Georges), much frequented by locals. By night it's a popular jazz venue.

From the Musée des Augustins, cross rue de Metz and head down rue des Arts, then turn left along rue Croix-Baragnin to place St-Etienne, site of both the city's oldest fountain, in marble (16th century), and of the cathedral of **St-Etienne,** erected in stages between the 13th and the 17th centuries. The nave and choir languished unfinished for a lack of funds; they look awkward because they are not properly aligned. A fine collection of 16th- and 17th-century tapestries traces the life of St. Stephen (Etienne, in French).

The broad allée François Verdier leads to the leafy, circular Grand Rond, flanked by the **Jardin Royal** (royal gardens) and **Jardin des Plantes** (botanical gardens)—home of the **Muséum d'Histoire Naturelle** (Natural History Museum) and its varied collection of stuffed birds and prehistoric exhibits. *35 allée Jules-Guesde. Gardens open daily dawn to dusk; admission free. Museum open daily 2–6; admission: 7 frs.*

Tour 2: Albi–Rocamadour–Montauban

Leave **Toulouse** by N88 and drive 53 kilometers (33 miles) northeast to **Gaillac,** an old town on the right bank of the Tarn and the center of a long-established vineyard renowned for its versatility. Dry, sweet, and lightly sparkling *(perlant)* white wine are all produced here, as are fruity reds; if you're in the mood to sample some, follow signs to a *dégustation* (tasting session). Some of the earliest winemakers, beginning in the 10th century, were Benedictine monks, whose abbey church stands alongside Pont St-Michel.

From Gaillac, head 24 kilometers (15 miles) north along D922 to the picture-book hilltop village of **Cordes,** built in 1222 by Count Raymond VII of Toulouse. When mists steal up from the Cérou Valley and enshroud the hillside, Cordes appears to hover in midair, hence its nickname, Cordes-sur-Ciel (Cordes in the Sky). Cordes is a typical *bastide*, a fortified medieval town built to a strict grid plan. Wander around the ancient streets and admire the restored medieval houses, many of which are peopled by artisans and craftsmen; the best crafts shops are found along the main street, **Grande-Rue.** The village's venerable **covered market,** supported by 24 octagonal stone pillars, is also noteworthy, while the nearby well is more than 300 feet deep.

Time Out Stop for a drink at one of the cafés on **Terrace de la Bride** and take in the view over the Cérou Valley. If you want something more substantial, try the delightful terrace of the **Hostellerie du Vieux Cordes;** the foie gras is superb. *Rue St-Michel.*

From Cordes, take pretty D600 to **Albi,** 25 kilometers (16 miles) away. This old town, with its narrow streets and redbrick buildings, has been tastefully preserved. In its heyday, Albi was a major center for Cathars, members of an ascetic religious sect that rejected earthly life as evil and criticized the worldly ways of the Catholic Church. Albi's huge cathedral of

Ste-Cécile, with its intimidating clifflike walls, resembles a cross between a castle, a power station, and an ocean liner and was meant to symbolize the Catholic Church's return to power after the crusade against the Cathars (or Albigensians, as they came to be known) at the start of the 13th century.

The cathedral's interior is an ornate reply to the massive austerity of the ocher outer walls. Every possible surface has been painted; the leading contributors were a 16th-century team of painters from Bologna, Italy, who splattered the main vault with saints and Old Testament *venerati*, then lined the bays with religious scenes and brightly colored patterns. The most striking fresco, however, is a 15th-century depiction of the Last Judgment, which extends across the west wall beneath the 18th-century organ loft. Unfortunately, its central section was smashed through in 1693, to make the St-Clair chapel.

Climb the stairway to the right of the altar up to the bell tower. Here the view takes in the rooftops of the old town and, between the cathedral and the Pont Vieux (Old Bridge) spanning the River Tarn, the **Palais de la Berbie.** Built in 1265 as the Bishop's Palace, it was later transformed first into a fortress, then into a museum honoring Albi's most famous son: Belle Epoque painter Henri de Toulouse-Lautrec (1864–1901).

Toulouse-Lautrec left Albi for Paris in 1882 and soon made his name with racy evocations of the bohemian glamour of the cabarets, music halls, bars, and cafés in and around Montmartre. Despite his aristocratic origins (Lautrec is a town not far from Toulouse), Henri cut a far-from-noble figure. He stood under five feet tall (his growth was stunted by a childhood riding accident) and pursued a decadent life that led to an early grave. The Albi exhibit is the country's largest collection of works by Toulouse-Lautrec. These works are beautifully presented, notably in the lengthy Galérie Ambrie (holding his earliest efforts) and in the rooms leading from the Salon Rose (portraits and lithographs). *Just off pl. Ste-Cécile. Admission: 20 frs. adults, 10 frs. children. Open Easter–Oct., daily 10–noon and 2–6; Nov.–Easter, Wed.–Mon. 10–noon and 2–5; closed Tues.*

Before leaving Albi, stroll around the old town to admire its pedestrian streets and elegant shops. You can also visit Lautrec's birthplace, **Maison Natale de Toulouse-Lautrec** (along boulevard Sibille from the cathedral), to see more of his early works, as well as his personal possessions and memorabilia. *14 rue Henri de Toulouse-Lautrec. Admission: 16 frs. adults, 10 frs. children. Open July–Aug., daily 10–noon and 3–7.*

⓱ Rodez, capital of the Aveyron *département*, sits on a windswept hill 78 kilometers (48 miles) northeast of Albi (via N88), halfway between the arid, limestone Causses plateau and the verdant Ségala hills. On top of the hill in Rodez towers the pink sandstone cathedral of **Notre-Dame,** built over the 13th to 15th centuries. Its awesome bulk is lightened by the decorative upper stories, completed in the 17th century, and by the magnificently elaborate 285-foot bell tower. The interior contains ornamental altarpieces, an elaborate 15th-century choir screen, and a 17th-century organ within an intricate wooden casing.

The old but renovated **Cité quarter,** once ruled by medieval bishops, lies behind the cathedral; attractive pedestrian zones have been created around place du Bourg. One of the city's finest medieval mansions can be found on the tiny place de l'Olmet, just off place du Bourg: the 16th-century **House of Armagnac,** with its open courtyard and ornate facade covered in the medallion emblems of the counts of Rodez.

Farther on, at place de la Madeleine, is the 18th-century church of **St-Amans,** featuring finely preserved Romanesque capitals and, inside, some colorful 16th-century tapestries. The extensively modernized **Musée Denys Puech,** an art gallery noted for works by local painters and sculptors, lies just beyond the wide boulevard that encircles the old town. *Pl. Clemenceau. Admission: 18 frs. adults, 12 frs. children under 18. Open Wed.–Sat. and Mon. 10–noon and 3–7; Sun. 3–7; closed Tues.*

18 From Rodez, head 35 kilometers (22 miles) up D901 to **Conques,** whose pretty, ocher-red houses harmonize perfectly with the surrounding rocky gorge. Conques is more than just a picturesque village, however. It holds one of the most outstanding religious monuments in southern France: the Romanesque church of **Ste-Foy.** The church was one of the four principal stopping points on the medieval pilgrimage route that left Le Puy, in central France, for the shrine of St. James at Santiago de Compostela in northwest Spain. Ste-Foy, begun in the early 11th century, enjoyed its heyday in the 12th and 13th centuries. Eventually, though, the flood of pilgrims dried up, taking with it a huge source of revenue for the church's upkeep. In 1561, Ste-Foy was devastated by Protestant hordes at the onset of the Wars of Religion; it then languished in neglect until the 19th century, when the writer and historic-monument enthusiast, Prosper Mérimée, stepped in with plans to salvage it.

Ste-Foy clings to a hill so steep that even driving and walking—let alone building—is a precarious business. Note the intensely dramatic *Last Judgment,* carved over the main portal during the 12th century. The church's interior is high and dignified; the ambulatory around the back was given a lot of wear and tear by medieval pilgrims who were keen on admiring the church's most precious relic: a 10th-century wooden statue of Ste-Foy herself, encrusted with gold and precious stones. Latterday visitors can admire the relic in the Treasury, situated off the recently restored cloisters. Other gold and silver relics testify to the presence of skilled metal workers in Conques from the 9th to the 14th century. The **Musée Docteur Joséph-Fau** (otherwise known as Trésor II), located in an old building opposite the pilgrims' fountain near the church, houses furniture, statues, tapestries, and sculpture. *Admission to Trésor and Musée Fau: 20 frs. adults, 15 frs. children. Open Sept.–June, Mon.–Sat. 9–noon and 2–6, Sun. 2–6; July–Aug., Mon.–Sat. 9–noon and 2–7, Sun. 2–7.*

Continue north on D901 for 8 kilometers (5 miles), then turn left onto D42 and wend your way along the beautiful Lot Valley **19** to **Figeac,** 48 kilometers (30 miles) away. Figeac, a charming old town with a lively Saturday-morning market, grew up around an abbey in the 9th century, becoming, in turn, a stopping point for pilgrims plodding from Conques to Compostela. Many houses in the older part of town date from the 13th, 14th, and 15th centuries and have been carefully restored. They retain their octagonal chimneys, rounded archways and arcades, and *soleilhos*, open attics used for drying flowers and stocking wood.

The 13th-century **Hôtel de la Monnaie,** a block in from the River Célé, is characteristic of such architecture, an elegant building probably used as a medieval money-changing office; these days, it houses the tourist office and a museum displaying fragments of sculpture and religious relics found in the town. *Pl. Vival. Admission free. Open July–Aug., daily 10–noon and 2:30–6:30; Sept.–June, Mon.–Sat. 3–5.*

Figeac was the birthplace of Jean-François Champollion (1790–1832), the first man to decipher Egyptian hieroglyphics. The **Musée Champollion,** in his house near place Champollion (walk right out of place Vival on rue 11-Novembre, take the first left and follow it around as it bends right), contains a casting of the Rosetta Stone, discovered in the Nile Delta; the stone's three inscriptions—two in Egyptian and one in ancient Greek—enabled the mysteries of the pharaonic dialect to be penetrated for the first time. On the ground floor of the museum, a film traces Champollion's life. *4 impasse Champollion. Admission: 18 frs. adults, 9 frs. children. Open May–Sept., Tues.–Sat. 10–noon and 2:30–6:30; and open Christmas and Easter holidays.*

N140 heads 43 kilometers (27 miles) northwest from Figeac, through the Causses de Gramat (an extensive limestone plateau), to **Rocamadour,** a medieval village that seems to defy the laws of gravity as it surges out of a cliff 1,500 feet above the Alzou River gorge.

Rocamadour first made its name in 1166, when chronicles recorded the miraculous discovery of the body of St-Amadour "quite whole" under a sanctuary. This was a major event: Amadour had died a thousand years earlier and, according to legend, was none other than Zaccheus, the tax collector of Jericho, who had come to live in Gaul as a hermit after Christ had persuaded him to give up his money-grubbing ways. Amadour's body was moved into the church, displayed to pilgrims, and began to work miracles. Its fame soon spread to Portugal, Spain, and Sicily, and pilgrims flocked to the site and climbed the 216-step staircase leading up to the church—on their knees. Making the climb on foot is a sufficient reminder of the medieval penchant for agonizing penance, and today an elevator assists weary souls.

The staircase (and elevator) starts from place de la Carreta; those making their way on foot can pause after the first 141 steps to admire the **Fort,** as the 14th-century Bishop's Palace is invitingly called. The remaining steps lead to tiny place St-Amadour and its seven sanctuaries: the basilica of **St-Sauveur** opposite the staircase; the **St-Amadour** crypt underneath the basilica; the chapel of **Notre-Dame** to the left; the chapels of **John the Baptist, St-Blaise,** and **Ste-Anne** to the right; and the Romanesque chapel of **St-Michel,** built into the overhanging cliff. St-Michel's two 12th-century frescoes—depicting the Annunciation and the Visitation—have survived in superb condition. *Centre d'Acceuil Notre-Dame. English-speaking guide available. Guided tours Mon.–Sat. 9–5; tips at visitors' discretion.*

The village itself boasts beautifully restored medieval houses. One of the finest is the 15th-century **Hôtel de Ville** (Town Hall), near the Porte Salmon, which also houses the tourist office and a fine collection of tapestries. *Admission free. Open Mon.–Sat. 10–noon and 3–8.*

Time Out Within the ancient stone walls of the **Beau-Site et Notre-Dame** hotel (Rue Roland-le-Preux) is an exceptionally cozy restaurant, serving richly flavored regional specialties as well as nouvelle dishes. The salmon *sashimi* is a good bet, but leave room for some of Madame Menot's homemade desserts.

From Rocamadour, D32/D39/D673 winds 19 kilometers (12 miles) down to St-Projet, there joining the N20 highway to **㉑ Cahors,** 26 miles farther. Cahors, once an opulent Gallo-Roman town, sits snugly in a loop formed by the River Lot. The town is perhaps best known for its tannic red wine—often, in fact, a deep purple, and known to the Romans as "black wine"—which you can taste at many of the small estates in the surrounding region. The finest sight in Cahors is the **Pont Valentré** bridge, a spellbinding feat of medieval engineering whose tall, elegant towers have loomed over the river since 1360.

Rue du Président-Wilson cuts across town from the bridge to the old quarter of Cahors around the Cathedral of **St-Etienne,** easily recognized by its cupolas and fortresslike appearance. The tympanum over the north door was sculpted around 1135 with figures portraying the Ascension and the life of St-Etienne (St. Stephen). The cloisters, to the right of the choir, contain a corner pillar embellished with a charmingly sculpted Annunciation Virgin with long, flowing hair. The cloisters connect with the courtyard of the archdeaconry, awash with Renaissance decoration and thronged with visitors viewing its temporary art exhibits.

N20 continues 63 kilometers (39 miles) south from Cahors to **㉒ Montauban,** birthplace of the great painter Jean Auguste Dominique Ingres (1780–1867). Ingres was the last of the great French Classicists, who took their cue from Raphaël, favoring line over color and taking much of their subject matter from the antique world. Ingres's personal dislike of Eugène Delacroix (the earliest and most important French Romantic painter), his sour personality, and (for some) his arid painting style, with its worship of line and technical draftsmanship, led many contemporaries to ridicule his work. These days, Ingres is undergoing a considerable revival in popularity; looking at the works in Montauban's Ingres museum, with their quasiphotographic realism, it's easy to see why.

The **Musée Ingres** is housed in the sturdy brick 17th-century Bishop's Palace overlooking the River Tarn. Ingres has the second floor to himself; note the contrast between his love of myth *(Ossian's Dream)* and his deadpan, uncompromising portraiture *(Madame Gonse),* underscored by a closet eroticism (silky-skinned nudes) that belies the staid reputation of academic art. The exhibit also includes hundreds of Ingres's drawings, plus some of his personal possessions—including his beloved violin.

Most of the paintings in the museum are from Ingres's excellent private collection, ranging from his followers (Théodore Chassériau) and precursors (Jacques Louis David) to Old Masters who were active between the 14th and the 18th centuries (displayed on the third floor). *Pl. Bourdelle. Admission: 12 frs. adults, 8 frs. students. Open July–Aug., Mon.–Sat. 9:30–*

noon and 1:30–6, Sun. 1:30–6; Sept.–June, Tues.–Sat. 10–noon and 2–6.

Take some time to explore the old streets of Montauban, especially the pedestrian zone around the restored place Nationale (home to a lively morning market). Check out the Classical cathedral of **Notre-Dame** on place Roosevelt: Its white stone is an eye-catching contrast to the pink brick of other buildings, while inside lurks a major Ingres painting, the *Vow of Louis XIII*.

㉓ From Montauban, D958/N113 heads west to **Moissac**, 29 kilometers (18 miles) away. Moissac holds one of the region's most remarkable abbey churches, **St-Pierre**. Little is left of the original 7th-century abbey, while religious wars laid waste its 11th-century replacement. Today's abbey, dating mostly from the 15th century, narrowly escaped demolition earlier in this century when the Bordeaux–Sète railroad was rerouted within feet of the cloisters, sparing the precious columns around the arcades, carved in different shades of marble. Each of the 76 capitals has its own unique pattern of animals, geometric motifs, and religious or historical scenes.

The museum, in the corner chapels, houses local religious sculpture and photographs of similar sculpture from throughout the Quercy region. The highlight of the abbey church is the 12th-century south portal, topped with carvings illustrating the Apocalypse. The sides and vaults of the porch are adorned with historical scenes sculpted in intricate detail. *6 bis rue de l'Abbaye. Admission to museum and cloisters: 18 frs. joint ticket. Open daily 9–noon and 2–5 (6 in June and Sept.; 7 in July and Aug.). Museum closed Tues. and Sun. morning.*

Tour 3: Gers

The rural Gers *département*, west of Toulouse, occupies the heart of the former dukedom of Gascony; it's studded with châteaus—from simple medieval fortresses to ambitious Classical residences—and tiny, isolated villages.

㉔ Take N124 west from Toulouse to **Gimont**, 54 kilometers (34 miles) away. You'll get a good idea of the area's gastronomic riches by browsing in the local shops: Armagnac brandy, *Floc de Gascogne* (an aperitif made with grape juice and Armagnac), goose and duck pâtés, preserves, and foie gras (Aux Ducs de Gascogne is one of France's leading producers of this rich delicacy).

㉕ **Auch,** the capital of Gers, is 24 kilometers (15 miles) west of Gimont via N124. Auch is best known for its Gothic cathedral and quaint alleyways, or *pousterles* (from the French for posterns—*poternes*, the gateways to the medieval fortifications).

The cathedral of **Ste-Marie,** in the center of town, dates from the 15th and 16th centuries. Most of the stained-glass windows in the choir are by Arnaud de Moles, who was working here around 1513, and portray biblical figures and handsome pagan sybils, or prophetesses. The oak choir stalls are especially interesting, carved with over 1,500 figures, both biblical and mythological; the stalls also date from the first half of the 16th century and took 50 years to complete. In June, Auch stages a festival in which concerts of classical music are held in the cathedral. *Pl. Salinis. Admission to stalls: 5 frs. Open daily 8–noon and 2–6.*

Cross place Salinis to the terrace overlooking the River Gers. A monumental flight of 232 steps leads down to the riverbank, and there is a statue of D'Artagnan, the musketeer immortalized by Alexandre Dumas, halfway down. Although Dumas set the action of his historical drama *The Three Musketeers* in the 1620s, the true D'Artagnan—Charles de Batz—was born in 1620, probably at Castlemore near Lupiac, and didn't become a musketeer until 1645. Batz adopted the nobler name of D'Artagnan from his mother's family, the Montesquieus, lords of Artagnan and one of the highest-ranking families in Gascony.

On the other side of the cathedral, behind the former Archbishop's Palace (now the Préfecture), is the **Musée des Jacobins**, showcasing one of the country's finest collections of Latin-American art and pre-Columbian pottery, gathered by 19th-century adventurer Guillaume Pujos. The museum also contains Gallo-Roman relics; look for the white-marble epitaph dedicated by a grief-stricken mistress to her dog Myia. *Rue Daumesnil. Admission: 6 frs. adults, 3 frs. children. Open May–Oct., Tues.–Sun. 10–noon and 2–6; Nov.–Apr., Tues.–Sat. 10–noon and 2–4.*

Leave Auch by N21 and follow the Gers Valley 35 kilometers (22 miles) north to Lectoure, via **Fleurance**, a *bastide* (fortified) town with a regimented street plan. The town's Gothic church of St-Laurent boasts three more stained-glass windows by Arnaud de Moles. Like Auch, **Lectoure** stands on a promontory above the Gers Valley and was once a Roman city and a fortified Gallic town. Archaeologists have a field day combing the area for ancient remains.

Although Lectoure was ravaged in 1473, when Louis XI attacked the fortress and established direct royal rule by killing the last count of Armagnac, there's still plenty to see in its old arched streets: the 13th-century **Fontaine Diane** (fountain) on rue Fontélie for starters. The nearby **Musée Municipal**, installed in the vaulted cellars of the former Episcopal Palace (now the Town Hall), complements the traditional marble tombs, mosaics, and vases with a dramatic collection of 20 pagan altars, discovered in 1640 under the choir of the cathedral. These altars feature Latin inscriptions and heads of the sacrificed bulls (or rams). *Hôtel de Ville. Admission: 21 frs. adults, 6 frs. children. Open daily 9–noon and 2–6.*

D7 heads west from Lectoure to **Condom,** 21 kilometers (13 miles) away. Condom, the town of seven churches, lies in the heart of Ténarèze, one of the three regions that produce Armagnac (the others: highly rated Bas-Armagnac, around Eauze to the west; and Haut-Armagnac, around Auch). Condom's location on the River Baïse made it an excellent base for exporting the local brandy to Bordeaux or Bayonne on the Atlantic coast.

The musty **Musée de l'Armagnac,** in an 18th-century annex of the former Bishop's Palace in the town center, details the production process from the grape harvest to the barrel. Armagnac is distilled only once (unlike cognac, which is distilled twice); you can inspect the copper stills, or *alambics*, used for distillation. *2 rue Jules-Ferry. Admission: 8 frs. adults, 4 frs. children. Open June–Sept., Tues.–Sun. 10–noon and 2–6; Oct.–May, Tues.–Sat. 10–noon and 2–4.*

Time Out The dining room of the **Table des Cordeliers** (a former monastery) is a converted 14th-century chapel, where you can enjoy foie gras, served with fresh pasta, or duck with peaches. *Av. Charles-de-Gaulle.*

㉙ Six kilometers (4 miles) southwest of Condom (take D931/D208) is the château of **Cassaigne,** once the country residence of the bishops of Condom. The vineyards surrounding this 13th-century manor house were originally cultivated for wine, with only the unconsumed leftovers distilled to make brandy (once prescribed by local pharmacists as a disinfectant!). By the 17th century, the English were importing Armagnac in large quantities; ever since, brandy production has been the château's main raison d'être.

Cassaigne has belonged to the same family since 1827. Today Elvire and Henri Faget organize tours of the château and visits to the 17th-century cellars, where the Armagnac is stored in oak barrels that give it an amber color. There's a small Armagnac museum, and you can taste and buy the brandy in the 16th-century vaulted kitchen. With luck, the slide show on the history of the house and the traditional methods of distillation will be in English as well as French by 1991. *Admission free. Open daily 9–noon and 2–7.*

D142 links Cassaigne to the 12th-century abbey of **Flaran,** just over 4 kilometers (2½ miles) away. In 1971, regional authorities took over the abbey, renovated it, and converted the guests' quarters into a cultural center for temporary exhibits. The abbey was built by Cistercian monks under St-Bernard; the monks' rooms on the second floor, overlooking the cloisters, remain largely unchanged.

The Cistercians preferred to build their abbeys in remote spots, next to a reliable water supply (here, the River Baïse). Have a look at the impressive sacristy, with its ribbed arches, resting on one central column, and at the storeroom, with its exhibit illustrating the medieval routes of pilgrims (two of which crossed the Gers) to Santiago de Compostela. *Valence-sur-Baïse. Admission: 15 frs. adults, 7 frs. children. Open July–Aug., daily 9:30–7; Sept.–June, Wed.–Mon, 9:30–noon and 2–6; closed Tues.*

Tour 4: The Pyrénées

㉚ The elegant town of **Pau,** 160 kilometers (100 miles) southwest of Toulouse, is the historic capital of Béarn, a state annexed to France in 1620. Pau rose to prominence after being "discovered" in 1815 by British officers who were returning from the Peninsular War in Spain and was soon launched as a winter resort. Fifty years later, English-speaking inhabitants made up one-third of Pau's population. They launched the Pont-Long steeplechase, still one of the most challenging in Europe, in 1841; created France's first golf course here, in 1856; and introduced fox hunting to the region.

Paying tribute to Pau's regal past is the **château,** begun in the 14th century by Gaston Phoebus, the flamboyant Count of Béarn. The building was transformed into a Renaissance palace in the 16th century by the beautiful Marguerite d'Angoulême, sister of French king François I. Marguerite's grandson, the future King Henri IV, was born in the château in 1553. Temporary exhibits connected to Henri's life and times are staged regularly here. His cradle—a giant turtle shell—is on show in his bedroom, one of the sumptuous, tapestry-lined royal apartments. Other highlights are the 16th-century kitchens and the imposing dining hall, which could seat up to 100 guests. *Rue du Château. Admission: 22 frs. (11 frs. Sun.). Open Apr.–Oct., daily 9:30–11:30 and 2–5:45; Nov.–Mar., daily 9:30–11:30 and 2–4:30.*

On the fourth floor of the château, the **Musée Béarnais** offers an overview of the region, encompassing everything from fauna to furniture to festival costumes. There is a reconstructed Béarn house and displays of such local crafts as cheese- and béret making. *Admission: 6 frs. adults, children free. Open Apr.–Oct., daily 9:30–12:30 and 2:30–6:30; Nov.–Mar., daily 9:30–12:30 and 2:30–5:30.*

31 The quickest and most scenic route from Pau to **Lourdes** (40 kilometers/25 miles southeast) is via N117/D940. More than 3 million pilgrims flock to Lourdes each year, many in quest of a miracle cure for their sickness or handicap. In February 1858, Bernadette Soubirous, a 14-year-old miller's daughter, claimed the Virgin Mary had appeared to her in the **Massabielle grotto** near the Gave de Pau river. The visions were repeated. During the ninth, Bernadette dug at the ground in the grotto, releasing a gush of water from a spot where no spring existed. From then on, pilgrims thronged the Massabielle rock in response to the water's supposed healing powers.

Church authorities reacted skeptically. It took four years of inquiry for the miracle to be authenticated by Rome and a sanctuary erected over the grotto. In 1864, the first organized procession was held. Today there are six official annual pilgrimages, the most important on August 15. In 1958, Lourdes celebrated the centenary of the apparitions by constructing the world's largest underground church, the basilica of **St-Pie X.** The basilica looks more like a parking lot than a church, but it can accommodate 20,000 people—more than the permanent population of the whole town. Above the basilica stand the neo-Byzantine basilica of **Rosaire** (1889) and the tall, white basilica of **Supérieure** (1871). Both are open throughout the day, but unfortunately, their spiritual function far outweighs their aesthetic appeal.

The area surrounding the churches and grotto (situated between the basilicas and the river) is woefully lacking in beauty. Out of season, the acres of parking space beneath the basilicas echo like mournful parade grounds to the steps of solitary visitors. Shops are shuttered and restaurants are closed. In season, a milling throng jostles for postcards, tacky souvenirs, and a glimpse of the famous grotto, lurking behind a forest of votive candles struggling to remain aflicker in the Pyrenean breeze.

The Pavillon Notre-Dame, across from the underground basilica, houses the **Musée Bernadette,** with mementoes of her life (she died at a convent in Nevers, Burgundy, in 1879) and illustrated history of the pilgrimages. In the basement is the **Musée d'Art Sacré du Gemmail,** *gemmail* being a modern approach to the stained-glass technique involving the assembly of broken glass, lit from behind, often by electric light. *72 rue de la Grotte. Admission free. Open July–Nov., daily 9:30–11:45 and*

2:30–6:15; Dec.–June, Wed.–Mon. 9:30–11:45 and 2:30–5:45; closed Tues.

Time Out   Stop in at the **Taverne de Bigorre**; (21 pl. du Champ Commun); Chef Claude Moreau prepares a filling stew of cabbage and bacon, or try one of his lighter fish dishes.

Just across the river are the **Moulin des Boly,** where Bernadette was born on January 7, 1844 (rue Bernadette-Soubirous; open Easter–mid-Oct., daily 9:30–11:45 and 2:30–5:45), and, close to the parish church where she was baptized, the **Cachot,** a shabby little room where Bernadette and her family lived. *15 rue des Petits-Fossés. Admission free. Open Easter–mid-Oct., daily 9:30–11:45 and 2:30–5:30; mid-Oct.–Easter, daily 2:30–5:30.*

Though the story of Bernadette is compelling, Lourdes is lucky to have an authentic historic attraction to complement the commercialized aura of its pilgrim sites. **Lourdes Castle** stands on a hill above the town and can be reached on foot or by escalator. In the 17th and 18th centuries, the castle was used as a prison; now it contains the **Musée Pyrénéen,** one of France's best provincial museums, devoted to popular customs and arts throughout the Pyrenees region, from Bayonne on the Atlantic to Perpignan by the Mediterranean. *Admission: 17.50 frs. adults, 7.50 frs. students, children free. Open Easter–mid-Oct., daily 9–noon and 2–7 (last admission at 6); mid-Oct.–Easter, Wed.–Mon. 9–noon and 2–7.*

32 Lourdes is close to several Pyrenean beauty spots. **Cauterets,** 30 kilometers (19 miles) south of Lourdes (via N21/D920), is a spa-resort set deep in the mountains, where you can sometimes ski until May. Ever since Roman times, Cauterets's thermal springs have been revered as a miracle cure for female sterility. Virile novelist Victor Hugo (1802–85) womanized here, and Lady Aurore Dudevant—better known as the writer George Sand (1804–76)—discovered the thrill of adultery. Poetic viscount François René Chateaubriand (1768–1848) stayed determinedly chaste, however, pining for his "inaccessible Occitan girl."

Continue south from Cauterets to the **Pont d'Espagne,** where steep-twisting D920 peters out. Continue on foot or by chairlift to the plateau and a view over the bright-blue **Lac de Gaube,** fed by the river of the same name.

33 Return via Cauterets to Pierrefitte-Nestalas and turn right along D921 and the Gorge de Luz to **Gavarnie,** 30 kilometers (19 miles) away at the foot of the **Cirque de Gavarnie,** one of the world's most remarkable examples of glacial erosion. When the upper snows melt, numerous streams whoosh down from the cliffs to form spectacular waterfalls; the greatest of them—the **Grande Cascade**—drops nearly 1,400 feet. The Cirque presents a daunting challenge to mountaineers; if you've forgotten your climbing boots, a horse or donkey can take you partway into the mountains from the village of Gavarnie.

34 Return along D921 as far as **Luz-St-Sauveur** and turn right along D918. The mountain scenery remains dramatic. The road
35 passes through the lively little spa town of **Barèges** and under the brow of the mighty Pic du Midi de Bigorre, towering nearly

10,000 feet above the Col du Tourmalet pass. Luz-St-Sauveur
36 lies just 18 miles from **Arreau** as the crow flies, but 61 kilometers (38 miles) as the tortuous D918 twists. The finest views—
and the sharpest curves—are found toward the Col d'Aspin
pass, whose panoramic views of the Pyrenees are unequalled.

Another spectacular road, D618, covers the 32 kilometers (20
miles), via the Col de Peyresourde, from Arreau southeast to
37 the largest and most fashionable Pyrenean spa, **Bagnères de
Luchon** (better known as just plain Luchon). Thermal waters
here cater to the vocal cords: Opera singers, lawyers, and politicians hoarse from electoral promises all pile in. Luchon lies at
the head of a lush valley, beneath the ski resort of
38 **Superbagnères,** reached by a serpentine 12-mile road (D46); on
the way up, admire the breathtaking views of the Maladeta
mountain range across the border in Spain. The Romans considered Luchon to rank second as a spa only to Naples. A
39 Roman road led directly from Luchon to **St-Bertrand de
Comminges** (then a huge town of 60,000), 32 kilometers (20
miles) north on D125/N125. This delightful village, whose inhabitants number just 500 today, is dwarfed beneath the imposing cathedral of **Ste-Marie,** largely 12th-century but
extended in the 13th by Bertrand de Got (later Pope Clement
V). Old houses, sloping alleyways, and crafts shops add to the
village's abundant charm.

What to See and Do with Children

At the **Rocher des Aigles** in Rocamadour a hundred different
species of birds of prey, including condors and vultures as well
as eagles, swoop high and low at the command of their expert
handlers. *Rte. du Château, tel. 65–33–65–45. Admission: 30
frs. adults, 15 frs. children. Open Apr.–mid-Nov. for demonstrations daily at 11, 3, 4, 5, and 6.*

The following attractions are described in the Exploring and
Off the Beaten Track sections:

Boat trip on the Rivière Souterraine, Labouiche, Off the Beaten
Track
Gouffre de Padirac, Off the Beaten Track
Grottes de Niaux, near Foix, Off the Beaten Track
Grande Cascade, Tour 4
Musée Béarnais, Pau, Tour 4
Muséum d'Histoire Naturelle (Natural History Museum), Tou-
louse, Tour 1

Off the Beaten Track

At first sight, the **Gouffre de Padirac,** 16 kilometers (10 miles)
northeast of Rocamadour via D673/D90, looks like an enormous
gaping hole; until the 19th century, locals took the terrifying
abyss to be the work of the devil. In 1889, a passage was found
leading to underground galleries, and since then, a 14-mile network has been discovered, littered with the bones of mam-
moths, rhinoceroses, and other mammals—some dating back
200,000 years. Elevators take you 200 feet down for an initial
encounter with a host of stalagmites, while, farther on, boats
cast off on a tour of the subterranean river through a mysterious underworld of chambers and lakes. *Admission: 32 frs.*

Open Apr.–July and Sept.–mid-Oct., daily 9–noon and 2–6; Aug., daily 7 AM–8 PM.

Carcassonne, 88 kilometers (55 miles) east of Toulouse along the A61 expressway, boasts Europe's lengthiest medieval town walls. The mighty circle of towers and battlements stands high on a hilltop above the River Aude: a fairy-tale sight, claimed as the setting for Charles Perrault's story *Puss in Boots.* The earliest sections of wall were built by the Romans in the 5th century, while the Visigoths enlarged the settlement into a true fortress. In the 13th century, French king St-Louis and his son, Philip the Bold, strengthened the fortifications and gave Carcassonne the appearance it has today. The old streets inside the walls are lined with souvenir shops, crafts boutiques, and restaurants. The **Château Comtal,** with its **Musée Lapidaire** (stone relics), is worth a visit; the view from the battlements toward the Pyrénées is stunning. *Château Comtal. Admission: 23 frs. adults, 12 frs. senior citizens, 5 frs. children. Open Apr.–Sept., daily 9–6; Oct.–Mar., daily 9:30–noon and 2–5.*

Six kilometers (4 miles) northwest of Foix (via D1) lies the **Rivière Souterraine** (underground river) of Labouiche, whose waters have tunneled through limestone cliffs. The 75-minute boat trip, past fantastically shaped and subtly lit stalactites and stalagmites, culminates in an encounter with a subterranean waterfall. *Admission: 30 frs. Open Easter–July and Sept., daily 9:30–noon and 2–5:30; Aug., daily 9:30–5:30.*

Lying 19 kilometers (12 miles) south of Foix (take D8 from Tarascon-sur-Ariège) are the superb **Grottes de Niaux,** caves containing scores of Magdalenian rock paintings dating to 20,000 BC. Stylized drawings of horses, deer, and bison line a natural gallery half a mile from the entrance. Now that the famous caves at Lascaux in the Dordogne can be seen only in reproduction, this is the finest assembly of prehistoric art open to the public in France. *Admission: July–Aug., 20 frs. adults, 10 frs. children; Sept.–June, 15 frs. adults, 7.50 frs. children. Open July–Sept., daily 8:30–12:30 and 1:30–5:15; Oct.–June, daily tours at 11, 3, and 4:30.*

Shopping

Gift Ideas Don't leave the Midi-Pyrénées without buying some of the region's renowned foie gras and preserved duck *(confit de canard).* Two manufacturers in particular, **Aux Ducs de Gascogne** (rte. de Mauvezin, Gimont) and **Comtesse de Barry** (rte. Touget, Gimont) offer beautifully packaged tins that make ideal gifts. You'll also find their products in most good grocery stores and general food shops throughout the region.

Spirits Armagnac brandy is distilled throughout the Gers *département.* You'll see signs for *dégustation* (tasting) just about everywhere in the area (you can buy as well as taste), but any good wine and liquor store will have plenty in stock. For a good selection, try **Caves de l'Hôtel de France** (rue d'Etigny) in Auch.

Stores and Boutiques As the area's largest city, Toulouse offers the widest range of shops. The downtown **Centre Commercial St-Georges** (rue du Rempart St-Etienne) is a frenetic, modern shopping mall offering a vast array of clothing, jewelry, books, records—and just about anything else you'd possibly want to buy or admire. For upscale clothes, try the chic shops on **rue St-Rome** and **rue**

d'Alsace-Lorraine, home to Toulouse's main department store, **Nouvelles Galeries,** which, like its sister store in Paris, Galeries Lafayette, provides a good range of services for foreign visitors (including overseas shipment and payment with any major credit card).

Sports and Fitness

Canoeing Canoeing is one of the region's most popular sports. Try canoe-kayaking in the rough waters of the Pyrenean torrents or the Tarn and Aveyron gorges, or make gentler progress in the peaceful Quercy rivers. The most important bases are at Millau, Rozier-Pyreleau, Najac, Penne, Midi-Pyrénées, Trébas, Burlats, Albi, St-Juéry, and Laguépie. Contact **Ligue de Canoë-Kayak** (16 rue Guillemin-Tarayre, 31000 Toulouse, tel. 61–62–65–05).

Fishing The rivers here teem with trout and salmon. Courses, for beginners and advanced fishermen, are run by **Loisirs Accueil** (Service Pêche, 14 rue Lazéma, 09000 Foix, tel. 61–65–01–15).

Hiking The Midi-Pyrénées offers more than 2,000 miles of marked paths for walkers and hikers, all designed to pass natural and historical sights. Local tourist offices have detailed maps, or, for advance information, contact **Comité de Randonnées Midi-Pyrénées** (CORAMIP, 12 rue Salammbô, 31200 Toulouse, tel. 61–47–11–12).

Horseback Riding There are more than 120 stables or horseback riding centers in the region; for a full listing, get in touch with **CORAMIP** (*see* Hiking, above). Two that we recommend are **Poney Club** (Association Vacances, Loisirs Nature, chemin St-Jean, Colomiers, near Toulouse) and the **Centre Equestre et Poney Club** (Degagnac, 46340 Salviac, north of Cahors via D6).

Skiing Skiing—both downhill and cross-country—is often more fun in the Pyrenees than in the Alps; resorts tend to be prettier and are certainly cheaper. There are 26 "stations" along the central part of the range. Contact **Comité Régional Pyrénées Est de sports d'hiver** (1 rue de la Charité, 31000 Toulouse, tel. 61–62–89–25).

Dining and Lodging

Dining

The cuisine in Toulouse and the southwest is rich and strongly seasoned, making generous use of garlic and goose fat. This is the land of foie gras, especially delicious when sautéed with grapes. The most famous regional dish is *cassoulet,* a succulent white-bean stew with *confit* (preserved goose), spicy sausage, pork, and sometimes lamb; there are a number of local versions around Toulouse and Carcassonne. Goose and duck dishes are legion: Try a *magret de canard* (a steak of duck breast). Cheaper specialties include *garbure,* mixed vegetables served as a broth or puree; *farci du lauragais,* a kind of pork pancake; and *gigot de sept heures,* a leg of lamb braised with garlic for no fewer than seven hours. Béarn, around Pau, is great eating country, famous for richly marinated stews made with wood pigeon *(civet de palombes)* or wild goat *(civet d'isnard).* The local *poule au pot* of stuffed chicken poached with vegetables is memorable.

Highly recommended restaurants are indicated by a star ★.

Category	Cost*
Very Expensive	over 350 francs
Expensive	200-350 francs
Moderate	100–200 francs
Inexpensive	under 100 francs

*per person for a three-course meal, including tax (18.6%) and tip but not wine

Lodging

Hotels in this vast region range from Mediterranean-style modern to Middle Ages baronial; most are small and cozy rather than luxurious. Toulouse, the area's only major town, has the usual range of big-city hotels; make reservations well ahead if you plan to visit in spring or fall. As with most of France, many of the hotels we list offer excellent eating opportunities.

Highly recommended hotels are indicated by a star ★.

Category	Cost*
Very Expensive	over 750 francs
Expensive	350–750 francs
Moderate	200–350 francs
Inexpensive	under 200 francs

*All prices are for a standard double room for two, including tax (18.6%) and service charge.

Albi
Dining

Le Jardin des Quatre Saisons. There are two reasons for this new restaurant's excellent reputation: value for the money and efficient service. Ask the wine waiter to help you choose a bottle from the extensive wine list to accompany one of the chef's fish dishes. House specialties include mussels baked with leeks, or *suprême de sandre* (a type of perch) in wine. Desserts are surprisingly light for this gastronomic region. Try for a table in the garden if the weather's fine. *19 blvd. de Strasbourg, tel. 63–60–77–76. Reservations advised. Jacket and tie required. AE, MC, V. Closed Mon., and Tues. lunch. Moderate.*

Dining and Lodging

La Réserve. A five-acre park surrounds this delightful hideaway of a hotel, a modern, hacienda-style building with arched windows and terraces extending the length of the facade. All the guest rooms are spacious, but those in the main building have the most charm, with elegant reproduction furniture and lots of pretty knickknacks. The restaurant offers tempting local specialties; the salmon with grapefruit and foie gras lightly fried with apples is a good bet. *Rte. de Cordes, 81000 Fonvialane (5 km/3 mi outside town), tel. 63–47–60–22. 24 rooms with bath. Facilities: restaurant, pool, tennis, park. Restaurant closed Nov.–Mar. AE, DC, MC, V. Expensive.*

Altéa. Ask for a room with a view in this converted 18th-centu-

ry windmill, opposite the cathedral and overlooking the River
Tarn. The ones on the second and fourth floor are best; those on
the third and top floors have tiny windows. The hotel's restaurant is a stylish place to try Jean-Paul Devisi's regional specialties, such as *fritons*—peanut-size chunks of duck lard in flaky
pastry with capers; they're a great deal more appetizing than
they sound. Dine on the terrace in summer. *41 rue Porta,
81000, tel. 63–47–66–66. 56 rooms with bath. Facilities: restaurant, terrace. AE, DC, MC, V. Moderate.*

Auch
Dining and Lodging
★
France. Be sure to pay a visit to this, the most celebrated restaurant in Gascony. Despite the building's sober facade, the
dining room's ambience is as warm and welcoming as at any corner bistro, with a bit of extra plush thrown in for good measure.
Renowned chef André Daguin creates traditional Gascon cuisine with a masterly touch; his best dishes include salad with
kid's liver and cod in flaky pastry accompanied by a whipped
liver sauce. Save room for dessert—chocolates in *Banyuls*
(warmed wine). There are 29 guest rooms as well, which
Andre's wife, Jocelyne, has decorated with great charm and individuality. *Pl. de la Libération, 32000, tel. 62–05–00–44. 29
rooms. Reservations required. Dress: neat but casual. Restaurant closed Jan., Sun. dinner, and Mon. AE, DC, MC, V. Expensive.*

Barbotan-les-Thermes
Dining and Lodging
La Bastide Gasconne. One of the country's leading food families—the Guérards—own and run this sumptuously decorated
18th-century manor house, now converted to a fine hotel-restaurant; it's located near an immense lake, close to the spa of
Barbotan and 36 kilometers (21 miles) west of Condom. Michel
Guérard presides over the magnificent, wood-beamed dining
room and dishes up exceptional nouvelle cuisine; try the fresh
foie gras cooked in muslin or ray-wing in a rich mushroom-and-
parsley sauce. Cognac or Armagnac and coffee by the open
hearth make a suitably grand finale. Guérard's wife, Christine,
is a talented interior decorator, and her elegant taste is shown
to advantage in the Gasconne's light, spacious decor. The guest
rooms feature a quaint-chic touch, and there are a pool and tennis courts. *Rue des Thermes, 32150, tel. 62–69–52–09. 36
rooms. Reservations required. Jacket and tie required. AE,
DC, MC, V. Closed Nov.–Mar. Expensive.*

Cabrerets
Dining and Lodging
La Pescalerie. In a gracious parkland setting on the banks of
the Célé (33 kilometers/20 miles northeast of Cahors), La
Pescalerie is run with precision by Hélène Combette, a former
psychiatrist, while Roger Belcour, a practicing surgeon, acts
as maître d'hôtel. Don't panic: The atmosphere is friendly and
welcoming and not in the least medicinal. The rustic manor
dates from the 16th and 17th centuries, and its shuttered stone
facade is cozily inviting. Each guest room features a different
decor and its own collection of contemporary paintings, and
some of the bathrooms are palatial; antiques are dotted
throughout. Rooms on the upper floor are charming, with
slanted ceilings and exposed beams. In the restaurant, try the
artichoke stew with thin slivers of duck; snails with nuts; and,
for dessert, peaches poached in wine. The Cahors wine list is
extensive. *A la Fontaine de la Pescalerie, 46330, tel. 65–31–22–
55. 10 rooms with bath. Facilities: restaurant, bar, park. AE,
DC, MC, V. Closed Nov.–Apr. Expensive.*

Cahors
Dining
Le Coq & La Pendule. This small, family-run café-restaurant,
in a pedestrian street near the cathedral, is a classic example of

homey French cooking in a down-to-earth setting. Space is tight, it's all hustle-bustle, but service is friendly, portions generous, and a five-course meal with wine and coffee won't cost much above 50 francs. *10 rue St-James, tel. 65–35–28–84. Dress: casual. No credit cards. Inexpensive.*

Dining and Lodging
★
Château de Mercuès. A graceful, curving staircase leads up to this majestic stone castle, whose corner towers reach high into the sky. The château, built in the 13th century and former home to the counts of Cahors, lies 8 kilometers (5 miles) outside town on the road to Villeneuve-sur-Lot. There are actually two hotels here: the Mercuès itself, whose guest rooms feature the sort of baronial splendor you'd expect in any self-respecting castle, and the new Cèdres annex, with contemporary furnishings and much less appeal (rooms here cost less, however, and you still get the same fantastic views of the countryside). Ask for the "*évêque*" (bishop) or "*donjon*" (turret) rooms. Duck, lamb, and truffles reign in the restaurant. *46090 Mercuès, tel. 65–20–00–01. 23 rooms with bath (plus 22 rooms with bath in annex). Facilities: restaurant, terrace, pool, tennis, helipad. AE, DC, MC, V. Closed Nov. and Jan.–Apr. Expensive–Very Expensive.*

Terminus. This small hotel is deep in the heart of truffle country, yet just two minutes' walk from Cahors train station; the restaurant, La Balandre, is the city's best. The decor is mainly Roaring Twenties and the atmosphere is stylishly jazzy, but the windows have turn-of-the-century stained glass. Gilles Marre and his wife, Jacqueline, specialize in truffles but also serve an exceptional fresh cod *brandade* (mousse) and foie gras in flaky pastry. There's a good range of local wines, and the service is sophisticated yet friendly. The guest rooms are cozily traditional in feel. *5 av. Charles de Freycinet 46000, tel. 65–35–24–50. 31 rooms. Reservations advised. Dress: neat but casual. AE, MC, V. Restaurant closed 2 weeks in Feb., 1 week in June, Sun. dinner, Mon., Jan.–Mar., and Sat. lunch, July–Aug. Moderate.*

Carcassonne Dining
★
Le Languedoc. Candlelight dinners on the Languedoc's terrace are romantic, elegant affairs. Maestro Didier Faugeras offers a range of delicacies, from artichoke hearts and chicken livers in warm vinegar to scallops with cucumbers and chive butter and seasonal game. The same family runs the Montségur, across the street. *32 allée d'Iéna, tel. 68–25–22–17. Reservations required. Jacket and tie required. AE, DC, MC, V. Closed mid-Dec.–mid-Jan., and Mon. and Sun. dinner, Sept.–June. Moderate–Expensive.*

Auberge du Pont-Levis. At the foot of the medieval city gateway, Porte Narbonnaise, the Pont-Levis provides a welcome shelter from the tourist crowds. Chef Henri Pautard serves traditional cassoulet stews and foie gras alongside a more inventive terrine marbled with artichokes and leeks, accompanied by a truffle vinaigrette. Otherwise, try the *méli-mélo du pêcheur*, a refreshing mix of seafood. In summer, you can eat on the terrace or in the pretty garden. *Porte Narbonnaise, tel. 68–25–55–23. Reservations advised. Jacket required. AE, DC, MC, V. Closed Nov., Feb., Sun. dinner, and Mon. Moderate.*

Lodging
★
Montségur. This pretty little town hotel lies just outside the old city walls. Rooms on the first two floors showcase elaborate Louis XV and XVI period furniture, while those above are more romantic, with gilt-iron bedsteads set under sloping oak

beams. *27 allée d'Iéna, 11000, tel. 68–25–31–41. 21 rooms with bath. DC, MC, V. Closed mid-Dec.–mid-Jan. Moderate.*

Dining and Lodging **Domaine d'Auriac.** Former rugby player Bernard Rigaudis has created a countrified atmosphere in this 19th-century manor house 2½ miles southwest of Carcassonne. Room prices vary according to the size and view; larger rooms look out over the magnificent park and vineyards. The dining room is festooned with copper pots and pans and offers traditional Languedoc cuisine. Feast on foie gras poached in Sauternes, anchovies with lemon in salmon *carpaccio*, or local game in season. *Rte. de St-Hilaire, 11330 Auriac, tel. 68–25–72–22. 23 rooms with bath. Facilities: restaurant, pool, garden, tennis, golf. AE, MC, V. Closed last 3 weeks in Jan.; restaurant closed Sun. dinner and Mon. lunch. Expensive.*

Castéra-Verduzan **Ténarèze.** The Ténarèze's restaurant, Le Florida, is fast ac-
Dining and Lodging quiring a reputation nearly as lofty as that of André Daguin's own establishment in Auch. The dining room's setting is unpretentious and completely upstaged by chef Bernard Ramounéda's creative flair. Ramounéda serves his foie gras with grapes, apples, or gooseberries and a glass of Sauterne; offers duck cooked in every possible manner; and presents a sumptuous range of desserts, including ice cream with prunes and Armagnac or peaches with spices. The hotel's inexpensive guest rooms are traditionally decorated, with heavy velvet drapes and lace trim. Castéra-Verduzan is a spa town featuring curative thermal springs. To get there, take tree-lined D930 25 kilometers (15 miles) northwest from Auch. *32410 Castéra-Verduzan, tel. 62–68–10–22. 24 rooms. Reservations required. Jacket and tie required. AE, DC, MC, V. Closed Mon., Sun. dinner, and Feb. Moderate.*

Cordes **Le Grand Ecuyer.** Dramatically set in one of the region's most
Dining and Lodging beautiful villages, Le Grand Ecuyer is a perfectly preserved
★ medieval mansion. The guest rooms contain period furnishings, and a few feature four-poster beds; only the bathrooms are contemporary. Yves Thuriès is one of the southwest's best chefs, and the dining room's elegant decor and ornate silverware provide a stylish background to his inventive recipes. Sample his salmon and sole twist in vanilla puree or the guinea fowl *suprême* in fragrant, flaky pastry. *Rue Voltaire, 81170, tel. 63–56–01–03. 13 rooms with bath. Facilities: restaurant. AE, DC, MC, V. Closed Nov.–Mar.; restaurant closed Mon., Sept.–June. Expensive.*

★ **L'Hostellerie du Vieux Cordes.** This magnificent 13th-century house, belonging to the same family as Le Grand Ecuyer, is set around a charming courtyard, shaded by overhanging trees and dotted with tiny white tables. Inside, the 21 guest rooms are richly decorated, but not nearly as opulent as the vast crimson dining rooms. Bernard Lafuente, Yves Thuriès's brother-in-law, is yet another accomplished chef. For a gastronomic blowout, go for his *Délices de Raymond VII*, a varying multi-course feast. Lighter—and more affordable—specialties include grilled goat cheese in honey, roast salmon with herb vinaigrette and marinated cucumbers, and young pigeon on a bed of red cabbage. *Rue St-Michel, 81170, tel. 63–56–00–12. 21 rooms. Reservations advised. Jacket required. AE, DC, MC, V. Closed Mon., Nov.–Easter; hotel closed mid-Jan.–mid-Feb. Moderate.*

Toulouse
Dining
★

Vanel. French gastronomes have long rated Vanel the top restaurant in Toulouse, and one of the country's finest. Lucien Vanel, now in his sixties and gradually passing control to his talented protégés, is known for his imagination; he's capable of changing the menu completely, overnight. You'll never be disappointed. The decor was more comfortable than exciting until a recent renovation transformed its Belle Epoque fustiness into modern chic. *22 rue Maurice-Fonvielle, tel. 61–21–51–82. Reservations required. Jacket and tie required. AE, MC, V. Closed part of Aug., Sun., and Mon. lunch. Expensive.*

La Belle Epoque. Owner Pierre Roudgé's approach to cooking is novel: Tell him what you don't like and he'll invent your menu on the spot. The ginger-spiced lobster in a flaky pastry is as good as it sounds, while other dishes include cod in leek butter and a light pastry stuffed with asparagus and foie gras. At press time, Roudgé was renovating the 1920s decor, so you'll be able to savor chef Pierre-Jean Ferrié's culinary efforts in a new setting. *3 rue Pargaminières, tel. 61–23–22–12. Reservations advised. Dress: casual. AE, DC, MC, V. Closed Sat. and Mon. lunch, Sun., and July. Moderate–Expensive.*

Chez Emile. There are two dining rooms at this restaurant, overlooking place St-Georges. The ground floor is modern and elegant, specializing in light, contemporary fish dishes that change daily; if it's on the menu, try the turbot in ginger. Upstairs is a cozy hideaway for those who appreciate a more traditional taste of Toulouse: *cassoulet, magrets de canard* (duck), and other filling fare. *13 pl. St-Georges, tel. 61–21–05–56. Reservations required. Dress: casual. AE, DC, MC, V. Closed last week in Aug., Sun., and Mon. Moderate.*

Dining and Lodging
★

Grand Hôtel de l'Opéra. This downtown doyen is conveniently located on Toulouse's place du Capitole. The guest rooms are comfortably plush, with calm, soothing colors and modern conveniences; make sure you're not given one of the smaller rooms—they are *very* small. Dominique Toulousy and his wife, Maryse, have made the hotel's Jardins de l'Opéra the most fashionable restaurant in town. Several intimate dining rooms and a covered terrace around a little pond make for undeniable, if slightly overcute, charm. The food is a successful mix of innovation and traditional Gascon fare; try the ravioli stuffed with foie gras and truffles or the *gambas* (jumbo shrimp) baked with artichokes and cheese. For dessert, there's a large selection of homemade patisserie. *1 pl. du Capitole, 31000, tel. 61–21–82–66. 63 rooms with bath. Facilities: restaurant, café, pool, garden. AE, DC, MC, V. Expensive.*

Lodging

Taur. If you want to be at the hub of things without paying Grand Hôtel prices, the Taur, just a stone's throw from the Capitole, is a workmanlike alternative: Its labyrinthine corridors have a faded, creaky charm, and the welcome is courteous. Be prepared, though, for soft mattresses, rooms without views, and gaudily florid wallpaper. *2 rue du Taur, 31000, tel. 62–21–17–54. 41 rooms, most with shower. AE, MC, V. Inexpensive.*

The Arts and Nightlife

The Arts

Toulouse, the region's cultural high spot, is also recognized as one of France's most arty cities. Its classical, lyrical, and chamber music orchestras, dramatic-arts center, and ballet are all listed as national companies—no mean feat in this arts-oriented country. So many opera singers have come to sing here at the Théâtre du Capitole or the Halle aux Grains that the city is known as the *capitale du bel canto.* The performing arts season lasts from October until late May, with occasional summer presentations. For information and advance bookings, contact **Théâtre du Capitole** (pl. du Capitole, 31000 Toulouse, tel. 61–23–21–35).

The medieval city of **Carcassonne** has a major arts festival in July, featuring dance, theater, classical music, and jazz; for details, contact the **Théâtre Municipal** (B.P. 236, rue Courtejaire, 11005 Carcassonne cedex, tel. 68–25–33–13).

Music   There are 50 music festivals a year in smaller towns throughout the region; the CRT and larger tourist offices can provide a list of dates and addresses, or contact **Délégation Musicale Régionale** (56 rue du Taur, 31000 Toulouse, tel. 61–23–20–39).

Toulouse is the hometown of Claude Nougaro, one of France's best jazz singers. If you're a blues or boogie buff, take in one of his slick, professional concerts.

Dance   Toulouse's **Ballet du Capitole** stages classical ballets, while the **Ballet-Théâtre Joseph Russilo** and **Compagnie Jean-Marc Matos** put on modern-dance performances. The **Centre National Chorégraphique de Toulouse** welcomes international companies each year in the St-Cyprien quarter. For a schedule of current programs, get in touch with the city tourist office (*see* Essential Information, above).

Theater   The main theaters in Toulouse are the **Théâtre du Capitole** (pl. du Capitole, tel. 61–23–21–35); **Théâtre de la Digue** (3 rue de la Digue, tel. 61–42–97–79); **Théâtre du Taur** (69 rue du Taur, tel. 61–21–77–13); **Halle Aux Grains** (pl. Dupuy, tel. 61–63–18–65); and **Théâtre Daniel Sorano** (35 allée Jules Guesde, tel. 61–25–66–87).

Nightlife

Toulouse stays up late. For a complete list of clubs and discos, buy a copy of *Toulouse Pratique,* available at any bookshop or newspaper stand.

Nightclubs   **L'Art Club** (1 rue de l'Echarpe) is a trendy, elegant vaulted brick cellar in the Esquirol quarter; if you like a more intimate setting, try **La Cendrée** (15 rue des Tourneurs), which has lots of cozy nooks and crannies. **L'Ubu** (16 rue St-Rome) has been the city's top night spot for 20 years, where the local glitterati and concert and theater stars come to relax. **Victory Clippers Club** (Canal de Brienne, 90 allée de Barcelone) may be a bit daring for some, but liberated couples love it.

Jazz Clubs   **Le Café des Allées** (64 allée Charles-de-Fitte) is a regular hothouse of local musicians. **Café Le Griot** (34 rue des Blanchers) features jazz, blues, and a number of American duos and trios. **Le Père Bacchus** (20 pl. St.-Georges) is the trendiest spot on the city's trendiest square.

16 The Atlantic Coast

Bordeaux, Biarritz

Introduction

If there's a formula for enjoying the Atlantic Coast of France and its hinterland, it should include cultural exploration, wine tasting, eating oysters, and relaxing by the sea. Swaths of sandy beaches line the coast: Well-heeled resorts, such as Biarritz, down by the Spanish border, are thronged with glistening bodies baking in the sun, although visitors who prefer more solitude won't have any trouble discovering vast, semideserted stretches.

For three centuries of the medieval era, this region was a battlefield in the wars between the French and the English, and the Dordogne and Périgord regions were on the front line. As a result, castles and châteaus—some ruined, some domesticated—stud the area, with Biron, Hautefort, and Beynac among the best. Robust Romanesque architecture is more characteristic of this area than the airy Gothic style found elsewhere in France: Poitiers showcases the best examples, notably Notre-Dame-la-Grande with its richly worked facade, but Romanesque on the grand scale can also be admired at nearby St-Savin abbey or at the cathedrals of Angoulême and Périgueux. Humble village churches, with distinctive, sturdy towers perch on verdant hills between Poitiers and Bordeaux, and generations of painters have been inspired by La Rochelle's harbor and imposing fortress-towers.

It's hard not to eat well while visiting the Atlantic Coast. Truffles, walnuts, plums, trout, eel, and myriad succulent species of mushrooms jostle for attention on restaurant menus. The goose market in the quaint old town of Sarlat is proof of the local addiction for foie gras. The River Dordogne is home to that rarest of western European fish, sturgeon, whose eggs—better known as caviar—surpass even foie gras as a sought-after delicacy.

The elegant 18th-century city of Bordeaux has tried to diversify its tourist appeal—its May music festival is a major crowd puller—but the city remains synonymous with the wine trade: The vineyards of Médoc, Sauternes, Graves, Entre-Deux-Mers, and St-Emilion are all within a short drive. Proud châteaus, standing resplendent among the vines, can be visited, although opening hours are irritatingly variable. Wine enthusiasts should note that the *vendanges* (grape harvests) usually begin about mid-September in the Bordelais (though you can't visit the wineries at this time). Harvests begin two weeks later in the Cognac region to the north, famed for its brandy.

In the Gironde *département* around Bordeaux the area of forest outstrips the area under vines by four to one; the great Landes pine forest extends all the way from Bordeaux to Spain. Farther north lies the Marais Poitevin, an extraordinary region whose marshy network of rivers and canals is nicknamed Green Venice.

Essential Information

Important Addresses and Numbers

Tourist Information Suggestions about wine tours and tastings, as well as information on local and regional sights, are available at the **Bordeaux**

Office de Tourisme, which also provides a round-the-clock answering service in English (12 cours du XXX Juillet, tel. 56–48–04–61).

The addresses of other tourist offices in towns mentioned on this tour are as follows: **Angoulême** (pl. de la Gare, tel. 45–92–27–57), **Bergerac** (97 rue Neuve d'Argenson, tel. 53–57–03–11), **Biarritz** (1 sq. Ixelles, tel. 59–24–20–24), **Cognac** (16 rue du XIV-Juillet, tel. 45–82–10–71), **Niort** (rue Ernest-Pérochon, tel. 49–24–18–79), **Poitiers** (11 rue Victor-Hugo, tel. 49–41–58–22), **La Rochelle** (10 rue Fleuriau, tel. 46–41–14–68), **St-Emilion** (pl. des Crénaux, tel. 57–24–72–03), **Saintes** (62 cours National, tel. 46–74–23–82), and **Sarlat** (pl. de la Liberté, tel. 53–59–27–67).

Travel Agencies   **American Express** (14 cours de l'Intendance, Bordeaux, tel. 56–81–70–02) and **Wagons-Lits** (28 cours de l'Intendance, tel. 56–52–92–70).

Car Rental   **Avis** (59 rue Peyronnet, Bordeaux, tel. 56–92–69–38; 133 blvd. du Grand-Cerf, tel. 49–58–13–00; and 166 blvd. Joffre, La Rochelle, tel. 46–41–13–55), **Hertz** (pl. de la Gare, Bergerac, tel. 53–57–19–27; and 107 blvd. du Grand Cerf, Poitiers, tel. 49–58–24–24).

Getting Around

By Plane   There are weekly flights from London to Bordeaux and Biarritz and a purely domestic airport at Limoges.

By Car   As capital of southwest France, Bordeaux boasts superb transport links with Paris, Spain, and even the Mediterranean (A62 expressway via Toulouse). The A10 Paris–Bordeaux expressway passes close to Poitiers, Niort (exit 23 for La Rochelle), and Saintes before continuing toward Spain as A63. Fast N137 connects La Rochelle with Saintes via Rochefort; Angoulême is linked to Bordeaux and Poitiers by the rapid N10; St-Emilion lies 32 kilometers (20 miles) east of Bordeaux; and D936 runs along the Dordogne Valley to Bergerac.

By Train   The new superfast TGV Atlantique service linking Paris (Gare Montparnasse) to Bordeaux—584 kilometers (365 miles) in 3 hours—stops at Poitiers (change for Niort, La Rochelle, and Rochefort) and Angoulême (change for Jarnac, Cognac, and Saintes). Trains run regularly from Bordeaux to Bergerac (80-minute journey), with occasional stops at St-Emilion, and, just three times daily, to Sarlat (nearly three hours). The main Paris–northern Spain train line covers the 800 kilometers (500 miles) to Biarritz in 5½ hours.

Guided Tours

Bus Excursions   **Horizons Européens** (France Tourisme, 3 rue d'Alger, 75001 Paris, tel. 42–60–31–25) organizes a seven-day bus tour of Dordogne and Périgord, leaving from Paris and taking in Limoges, castles, wine tastings, and grottoes; cost is about 4,000 francs inclusive. Day trips in a seven-seater minibus are organized Easter through November from Sarlat by **Hep Excursion** (tel. 53–59–05–48); cost is about 160 francs.

Boat Trips   The canal-crossed Marais Poitevin area has been described as a rural version of Venice. You can tour the area by boat, starting at the Benedictine **Abbey of Maillezais;** the 45-minute trip has

departures between 9 and noon and 2 and 7 from Easter
through October, for a cost of 60 francs per boat.

To get a feel for the historic port of **Bordeaux,** the region's largest city, take the 90-minute boat tour that leaves weekdays
from the Embarcadères des Quinconces at around 3; cost is
about 40 francs.

Special-Interest Tours of the pretty St-Emilion vineyard (including wine tastings) are organized by the **St-Emilion tourist office** (1 pl.
Créneaux, tel. 57–24–72–03). Tours last two hours and depart
weekdays during summer months from the tourist office at 2
and 4:15; cost is 45 francs.

Walking Tours The tourist office in **Sarlat** (pl. de la Liberté, tel. 53–59–27–67)
offers a one-hour walking tour of the town; cost is 15 francs.

Exploring the Atlantic Coast

*Numbers in the margin correspond with points of interest on
the Atlantic Coast map.*

Orientation

We've divided the region into three tours. The first begins in
Poitou-Charentes, a rural area north of Bordeaux, and explores the countryside from St-Savin to the seacoast town of La
Rochelle and back inland again to Cognac country. Our second
tour explores the scenic provinces of Dordogne and Périgord.
The vineyards surrounding Bordeaux form the basis of the
third tour, which continues south through sand dunes and
forested scenery to the coastal resort of Biarritz, near the
Spanish border.

Highlights for First-time Visitors

Beynac Castle, Tour 2
Biarritz, Tour 3
Bordeaux, Tour 3
Marais Poitevin, Tour 1
Poitiers, Tour 1
La Rochelle, Tour 1
St-Emilion, Tour 2
Sarlat, Tour 2

Tour 1: Poitou-Charentes

The region of Poitou-Charentes occupies the middle band of
France's Atlantic coast. Our tour starts just about as far from
the sea as regional boundaries will allow: at the tiny village of
1 **St-Savin,** 40 kilometers (25 miles) east of Poitiers.

The large **abbey of St-Savin,** which dates to the 11th century, is
impressive enough from the outside. But it is the interior that
beckons, partly for the sculpted ornament—monsters run riot
on the column capitals—and mainly for the extensive wall
paintings in restrained but skillfully contrasted hues of green
and ocher. These frescoes, dating from the building's construction, were painted directly onto the walls, and it's surprising

The Atlantic Coast

La Roche-sur-Yon
Les Sables-d'Olonne
Parthenay
Le Blanc
Poitiers ❷
Chauvigny
St-Savin ❶
Lussac-les-Châteaux
Fontenay-le-Comte
Maillezais
Marans
St-Martin-de-Ré
Niort ❸
Coulon ❹ ❸
Melle
Civray
Ile de Ré ❻ ❺
La Rochelle
Surgères
Aulnay
Ruffec
Mansle
Confolens
St-Junien
Limoges
Ile d'Oléron ❽
Rochefort-sur-Mer
St-Jean-d'Angély
Aigre
Rochechouart
Brouage ❼
Marennes
Saintes ⓫
Cognac ⓬
Jarnac
Angoulême ⓭
Châlus
Royan ❾
Pointe de Grave ㊶
Soulac-sur-Mer ㊷
Gironde
Talmont ❿
Mirambeau
Barbezieux-St-Hilaire
Brantôme
Thiviers
Hautefort ㉕
Hourtin
Blaye
Chalais
Ribérac
Périgueux ㉖
Montignac
Lacanau
Margaux ㊵ ⓮
Bourg
Libourne
Isle
Grotte of Lascaux
Les Eyzies-de-Tayac
Sarlat ㉔
Bordeaux
㉗ – ㊱
Pessac
St-Emilion ⓯
Bergerac
㉓ Beynac ㉒ ㉑
Arcachon
Léognan ㊴
Langoiran
Monbazillac
㉒ ⓲ Lanquais
Domme
La Roque-Gageac
Cazaux
Labrède
Cadillac
Haut-Bénauge ㊳
Loupiac
Monpazier ⓳
Biron ⓴
Biscarosse
Barsac
Ste-Croix-du-Mont
Langon
Eymet
Monflanquin
Parentis-en-Born
Sauternes ㊲
Bazas
Mimizan
Casteljaloux
Damazan
Sabres
Agen
Nérac
Moissac
St-Julien-en-Born
Lévignacq
Morcenx
Roquefort
Cazaubon
Condom
Castelsarrasin
Mont-de-Marsan
Tartas
Villeneuve-de-Marsan
Eauze
Fleurance
Grenade
Dax ㊸
St-Sever
Nogaro
Auch
Gimont
Leguevin
Muret
Biarritz
Bayonne ㊻ ㊺
St-Jean-de-Luz ㊼
TO HENDAYE, IRUN
Orthez
Maubourguet
Mirande
Rieumes
Sauveterre-de-Béarn
Pau
Tarbes
Boulogne-S.-Gesse

Bay of Biscay

SPAIN

0 — 20 miles
0 — 30 km

that the thin film of paint has survived the centuries in such fine condition. Swaying folds of cloth and enormous, expressive hands lend life and expression to the numerous figures enacting biblical stories.

❷ Leave St-Savin to the west along N151, making for **Poitiers.** Thanks to its majestic hilltop setting above the River Clain, and its position halfway along the Bordeaux–Paris trade route, Poitiers became an important commercial, religious, and university town in the Middle Ages. Since the 17th century, however, not much has happened in Poitiers, but visitors will find that this is not such a bad thing; stagnation equals preservation, and Poitier's architectural heritage is correspondingly rich.

The church of **Notre-Dame-la-Grande,** in the town center, is one of the most impressive examples of the Romanesque architecture so common in western France. Its 12th-century facade is framed by rounded arches of various sizes and decorated with a multitude of bas-reliefs and sculptures. The interior is dark. Its painted walls and pillars are not original; such decoration was a frequent ploy of mid-19th century clerics keen to brighten up their otherwise austere churches. *Rue des Cordeliers.*

Just off Grand'Rue, a few hundred yards beyond Notre-Dame-la-Grande, is the cathedral of **St-Pierre,** built during the 13th and 14th centuries. The largest church in Poitiers, it has a distinctive facade featuring two asymmetrical towers, as well as the usual rose window and carved portals. The imposing interior is noted for its 12th-century stained glass, especially the Crucifixion in the chancel, and 13th-century wooden choir stalls, thought to be the oldest in France. *Pl. de la Cathédrale.*

Head down Grand'Rue, taking the second left and first right into rue Jean-Jaurès. The town museum, **Musée Ste-Croix,** is a modern building housing archaeological discoveries and European paintings from the 15th to the 19th centuries; these are of good, though not outstanding, quality. *Rue St-Simplicien. Admission free. Open Wed.–Mon. 10–11:30 and 2–5:30; closed Tues.*

Next to the museum is the 4th-century **Baptistère St-Jean,** the oldest Christian building in France. Its heavy stone bulk is sunk some 12 feet beneath ground level and consists of a rectangular chamber, used for baptisms, and an eastern end added during the 6th and 7th centuries. The porch, or narthex (restored in the 10th century), is linked to the main building by three archways. Go inside to see the octagonal basin, a larger version of a font for baptism by total immersion, and a collection of sarcophagi and works of sculpture. *Rue Jean-Jaurès. Admission: 8 frs. Open Mar.–Jan., daily 10–12:30 and 2:30–4; Feb., Thurs.–Tues. 10–12:30 and 2:30–4.*

Make your way back into the town center, pausing to admire the beautifully preserved houses lining the way, and turn left into rue Carnot. Shortly after this street has become rue de la Tranchée, the oldest of Poitiers's churches, **St-Hilaire-le-Grand,** appears to the right. Parts of St-Hilaire date from the early 11th century. Unfortunately, the original church had to be reduced in width in the 12th century when its roof was destroyed by fire; local masons lacked the engineering know-how to cover large expanses with the fireproof stone vaults chosen as a replacement. The semicircular, mosaic-floor choir rises high above the level of the nave. Cupolas, mighty columns, frescoes, and finely carved capitals add to the church's interest. *Rue St-Hilaire.*

❸ Niort, 72 kilometers (45 miles) down A10, is a complacent, middle-class town best known as the capital of the French insurance business. The massive keep, with its two square towers dominating the River Sèvre, is all that remains of the **castle** built at the end of the 12th century by English kings Henry II and Richard the Lionheart. Inside there is a museum with an extensive collection of arms and local costumes. *Next to the Vieux-Ponts (Old Bridges). Admission: 13 frs. Open Apr.–Oct., Wed.–Mon 9–noon and 2–6; Nov.–Mar., Wed.–Mon. 9–noon and 2–5; closed Tues.*

Just off the nearby rue Victor-Hugo is the old town hall, a triangular building completed in 1535. It now houses the **Musée du Pilori,** with its collection of local archaeological finds and Renaissance artifacts. The highlight is an ebony chest encrusted with gold and silver. *Just off rue Victor-Hugo. Admission: 10 frs. Open Apr.–Oct., Wed.–Mon. 9–noon and 2–6; Nov.–Mar., Wed.–Mon. 9–noon and 2–5; closed Tues.*

Do an about-face and amble down rue St-Jean, the oldest street in Niort, to the **Musée des Beaux-Arts** (Fine Arts Museum), where tapestries, gold and enamelware, wooden statues and effigies, and 17th- to 18th-century paintings are on display. *Rue St-Jean. Admission: 10 frs. Open Wed.–Thurs. 9–noon and 2–6 (5 in winter).*

West of Niort is the **Marais Poitevin,** an extraordinary region nicknamed Green Venice because of its hundreds of canals, lush fields, and rows of hedges. The only way to explore the Marais proper is by rowboat—or, more typically, on one of the odd-looking local punts (flat, narrow boats maneuvered with a long **❹** pole); you can find them in **Coulon,** a picturesque village on the Sèvre Niortaise River 11 kilometers (7 miles) west of Niort along D9. (They cost about 90 francs per hour per boat, maximum six persons.) A guide will fill you in on local lore as he steers sedately around the canals; be aware, though, that not all guides speak much English. To explore the region by car or bicycle, a detailed map and sound sense of direction are advisable.

Willows, ash, and alder trees line the rivers and canals; artichokes, onions, melons, and garlic are grown in the fields alongside. There is little but the occasional very pretty village in the way of man-made embellishment, apart from the ruins of the once-mighty Benedictine **Abbaye de Maillezais,** 13 kilometers (8 miles) northwest of Coulon via D9. Maillezais used to be a bishop's seat (transferred to La Rochelle), as well as a powerful monastery. The ruins include the 14th-century cloister and refectory, the 11th-century porch, and the 15th-century transept. There is a fine view from the top of one of the towers. *Admission: 14 frs. Open Nov.–Mar., daily 9–12:30 and 1:30–6; Apr.–Oct., daily 9–8.*

As you leave the abbey, head right, down to the waterside. Boats leave here for 45-minute trips through the Marais Poitevin from Easter until the end of October *(see* Guided Tours in Essential Information, above).

Time Out Before or after your trip, pause at the rustic café nearby; its stone walls, wood beams, and open fireplace have great character.

Between Maillezais and the Atlantic coast, the Marais Mouillé (wet marsh) gradually dries up and a flat, barren, eerie landscape appears: the Marais Desséché, or dried-out marsh. From Maillezais, head south along D15, then turn right after La Ronde into narrow D262, which hugs the straight banks of the Canal de la Branche as far as Marans, once a thriving seaport but now linked to the sea only by canal. D105 sneaks seaward from Marans. At the first major crossroad, 8 kilometers (5 miles) past Marans, turn left along D9 toward La Rochelle, 16 kilometers (10 miles) away.

⑤ La Rochelle is an appealing old town; its ancient streets are centered on its harbor, the remarkably picturesque Vieux Port. Standing sentinel on either side of the harbor are the fortresslike 14th-century towers known as **Tour St-Nicholas** (to the left) and the **Tour de la Chaîne** (to the right). From the top of Tour St-Nicholas, visitors can admire the view over the surrounding bay toward the Ile d'Aix. *Admission: 14 frs.; joint ticket with nearby Tour de la Lanterne, 22 frs. Open Easter–Oct., Wed.–Mon. 10–12:30 and 2:30–6; Nov.–Easter, Wed.–Mon. 2–5; closed Tues.*

Boats leave La Rochelle harbor daily in summer for the nearby islands of **Ré** (70 frs. adults, 49 frs. children, round-trip), **Aix** (120/84 frs.), and **Oléron** (135/95 frs.).

Time Out Close to the harbor, in the shadow of the Tour de la Chaîne, **Le Crystal Piano Bar** serves up refreshing sorbets and cocktails against a background of piano music. *54 cours des Dames.*

Take cours des Dames, a spacious avenue lined with sturdy trees and 18th-century houses, back to the Porte de la Grosse Horologe, a massive stone gate marking the entrance to the straight, narrow, bustling streets of the old town. Head down rue du Palais and into rue Gargoulleau. Halfway down on the left is the 18th-century Bishop's Palace, now home to a museum of paintings. Opposite is the **Musée Lafaille,** housed in an elegant mansion and containing extensive collections of rocks, coral, and shellwork. Other items range from a tribal idol from Easter Island in the South Pacific to a giraffe (now stuffed) given as a gift to King Charles X (1824–30). *28 rue Albert-Ier. Admission: 7 frs. Open Apr.–Oct., Tues.–Sun. 10–noon and 2–6; Nov.–Mar., Tues.–Sun. 10–noon and 2–5.*

Farther down rue du Palais (which becomes rue Albert-Ier) is another 18th-century building containing the **Musée du Nouveau-Monde** (New World Museum). Old maps, engravings, watercolors, and even wallpaper evoke the commercial links between La Rochelle and the New World. *10 rue Fleuriau. Admission: 11 frs. Open Wed.–Mon. 10–6; closed Tues.*

A bridge curves across from La Rochelle to a cheerful island, **⑥** known as **Ile de Ré,** just 26 kilometers (16 miles) long and never more than 6 kilometers (4 miles) wide. Vineyards sweep over the eastern part of the island while oyster beds straddle the shallow waters to the west. The largest village, **St-Martin de Ré** (population 3,000), has a lively harbor and a citadel built by ace military architect Sébastien de Vauban in 1681. Many of its streets also date from the 17th century, and the villagers' low, white houses, often embellished with window boxes full of flowers, are typical of the island as a whole.

Head down to the far end of the island to climb up the **Phare de la Baleine** (lighthouse) for sweeping views, and check out the village of **Ars,** with its black-and-white church spire and cute harbor.

Time Out The **Café de la Phare,** at the foot of the lighthouse, serves excellent meals and snacks in a surprising, art-deco setting full of arty '30s lamps. Try the *poutargue,* a local specialty made from smoked cod roe and served with shallots and sour cream.

The wide, fast N137 speeds down the coast from La Rochelle to Rochefort-sur-Mer, 32 kilometers (20 miles) away and home to the 400-yard-long Corderie Royale—a rope-making factory built for Louis XIV's fleet in 1666. From Rochefort head southwest along D3, via the ancient town of·**Brouage,** whose 17th-century walls loom sullenly above deserted marshland. Samuel de Champlain, who founded Quebec in 1608, was born in Brouage—then a major port. You can stroll freely around the walls and gaze across the marsh toward the sea—now over 2 miles away—and then visit the village church to learn more of Champlain's tale (Quebec flags flutter proudly in the main street). You can also muse on the fate of Louis XIV's sweetheart Marie Mancini, who retired here in 1659 after learning that her regal suitor had wed the Infanta of Spain for reasons of state.

Head on toward Marennes and its mighty, 280-foot spire, turning right into D26 and crossing a modern, 3 kilometer (2-mile) bridge to the **Ile d'Oléron,** France's largest island after Corsica, measuring 30 kilometers (19 miles) from end to end and up to 11 kilometers (7 miles) across. Sand dunes ring the island to the north and west, while oyster beds line the eastern shores, notably along the route des Huîtres north of the Château d'Oléron, a ruined 17th-century castle. Mainland activity is dominated by the vine; the tangy sweet aperitif, known as *Pineau des Charentes,* is produced by mixing unfermented grape juice with cognac.

Back on the mainland, take D25 across the Baie de la Seudre and its quilt-like pattern of oyster beds, and continue around the coast to **Royan,** a commercialized resort town that was rebuilt—largely in concrete—after being pounded to bits by Nazi shells in 1945. The Royan skyline is dominated by the tower of the **Eglise Notre-Dame,** an enormous concrete church with a breathtaking oval interior; the huge sweep of its curved ceiling, unsupported by any pillar, is a technical tour de force.

Royan's vast seafront is packed to the gills in summer, although there are prettier beaches just north (Pontaillac and St-Palais). A car ferry (follow signs to the BAC) plows across the Gironde estuary to the Médoc peninsula several times daily from Royan harbor (*see* Tour 3, below).

Head down the coast from Royan along D25 to the pleasant resort of St-Georges-de-Didonne, then continue through a landscape of pine forest and chalky grottoes (via D145) to Meschers and **Talmont,** an unspoiled village renowned for its gently proportioned, 12th-century church jutting out over the waters on a rocky promontory.

Time Out On your way from Royan to Talmont, stop off in Meschers at **Les Grottes de Matata,** where you can sip tea or eat ice cream on a flower-decked terrace overlooking the estuary. *Open daily May–Sept.*

⓫ From Talmont head inland along D114 to **Saintes,** a city of stately serenity. Its **cathedral** seems to stagger beneath the weight of its chunky tower, which climbs above the red roofs of the old town. Engineering caution foiled plans for the traditional pointed spire, so the tower was given a shallow dome—incongruous, perhaps, but distinctive. Angels, prophets, and saints decorate the Flamboyant Gothic main door of the cathedral, while the austere 16th-century interior is lined with circular pillars of formidable circumference.

The narrow pedestrian streets clustered around the cathedral contrast with the broad boulevards that slice through the town and over the River Charente, but both are full of life and color. Just across the bridge, to the right, is the impressive Roman **Arc de Germanicus,** built in AD 19. Ahead, reached by rue de l'Arc de Triomphe, is the sturdy octagonal tower of the **Abbaye aux Dames.** Consecrated in 1047, this abbey church is fronted by an exquisite, arcaded facade, whose portals and capitals, carved with fantastic beasts, deserve more than a quick look. Although the Romanesque choir remains largely in its original form, the rest of the interior is less harmonious, having been periodically restored.

Time Out The abbey complex was reopened in 1989 after a thorough overhaul. One consequence: a brasserie opposite the abbey portals that offers state-of-the-art design and astounding lunchtime menus (55 and 90 francs). Try the broccoli flan.

Saintes owes its development to the salt marshes that first attracted the Romans to the area some 2,000 years ago. The Romans left their mark with an arch, which we've already seen, and with an impressively restored amphitheater: There are several better-preserved examples in France, but few as old. To reach the amphitheater, take the boulevard back across the river and veer left into cours Reverseaux. *Access via rue St-Eutrope.*

⓬ Leave Saintes to the east along D24, making for the black-walled town of **Cognac,** 27 kilometers (17 miles) away. Compared with Saintes, Cognac seems dull and an unlikely hometown for one of the world's most successful drink trades. You may be disappointed initially by the town's unpretentious appearance, but, like the drink, it tends to grow on you. Cognac owed its early development to the transport of salt and wine along the River Charente. When 16th-century Dutch merchants discovered that the local wine was both tastier and easier to transport if distilled, the town became the heart of the brandy industry and remains so to this day.

The leading monument in Cognac is its former **castle,** now part of the premises of Otard Cognac, a leading merchant. Volatile Renaissance monarch François I was born here in 1494. The castle has changed quite a bit since then. The remaining buildings are something of a hodge-podge, though the stocky towers that survey the Charente recall the site's fortified origins. The tour of Otard Cognac combines its own propaganda with historical comment on the drink itself. The slick audiovisuals are tastefully done, and you will visit some interesting rooms and receive a free taste of the firm's product, which is available for sale at vastly reduced prices. *Admission free. Guided tours daily on the hour 10–noon and 2–5 (except Sun. during Oct.– May).*

Most cognac houses organize visits of their premises and *chais* (warehouses). **Hennessy,** a little farther along the banks of the Charente (note the company's mercenary emblem: an ax-wielding arm carved in stone), and **Martell** both give polished guided tours, an ideal introduction to the mysteries of cognac. Martell's *chais* are perhaps more picturesque, but the Hennessy tour includes a cheerful jaunt across the Charente in old-fashioned boats. Wherever you decide to go, you will literally soak up the atmosphere of cognac; 3% of the precious caskbound liquid evaporates every year! This has two consequences: Each *chais* smells delicious, and a small, black, funguslike mushroom, which feeds on cognac's alcoholic fumes, forms on walls throughout the town. *Hennessy, rue Richonne, tel. 45–82–52–22. Martell, pl. Martell, tel. 45–82–44–44.*

Rue Saulnier, alongside the Hennessy premises, is the most atmospheric of the somber, sloping, cobbled streets that compose the core of Cognac, dominated by the tower of **St-Léger,** a church with a notably large Flamboyant Gothic rose window. Busy boulevard Denfert-Rochereau twines around the old town, passing in front of the manicured lawns of the town hall and the gravelly drive of the neighboring **Musée du Cognac,** which contains good ceramics and Art Nouveau glass but is worth visiting mainly for its section on cognac itself. The history and production of cognac are clearly explained, and one room is devoted to amusing early advertising posters. *48 blvd. Denfert-Rochereau. Admission 15 frs. Open Wed.–Mon. 10– noon and 2:30–5:30; closed Tues.*

Several cognac firms are found 16 kilometers (10 miles) upriver at the charming village of **Jarnac. Hine** (quai de l'Orangerie, tel. 45–81–11–38) and **Courvoisier** (pl. du Château, tel. 45–35– 55–55) organize visits of their riverbank premises, though Hine's cozy buildings in local chalky stone have more appeal than does Courvoisier's bombastic redbrick factory by the bridge. Jarnac is also famous as the birthplace of French president François Mitterrand.

Twenty-six kilometers (16 miles) east of Jarnac along N141 is **Angoulême,** divided, like many French towns, between an old, picturesque sector perched around a hilltop cathedral and a modern, industrial part sprawling along the valley and railroad below.

Angoulême Cathedral, in place St-Pierre, bears little resemblance to the majority of its French counterparts because of a flattened dome that lends it an Oriental appearance. The cathedral dates from the 12th century, though it was partly destroyed by Calvinists in 1562, then restored in a heavy-handed manner in 1634 and 1866. Its principal attraction is the magnificent Romanesque facade, whose layers of rounded arches boast 70 stone statues and bas-reliefs illustrating the Last Judgment. The interior is austere and massive but of no great interest.

The cathedral dominates the *ville haute* (upper town), known as the "plateau." There are stunning views from the ramparts alongside, and a warren of quaint old streets to explore in the shadow of the Hôtel de Ville (Town Hall), with its colorful garden. Literary enthusiasts may like to note that 19th-century novelist Honoré de Balzac is one of the town's adopted sons; Balzac described Angoulême in his novel *Lost Illusions*.

Tour 2: Dordogne and Périgord

On the first half of this tour, we follow one of the country's longest rivers, the Dordogne, as it meanders inland to Sarlat from its confluence with the River Garonne. The two rivers merge to form the Gironde between Bourg and Blaye, two lesser-known sectors of the Bordeaux vineyard that produce cheerful, light reds and tiny quantities of dry white wine. The small harbor town of **Blaye** (pronounced "bly"), 48 kilometers (30 miles) north of Bordeaux, is worth a visit, chiefly for its vast riverside **citadel,** over half a mile across, erected by Sébastien de Vauban in the 1680s. From a vantage point at the top of the citadel's Tour de l'Aiguillette, the roving gaze can survey the mighty Gironde estuary and the beginnings of the Atlantic Ocean. Close by are two other towers, all that remain of the medieval Château des Rudel. Ditches and ramparts surround the citadel on the landward side. Beyond, the streets of Blaye soon give way to the Côtes de Blaye vineyard, which extends north to the limits of Cognac country.

D669 runs 14 kilometers (9 miles) along the banks of the Gironde estuary from Blaye to **Bourg,** with its once-fortified *ville haute* perched on top of a chalky cliff and linked by stone stairs to the *ville basse* (lower town), with its harbor on the River Dordogne. There is a fine wooded garden around the **Château de la Citadelle** (former summer residence of the bishops of Bordeaux) and a broad view over the Côtes de Bourg vineyard from its terrace.

Follow D670 southeast of Bourg to **Libourne,** 30 kilometers (19 miles) away and surrounded by some famous vineyards. The tiny vineyards of Fronsac and Canon-Fronsac (producing robust, spicy reds) greet you on your approach from the west. Scattered across the banks of the Dordogne are the vines of Entre-Deux-Mers, which yield crisp, dry, good-value whites. The best is produced beneath the ruins of the Château of Haut-Bénauge near Cadillac (*see* Tour 3, below).

From Libourne, take D244 east to approach the pretty town of St-Emilion across the sun-fired flatness of Pomerol, a land of tiny, twisty lanes and ubiquitous grapevines. The occasional hamlet apologetically interrupts, with scruffy gardens and scraggly dogs. All the wealth is in the earth. Locally produced Château Petrus, made exclusively from Merlot grapes, claims to be the world's most expensive red wine, while the nearby Cheval Blanc vineyard produces one of the two top-ranking St-Emilion wines.

Without any warning, the flatlands break into hills to send you tumbling into **St-Emilion.** This jewel of a town has old buildings of golden stone, ruined town walls, well-kept ramparts offering charming views, and a church hewn into a cliff. Sloping vines invade from all sides, and lots and lots of tourists invade down the middle.

The medieval streets are filled with wine stores and crafts shops. Macaroons are a specialty. The local wines offer the twin advantages of reaching maturity earlier than other Bordeaux reds and representing better value for the money. Tours of the pretty **St-Emilion vineyard,** including wine tastings, are organized by the *Syndicat d'Initiative* (tourist office) on place des Créneaux, a bulky square with a terrace overlooking the lower part of St-Emilion. A stroll along the 13th-century ramparts helps you appreciate St-Emilion's ancient, unspoiled stonewalled houses, and soon brings you to the Royal Castle, or **Château du Roi,** built by occupying sovereign Henry III of England (1216–72).

Steps lead down from the ramparts to place du Marché, a wooded square where cafés remain open late into the balmy summer night. Lining one side are the east windows of the **Eglise Monolithe,** one of France's largest underground churches, hewn out of the rock face between the 9th and 12th century. *Visits organized by the Syndicat d'Initiative.*

Just south of the town walls is **Château Ausone,** an estate that is ranked with Cheval Blanc as producing the finest wine of St-Emilion.

As you continue east along D243, you'll soon find yourself amid the vines of the Côtes de Castillon; the Côtes de Castillon wine is a cheaper and more than palatable alternative to St-Emilion. We are now at the beginning of what English speakers often refer to simply as "The Dordogne," those magical words conjuring up French gastronomy and romantic castles perched above steep valleys.

⑯ D936 chugs along the north bank of the river, bypassing the old bastide town of Sainte-Foy-la-Grande, to **Bergerac.** Vines are cultivated here, too, though less expected is the presence of tobacco plantations. Learn about this local industry at the **Musée du Tabac,** a museum housed in the haughty 17th-century Maison Peyrarède near the quayside. The manufacture, uses, and history of tobacco, from its American origins to its spread worldwide, are explained with the help of maps, pictures, documents, and other exhibits, including a collection of pipes and snuff bottles. *Rue de l'Ancien Pont. Admission: 12 frs. Open Tues.–Fri. 10–noon and 2–6, Sat. 10–noon and 2–5, Sun. 2:30–6:30.*

Head left from the tobacco museum, past place de la Myrpe, to the **Couvent des Récollets,** a former convent. The convent's stone-and-brick buildings range in date from the 12th to the 17th centuries and include galleries, a large, vaulted cellar, and a cloister, where the Maison du Vin dishes out information on—and samples of—local wines. From the first floor of the convent, treat yourself to a view of the sloping vineyards of Monbazillac across the Dordogne. *Just off pl. de la Myrpe. Admission: 12 frs. Visits July–Aug., every hour from 10:30–11:30, and 1:30–5:30; mid-May–June and Sept.–mid-Oct., at 3:30 and 4:30. Closed Mon. and Sun., mid-May–June and Sept.–mid-Oct.*

The regional wines of Bergerac range from red and rosé to dry and sweet whites. While you're in town, you might like to purchase a bottle or two of the town's most famous vintage: Monbazillac, a sweet wine made from overripe grapes that enjoyed an international reputation long before its Bordeaux rival, Sauternes.

D13 heads south 8 kilometers (5 miles) from Bergerac to the ⓱ 16th-century château of **Monbazillac.** Vines grow up to the very doors of this beautifully proportioned, gray-stone building whose squat corner towers pay tribute to the fortress tradition of the Middle Ages but whose large windows and sloping roofs reveal the domesticating influence of the Renaissance. Regional furniture and an ornate, early 17th-century bedchamber enliven the interior. A tasting is provided at the end of your tour. *Admission: 20 frs. Open Apr.–Oct., daily 9:30–noon and 2–6:30; Nov.–Mar., 9:30–noon and 2–5:30.*

From Monbazillac, head back toward Bergerac and take D37 east along the banks of the Dordogne to the village and tur- ⓲ reted château of **Lanquais** (15th–17th century), surrounded by a large garden. The interior is richly furnished throughout and features majestic Italian fireplaces on loan from the Louvre. *Admission: 12 frs. Open Apr.–Oct., Fri.–Wed. 9:30–noon and 2:30–7; closed Thurs.*

On the opposite side of the Dordogne loom the towers of Baneuil Castle. Stay on the south bank and turn right at Couze ⓳ along D660, making for the tiny town of **Monpazier,** 27 kilometers (17 miles) away. Monpazier is one of France's best-preserved *bastides* (fortified medieval towns with regimented street plans), built in ocher-colored stone by English king Edward I in 1284 to protect the southern flank of his French possessions. The *bastide* features three stone gateways (of an original six), a large central square, and the church of **St-Dominique,** housing 35 carved wooden choir stalls and a relic of the True Cross. Opposite the church is the finest medieval building in Monpazier, the **Maison du Chapître** (chapter house), once used as a barn for storing grain. Its wood-beam roof is constructed of chestnut to repel web-spinning spiders.

⓴ Five miles south of Monpazier is the hilltop château of **Biron;** its keep, square tower, and chapel date from the Middle Ages, while the Classical buildings were completed in 1730. Highlights of a visit here include monumental staircases, the kitchen with its huge stone slabs, and the tomb of a former owner, Pons de Gontaut-Biron (who died in 1524). English Romantic poet Lord Byron (1788–1824) is claimed as a distant descendant of the Gontaut-Biron family, which lived here for 14 generations. *Admission: 20 frs. Open Feb.–June and Sept.–Nov., Wed.–Mon. 9–11:30 and 2–6; July–Aug., daily 9–11:30 and 2–6.*

Return to Monpazier and go northeast on D53, which passes by the château of **Les Milandes,** once owned by the American-born cabaret star of Roaring-Twenties Paris, Josephine Baker (open May–Oct., daily 9:30–11:30 and 2–6). D53 goes by the ruined castle of **Castlenaud** (open May–Nov., daily 10–7). From here, D57 crosses over the Dordogne; turn onto D703, passing the ㉑ 13th-century castle of **Beynac,** daringly perched atop a sheer cliff face beside an abrupt bend in the Dordogne. Restoration of this privately owned castle is an ongoing process, but its muscular architecture and the staggering views from its battlements make a visit imperative. *Admission: 22 frs. Open daily Apr.–Oct. 9:30–noon and 2–7; Nov.–Mar. 10–noon and 2:30–5.*

A short distance upriver, huddled beneath a towering gray cliff, is **La Roque-Gageac,** one of the prettiest and best-restored villages in the Dordogne Valley. Craft shops line its low, narrow streets, which are dominated by the outlines of the 19th-century, mock-medieval Château de Malartrie and the Manoir de Tarde, with its cylindrical turret.

㉒ D46 now heads a few miles north to another Dordogne gem, the small town of **Sarlat.** To do justice to its golden-stone splendor, you may want to take advantage of the guided tour offered by the tourist office on place de la Liberté *(see* Guided Tours in Essential Information, above). Rue de la Liberté leads to place du Payrou, occupied on one corner by the pointed-gabled Renaissance house where writer-orator Etienne de la Boétie (1530–63) was born. Diagonally opposite is the entrance to **Sarlat Cathedral.** An elaborate turret-topped tower, begun in the 12th century, is the oldest part of the building and, along with the choir, all that remains of the original Romanesque church. A sloping garden behind the cathedral, the Cour de l'Evêché, affords good views of the choir and contains a strange, conical tower known as the **Lanterne des Morts** (Lantern of the Dead), which was occasionally used as a funeral chapel.

Rue d'Albusse, adjoining the garden, and rue de la Salamandre are narrow, twisty streets that head back to place de la Liberté and the 17th-century town hall. Opposite the town hall is the rickety former church of St-Marie, overlooking place des Oies and pointing the way to Sarlat's most interesting street, **rue des Consuls.** Among its medieval buildings are the Hôtel Plamon, with broad windows that resemble those of a Gothic church, and, opposite, the 15th-century Hôtel de Vassal.

Time Out If you feel like lunch or a snack, make your way to the **Jardin des Consuls** (4 rue des Consuls), in the heart of old Sarlat. It's part restaurant, part tearoom serving sorbets and pancakes. The stone-walled dining room is pleasant enough, but in sunny weather, cross through it to the idyllic courtyard in back. Soups and *cassoulet* stews head the filling 100-franc menu, best accompanied by a young, *gouleyant* (fruity) Cahors.

Across the undistinguished rue de la République, which slices Sarlat in two, is the Quartier Ouest, many of whose streets are too narrow to be used by cars. Rue Rousseau saunters past the Chapelle des Récollets and Abbaye St-Claire to the 16th-century Tour du Bourreau and a remnant of the former town walls.

㉓ From Sarlat, D47 twists 21 kilometers (13 miles) west to **Les Eyzies-de-Tayac,** passing the elegant **Château of Puymartin** (open July–Sept., daily 10–noon and 2–6) on the way. Many signs of prehistoric man have been discovered in the vicinity of Les Eyzies; a number of excavated caves and grottoes, some with wall paintings, are open for public viewing. Ask for details of possible visits at the **Musée Nationale de Préhistoire,** where you can also examine many artifacts. The museum's primitive sculpture, furniture, and work tools are presented in an appealing setting: a restored, mainly Renaissance, château. *Admission: 14 frs., 7 frs. Sun., free Wed. Open Apr.–Oct., Wed.–Mon.*

9:30–noon and 2–6; Nov.–Mar., Wed.–Mon. 9:30–noon and 2–5; closed Tues.

㉔ Take D706 up the Vézère Valley to Montignac. Six kilometers (4 miles) away is the famous **Grotto of Lascaux,** whose hundreds of mesmerizing prehistoric wall paintings, thought to be at least 20,000 years old, were discovered by chance in 1940. Unfortunately, the caves have been sealed off to prevent irreparable damage, though portions are reproduced in the Lascaux 2 exhibition center in Montignac. *Admission: 40 frs. Open Tues.–Sun. 10–noon and 2–5:30.*

㉕ Continue north via D65 and D704 until you reach the château of **Hautefort,** a vast castle surrounded by gardens and presenting a disarmingly arrogant face to the world. The castle's skyline bristles with high roofs, domes, chimneys, and cupolas. The square-lined Renaissance left wing clashes with the muscular, round towers of the right wing, as the only surviving section of the original medieval castle—the gateway and drawbridge—referees in the middle. Most of the buildings date from the 17th century, and furniture and tapestries of that period adorn the interior. *Admission: 22 frs. Open May–Nov., daily 9–noon and 2–6; Dec.–Apr., Sun. 2–5.*

㉖ **Périgueux,** lying 40 kilometers (25 miles) west via D704/705 (which joins N89), is famous not for a château but for its weird-looking cathedral. The **Cathédrale St-Front** (finished in 1173 but comprehensively restored in the last century) could be on loan from Constantinople, given its shallow, scale-patterned domes and small, elongated, conical cupolas sprouting from the roof like baby minarets. The 200-foot Romanesque tower, one of the finest in southern France, is also topped by a conical dome. You may be struck by similarities with the Byzantine-style Sacré-Coeur in Paris; that's no coincidence—architect Paul Abadie (1812–84) worked on both sites. The interior is cool, vast, and relatively dark. *Pl. de la Clautre.*

From Périgueux, head 27 kilometers (17 miles) up D939 to the beautiful old town of Brantôme, beside the sparkling waters of the River Dronne.

Tour 3: Bordeaux to Biarritz

㉗ **Bordeaux,** the capital of southwest France, is renowned worldwide for its wines. Vineyards extend on all sides: Graves and pretty Sauternes to the south; flat, dusty Médoc to the west; and Pomerol and St-Emilion to the east. Stylish châteaus loom above the most famous vines, but much of the wine-making area is unimpressive, with little sign of the extraordinary regional affluence it promotes.

Numbers in the margin correspond with points of interest on the Bordeaux map.

There are signs enough in the city itself, however, where wine shippers have long based their headquarters along the banks of the Garonne. An aura of 18th-century elegance permeates the downtown area, whose fine shops and pedestrian precincts invite leisurely exploration. Take time to head south of the center ㉘ into the **old dockland,** with its narrow, sturdy, low-terraced streets. There is a forbidding feel here and, indeed, Bordeaux as a whole is a less exuberant city than most in France, with an almost British reserve. For a better view of the picturesque

Cathédrale
St-André, **34**

Cité Mondiale
du Vin, **32**

CIVB, **31**

Grand Théâtre, **30**

Hôtel de Ville, **35**

Musée des
Beaux-Arts, **36**

Old dockland, **28**

Place de la Bourse, **33**

Pont de Pierre, **29**

Bordeaux

29 quayside, stroll across the **Pont de Pierre** bridge spanning the Garonne; built by Napoleon at the start of the 19th century, the bridge makes spectacular viewing itself, thanks to a gracefully curving multitude of arches.

Two blocks from the riverbank, along cours Chapeau-Rouge, is **30** the city's leading 18th-century monument: the **Grand Théâtre,** built between 1773 and 1780 to the plans of architect Victor Louis. Its elegant exterior is ringed by graceful Corinthian columns and pilasters. The majestic foyer, with its two-winged staircase and cupola, inspired Charles Garnier's design for the Paris Opera. The theater-hall itself has a frescoed ceiling and a shimmering chandelier composed of 14,000 Bohemian crystals; the acoustics are said to be perfect. (Be aware that the theater is scheduled for renovation in 1992.) *Pl. de la Comédie. Admission: 12 frs. Guided tours mid-July–Sept., Tues.–Fri. at 10:30, 3, and 4:30; Oct.–mid-July, Sat. at 3 and 4.*

The allées de Tourny and cours du 30-Juillet, haughty tree-lined boulevards, reel off north from the Grand Théâtre. At the **31** start of the cours du 30-Juillet is the **CIVB,** headquarters of the Bordeaux wine trade, where information can be had and samples tasted. The **Vinothèque,** opposite, sells Bordeaux by the bottle to suit every purse. At the far end of the cours is the **Esplanade des Quinconces,** a vast 400-yard-long square overlooking the Garonne.

Turn left from the esplanade and head 400 yards along the **32** quayside to the **Cité Mondiale du Vin** (entry 25 quai des Chartrons). This ambitious complex, opened in 1991, is part office block, part shopping mall, and part culture center; a museum, bars, and exhibition hall all have a common theme: the world of wine.

㉝ Head back along the river, past the esplanade, as far as **place de la Bourse,** the city's second most important 18th-century landmark after the Grand Théâtre. A provincial reply to Paris's celebrated place Vendôme, the square (built 1730–55) features airy, large-windowed buildings designed by the country's most esteemed architect of the era, Jacques Ange Gabriel.

Time Out Head two blocks down rue F-Philippart to the 18th-century **place du Parlement,** and you'll have no problem finding a promising-looking lunch spot. No fewer than six bistros and restaurants, some with outdoor tables, line the square. Among them are bustling **L'Ombrière** (no. 14); **La Ténarèze** (no. 18), providing rich dishes from Gascony; and expensive **Chez Philippe** (no. 1), one of the city's top fish restaurants. *Most restaurants closed Sun. and Mon.*

A maze of narrow streets wend their way from the river to the **㉞** **Cathédrale St-André,** located in place Pey-Berland. This hefty edifice, 135 yards long, isn't one of France's better Gothic cathedrals, and the outside has a dirty, neglected look. The interior, though, rewards your scrutiny as the soaring 14th-century chancel makes an interesting contrast with the earlier, more severe nave. Excellent—albeit grimy—stone carvings adorn the facade (notably that of the Porte Royale, to the right), as well as the 15th-century Pey-Berland Tower that stands nearby.

㉟ Across the tidy gardens of the luxurious **Hôtel de Ville** (Town Hall) opposite the cathedral is the busy cours d'Albret and the **㊱** **Musée des Beaux-Arts.** This fine-arts museum has a notable collection of works spanning the 15th–20th centuries, with important paintings by Paolo Veronese *(Apostle's Head)*, Camille Corot *(Bath of Diana)*, and Odilon Redon *(Chariot of Apollo)*, and sculptures by Auguste Rodin. *20 cours d'Albret. Admission: 12 frs. Open Wed.–Mon. 10–noon and 2–6; closed Tues.*

You can find one of the region's most famous châteaus without even leaving the city. Follow N250 from central Bordeaux (direction Arcachon) for a couple of miles to the district of Pessac, home to the flagship of the Graves vineyard: **Haut-Brion,** producer of the only non-Médoc wine to be ranked a *Premier Cru* (the most elite wine classification). The white, Classical château surveys pebbly soil whose vines yield a celebrated red wine, plus tiny quantities of white. The wines produced at La Mission-Haut Brion, literally across the road, are equally sought after.

Numbers in the margin correspond with points of interest on the Atlantic Coast map.

Continue from Pessac to the A630 expressway that encircles Bordeaux, then head 32 kilometers (20 miles) south via A62 as far as the Barsac exit. Barsac, a small, innocuous town on the banks of the Garonne, lies 13 kilometers (8 miles) north of the **㊲** tiny village of **Sauternes.**

Nothing here would tell you that mind-boggling wealth lurks amid the picturesque vine-laden slopes and hollows. Grubby

Sauternes has a wine shop where bottles of the celebrated Château d'Yquem gather dust on rickety shelves, next to handwritten pricetags demanding 1,000 francs apiece (about $200 at 1991 exchange rates). The bottles do not seem to have been disturbed for years, which, at that price, is hardly surprising.

Making Sauternes is a tricky business. Autumn mists that steal up the valleys promote a form of rot called *pourriture noble*, which sucks moisture out of the grapes, leaving a high proportion of sugar. Not all grapes achieve the required degree of overripeness simultaneously; up to seven successive harvests are undertaken at Château d'Yquem, one mile north of Sauternes village, to assure the optimum selection. This painstaking attention to detail, added to a centuries-old reputation and soil ideally suited to making sweet white wine, enables bottles of d'Yquem to obtain prices more appropriate to liquid gold. If you do splurge on a recent vintage, you may as well lock it away; Château d' Yquem needs to wait a good 10 years before coming into its own and will reward decades of patience.

From Sauternes, take D8 to Langon, cross the Garonne, and head north up the attractive D10, sandwiched between the river and the vineyards of Sainte-Croix-du-Mont, Loupiac, and Cadillac. These picturesque villages also produce excellent sweet wines, at a fraction of the cost of prestigious Sauternes.

Meanwhile, 8 kilometers (5 miles) north of Cadillac via D11, a different style of wine is produced beneath the ruins of the **38** Château of **Haut-Bénauge.** The vines here are too far from the Garonne to benefit from the rising early morning damp of the river valley; their grapes prove more suitable for dry white wine—excellent dry white, in fact. Officially, it's the best of the Entre-Deux-Mers region that stretches northeast toward the River Dordogne.

Cross back over the Garonne at Langoiran and head toward Bordeaux (via Labrède and Léognan) through the vineyards of the **Graves** region, so called because of its gravelly soil. The Graves encircles western Bordeaux and is the region's most historic appellation; a lightish red wine known as Clairet (origin of the word "claret," meaning red Bordeaux) was esteemed by English occupiers back in the Middle Ages. White wine—both dry and sweet—is also produced, some of the best at the **39** tiny Domaine de Chevalier in **Léognan.**

A630 skirts Bordeaux, with the N215 exit swiftly announcing the Wine Road, or D2, which slips off north toward Médoc.

Médoc is strange, dusty territory. Even the vines look dusty, **40** and so does the ugly town of **Margaux,** the area's unofficial capital. Yet the soil hereabouts is sown with the seeds of grandeur. The small, arid communes and châteaux of Haut-Médoc feature such venerable names as Margaux, St-Julien, Pauillac, and St-Estèphe. Château Margaux, an elegant, coolly restrained Classical building of 1802, and three wineries at Pauillac—Lafite-Rothschild, Latour, and Mouton-Rothschild—are recognized as producers of *Premiers Crus*, their wines qualifying with Graves's Haut-Brion as Bordeaux's top five reds.

D2 chugs through the less prestigious wine fields of northern, **41** or Bas, Médoc, before merging with N215. **Pointe de Grave,** at the tip of the Médoc peninsula, is the site of an American memorial commemorating the landing of U.S. troops in 1917.

From the surrounding sand dunes, there are views over the Gironde estuary to Royan and back across the Atlantic. A carferry plows across to Royan four times daily (cost: 110 frs. per car, 30 frs. per passenger).

42 Just south of Pointe de Grave is **Soulac-sur-Mer.** The 12th-century basilica of **Notre-Dame de la Fin-des-Terres** deserves to have an outlandish history, given its name—Our Lady of the Ends of the Earth. It does: By 1800 it had been almost completely embedded in drifting sands and was dug out and restored only 100 years ago.

The entire coast, which stretches down to Spain in a straight line, was once subject to drifting sands. Today the highest dunes in Europe pile up behind uninterrupted miles of sandy beach. The sands' unpredictable inland advance used to go on at the alarming rate of several yards a year. At the start of the 19th century, efforts were made to stop the sandy invasion by planting a frontline of sturdy beach grass with pine trees to the rear. The resulting forest has transformed the hinterland region. The name **Landes,** now synonymous with "enormous pine forest," originally implied a wasteland. This is precisely what the region once was: part sandy desert, part marshy wilderness, whose eccentric inhabitants sported sheepskin jackets and stomped around on stilts. Some still do, mainly for the benefit of the tourists who are attracted to the area by the healthy climate and by the variety of sports activities offered—hiking, fishing, canoeing, sand-skiing, golf, tennis, surfing, sailing, bathing, and water sports of all kinds.

At the start of the century, the coast adopted the name Côte d'Argent, or Silver Coast, in a bid to consolidate its new image. Parallel to this silver coast, a few miles inland, is a chain of lakes connected by streams and canals. The first lake we encounter (take D101 from Soulac) is France's largest: the wild, 12-mile-long **Lac d'Hourtin-Carcans.** The small town of Hourtin, with a marina and 460-yard jetty, stands on its northern shore.

After Hourtin, D3 continues south as the Lake Road to the smaller Lac de Lacanau, which teems with pike, perch, and eel and is linked by the Canal de Lège to the Bassin d'Arcachon, a vast triangular bay named after the town on its southern flank. The bay is renowned both for its rich variety of migratory birds and for its excellent oysters. Many of the oyster beds cluster around the Ile aux Oiseaux, a small island in the middle of the bay.

43 **Arcachon** was "created"—at least as a resort—in the 1850s, when the new railroad connected it with Bordeaux, 64 kilometers (40 miles) away. These days, Arcachon is a lively boating center, with three jetties protruding over its sandy beaches. From boulevard de la Mer, there are good views toward Cap Ferret, across the narrow straits that mark the divide between bay and ocean.

A small lake, 13 kilometers (8 miles) south of Arcachon, the Etang de Cazaux, marks the boundary between the Gironde and Landes *départements*. Oil has been found at Parentis-en-Born, on the eastern shore of the neighboring Etang de Biscarosse. Mimizan, on the southern shore of the Etang d'Aureilhan (the next lake along), was swamped in roving sand during the 18th century; sand still surrounds its ruined Benedictine abbey. Take D652 down to St-Julien-en-Born, then D41 to the charming old village of Lévignacq, with its fortified church and low houses that are typical of the region.

④④ D41 joins N10, which branches off toward Dax (as D947) at Castets. **Dax,** known in Roman times as Aquae Tarbellicae, has been famous for 2,000 years on account of its thermal springs. The daughter of Caesar Augustus came here to soothe her aches and pains, and was the first in a long line of seasonal guests whose numbers have swollen to 50,000 each year, making Dax the country's premier warm-water spa. Steaming water gushes out of the lion-headed Néhé fountain in the center of town. The local mud (containing radioactive algae) is also reputed to have healing qualities.

Dax is an airy town, offering pleasant walks through its parks and gardens and along the banks of the River Adour. Eleventh-century bas-reliefs adorn the east end of the church of St-Paulles-Dax, while the 17th-century cathedral, built in the Classical style, boasts a variety of fine sculpture, some inherited from the previous Gothic building.

④⑤ **Bayonne,** 48 kilometers (30 miles) southwest of Dax via N124 and N10, is the gateway to Basque country, a territory stretching across the Pyrenees to Bilbao in Spain. Bayonne stands at the confluence of the Rivers Adour and Nive; the port of Bayonne extends along the valley to the sea 3 miles away. You could easily spend an enjoyable few hours here, admiring the town's 13th-century cathedral, cloisters, old houses, and 17th-century ramparts. The airy, modernized **Musée Bonnat** houses a notable collection of 19th-century paintings. *5 rue Jacques-Lafitte. Open Wed.–Mon. 10–noon and 3–7. Admission: 11 frs.*

④⑥ The celebrated resort of **Biarritz** lies 8 kilometers (5 miles) west of Bayonne on a particularly sheltered part of the Atlantic coast. Biarritz rose to prominence in the 19th century when upstart Emperor Napoleon III took to spending his holidays here. You'll soon understand why: The crowded Grande Plage and neighboring Miramar Beach provide fine sand and friendly breakers amid a setting of craggy natural beauty. Biarritz remains a high-brow resort, with no shortage of deluxe hotels or bow-tied gamblers ambling over to the casino. Yet the old down-to-earth charm of the former fishing village remains to counterbalance the uppercrust ambience. The narrow streets around the cozy 16th-century church of St-Martin are delightful to stroll and, together with the harbor of Port des Pêcheurs, offer a tantalizing glimpse of the Biarritz of old.

④⑦ A 26-kilometer (16-mile) drive along the coast, through the pretty villages of St-Jean-de-Luz and Hendaye, leads to Irun on the Spanish border. **St-Jean-de-Luz,** in particular, deserves a visit, for its old streets, curious church, colorful harbor, and elegant beach. The tree-lined place Louis-XIV, alongside the Hôtel de Ville (Town Hall) with its narrow courtyard and dainty statue of Louis XIV on horseback, is the quaint hub of the town. Nearby are the Eglise St-Jean-Baptiste, where unusual wooden galleries line one wall to create a theater-like effect, and the Maison de l'Infante, where Maria Teresa of Spain stayed prior to her wedding to the Sun King (*see* Brouage, above). The foursquare mansion contains worthy 17th-century furnishings. *Quai de l'Infante. Admission: 15 frs. Open June–Sept. 10:30–noon and 3–6:30. Closed Sun. AM.*

What to See and Do with Children

The Atlantic coast is lined with an almost uninterrupted run of
fine, large, sandy **beaches** that are ideal for swimming and sun-
bathing. Popular resorts are Biarritz and Arcachon (Tour 3),
and Royan (Tour 1), though you'll undoubtedly discover less
crowded spots for yourself (also *see* Sports and Fitness, below).

Harbor, Musée Lafaille, and **Musée du Nouveau-Monde** (New
World Museum), La Rochelle, Tour 1.

Hennessy tour (including boat trip), Cognac, Tour 1.

Boat trip through the **Marais Poitevin** (*see* Guided Tours in Essential Information; also Tour 1, above).

Sarlat Aquarium gives a thorough presentation of the fish found
in the local rivers: salmon, eel, pike, perch, trout, and even
sturgeon, a fish famous for its eggs (caviar) but rarely found
outside the waters of the Caspian Sea. *Rue du Commandant-
Maratuel. Admission: 18 frs. adults, 11 frs. children. Open
mid-June–mid-Sept., daily 10–7; mid-Sept.–mid-June, daily
10–noon and 2:30–6; closed mornings, Nov.–Mar.*

Off the Beaten Track

Limoges is the porcelain collector's mecca, and, at 120 kilometers (75 miles) from Poitiers and 102 kilometers (64 miles) from
Angoulême (direct route on N141), it is well worth the detour
toward the center of France. In addition to shops filled with
Limoges's delicate porcelain, visit the **St-Etienne Cathedral,**
the **Adrien Dubouché Museum** (ceramics), the **Palais Episcopal,**
and the **Municipal Museum,** with samples of Limoges china
from the 12th century to the present day. Limoges is also the
base of David Haviland's **porcelain factory.** This smart American entrepreneur set up shop here in the mid-19th century, and
the Haviland hallmark is now synonymous with some of the
finest china in Europe. Samples of the group of Limoges porcelain factories and enamel workshops can be seen at the **Limo-
ges-Castel Demonstration Center.** *Pavillon de la Porcelaine,
av. John-Kennedy, Zone Industrielle Magré. Open mid-
Apr.–mid-Oct., daily 8:30–6; mid-Oct.–mid-Apr., Mon.–Sat.
8:30–6.*

The historic clifftop village of **Domme** lies across the River
Dordogne from La Roque-Gageac. Domme is famous for its
grottes (caves), where prehistoric bison and rhinoceros bones
have been discovered. You can visit the 500-yard-long illuminated galleries, which are lined with stalagmites and
stalactites. *Entrance on pl. de la Halle. Admission: 18 frs.
Open Apr.–Sept., daily 9–noon and 2–6.*

Shopping

The city of Bordeaux abounds with stylish shops in its commercial heart between the cathedral and Grand Théâtre, where
you'll find numerous pleasant pedestrian streets. Other than
this section, however, serious shoppers should keep their eyes
peeled for likely-looking shops in every small town and village.

Food Items The Périgord region owes much of its fame to such gastronomic
specialties as truffles, *fruits confits* (fruit preserved in brandy), and foie gras (ask for a sealed can rather than a glass jar,

and it will last for months). Similar local goods are found at **La Maison des Produits Régionaux,** in the Cestras complex on N250 outside Arcachon. For an exceptional selection of cheeses, go to **Jean d'Alos** in Bordeaux (4 rue Montesquieu). If you feel like giving yourself a present that definitely won't last, try some of "the best butter in the world"—available from the **Laiterie Co-Opérative** at Echiré, just north of Niort.

Gift Ideas Regional gifts include embroidery, wooden models, and, more exceptionally, the small green animals made from the stems of the wild angelica found around Poitiers and Niort.

Wine and Spirits An old bottle of cognac makes a fine souvenir; try **La Cognathèque** in Cognac itself (10 pl. Jean-Monnet). You'll find the same stuff, but infinitely cheaper, at any local producer. A top-ranking Bordeaux is less likely to represent top value, though at the **Vinothèque** in Bordeaux (8 cours du XXX-Juillet) or the **Maison de Tourisme et du Vin** in Pauillac (north of Bordeaux), you'll have a wide choice.

Sports and Fitness

Beaches and Water Sports The Atlantic coast presents an outstanding, uninterrupted vista of sandy beaches from Rochefort to Royan and from the Pointe de Grave to Biarritz (a stretch known as the **Côte d'Argent:** Silver Coast). Major resorts, offering a welter of sports facilities, are **Royan, Soulac, Carcans, Lacanau,** and **Arcachon.** The **Aquacity** complex (off N250 south of Arcachon, tel. 56–66–39–39), with water slides, wave-machine, and warm-water swimming pool, offers fun for all the family (admission: 80 frs. adults, 60 frs. children under 12).

The lakes that dot the **Landes pine forest** some 30 kilometers (20 miles) from the coast offer various water sports (such as waterskiing or canoeing), as does the stretch of water at **Siorac** between Bergerac and Sarlat.

Bullfighting As you approach the Pyrénées, you step into Basque country, where bullfights are a major sporting occupation. Bullfights are held at **Dax, Mont-de-Marsan,** and **Bayonne;** if you're in the area during the summer months, you can't miss the colorful posters announcing them.

Golf There are courses at **Biarritz** (tel. 59–03–71–80), **Lacanau** (tel. 56–26–35–50), **Bordeaux** (tel. 56–39–10–02), **Arcachon** (tel. 56–54–44–00), and **Cognac** (tel. 45–32–18–17).

Dining and Lodging

Dining

The cuisine of this ocean-facing region centers on fish and seafood. Oysters and mussels are major industries, while carp, eel, sardines, sole, and even sturgeon form the basis of menus in fish restaurants. Heading inland into Périgord, along the Dordogne Valley, you'll find that the cooking becomes richer. Truffles and foie gras lead the way, followed by many types of game, fowl, and mushrooms. The versatile wines of Bordeaux make fine accompaniments to most regional dishes, but don't overlook their less prestigious cousins (Bergerac, Pécharmant,

Fiefs Vendéens, Monbazillac, Charentes). Cognac is de rigueur to finish a meal.

Highly recommended restaurants are indicated by a star ★.

Category	Cost*
Very Expensive	over 350 francs
Expensive	200–350 francs
Moderate	100–200 francs
Inexpensive	under 100 francs

*per person for a three-course meal, including tax (18.6%) and tip but not wine

Lodging

In summer, France's western coast provides extreme contrasts of crowds and calm. Vacationers flock to La Rochelle, Royan, Arcachon, Biarritz, and the offshore islands of Ré and Oléron, and for miles around, hotels are booked solid months in advance. Farther inland the situation is easier, but note the dearth of hotel accommodations in Bordeaux. Advance booking is recommended here and in Périgord, whose few towns—Sarlat, Périgueux, and Brantôme—fill up quickly in mid-summer.

Highly recommended hotels are indicated by a star ★.

Category	Cost*
Very Expensive	over 750 francs
Expensive	350–750 francs
Moderate	200–350 francs
Inexpensive	under 200 francs

*All prices are for a standard double room for two, including tax (18.6%) and service charge.

Angoulême
Dining and Lodging

Hôtel de France. Set in an old building (part 17th-century), Hôtel de France retains a rustic atmosphere, with lots of wood and stone in evidence. It is extremely well located in the Ville Haute, and there are fine views from the garden. The service is distant, though efficient, and the staff is accustomed to English-speaking visitors. The restaurant serves solid, unpretentious regional cuisine. *1 pl. des Halles, 16000, tel. 45–95–47–95. 90 rooms with bath. Facilities: restaurant, bar, garden. AE, DC, V. Restaurant closed Christmas, New Year's, Sun. lunch; and Sat. during Sept.–May. Moderate.*

Bergerac
Dining and Lodging

Bordeaux. You'll find a curious mixture here: Bordeaux is part typical French provincial hotel, with stocky furniture and absurdly spacious rooms, and part city slicker, with the would-be modern design of the facade and reception area that might have worked a few decades ago but looks strangely unconvincing in a quiet square in a small country town. The recently refitted bathrooms, however, are just fine. The admirable restaurant serves regional dishes with nouvelle inventiveness, though guests are not obliged to eat here. English and American visitors are warmly and frequently welcomed. Rooms facing the garden/courtyard are preferable to those with a view across undistinguished place Gambetta. *38 pl. Gambetta, 24100, tel. 53–57–12–83. 42 rooms with bath. Facilities: restaurant, pool, garden. AE, DC, MC, V. Closed Jan. Restaurant closed Mon. and Sat. during Nov.–Mar. Moderate.*

Biarritz
Dining
★

Café de Paris. This is the most elegant dining room in Biarritz. There is a moderately priced set menu, but most of chef Pierre Laporte's specialties, including grilled duck liver and *ris de veau* (calf's sweetbreads) can be ordered only à la carte, and you will pay handsomely for that privilege. Fish and meats are also available, served with an imaginative nouvelle touch that contrasts with the complacent, fading glory of the Belle Epoque decor. The reasonably priced wine list is strong on Bordeaux. The **Alambic** (tel. 59–24–53–41), at the same address, is a brasserie-type sister restaurant that provides a less costly alternative. *5 pl. Bellevue, tel. 59–24–19–53. Closed Sun. dinner, Mon. except during July–Sept., and Nov.–Apr. Reservations required. Jacket and tie required. AE, DC, V. Expensive–Very Expensive.*

Lodging
★

Palais. This majestic redbrick hotel exudes a stylish, somewhat pompous air. Empress Eugénie, wife of Napoleon III, left her mark here a century ago when she discovered the then-little-known resort of Biarritz. An immense driveway, lawns, and a richly furnished, many-mirrored, semicircular dining room overlooking the sea and superb sandy beach embody a style and luxury that stops just short of decadence. Chef Grégoire Sein creates deft, innovative fare that takes full advantage of subtle herbs and textures. There's also a poolside terrace serving lunch and cocktails. The only drawback is the smallness of some of the rooms. *1 av. de l'Impératrice, 64200, tel. 59–24–09–40. 117 rooms with bath. Facilities: restaurant, 2 bars, pool, sauna, solarium, terrace. AE, DC, MC, V. Closed Nov.–Easter. Very Expensive.*

Miramar. If you can't get into the Palais, or prefer luxury of a slicker kind, make for the modern Miramar next door. It has less atmosphere perhaps, but some find the service less pretentious, and you can enjoy the same sea views plus the special low-calorie meals in which the restaurant specializes. *13 rue Louison-Bobet, 64200, tel. 59–41–30–00. 143 rooms with bath. Facilities: restaurant, bar, pool. AE, DC, MC, V. Expensive.*

Windsor. Built in the 1920s, this hotel is handy for the casino and beach and boasts its own restaurant (fish predominates; the cheapest menu is around 100 francs). The guest rooms are modernized and cozy, and some offer sea views. Guests, including many foreigners, tend to come here because they can't afford the Palais or Miramar. *19 blvd. du Général-de-Gaulle, 64200, tel. 59–24–08–52. 37 rooms with bath. Facilities: restaurant. AE, MC, V. Closed mid-Nov.–mid Mar. Moderate–Expensive.*

Bordeaux
Dining
★

Clavel. The recently opened sister restaurant to a center-city establishment of the same name adds a good-value gastronomic note to the undistinguished St-Jean *quartier* near the train station. It is one of the few places in town where you can sample claret by the glass, though any number of fruity young Bordeaux are available by the bottle for under 100 francs. The squeaky-clean modern-rustic decor, varied cuisine (including salmon, pig's feet, and lobster) and true bistro prices—make this an excellent choice. *44 rue Charles-Domercq, tel. 56–92–91–52. Reservations advised. Dress: casual. MC, V. Closed Sun., Mon., and second half of July. Moderate.*

★ **Vieux Bordeaux.** This much-acclaimed nouvelle cuisine haunt lies on the fringe of the old town. Chef Michel Bordage concentrates on fresh produce. His menu is therefore short but of high quality, complemented by three set-price menus. His fish dishes are particularly good; try the steamed turbot. The wine is good value, the decor modern, and the ambience lively. *27 rue Buhan, tel. 56–52–94–36. Reservations advised. Dress: casual. AE, MC, V. Closed Sat. lunch, Sun., Aug., and 1 week in Feb. Moderate.*

Ombrière. The friendly Ombrière looks out over one of the finest squares in old Bordeaux; during summer months, you can eat outside. The food is pleasant in an unexciting, brasserie sort of way (steak and fries) but, for central Bordeaux, its set menu is fairly priced, and even a choice à la carte dinner won't seem extravagant. *14 pl. du Parlement, tel. 56–44–82–69. Dress: casual. MC, V. Closed Sun., Mon., and Aug. Inexpensive.*

Lodging **Pyrénées.** Located in a turn-of-the-century building close to theater and old town, Pyrénées provides typically earnest provincial comfort (deep, slightly worn armchairs and effusive decor). American and British guests are common. There is no restaurant. *12 rue St-Rémi, 33000, tel. 56–81–66–58. 18 rooms with bath. AE, V. Closed second half Aug. and Christmas–New Year's. Moderate.*

Royal Médoc. This Bordeaux hotel is admirably situated near the majestic Esplanade de Quinconces in the city center, in a building that dates from 1720. English-speaking guests form the backbone of the foreign clientele, attracted by the elegant, neoclassical architecture and cheerful, efficient service. There is no restaurant. *5 rue de Sèze, 33000, tel. 56–81–72–42. 45 rooms, many with bath. AE, MC, V. Moderate.*

Brouage **Brouage.** This cheerful, recently modernized hotel-restaurant
Dining and Lodging on the main street doubles as the village bar, where colorful locals put the world to rights over beer and *pastis*. You'll soon feel one of the family—and be sure of a top-value meal featuring regional specialties like oysters and eel fricassee (with huge chunks of pâté served "while you wait"). *Rue de Québec, 17320 Hiers-Brouage, tel. 46–85–03–06. 7 rooms with bath or shower. V. Inexpensive.*

Cognac **Pigeons Blancs.** "White Pigeons," a converted and modernized
Dining and Lodging coaching inn standing in spacious grounds, has been owned by the same family since the 17th century. The welcome is warm, and the hotel is comfortable and intimate. The restaurant is highly rated, offering a choice of three menus of varying sophistication. The most expensive will not only titillate your tastebuds but will keep you going for about a week! *110 rue Jules-Brisson, tel. 45–82–16–36. 10 rooms with bath. Facilities: restaurant. AE, DC, MC, V. Closed Sun. dinner and first half of Jan. Moderate.*

Auberge. The two-story Auberge occupies an old building on a quiet street in the heart of Cognac. The emphasis is on bourgeois comfort; the restaurant, decked out in earnest, mock-18th century (Louis XVI) style, sets the tone. The food has a similarly serious ring to it: copious but unexceptional. *13 rue Plumejeau, 16100, tel. 45–32–08–70. 27 rooms, 20 with bath.*

Facilities: restaurant. AE, MC, V. Hotel closed Christmas–
New Year's; restaurant closed Sat. Inexpensive.

Coulon
Dining and Lodging

Au Marais. The old village of Coulon is a sound base for exploring the Marais Poitevin, and Au Marais, with its waterside setting and bulky, regional wooden furniture, is its most authentic
hotel. The restaurant provides fresh, locally caught eels and
snails. English, Belgian, and German guests are frequent. *48
quai Louis-Tardy, 79270, tel. 49–35–90–43. 11 rooms with
bath. V. Closed mid-Dec.–mid-Mar.; restaurant closed Sun.
dinner and Mon., Sept.–June. Moderate.*

Domme
Dining and Lodging

L'Esplanade. Make sure your room has an expansive view over
the Dordogne, because it's the view that makes this hotel special. The rooms are small but modernized, and the service English-speaking. Salmon and trout top the menu, but dining à la
carte can be pricey. *24250 Domme, tel. 53–28–31–41. 19 rooms
with bath. AE, MC, V. Closed mid-Nov.–mid-Feb. and Sun./
Mon. out of season. Moderate.*

Eymet
Dining and Lodging

Les Fauchés. Visitors to Bergerac and Monbazillac should head
a few miles south to Razac d'Eymet, where English couple Guy
and Lynne Feltham have transformed an old country house into
a modern hotel full of local character (tiled floors, for instance),
and serve up a not unappealing brand of Anglo-French cuisine.
Peas—ignored by most French chefs—are king vegetable
here. *24500 Razac d'Eymet, tel. 53–24–69–27, 10 rooms with
bath. Facilities: pool, dining-room, Ping-Pong. V. Inexpensive–Moderate.*

Les Eyzies
Dining and Lodging
★

Le Centenaire. Although its hotel is stylish, modern, comfortable, and offers numerous amenities, Le Centenaire is known
first and foremost as a restaurant. Roland Mazère is rated one
of the most accomplished chefs in the whole of Périgord. He
adds flair and imagination to the preparation of local specialties: risotto with truffles, foie gras and scampi, and snails with
ravioli and gazpacho. The dining room, with its gold-colored
stone and wooden beams, retains local character, too, and commands pleasant views across the countryside. *24620 Les
Eyziesde-Tayac, tel. 53–06–97–18. 29 rooms with bath. Facilities: restaurant, pool, sauna, health club, shopping arcade,
garden. Restaurant reservations advised. Jacket required.
MC, V. Closed Tues. lunch and Nov.–Mar. Expensive.*

Monflanquin
Dining and Lodging

Prince Noir. This 13th-century house in the bastide town of
Monflanquin, close to the Château de Biron, comes reader-recommended for renovated comfort and regional cuisine (foie
gras and steak). The second-floor restaurant has a section for
nonsmokers. *Pl. des Arcades, 47150, tel. 53–36–50–25. 11
rooms with bath or shower. MC, V. Moderate.*

Poitiers
Dining

Maxime. This crowd-pleaser lives up to its famous name,
thanks to a wide choice of set menus, the personal recipes of
chef Christian Rougier (foie gras and duck salad, for instance),
and a pastel-toned decor featuring interwar frescoes. *4 rue St-
Nicolas, tel. 49–41–09–55. Reservations required. Dress: casual. AE, MC, V. Closed Sat., Sun., and much of July and
Aug. Moderate.*

Lodging

Europe. An early 19th-century building in the middle of town
holds this unpretentious hotel, though some rooms occupy a
modern extension. Foreign visitors often stay here, attracted
by the traditional decor and competitive prices. There is no res-

taurant. *39 rue Carnot, 86000, tel. 49–88–12–00. 78 rooms, some with bath. V. Inexpensive.*

Pons
Dining and Lodging
★

Moulin de Marcouze. You, too, can feast like a brandy baron—if your take the 30-minute drive from Cognac or Saintes to the village of Mosnac (11 km south of Pons). Dominique Bouchet (of Tour d'Argent in Paris) has transformed an old mill (complete with stream and waterwheel) into a sophisticated restaurant in a picturesque country setting. The style is understated: spacious layout, original paintings, and food that innovates without flash (sauteed sole fillet or duck pie with truffles). At midday, local drink executives and their clients pile in for power lunches, but if you come for dinner or book one of the guestrooms you can linger over a peaceful meal. The waiters will gladly steer you to the bargain end of the extensive wine list. *17240 Mosnac, tel. 46–70–46–16. 10 rooms with bath. Facilities: pool, helipad. Jacket and tie required. AE, DC, MC, V. Closed Feb. and Tues. and Wed. lunch out of season. Moderate–Expensive.*

André. The salty decor is somewhat excessive—fishing nets flutter overhead, and posters of ocean liners billow from the walls—but the food and service have such gusto that you'll be caught up in the mood, especially if you order a monumental seafood platter (washed down with white Charentes wine). *5 rue St-Jean, tel. 46–41–28–24. Reservations advised. Dress: casual. MC, V. Moderate.*

La Rochelle
Dining

Pré Vert. Decorated throughout in shades of green, this restaurant is hidden down a discreet pedestrian street close to the harbor. It offers three inexpensive menus and regional specialties, such as foie gras, eel, and duck. *45 rue St-Nicolas, tel. 46–41–24–43. Reservations advised in summer. Dress: casual. AE, DC, MC, V. Closed Sun., Nov.–Feb. Inexpensive.*

Lodging

Tour de Nesle. This modernized hotel may be a bit cramped, but it is clean, cheerful, and ideally placed for exploring the harbor and the old town. Ask for a room with a view across the canal toward St-Sauveur church. Parking, a major headache in La Rochelle, is usually possible along the street in front. *2 quai Louis-Durand, 17000, tel. 46–41–30–72. 28 rooms with shower or bath. MC, V. Moderate.*

St-Emilion
Dining

Germaine. Family cooking and regional dishes are featured at this central St-Emilion eatery. The stylish upstairs dining room, candlelit and adorned with flowers, is a pleasant place in which to enjoy the reasonably priced set menus. Grilled meats and fish are house specialties; for dessert, try the almond macaroons. There's also a terrace for outdoor eating. *Pl. des Crénaux, tel. 57–24–70–88. Reservations advised. Dress: casual. DC, V. Closed Sun., Mon., and mid-Dec.–mid-Jan. Moderate.*

Dining and Lodging
★

Auberge de la Commanderie. For such a pretty town, St-Emilion is a bit short on accommodations. Luckily, this two-story, 19th-century hotel is admirable in every sense. It is close to the ramparts and has its own garden and views of the vineyards. The rooms are small but clean and individually decorated. The attractive restaurant is often frequented by nonresidents and boasts a good selection of local wines. *Rue des Cordeliers, 33300, tel. 57–24–70–19. 15 rooms, most with bath. Facilities: restaurant, garden. MC, V. Closed Dec.–Jan.; restaurant closed Tues., Sept.–June. Moderate.*

Sarlat
Dining and Lodging

St-Albert. At the edge of the old town, St-Albert provides functional accommodations and a friendly welcome from owner Michel Garrigou. The old-fashioned restaurant, with four moderately priced set menus, provides some of the best-value meals in small, pretty Sarlat, though the cooking can be on the heavy side. House specialties include duck foie gras with shallots, and *la mique,* a dumpling dish served with pork and vegetables. *10 pl. Pasteur, 24200, tel. 56–59–01–09. 56 rooms, some with bath. AE, DC, MC, V. Restaurant closed Sun. dinner and Mon., Nov.–mid-Apr. Inexpensive–Moderate.*

The Arts and Nightlife

The Arts

The major festival activities in this ocean-bordered region are inspired by the sea. "Fêtes de la Mer"—sometimes including carnival parades—are frequent, with the biggest at **La Rochelle** at Pentecost, **Royan** in late June, and **Arcachon** in mid-August. Drama and music combine to make up the **Festival International de l'Entre-Deux-Mers** (for information, call 56–71–51–35). A Bande Dessinée (comic book) festival takes place in **Angoulême** in January, and there's a Crime Film festival in **Cognac** each September.

Theater

The region's principal theaters—inevitably devoted to works in the French language—are at **Poitiers** (1 pl. du Maréchal-Leclerc, tel. 49–41–28–33) and **Bordeaux** (Grand Théâtre, pl. de la Comédie, tel. 56–90–91–60).

Concerts

A wide range of music is available during **Bordeaux's International Musical May,** a leading event on France's cultural calendar. Smaller summer festivals are held at **Saintes** (the **Festival de la Musique Ancienne,** early July) and **Arcachon** (the **International Guitar Festival** in July). Modern music gets a week-long airing at **La Rochelle's Franco-Folies** festival in July.

Opera

There are occasional operatic performances at the **Grand Théâtre** in **Bordeaux** *(see* above).

Nightlife

Bars and Nightclubs

Try **L'Aztecal** (61 rue du Pas-St-Georges) or **Cabaret Andalucia** (7 quai Bacalan) in Bordeaux. **Le Vaudeville** (13 quai de la République) in Saintes has a homey English atmosphere and a tongue-tingling array of old whiskies.

Jazz Clubs

Les Argentiers (7 rue Teulère) is a respected and long-established Bordeaux hangout.

Rock Clubs

A late-night venue for raunchy music, complete with videos, is **Le Chat-Bleu** in Bordeaux (122 quai Bacalan).

Discos

In Bordeaux, try **Sénéchal** (57 bis quai de Paludate); in Arcachon, **Cyclone** (177 blvd. de la Plage) or **Cotton Club** (4 blvd. Mestrezat); in Niort, **Le Niagara** (469 av. de Limoges) or **Club St-Gelais** (43 rue St-Gelais); in Sarlat, **Le Bas Roc** (av. de la Dordogne); in Cognac, **New Orleans** (2 impasse du Moulin); and in Poitiers, **Black House** (195 av. du 8-mai-1945) or the split-level **La Grand' goule** (46 rue du Pigeon-Blanc).

Casinos There are casinos in **Biarritz, Royan, Arcachon,** and on the is-land of **Oléron.**

Conversion Tables

Clothing Sizes

Men
Suits To change American suit sizes to French suit sizes, add 10 to the American suit size.
To change French suit sizes to American suit sizes, subtract 10 from the French suit size.

U.S.	36	38	40	42	44	46	48
French	46	48	50	52	54	56	58

Shirts To change American shirt sizes to French shirt sizes, multiply the American shirt size by 2 and add 8.
To change French shirt sizes to American shirt sizes, subtract 8 from the French shirt size and divide by 2.

U.S.	14	14½	15	15½	16	16½	17	17½
French	36	37	38	39	40	41	42	43

Shoes French shoe sizes vary in their relation to American shoe sizes.

U.S.	6½	7	8	9	10	10½	11
French	39	40	41	42	43	44	45

Women
Dresses and Coats To change U.S. dress/coat sizes to French dress/coat sizes, add 28 to the U.S. dress/coat size.
To change French dress/coat sizes to U.S. dress/coat sizes, subtract 28 from the French dress/coat size.

U.S.	4	6	8	10	12	14	16
French	32	34	36	38	40	42	44

Blouses and Sweaters To change U.S. blouse/sweater sizes to French blouse/sweater sizes, add 8 to the U.S. blouse/sweater size.
To change French blouse/sweater sizes to U.S. blouse/sweater sizes, subtract 8 from the French blouse/sweater size.

U.S.	30	32	34	36	38	40	42
French	38	40	42	44	46	48	50

Shoes To change U.S. shoe sizes to French shoe sizes, add 32 to the U.S. shoe size.
To change French shoe sizes to U.S. shoe sizes, subtract 32 from the French shoe size.

U.S.	4	5	6	7	8	9	10
French	36	37	38	39	40	41	42

French Vocabulary

Words and Phrases

	English	French	Pronunciation
Basics	Yes/no	Oui/non	wee/no
	Please	S'il vous plaît	seel voo play
	Thank you	Merci	mare-**see**
	You're welcome	De rien	deh ree-**en**
	Excuse me, sorry	Pardon	pahr-**doan**
	Sorry!	Désolé(e)	day-zoh-**lay**
	Good morning/ afternoon	Bonjour	bone-**joor**
	Good evening	Bonsoir	bone-**swar**
	Goodbye	Au revoir	o ruh-**vwar**
	Mr. (Sir)	Monsieur	mih-see-**oor**
	Mrs. (Ma'am)	Madame	ma-dam
	Miss	Mademoiselle	mad-mwa-**zel**
	Pleased to meet you	Enchanté(e)	on-shahn-**tay**
	How are you?	Comment allez-vous?	ko-men-tahl-ay-**voo**
Numbers	one	un	un
	two	deux	dew
	three	trois	twa
	four	quatre	**cat**-ruh
	five	cinq	sank
	six	six	seess
	seven	sept	set
	eight	huit	wheat
	nine	neuf	nuf
	ten	dix	deess
	eleven	onze	owns
	twelve	douze	dooz
	thirteen	treize	trays
	fourteen	quatorze	ka-torz
	fifteen	quinze	cans
	sixteen	seize	sez
	seventeen	dix-sept	deess-**set**
	eighteen	dix-huit	deess-**wheat**
	nineteen	dix-neuf	deess-**nuf**
	twenty	vingt	vant
	twenty-one	vingt-et-un	vant-ay-**un**
	thirty	trente	trahnt
	forty	quarante	ka-**rahnt**
	fifty	cinquante	sang-**kahnt**
	sixty	soixante	swa-**sahnt**
	seventy	soixante-dix	swa-sahnt-**deess**
	eighty	quatre-vingts	cat-ruh-**vant**
	ninety	quatre-vingt-dix	cat-ruh-vant-**deess**
	one-hundred	cent	sahnt
	one-thousand	mille	meel

Colors	black	noir	nwar
	blue	bleu	blu
	brown	brun/marron	brun
	green	vert	vair
	orange	orange	o-**ranj**
	red	rouge	rouge
	white	blanc	blahn
	yellow	jaune	jone
Days of the Week	Sunday	dimanche	dee-**mahnsh**
	Monday	lundi	lewn-**dee**
	Tuesday	mardi	mar-**dee**
	Wednesday	mercredi	mare-kruh-**dee**
	Thursday	jeudi	juh-**dee**
	Friday	vendredi	van-dra-**dee**
	Saturday	samedi	sam-**dee**
Months	January	janvier	jan-**vyay**
	February	février	feh-vree-**ay**
	March	mars	marce
	April	avril	a-**vreel**
	May	mai	meh
	June	juin	jwan
	July	juillet	jwee-**ay**
	August	août	oot
	September	septembre	sep-**tahm**-bruh
	October	octobre	oak-**toe**-bruh
	November	novembre	no-**vahm**-bruh
	December	décembre	day-**sahm**-bruh
Useful Phrases	Do you speak English?	Parlez-vous anglais?	par-lay vooz ahng-**glay**
	I don't speak French	Je ne parle pas français	jeh nuh parl pah fraun-**say**
	I don't understand	Je ne comprends pas	jeh nuh kohm-prahn **pah**
	I understand	Je comprends	jeh kohm-**prahn**
	I don't know	Je ne sais pas	jeh nuh say **pah**
	I'm American/ British	Je suis américain/ anglais	jeh sweez a-may-ree-**can**/ahng-**glay**
	What's your name?	Comment vous appelez-vous?	ko-mahn voo za-pel-ay-**voo**
	My name is . . .	Je m'appelle . . .	jeh muh-**pel** . . .
	What time is it?	Quelle heure est-il?	kel ur et-**il**
	How?	Comment?	ko-**mahn**
	When?	Quand?	kahnd
	Yesterday	Hier	yair
	Today	Aujourd'hui	o-zhoor-**dwee**
	Tomorrow	Demain	deh-**man**
	This morning/ afternoon	Ce matin/cet après-midi	seh ma-**tanh**/set ah-pray-mee-**dee**

Tonight	Ce soir	seh **swar**
What?	Quoi?	kwah
What is it?	Qu'est-ce que c'est?	kess-kuh-**say**
Why?	Pourquoi?	poor-**kwa**
Who?	Qui?	kee
Where is . . .	Où est . . .	oo ay
the train station?	la gare?	la gar
the subway station?	la station de métro?	la sta-syon deh may-**tro**
the bus stop?	l'arrêt de bus?	la-ray deh **booss**
the terminal (airport)?	l'aérogare?	lay-ro-**gar**
the post office?	la poste?	la post
the bank?	la banque?	la bahnk
the . . . hotel?	l'hôtel . . . ?	low-**tel**
the . . . museum?	le musée . . . ?	leh mew-**zay**
the hospital?	l'hôpital?	low-pee-**tahl**
the elevator?	l'ascenseur?	la-sahn-**seur**
the telephone?	le téléphone?	leh te-le-**phone**
Where are the restrooms?	Où sont les toilettes?	oo son lay twah-**let**
Here/there	Ici/lá	ee-**see**/la
Left/right	A gauche/à droite	a goash/a drwat
Is it near/far?	C'est près/loin?	say pray/lwan
I'd like . . .	Je voudrais . . .	jeh voo-**dray**
a room	une chambre	ewn **shahm**-bra
the key	la clé	la clay
a newspaper	un journal	un joor-**nahl**
a stamp	un timbre	un **tam**-bruh
I'd like to buy . . .	Je voudrais acheter . . .	jeh voo-**dray** ahsh-**tay**
cigarettes	des cigarettes	day see-ga-**ret**
matches	des allumettes	days a-loo-**met**
city plan	un plan de ville	un plahn de la **veel**
road map	une carte routière	ewn cart roo-tee-**air**
magazine	une revue	ewn reh-**view**
envelopes	des enveloppes	dayz ahn-veh-**lope**
writing paper	du papier à lettres	deh-pa-pee-ay a **let**-ruh
airmail writing paper	du papier avion	deh pa-pee-ay a-vee-**own**
postcard	une carte postale	ewn cart post-**al**
How much is it?	C'est combien?	say comb-bee-**en**
It's expensive/cheap	C'est cher/pas cher	say sher/pa sher
A little/a lot	Un peu/beaucoup	un puh/bo-**koo**
More/less	Plus/moins	ploo/mwa

Enough/too (much)	Assez/trop	a-**say**/tro
I am ill/sick	Je suis malade	jeh swee ma-**lahd**
Call a doctor	Appelez un docteur	a-pe-lay un dohk-**tore**
Help!	Au secours!	o say-**koor**
Stop!	Arrêtez!	a-ruh-**tay**

Dining Out

A bottle of . . .	une bouteille de . . .	ewn boo-**tay** deh
A cup of . . .	une tasse de . . .	ewn tass deh
A glass of . . .	un verre de . . .	un vair deh
Ashtray	un cendrier	un sahn-dree-**ay**
Bill/check	l'addition	la-dee-see-**own**
Bread	du pain	due pan
Breakfast	le petit déjeuner	leh pet-**ee** day-zhu-**nay**
Butter	du beurre	due bur
Cocktail/aperitif	un apéritif	un ah-pay-ree-**teef**
Dinner	le dîner	leh dee-**nay**
Fixed-price menu	le menu	leh may-**new**
Fork	une fourchette	ewn four-**shet**
I am on a diet	Je suis au régime	jeh sweez o ray-**jeem**
I am vegetarian	Je suis végétarien(ne)	jeh swee vay-jay-ta-ree-**en**
I cannot eat . . .	Je ne peux pas manger de . . .	jeh nuh puh pah mahn-**jay** deh
I'd like to order	Je voudrais commander	jeh voo-**dray** ko-mahn-**day**
I'd like . . .	Je voudrais . . .	jeh voo-**dray**
I'm hungry/thirsty	J'ai faim/soif	jay fam/swahf
Is service/the tip included?	Est-ce que le service est compris?	ess keh leh sair-veess ay comb-**pree**
It's good/bad	C'est bon/mauvais	say bon/mo-**vay**
It's hot/cold	C'est chaud/froid	say sho/frwah
Knife	un couteau	un koo-**toe**
Lunch	le déjeuner	leh day-juh-**nay**
Menu	la carte	la cart
Napkin	une serviette	ewn sair-vee-**et**
Pepper	du poivre	due **pwah**-vruh
Plate	une assiette	ewn a-see-**et**
Please give me . . .	Donnez-moi . . .	doe-nay-**mwah**

Salt	du sel	dew sell
Spoon	une cuillère	ewn kwee-**air**
Sugar	du sucre	due **sook**-ruh
Wine list	la carte des vins	la cart day **van**

Menu Guide

English	*French*
Set menu	Menu à prix fixe
Dish of the day	Plat du jour
Drink included	Boisson comprise
Local specialties	Spécialités locales
Choice of vegetable accompaniment	Garniture au choix
Made to order	Sur commande
Extra charge	Supplément/En sus
When available	Selon arrivage

Breakfast

Jam	Confiture
Croissants	Croissants
Honey	Miel
Boiled egg	Oeuf à la coque
Bacon and eggs	Oeufs au bacon
Ham and eggs	Oeufs au jambon
Fried eggs	Oeufs sur le plat
Scrambled eggs	Oeufs brouillés
(Plain) omelet	Omelette (nature)
Rolls	Petits pains

Starters

Anchovies	Anchois
Chitterling sausage	Andouille(tte)
Assorted cold cuts	Assiette anglaise
Assorted pork products	Assiette de charcuterie
Small, highly seasoned sausage	Crépinette
Mixed raw vegetable salad	Crudités
Snails	Escargots
Ham (Bayonne)	Jambon (de Bayonne)
Bologna sausage	Mortadelle
Devilled eggs	Oeufs à la diable
Liver purée blended with other meat	Pâté
Tart with a rich, creamy filling of cheese, vegetables, meat or seafood	Quiche (lorraine)
Cold sausage	Saucisson
Pâté sliced and served from an earthenware pot	Terrine
Cured dried beef	Viande séchée

Salads

Diced vegetable salad	Salade russe
Endive salad	Salade d'endives
Green salad	Salade verte
Mixed salad	Salade panachée
Tuna salad	Salade de thon

Soups

Cold leek and potato cream soup	Vichyssoise
Cream of . . .	Crème de . . .
Cream of . . .	Velouté de . . .
Hearty soup	Soupe
day's soup	*du jour*
French onion soup	à l'oignon
Provençal vegetable soup	au pistou
Light soup	Potage
mashed red beans	*condé*
shredded vegetables	julienne
potato	parmentier
Fish and seafood stew	Bouillabaisse
Seafood stew (chowder)	Bisque
Stew of meat and vegetables	Pot-au-feu

Fish and Seafood

Bass	Bar
Carp	Carpe
Clams	Palourdes
Cod	Morue
Creamed salt cod	Brandade de morue
Crab	Crabe
Crayfish	Ecrevisses
Eel	Anguille
Fish stew from Marseilles	Bourride
Fish stew in wine	Matelote
Frog's legs	Cuisses de grenouilles
Herring	Harengs
Lobster	Homard
Mackerel	Maquereau
Mussels	Moules
Octopus	Poulpe
Oysters	Huîtres
Perch	Perche
Pike	Brochet
Dublin bay prawns (scampi)	Langoustines
Red mullet	Rouget
Salmon	Saumon
Scallops in creamy sauce	Coquilles St-Jacques
Sea bream	Daurade
Shrimps	Crevettes
Sole	Sole
Squid	Calmar
Trout	Truite
Tuna	Thon
Whiting	Merlan

Methods of Preparation

Baked	Au four
Fried	Frit
Grilled	Grillé
Marinated	Mariné
Poached	Poché
Sautéed	Sauté
Smoked	Fumé
Steamed	Cuit à la vapeur

Meat

Beef	Boeuf
Beef stew with vegetables, braised in red Burgundy wine	Boeuf bourguignon
Brains	Cervelle
Chops	Côtelettes
Cutlet	Escalope
Double fillet steak	Chateaubriand
Kabob	Brochette
Kidneys	Rognons
Lamb	Agneau
Leg	Gigot
Liver	Foie
Meatballs	Boulettes de viande
Pig's feet (trotters)	Pieds de cochon
Pork	Porc
Rib	Côte
Rib or rib-eye steak	Entrecôte
Sausages	Saucisses
Sausages and cured pork served with sauerkraut	Choucroute garnie
Steak (always beef)	Steak/steack
Stew	Ragoût
T-bone steak	Côte de boeuf
Tenderloin steak	Médaillon
Tenderloin of T-bone steak	Tournedos
Tongue	Langue
Veal	Veau
Veal sweetbreads	Ris de veau

Methods of Preparation

Very rare	Bleu
Rare	Saignant
Medium	A point
Well-done	Bien cuit
Baked	Au four
Boiled	Bouilli
Braised	Braisé
Fried	Frit
Grilled	Grillé
Roast	Rôti
Sautéed	Sauté
Stewed	A l'étouffée

Game and Poultry

Chicken	Poulet
Chicken breast	Suprême de volaille
Chicken stewed in red wine	Coq au vin
Chicken stewed with vegetables	Poule au pot
Spring chicken	Poussin
Duck/duckling	Canard/caneton
Duck braised with oranges and orange liqueur	Canard à l'orange
Fattened pullet	Poularde
Fowl	Volaille
Guinea fowl/young guinea fowl	Pintade/pintadeau
Goose	Oie

Partridge/young partridge	Perdrix/perdreau
Pheasant	Faisan
Pigeon/squab	Pigeon/pigeonneau
Quail	Caille
Rabbit	Lapin
Turkey/young turkey	Dinde/dindonneau
Venison (red/roe)	Cerf/chevreuil

Vegetables

Artichoke	Artichaut
Asparagus	Asperge
Brussels sprouts	Choux de Bruxelles
Cabbage (red)	Chou (rouge)
Carrots	Carottes
Cauliflower	Chou-fleur
Eggplant	Aubergines
Endive	Endives
Leeks	Poireaux
Lettuce	Laitue
Mushrooms	Champignons
Onions	Oignons
Peas	Petits pois
Peppers	Poivrons
Radishes	Radis
Spinach	Epinards
Tomatoes	Tomates
Watercress	Cresson
Zucchini	Courgette
White kidney/French beans	Haricots blancs/verts
Casserole of stewed eggplant, onions, green peppers, and zucchini	Ratatouille

Spices and Herbs

Bay leaf	Laurier
Chervil	Cerfeuil
Garlic	Ail
Marjoram	Marjolaine
Mustard	Moutarde
Parsley	Persil
Pepper	Poivre
Rosemary	Romarin
Tarragon	Estragon
Mixture of herbs	Fines herbes

Potatoes, Rice, and Noodles

Noodles	Nouilles
Pasta	Pâtes
Potatoes	Pommes (de terre)
matchsticks	*allumettes*
mashed and deep-fried	*dauphine*
mashed with butter and egg yolks	*duchesse*
in their jackets	*en robe des champs*
french fries	*frites*
mashed	*mousseline*
boiled/steamed	*nature/vapeur*

Rice	Riz
boiled in bouillon with onions	*pilaf*

Sauces and Preparations

Brown butter, parsley, lemon juice	Meunière
Curry	Indienne
Egg yolks, butter, vinegar	Hollandaise
Hot pepper	Diable
Mayonnaise flavored with	
mustard and herbs	Tartare
Mushrooms, red wine, shallots,	
beef marrow	Bordelaise
Onions, tomatoes, garlic	Provençale
Pepper sauce	Poivrade
Red wine, herbs	Bourguignon
Vinegar, egg yolks, white wine,	
shallots, tarragon	Béarnaise
Vinegar dressing	Vinaigrette
White sauce	Béchamel
White wine, mussel broth, egg	
yolks	Marinière
Wine, mushrooms, onions, shallots	Chasseur
With goose or duck liver purée and	
truffles	Périgueux
With Madeira wine	Madère

Cheeses

Mild:	Beaufort
	Beaumont
	Belle étoile
	Boursin
	Brie
	Cantal
	Comté
	Reblochon
	St-Paulin
	Tomme de Savoie
Sharp:	Bleu de Bresse
	Camembert
	Livarot
	Fromage au marc
	Munster
	Pont-l'Évêque
	Roquefort
Swiss:	Emmenthal
	Gruyère
	Vacherin
Goat's milk:	St-Marcellin
	Crottin de Chavignol Valençay
Cheese tart	Tarte au fromage
Small cheese tart	Ramequin
Toasted ham and cheese sandwich	Croque-monsieur

Fruits and Nuts

Almonds	Amandes
Apple	Pomme
Apricot	Abricot
Banana	Banane
Blackberries	Mûres
Blackcurrants	Cassis
Blueberries	Myrtilles
Cherries	Cerises
Chestnuts	Marrons
Coconut	Noix de coco
Dates	Dattes
Dried fruit	Fruits secs
Figs	Figues
Grapefruit	Pamplemousse
Grapes green/blue	Raisin blanc/noir
Hazelnuts	Noisettes
Lemon	Citron
Melon	Melon
Orange	Orange
Peach	Pêche
Peanuts	Cacahouètes
Pear	Poire
Pineapple	Ananas
Plums	Prunes
Prunes	Pruneaux
Raisins	Raisins secs
Raspberries	Framboises
Strawberries	Fraises
Tangerine	Mandarine
Walnuts	Noix
Watermelon	Pastèque

Desserts

Apple pie	Tarte aux pommes
Baked Alaska	Omelette norvégienne
Caramel pudding	Crème caramel
Chocolate cake	Gâteau au chocolat
Chocolate pudding	Mousse au chocolat
Custard tart	Flan
Custard	Creme anglaise
Ice cream	Glace
Layer cake	Tourte
Pear with vanilla ice cream and chocolate sauce	Poire Belle Hélène
Soufflé made with orange liqueur	Soufflé au Grand-Marnier
Sundae	Coupe (glacée)
Water ice	Sorbet
Whipped cream	Crème Chantilly
Creamy dessert of egg yolks, wine, sugar, and flavoring	Sabayon
Puff pastry filled with whipped cream or custard	Profiterole

Index

Abbaye aux Hommes (Caen), *235*
Abbeville, *263*
Abbey Palace (Paris), *93–94*
Académie Francaise (Paris), *93*
Accident insurance, *13*
Accommodations, *32–33*
in Alsace-Lorraine, *303–308*
on Atlantic Coast, *507–513*
in Brittany, *217–222*
in Burgundy, *330–336*
in Champagne, *271–276*
for children, *18*
on Corsica, *450–455*
in Ile de France, *159–165*
in Loire Valley, *189–195*
in Lyon and the Alps, *358–364*
in Normandy, *243–251*
for older travelers, *20–21*
in Paris, *125–132*
in Provence, *392–399*
on Riviera, *425–433*
tipping in, *29–30*
in Toulouse and Midi-Pyrénées, *477–482*
Agay, *407*
Aigues-Mortes, *375*
Air travel, *22–23*
to Alsace-Lorraine, *280*
to Atlantic Coast, *487*
to Burgundy, *312*
to Champagne, *254*
with children, *18–19*
to Corsica, *437*
within France, *26*
from Great Britain to France, *24*
to Ile de France, *136*
to Lyon and the Alps, *339*
to Normandy, *225*
to Paris, *67–68*

to Provence, *368*
to Toulouse and Midi-Pyrénées, *458*
Aître St-Maclou (Rouen), *230–231*
Aix-en-Provence, *384–385, 393–394*
Aix-les-Bains, *355*
Ajaccio, *444–445, 451*
Albi, *465–466, 478–479*
Alençon, *240*
Alèria, *446–448*
Alps, *338–365 See also Lyon*,
arts and entertainment in, *364–365*
children's activities in, *356*
dining and lodging in, *358–364*
Grenoble and, *353–356*
Rhône Valley, *350–353*
shopping, *357–358*
sports in, *358*
tours and sightseeing in, *339–356*
transportation to and in, *339*
Alsace, *288–294*
Alsace-Lorraine, *279–309*
Alsace, *288–294*
arts and entertainment in, *308–309*
children's activities in, *301*
dining and lodging in, *303–308*
Lorraine, *294–301*
shopping in, *302–304*
sports, *303*
Strasbourg, *281–288*
tours and sightseeing in, *281–302*
transportation to and in, *280*
Amboise, *178–179, 190*
American Association of Retired Persons (AARP), *20*
American Cathedral

of the Holy Trinity (Paris), *87*
American Express MoneyGrams, *8*
American Institute for Foreign Study, *17*
American Star Lines, *24*
Amiens, *258–259, 272*
Amusement parks
Mirapolis Amusement Park (Cergy), *157*
O.K. Corral, *390*
in Paris, *102*
Park Asterix, *157*
Ancy-le-Franc, *320*
Andelys, Les, *227*
Andlau, *290*
Anet, *146*
Angers, *169–171*
Angoulême, *495–496, 508*
Annecy, *355*
Annonay, *352*
Antibes, *409–410*
Antiques
in Burgundy, *329*
in Champagne, *270*
in Ile de France, *158*
in Loire Valley, *187*
in Normandy, *242*
in Paris, *114*
APEX airfares, *22*
Aquariums
Marineland, *410*
in Paris, *102*
at Sarlat, *506*
Arcachon, *504–505*
Architecture, *54–58*
in Châlons-sur-Marne, *268*
of Fontainebleau, *153–154*
in Ile de France, *135*
Archives Nationales (Paris), *83*
Arc de Triomphe (Paris), *86*
Arènes, *372*
Arles, *376–379, 394–395*
Arnay-le-Duc, *331*
Arras, *259, 272*
Arromanches,

237–238
Arts
in Alsace-Lorraine, *308–309*
on Atlantic Coast, *513*
in Brittany, *222*
in Burgundy, *328*
in Champagne, *277*
on Corsica, *454–455*
in Ile de France, *165*
in Loire Valley, *195*
in Lyon and the Alps, *364–365*
in Normandy, *251*
in Paris, *131–132*
in Provence, *399*
on Riviera, *433–434*
in Toulouse and Midi-Pyrénées, *483–484*
Asco Valley, *443*
Atlantic Coast, *486–514*
arts and entertainment on, *513*
Bordeaux to Biarritz, *500–505*
children's activities on, *506*
dining and lodging on, *507–513*
Dordogne and Périgord, *496–500*
Poitou-Charentes, *488–496*
shopping on, *506–507*
sports, *507*
tours and sightseeing on, *487–505*
transportation to and on, *487*
Aubagne, *388*
Auberge de l'Abbaye, *245*
Auch, *470–471, 479*
Automobiles
in Alsace-Lorraine, *280*
on Atlantic Coast, *487*
in Burgundy, *312*
in Champagne, *254*
on Corsica, *437*
English Channel crossings for, *25*
within France, *27–28*

Automobiles
(continued)
in Ile de France, *136*
in Loire Valley, *168*
in Normandy, *197*
to Paris, *68*
in Provence, *368*
renting and leasing, *14–15*
on Riviera, *402*
in Toulouse and Midi-Pyrénées, *458*
Autun, *321, 331*
Auverssur-Oise, *150–151*
Auxerre, *319, 331*
Avallon, *323, 331–332*
Avignon, *395*
Avioth, *294*
Azay-le-Rideau, *174–175, 191*

Babylone Bar, *203*
Baby-sitting services, *19*
Bagnères de Luchon, *475*
Bagnoles-de-l'Orne, *240, 244–245*
Bains, Les (Paris), *133*
Balagne, *441*
Ballet, *433*
Banks, *30*
Barbizon, *154, 160*
Barbotan-les-Thermes, *479*
Barr, *289*
Bars
in Alsace-Lorraine, *309*
in Brittany, *222*
in Champagne, *276*
in Lyon, *365*
in Normandy, *251*
in Paris, *132–133*
Basilique du Sacré Coeur (Paris), *100*
Bastia, *439–441, 451–452*
Bastille (Paris), *85*
Bateau-Lavoir (Paris), *99*
Baule, La, *212, 218*
Baux-de-Provence, Les, *378, 396*
Bayeux, *236–237, 245*
Bayeux Tapestry, *236*
Bayonne, *505*
Bazar de l'Hôtel de

Ville (Paris), *82*
Beaches, *31*
on Atlantic Coast, *507*
in Brittany, *216*
in Champagne, *269, 270–271*
on Corsica, *449–450*
in Normandy, *242*
on Riviera, *425*
at St-Tropez, *406*
Beaubourg (Centre National d'Art et de Culture Georges Pompidou; Paris), *82–83, 102*
Beaulieu, *417*
Beaumont-sur-Oise, *151*
Beaune, *326, 332*
Beauvais, *255, 258*
Bec-Hellouin, Le, *241, 245*
Bed-and-breakfasts, *33*
Belle-Ile, *211, 218*
Bénouville, *245*
Bergerac, *497, 508–509*
Biarritz, *505, 509*
Bibliothèque Forney (Paris), *85*
Bibliothèque Humaniste (Sélestate), *290*
Bibliothèque Nationale (Paris), *80*
Bicycling, *28*
in Alsace-Lorraine, *303*
in Brittany, *217*
in Burgundy, *329*
in Champagne, *270*
on Corsica, *449*
in Ile de France, *159*
in Loire Valley, *168, 188*
in Normandy, *242*
in Paris, *69, 115*
in Provence, *391–392*
on Riviera, *424*
Biot, *410*
Biron, *498*
Blaye, *496*
Blois, *181, 191*
Boating, *102*
Boats
on Atlantic Coast, *487–488*
in Brittany, *214*
on Corsica, *438*
within France, *28*

to Normandy, *197*
Paris tours by, *72*
on Riviera, *402*
trips in Paris in, *102*
Boersch, *288*
Bois Préau, *101*
Bonifacio, *447*
Bonnieux, *384*
Bonsecours, *227, 246*
Books on France, *21–22*
Bookstores, *72*
Bordeaux, *500–505, 509–510*
Boulogne, *262*
Boulogne-sur-Mer, *273*
Bourbansais, La *204*
Bourg, *496*
Bourg-en-Bresse, *349, 360*
Bourges, *328–329*
Bourse du Commerce (Paris), *80*
Brasserie Georges, *348*
Brasserie Liégoise, *273*
Brasserie Royale, *394*
Brest, *208–209*
Breteuil, *143*
Brioude, *357*
British travelers, *10, 11, 24–26*
Brittany, *197–222*
arts and entertainment in, *222*
children's activities, *214–215*
dining and lodging in, *217–222*
Northeast Brittany, *199–207*
shopping in, *216*
sports, *216–217*
tours and sightseeing in, *198–216*
transportation to and in, *198*
west coast of, *207–214*
Burgundy, *311–336*
arts and entertainment in, *336*
children's activities in, *328*
dining and lodging in, *330–336*
northern and western, *313–323*
shopping in, *329*

sports, *329–330*
tours and sightseeing in, *322–398*
transportation to and within, *312*
wine country, *323–328*
Buses
in Alsace-Lorraine, *280–281*
on Atlantic Coast, *487*
in Champagne, *254–255*
from Charles de Gaulle (Roissy) Airport, *67*
on Corsica, *438*
within France, *27*
from Great Britain to France, *25–26*
in Loire Valley, *168*
in Normandy, *225*
from Orly Airport, *67–68*
to Paris, *68*
in Paris, *69*
in Provence, *369*
on Riviera, *402*
Buttes-Chaumont (Paris), *103*

Cabarets, *132, 277, 309, 455*
Cabourg, *235, 246*
Cabrerets, *479*
Caen, *235, 246–247*
Café Beaubourg, *83*
Café de la Bourse, *221*
Café de Flore, *94*
Café des Federations, *361*
Café du Palais, *266*
Café de Paris (Biarritz), *509*
Cagnes-sur-Mer, *412–413*
Cahors, *469, 479–480*
Calais, *261–262, 273*
Calenzana, *442*
Calvi, *442–443, 452–453*
Camargue, *375*
Cambrai, *269*
Canadian travelers, *9, 11*
Cancale, *207, 218*
Cannes, *408, 427–428*
Canoeing, *477*
Cap d'Antibes, *409*

Cap Corse peninsula, 448

Caradeuc, 204

Carcassonne, 476, 480–481

Carnac, 211

Carrefour de Buci (Paris), 92

Cars. *See* Automobiles

Casinos, 222, 251, 277, 514

in Monte Carlo, 421

on Riviera, 434

Cassaigne, 472

Cassis, 388–389

Castéra-Verduzan, 481

Catacombes, Les (Paris), 103

Cateau-Cambrésis, Le, 269

Cathedrals

American Cathedral of the Holy Trinity (Paris), 87

Ancienne (St-Pol-del-Leon), 208

of Angoulême, 495–496

architecture of, 55–56

of Arènes, 373

of Autun, 321

of Avignon, 395

Chartres, 144

on Corsica, 444

of Fréjus, 407

of Marseille, 387

of Nancy, 297

Notre-Dame (Amiens), 258

Notre-Dame (Bayeux), 237

Notre-Dame (Eveux), 227

Notre-Dame (Laon), 265

Notre-Dame (Paris), 81

Notre-Dame (Reims), 266

Notre-Dame (Rodez), 466–467

Notre-Dame (Rouen), 227, 230

Notre-Dame (Senlis), 152

Notre-Dame (Strasbourg), 382–383

Notre-Dane-dy-Puy, 357

Primatiale St-Jean (Lyon), 341

St-André (Bordeaux), 502

St-Apollinaire (Valance), 352

St-Corentin (Quimper), 210

Ste-Croix (Orléans), 183–184

St-Eloi (Noyon), 264

Ste-Marie (Auch), 470–471

of Saintes, 494

St-Etienne (Bourges), 328–329

St-Etienne (Cahors), 469

St-Etienne (Châlons-sur-Marne), 268

St-Etienne (Metz), 296

St-Etienne (Pontigny), 319

St-Etienne (Sens), 313

St-Etienne (Toulouse), 465

St-Front (Périgueux), 500

St-Gatien (Tours), 176

St-Louis (Versailles), 142

of St-Maclou (Pontoise), 150

St-Maurice (Angers), 171

St-Maurice (Vienne), 351

St-Pierre (Beauvais), 258

St-Pierre (Lisieux), 234

St-Pierre (Nantes), 213

St-Pierre (Poiters), 490

St-Pierre (Rennes), 203

St-Pierre (Vannes), 212

St-Pierre St-Paul (Troyes), 315

St-Samson (Dol-de-Bretagne), 204

St-Sauveur (Aix-en-Provence), 385

St-Vaast (Arras), 259

St-Vulfran's Abbeville, 263

of Sarlat, 499

of Toul, 297

of Vence, 412

of Verdun, 296

Caudebec-en-Caux, 232

Cauria, 446–447

Cauterets, 474

Caveau de la Huchette (Paris), 133

Caveau des Oubliettes (Paris), 132

Centre National d'Art et de Culture Georges Pompidou (Beaubourg; Paris), 82–83

Centuri, 453

Chaalis, 152–153

Chablis, 319

Chagny, 333

Châlons-sur-Marne, 268, 273

Chalon-sur-Saône, 327

Chambery, 355

Chambord, 182, 186, 191

Chamonix, 356, 359

Champagne, 253–277

arts and entertainment in, 277

Champagne Country, 263–268

children's activities, 269

dining and lodging in, 271–276

North France and, 255–263

shopping in, 270

sports, 270–271

tours and sightseeing in, 254–269

transportation to and in, 254

Champigny-sur-Veude, 187

Champs-Elysées (Paris), 86–87

Chantilly, 151–152, 161

Chapelle de Martyre (Paris), 99

Chapelle Royale de St-Louis, 145–146

Charité-sur-Loire, La, 322

Charles de Gaulle (Roissy) Airport, 67, 136

Charter flights, 22

Chartres, 144–145, 161–162

Château (Angers), 172

Château-Chinon, 321

Château de Corcelles, 348

Château de Gaillard, 227

Château des Ducs de Bretagne, 213

Châteaudun, 187

Châteauneuf-du-Pape, 382

Château de Serrant, 187

Château-Theirry, 269

Chaumont-sur-Loire, 191–192

Chenonceaux, 179, 192

Children's activities

in Alsace-Lorraine, 301

on Atlantic Coast, 506

in Brittany, 214–215

in Burgundy, 328

in Champagne, 269

on Corsica, 448

Haut Vivarais Safari Park, 351–352

in Ile de France, 157

Jardin a l'Anglaise (Thoiry), 148

in Loire Valley, 186

in Lyon and the Alps, 356

in Normandy, 241

in Paris, 102–103

in Provence, 390

on Riviera, 422–423

in Toulouse and Midi-Pyrénées, 475

travel with, 17–19

Chinon, 173–174, 192

Churches, *See also* Cathedrals

architecture of, 55–56

Circuses, 102–103

Cité des Sciences et de l'Industrie de la Villette (Paris), 103

Clairère de
l'Armistice, *264*
Clamecy, *322, 333*
Clécy, *240*
Clermont-Ferrand,
357
Climate, *4*
Clothing
to bring, *6–7*
shopping for, *115,
329, 357, 424*
Club 79 (Paris), *132*
Club Zed (Paris), *133*
Cluny, *333*
Cognac, *494–495,
510–511*
Colmar, *304–305*
Colonne de Juillet
(Paris), *85*
Combourg, *204*
Comédie-Francaise
(Paris), *79*
Compiègne, *264, 273*
Concarneau,
210–211, 218–219
Conciergerie (Paris),
81
Condom, *471–472*
Conflans-Sainte-
Honorine, *150*
Conques, *467*
Corbara, *442*
Cordes, *465, 481*
Correrie, La, *354*
Corsica, *436–455*
Ajaccio, *443–445*
Alèria, *446–448*
arts and
entertainment on,
454–455
beaches, *449–450*
children's activities,
448
dining and lodging on,
450–455
northern coast of,
439–443
shopping on, *448–449*
sports on, *449*
tours and sightseeing
on, *438–448*
transportation to and
on, *437–438*
Corte, *443, 453*
Costs, *8–9*
Coulon, *491–492, 511*
Council on
International
Educational
Exchange (CIEE),

16–17, 22
Council Travel, *16–17*
Cour Carré (Paris),
78
Cour-Cheverny, *181*
Credit cards, *7–8, 33*
Cruises, *23–24*
Crystal Piano Bar,
La, *492*
Cunard Line, *24*
Currency, *8*
Customs and duties,
10–11

Dambach-la-Ville,
290
Dampierre, *142*
Dance, *132, 483*
David, Jean-Pierre,
171
Dax, *505*
Deauville, *234–235,
247*
Department stores,
111
Dieppe, *233–234, 247*
Dijon, *323–324, 334*
Dinan, *205–206, 219*
Dinard, *206–207, 219*
Dining. See also
Restaurants
French cooking, *48–53*
French wines, *59–65*
Disabled travelers,
19–20
Discos
in Alsace-Lorraine,
309
on Atlantic Coast, *513*
in Brittany, *222*
In Champagne, *277*
in Lyon, *365*
in Paris, *133*
on Riviera, *434*
Dol-de-Bretagne,
204–205, 219
Domme, *506, 511*
Dordogne, *496–500*
Douarnenez, *209*
Dreux, *145–146, 162*
Duclair, *247*
Duties, *10–11*

Ecole Nationale des
Beaux-Arts (Paris),
93
Ecouen, *157–158*
Educational Travel
Center, *17*
Eglise du Dome

(Paris), *90*
Eglise Jeanne d'Arc
(Rouen), *231*
Eglise de la
Madeleine (Paris),
88
Eglise Notre-Dame
(Versailles), *142*
Eglise St-Aignan
(Chartres), *145*
Eglise St-Maclou
(Rouen), *230*
Eglise St-Pierre
(Chartes), *145*
Eglise de la
Sorbonne (Paris), *95*
Eglise La Trinité
(Fécamp), *248*
Eiffel Tower (Paris),
90
Elderhostel, *20*
Elderly travelers,
20–21, 27
Embassies, *69*
Emergency telephone
numbers, *72*
English language, *12*
Entertainment
in Alsace-Lorraine,
308–309
on Atlantic Coast, *513*
in Brittany, *222*
in Burgundy, *328*
in Champagne, *277*
on Corsica, *454–455*
in Ile de France, *165*
in Loire Valley, *195*
in Lyon and the Alps,
364–365
in Normandy, *251*
in Paris, *131–132*
in Provence, *399*
on Riviera, *433–434*
in Toulouse and
Midi-Pyrénées,
483–484
Epernay, *268*
Ermenonville, *161*
Etretat, *233, 247–248*
EurailPass, *15*
Eurolines (bus
travel), *25*
Eveux, *226–227*
Evian-les-Bains, *355*
Eyzies, Les, *511*
Eyzies-de-Tayac,
499–500
Eze, *418, 428–429*

Fécamp, *248*

Fermont, *295*
Festivals, *5–6*
in Burgundy, *336*
on Corsica, *454–455*
in Lyon and the Alps,
364
in Loire Valley, *195*
in Normandy, *251*
on Riviera, *433*
Figeac, *467–468*
Filitosa, *446*
Films
in Normandy, *251*
in Paris, *132*
Fishing, *188, 477*
Fitness centers,
115–116
Folgoët, Le, *208*
Folies-Bergère
(Paris), *132*
Fontainebleau, *154,
162*
Fontaine-de-Vaucluse,
383
Fontenay, *320*
Fontevraud, *173*
Fontvielle, *378*
Fortress of Largoet,
215
Fort of Six-Fours,
390
Forum des Halles
(Paris), *80*
Fougères, *202*
France
cooking of, *48–53*
history of, *42–47*
Free activities,
101–102
Fréjus, *407*
French cooking,
48–53
French Government
Tourist Offices, *2*
French language, *12*
French National
Railways (SNFC),
15–16, 26–27
children on, *19*
French wines, *59–65*

Gaillac, *465*
Gardens, See Parks
and gardens
Gassin, *407*
Gavarnie, *474*
Germigny, *185*
Gers, *470–472*
Gimont, *470*
Giverny, *146–147*

Glass pyramid
(Paris), *78*
Golf, *159, 242, 271,
358, 392, 424, 507*
Gordes, *384, 396*
Gouffre de Padirac,
475–476
Grande Motte, La,
374
**Grand Hôtel des
Beaux-Arts**, *361–362*
**Grand Hôtel de Cala
Rossa**, *447*
**Grand Hôtel de
l'Opera**, *482*
**Grand Hôtel de la
Reine**, *306*
Grand Palais (Paris),
87
Grand Trianon, *139*
Grasse, *410–411, 429*
Grenoble, *353–356*
Grottes de Niaux, *476*
Grotto of Lascaux,
500
Guebwiller, *292–293*
Gué-Péan, *186*
Guided tours, *See*
Tours and
sightseeing

**Handicapped
travelers**, *19–20*
Harry's Bar (Paris),
132
Hautefort, *500*
Hauterives, *356–357,
360–362*
Haut-Koenigsbourg,
290–291
Hautvillers, *268*
**Haut Vivarais Safari
Park**, *351–352*
Havre, Le, *232–233*
Health, *12–13*
Health insurance, *13*
Hiking, *159, 188,
243, 303, 329, 392,
449, 477*
Hirtzbach, *305*
**Historic sites and
houses**. *See also*
Monuments
in Amboise, *179–180*
architecture and,
54–58
Bastille, *85*
Clairère de
l'Armistice, *264*
Eiffel Tower, *90*

in Paris, *73–82*
in Verdun, *295–296*
Versailles, *138–142*
History of France,
42–47
Holidays, *4–5*
Home exchanges, *18*
Honfleur, *234,
248–249*
Horseback riding
in Alsace-Lorraine,
303
in Brittany, *217*
in Burgundy, *329–330*
in Champagne, *271*
on Corsica, *449*
in Ile de France, *159*
in Loire Valley, *188*
in Lyon and the Alps,
358
in Normandy, *243*
in Provence, *369, 392*
on Riviera, *424*
in Toulouse and
Midi-Pyrénées, *477*
Hospitaliers, Les, *362*
Hospitals, *72*
Hôtel de Berny, *258*
Hôtel Carnavalet, *84*
Hôtel Crillon, *88*
Hôtel des Invalides,
90
Hôtel des Monnaies
(national mint,
Paris), *92*
Hôtel de Montmor,
83
Hôtel Negresco, *415*
Hotels. *See*
Accommodations
Hôtel de Sens, *85*
Hôtel de Ville
(Paris), *82*
Hôtel de Ville
(Ramouillet), *143*
Hugo, Victor, *232*

Ile de la Cité (Paris),
73, 80
Ile de France,
135–165
accommodations in,
159–165
arts and
entertainment in, *165*
children's activities in,
157
Fontainebleau,
153–156
restaurants in,

159–165
St-Germain-en-Laye
and Chantilly,
148–153
shopping in, *158*
sports and fitness in,
159
transportation in,
136–137
Versailles, Chartres,
Giverny and Thoiry,
138–148
Ile-d'Oléron, *493*
Ile de Porquerolles,
396
Ile de Ré, *492*
Ile St-Louis (Paris),
86
Iles de Lérins, *408*
**Information Center
for Individuals with
Disabilities**, *20*
Information sources
for Alsace-Lorraine,
281
for Atlantic Coast,
486–487
for Brittany, *197–198*
for Burgundy,
311–312
for Champagne,
253–254
for Corsica, *437*
for Ile de France, *136*
for Loire Valley, *167*
for Lyon and the
Alps, *338–339*
for Normandy, *224*
for Paris, *69*
for Provence, *368*
reading materials,
21–22
for Riviera, *401*
for Toulouse and
Midi-Pyrénées, *457*
Institut de France
(Paris), *93*
**Institute for
International Travel
(IEE)**, *17*
Insurance, *13–14*
**International
Association for
Medical Assistance
to Travelers
(IAMAT)**, *13*
**International Driving
Permit**, *14*
**International
Express** (bus travel),

26
**International
Student Identity
Card**, *16*
**International
telephone calls**, *29*
**International Youth
Hostels**, *16*
Isle-Adam, L', *151,
162–163*
**Isle-sur-la-Sorgue,
L'**, *383*

Jardin. . . . *See* Parks
and gardens
Jarnac, *495*
Jazz clubs, *133, 222,
309, 483–484, 513*
Jeu de Paume
(Paris), *88*
Jogging, *116*
Josselin, *215*
Juan-les-Pins, *409,
426*
Jumièges, *232*

Kerjean, *208*

Languages, *12*
Lanquais, *498*
Laon, *264–265,
274*
Lapin Agile, Le
(bar-cabaret), *100,
133*
Latin Quarter
(Paris), *91–92,
132–133*
Leasing cars, *15*
Lectoure, *471*
Left Bank (Paris),
89–90, 91–96, 110
Lewarde, *260*
Libourne, *496*
Libraries
Bibliothèque Forney,
85
Bibliothèque
Humaniste
(Sèlestate), *290*
Bibliothèque
Nationale, *80*
Lille, *260–261, 274*
Limoges, *506*
Lisieux, *234*
Loches, *179–180*
Lodging. *See*
Accommodations
Logis Royaux
(Loches), *180*

Loire Valley, *167–195*
arts and
  entertainment in, *195*
children's activities in,
  186
dining and lodging in,
  189–195
Eastern, *178–186*
shopping in, *187–188*
sports in, *188*
tours and sightseeing
  in, *168–187*
transportation in, *168*
Western, *169–178*
Longuyon, *305*
Lorraine, *294–301*
  See also
  Alsace-Lorraine
Lost luggage, *13*
Lourdes, *473–474*
Louviers, *227*
Louvre (Paris), *78–79*
Luggage, *7*
lost, *13*
Lyon, *338–365. See*
  also Alps
arts and
  entertainment in,
  364–365
children's activities in,
  356
dining and lodging in,
  358–364
shopping in, *357–358*
sports in, *358*
tours and sightseeing
  in, *339–356*
transportation to and
  in, *339*

Mâcon, *328*
Mail, *29*
Maintenon, *144, 163*
Maisons-Laffitte, *150*
**Maison de Victor
  Hugo** (Paris), *85*
Malaucène, *383*
Malmaison, La, *101*
Mantes-la-Jolie, *147*
Marais (Paris), *82–83*
Marais, Le, *158*
Marais Poitevin, *491*
Marché aux Fleurs
  (Paris), *82*
Margaux, *503*
Markets, *111, 114,*
  424
Marlenheim, *288*
Marseille, *384–390,*
  396–397

Médan, *157*
Médoc, *503*
Memorials. *See*
  Monuments
Menton, *422, 429*
Mercier (Epernay),
  268
Métro (Paris
  subway), *68–69*
Metz, *296–297,*
  305–306
Meung-sur-Loire,
  183, 185, 192–193
Midi-Pyrénées,
  457–484
Albi, Rocamadour and
  Montauban, *465–470*
arts and
  entertainment in,
  483–484
children's activities in,
  475
dining and lodging in,
  477–482
Gers, *470–472*
Pyrénées, *472–475*
shopping in, *476–477*
sports in, *477*
Toulouse and, *460–465*
tours and sightseeing
  in, *458–475*
transportation to and
  in, *458*
**Mirapolis
  Amusement Park**
  (Cergy), *157*
Missillac, *212*
Moint Ste-Odile, *289*
Moissac, *470*
Monaco, *418–419*
Monbazillac, *498*
Monet, Claude,
  146–147
Monpazier, *498*
Montauban, *469*
Montbazon, *193*
Monte Carlo,
  419–421, 429–430
Montélimar, *353, 362*
Montemaggiore, *442*
Montmarte (Paris),
  97–100
Montmarte cemetery
  (Paris), *97*
Montmuran, *204*
Montpellier, *373–374,*
  397
Montreuil-Bellay, *173*
Montreuil-sur-Mer,

  263
Mont St-Eloi, *260*
Mont-St-Michel,
  238–239, 249–250
Monuments
in Amiens, *259*
des Bourgeois de
  Calais, *262*
at Brest, *209*
in Carnac, *211*
Mont-St-Michel,
  238–239
to Normandy
  invasion, *238*
Vimy Ridge, *260*
Moret-sur-Loing, *156*
Morlaix, *207–208,*
  219–220
Mosquée, La (Paris),
  96
Mougins, *410, 430*
Moulin de la Galette
  (Paris), *97*
Moulin Rouge
  (Paris), *97, 132*
Mulhouse, *293–294*
Museums
in Aix-en-Provence,
  385–386
in Alençon, *240–241*
in Angers, *171, 172*
in Annonay, *352*
in Antibes, *409*
Archives Nationales,
  83–84
in Arènes, *372–373*
in Arles, *376–377*
in Arras, *259*
Auberge du Pere
  Ganne, *154*
automotive, *180–181,*
  241, 293
in Autun, *321*
in Avignon, *395*
Balzac museum, *175*
in Bastia, *439, 441*
in Bayeux, *236–237*
in Beauvais, *255, 258*
in Blois, *182*
in Boersch, *288*
in Bordeaux, *502*
in Brest, *209*
in Calais, *262*
Centre National d'Art
  et de Culture
  Georges Pompidou
  (Beaubourg), *82–83*
in Chalon-sur-Saône,
  327
in Chantilly, *152*

in Chartres, *146*
for children, *103*
Cocteau Museum, *422*
in Cognac, *495*
in Colmar, *304*
in Compiègne, *264*
in Condom, *471–472*
in Conques, *467*
on Corsica, *439, 441*
in Dijon, *324, 326*
in Dinard, *206*
in Eyzies-de-Tayac,
  499–500
of Folklore, *321–322*
Fondation Maeght,
  412
in Fougères, *202*
of Gastronmy, *148*
in Grasse, *411*
in Grenoble, *356*
in Guebwiller, *293*
in Le Havre, *232, 233*
Hôtel et Musée de
  Cluny, *95*
in Lille, *261*
Louvre, *78–79*
in Lyon, *344, 347–348*
in Marseille, *386–388*
in Metz, *296–297*
Mining Museum, *260*
in Montauban, *469*
in Monte Carlo, *421,*
  422
in Montpellier, *374*
in Moret-sur-Loing,
  156
in Morlaix, *236*
**Musée des Antiquités
  National,** *149*
Musée de l'Armée,
  90
Musée le l'Art Juif,
  100
**Musée de la Bataille
  de Normandie,** *237*
**Musée de la
  Bénédictine,** *233*
**Musée Bricard de la
  Surrure,** *84*
**Musée de
  Debarquement,** *238*
**Musée des
  Equipages,** *152–154*
**Musée Eugène
  Delacroix,** *93*
**Musée de la Folie
  Marco,** *289*
Musée Guimet, *91*
**Musée de l'Histoire
  de Paris,** *84*

Musée Historique, *149*

Musée Lambinet, *142*

Musée de la Mode et Costume, *91*

Musée Monétaire, *92–93*

Musée Notre-Dame, *82*

Musée d'Orsay, *89*

Musée de la Pêche, *200*

Musée Picasso, *84*

Musée des Plans-Reliefs, *90*

Musée Poulain, *146*

Musée du Prieuré, *149–150*

Musée Rodin, *89–90*

Musée Victor Hugo, *232*

Musée du Vieux Montmarte, *100*

in Nancy, *298–299, 300–301*

in Nantes, *213*

in Nevers, *322*

in Nice, *415–416*

in Niort, *491*

opening and closing times for, *30*

Opéra museum, *89*

in Orléans, *184–185*

in Palais de Chaillot, *90–91*

in Pau, *473*

in Poitiers, *490*

in Quimper, *209*

in Reims, *266*

in Rennes, *203*

in La Rochelle, *492*

in Rodez, *402*

in Rouen, *231*

in St-Jean-Cap-Ferrat, *467*

in St-Malo, *207*

in St-Rémy de Provence, *379*

in Saumur, *172*

in Strasbourg, *283, 286*

in Toul, *297*

in Toulouse, *461, 464, 467*

in Tournon, *352*

in Tours, *177*

in Troyes, *316–317*

in Ungersheim, *293*

in Valance, *352*

in Versailles, *142*

Music

in Alsace-Lorraine, *308*

on Corsica, *454–455*

in Lyon, *364*

in Normandy, *251*

in Paris, *131–132*

in Provence, *399*

on Riviera, *433*

in Toulouse and Midi-Pyrénées, *483*

Nancy, *297–298, 306*

Nantes, *212–213, 220*

Napoule, La, *407, 430–431*

National Council of Senior Citizens, *21*

Nevers, *322*

New Morning (Paris), *133*

Nice, *413–417, 430–431*

Nightclubs

in Alsace-Lorraine, *309*

in Brittany, *222*

in Champagne, *276*

in Loire Valley, *195*

in Lyon, *365*

in Normandy, *251*

in Paris, *132–133*

on Riviera, *434*

in Toulouse, *484*

Nightlife, *See* Entertainment

Nimes, *370–380, 398*

Niort, *491*

Normandy, *224–251*

arts and entertainment in, *251*

beaches, *242*

Calvados Coast and Mont-St-Michel, *234–239*

children's activities in, *241*

dining and lodging in, *243–251*

shopping in, *241–242*

sports in, *242–243*

Suisse Normandie, *239–241*

tours and sightseeing in, *225–241*

transportation to and in, *225*

Upper Normandy, *226–234*

Normandy, Battle of, *238*

Notre-Dame, Cathedral of (Paris), *81–82*

Notre-Dame, Cathedral of (Senlis), *152*

Notre-Dame (church, Mantes-la-Jolie), *147*

Notre-Dame (church, Vernon), *146*

Nouveau Monde des Schtroumpfs (theme park), *301*

Novotel (hotel chain), *18*

Noyon, *264, 274*

Obernai, *288*

Océanopolis (Brest), *209*

Odenas, *348*

O. K. Corral (amusement park), *390*

Older travelers, *20–21, 27*

Omaha Beach, *238*

Opéra (Paris), *89, 131–132*

Opera, *131–132, 277, 433, 513*

Orange, *398*

Orangerie (Paris), *88*

Orge Valley, *158*

Orléans, *183–185, 193–194*

Orly Airport, *67, 136*

Ottrott, *306*

Palais Bourbon (Paris), *89*

Palais de Chaillot (Paris), *90*

Palais Dobrée, *242*

Palais de l'Elyseés (Paris), *87*

Palais Galliera (Paris), *91*

Palais Idéal, *356–357*

Palais de Justice (Paris), *81*

Palais de la Mutualité, *96*

Palais Royal (Paris), *79*

Palais Synodal (Sens), *315*

Panthéon (Paris), *95*

Parc des Oiseaux (Villars-les-Dombes), *349–350*

Paris, *67–133*

accommodations in, *125–131*

Arc de Triomphe to Opéra walking tour of, *86–89*

architecture of, *56*

arts in, *131–132*

cemeteries, *110*

children's activities in, *102–103*

churches, *107–109*

free activities in, *101–102*

historic buildings and sites, *104*

historic heart walking tour of, *73–82*

Left Bank walking tour of, *91–96*

Marais and Ile St-Louis walking tour of, *82–86*

Montmartre walking tour of, *97–100*

museums and galleries, *105–107*

nightlife in, *132–133*

Orsay to Trocadero walking tour of, *89–91*

parks and gardens, *109–110*

restaurants in, *116–124*

Rueil-Malmaison, excursion to, *101*

shopping in, *110–115*

sports in, *115–116*

tours and sightseeing in, *72–100*

transportation to and within, *67–69*

Park Astérix (theme park), *157*

Parks and gardens

in Arènes, *372*

in Arles, *379*

Buttes-Chaumont (Paris), *109*

in Chantilly, *151–152*

in Chartes, *145*

in Dinan, *205*

in Giverny, *148*

Jardin du Luxembourg (Paris), *94*

Jardin des Plantes

Parks and gardens
(continued)
(Paris), *96*
Jardin des Plantes
(Paris), *96*
Jardin Thuret, *410*
Jardin des Tuileries
(Paris), *109*
in Lyon, *345, 346–347*
in Montpellier, *374*
in Orléans, *186*
in Palais Royal, *79*
Parc de la Colline
St-Eutrope, *382–383*
in Provins, *156*
in Thoiry, *148*
in Toulouse, *465*
in Vendôme, *186*
in Versailles, *139*
Passavant-la-Rochère,
301
Passports and visas,
9–10
Patrimonio, *441*
Pau, *472–473*
Pavillon de l'Horloge
(Paris), *78*
Peillon, *418*
Pen pals, *19*
Perfume, *115*
Périgueux, *500*
Périgord, *496–500*
Perogues, *350, 362*
Personal guides
in Champagne, *255*
in Ile de France, *137*
in Loire Valley, *169*
in Normandy, *226*
in Paris, *73*
Petit Opportun, Le
(Paris), *133*
Petit Palais (Paris),
87
Petit Trianon, *139*
Photography, *11–12*
Piana, *453*
Picasso Museum
(Paris), *84*
Pierrefonds, *263–264,*
274–275
Place des Abbesses
(Paris), *97*
Place André-Malraux
(Paris), *79*
Place de la Bastille
(Paris), *85*
Place Blanche
(Paris), *97*
Place de la Concorde
(Paris), *88*

Place Jean-Baptiste
Celement, *99*
Place des Pyramides
(Paris), *79*
Place St-Michel
(Paris), *92*
Place du Terte
(Paris), *99*
Place Vendôme,
88–89
Place des Victoires
(Paris), *80*
Plessis-Bourré, *172*
Poitiers, *490, 511–512*
Poitou-Charentes,
488–496
Pont-Aven, *220*
Ponte Leccia, *443*
Pont du Gard, *370*
Pontigny, *318–319*
Pont Neuf (Paris), *78*
Pontoise, *150*
Pont d'Ouilly, *240*
Port-Grimaud,
406–407
Porticcio, *453–454*
Porto-Vecchio, *447,*
454
Postal service, *29*
Privas, *362*
Provence, *367–399*
arts and
entertainment in, *399*
children's activities in,
390
dining and lodging in,
392–399
Marseille, *384–390*
Nîmes and Camargue,
370–380
shopping in, *391*
sports in, *391–392*
tours and sightseeing
in, *369–390*
transportation to and
in, *368–369*
Vaucluse, *380–384*
Provins, *156, 163*
Puppet shows, *103*
Puy, Le, *357*
Pyrénées, *472–475*
See also
Midi-Pyrénées

Quartier de
L'Horloge (Paris),
83
Quimper, *209*

Rabodanges, *240*

Railroads
in Alsace-Lorraine,
280
on Atlantic Coast, *487*
in Brittany, *198*
in Burgundy, *312*
in Champagne, *254*
from Charles de
Gaulle (Roissy)
Airport, *67*
children on, *19*
on Corsica, *437–438*
within France, *26–27*
from Great Britain to
France, *25*
in Ile de France, *136*
in Loire Valley, *168*
in Lyon and the Alps,
339
métro (Paris subway),
68–69
to and in Normandy,
197
to Paris, *68*
in Provence, *368, 369*
rail passes for, *15–16*
on Riviera, *402*
in Toulouse and
Midi-Pyrénées, *458*
Ramatuelle, *407*
Rambouillet, *143, 163*
Reading materials on
France, *21–22*
Redon, *212*
Reims, *265–268, 275*
Rennes, *203–204,*
220–221
Rentals
cars, *14–15, 136, 168,*
198, 339, 368, 380,
458, 487
villas, *18–33*
Restaurants, *31–32*
in Alsace-Lorraine,
303–308
on Atlantic Coast,
507–513
in Brittany, *217–222*
in Burgundy, *330–336*
in Champagne,
271–276
on Corsica, *450–455*
in Ile de France,
159–165
in Loire Valley,
189–195
in Lyon and the Alps,
358–364
in Normandy,
243–251

in Paris, *116–124*
in Provence, *392–399*
on Riviera, *425–433*
tipping in, *29–30*
in Toulouse and
Midi-Pyrénées,
477–482
Rhône Valley,
350–353
Riems, *275*
Right Bank (Paris),
111
Riviera, *401–434*
arts and
entertainment on,
433–434
beaches, *425*
children's activities
on, *422–423*
dining and lodging on,
425–433
dining and lodging on,
425–433
Grasse to Menton,
410–422
St-Tropez to Antibes,
403–410
shopping on, *424*
sports, *424*
tours and sightseeing
in, *402–422*
transportation to and
in, *402*
Rivière Souterraine,
476
Rocamadour,
468–469
Rochefort-en-Terre,
215
Roche-Guyon, La,
147
Rochelle, La, *492,*
512
Rock climbing, *159,*
207, 221, 243
Rodez, *466–467*
Roque-Gageac, La,
499
Rosheim, *288*
Rôtisserie de
l'Abbaye, La (Paris),
133
Rouen, *227, 250*
Roussillon, *384*
Royal Viking Line,
24
Royan, *493*
Rue du Faubourg
St-Honoré (Paris),
87

Rueil-Malmaison,
101
Rue Visconti (Paris),
93
Rue Yvonne-le-Tac
(Paris), *97, 99*

Saché, *175*
St-Benoit-sur-Loire,
185
St-Cloud, *148–149*
Sainte Chapelle
(Paris), *81*
Ste-Marguerite, *408*
St-Emilion, *496–497,*
512
Saintes, *494*
Saintes-Maries-de-
la-Mer, *375*
St-Eustache, church
of (Paris), *80*
St-Florent, *441*
St-Germain-des-Pres
(church, Paris), *93*
St-Germain-en-Laye,
149–150, 163–164
St-Germain-
l'Auxerrois, church
of (Paris), *78*
St-Gervais-St.-Protais,
church of (Paris), *85*
St-Honorat, *409*
St-Jean-Cap-Ferrat,
418
St-Julien-le-Pauvre,
church of (Paris), *96*
St.-Laurent, church
of
(Beaumont-sur-Oise),
151
St-Lô, *238*
St-Malo, *207, 221*
St-Omer, *261,*
275–276
St-Paul-de-Vence,
412, 431–432
St-Pierre, church of
(Senlis), *152*
St-Pol-del-Léon, *208*
St-Quirace (church
Provins), *156*
St-Raphaël, *407*
St-Rémy-de-Provence,
379, 398–399
St-Roch, church of
(Paris), *79*
St-Savin, *488*
St-Séverin, church of
(Paris), *95–96*
St-Tropez, *403–406,*

432–433
St-Vincent Cemetery
(Paris), *100*
St-Wandrille, *232*
Sanary, *389*
Santa Giulia, *454*
Sarlat, *499, 513*
Sartène, *446*
Saulieu, *320*
Saumur, *172, 194*
Sauternes, *502–503*
Saverne, *288*
Seasonal events, *5–6*
in Loire Valley, *195*
Sélestat, *290*
Senior citizens,
20–21
rail fare discounts for,
27
Senlis, *152, 164*
Sens, *313–315, 335*
Serrières, *351–352,*
363
Service charges
(tips), *9*
Ships, *23–24*
Shooting, *188*
Shopping, *30*
in Alsace-Lorraine,
302–304
on Atlantic Coast,
506–507
in Brittany, *216*
in Burgundy, *329*
in Champagne, *270*
on Corsica, *448–449*
in Ile de France, *158*
in Loire Valley,
187–188
in Lyon and the Alps,
357–358
in Normandy,
241–242
in Paris, *110–115*
in Provence, *391*
on Riviera, *424*
in Toulouse and
Midi-Pyrénées,
476–477
Sightseeing. *See*
Tours and
sightseeing
Skiing, *303, 358, 477*
Society for the
Advancement of
Travel for the
Handicapped, *20*
Son-et-lumière, *195*
Sorbonne (Paris), *95*
Soulac-sur-Mer, *504*

Special-interest
tours, *3*
of Atlantic Coast, *488*
in Burgundy, *312*
in Champagne, *255*
in Loire Valley,
168–169
in Lyon and the Alps,
339–340
in Normandy, *226*
in Paris, *72*
in Provence, *369*
on Riviera, *402*
Sports, *30–31*
in Alsace-Lorraine,
303
on Atlantic Coast, *507*
in Brittany, *216–217*
in Burgundy, *329–330*
in Champagne,
270–271
on Corsica, *449*
in Ile de France, *159*
in Loire Valley, *188*
in Lyon and the Alps,
358
in Normandy,
242–243
in Paris, *115–116*
in Provence, *391–392*
on Riviera, *424*
in Toulouse and
Midi-Pyrénées, *477*
Square du Vert
Galant (Paris),
73–74
Strasbourg, *281–288,*
307
Struthof, Le, *294*
Struthof, Le, *294*
Students, *16–17*
Studio 28 (Paris), *97*
Suisse Normandie
(Swiss Normandy),
239–241
Sully, *321*
Swimming, *159, 358*

Tabou jazz club
(Paris), *92*
Tanlay, *319–320*
Tarascon, *379–380*
Taxes, *9*
Taxis, *67, 69*
Telephones, *28–29*
Tennis, *116*
Thann, *294*
Theater
in Alsace-Lorraine,
308

on Atlantic Coast, *513*
in Brittany, *222*
in Champagne, *277*
in Lyon, *345, 364*
in Paris, *131*
in Provence, *377, 382,*
399
on Riviera, *433*
in Toulouse, *483*
Théâtre Libre
(Paris), *97*
Thoiry, *147, 164*
Thonon-les-Bains,
355
Thury-Harcourt, *240*
Tipping, *29–30*
Tonnerre, *319*
Toul, *297, 307–308*
Toulon, *389*
Toulouse, *457–484*
arts and
entertainment in,
483–484
dining and lodging in,
477–482
tours and sightseeing
in, *458–475*
transportation to and
in, *458*
Touquet, Le, *263, 276*
Tourette-sur-Loup,
411–412
Tour
Maine-Montparnasse
(Paris), *94*
Tournon, *352, 363*
Tournus, *327*
Tours (city), *176, 194*
Tours and
sightseeing, *2–3*
in Alsace-Lorraine,
281–302
of Atlantic Coast,
487–505
in Brittany, *198–216*
in Burgundy, *312–328*
in Champagne,
254–269
on Corsica, *449*
in Ile de France, *137*
in Loire Valley,
168–169
in Lyon and the Alps,
339–356
in Normandy,
225–241
in Paris, *72–73*
in Provence, *369–390*
on Riviera, *402–422*
in Toulouse and

**Tours and sight-
seeing** *(continued)*
Midi-Pyrénées,
458–475
Trains. *See* Railroads
Transportation
air travel, *22–24*
in Alsace-Lorraine,
280
on Atlantic Coast,
487
to and within
Brittany, *198*
to and in Burgundy,
312
to and within
Champagne, *254*
for children, *18–19*
to and on Corsica,
437–438
within France,
26–28
in Ile de France, *136*
in Loire Valley, *168*
in Lyon and the Alps,
339
to and within
Normandy, *225*
to and within Paris,
67–69
to and within

Provence, *368–369*
rail passes for, *15–16*
renting and leasing
cars, *14–15*
to and on Riviera,
402
by ship, *23–24*
to and within
Toulouse and
Midi-Pyrénées, *458*
Travel clubs, *23*
Traveler's checks,
7–8
Traveler's diarrhea,
12
**Travel Industry and
Disabled Exchange,**
20
Treasury (Paris),
82
**Trip cancellation
insurance,** *13*
Trouville, *234–235,
251*
Troyes, *315, 335*
TWYCH (Travel with
Your Children), *17*

Ungersheim, *293*

Vaison-la-Romaine,

383
Valance, *352, 363*
Valençay, *180, 194*
Vallauris, *409*
Vallée d'Auge, *241*
Vannes, *212, 221*
Varengeville-sur-Mer,
233
Vaucluse, *380–384*
Vaux-le-Vicomte,
153
Vence, *412, 433*
Vendôme, *186*
Ventimiglia, *423*
Verdun, *295–296, 308*
Vernon, *146, 164, 250*
Versailles, *138–148,
164–165*
Vézelay, *323,
335–336*
Vienne, *350–351, 363*
Villandry, *175, 195*
Villa rentals, *18, 33*
Ville Close, *210*
**Villefranche-sur-
Saône,** *348*
Villa Morte, *378*
Villeneuve-Loubet,
413
**Villeon, Emmanuel
de La,** *202*

Villequier, *232*
Vimy Ridge, *260*
Visas, *9–10*
Vitré, *199, 202–222*
Vonnas, *364*
Vougeot, *326*

Water sports, *188,
216, 243, 263, 270,
392, 424, 449, 507*
on Riviera, *424*
Western Union, *8*
Wines, *59–65*

Youth hostels, *16*
**Youth International
Educational
Exchange Card,** *16*
Youth travel, *16–17*

Zoos and aquariums
Haut Vivarais Safari
Park, *351–352*
in Loire Valley, *186*
Marineland, *410*
in Normandy, *241*
Parc Ornithologique,
375–376
in Paris, *103*
Sarlat Aquarium, *506*
in Thoiry, *148*

Personal Itinerary

Departure *Date*

Time

Transportation

Arrival *Date*   *Time*

Departure *Date*   *Time*

Transportation

Accommodations

Arrival *Date*   *Time*

Departure *Date*   *Time*

Transportation

Accommodations

Arrival *Date*   *Time*

Departure *Date*   *Time*

Transportation

Accommodations

Personal Itinerary

Arrival *Date*   *Time*

Departure *Date*   *Time*

Transportation

Accommodations

Arrival *Date*   *Time*

Departure *Date*   *Time*

Transportation

Accommodations

Arrival *Date*   *Time*

Departure *Date*   *Time*

Transportation

Accommodations

Arrival *Date*   *Time*

Departure *Date*   *Time*

Transportation

Accommodations

Personal Itinerary

Arrival   *Date*   *Time*

Departure   *Date*   *Time*

Transportation

Accommodations

Arrival   *Date*   *Time*

Departure   *Date*   *Time*

Transportation

Accommodations

Arrival   *Date*   *Time*

Departure   *Date*   *Time*

Transportation

Accommodations

Arrival   *Date*   *Time*

Departure   *Date*   *Time*

Transportation

Accommodations

Personal Itinerary

Arrival *Date*   *Time*

Departure *Date*   *Time*

Transportation

Accommodations

Arrival *Date*   *Time*

Departure *Date*   *Time*

Transportation

Accommodations

Arrival *Date*   *Time*

Departure *Date*   *Time*

Transportation

Accommodations

Arrival *Date*   *Time*

Departure *Date*   *Time*

Transportation

Accommodations

Personal Itinerary

Arrival *Date* *Time*

Departure *Date* *Time*

Transportation

Accommodations

Arrival *Date* *Time*

Departure *Date* *Time*

Transportation

Accommodations

Arrival *Date* *Time*

Departure *Date* *Time*

Transportation

Accommodations

Arrival *Date* *Time*

Departure *Date* *Time*

Transportation

Accommodations

Addresses

Name	*Name*
Address	*Address*
Telephone	*Telephone*
Name	*Name*
Address	*Address*
Telephone	*Telephone*
Name	*Name*
Address	*Address*
Telephone	*Telephone*
Name	*Name*
Address	*Address*
Telephone	*Telephone*
Name	*Name*
Address	*Address*
Telephone	*Telephone*
Name	*Name*
Address	*Address*
Telephone	*Telephone*
Name	*Name*
Address	*Address*
Telephone	*Telephone*
Name	*Name*
Address	*Address*
Telephone	*Telephone*

Addresses

Name	Name
Address	Address
Telephone	Telephone
Name	Name
Address	Address
Telephone	Telephone
Name	Name
Address	Address
Telephone	Telephone
Name	Name
Address	Address
Telephone	Telephone
Name	Name
Address	Address
Telephone	Telephone
Name	Name
Address	Address
Telephone	Telephone
Name	Name
Address	Address
Telephone	Telephone
Name	Name
Address	Address
Telephone	Telephone

Notes

Fodor's Travel Guides

U.S. Guides

Alaska
Arizona
Boston
California
Cape Cod, Martha's Vineyard, Nantucket
The Carolinas & the Georgia Coast
The Chesapeake Region
Chicago
Colorado
Disney World & the Orlando Area
Florida
Hawaii

Las Vegas, Reno, Tahoe
Los Angeles
Maine, Vermont, New Hampshire
Maui
Miami & the Keys
National Parks of the West
New England
New Mexico
New Orleans
New York City
New York City (Pocket Guide)

Pacific North Coast
Philadelphia & the Pennsylvania Dutch Country
Puerto Rico (Pocket Guide)
The Rockies
San Diego
San Francisco
San Francisco (Pocket Guide)
The South
Santa Fe, Taos, Albuquerque
Seattle & Vancouver

Texas
USA
The U. S. & British Virgin Islands
The Upper Great Lakes Region
Vacations in New York State
Vacations on the Jersey Shore
Virginia & Maryland
Waikiki
Washington, D.C.
Washington, D.C. (Pocket Guide)

Foreign Guides

Acapulco
Amsterdam
Australia
Austria
The Bahamas
The Bahamas (Pocket Guide)
Baja & Mexico's Pacific Coast Resorts
Barbados
Barcelona, Madrid, Seville
Belgium & Luxembourg
Berlin
Bermuda
Brazil
Budapest
Budget Europe
Canada
Canada's Atlantic Provinces

Cancun, Cozumel, Yucatan Peninsula
Caribbean
Central America
China
Czechoslovakia
Eastern Europe
Egypt
Europe
Europe's Great Cities
France
Germany
Great Britain
Greece
The Himalayan Countries
Holland
Hong Kong
India
Ireland
Israel
Italy

Italy 's Great Cities
Jamaica
Japan
Kenya, Tanzania, Seychelles
Korea
London
London (Pocket Guide)
London Companion
Mexico
Mexico City
Montreal & Quebec City
Morocco
New Zealand
Norway
Nova Scotia, New Brunswick, Prince Edward Island
Paris

Paris (Pocket Guide)
Portugal
Rome
Scandinavia
Scandinavian Cities
Scotland
Singapore
South America
South Pacific
Southeast Asia
Soviet Union
Spain
Sweden
Switzerland
Sydney
Thailand
Tokyo
Toronto
Turkey
Vienna & the Danube Valley
Yugoslavia

Wall Street Journal Guides to Business Travel

Europe

International Cities

Pacific Rim

USA & Canada

Special-Interest Guides

Bed & Breakfast and Country Inn Guides:
Mid-Atlantic Region
New England
The South
The West

Cruises and Ports of Call
Healthy Escapes
Fodor's Flashmaps New York

Fodor's Flashmaps Washington, D.C.
Shopping in Europe
Skiing in the USA & Canada

Smart Shopper's Guide to London
Sunday in New York
Touring Europe
Touring USA